Organization Development and Transformation

Managing Effective Change

Sixth Edition

Wendell L. French
Graduate School of Business Administration
University of Washington

Cecil H. Bell, Jr.
Graduate School of Business Administration
University of Washington

Robert A. Zawacki
Graduate School of Business Administration
University of Colorado, Colorado Springs

McGraw-Hill Irwin

Boston   Burr Ridge, IL   Dubuque, IA   Madison, WI   New York   San Francisco   St. Louis
Bangkok   Bogotá   Caracas   Kuala Lumpur   Lisbon   London   Madrid   Mexico City
Milan   Montreal   New Delhi   Santiago   Seoul   Singapore   Sydney   Taipei   Toronto

McGraw-Hill Irwin

ORGANIZATION DEVELOPMENT AND TRANSFORMATION: MANAGING EFFECTIVE CHANGE
Published by McGraw-Hill/Irwin, a business unit of The McGraw-Hill Companies, Inc., 1221 Avenue of the Americas, New York, NY, 10020. Copyright © 2005, 2000, 1994, 1989, 1983, and 1978 by The McGraw-Hill Companies, Inc. All rights reserved. No part of this publication may be reproduced or distributed in any form or by any means, or stored in a database or retrieval system, without the prior written consent of The McGraw-Hill Companies, Inc., including, but not limited to, in any network or other electronic storage or transmission, or broadcast for distance learning.

Some ancillaries, including electronic and print components, may not be available to customers outside the United States.

This book is printed on acid-free paper.

domestic 1 2 3 4 5 6 7 8 9 0 DOC/DOC 0 9 8 7 6 5 4
international 1 2 3 4 5 6 7 8 9 0 DOC/DOC 0 9 8 7 6 5 4

ISBN 0-07-248167-6

Vice president and editor-in-chief: *Robin J. Zwettler*
Editorial director: *John E. Biernat*
Executive editor: *John Weimeister*
Editorial coordinator: *Trina Hauger*
Marketing manager: *Lisa Nicks*
Media producer: *Mark Molsky*
Lead project manager: *Pat Frederickson*
Freelance project manager: *Stacey C. Sawyer, Sawyer & Williams*
Senior production supervisor: *Sesha Bolisetty*
Designer: *Mary E. Kazak*
Senior digital content specialist: *Brian Nacik*
Typeface: *10.5/12 Times New Roman*
Compositor: *Shepherd Inc.*
Printer: *R. R. Donnelley*

Library of Congress Cataloging-in-Publication Data

Organization development and transformation : managing effective change / edited by
   Wendell L. French, Cecil H. Bell, Jr., Robert A. Zawacki. — 6th ed.
     p. cm.
   Includes bibliographical references and index.
   ISBN 0-07-248167-6 (alk. paper)
   1. Organizational change. I. French, Wendell L., 1923– . II. Bell, Cecil, 1935– .
   III. Zawacki, Robert A.
  HD58.8.O724 2005
  658.4'06—dc22   2003067469

INTERNATIONAL EDITION ISBN 0-07-111266-9

Copyright © 2005. Exclusive rights by The McGraw-Hill Companies, Inc. for manufacture and export. This book cannot be re-exported from the country to which it is sold by McGraw-Hill.

The International Edition is not available in North America.

http://www.mhhe.com

From Wendell to Andy, Tom, and Amy
From Cecil to Dianne and Annie
From Bob to Jimmie

Contents

Preface to the Instructor

Organization development is an organizational improvement strategy that uses behavioral science principles and practices to increase individual and organizational effectiveness. The field of organization development (or OD as it is called) continues to gain practitioners, clients, theorists, researchers, and new technologies. It is applied in a wide range of settings and has become a preferred strategy for facilitating change in organizations.

What began as isolated experiments for improving organizational dynamics and management practices in the 1950s evolved into the coherent discipline we know today as organization development. And the field of OD continues to evolve. For example, in the 1980s as the pace and scope of environmental changes increased, new theories and techniques were developed to help leaders direct large-scale, systemwide changes. These efforts, called "organizational transformation," (OT) represent a variant of OD in which organizations are transformed in fundamental ways. These transformations often involve paradigm shifts—radical changes in management philosophy, ways of organizing the work, and ways of relating to employees and customers. Organization development and transformation focus on how people *and* organizations and people *in* organizations function, and how to make them function better.

The field of organization development offers a prescription for improving the "goodness of fit" between individuals and organizations and between organizations and environments. Ingredients of that prescription include a focus on the organization's culture and processes; guidelines for designing and implementing action programs; conceptualizing the organization and its environment in system theory terms; and creating change processes that empower individuals through involvement, participation, and commitment.

OD is the applied domain of organizational psychology and sociology. It is the engineering side of the organizational sciences. Planned change involves common sense; hard work applied diligently over time; a systematic and goal-oriented approach; and valid knowledge about organizational dynamics and how to change them. The valid knowledge comes from basic and applied behavioral science. The total prescription comes from five decades of practice in discovering what works in organizations and why.

The aim of organization development and transformation is to help individuals and organizations function better in today's increasingly interdependent, complex, and competitive world. The aim of this book is to present a clear, comprehensive picture of organization development and transformation so that the reader may acquire the knowledge and skill to manage change more effectively.

We wish to thank the authors whose writings we have included. We acknowledge our debt to the hundreds of talented contributors to the field of OD.

Wendell L. French

Cecil H. Bell, Jr.

Robert A. Zawacki

Preface to the Student

What Is Organization Development

Organization development (OD) is a powerful set of concepts and techniques for improving organizational effectiveness and individual well-being that had its genesis in the behavioral sciences and was tested in the laboratory of real-world organizations. OD addresses the opportunities and problems involved in improving human dynamics in organizations. It offers solutions that have been shown to work. Organization development consists of intervention techniques, theories, principles, and values that show how to implement planned change efforts and achieve success.

What Is Organization Transformation

Organization transformation (OT) is a recent extension of organization development that seeks to create far-reaching changes in an organization's structures, processes, culture, and orientation to its environment. Organization transformation applies behavioral science theory and practice to effect large-scale, paradigm-shifting organizational change. An organizational transformation usually results in totally new paradigms or models for organizing and performing work. Organization transformation has been referred to as "second-generation organization development." The demands on today's organizations for constant change and adaptation are so great that new responses were required. OT represents one of those responses. But simultaneously improving organizational effectiveness and individual well-being is still the goal. Both OD and OT are means to accomplish that goal.

Why Study Organization Development

Understanding what OD is and how it is practiced is important for several reasons. **First,** it works. Organization development programs can improve individual performance, create better morale, and increase organizational profitability. Many chronic problems in organizations can be cured by OD techniques. Many unrealized opportunities in organizations can be accomplished through OD techniques.

Second, the use of organization development is growing. The approach and methods of OD are applied throughout the gamut of today's organizations and industries. Manufacturing and service companies, high-technology and low-technology organizations, and public- and private-sector institutions all have sponsored successful OD programs.

Third, it is now recognized that the most important assets of organizations are human assets—the men and women who produce the goods and make the decisions. Finding ways to protect, enhance, and mobilize human assets doesn't just make good human-relations sense, it makes good economic sense. OD offers a variety of methods to strengthen the human side of organizations to the benefit of both the individual and the organization.

Fourth, OD is a critical managerial tool. We believe that the concepts and techniques of organization development will soon be as much a part of the well-trained manager's repertoire as knowledge of accounting, marketing, and finance. We predict that a significant period of transition lies just ahead in which the charter and boundaries of organization development will be expanded; specifically, the practice of OD will be incorporated within the art and science of management. Organization development offers a set of generic tools available to any managers and members of organizations who want to improve goal achievement. Today's managers manage change, and OD is a prescription for managing change. Managers need to know what OD is and how to use it. A good understanding of organization development has great practical value for present and future managers and leaders.

This collection of readings tells the story of OD's and OT's theory, practice, and research foundations. Articles by prominent authors in the field present a comprehensive portrait that we believe will be useful to managers, students of organizational dynamics, and professionals in the fields of human resource management and organization development and transformation.

The field of organization development is fun and exciting. We hope this anthology will convey some of that sense of excitement.

An Overview of the Book

This sixth edition continues the tradition of its predecessors. Our goal is to present classic statements about the field of organization development and transformation and also provide timely articles describing innovations and new directions. The field of organization development is constantly evolving, and this anthology evolves with it. In creating this edition, we deleted 13 articles, added 11 new articles, and retained a core of 33 articles. We strengthened our coverage of large-scale system change, appreciative inquiry, "future search" conferences, coaching, and "Fast Cycle OD." The book deals with theory and practice, history and the future, and problems and opportunities related to organization development and transformation.

Part 1, Mapping the Territory, provides an introduction and overview of the field. Early definitions and descriptions of organization development along with an historical look at the origins of OD begin the story. Next, the concepts of change and changing are examined, followed by a description of how OD was evolving in the mid-1980s. Excerpts from a comprehensive review of organization development and organization transformation convey a summary of contemporary thought and practice in the 1990s. A look at some of the major influences on the development of management thought reveals that many of these same influences helped shape the theory and practice of organization development.

Part 2, Foundations of Organization Development and Transformation, describes several theoretical and practice underpinnings of the field. Articles on intervention theory, sociotechnical systems theory, intergroup problems in organizations, and organizational culture describe some of the building blocks OD practitioners rely upon as they seek to understand organizational dynamics.

Most of the actual work in organization development is accomplished through "interventions"—structured sets of activities designed to cause learning and change. The interventions presented in **Part 3, Fundamental Interventions,** were some of the early tools in the OD practitioner's "kit bag." The interventions shown here are designed to diagnose organizational dynamics, clarify role expectations, resolve interpersonal conflict, improve intergroup relations, and enhance planning and decision-making procedures. This section of the book shows what OD practitioners actually do as they work with organization members to increase individual and organizational effectiveness. These interventions have been shown to be effective in a variety of settings and organizations.

Part 4, Cutting-Edge Change Strategies, continues the exploration of ways to intervene in organizations to produce learning and change, but shifts the discussion to the level of "change programs" or "grand strategies" for bringing about desired change. Articles in this section describe recent approaches for transforming organizations. Included are reports on self-directed teams, appreciative inquiry, future search conferences, centers of excellence, and fast cycle organization development. These approaches are currently a "hot" area in OD and OT practice. Underlying concepts and how to implement them are discussed.

Part 5, Implementation Guidelines and Issues, offers suggestions for increasing the likelihood of success in OD and OT programs. What are the ingredients of successful consulting? What are the critical success factors involved in managing long-term change projects? These questions are addressed in this section. Articles cover such topics as creating readiness for change, considering the role of power and politics in organizational change, choosing the depth of interventions to be used, reflecting on some cogent "rules of thumb" for practitioners, and enhancing the effectiveness of change efforts through coaching.

Part 6, Examples and Special Situations, reports on organization development programs at British Airways, the Veterans Health Administration, Ford Motor Company, Boeing Company, and NASA. Issues and challenges involved in executing such programs show how complicated organizational change can be. Articles on the relevance of OD for entrepreneurial firms and for turnaround situations demonstrate the wide range of settings where OD and OT programs can be applied.

Part 7, Challenges and Opportunities for the Future, completes the anthology. We selected articles on empowering self-directed teams, ethics, managing discontinuous change, implementing effective human resource practices, a proposed agenda for OD in the near-term future, and a discussion of OD's relevance in light of today's fast-paced changes in a digital, globalized, hyper-competitive environment. There are indeed plenty of challenges and opportunities for the field. But if the past is a good predictor of the future, new theories and techniques will be developed, tested, and proven—and these will show up in future editions of this book.

The need for organization development and transformation has never been greater. We believe organization development offers a way to achieve organizational and individual effectiveness in a rapidly changing world. Again, we express our thanks to the authors of these articles for their insights. The "present" is an exciting time, and organization development is an exciting field.

Mapping the Territory

The subject matter of this book of readings is organization development and transformation. The aim of the book is to present a well-rounded exposition of the field so the reader has a thorough understanding of its nature, technologies, theory, research underpinnings, and applications.

Organization development is the applied behavioral science discipline dedicated to improving organizations and the people in them using the theory and practice of planned change. OD is an improvement strategy—a means for "bettering" organizations and the people in them. Organization development activities focus on the "human side" of organizations—people, relationships, policies, procedures, processes, norms, culture, and organization design. OD practitioners view organizations as human systems created to achieve certain purposes or goals. "Improvement" in organizations occurs through planned changes, and that is accomplished in a variety of ways: by "fixing" problems, by seizing unrealized opportunities, by taking actions to create desired future states not currently in existence.

Organization development came into being in the 1950s and 1960s as a means to enhance organizational effectiveness and improve the quality of work life for organizational members. Following World War II there was a tremendous growth in knowledge, research, and theories concerning organizations. This was derived from research in organizational behavior, organization theory, management, human resources management, and "strategic management." Along with increased interest in how organizations work came the emergence of organization development as a way to help them function better. Porras and Robertson capture this development as follows: "Organizational development (OD) is the practical application of the science of organizations. Drawing from several disciplines for its models, strategies, and techniques, OD focuses on the planned change of human systems and contributes to organization science through the knowledge gained from its study of complex change dynamics."[1] The constant interchange between OD and the science of organizations will be apparent throughout this book.

In Part 1 we map the territory of organization development and transformation. What is OD? What is organization transformation (OT)? What makes OD different from other improvement strategies? What are some of the varieties of OD and OT?

Toward a Definition of Organization Development

No generally accepted, single definition of organization development exists. But there is substantial agreement on what the field is all about. Let's examine several definitions from the early OD literature to see what people say it is.

Organization development is an effort (1) *planned,* (2) *organizationwide,* and (3) *managed* from the *top,* to (4) *increase organization effectiveness* and *health* through (5) *planned interventions* in the organization's "processes," using *behavioral-science* knowledge.[2]

Organization development (OD) is a response to change, a complex educational strategy intended to change the beliefs, attitudes, values, and structure of organizations so that they can better adapt to new technologies, markets, and challenges, and the dizzying rate of change itself.[3]

Organization development is the strengthening of those human processes in organizations which improve the functioning of the organic system so as to achieve its objectives.[4]

Organization renewal is the process of initiating, creating and confronting needed changes so as to make it possible for organizations to become or remain viable, to adapt to new conditions, to solve problems, to learn from experiences, and to move toward greater organizational maturity.[5]

OD can be defined as a planned and sustained effort to apply behavioral science for system improvement, using reflexive, self-analytic methods.[6]

Organization development is a process of planned change—change of an organization's culture from one which avoids an examination of social processes (especially decision making, planning, and communication) to one which institutionalizes and legitimizes this examination.[7]

In the behavioral science, and perhaps ideal, sense of the term, *organization development is a long-range effort to improve an organization's problem-solving and renewal processes, particularly through a more effective and collaborative management of organization culture—with special emphasis on the culture of formal work teams—with the assistance of a change agent, or catalyst, and the use of the theory and technology of applied behavioral science, including action research.*[8]

[Italics in the original.]

Analysis of these definitions suggests that organization development is *not* just "anything done to better an organization"; it is a particular kind of change process designed to bring about a particular kind of end result. In Table 1 the definitions are dissected and put into an analytic framework to show the particular kind of change processes and the particular kind of end results desired.

Examination of Table 1 suggests the following conclusion. Organization development (OD) is a prescription for a process of planned change in organizations in which the key prescriptive elements relate to (1) the nature of the effort or program (it is a long-range, planned, systemwide process); (2) the nature of the change activities (they utilize behavioral science interventions of an educational, reflexive, self-examining, learn-to-do-it-yourself nature); (3) the targets of the change activities (they are directed toward the human and social processes of organizations, specifically individuals' beliefs, attitudes, and values, the culture and processes of work groups—viewed as basic building blocks of the organization—and the processes and culture of the total organization); and (4) the desired outcomes of the change activities (the goals are *needed changes* in the targets of the interventions that cause the organization to be better able to adapt, cope, solve its problems, and renew itself). Organization development thus represents a unique strategy for system change, a strategy largely based in the theory and research of the behavioral sciences, and a strategy having a substantial prescriptive character. Organization development is thus a normative discipline that prescribes how planned change in organizations should be approached and carried out if organization improvement is to be obtained.

Organization development attempts to make organizations (viewed as social-technical systems) better able to attain their short- and long-term objectives. This is achieved by teaching the organization members to manage their organization processes, structures, and culture more effectively. A basic belief of OD theorists and practitioners is that for effective, lasting change to take place, the system members must grow in the competence to master their own fates.

Finally, it is important to note that OD has two broad goals: organization development and individual development. Although it is not stated explicitly in the above definitions, improving the quality of life for individuals in organizations is a primary goal of organization development. Enhancing individual development is a key value of OD practitioners and, we believe, a key outcome of most OD programs.

A definition of OD by Porras and Robertson makes this clear: "Organizational development is a set of behavioral science-based theories, values, strategies, and techniques aimed at the planned change of the organizational work setting for the purpose of enhancing individual development and improving organizational performance, through the alteration of organizational members' on-the-job behaviors."[9]

They say further: "[W]e maintain that OD has two primary purposes. One is improvement in the organization's ability to perform. . . . The second is improvement in the development of the organization's members—that is, in their psychological well-being, their level of self-actualization or realization, and their capabilities."[10]

OD: A Unique Change Strategy

Consulting to organizations can take many forms. For example, Edgar Schein describes three consulting models: the "purchase of expertise model"; the "doctor-patient model"; and the "process consultation model." The process consultation model is typical of the OD approach, while the other two are not.

TABLE 1 An Analysis of Selected Definitions of Organization Development

	Components of the Organization Development Process				
Author	Nature and Scope of the Effort	Nature of Activities/Interventions	Targets of Interaction/Activities	Knowledge Base	Desired Goals, Outcomes, or End States of Organization Development Effort
Beckard	Planned. Organizationwide. Managed from the top. Complex educational strategy. A response to change.	Planned intervention in the organization's "processes." Educational. Change-oriented.	catalyst. Total organization. Organization's "processes."	Behavioral science knowledge.	Increased organization effectiveness and health.
Bennis			Beliefs, attitudes, values, and structures of organizations.		Better ability to adapt to new technologies, markets, and challenges, and the dizzying rate of change itself.
Gordon Lippitt (on OD)		Designed to strengthen human processes in organizations.	Those human processes in organizations that improve the organic system.		Enable the organization to achieve its objectives (through improved functioning of the organic system).
Gordon Lippitt (on organization renewal)	A process.	A process of initiating, creating, and confronting needed changes.	[Implied] total organization.		Enhance the ability of the organization to: Become or remain viable. Adapt to new conditions. Solve problems Learn from experience. Move toward greater organizational maturity.
Schmuck and Miles	A planned and sustained effort.	Apply behavioral science for system improvement. Using reflexive, self-analytic methods.	Total System (organization).	Behavioral science.	System improvement. [implied] continued self-analysis and reflection.

Burke and Hornstein	A process of planned change.	Change-oriented and self-examining oriented; specifically change of an organization's culture from one which avoids an examination of social processes in organization . . . to one which institutionalizes and legitimizes this examination.	The organization's culture and the social processes in organization, especially decision making, planning, and communication.		[Self-examination] of social processes in organization, especially decision making, planning, and communication.
French and Bell	A long-range effort.	Designed to bring about a more effective and collaborative management of organization culture; using assistance of change agent, or	Organization culture. Culture of formal work teams. Organization's problem-solving and renewal processes.	The theory and technology of applied behavioral science, including action research.	Improve an organization's problem-solving and renewal processes.

In the "purchase of expertise model," a leader or group identifies a need for information or expertise that the organization cannot supply. The leader hires a consultant to obtain the information and make a report, often including recommendations for action. Examples would be (1) surveying consumers or employees about some matter, (2) finding out how best to organize the company after a merger, or (3) developing a marketing strategy for a new product. This is a typical consulting approach that is widely used.

In the "doctor-patient model," a leader or group detects symptoms of ill health in some part of the organization, and calls in a consultant who diagnoses the situation, identifies the causes of problems and then, like a physician, prescribes a cure. Examples would be calling in "the doctor" to examine (1) low morale at a particular plant, (2) being over budget and behind schedule on a major project, or (3) a high-performing manager who suddenly becomes a low-performer. This too is a well-known, traditional approach to consultation.

In the "process consultation model," the consultant *works with* the leader and group to diagnose strengths and weaknesses, identify problems and opportunities, and develop action plans and methods for reaching desired goals. In this model the consultant assists the client organization in becoming more effective at examining and improving its own processes of problem solving, decision making, and action taking. This third model, typical in OD, encourages greater collaboration between clients and consultant, engages the resources and talents of the clients, and strengthens clients' abilities to improve their work processes. Examples would include working on any of the previously mentioned problems, but using a collaborative, participative, you-can-figure-out-the-right-answers-yourselves approach. An organization development consultant typically suggests general processes and procedures for addressing problems and issues. The consultant helps the clients generate valid data and learn from the data. The OD consultant is an expert on *process*—how to "go about" effective problem solving and decision making.

Thus, OD differs substantially from traditional "expert" models of consulting in its overall *approach.* Likewise, OD practitioners have different *goals* and focus on different *targets* compared with other consulting models. Here is a list of "primary distinguishing characteristics of organization development" proposed in the literature:

1. OD focuses on culture and processes.
2. Specifically, OD encourages collaboration between organization leaders and members in managing culture and processes.
3. Teams of all kinds are particularly important for accomplishing tasks and are targets for OD activities.
4. OD focuses on the human and social side of the organization and in so doing, also intervenes in the technological and structural sides.

5. Participation and involvement in problem solving and decision making by all levels of the organization are hallmarks of OD.

6. OD focuses on total system change and views organizations as complex social systems.

7. OD practitioners are facilitators, collaborators, and co-learners with the client system.

8. An overarching goal is to make the client system able to solve its problems on its own by teaching the skills and knowledge of continuous learning through self-analytical methods. OD views organization improvement as an ongoing process in the context of a constantly changing environment.

9. OD relies on an action research model with extensive participation by client system members.

10. OD takes a developmental view that seeks the betterment of both individuals and the organization. Attempting to create "win-win" solutions is standard practice in OD programs.[11]

These distinctive features of OD suggest why it is such a powerful change strategy. The participative, collaborative, problem-focused nature of OD marshals the experience and expertise of organization members as they work on their most important problems and opportunities in ways designed to lead to successful outcomes.

The Emergence of Organization Transformation (OT)

The preceding discussion describes classical organization development, which began in the mid-1950s and continues to the present. Over the years the practice of OD has evolved and matured, clarifying its values, theories, methods, and interventions, as well as adding new values, theories, and so forth. Beginning in the 1980s, articles and books appeared that described change programs designed to cause large-scale, radical, and fundamental changes in organizations. These paradigm-shifting changes were referred to as "organization transformation" or "organizational transformation." Some authors believe OT is an extension of OD; others believe OT represents a new discipline in its own right. It is too early to categorize organization transformation; for now, we see it as an extension of OD. Some forces leading to the emergence of OT can be identified, however.

In the 1960s and 1970s OD focused on improving the internal working of organizations through the use of role clarification, improved communication, team building, intergroup team building, and the like. The organization was conceptualized as an open system in interaction with its environment, but primary attention was directed toward making the parts and the whole function better. In the 1970s new work arrangements were tested in the form of sociotechnical systems theory experiments and quality of work life experiments. Sociotechnical systems theory

(STS) postulates that an organization comprises both a social system and a technical system, and that these two systems must be jointly optimized for best results.[12] One result of STS experimentation was the discovery that "autonomous work groups" (similar to today's self-managed teams and self-directed teams) constituted a better working arrangement than the usual isolated individuals with a boss to tell them what to do. This was an important discovery, and autonomous work groups and self-managed teams proliferated in a variety of settings. Quality of work life experiments led to similar discoveries about the value of self-directed teams, and they additionally produced new ways for labor and management to work together to lessen adversarial relations.[13] These experiments and others in work redesign and reorganization called into question old paradigms (beliefs and assumptions) about working arrangements and authority relations in organizations.

In the 1980s strategic management achieved prominence in managerial thinking, and attention was directed toward the fit between the environment with its "threats" and "opportunities" and the organization with its "strengths" and "weaknesses." Considerable effort was directed toward defining the mission, purpose, vision, and strategy of organizations. OD practitioners developed interventions to facilitate strategic management by the organization's executives. It was soon realized that a clear, articulated vision was a powerful component of organizational effectiveness.

Also in the 1980s the demands on organizations intensified: competition increased; customers demanded better products and services; the total quality movement created winners and losers; information technology exploded; economic and political changes occurred. Organizations had to change—fast—to survive. The old ways of doing things were no longer good enough; the old belief systems were no longer adequate. Organizations had to be transformed, not just "tweaked." Paradigms had to be changed, not just adjusted. All these conditions and more gave rise to explorations in the theory and practice of organization transformation.

Porras and Silvers state in Reading 5: "Planned change interventions can be divided into two general types. The first comprises the more traditional approach, Organization Development (OD), which until recently was synonymous with the term *planned change*. The second, Organization Transformation (OT), is the cutting edge of planned change and may be called 'second generation OD.'" These authors emphasize the importance of "vision," "guiding beliefs and principles," "purpose," and "mission" as major features of OT interventions.

Cummings and Worley describe OT as follows:

> Organization transformations can occur in response to or in anticipation of major changes in the organization's environment or technology. In addition, these changes are often associated with significant alterations in the firm's business strategy, which, in turn, may require modifying corporate culture as well as internal structures and processes to support the new direction. Such fundamental change entails a new paradigm for organizing and managing organizations. It involves qualitatively different ways of perceiving, thinking, and behaving in organizations.[14]

They suggest three interventions to facilitate organization transformations: culture change, strategic change, and self-designing organizations.

Clearly the phenomenon of organization transformation is important, real, and here to stay. The task for OD and OT practitioners is to develop behavioral science theories, models, practices, and interventions to facilitate the transformations.

Readings in Part 1

The readings in this part range from early statements about the nature and characteristics of organization development to recent articles describing both OD and organization transformation.

The first selection is by Richard Beckhard, an early OD practitioner and theorist. Beckhard asks and answers the question: What is organization development? His operational definition, operational goals of OD, and characteristics of OD efforts combine to make this one of the best statements available on what OD is all about. He is pithy, to the point, and right on target. He identifies several distinguishing features about OD that are not found in other organizational change approaches. This selection is taken from his little book titled *Organization Development: Strategies and Models* that appeared in 1969. In that year Addison-Wesley Publishing Company published six little paperback books on OD, all packaged together. These came to be known as "The Addison-Wesley OD Six Pack" among practitioners. Collectively these books defined the field of OD at that time. Other authors and titles in the "Six Pack" were Warren Bennis, *Organization Development: Its Nature, Origins, and Prospects;* Paul Lawrence and Jay Lorsch, *Developing Organizations: Diagnosis and Action;* Edgar Schein, *Process Consultation: Its Role in Organization Development;* Richard Walton, *Interpersonal Peacemaking: Confrontations and Third-Party Consultation;* and Robert Blake and Jane Srygley Mouton, *Building a Dynamic Corporation through Grid Organization Development.*

The roots, birth, and major milestones in the development of the field of organization development are described in the next article. Wendell French has been intrigued with tracing the history of OD for many years. The selection was written by him; it appears in a book on organization development by Wendell French and Cecil Bell.[15] French points to the importance of Kurt Lewin as a prime contributor to events leading up to the emergence of OD, and to four mainstreams of activities as precursors of OD—laboratory training, survey research and feedback, action research, and the sociotechnical and socioclinical approaches of the Tavistock Clinic in England. Early projects and the people involved in them are described, using as source materials both published accounts and extensive correspondence with the individuals who were in the forefront of the new applied behavioral science developments at that time—Robert Blake, Herbert Shepard, Ronald Lippitt, Eva Schindler-Rainman, Richard Beckhard, and others.

An article on the history of OD by Michael McGill, not included in this reader, gives a somewhat different view of early events.[16] McGill goes back to just after World War II to search for the beginnings of OD and, in so doing, finds reason to include the activities, writings, and conceptualizations of Leland Bradford and Neely Gardner as important foundations. Both Bradford and Gardner were engaged in training and development activities in large organizations and conceived the necessity to develop *both* the individual and the organization. Bradford has been intimately involved with most of the applied behavioral science developments in the United States because he was the director of the National Training Laboratory in Group Development (NTL) from its inception in 1947 to his retirement in 1970. NTL (now the NTL—Institute for Applied Behavioral Science) was both a source of support for the fledgling organization development movement and also a source of most of the OD practitioners.[17]

The article by Robert Chin and Kenneth D. Benne describes three broad general strategies for effecting changes in human systems—the empirical-rational strategy, the normative-reeducative strategy, and the power-coercive strategy. This elegant and erudite essay was written for the book *The Planning of Change,* edited by Warren Bennis, Kenneth Benne, and Robert Chin. The historical development of the three strategies of change is traced in detail, and examples of each strategy in operation are given. It is our opinion that organization development rests primarily on a normative-reeducative strategy and secondarily on an empirical-rational strategy. For this reason, understanding the three general strategies for change is important for the OD practitioner as well as for leaders who may be interested in OD efforts in their organizations.

The selection by Marvin Weisbord sets the stage for thinking about organization transformations and how a consultant can help. Weisbord ponders the differences between traditional organization development thinking and practice and the thinking and practice required in a "third-wave" world as described by futurist Alvin Toffler. New times require new paradigms. Weisbord supplies some. His "four useful practices" suggest new ways consultants can facilitate organization transformation. His discussion of the "four-room apartment" provides great insights. These are important issues for leaders, managers, and OD consultants.

The selection by Jerry Porras and Robert Silvers is taken from the *Annual Review of Psychology.* About every four years the latest developments in the field of OD (and now, OT) are summarized by prominent theorists/practitioners in that publication. This article represents the first time that organization transformation was featured. An especially important contribution of this reading is its model of planned change. Organization development and transformation need better theoretical underpinnings, and this article addresses that deficiency. Porras and Silvers present a thorough review of contemporary research and thinking in the field of organization development and transformation.

The final reading in Part 1 lists the 25 most influential management books of the last century as nominated by the Fellows of the Academy of Management. These books and other important works reflect major milestones in the development of organization science. We include this selection to show the evolution of knowledge about organizations and the people in them. Several of the authors (McGregor, Argyris, Likert) made important contributions to OD, as you will see in Reading 2, "A History of Organization Development."

These selections should give the reader a good understanding of what organization development and transformation are all about. Subsequent sections of the book will develop these themes in detail.

Endnotes

1. Jerry I. Porras and Peter J. Robertson, "Organizational Development: Theory, Practice, and Research," in Marvin D. Dunnette and Leaetta M. Hough, eds., *Handbook of Industrial and Organizational Psychology,* 2nd ed., vol. 3 (Palo Alto, CA.: Consulting Psychologists Press, 1992), p. 720.

2. Richard Beckhard, *Organization Development: Strategies and Models* (Reading, Mass.: Addison-Wesley Publishing, 1969), p. 9.

3. Warren G. Bennis, *Organization Development: Its Nature, Origins, and Prospects* (Reading, Mass.: Addison-Wesley Publishing, 1969), p. 2.

4. Gordon L. Lippitt, *Organization Renewal* (New York: Appleton-Century-Croft, 1969), p. 1.

5. Ibid., p. 4.

6. Richard Schmuck and Matthew Miles, *Organization Development in Schools* (Palo Alto, Calif.; National Press Books, 1971), p. 2.

7. Warner Burke and Harvey A. Hornstein, *The Social Technology of Organization Development* (Fairfax, Va.: Learning Resources Corp., 1972), p. xi.

8. Wendell L. French and Cecil H. Bell, Jr., *Organization Development,* 2nd ed. (Englewood Cliffs, N.J.: Prentice Hall, 1978), p. 14.

9. Porras and Robertson, p. 722.

10. Ibid., pp. 722–23.

11. Wendell L. French and Cecil H. Bell, Jr., *Organization Development,* 6th ed. (Upper Saddle River, N.J.: Prentice Hall, Inc., 1999), pp. 29.

12. E. Trist and K. Bamforth, "Some Social and Psychological Consequences of the Longwall Method of Goal-Getting," *Human Relations* 4 (January 1951), pp. 1–38.

13. R. E. Walton, "Quality of Working Life: What Is It?" *Sloan Management Review,* Fall 1973, pp. 11–21.

14. T. G. Cummings and C. G. Worley, *Organization Development and Change,* 6th ed. (Minneapolis, Minn.: West Publishing Co., 1993), p. 520.

15. French and Bell, 6th ed; see Chapter 3.

16. Michael E. McGill, "The Evolution of Organization Development: 1947–1960," *Public Administration Review,* March–April 1974, pp. 98–105.

17. Leland P. Bradford, *National Training Laboratories—Its History: 1947–1970.* Copyright 1974 by Leland P. Bradford, Bethel, Maine.

Reading 1

What Is Organization Development?

Richard Beckhard

Definition. Organization development is an effort (1) *planned,* (2) *organizationwide,* and (3) *managed* from the *top,* to (4) increase *organization effectiveness* and *health* through (5) *planned interventions in* the organization's "processes," using *behavioral-science* knowledge.

1. It is a *planned change* effort.

   An OD program involves a systematic diagnosis of the organization, the development of a strategic plan for improvement, and the mobilization of resources to carry out the effort.

2. It involves the total "*system.*"

   An organization development effort is related to a total organization change such as a change in the culture or the reward systems or the total managerial strategy. There may be tactical efforts which work with subparts of the organization but the "system" to be changed is a total, relatively autonomous organization. This is not necessarily a total corporation, or an entire government, but refers to a system which is relatively free to determine its own plans and future within very *general* constraints from the environment.

3. *It is managed from the top.*

   In an organization development effort, the top management of the system has a personal investment in the program and its outcomes. They actively participate in the *management* of the effort. This does not mean they must par-

ticipate in the same *activities* as others, but it does mean that they must have both knowledge and *commitment* to the goals of the program and must actively support the methods used to achieve the goals.

4. It is designed to *increase organization effectiveness* and *health.*

   To understand the goals of organization development, it is necessary to have some picture of what an "ideal" effective, healthy organization would look like. What would be its characteristics? Numbers of writers and practitioners in the field have proposed definitions which, although they differ in detail, indicate a strong consensus of what a healthy operating organization is. Let me start with my own definition. An effective organization is one in which:

   a. The total organization, the significant subparts, and individuals, manage their work against *goals* and *plans* for achievement of these goals.

   b. Form follows function (the problem, or task, or project, determines how the human resources are organized).

   c. Decisions are made by and near the sources of information regardless of where these sources are located on the organization chart.

   d. The reward system is such that managers and supervisors are rewarded (and punished) comparably for:

   Short-term profit or production performance.

   Growth and development of their subordinates.

   Creating a viable working group.

   e. Communication laterally and vertically is *relatively* undistorted. People are generally

Source: Richard Beckhard, *Organization Development; Strategies and Models,* pp. 9, 10, 14, ©1969 Addison-Wesley Longman Inc. Reprinted by permission of Addison-Wesley Longman.

open and confronting. They share all the relevant facts including feelings.

f. There is a minimum amount of inappropriate win/lose activities between individuals and groups. Constant effort exists at all levels to treat conflict, and conflict situations, as *problems* subject to problem-solving methods.

g. There is high "conflict" (clash of ideas) about tasks and projects, and relatively little energy spent in clashing over *interpersonal* difficulties because they have been generally worked through.

h. The organization and its parts see themselves as interacting with each other *and* with a *larger* environment. The organization is an "open system."

i. There is a shared value, and management strategy to support it, of trying to help each person (or unit) in the organization maintain his (or its) integrity and uniqueness in an interdependent environment.

j. The organization and its members operate in an "action-research" way. General practice is to build in *feedback mechanisms* so that individuals and groups can learn from their own experience.

Another definition is found in John Gardner's set of rules for an effective organization. He describes an effective organization as one which is *self-renewing* and then lists the rules:

The *first rule* is that the organization must have an effective program for the recruitment and development of talent.

The *second rule* for the organization capable of continuous renewal is that it must be a hospitable environment for the individual.

The *third rule* is that the organization must have built-in provisions for self-criticism.

The *fourth rule* is that there must be fluidity in the internal structure.

The *fifth rule* is that the organization must have some means of combating the process

by which men become prisoners of their procedures.[1]

Edgar Schein defines organization effectiveness in relation to what he calls "the adaptive coping cycle," that is, an organization that can effectively adapt and cope with the changes in its environment. Specifically, he says:

The sequence of activities or processes which begins with some change in the internal or external environment and ends with a more adaptive, dynamic equilibrium for dealing with the change, is the organization's "adaptive coping cycle." If we identify the various stages or processes of this cycle, we shall also be able to identify the points where organizations typically may fail to cope adequately and where, therefore, consultants and researchers have been able in a variety of ways to help increase organization effectiveness.[2]

The organization conditions necessary for effective coping, according to Schein, are:

The ability to take in and communicate information reliably and validly.

Internal flexibility and creativity to make the changes which are demanded by the information obtained (including structural flexibility).

Integration and commitment to the goals of the organization from which comes the willingness to change.

An internal climate of support and freedom from threat, since being threatened undermines good communication, reduces flexibility, and stimulates self-protection rather than concern for the total system.

Miles et al. (1966) define the healthy organization in three broad areas—those concerned with task accomplishment, those concerned with internal integration, and those involving mutual adaptation of the organization and its environment. The following dimensional conditions are listed for each area:

In the task-accomplishment area, a healthy organization would be one with (1) reasonably clear, accepted, achievable and appropriate goals; (2) relatively understood communications flow; (3) optimal power equalization.

In the area of internal integration, a healthy organization would be one with (4) resource utilization and individuals' *good fit* between personal disposition and role demands; (5) a reasonable degree of cohesiveness and "organization identity," clear and attractive enough so that persons feel actively connected to it; (6) high morale. In order to have growth and active changefulness, a healthy organization would be one with innovativeness, autonomy, adaptation, and problem-solving adequacy.[3]

Lou Morse, in his recent thesis on organization development, writes that:

The commonality of goals are cooperative group relations, consensus, integration, and commitment to the goals of the organization (task accomplishment), creativity, authentic behavior, freedom from threat, full utilization of a person's capabilities, and organizational flexibility.[4]

5. Organization development achieves its goals through *planned interventions* using behavioral science knowledge.

A strategy is developed of intervening or moving into the existing organization and helping it, in effect, "stop the music," examine its present ways of work, norms, and values, and look at alternative ways of working, or relating, or rewarding. . . . The interventions used draw on the knowledge and technology of the behavioral sciences about such processes as individual motivation, power, communications, perception, cultural norms, problem solving, goal setting, interpersonal relationships, intergroup relationships, and conflict management.

Some Operational Goals in an Organization-Development Effort

To move toward the kind of organization conditions described in the above definitions, OD efforts usually have some of the following operational goals:

1. To develop a self-renewing, *viable system* that can organize in a variety of ways depending on tasks. This means systematic efforts to change and loosen up the way the organization operates, so that it organizes differently depending on the nature of the task. There is movement toward a concept of "form follows function," rather than that *tasks* must *fit* into existing structures.

2. To optimize the effectiveness of both the stable (the basic organization chart) and the temporary systems (the many projects, committees, et cetera, through which much of the organization's work is accomplished) by built-in, *continuous improvement mechanisms*. This means the introduction of procedures for analyzing work tasks and resource distribution, and for building in continuous "feedback" regarding the way a system or sub-system is operating.

3. To move toward *high collaboration* and *low competition* between interdependent units. One of the major obstacles to effective organizations is the amount of dysfunctional energy spent in inappropriate competition—energy that is not, therefore, available for the accomplishment of tasks. If all of the energy that is used by, let's say, manufacturing people disliking or wanting to "get those sales people," or vice versa, were available to improve organization output, productivity would increase tremendously.

4. To create conditions where conflict is brought out and managed. One of the fundamental problems in unhealthy (or less than healthy) organizations is the amount of energy that is dysfunctionally used trying to work around, or avoid, or cover up, conflicts which are inevitable in a complex organization. The goal is to move the organization towards seeing conflict as an inevitable condition and as problems that need to be *worked* before adequate decisions can be made.

5. To reach the point where decisions are made on the basis of information source rather than organizational role. This means the need to

move toward a *norm* of the *authority of knowledge* as well as the authority of role. It does not only mean that decisions should be moved down in the organization; it means that the organization manager should determine which is the best source of information (or combination of sources of information) to work a particular problem, and it is there that the decision making should be located.

Endnotes

1. J. W. Gardner, "How to Prevent Organizational Dry Rot," *Harper's Magazine,* October 1965.

2. E. H. Schein, *Organizational Psychology* (Englewood Cliffs, N.J.: Prentice Hall, 1965.)

3. M. B. Miles et al., "Data Feedback and Organization Change in a School System." (Paper given at a meeting of the American Sociological Association, August 27, 1966.)

4. L. H. Morse, "Task-Centered Organization Development," (Master's thesis, Sloan School of Management, MIT, June 1968.)

Reading 2

A History of Organization Development

Wendell L. French
Cecil H. Bell, Jr.

The history of organization development is rich with the contributions of behavioral scientists and practitioners, many of whom are well known, as well as the contributions of many people in client organizations. Even if we were aware of all the significant contributors, which we are not, we could not do justice to the richness of this history in a short essay. Therefore, all we can do is write about what we believe to be the central thrusts of that history, based on our research to date, and hope that the many people who are not mentioned will not be offended by our incompleteness. Our focus will be largely the origins of OD plus some discussion of current trends and the current extent of application.

Systematic organization development activities have a recent history and, to use the analogy of a mangrove tree, have at least four important trunk stems. One trunk stem consists of innovations in applying laboratory training insights to complex organizations. A second major stem is survey research and feedback methodology. Both stems are intertwined with a third, the emergence of action research. Paralleling these stems, and to some extent linked, is a fourth stem—the emergence of the Tavistock sociotechnical and socioclinical approaches. The key actors in these stems interact with each other and are influenced by experiences and concepts from many fields, as we will see.

Source: Wendell L. French and Cecil H. Bell, Jr., *Organization Development: Behavioral Science Interventions for Organization Improvement,* 6th ed. (Upper Saddle River, N.J.: Prentice Hall, 1999), pp. 32–61. Copyright ©1999. Reprinted by permission of Prentice Hall.

The Laboratory Training Stem

The T-Group

Laboratory training, essentially unstructured small-group situations in which participants learn from their own actions and the group's evolving dynamics, began to develop about 1946 from various experiments in using discussion groups to achieve changes in behavior in back-home situations. In particular, an Inter-Group Relations workshop held at the State Teachers College in New Britain, Connecticut, in the summer of 1946 influenced the emergence of laboratory training. This workshop was sponsored by the Connecticut Interracial Commission and the Research Center for Group Dynamics, then at MIT.

The Research Center for Group Dynamics (RCGD) was founded in 1945 under the direction of Kurt Lewin, a prolific theorist, researcher, and practitioner in interpersonal, group, intergroup, and community relationships.[1] Lewin had been recruited to MIT largely through the efforts of Douglas McGregor of the Sloan School of Management, who had convinced MIT President Carl Compton of the wisdom of establishing a center for group dynamics. Lewin's original staff included Marian Radke, Leon Festinger, Ronald Lippitt, and Dorwin Cartwright.[2] Lewin's field theory and his conceptualizing about group dynamics, change processes, and action research profoundly influenced the people associated with the various stems of OD.

Through a series of events at the New Britain workshop of 1946, what was later to be called the "T-group" ("T" for "training") began to emerge. The workshop staff consisted of Kurt Lewin,

Kenneth Benne, Leland Bradford, and Ronald Lippitt. The latter three served as leaders of "learning groups" (sometimes called "L-groups"). Each group, in addition to group members and a leader, had an observer who made notes about interactions among members. At the end of each day, the observers met with the staff and reported what they had seen. At the second or third evening session, three members of the workshop asked if they could sit in on the reporting session, and were encouraged to do so. One woman disagreed with the observer about the meaning of her behavior during the day's sessions, and a lively discussion ensued. The three workshop members then asked to return to the next reporting session, and, because of the lively and rich discussion, Lewin and the staff enthusiastically agreed. By the next evening, about half of the 50–60 members of the workshop attended the feedback session. These sessions soon became the most significant learning experiences of the conference.[3]

This experience led to the National Training Laboratory in Group Development, organized by Benne, Bradford, and Lippitt (Lewin died in early 1947). They held a three-week session during the summer of 1947 at the Gould Academy in Bethel, Maine.[4] Participants met with a trainer and an observer in Basic Skill Training Groups (later called T-groups) for a major part of each day. The 1947 laboratory was sponsored by the Research Center for Group Dynamics (MIT), the National Education Association (NEA), Teachers College of Columbia University, University of California at Los Angeles (UCLA), Springfield College, and Cornell University. The work of that summer evolved into the National Training Laboratory, later called NTL Institute for Applied Behavioral Science, and into contemporary T-group training. Out of the Bethel experiences and NTL grew a significant number of laboratory training centers sponsored by universities. One of the first was the Western Training Laboratory, headed by Paul Sheats and sponsored by UCLA. The Western Training Laboratory offered its first program in 1952.

In addition to Lewin and his work, extensive experience with role playing and Moreno's psychodrama influenced Bradford, Lippitt, and Benne's invention of the T-group and the subsequent emergence of OD.[5] Further, Bradford and Benne were influenced by John Dewey's philosophy of education, including concepts about learning and change and about the transactional nature of humans and their environment.[6] Benne, in collaboration with R. Bruce Raup and others, built on Dewey's philosophy, focusing on the processes by which people who differ reach policy agreements.[7] In addition, Benne was influenced by the works of Mary Follett, an early management theorist, including her ideas about integrative solutions to problems in organizations.[8]

As a footnote to the emergence of the T-group, the widespread use of flip-chart paper as a convenient way to record, retrieve, and display data in OD activities and in training sessions was invented by Ronald Lippitt and Lee Bradford during the 1946 New Britain sessions. Lippitt reports,

> The blackboards were very inadequate, and we needed to preserve a lot of the material we produced. So I went down to the local newspaper and got a donation of the end of press runs. The paper was still on the rollers. We had a "cutting bee" of Lee, Ken, myself and several others to roll the sheets out and cut them into standard sizes that we could put up in quantity with masking tape on the blackboards and walls of the classrooms. We took the practice back to MIT and I had the shop make some boards with clamps across the top. We hung them in our offices and the seminar room, and Lee did the same thing at the NEA in Washington. . . . The next summer at Bethel we had a large supply of cut newsprint and used some of the boards on easels, as well as using the walls.[9]

Bradford also reports that he and Ronald Lippitt used "strips of butcher paper" in their early work with organizations.[10]

In a sense, the T-group emerged from an awareness that had been growing for a decade or more, awareness of the importance of helping groups and group leaders focus on group and leadership *processes*. This growing awareness was particularly evident in adult education and group therapy.[11] As the use of the laboratory method evolved, stated goals of T-group experiences tended to include such statements as "(1) self-insight . . . , (2) understanding the conditions which inhibit or facilitate group functioning, (3) understanding interpersonal operations in groups, and (4) developing skills for diagnosing individual, group, and organizational behavior."[12]

While these insights and skills were practical and relevant for most participants, one driving force for the rapidly growing popularity of T-groups was probably their spiritual and therapeutic (therapy for normals) aspects. Art Kleiner captures these aspects:

> . . . toward the end of the two weeks (or three, or one), something wonderful and unfathomable would happen. It was rarely written down in the voluminous scholarly literature that NTLers created about T-Groups, but it kept drawing people back, session after session, and it prodded some participants to drop out of their management jobs to become educators and psychologists. After two or three weeks of soul-baring in a group of soul-barers, each person in the room would reach a moment when he or she discovered some core of redemption, some inner worth, deep within. The same feeling surged in those moments that, perhaps, surged when crowds gathered around Pelagius in Rome, and that surges whenever people gather to understand the deepest ties they hold in common.
>
> Some of the NLT participants described the experience as "unconditional love"; others, as "pure joy"; others, as a kind of mystical breakthrough or peak experience. . . . After you experienced that peak, you knew that the unconscious was not a Freudian cesspool spewing forth bitter legacies of childhood traumas. It was a source of Pelagian grace and hidden value, terrifying in its power and yet delightful in its beauty. It could only come forward when people learned, in a trusting, empathic environment like a T-Group, how to break free of their old ways of talking and thinking.

> A few NLT participants never felt the Pelagian grace rise within them. They sat in their T-Groups, puzzled and mildly disappointed, while everyone around them was swept up in a contact conversational high.[13]

Over the next decade, as trainers began to work with social systems of more permanency and complexity than T-groups, they began to experience considerable frustration in transferring laboratory behavioral skills and insights of individuals into solving problems in organizations. Personal skills learned in the "stranger" T-groups setting were difficult to transfer to complex organizations. However, the training of "teams" from the same organization emerged early at Bethel and undoubtedly was a link to the total organizational focus of Douglas McGregor, Herbert Shepard, Robert Blake, and Jane Mouton and subsequently the focus of Richard Beckhard, Chris Argyris, Jack Gibb, Warren Bennis, Eva Schindler-Rainman, and others.[14] All had been T-group trainers in NTL programs.

Robert Tannenbaum

Some of the earliest sessions of what would now be called "team building" were conducted by Robert Tannenbaum in 1952 and 1953 at the U.S. Naval Ordnance Test Station at China Lake, California.[15] According to Tannenbaum, the term *vertically structured groups* was used with groups dealing with "personal topics (such as departmental sociometrics, interpersonal relationships, communication, and self-analysis), and with organizational topics (such as deadlines, duties and responsibilities, policies and procedures, and—quite extensively—with interorganizational-group relations)."[16] These sessions, which stimulated a 1954 *Personnel* article by Tannenbaum, Kallejian, and Weschler, were conducted "with all managers of a given organizational unit present."[17] The more personally oriented dynamics of such sessions were described in a 1955 *Harvard Business Review* article by the same authors.[18]

Tannenbaum, along with Art Shedlin, also led what appears to be the first nondegree training program in OD, the Learning Community in Organizational Development at UCLA. This annual program was first offered as a full-time, ten-week, residential program, January–March 1967.[19]

Tannenbaum, who held a Ph.D. in Industrial Relations from the School of Business at the University of Chicago, was influenced early by Mary Parker Follett in management theory, V. V. Anderson's *Psychiatry in Industry,* Roethlisberger and Dickson's *Management and the Worker,* and Burleigh Gardner's *Human Relations in Industry.* He was on the planning committee for the Western Training Laboratory (WTL) and a staff member for the first session (1952). During that first session he co-trained with a psychiatric social worker who had attended a Bethel program, and in subsequent sessions, in his words, "co-trained with a psychiatrist, an educator, a clinical psychologist . . . and I learned much from them."[20]

Chris Argyris

In 1957, Chris Argyris, then a faculty member at Yale University (later at Harvard), was one of the first to conduct team building sessions with a CEO and the top executive team. Two of Argyris's early clients were IBM and Exxon. His early research and interventions with a top executive group are reported in his 1962 book *Interpersonal Competence and Organizational Effectiveness.*[21]

In 1950, while working on a Ph.D. at Cornell University, Argyris visited Bethel as a member of NTL's research staff in order to study T-groups. In his words, "I became fascinated with what I saw, and wanted to become a trainer. Several years later . . . I was invited to become a staff member."[22]

Argyris was later to make extensive contributions to theory and research on laboratory training, OD, and organizational learning. One of his several books on OD, *Intervention Theory and Method,* stands as a classic in the field.[23]

According to Argyris, three people had the greatest impact on his early career:

> Number one was Kurt Lewin.[24] . . . I was at
> Clark, finishing my undergraduate degree. I would
> go over (to MIT) and sit in on his seminars.[25] . . .

But his writings . . . had the greatest impact.[26] Next came Roger Barker, and his studies on psychological ecology and behavioral settings. I worked with Roger for several years. His greatest impact was not only on helping me to understand how to study behavioral settings more rigorously, but his whole approach to knowledge, which was to explore, to enquire, and to experiment. Finally, there was Bill Whyte at Cornell University, with whom I received my Ph.D. (in organizational behavior). Bill was not only a very thoughtful and encouraging advisor, but he was very smart and learned about field work. He had a sensitivity for what it meant to be an ethnographer that helped me to learn a lot about what to do in the field.[27]

Argyris interacted with many of the early leaders in the T-group and OD fields. For example, in referring to Douglas McGregor, he states, "I had many wonderful discussions with him in the advanced president's programs at Bethel and in Florida." In referring to Bradford, with whom he worked numerous times from 1950 on, he states that "he was, without any doubt, the person who helped make NTL come alive."[28]

Douglas McGregor

Beginning about 1957, Douglas McGregor, as a professor-consultant, working with Union Carbide, was one of the first behavioral scientists to address the transfer problem and to talk systematically about and to help implement the application of T-group skills in complex organizations.[29] John Paul Jones, who had come up through industrial relations at Union Carbide, in collaboration with McGregor and with the support of a corporate executive vice president and director, Birny Mason, Jr. (later president of the corporation), established a small internal consulting group. In large part, this group used behavioral science knowledge to help line managers and their subordinates learn how to be more effective in groups. McGregor's ideas were a dominant force in this consulting group; other behavioral scientists who influenced Jones's thinking were Rensis Likert and Mason Haire. Jones's organization was later called an "organization development group."[30]

Among the many influences on Douglas Mc-Gregor, of course, was Kurt Lewin, a colleague at MIT whom McGregor had helped recruit. It is also clear that he was influenced by Leland Bradford, Edwin Boring, Irving Knickerbocker, Jay Forrester, and Gordon Allport.[31] McGregor also must have been influenced by Carl Rogers, the leading theorist and practitioner in client-centered therapy, because McGregor assigned Rogers' writings to his classes at MIT.[32] McGregor's classic work, *The Human Side of Enterprise,* which has had a great impact on managers since its publication in 1960, cites an extensive list of psychologists, sociologists, and management theorists, including Peter Drucker.[33] (See the discussion of Richard Beckhard, which refers to the influence of McGregor's consulting work at General Mills on *The Human Side of Enterprise.*) (As a historical footnote, McGregor was president of Antioch College from 1948 to 1954 after his first tour as a professor at MIT. Subsequent to this college presidency, McGregor returned to MIT to start a program in organizational studies.[34])

Herbert Shepard

During the same year, 1957, introductions by Douglas McGregor led to Herbert Shepard's joining the employee relations department of Esso Standard Oil (now Exxon) as a research associate. Shepard was to have a major impact on the emergence of OD. Although we will focus mainly on Shepard's work at Esso, we also want to note that Shepard was later involved in community development activities and, in 1960, at the Case Institute of Technology, founded the first doctoral program devoted to training OD specialists.

Before joining Esso, Shepard had completed his doctorate at MIT and stayed for a time as a faculty member in the Industrial Relations Section. Among influences on Shepard were Roethlisberger and Dickson's *Management and the Worker* (1939) and a biography of Clarence Hicks. (As a consultant to Standard Oil, Hicks had helped develop participative approaches to personnel management and labor relations.) Shepard was also influenced by Farrell Toombs,

who had been a counselor at the Hawthorne plant and had trained under Carl Rogers. In addition, Shepard was heavily influenced by the writings of Kurt Lewin and others of NTL. He attended an NTL lab in 1950 and subsequently was a staff member in many of its programs.[35]

In 1958 and 1959 Shepard launched three experiments in organization development at major Esso refineries: Bayonne, New Jersey; Baton Rouge, Louisiana; and Bayway, Texas. At Bayonne, he conducted an interview survey that was discussed with top management. The survey was followed by a series of three-day laboratories for all members of management.[36] Paul Buchanan, who had worked earlier at the Naval Ordnance Test Station and more recently had been using a somewhat similar approach in Republic Aviation, collaborated with Shepard at Bayonne and subsequently joined the Esso staff.

Herbert Shepard and Robert Blake

At Baton Rouge, Robert Blake joined Shepard, and the two initiated a series of two-week laboratories attended by all members of "middle" management. At first, they tried to combine the case method with the laboratory method, but their designs soon emphasized T-groups, organizational exercises, and lectures. One innovation in this training program was an emphasis on intergroup as well as interpersonal relations. Although working on interpersonal problems affecting work performance was clearly an organizational effort, between-group problem solving had even greater organization development implications because it involved a broader and more complex segment of the organization.

At Baton Rouge, efforts to involve top management failed, and as a result follow-up resources for implementing organization development were not available. By the time the Bayway program started, two fundamental OD lessons had been learned: the requirement for top management's active involvement in and leadership of the program and the need for on-the-job application.

Bayway brought two significant innovations. First, Shepard, Blake, and Murray Horwitz used the instrumented laboratory, which Blake and Jane Mouton had been developing in social psychology classes at the University of Texas and which they later developed into the Managerial Grid approach to organization development.[37] (An essential dimension of the instrumented lab is feedback based on measurements of group and individual behavior during sessions.[38]) Second, at Bayway more resources were devoted to team development, consultation, intergroup conflict resolution, and so forth than were devoted to laboratory training of "cousins," that is, organization members from different departments. As Robert Blake stated, "It was learning to *reject* T-group stranger-type labs that permitted OD to come into focus," and it was intergroup projects, in particular, that "triggered real OD."[39]

Robert Blake and Jane Mouton

Several influences on Robert Blake up to that point were important in the emergence of OD. While at Berea College majoring in psychology and philosophy (later an M.A., University of Virginia, and a Ph.D., University of Texas), Blake was strongly influenced by the works of Korzybski and the general semanticists and found that "seeing discrete things as representative of a continuous series was much more stimulating and rewarding than just seeing two things as 'opposites.'" This thinking contributed in later years to Blake's conceptualization of the Managerial Grid with Jane Mouton and to their intergroup research on win-lose dynamics. This intergroup research and the subsequent design of their intergroup conflict management workshops were also heavily influenced by Muzafer Sherif's fundamental research on intergroup dynamics.[40] Jane Mouton's influence on Blake's thinking and on the development of the Grid stemmed partly, in her words, "from my undergraduate work (at Texas) in pure mathematics and physics which emphasized the significance of measurement, experimental design, and a scientific approach to phenomena."[41] (Mouton later attained an M.A. from the University of Virginia and a Ph.D. from the University of Texas.)

During World War II, Blake served in the Psychological Research Unit of the Army Air Force where he interacted with many behavioral scientists, including sociologists. This experience contributed to his interest in "looking at the system rather than the individuals within the system on an isolated one-by-one basis."[42] (This system-wide approach is probably one of many links between systems concepts or systems theory and OD.)

Another major influence on Blake was the work of John Bowlby, a medical member of the Tavistock Clinic in London, who was working in family group therapy. After completing his Ph.D. work in clinical psychology, Blake went to England for 16 months in 1948 and 1949 to study, observe, and do research at Tavistock. As Blake states it,

> Bowlby had the clear notion that treating mental illness of an individual out of context was an . . . ineffective way of aiding a person. . . . As a result, John was unprepared to see patients, particularly children, in isolation from their family settings. He would see the intact family: mother, father, siblings. . . . I am sure you can see from what I have said that if you substitute the word organization for family and substitute the concept of development for therapy, the natural next step in my mind was organization development.[43]

Among others at Tavistock who influenced Blake were Wilfred Bion, Henry Ezriel, Eric Trist, and Elliott Jaques.

After returning from Tavistock and taking an appointment at Harvard, Blake joined the staff for the summer NTL programs at Bethel. His first assignment was joint responsibility for a T-group with John R. P. French. Blake was a member of the Bethel staff from 1951 to 1957 and continued after that with NTL labs for managers at Harriman House, Harriman, New York. Among other influences on Blake were Jacob Moreno's action orientation to training through the use of psychodrama and sociodrama and E. C. Tolman's notions of purposive behavior in humans.[44]

Richard Beckhard

Richard Beckhard, another major figure in the emergence and extension of the OD field, came from a career in the theater. In his words,

I came out of a whole different world—the theater—and went to NTL in 1950 as a result of some discussions with Lee Bradford and Ron Lippitt. At that time they were interested in improving the effectiveness of the communications in large meetings and I became involved as head of the general sessions program. But I also got hooked on the whole movement. I made a career change and set up the meetings organization, "Conference Counselors." My first major contact was the staging of the 1950 White House conference on children and youth. . . . I was brought in to stage the large general sessions with six thousand people. . . . I had been doing a lot of large convention participative discussion type things and had written on the subject. . . . At the same time I joined the NTL summer staff. . . . My mentors in the field were Lee Bradford, in the early days, and Ron Lippitt and later, Ren Likert, and very particularly, Doug McGregor, who became both mentor, friend, father figure. . . . and in the later years, brother. Doug had left MIT and was at Antioch as president. . . . Doug and I began appearing on similar programs. One day coming back on the train from Cincinnati to Boston, Doug asked if I was interested in joining MIT. . . .

In the period 1958–63, I had worked with him (McGregor) on two or three projects. He brought me to Union Carbide, where I replaced him in working with John Paul Jones, and later, George Murray and the group. We (also) worked together at . . . Pennsylvania Bell and . . . at General Mills.[45]

Beckhard worked with McGregor at General Mills in 1959 or 1960, where McGregor was working with Dewey Balsch, vice president of personnel and industrial relations, in an attempt to facilitate "a total organizational culture change program which today might be called quality of work life or OD." Beckhard goes on to say, "The issues that were being worked were relationships between workers and supervision; roles of super-

vision and management at various levels; participative management for real. . . . This experience was one of the influences on Doug's original paper, 'The Human Side of Enterprise' . . . and from which the book emerged a year or so later."[46]

Beckhard developed one of the first major nondegree training programs in OD, NTL's Program for Specialists in Organizational Training and Development (PSOTD). The first program was an intensive four-week session held in the summer of 1967 at Bethel, Maine, the same year that UCLA launched its Learning Community in OD. Core staff members the first year in the NTL program were Beckhard as dean, Warner Burke, and Fritz Steele. Additional resource persons the first year were Herbert Shepard, Sheldon Davis, and Chris Argyris.

In addition, Beckhard along with McGregor, Rensis Likert, Chris Argyris, Robert Blake, Lee Bradford, and Jack Gibb, founded NTL's Management Work Conferences. These conferences are essentially laboratory training experiences for middle managers. As an extension of this program, Beckhard was also active in developing and conducting NTL's senior executive conferences and presidents' labs.[47]

Warren Bennis

One of the major figures associated with the evolution of the OD field has been Warren Bennis. As described in Art Kleiner's book, *The Age of Heretics,* Warren Bennis has been a ". . . lecturer, professor, essayist, university president, author of prominent books on leadership, dreamer of grand visions, and the only NTLer to actually take the helm of a large organization and try to reshape it from the top." Bennis had been an industrial management professor in Douglas McGregor's department at MIT, a T-group trainer, and a participant in a number of the early major OD consulting projects, including one at the U.S. State Department.[48]

During his career, Bennis became vice president for academic affairs at State University of New York at Buffalo, and then president of the

University of Cincinnati. His associates and mentors, particularly in the earlier years, included Douglas McGregor, Ed Schein, Mason Haire, Abraham Maslow, Carl Rogers, Kenneth Benne, Herb Shepard, Leland Bradford, Peter Drucker, and Robert Chin.[49] He was also influenced by the labor economist George Schultz (later to be Secretary of Labor and Secretary of State), Elton Mayo, and Henry Stack Sullivan. Some of his more notable publications include the book *The Planning of Change,*[50] written with Kenneth Benne and Robert Chin, and the essay "Democracy Is Inevitable,"[51] coauthored with Philip Slater.

Eva Schindler-Rainman

Probably one of the first persons to be an NLT staff member doing OD work and having been trained almost exclusively in the social work field was Eva Schindler-Rainman. Schindler-Rainman was awarded both a masters and doctorate from the University of Southern California with specialties in group work, organizational behavior, and community organization. While employed as director of personnel and training for the Los Angeles Girl Scouts Council, in the early 1950s she attended one of the first events of the Western Training Laboratory. Her T-group trainers there were Gordon Hearn and Marguerite Vanderworker.

About 1959, Schindler-Rainman was on the staff of an NTL-sponsored Community Development Laboratory at UCLA's Arrowhead Conference Center where she was a T-group co-trainer with Leland Bradford. Others on the staff were Warren Schmidt, Kenneth Benne, and Max Birnbaum.

Reflecting on transferring her social work, community development experiences, and T-group training to the emerging field of OD, Schindler-Rainman observes

> . . . I would say that I began consciously doing OD work when I was the Director of Training and Personnel for the Girl Scouts. . . . I did OD-type work with school districts, organizing a coordinating council that made it possible to bring in-service classes from UCLA to teachers from all of those districts.[52]

Schindler-Rainman goes on to describe her work with the Health Department in Los Angeles, and the Education Extension department at UCLA where she was at one time assistant director. Along with Charles Ferguson, she later became one of the associate directors of the Department of Conferences at UCLA, headed by Warren Schmidt. She also worked with Robert Tannenbaum, Irv Weschler, Joan Lasko, and Jerry Reisel. In addition, she worked with Richard Beckhard, who was doing a series of interventions with the California Cancer Society.

Schindler-Rainman's formal link to NTL came with a staff assignment at Bethel about 1966. Ronald Lippitt was the dean. Other staff members included Dorothy Mial, Cyril Mill, and Matthew Miles. Some of the other women with whom Schindler-Rainman worked, in addition to Dorothy Mial, were Edith Seashore, Miriam Ritvo, and Peggy Lippitt. Referring to the women in the field, Schindler-Rainman recounts, "Edie [Edith Seashore] was the person doing more OD interventions than anybody else as far as I know."[53] (For more on Edith Seashore, see Kleiner, *The Age of Heretics.*[54])

Schindler-Rainman worked with a wide range of clients, both in the United States and internationally. A few of her well-known publications are *The Creative Volunteer Community: A Collection of Writings,*[55] *Building the Collaborative Community,*[56] *The Volunteer Community,*[57] and *Team Training for Community Change.*[58] (The latter three were coauthored with Ronald Lippitt.) Schindler-Rainman's extensive professional training, her collaboration with a number of key men and women in the early days of NTL and the OD movement, and her early and extensive contribution to the community development movement clearly identify her as one of the pioneers in the laboratory training stem of OD.

The Term *Organization Development*

It is not entirely clear who coined the term *organization development,* but the term likely emerged more or less simultaneously in two or three places through the works of Robert Blake, Herbert Shepard, Jane Mouton, Douglas McGregor, and Richard Beckhard.[59] The phrase *development group* had been used earlier by Blake and Mouton in connection with human relations training at the University of Texas, and it appeared in their 1956 document distributed for use in the Baton Rouge experiment.[60] (The same phrase appeared in a Mouton and Blake article first published in the journal *Group Psychotherapy* in 1957.[61]) The Baton Rouge T-groups run by Shepard and Blake were called *development groups,*[62] and this program of T-groups was called "organization development" to distinguish it from the complementary management development programs already underway.[63]

Referring to his consulting with McGregor at General Mills, Beckhard gives this account of the term emerging there:

> At that time we wanted to put a label on the program at General Mills. . . . We clearly didn't want to call it management development because it was total organization-wide, nor was it human relations training although there was a component of that in it. We didn't want to call it organization improvement because that's a static term, so we labeled the program "Organization Development," meaning system-wide change effort.[64]

Thus, the term emerged as a way of distinguishing a different mode of working with organizations and as a way of highlighting its developmental, systemwide, dynamic thrust.

The Role of Human Resources Executives

It is of considerable significance that organization development efforts in three of the first corporations to be extensively involved, Union Carbide, Esso, and General Mills, included human resources people seeing themselves in new roles. At Union Carbide, John Paul Jones, in industrial relations, now saw himself as a behavioral science consultant to other managers.[65] At Esso, the headquarters human relations research division began to view itself as an internal consulting group offering services to field managers rather than as a research group developing reports for top management.[66] At General Mills, the vice president of personnel and industrial relations, Dewey Balsch, saw his role as including leadership in conceptualizing and coordinating changes in the culture of the total organization.[67] Thus, in the history of OD we see both external consultants and internal staff departments departing from their traditional roles and collaborating in a new approach to organization improvement.

The Survey Research and Feedback Stem

Survey research and feedback,[68] a specialized form of action research (see Chapter 7) constitutes the second major stem in the history of organization development. The history of this stem revolves around the techniques and approach developed over a period of years by staff members at the Survey Research Center (SRC) of the University of Michigan.

Rensis Likert

The SRC was founded in 1946 after Rensis Likert, director of the Division of Program Surveys of the Federal Bureau of Agricultural Economics, and other key members of the division moved to Michigan. Likert held a Ph.D. in psychology from Columbia, and his dissertation, *A Technique for the Measurement of Attitudes,* was the classic study that developed the widely used five-point Likert scale. After completing his degree and teaching at Columbia for awhile, Likert worked for the Life Insurance Agency Management Association. There he conducted research on leadership, motivation, morale, and productivity. He then moved to the U.S. Department of Agriculture, where his Division of Program Surveys furthered a more scientific approach to survey research in its work with various federal departments, including the Office of War Information.[69] In 1948 after helping to develop and direct the Survey Research Center, Likert became the director of a new Institute for Social Research, which included both the SRC and the Research Center for Group Dynamics. The latter had moved to Michigan from MIT after Lewin's death.

Floyd Mann, Rensis Likert, and Others

Part of the emergence of survey research and feedback was based on refinements made by SRC staff members in survey methodology. Another part was the evolution of feedback methodology. As related by Rensis Likert,

> In 1947, I was able to interest the Detroit Edison Company in a company-wide study of employee perceptions, behavior, reactions and attitudes which was conducted in 1948. Floyd Mann, who had joined the SRC staff in 1947, was the study director on the project. I provided general direction. Three persons from D.E.: Blair Swartz, Sylvanus Leahy and Robert Schwab with Mann and me worked on the problem of how the company could best use the data from the survey to bring improvement in management and performance. This led to the development and use of the survey-feedback method. Floyd particularly played a key role in this development. He found that when the survey data were reported to a manager (or supervisor) and he or she failed to discuss the results with subordinates and failed to plan with them what the manager and others should do to bring improvement, little change occurred. On the other hand, when the manager discussed the results with subordinates and planned with them what to do to bring improvement, substantial favorable changes occurred.[70]

Another aspect of the Detroit Edison study was the process of feeding back data from an attitude survey to the participating departments in what Mann calls an "interlocking chain of conferences."[71] Additional insights are provided by Baumgartel, who participated in the project and who drew the following conclusions from the Detroit Edison study:

> The results of this experimental study lend support to the idea that an intensive, group discussion procedure for utilizing the results of an employee questionnaire survey can be an effective tool for introducing positive change in a business organization. It may be that the effectiveness of this method, in comparison to traditional training courses, is that it deals with the system of human relationships as a whole (superior and subordinate can change together) and it deals with each manager, supervisor, and employee in the context of his own job, his own problems, and his own work relationships.[72]

Links between the Laboratory Training Stem and the Survey Feedback Stem

As early as 1940, links occurred between people who were later to be key figures in the laboratory training stem of OD and people who were to be key figures in the survey feedback stem. These links, which continued over the years, were undoubtedly of significance in the evolution of both stems. Of particular interest are the links between Likert and Lewin and between Likert and key figures in the laboratory training stem of OD. As Likert states, "I met Lewin at the APA annual meeting at State College, Pa., I believe in 1940. When he came to Washington during the War, I saw him several times and got to know him and his family quite well."[73] In 1944 Likert arranged a dinner at which Douglas McGregor and Kurt Lewin explored the feasibility of a group dynamics center at MIT.[74]

Likert further refers to McGregor: "I met McGregor during the war and came to know him very well after Lewin had set up the RCGD at MIT. After the War, Doug became very interested in the research on leadership and organizations that we were doing in the Institute for Social Research. He visited us frequently and I saw him often at Antioch and at MIT after he returned." Likert goes on to refer to the first NTL lab for managers held at Arden House in 1956: "Douglas McGregor and I helped Lee Bradford launch it. . . . Staff members in the 1956 lab were: Beckhard, Benne, Bradford, Gordon Lippitt, Malott, Shepard and I. Argyris, Blake and McGregor joined the staff for the 1957 Arden House lab."[75]

Argyris refers to Likert:

Rensis Likert was also a leader in the field when I was a graduate student, and I had the highest respect for him and his commitment to trying to connect theory with practice. Indeed, I've always been a bit sad to see how many of his colleagues, who saw themselves as mere researchers, at times would downplay Rensis' commitment to practice. They saw him as being too . . . committed to the world of practice. I never felt that. I felt that it was the combination of practice and theory that made him an important member of our community. I would put Lewin first on that dimension, and Ren Likert and Doug McGregor next, each in his own way making important contributions.[76]

Links between group dynamics and survey feedback people were extensive, of course, after the RCGD moved to Michigan with the encouragement of Rensis Likert and members of the SRC. Among the top people in the RCGD who moved to Michigan were Leon Festinger, Dorwin Cartwright, Ronald Lippitt, and John R. P. French, Jr. Cartwright, selected by the group to be the director of the RCGD, was particularly knowledgeable about survey research, since he had been on the staff of the Division of Program Surveys with Rensis Likert and others during World War II.[77]

The Action Research Stem

In earlier chapters we briefly described action research as a collaborative, client-consultant inquiry. Chapter 7 describes four versions of action research, one of which, participant action research, is used with the most frequency in OD. The laboratory training stem in the history of OD has a heavy component of action research; the survey feedback stem is the history of a specialized form of action research; and Tavistock projects have had a strong action research thrust, as we will discuss shortly.

Because we will treat the history of action research in some detail later, we will mention only a few aspects here. For example, William F. Whyte and Edith L. Hamilton used action research in their work with Chicago's Tremont Hotel in 1945

and 1956; John Collier, commissioner of Indian Affairs, described action research in a 1945 publication; Kurt Lewin and his students conducted numerous action research projects in the mid-1940s and early 1950s. The work of these and other scholars and practitioners in inventing and utilizing action research was basic in the evolution of OD.

The Sociotechnical and Socioclinical Stem

A fourth stem in the history of OD is the evolution of socioclinical and sociotechnical approaches to helping groups and organizations. Parallel to the work of the RCGD, the SRC, and NTL was the work of the Tavistock Clinic in England. The clinic was founded in 1920 as an outpatient facility to provide psychotherapy based on psychoanalytic theory and insights from the treatment of battle neurosis in World War I. A group focus emerged early in the work of Tavistock in the context of family therapy in which the child and the parent received treatment simultaneously.[78] (See the reference earlier in this chapter to John Bowlby's influence on Robert Blake and, in turn, the emergence of the concept of "organization development.") The action research mode also emerged at Tavistock in attempts to give practical help to families, organizations, and communities.

W. R. Bion, John Rickman, and Others

The professional staff of the Tavistock Clinic was extensively influenced by such innovations as World War II applications of social psychology to psychiatry, the work of W. R. Bion and John Rickman and others in group therapy, Lewin's notions about the "social field" in which a problem was occurring, and Lewin's theory and experience with action research. Bion, Rickman, and others had been involved with the six-week "Northfield Experiment" at a military hospital near Birmingham during World War II. In this experiment each soldier was required to join a group that performed some tasks such as handicraft or map reading as well as discussed feelings, interpersonal relations, and administrative and managerial problems. Insights from this experiment carried over into Bion's theory of group behavior.[79]

Eric Trist

A clear historical and conceptual connection can be made between the group dynamics field and the sociotechnical approaches to assisting organizations. Tavistock's sociotechnical approach is particularly significant in that it grew out of Eric Trist's 1947 visit to a British coal mine at Haighmoor; his insights as to the relevance of Lewin's work on group dynamics and Bion's work on leaderless groups resulted in a new approach to solving mine problems.[80] Trist was also influenced by the systems concepts of Von Bertalanffy and Andras Angyal.[81]

At Haighmoor, Trist observed miners working in teams—teams that the miners themselves had organized—which was in stark contrast to the typical assembly-line structure in the mines of that day. According to Kleiner, each team ran the job and sold the coal, and would take care of team members' families in the case of an accident. Each miner might handle several different jobs, and team members were compensated on the basis of the team tonnage produced. The results of the team approach were remarkable in terms of safety and productivity.[82]

Trist's subsequent experiments in work design and the use of semiautonomous work teams in coal mining were the forerunners of other work redesign experiments in various industries in Europe, India, Australia, and the United States. In these experiments, terms such as *industrial democracy, open systems,* and *sociotechnical systems* were used by Trist and his colleagues, including Fred Emery.[83] (Emery's extensive collaboration with Eric Trist includes the development of "Search Conferences," to be discussed later.)

Tavistock–U.S. Links

Tavistock leaders, including Trist and Bion, had frequent contact with Kurt Lewin, Rensis Likert, Chris Argyris, and others in the United States.

One product of this collaboration was the decision to publish the journal *Human Relations* as a joint publication between Tavistock and MIT's Research Center for Group Dynamics.[84] Some Americans prominent in the emergence and evolution of the OD field, for example, Robert Blake, as we noted earlier, and Warren Bennis,[85] studied at Tavistock. Chris Argyris held several seminars with Tavistock leaders in 1954.[86]

The sociotechnical approach focused on the nonexecutive ranks of organizations and especially the redesign of work. The focus on teams and the use of action research and participation was consistent with evolving OD approaches. Some contemporary quality of work life (QWL) and some total quality management (TQM) programs are amalgamations of OD, sociotechnical, and other approaches.

The Changing Context

Even though it is important to understand how OD emerged, it is also important to understand the changing milieu in which contemporary OD activities are occurring. That context has changed dramatically throughout the 1980s and 1990s. As authors are prone to say, the environment has become increasingly "turbulent." In the United States, the pace of technological innovation, company mergers, acquisitions, leveraged buyouts, bankruptcies, success stories, downsizings, and changes in law has intensified. At the same time, thousands of small companies are born each year. Globalization of companies is commonplace. Worldwide, many previously centralized and autocratic societies are moving toward creating democratic institutions and privatizing business and industry. These changes create opportunities for OD applications, but also stretch the capabilities of leaders and OD practitioners to the utmost.

In this context what might be called *second-generation OD* is evolving. Practitioners still rely on the first-generation techniques of OD that are highly relevant to adaptive, incremental change, such as action research, a focus on teams, team building, the use of facilitators, process consultation, survey feedback, intergroup problem solving, sociotechnical systems approaches to job design, and participative management. Indeed, theory building and/or research as well as application relative to all of these OD basics is growing. But the field is reaching far beyond these first-generation approaches in the sense that many applications of OD are now more complicated and more multifaceted.

Second-Generation OD

Practitioners and researchers are giving considerable attention to emerging concepts, interventions, and areas of application that might be called second-generation OD. Each, to some extent, overlaps with some or all of the others. Second-generation OD, in particular, has a focus on organizational transformation.

Interest in Organizational Transformation

More and more, practitioners and scholars are talking and writing about "organizational transformation." Amir Levy and Uri Merry give one of the most complete explorations of this topic in their book, *Organizational Transformation.* They define the term as follows: "Second-order change (organization transformation) is a multidimensional, multi-level, qualitative, discontinuous, radical organizational change involving a paradigmatic shift."[87]

Increasingly, OD professionals distinguish between the more modest, or evolutionary, efforts toward organization improvement and those that are massive and, in a sense, revolutionary. For example, Nadler and Tushman refer to "transitions" on the one hand, and "frame bending" on the other.[88] Goodstein and Burke contrast "fine tuning" and "fundamental, large-scale change in the organization's strategy and culture."[89] Barczak, Smith, and Wilemon differentiate "adaptive, incremental change" from "large-scale change."[90] Beckhard and Pritchard contrast "incremental" change strategies and "fundamental" change strategies.[91] Organizational transformation is seen as requiring more demands on top leadership, more visioning, more experimenting, more time, and the simultaneous management of many additional variables.

Interest in Organizational Culture

Efforts to define, measure, and change organizational culture have become more sophisticated. Schein in particular has written extensively about culture.[92] He has devised interventions to help leaders and employees identify those cultural assumptions that will assist the organization in attaining its goals and those that hinder goal attainment. Making such distinctions is done through a joint exploration to identify sequentially the organization's *artifacts,* such as office layout and status symbols; the *values* underlying these artifacts; and the *assumptions* behind those values.[93] Others have helped organizations focus on culture through the use of questionnaires aimed at identifying actual and desired norms. Participants then make agreements about new norms and how to monitor and reinforce the changes.[94] (For greater detail, see Chapter 11.)

Interest in the Learning Organization

The works of Argyris,[95] Argyris and Schon,[96] and Senge have stimulated considerable interest in the conditions under which individuals, teams, and organizations learn. Argyris, for example, has focused on the defensive routines of organizational members, or "master programs in their heads that tell them how to deal with embarrassment and threat." Basically, according to Argyris, individuals tend to follow these rules:

1. Bypass embarrassment and threat whenever possible.
2. Act as though you are not bypassing them.
3. Don't discuss steps 1 and 2 while they are happening.
4. Don't discuss the undiscussability of the undiscussable.[97]

Workshops with top management teams are designed to tackle simultaneously major tasks such as strategy formulation plus learning how to recognize defensive routines that hinder improvements in communications and the quality of team decision making.[98]

Senge writes extensively about the importance of systems thinking ("the fifth discipline") in organizations, and about the learning disabilities that plague organizations. One learning disability, for example, is focusing on one's own job exclusively with little sense of responsibility for the collective product. Another is blaming the "enemy out there" for things that are wrong, whether it's another department in the same organization or a competitor overseas.[99] Senge is noted for workshops in which he uses games and exercises to create an awareness of these disabilities and to develop different ways of thinking about complex problems.[100]

Intensified Interest in Teams

A focus on intact work teams and other team configurations has been central to OD since the emergence of the field, but recent years have seen a widening and deepening interest in teams, especially what are called high-performance teams, cross-functional teams, and self-managed teams. Interest has intensified particularly in self-managed or self-directed teams. This interest has accelerated due to converging pressures on organizations to improve quality, to become more flexible, to reduce layers of management, and to enhance employee morale.[101]

Laboratory training methods have proved highly useful in training team members in effective membership and leadership behaviors, and in training supervisors and managers in the arts of delegation and empowerment. Furthermore, many organizations use team-building approaches to help self-managed teams and cross-functional teams get started. In addition, as self-managed teams have assumed many functions previously performed by management, supervisors and middle managers have used team-building approaches

within their own ranks to help reconceptualize their own roles.

Interest in Total Quality Management (TQM)

The past decade has seen a mushrooming of interest in total quality management worldwide, and then perhaps some decline in application as both successes and failures have been reported. Applications that have been successful appear to have some ingredients in common with OD efforts.

Ciampa, who acknowledges the pioneering contributions of Joseph Juran, W. Edwards Deming, and Armand Feigenbaum to the development of TQM,[102] provides a clear statement on the relationship between TQM and OD. First, his definition: "Total Quality is typically a companywide effort seeking to install and make permanent a climate where employees continuously improve their ability to provide on demand products and services that customers will find of particular value."[103] He then goes on to say that one element that separates successful TQ efforts from less successful ones is

> . . . a particular set of values about the individual and the individual's role in the organization. TQ efforts in these companies encourage true employee involvement, demand teamwork, seek to push decision-making power to lower levels in the company, and reduce barriers between people. . . . These values are at the core of Organization Development (OD), as well.[104]

Burke also comments on the contribution OD can make to TQM efforts. Focusing on the OD practitioner, he states: ". . . the quality movement, to be successful, is highly dependent on effective process—and process is the OD practitioner's most important product."[105] (For more on OD and TQM, see Chapter 12.)

Interest in Visioning and Future Search

Interventions designed to help organizational members look to the future—visioning—are not new to OD, but renewed interest has developed using interventions to look at trends projected into the future and their organizational implications. Marvin Weisbord, for example, has built on the work and experience of Ronald Lippitt and Edward Lindaman,[106] Ronald Fox, Ronald Lippitt, and Eva Schindler-Rainman,[107] and Eric Trist and Fred Emery[108] to develop "future search conferences." In a two- or three-day conference, participants are asked to "(a) build a data base, (b) look at it together, (c) interpret what they find, and (d) draw conclusions for action."[109] This last part of the conference asks participants to develop next action steps and a structure for carrying them out, including task forces and specific assignments.[110]

Senge believes that "the origin of the vision is much less important than the process whereby it comes to be shared." He strongly urges that "shared visions" be based on encouraging organizational members to develop and share their own personal visions, and he claims that a vision is not truly shared "until it connects with the personal visions of people throughout the organization."[111] This type of connection obviously requires OD-like processes to implement.

Rediscovering Large Meetings and Getting the "Whole System" in the Room

As described earlier, one contributing factor in the emergence of the OD movement was the experience of people such as Leland Bradford, Ronald Lippitt, and Richard Beckhard in improving the effectiveness of large meetings. Early on, Beckhard wrote an article entitled "The Confrontation Meeting," which was really about getting the total management group of an organization together in a one-day session to diagnose the state of the system and to make plans for quickly improving conditions.[112] In recent years, Marvin Weisbord and others have written about the importance of OD consultants "getting the whole system in the room." For example, with reference to future search conferences, he advises that such conferences involve all of top

management and "people from as many functions and levels as feasible." Again, the final products are action plans and specific assignments to carry the process forward.[113]

Other Directions and Areas of Interest

Several other areas are notable in second-generation OD. Assistance in developing diversity awareness workshops and in "managing" and "valuing" diversity has been much in evidence recently. Expanded interest in sociotechnical systems design, interrelated with interest in self-managed teams and in total quality management, has been apparent. OD applications to quality of work life (QWL) programs have continued but are less evident because of the heightened attention to TQM. Partially as a result of a focus on teams and teamwork, a great deal of attention has been directed toward developing congruent reward systems, including productivity gainsharing plans and skills-based pay plans. Research and conceptualizing about action research, process consultation, and third-party roles have continued and perhaps increased. There is renewed interest in the concept of community as well as spirituality relative to organizational transformation and high-performance organizations. Considerable work has been done with "appreciative inquiry" workshops. (In these sessions, participants focus on the best of "what is" and use these themes as a springboard for focusing on "what might be.")[114] Interest in physical settings continues among OD practitioners.

Widespread business and media interest in *reengineering*—called by various names such as *business process reengineering* and *core process redesign*[115]—has caught the attention of OD practitioners and theorists. OD processes and values appear *not* to underly most reengineering efforts, and the almost-stampede by business and industry to embrace reengineering raises a number of issues pertaining to the role that OD practitioners should or should not play relative to this phenomenon. (See Chapter 12.)

All these areas are fruitful areas for OD theory, research, and practice. However, with the diffusion of OD techniques into so many areas, identifying what is and what is not OD becomes more difficult. Thus, the importance of examining the assumptions and the processes underlying various improvement efforts cannot be overstated—not because OD or the term "OD" is inherently sacred—because the fundamental building blocks of OD as defined in this book are vital ingredients, we believe, to long-term organizational effectiveness and to participant satisfaction and development.

Extent of Application

Applications emerging from one or more of the stems described previously are evident in contemporary organization development efforts occurring in many countries, including England, Japan, Norway, Italy, Belgium, Switzerland, Canada, Sweden, Germany, Finland, Australia, New Zealand, the Philippines, Mexico, France, Venezuela, and the Netherlands, as well as in the United States. Among the large number of organizations in America that have at one time or another embarked on organization development efforts are Union Carbide and Exxon (the first two companies), Connecticut General Insurance Company, Hewlett-Packard, Tektronix, Graphic Controls, Equitable Life Assurance Company, Digital Equipment Corporation, Procter & Gamble, Microelectronics and Computer Technology Corporation (MCC), Mountain Bell Telephone, Searle Laboratories, the Boeing Company, Bankers Trust, Ford Motor Company, Heinz Foods, Polaroid, Sun Oil, and TRW Inc.

Applications have varied, with the total organization involved in many instances, but with only some divisions or plants in others. Further, some efforts have moved ahead rapidly, only to flounder at a later time. In many situations, OD approaches have become an ongoing way of managing with little program visibility and under different terminology. Thus, the extent of application is sometimes difficult to report with any precision.

Applications at TRW Space & Electronics Group (S&EG) were of major significance in the emergence and history of OD. Among the key figures in the beginnings of OD there in the early 1960s (then called TRW Systems Group) were Jim Dunlap, director of industrial relations; Shel Davis, who was later promoted to that position; Ruben Mettler, president; and Herb Shepard. T-group labs conducted by internal trainers, NTL, and UCLA staff members were also important in providing impetus to the effort in its early phases. Early applications of OD at TRW Systems included team building, intergroup team building, interface laboratories between departments and between company and customers, laboratory training, career assessment workshops, and organization redesign and structuring for improved productivity and quality of working life.[116] (For more on the life of Shel Davis and his contribution to the OD field, see the essay by Celeste A. Coruzzi. In that essay, Warner Burke refers to him as "the pioneer internal OD consultant."[117])

After successful applications in the 1960s, OD activities at TRW declined during the 1970s and 1980s. However, according to Michael Thiel, director of leadership and organization effectiveness at S&EG, "radical structural change within the defense industry has forced TRW (and other defense contractors) to critically examine and shift basic operating paradigms."[118] Thiel goes on to say:

> This has led to the rebirth of "OD-like" activities as part of cultural change and organization transformation efforts. Since 1989, S&EG has been actively pursuing the creation/implementation of a total quality culture, incorporating continuous process improvement, employee empowerment, performance management, and the use of concurrent engineering/integrated product development with cross-functional teams. OD methodologies such as organizational diagnosis, values clarification, offsite meetings, sensing, etc. have been used where appropriate in these activities. Other tools include team facilitation, team-based experimental education and survey/feedback systems.

Most of these "organization effectiveness" interventions are spearheaded by the Human Resources organization, either HR generalists, or specialists from my office. In addition, there are a number of line/technical managers involved in various facets (specifically team facilitation/process improvement, and self-managed work teams).[119]

Business and industrial organizations are by no means the only kinds of institutions involved. Applications can be made, for example, in public school systems; colleges; medical schools; social welfare agencies; police departments; professional associations; governmental units at the local, county, state, and national levels; the White House;[120] various health care delivery systems; churches; Native American tribes; and the U.S. military.

The history of OD in the U.S. military is beyond the scope of this book, but OD activities in the military services have been extensive. For example, at one time, the Army ran an Organizational Effectiveness Center at Fort Ord, California, and graduated some 1,702 officers as internal consultants between 1975 and 1985.[121] In 1977, the Navy was utilizing 300 full-time OD specialists.[122] Further, during that period, the Naval Postgraduate School offered a master's degree in human resources management, which was essentially a master's degree in OD. Students in that program included active duty officers from the Air Force, Coast Guard, and Army in addition to Navy officers.[123]

Some community development strategies share a number of elements in common with organization development, such as the use of action research, the use of a change agent, and an emphasis on facilitating decision-making and problem-solving processes.[124] Undoubtedly, some of the commonality stems from OD practitioners working in the community development field. For example, in 1961 Herbert Shepard conducted community development laboratories at China Lake, California, sponsored by the Naval Ordnance Test Station. These one-week labs involved military persons and civilians of all ages and so-cioeconomic levels. Outcomes included the resolution of some community and intercommunity issues.[125] In later years, such conferences have been called *search conferences* or *future search conferences.*

In addition to emphasizing the diversity of systems using OD consultants, we want to emphasize that intraorganization development efforts have not focused on just top management teams, although the importance of top management involvement will be discussed in later chapters. The range of occupational roles that have been involved in OD is almost limitless and has included production workers,[126] managers, soldiers, military officers, miners, scientists and engineers, ministers, psychologists, geologists, lawyers, accountants, nurses, physicians, teachers, computer specialists, foresters, technicians, secretaries, clerical employees, board members, and flight crews.

The emergence and growth of the OD Network indicates the widespread application of organization development concepts. The OD Network began in 1964 and by 1998 had a membership of about 34,000 and 46 regional networks. Most members either have major roles in the OD efforts of organizations or are scholar-practitioners in the OD field. Although most network members reside in the United States, in 1998 the Network included 184 international members, the majority from Canada. Thirty-one countries were represented in addition to the United States.

The OD Network began with discussions at the Case Institute of Technology between Herbert Shepard, Sheldon Davis of TRW Systems, and Floyd Mann of the University of Michigan,[127] and through the initiative of Leland Bradford and Jerry Harvey of NTL and a number of industrial people who had attended labs at Bethel. Among the industrial founders of the organization, originally called the Industrial Trainers Network, were Sheldon Davis of TRW Systems, George Murray of Union Carbide, John Vail of Dow Chemical, and Carl Albers of the Hotel Corporation of America. Other early members were from Procter & Gamble, Weyerhaeuser, Bankers Trust, West

Virginia Pulp and Paper Company, The U.S. State Department, the U.S. National Security Agency, Pillsbury, Eli Lilly, Polaroid, Esso, Parker Pen, American Airlines, Goodrich-Gulf Chemicals, RCA, Sandia, National Association of Manufacturers, General Foods, Armour & Company, Heublein, and Du Pont. Jerry Harvey was the first secretary/coordinator of the emerging organization, and Warner Burke assumed that role in 1967 shortly after joining NTL full-time. At that time the Network had fewer than 50 members; when Warner Burke stepped aside as executive director in 1975, it had approximately 1,400 members.[128] That same year the OD Network became independent of NTL.

The Academy of Management, whose members are mostly professors in management and related areas, established a Division of Organization Development within its structure in 1971. This unit, renamed The Division of Organization Development and Change, had 1,601 members by 1998. The OD Forum of the American Society for Training and Development had 11,374 members at the beginning of that year. The Society of Industrial-Organizational Psychology of the American Psychological Association has held workshops on organization development at the annual APA conventions; several annual conventions going back at least to 1965 have included papers or symposia on organization development or related topics.[129] In 1974 the *Annual Review of Psychology* for the first time devoted a chapter entirely to a review of research on organization development.[130] Chapters on OD have appeared at other times, for example, 1977,[131] 1982, 1987,[132] and 1991.[133] The 1982 chapter was written by authors from the Netherlands and France, indicative of OD's international applications.[134]

The first doctoral program devoted to training OD specialists was founded by Herbert Shepard in 1960 at the Case Institute of Technology. Originally called The Organizational Behavior Group, this program is now part of the Department of Organizational Behavior, School of Management, Case Western Reserve University. UCLA also has a program at the doctoral level. Pepperdine offers

Doctor of Education in Organization Change (Ed-DOC), and Benedictine University offers a Ph.D. in Organization Development.

Masters degree programs in organization development or masters programs with concentrations in OD have been offered in recent years by several universities, including New York University, Brigham Young, Pepperdine, Loyola, Bowling Green, New Hampshire, Central Washington University, Columbia, Case Western Reserve, Antioch, University of South Florida, University of San Francisco, Sonoma State University, California School of Professional Psychology, Fielding Institute, Eastern Michigan University, and Sheffield Polytechnic in England. The American University and NTL Institute jointly offer a master of science in organization development. The John F. Kennedy University and NTL cosponsor a masters program that has organization development and change as a major component. Many other major U.S. universities, if not most, now have graduate courses concentrating on organization development, including UCLA, Stanford, Harvard, University of Washington, University of Southern California, Hawaii, Oklahoma, Colorado, Indiana, and Purdue. In England, such courses are found at the University of Manchester Institute of Science and Technology and the University of Bath.[135]

This rapid growth in OD interest and attention has been given impetus by special programs in OD, particularly NTL Institute's Program for Specialists in OD (PSOD), now called Integrating OD Theory and Practice. Other NTL OD programs include such offerings as What is OD?, Facilitating and Managing Complex Systems Change, Consultation Skills, Diversity and OD, Group Process Consultation, Team Building, Managing Conflict, and Creating and Sustaining High-Performing Teams. Another strong source of OD education and training is Teachers College at Columbia University. As part of its organizational psychology program, Columbia offers both a two-part Principles of Organization Development Program and a three-part Advanced Program in Organization Development and Human Resources Management.

Another organization, the Organization Development Institute, offers numerous workshops, and sponsors an Organization Development World Congress held in a different country each year. Other professional programs in OD have been or are now being offered in the United States, Canada, the United Kingdom, Australia, New Zealand, and elsewhere under the sponsorship of universities, foundations, professional associations, and other institutions.

Concluding Comments

Organization development emerged largely from applied behavioral sciences and has four major stems: (1) the invention of the T-group and innovations in the application of laboratory training insights to complex organizations, (2) the invention of survey feedback technology, (3) the emergence of action research, and (4) the evolution of the Tavistock sociotechnical and socioclinical approaches.

Key figures in this early history interacted with each other across these stems and were influenced by concepts and experiences from a wide variety of disciplines and settings. These disciplines included social psychology, clinical psychology, family group therapy, ethnography, military psychology and psychiatry, the theater, general semantics, social work, systems theory, mathematics and physics, philosophy, psychodrama, client-centered therapy, survey methodology, experimental and action research, human resources management, organizational behavior, general management theory, and large conference management.

The context for applying OD approaches has changed to an increasingly turbulent environment. While practitioners still rely on OD basics, they are giving considerable attention to new concepts, interventions, and areas of application. Among the directions of interest in second-generation OD are organizational transformation, organizational culture, the learning organization, high-performance teams, total quality management, "getting the whole system in the room,"

future search, and the role OD practitioners should play in reengineering.

The field of OD is emergent in that a rapidly increasing number of behavioral scientists and practitioners are building on the research and insights of the past as well as rediscovering the utility of some of the earlier insights. These efforts, often under different terminology, are now expanding and include a wide range of organizations, types of institutions, occupational categories, and geographical locations.

In the chapters that follow, the assumptions, theory, and techniques of organization development, as well as problems with implementing OD processes, will be examined in considerable depth. We will also speculate on the future viability of OD or OD-like processes.

Endnotes

1. The phrase *group dynamics* was coined by Kurt Lewin in 1939. See Warren Bennis, address to the Academy of Management, San Diego, California, August 3, 1981.

2. This and the next paragraph are based on Kenneth D. Benne, Leland P. Bradford, Jack R. Gibb, and Ronald O. Lippitt, eds., *The Laboratory Method for Changing and Learning: Theory and Application* (Palo Alto, CA: Science and Behavior Books, 1975), pp. 1–6; and Alfred J. Marrow, *The Practical Theorist: The Life and Work of Kurt Lewin* (New York: Basic Books, 1969), pp. 210–214. For additional history, see Leland P. Bradford, "Biography of an Institution," *Journal of Applied Behavioral Science,* 3 (April–June 1967), pp. 127–143; and Alvin Zander, "The Study of Group Behavior during Four Decades," *Journal of Applied Behavioral Science,* 15 (July–September 1979), pp. 272–282. We are indebted to Ronald Lippitt for his correspondence, which helped to clarify this and the following paragraph.

3. Jerrold I. Hirsch, *The History of the National Training Laboratories 1947–1986* (New York: Peter Lang publishing, 1987), pp. 17–18; and address by Ronald Lippitt, Academy of Management annual conference, Chicago, Illinois, August 1986. For more on Bradford, see David L. Bradford, "A Biography of Leland P. Bradford," *Journal of Applied Behavioral Science,* 26, no. 1 (1990), p. viii.

4. See also Nancie Coan, "A History of NTL Institute in Bethel," *NTL Institute News & Views* (February 1991), pp. 11–15.

5. Peter B. Smith, ed., *Small Groups and Personal Change* (London: Methuen & Co. 1980), pp. 8–9.

6. Robert Chin and Kenneth D. Benne, "General Strategies for Effecting Changes in Human Systems," in Warren G. Bennis, Kenneth D. Benne, and Robert Chin, eds., *The Planning of Change,* 2d ed. (New York: Holt, Rinehardt and Winston, 1969), pp. 100–102.

7. Correspondence with Kenneth Benne. Raup was Benne's Ph.D. major professor at Columbia. Benne states that he was also influenced by Edward Lindeman. For more on Benne, see Paul Nash, "Biography of Kenneth D. Benne," *Journal of Applied Behavioral Science,* 28 (June 1992), p. 167.

8. Chin and Benne, op cit., p. 102.

9. Correspondence with Ronald Lippitt.

10. Conversation with Lee Bradford, conference on current theory and practice in organization development, San Francisco, March 16, 1978.

11. See, for example, S. R. Slavson, *An Introduction to Group Therapy* (New York: The Commonwealth Fund, 1943); and S. R. Slavson, *Creative Group Education* (New York: Association Press, 1937), especially Chapter 1.

12. Edgar H. Schein and Warren G. Bennis, *Personal and Organizational Change through Group Methods: The Laboratory Approach* (New York: John Wiley & Sons, 1965), p. 35.

13. Art Kleiner, *The Age of Heretics* (New York: Currency and Doubleday, 1996), pp. 41–42.

14. Based largely on correspondence with Ronald Lippitt. According to Lippitt, as early as 1945 Bradford and Lippitt were conducting "three-level training" at Freedman's Hospital in Washington, D.C., in an effort "to induce interdependent changes in all parts of the same system." Lippitt also reports that Leland Bradford very early was acting on a basic concept of "multiple entry," that is, simultaneously training and working with several groups in the organization.

15. Correspondence with Robert Tannenbaum.

16. Tannenbaum correspondence; memorandum of May 12, 1952, U.S. Naval Ordnance Test Station from E. R. Toporeck to "Office, Division and Branch Heads, Test Department," and "Minutes, Test Department Management Seminar, 5 March 1953."

17. Robert Tannenbaum, Verne Kallejian, and Irving R. Weschler, "Training Managers for Leadership," *Personnel,* 30 (January 1954), p. 3.

18. Verne J. Kallejian, Irving R. Weschler, and Robert Tannenbaum, "Managers in Transition," *Harvard Business Review,* 33 (July–August 1955), pp. 55–64.

19. Tannenbaum correspondence.

20. Ibid.

21. Correspondence with Chris Argyris; and Chris Argyris, *Interpersonal Competence and Organizational Effectiveness* (Homewood, IL: Richard D. Irwin, 1962).

22. Argyris correspondence.

23. Chris Argyris, *Intervention Theory and Method* (Reading, MA: Addison-Wesley, 1970).

24. Argyris correspondence.

25. Donald D. Bowen, "Competence and Justice: A Conversation with Chris Argyris," p. 42 of a manuscript accepted for publication in the 1988 *OD Annual.*

26. Argyris correspondence.

27. Ibid. Argyris's Ph.D. in organizational behavior may have been the first ever awarded.

28. Argyris correspondence.

29. See Richard Beckhard, W. Warner Burke, and Fred I. Steele, "The Program for Specialists in Organization Training and Development," p. ii, mimeographed paper (NTL Institute for Applied Behavioral Science, December 1967); and John Paul Jones, "What's Wrong with Work?" in *What's Wrong with Work?* (New York: National Association of Manufacturers, 1967), p. 8. According to correspondence with Rensis Likert, the link between McGregor and John Paul Jones occurred in the summer of 1957. Discussion took place between the two when Jones attended one of the annual two-week seminars at Aspen, Colorado, organized by Hollis Peter of the Foundation for Research on Human Behavior and conducted by Douglas McGregor, Mason Haire, and Rensis Likert.

30. Gilbert Burck, "Union Carbide's Patient Schemers," *Fortune,* 72 (December 1965), pp. 147–149. For McGregor's account, see "Team Building at Union Carbide," in Douglas McGregor, *The Professional Manager* (New York: McGraw-Hill, 1967), pp. 106–110.

31. See the Editor's Preface to Douglas McGregor, *The Professional Manager* (New York: McGraw-Hill, 1967), p. viii.

32. Conversation with George Strauss, Western Division of the Academy of Management conference, San Diego, California, March 1985. For a brief overview of Rogers's life and career, see "Carl Rogers (1902–1987)," *American Psychologist,* 43 (February 1988), pp. 127–128. Carl Rogers was also on the staff of several NTL president's labs in the early days. Seminar with Carl Rogers, Western Division of the Academy of Management conference, San Diego, California, March 1985.

33. Douglas McGregor, *The Human Side of Enterprise* (New York: McGraw-Hill, 1960). For more on McGregor, see Marvin R. Weisbord, *Productive Workplaces* (San Francisco: Jossey-Bass Publishers, 1987), pp. 106–122.

34. Warren Bennis, *An Invented Life: Reflections on Leadership and Change* (Reading, MA: Addison-Wesley, 1993), p. 14.

35. This paragraph is based on interviews with Herbert Shepard, August 3, 1981. For a brief discussion of the career of Clarence Hicks, see Wendell French, *The Personnel Management Process,* 6th ed. (Boston: Houghton Mifflin, 1987), Chapter 2.

36. Much of the historical account in this paragraph and the following three paragraphs is based on correspondence and interviews with Herbert Shepard, with some information added from correspondence with Robert Blake.

37. Correspondence with Robert Blake and Herbert Shepard. For further reference to Murray Horowitz and Paul Buchanan, as well as to comments about the innovative contributions of Michael Blansfield, see Herbert A. Shepard, "Explorations in Observant Participation," in Bradford, Gibb, and Benne, eds., *T-Group Theory,* pp. 382–383. See also Marshall Sashkin, "Interview with Robert R. Blake and Jane Srygley Mouton," *Group and Organization Studies,* 3 (December 1978), pp. 401–407.

38. See Robert Blake and Jane Srygley Mouton, "The Instrumented Training Laboratory," in Irving R. Weschler and Edgar M. Schein, eds., *Selected Readings Series Five: Issues in Training* (Washington, DC: National Training Laboratories, 1962), pp. 61–85. In this chapter, Blake and Mouton credit Muzafer and Carolyn Sherif with important contributions to early intergroup experiments. Reference is also made to the contributions of Frank Cassens of Humble Oil and Refinery in the early phases of the Esso program. For a brief description of the development of the two-dimensional Managerial Grid, see Robert Blake and Jane Srygley Mouton, *Diary of an OD Man* (Houston: Gulf 1976), pp. 332–336. For more on Sherif, see O. J. Harvey, "Muzafer Sherif (1906–1988)," *American Psychologist,* 44 (October 1989), pp. 1325–1326.

39. Based on correspondence with Robert Blake. See also Robert R. Blake and Jane Srygley Mouton, "Why the OD Movement is 'Stuck' and How to Break It Loose," *Training and Development Journal,* 33 (September 1979), pp. 12–20.

40. Blake correspondence.

41. Mouton correspondence.

42. Blake correspondence.

43. Ibid. For more on Bowlby, see Mary D. Salter Ainsworth, "John Bowlby (1907–1993)," *American Psychologist,* 47 (May 1992), p. 668.

44. Blake correspondence.

45. Correspondence with Richard Beckhard.

46. Ibid.

47. Based on Beckhard correspondence and other sources.

48. Kleiner, *The Age of Heretics,* p. 223.

49. Bennis, *An Invented Life: Reflections on Leadership and Change* pp. 15–29.

50. Warren G. Bennis, Kenneth D. Benne, and Robert Chin, *The Planning of Change,* 2d ed. (Holt, Rinehart and Winston, 1969).

51. Warren G. Bennis and Philip Slater, "Democracy Is Inevitable," *Harvard Business Review* (September–October 1990).

52. The previous three paragraphs and the following three are based on correspondence with Eva Schindler-Rainman. For additional material, see Anthony J. Reilly, "Interview" (with Eva Schindler-Rainman and Ron Lippitt) *Group & Organization Studies,* 2 (September 1977), pp. 265–281.

53. For more on Edith Seashore, see Charleen Alderfer, "A Biography of Edith Whitfield Seashore," *Journal of Applied Behavioral Science,* 28 (March 1992), pp. 7–8.

54. Kleiner, *The Age of Heretics,* pp. 223–225.

55. Eva Schindler-Rainman, *The Creative Volunteer Community: A Collection of Writings by Eva Schindler-Rainman,* D.S.W. (Vancouver, BC: Vancouver Volunteer Centre, 1987).

56. Eva Schindler-Rainman and Ronald Lippitt, *Building the Collaborative Community: Mobilizing Citizens for Action* (Riverside, CA: University of California

Extension, 1980.) (Third printing available through ENERGIZE, 5450 Wissahickon Avenue, Philadelphia, PA 19144.)

57. Eva Schindler-Rainman and Ronald Lippitt, *The Volunteer Community: Creative Use of Human Resources,* 2d ed. (San Diego: University Associates, 1975.) (Available through ENERGIZE.)

58. Eva Schindler-Rainman and Ronald Lippitt, *Team Training for Community Change: Concepts, Goals, Strategies and Skills* (Bethesda, MD: Development Publications, 1972). (Third printing, 1993, available through Dr. Eva Schindler-Rainman, 4267 San Rafael Avenue, Los Angeles, CA 90042.)

59. Interpretations of Blake correspondence, Shepard interview, Beckhard correspondence, and Larry Porter, "OD: Some Questions Some Answers—An Interview with Beckhard and Shepard," *OD Practitioner,* 6 (Autumn 1974), p. 1.

60. Blake correspondence.

61. Jane Srygley Mouton and Robert R. Blake, "University Training in Human Relations Skills," *Selected Readings Series Three: Forces in Learning* (Washington DC: National Training Laboratories, 1961), pp. 88–96, reprinted from *Group Psychotherapy,* 10 (1957), pp. 342–345.

62. Shepard and Blake correspondence.

63. Interview with Herbert Shepard, San Diego, California, August 3, 1981.

64. Beckhard correspondence.

65. Burck, "Union Carbide's Patient Schemers," p. 149.

66. Harry D. Kolb, "Introduction" to *An Action Research Program for Organization Improvement* (Ann Arbor, MI: Foundation for Research on Human Behavior, 1960), p. i. The phrase *organization development* is used several times in this monograph based on a 1959 meeting about the Esso programs and written by Kolb, Shepard, Blake, and others.

67. Based on Beckhard correspondence.

68. This history is based largely on correspondence with Rensis Likert and partially on "The Career of Rensis Likert," *ISR Newsletter* (Winter 1971); and *A Quarter Century of Social Research,* Institute for Social Research (1971). See also Charles Cannell and Robert Kahn, "Some Factors in the Origins and Development of The Institute for Social Research, The University of Michigan," *American Psychologist,* 39 (November 1984), pp. 1256–1266.

69. "Rensis Likert," *ISR newsletter,* p. 6.

70. Likert correspondence. Floyd Mann later became the first director of the Center for Research on the Utilization of Scientific Knowledge (CRUSK) when the center was established by ISR in 1964. See also Floyd C. Mann, "Studying and Creating Change," in Bennis, Benne, and Chin, eds., *Planning of Change,* pp. 605–613.

71. Mann, "Studying and Creating Change," p. 609.

72. Howard Baumgartel, "Using Employee Questionnaire Results for Improving Organizations: The Survey (Feedback) Experiment," *Kansas Business Review,* 12 (December 1959), pp. 2–6.

73. Likert correspondence.

74. Marrow, *The Practical Theorist,* p. 164. This book about the life and work of Kurt Lewin is rich with events that are important to the history of OD.

75. Likert correspondence.

76. Argyris correspondence.

77. Likert correspondence.

78. H. V. Dicks, *Fifty Years of the Tavistock Clinic* (London: Routledge & Kegan Paul, 1970), pp. 1, 32.

79. Based on ibid., 5, 7, 133, 140; and Robert DeBoard, *The Psychoanalysis of Organizations* (London: Tavistock 1978), pp. 35–43.

80. Eric Trist and Marshall Sashkin, "Interview," *Group & Organization Studies,* 5 (June 1980), pp. 150–151; and Kleiner, *The Age of Heretics,* pp. 63–64.

81. Trist and Sashkin, p. 155. See also William A. Pasmore and Guruder S. Khalsa, "The Contributions of Eric Trist to the Social Engagement of Social Science," *Academy of Management Review,* 18 (July 1993), pp. 546–569.

82. Kleiner, p. 64.

83. Ibid., p. 65.

84. Trist and Sashkin, pp. 144–151.

85. Bennis address, Academy of Management, August 3, 1981.

86. Argyris correspondence.

87. Amir Levy and Uri Merry, *Organizational Transformation* (New York: Praeger Publishers, 1986), p. 5.

88. David A. Nadler and Michael L. Tushman, "Organizational Frame Bending: Principles for Managing Reorientation," *The Academy of Management Executive,* 3 (August 1989), pp. 194–204.

89. Leonard D. Goodstein and W. Warner Burke, "Creating Successful Organization Change," *Organizational Dynamics,* 19 (Spring 1991), pp. 5–17.

90. Gloria Barczak, Charles Smith, and David Wilemon, "Managing Large-Scale Organizational Change," *Organizational Dynamics* (Autumn 1987), pp. 23–35.

91. Richard Beckhard and Wendy Pritchard, *Changing the Essence* (San Francisco: Jossey-Bass Publishers, 1992), p. 3; and Richard Beckhard, "Choosing and Leading a Fundamental Change," *Academy of Management ODC Newsletter* (Summer 1993), pp. 6–8.

92. Edgar H. Schein, *Organizational Culture and Leadership* (San Francisco: Jossey-Bass Publishers, 1985).

93. Edgar H. Schein, "Organization Development and the Study of Organizational Culture," *Academy of Management OD Newsletter* (Summer 1990), pp. 3–5.

94. Ralph H. Kilmann, "Five Steps for Closing Culture-Gaps," pp. 351–369; and Robert F. Allen, "Four Phases for Bringing about Cultural Change," pp. 332–350 in Ralph H. Kilmann, Mary J. Saxton, and Roy Serpa, eds. *Gaining Control of the Corporate Culture* (San Francisco: Jossey-Bass Publishers, 1985). See also William G. Ouchi and Raymond L. Price, "Hierarchies, Clans, and Theory Z: A New Perspective on Organization Development," *Organizational Dynamics,* 21 (Spring 1993), pp. 62–70.

95. Chris Argyris, *Overcoming Organizational Defensive Routines* (Boston: Allyn and Bacon, 1990).

96. Chris Argyris and Donald Schon, *Organizational Learning* (Reading, MA: Addison-Wesley, 1976).

97. Chris Argyris, "Strategy Implementation and Experience in Learning," *Organizational Dynamics,* 18 (Autumn 1989), pp. 8, 9.

98. Ibid., pp. 5–15; and Chris Argyris, "Teaching Smart People How to Learn," *Harvard Business Review,* 69 (May–June 1991), pp. 99–109.

99. Peter M. Senge, *The Fifth Discipline: The Art and Practice of the Learning Organization* (New York: Doubleday/Currency, 1990), pp. 12, 18, 19, 44.

100. John A. Byrne, "Management's New Gurus," *Business Week,* August 31, 1992, pp. 44–52.

101. For more on teams, see Jon R. Katzenbach and Douglas K. Smith, *The Wisdom of Teams* (Boston: Harvard Business School Press, 1993); Richard S. Wellins, William C. Byham, and Jeanne M. Wilson, *Empowered Teams* (San Francisco: Jossey-Bass Publishers, 1991); David Barry, "Managing the Bossless Team: Lessons in Distributed Leadership," *Organizational Dynamics,* 20 (Summer 1991), pp. 31–46; Eric Sundstrom, Kenneth P. De Meuse, and David Futrell, "Work Teams Applications and Effectiveness," *American Psychologist,* 45 (February 1990), pp. 120–133. Glenn M. Parker, *Team Players and Teamwork* (San Francisco: Jossey-Bass Publishers, 1990); and Larry Hirschhorn, *Managing in the New Team Environment* (Reading, MA: Addison-Wesley Publishing Company, 1991).

102. Dan Ciampa, *Total Quality* (Reading, MA: Addison-Wesley Publishing Company, 1992), p. xxi. See also Marshall Sashkin and Kenneth J. Kiser, *Total Quality Management* (Seabrook, MD: Ducochon Press, 1991).

103. Ciampa, *Total Quality,* p. xxii.

104. Ibid., p. xxiv.

105. W. Warner Burke, *Organization Development: A Process of Learning and Changing* (Reading, MA: Addison-Wesley Publishing Company, 1994), p. 199.

106. Edward Lindaman and Ronald Lippitt, *Choosing the Future You Prefer* (Washington, DC: Development Publications, 1979).

107. Ronald Fox, Ronald Lippitt, and Eva Schindler-Rainman, *The Humanized Future: Some New Images* (LaJolla, CA: University Associates, 1973).

108. Merrelyn Emery, *Searching: For New Directions, in New Ways for New Times* (Canberra: Centre for Continuing Education, Australian National University, 1982).

109. Marvin R. Weisbord, "Future Search: Toward Strategic Integration," in Walter Sikes, Allan Drexler, and Jack Gant, eds., *The Emerging Practice of Organization Development* (Alexandria, VA: NTL Institute for Applied Behavioral Science, and San Diego, CA: University Associates, 1989), p. 171; and Marvin R. Weisbord, "Future Search: Innovative Business Conference," *Planning Review,* 12 (July 1984), pp. 16–20.

110. Marvin R. Weisbord, *Productive Workplaces* (San Francisco: Jossey-Bass Publishers, 1987), pp. 289–292.

111. Senge, *The Fifth Discipline,* p. 214.

112. Richard Beckhard, "The Confrontation Meeting," *Harvard Business Review,* 45 (March–April 1967), pp. 149–155. See also W. Warner Burke and Richard Beckhard, *Conference Planning,* 2d ed. (San Diego: University Associates, 1970).

113. Marvin R. Weisbord, "Toward Third-Wave Managing and Consulting," *Organizational Dynamics,* 15 (Winter 1987), pp. 19–20.

114. See Frank J. Barrett and David L. Cooperrider, "Generative Metaphor Intervention: A New Approach for Working with Systems Divided by Conflict and Caught in Defensive Perception," *Journal of Applied Behavioral Science,* 26, no. 2 (1990), 219–239; and Rita F. Williams, "Survey Guided Appreciative Inquiry: A Case Study," *OD Practitioner,* 28, nos. 1, 2 (1996), pp. 43–51.

115. Gerard Burke and Joe Peppard, *Examining Business Process Re-Engineering: Current Perspectives and Research Directions* (London: Kogan Page, 1995), p. 25.

116. Interview with Sam Shirley, February 4, 1982; correspondence with Sheldon A. Davis; Sheldon A. Davis, "An Organic Problem-Solving Method of Organizational Change," *Journal of Applied Behavioral Science,* 3 (November 1, 1967), pp. 3–21; and the case study of the TRW Systems Group in Gene Dalton, Paul Lawrence, and Larry Greiner, *Organizational Change and Development* (Homewood, IL: Irwin-Dorsey, 1970), pp. 4–153.

117. Celeste A. Coruzzi, "Remembering Shel Davis," *OD Practitioner,* 27, nos. 2, 3 (1995), pp. 19–21.

118. Correspondence with Michael Thiel, June 1993.

119. Ibid.

120. *The Wall Street Journal,* March 5, 1993, p. B7A.

121. Mel R. Spehn, "Reflections on the Organizational Effectiveness Center and School," mimeographed paper, compiled in the summer/fall of 1985, Fort Ord, CA, p. 3.

122. Ibid., p. 11.

123. Correspondence from Ray L. Forbes, Jr., Franklin University Graduate School of Business, June 5, 1995; and Raymond L. Forbes, Jr., "Organization Development: An Analysis of the U.S. Navy Experience," a human resource management working paper, Department of Administrative Sciences, Naval Postgraduate School, Monterey, California, June 30, 1977.

124. See Eva Schindler-Rainman, "Community Development Through Laboratory Methods," in Benne, Bradford, Gibb, and Lippitt, eds., *Laboratory Method of Changing and Learning,* pp. 445–463. See also John W. Selsky, "Lessons in Community Development," *Journal of Applied Behavioral Science,* 27 (March 1991), pp. 91–115.

125. Shepard correspondence. Starting in 1967, Herbert Shepard was involved in the applications of OD to community problems in Middletown, CT.

126. See Scott Myers, "Overcoming Union Opposition to Job Enrichment," *Harvard Business Review,* 49 (May–June 1971), pp. 37–49; and Robert Blake, Herbert Shepard, and Jane Mouton, *Managing Intergroup Conflict in Industry* (Houston: Gulf, 1964), pp. 122–138.

127. Shepard correspondence.

128. Correspondence with W. Warner Burke and memoranda and attendance lists pertaining to 1967–1969 Network meetings furnished by Burke.

129. For example, the following topics were included in the program of the 1965 convention: "Strategies for Organization Improvement: Research and Consultation," "Managerial Grid Organization Development," and "The Impact of Laboratory Training in Research and Development Environment," *American Psychologist,* 20 (July 1965), pp. 549, 562, 565.

130. Frank Friedlander and L. Dave Brown, "Organization Development," *Annual Review of Psychology,* 25 (1974), pp. 313–341.

131. Clay Alderfer, "Organization Development," *Annual Review of Psychology,* 28 (1977), pp. 197–223.

132. Michael Beer and Anna Elise Walton, "Organizational Change and Development," *Annual Review of Psychology,* 38 (1987), pp. 339–367.

133. Jerry I. Porras and Robert C. Silvers, "Organization Development and Transformation," *Annual Review of Psychology,* 42 (1991), pp. 51–78.

134. Claude Faucheux, Gilles Amada, and André Laurent, "Organizational Development and Change," *Annual Review of Psychology,* 33 (1982), pp. 343–370.

135. D. D. Warrick, ed., *OD Newsletter,* OD Division, Academy of Management (Spring 1979), p. 7. Also various sources, including "Academic Program Reviews," *OD Practitioner,* 28, nos. 1, 2 (1996), pp. 61–67.

General Strategies for Effecting Changes in Human Systems

Robert Chin
Kenneth D. Benne

Discussing general strategies and procedures for effecting change requires that we set limits to the discussion. For, under a liberal interpretation of the title, we would need to deal with much of the literature of contemporary social and behavioral science, basic and applied.

Therefore we shall limit our discussion to those changes which are planned changes—in which attempts to bring about change are conscious, deliberate, and intended, at least on the part of one or more agents related to the change attempt. We shall also attempt to categorize strategies and procedures which have a few important elements in common but which, in fact, differ widely in other respects. And we shall neglect many of these differences. In addition, we shall look beyond the description of procedures in commonsense terms and seek some genotypic characteristics of change strategies. We shall seek the roots of the main strategies discussed, including their variants, in ideas and idea systems prominent in contemporary and recent social and psychological thought.

One element in all approaches to planned change is the conscious utilization and application of knowledge as an instrument or tool for modifying patterns and institutions of practice. The knowledge or related technology to be applied may be knowledge of the nonhuman environment in which practice goes on or of some knowledge-based "thing technology" for controlling one or another feature of the practice environment. In educational practice, for example, technologies of communication and calculation, based upon new knowledge of electronics—audiovisual devices, television, computers, teaching machines—loom large among the knowledges and technologies that promise greater efficiency and economy in handling various practices in formal education. As attempts are made to introduce these new thing technologies into school situations, the change problem shifts to the human problems of dealing with the resistances, anxieties, threats to morale, conflicts, disrupted interpersonal communications, and so on, which prospective changes in patterns of practice evoke in the people affected by the change. So the change agent, even though focally and initially concerned with modifications in the thing technology of education, finds himself in need of more adequate knowledge of human behavior, individual and social, and in need of developed "people technologies," based on behavioral knowledge, for dealing effectively with the human aspects of deliberate change.

The knowledge which suggests improvements in educational practice may, on the other hand, be behavioral knowledge in the first instance—knowledge about participative learning, about attitude change, about family disruption in inner-city communities, about the cognitive and skill requirements of new careers, and so forth. Such knowledge may suggest changes in school grouping, in the relations between teachers and students, in the relations of teachers and principals to

Source: "General Strategies for Effecting Changes in Human Systems" from *The Planning of Change,* 3rd ed., by Warren G. Bennis, Kenneth D. Benne, Robert Chin, and Kenneth E. Corey, copyright © 1976 by Holt, Rinehart, and Winston, Inc. Reprinted by permission of the publisher.

parents, and in counseling practices. Here change agents, initially focused on application of behavioral knowledge and the improvement of people technologies in school settings, must face the problems of using people technologies in planning, installing, and evaluating such changes in educational practice. The new people technologies must be experienced, understood, and accepted by teachers and administrators before they can be used effectively with students.

This line of reasoning suggests that, whether the focus of planned change is in the introduction of more effective thing technologies or people technologies into institutionalized practice, processes of introducing such changes must be based on behavioral knowledge of change and must utilize people technologies based on such knowledge.

Types of Strategies for Changing

Our further analysis is based on three types or groups of strategies. The first of these, and probably the most frequently employed by men of knowledge in America and Western Europe, are those we call empirical-rational strategies. One fundamental assumption underlying these strategies is that men are rational. Another assumption is that men will follow their rational self-interest once this is revealed to them. A change is proposed by some person or group which knows of a situation that is desirable, effective, and in line with the self-interest of the person, group, organization, or community which will be affected by the change. Because the person (or group) is assumed to be rational and moved by self-interest, it is assumed that he (or they) will adopt the proposed change if it can be rationally justified and if it can be shown by the proposer(s) that he (or they) will gain by the change.

A second group of strategies we call normative-reeducative. These strategies build upon assumptions about human motivation different from those underlying the first. The rationality and in-

telligence of men are not denied. Patterns of action and practice are supported by sociocultural norms and by commitments on the part of individuals to these norms. Sociocultural norms are supported by the attitude and value systems of individuals—normative outlooks which undergird their commitments. Change in a pattern of practice or action, according to this view, will occur only as the persons involved are brought to change their normative orientations to old patterns and develop commitments to new ones. And changes in normative orientations involve changes in attitudes, values, skills, and significant relationships, not just changes in knowledge, information, or intellectual rationales for action and practice.

The third group of strategies is based on the application of power in some form, political or otherwise. The influence process involved is basically that of compliance of those with less power to the plans, directions, and leadership of those with greater power. Often the power to be applied is legitimate power or authority. Thus the strategy may involve getting the authority of law or administrative policy behind the change to be effected. Some power strategies may appeal less to the use of authoritative power to effect change than to the massing of coercive power, legitimate or not, in support of the change sought.[1]

Empirical-Rational Strategies

A variety of specific strategies are included in what we are calling the empirical-rational approach to effecting change. As we have already pointed out, the rationale underlying most of these is an assumption that men are guided by reason and that they will utilize some rational calculus of self-interest in determining needed changes in behavior.

It is difficult to point to any one person whose ideas express or articulate the orientation underlying commitment to empirical-rational strategies of changing. In Western Europe and America, this orientation might be better identified with the general social orientation of the enlightenment and of classical liberalism than with the ideas of any one man. On this view, the chief foes of human rationality and to change or progress based on rationality were ignorance and superstition. Scientific investigation and research represented the chief ways of extending knowledge and reducing the limitations of ignorance. A corollary of this optimistic view of man and his future was an advocacy of education as a way of disseminating scientific knowledge and of freeing men and women from the shackles of superstition. Although elitist notions played a part in the thinking of many classic liberals, the increasing trend during the 19th century was toward the universalization of educational opportunity. The common and universal school, open to all men and women, was the principal instrument by which knowledge would replace ignorance and superstition in the minds of people and become a principal agent in the spread of reason, knowledge, and knowledge-based action and practice (progress) in human society. In American experience, Jefferson may be taken as a principal, early advocate of research and of education as agencies of human progress. And Horace Mann may be taken as the prophet of progress through the institutionalization of universal education opportunity through the common school.[2]

Basic Research and Dissemination of Knowledge through General Education

The strategy of encouraging basic knowledge building and of depending on general education to diffuse the results of research into the minds and thinking of men and women is still by far the most appealing strategy of change to most academic men of knowledge and to large segments of the American population as well. Basic researchers are quite likely to appeal for time for further research when confronted by some unmet need. And many people find this appeal convincing. Both of these facts are well illustrated by difficulties with diseases for which no adequate control measure or cures are available—poliomyelitis, for example. Medical researchers asked

for more time and funds for research and people responded with funds for research, both through voluntary channels and through legislative appropriations. And the control measures were forthcoming. The educational problem then shifted to inducing people to comply with immunization procedures based on research findings.

This appeal to a combination of research and education of the public has worked in many areas of new knowledge-based thing technologies where almost universal readiness for accepting the new technology was already present in the population. Where such readiness is not available, as in the case of fluoridation technologies in the management of dental cavities, the general strategy of basic research plus educational (informational) campaigns to spread knowledge of the findings do not work well. The cases of its inadequacy as a single strategy of change have multiplied, especially where "engineering" problems, which involve a divided and conflicting public or deep resistances due to the threat by the new technology to traditional attitudes and values, have thwarted its effectiveness. But these cases, while they demand attention to other strategies of changing, do not disprove the importance of basic research and of general educational opportunity as elements in a progressive and self-renewing society.

We have noted that the strategy under discussion has worked best in grounding and diffusing generally acceptable thing technologies in society. Some have argued that the main reason the strategy has not worked in the area of people technologies is a relative lack of basic research on people and their behavior, relationships, and institutions and a corresponding lack of emphasis upon social and psychological knowledges in school and college curricula. It would follow in this view that increased basic research on human affairs and relationships and increased efforts to diffuse the results of such research through public education are the ways of making the general strategy work better. Auguste Comte, with his emphasis on positivistic sociology in the reorganization of society, and Lester F. Ward in America may be taken as late 19th-century representatives of this view. And the spirit of Comte and Ward is by no means dead in American academia or in influential segments of the American public.

Personnel Selection and Replacement

Difficulties in getting knowledge effectively into practice may be seen as lying primarily in the lack of fitness of persons occupying positions with job responsibilities for improving practice. The argument goes that we need the right person in the right position, if knowledge is to be optimally applied and if rationally based changes are to become the expectation in organizational and societal affairs. This fits with the liberal reformers' frequently voiced and enacted plea to drive the unfit from office and to replace them with those more fit as a condition of social progress.

That reformers' programs have so often failed has sobered but by no means destroyed the zeal of those who regard personnel selection, assessment, and replacement as a major key to program improvement in education or in other enterprises as well. This strategy was given a scientific boost by the development of scientific testing of potentialities and aptitudes. We will use Binet as a prototype of psychological testing and Moreno as a prototype in sociometric testing, while recognizing the extensive differentiation and elaboration which have occurred in psychometrics and sociometrics since their original work. We recognize, too, the elaborated modes of practice in personnel work which have been built around psychometric and sociometric tools and techniques. We do not discount their limited value as actual and potential tools for change, while making two observations on the way they have often been used. First, they have been used more often in the interest of system maintenance rather than of system change, since the job descriptions personnel workers seek to fill are defined in terms of system requirements as established. Second, by focusing on the role occupant as the principal barrier to improvement, personnel selection and replacement strategies have tended not to reveal the social and cultural system difficulties which may be in need of change if improvement is to take place.

Systems Analysts as Staff and Consultants

Personnel workers in government, industry, and education have typically worked in staff relations to line management, reflecting the bureaucratic, line-staff form of organization which has flourished in the large-scale organization of effort and enterprise in the 20th century. And other expert workers—systems analysts—more attuned to system difficulties than to the adequacies or inadequacies of persons as role occupants within the system, have found their way into the staff resources of line management in contemporary organizations.

There is no reason why the expert resources of personnel workers and systems analysts might not be used in nonbureaucratic organizations or in processes of moving bureaucratic organizations toward nonbureaucratic forms. But the fact remains that their use has been shaped, for the most part, in the image of the scientific management of bureaucratically organized enterprises. So we have placed the systems analysts in our chart under Frederick Taylor, the father of scientific management in America.

The line management of an enterprise seeks to organize human and technical effort toward the most efficient service of organizational goals. And these goals are defined in terms of the production of some mandated product, whether a tangible product or a less tangible good or service. In pursuing this quest for efficiency, line management employs experts in the analysis of sociotechnical systems and in the laying out of more efficient systems. The experts employed may work as external consultants or as an internal staff unit. Behavioral scientists have recently found their way, along with mathematicians and engineers, into systems analysis work.

It is interesting to note that the role of these experts is becoming embroiled in discussions of whether or not behavioral science research should be used to sensitize administrators to new organizational possibilities, to new goals, or primarily to implement efficient operation within perspectives and goals as currently defined. Jean Hills has raised the question of whether behavioral science when applied to organizational problems tends to perpetuate established ideology and system relations because of blinders imposed by their being "problem centered" and by their limited definition of what is "a problem."[3]

We see an emerging strategy, in the use of behavioral scientists as systems analysts and engineers, toward viewing the problem of organizational change and changing as a wide-angled problem, one in which all the input and output features and components of a large-scale system are considered. It is foreseeable that with the use of high-speed and high-capacity computers, and with the growth of substantial theories and hypotheses about how parts of an educational system operate, we shall find more and more applications for systems analysis and operations research in programs of educational change. In fact, it is precisely the quasi-mathematical character of these modes of research that will make possible the rational analysis of qualitatively different aspects of educational work and will bring them into the range of rational planning—masses of students, massive problems of poverty and educational and cultural deprivation, and so on. We see no necessary incompatibility between an ideology which emphasizes the individuality of the student and the use of systems analysis and computers in strategizing the problems of the total system. The actual incompatibilities may lie in the limited uses to which existing organizers and administrators of educational efforts put these technical resources.

Applied Research and Linkage Systems for Diffusion of Research Results

The American development of applied research of a planned system for linking applied researchers with professional practitioners and both of these with centers for basic research and with organized consumers of applied research has been strongly influenced by two distinctive American inventions—the land-grant university and the agricultural extension system. We, therefore, have put the name of Justin Morrill, author of the land-grant college act and of the act which established the cooperative agricultural extension system, on our chart. The land-grant colleges or universities were dedicated to doing applied research in the service of agriculture and the mechanic arts. These colleges and universities developed research programs in basic sciences as well and experimental stations for the development and refinement of knowledge-based technologies for use in engineering and agriculture. As the extension services developed, county agents—practitioners—were attached to the state land-grant college or university that received financial support from both state and federal governments. The county agent and his staff developed local organizations of adult farm men and women and of farm youth to provide both a channel toward informing consumers concerning new and better agricultural practices and toward getting awareness of unmet consumer needs and unsolved problems back to centers of knowledge and research. Garth Jones has made one of the more comprehensive studies of the strategies of changing involved in large-scale demonstration.[4]

All applied research has not occurred within a planned system for knowledge discovery, development, and utilization like the one briefly described above. The system has worked better in developing and diffusing thing technologies than in developing and diffusing people technologies, though the development of rural sociology and of agricultural economics shows that extension workers were by no means unaware of the behavioral dimensions of change problems. But the large-scale demonstration, through the land-grant university cooperative extension service, of the stupendous changes which can result from a planned approach to knowledge discovery, development, diffusion, and utilization is a part of the consciousness of all Americans concerned with planned change.[5]

Applied research and development is an honored part of the tradition of engineering approaches to problem identification and solution. The pioneering work of E. L. Thorndike in applied research in education should be noted on our chart. The processes and slow tempo of diffusion and utilization of research findings and inventions in public education are well illustrated in studies by Paul Mort and his students.[6] More recently, applied research, in its product development aspect, has been utilized in a massive way to contribute curriculum materials and designs for science instruction (as well as in other subjects). When we assess this situation to find reasons why such researches have not been more effective in producing changes in instruction, the answers seem to lie both in the plans of the studies which produced the materials and designs and in the potential users of the findings. Adequate linkage between consumers and researchers was frequently not established. Planned and evaluated demonstrations and experimentations connected with the use of materials were frequently slighted. And training of consumer teachers to use the new materials adaptively and creatively was frequently missing.

Such observations have led to a fresh spurt of interest in evaluation research addressed to educational programs. The fear persists that this, too, may lead to disappointment if it is not focused for two-way communication between researchers and teachers and if it does not involve collaboratively the ultimate consumers of the results of such research—the students. Evaluation researches conducted in the spirit of justifying a program developed by expert applied researchers will not help to guide teachers and students in their quest for improved practices of teaching and learning, if the concerns of the latter have not been taken centrally into account in the evaluation process.[7]

Recently, attempts have been made to link applied research activities in education with basic researchers on the one hand and with persons in action and practice settings on the other through some system of interlocking roles similar to those suggested in the description of the land-grant extension systems in agriculture or in other fields where applied and development researches have flourished.

The linking of research-development efforts with diffusion-innovation efforts has been gaining headway in the field of education with the emergence of federally supported research and development centers based in universities, regional laboratories connected with state departments of education, colleges and universities in a geographic area, and with various consortia and institutes confronting problems of educational change and changing. The strategy of change here usually includes a well-researched innovation which seems feasible to install in practice settings. Attention is directed to the question of whether or not the innovation will bring about a desired result, and with what it can accomplish, if given a trial in one or more practice settings. The questions of *how* to get a fair trial and *how* to install an innovation in an already going and crowded school system are ordinarily not built centrally into the strategy. The rationalistic assumption usually precludes research attention to these questions. For, if the invention can be rationally shown to have achieved desirable results in some situations, it is assumed that people in other situations will adopt it once they know these results and the rationale behind them. The neglect of the above questions has led to a wastage of much applied research effort in the past.

Attention has been given recently to the roles, communication mechanisms, and processes necessary for innovation and diffusion of improved education practices.[8] Clark and Guba have formulated very specific processes related to and necessary for change in educational practice following upon research. For them, the necessary processes are: *development,* including invention and design; *diffusion,* including dissemination and demonstration; *adoption,* including trial, installation, and institutionalization. Clark's earnest conviction is summed up in this statement: "In a sense, the education research community will be the educational community, and the route to educational progress will self-evidently be research and development."[9]

The approach of Havelock and Benne is concerned with the intersystem relationships between basic researchers, applied researchers, practitioners, and consumers in an evolved and evolving organization for knowledge utilization.

They are concerned especially with the communication difficulties and role conflicts that occur at points of intersystem exchange. These conflicts are important because they illuminate the normative issues at stake between basic researchers and applied researchers, between applied researchers and practitioners (teachers and administrators), between practitioners and consumers (students). The lines of strategy suggested by their analysis for solving role conflicts and communication difficulties call for transactional and collaborative exchanges across the lines of varied organized interests and orientations within the process of utilization. This brings their analysis into the range of normative-reeducative strategies to be discussed later.

The concepts from the behavioral sciences upon which these strategies of diffusion rest come mainly from two traditions. The first is from studies of the diffusion of traits of culture from one cultural system to another, initiated by the American anthropologist, Franz Boas. This type of study has been carried on by Rogers in his work on innovation and diffusion of innovations in contemporary culture and is reflected in a number of recent writers, such as Katz and Carlson.[10] The second scientific tradition is in studies of influence in mass communication associated with Carl Hovland and his students.[11] Both traditions have assumed a *relatively passive recipient of input* in diffusion situations. And actions within the process of diffusion are interpreted from the standpoint of an observer of the process. Bauer has pointed out that scientific studies have exaggerated the effectiveness of mass persuasion since they have compared the total number in the audience to the communications with the much smaller proportion of the audience persuaded by the communication.[12] A clearer view of processes of diffusion must include the actions of the receiver as well as those of the transmitter in the transactional events which are the units of diffusion process. And strategies for making diffusion processes more effective must be transactional and collaborative by design.

Utopian Thinking as a Strategy of Changing

It may seem strange to include the projection of utopias as a rational-empirical strategy of changing. Yet inventing and designing the shape of the future by extrapolating what we know of in the present is to envision a direction for planning and action in the present. If the image of a potential future is convincing and rationally persuasive to men in the present, the image may become part of the dynamics and motivation of present action. The liberal tradition is not devoid of its utopias. When we think of utopias quickened by an effort to extrapolate from the sciences of man to a future vision of society, the utopia of B. F. Skinner comes to mind.[13] The title of the Eight State Project, "Designing Education for the Future," for which this paper was prepared, reveals a utopian intent and aspiration and illustrates an attempt to employ utopian thinking for practical purposes.[14]

Yet it may be somewhat disheartening to others as it is to us to note the absence of rousing and beckoning normative statements of what both can and ought to be in man's future in most current liberal-democratic utopias, whether these be based on psychological, sociological, political, or philosophical findings and assumptions. The absence of utopias in current society, in this sense, and in the sense that Mannheim studied them in his now classical study,[15] tends to make the forecasting of future directions a problem of technical prediction, rather than equally a process of projecting value orientations and preferences into the shaping of a better future.

Perceptual and Conceptual Reorganization through the Clarification of Language

In classical liberalism, one perceived foe of rational change and progress was superstition. And superstitions are carried from man to man and from generation to generation through the agency of unclear and mythical language. British utilitarianism was one important strand of classical liberalism, and one of utilitarianism's important figures, Jeremy Bentham, sought to purify language of its dangerous mystique through his study of fictions.

More recently, Alfred Korzybski and S. I. Hayakawa, in the general semantics movement, have sought a way of clarifying and rectifying the names of things and processes.[16] While their main applied concern was with personal therapy, both, and especially Hayakawa, were also concerned with bringing about changes in social systems as well. People disciplined in general semantics, it was hoped, would see more correctly, communicate more adequately, and reason more effectively and thus lay a realistic common basis for action and changing. The strategies of changing associated with general semantics overlap with our next family of strategies, the normative-reeducative, because of their emphasis upon the importance of interpersonal relationships and social contexts within the communication process.

Normative-Reeducative Strategies of Changing

We have already suggested that this family of strategies rests on assumptions and hypotheses about man and his motivation which contrast significantly at points with the assumptions and hypotheses of those committed to what we have called rational-empirical strategies. Men are seen as inherently active, in quest of impulsive and need satisfaction. The relation between man and his environment is essentially transactional, as Dewey[17] made clear in his famous article on "The Reflex-Arc Concept." Man, the organism, does not passively await given stimuli from his environment in order to respond. He takes stimuli as furthering or thwarting the goals of his ongoing action. Intelligence arises in the process of shaping organism-environmental relations toward more adequate fitting and joining of organismic demands and environmental resources.

Intelligence is social, rather than narrowly individual. Men are guided in their actions by socially funded and communicated meanings, norms, and institutions, in brief by a normative culture. At the personal level, men are guided by internalized meanings, habits, and values. Changes in patterns of action or practice are, therefore, changes, not alone in the rational information equipment of men, but at the personal level, in habits and values as well and, at the sociocultural level, changes are alterations in normative structures and in institutionalized roles and relationships, as well as in cognitive and perceptual orientations.

For Dewey, the prototype of intelligence in action is the scientific method. And he saw a broadened and humanized scientific method as man's best hope for progress, if men could learn to utilize such a method in facing all of the problematic situations of their lives. *Intelligence*, so conceived, rather than *reason* as defined in classical liberalism, was the key to Dewey's hope for the invention, development, and testing of adequate strategies of changing in human affairs.

Lewin's contribution to normative-reeducative strategies of changing stemmed from his vision of required interrelations between research, training, and action (and, for him, this meant collaborative relationships, often now lacking, between researchers, educators, and activists) in the solution of human problems, in the identification of needs for change, and in the working out of improved knowledge, technology, and patterns of action in meeting these needs. Man must participate in his own reeducation if he is to be reeducated at all. And reeducation is a normative change as well as a cognitive and perceptual change. These convictions led Lewin[18] to emphasize action research as a strategy of changing, and participation in groups as a medium of reeducation.

Freud's main contributions to normative-reeducative strategies of changing are two. First, he sought to demonstrate the unconscious and preconscious bases of man's actions. Only as a man finds ways of becoming aware of these nonconscious wellsprings of his attitudes and actions will he be able to bring them into conscious self-control. And Freud devoted much of his magnificent genius to developing ways of helping men to become conscious of the mainsprings of their actions and so capable of freedom. Second, in developing therapeutic methods, he discovered and developed ways of utilizing the relationships between change agent (therapist) and client (patient) as a major tool in reeducating the client toward expanded self-awareness, self-understanding, and self-control. Emphasis upon the collaborative relationship in therapeutic change was a major contribution by Freud and his students and colleagues to normative-reeducative strategies of changing in human affairs.[19]

Normative-reeducative approaches to effecting change bring direct interventions by change agents, interventions based on a consciously worked out theory of change and of changing, into the life of a client system, be that system a person, a small group, an organization, or a community. The theory of changing is still crude, but it is probably as explicitly stated as possible, granted our present state of knowledge about planned change.[20]

Some of the common elements among variants within this family of change strategies are the following. First, all emphasize the client system and his (or its) involvement in working out programs of change and improvement for himself (or itself). The way the client sees himself and his problem must be brought into dialogic relationship with the way in which he and his problem are seen by the change agent, whether the latter is functioning as researcher, consultant, trainer, therapist, or friend in relation to the client. Second, the problem confronting the client is not assumed a priori to be one which can be met by more adequate technical information, though this possibility is not ruled out. The problem may lie rather in the attitudes, values, norms, and the external and internal relationships of the client system and may require alteration or reeducation of these as a condition of its solution. Third, the change agent must learn to intervene mutually and collaboratively along with the client into efforts to define and solve the client's problem(s). The here and now experience of the two provide an important basis

for diagnosing the problem and for locating needs for reeducation in the interest of solving it. Fourth, nonconscious elements which impede problem solution must be brought into consciousness and publicly examined and reconstructed. Fifth, the methods and concepts of the behavioral sciences are resources which change agent and client learn to use selectively, relevantly, and appropriately in learning to deal with the confronting problem and with problems of a similar kind in the future.

These approaches center in the notion that people technology is just as necessary as thing technology in working out desirable changes in human affairs. Put in this bold fashion, it is obvious that for the normative-reeducative change agent, clarification and reconstruction of values is of pivotal importance in changing. By getting the values of various parts of the client system, along with his own, openly into the arena of change, and by working through value conflicts responsibly, the change agent seeks to avoid manipulation and indoctrination of the client, in the morally reprehensible meanings of these terms.

We may use the organization of the National Training Laboratories (NTL) in 1947 as a milestone in the development of normative-reeducative approaches to changing in America. The first summer laboratory program grew out of earlier collaborations among Kurt Lewin, Ronald Lippitt, Leland Bradford, and Kenneth Benne. The idea behind the laboratory was that participants, staff, and students would learn about themselves and their back-home problems by collaboratively building a laboratory in which participants would become both experimenters and subjects in the study of their own developing interpersonal and group behavior within the laboratory setting. It seems evident that the five conditions of a normative-reeducative approach to changing were met in the conception of the training laboratory. Kurt Lewin died before the 1947 session of the training laboratory opened. Ronald Lippitt was a student of Lewin's and carried many of Lewin's orientations with him into the laboratory staff. Leland Bradford and Kenneth Benne were both students of John Dewey's philosophy of education. Bradford had invented several technologies for participative learning and self-study in his work in WPA adult education programs and as training officer in several agencies of the federal government. Benne came out of a background in educational philosophy and had collaborated with colleagues prior to 1943 in developing a methodology for policy and decision making and for the reconstruction of normative orientations, a methodology which sought to fuse democratic and scientific values and to translate these into principles for resolving conflicting and problematic situations at personal and community levels of human organization.[21] Benne and his colleagues had been much influenced by the work of Mary Follett,[22] her studies of integrative solutions to conflicts in settings of public and business administration, and by the work of Karl Mannheim[23] on the ideology and methodology of planning changes in human affairs, as well as by the work of John Dewey and his colleagues.

The work of the National Training Laboratories has encompassed development and testing of various approaches to changing in institutional settings, in America and abroad, since its beginning. One parallel development in England which grew out of Freud's thinking should be noted. This work developed in efforts at Tavistock Clinic to apply therapeutic approaches to problems of change in industrial organizations and in communities. This work is reported in statements by Elliot Jaques[24] and in this volume by Eric Trist. Another parallel development is represented by the efforts of Roethlisberger and Dickson to use personal counseling in industry as a strategy of organizational change.[25] Roethlisberger and Dickson had been strongly influenced by the pioneer work of Elton Mayo in industrial sociology[26] as well as by the counseling theories and methodologies of Carl Rogers.

Various refinements of methodologies for changing have been developed and tested since the establishment of the National Training Laborato-

ries in 1947, both under its auspices and under other auspices as well. For us, the modal developments are worthy of further discussion here. One set of approaches is oriented focally to the improvement of the problem-solving processes utilized by a client-system. The other set focuses on helping members of client systems to become aware of their attitude and value orientations and relationship difficulties through a probing of feelings, manifest and latent, involved in the functioning and operation of the client system.[27] Both approaches use the development of "temporary systems" as a medium of reeducation of persons and of role occupants in various ongoing social systems.[28]

Improving the Problem-Solving Capabilities of a System

This family of approaches to changing rests on several assumptions about change in human systems. Changes in a system, when they are reality oriented, take the form of problem solving. A system to achieve optimum reality orientation in its adaptations to its changing internal and external environments must develop and institutionalize its own problem-solving structures and processes. These structures and processes must be tuned both to human problems of relationship and morale and to technical problems of meeting the system's task requirements, set by its goals of production, distribution, and so on.[29] System problems are typically not social *or* technical but actually sociotechnical.[30] The problem-solving structures and processes of a human system must be developed to deal with a range of sociotechnical difficulties, converting them into problems and organizing the relevant processes of the data collection, planning, invention, and tryout of solutions, evaluation and feedback of results, replanning, and so forth, which are required for the solution of the problems.

The human parts of the system must learn to function collaboratively in these processes of problem identification and solution and the system must develop institutionalized support and mechanisms for maintaining and improving these processes. Actually, the model of changing in these approaches is a cooperative, action-research model. This model was suggested by Lewin and developed most elaborately for use in educational settings by Stephen M. Corey.[31]

The range of interventions by outside change agents in implementing this approach to changing is rather wide. It has been most fully elaborated in relation to organizational development programs. Within such programs, intervention methods have been most comprehensively tested in industrial settings. Some of these more or less tested intervention methods are listed below. A design for any organizational development program, of course, normally uses a number of these in succession or combination.

1. Collection of data about organizational functioning and feedback of data into processes of data interpretation and of planning ways of correcting revealed dysfunctions by system managers and data collectors in collaboration.[32]

2. Training of managers and working organizational units in methods of problem solving through self-examination of present ways of dealing with difficulties and through development and tryout of better ways with consultation by outside and/or inside change agents. Usually, the working unit leaves its working place for parts of its training. These laboratory sessions are ordinarily interspersed with on-the-job consultations.

3. Developing acceptance of feedback (research and development) roles and functions within the organization, training persons to fill these roles, and relating such roles strategically to the ongoing management of the organization.

4. Training internal change agents to function within the organization in carrying on needed applied research, consultation, and training.[33]

Whatever specific strategies of intervention may be employed in developing the system's capabilities for problem solving, change efforts are designed to help the system in developing ways of scanning its operations to detect problems, of diagnosing these problems to determine relevant changeable factors in them, and of moving toward collaboratively determined solutions to the problems.

Releasing and Fostering Growth in the Persons Who Make Up the System to Be Changed

Those committed to this family of approaches to changing tend to see the person as the basic unit of social organization. Persons, it is believed, are capable of creative, life-affirming, self- and other-regarding and respecting responses, choices, and actions, if conditions which thwart these kinds of responses are removed and other supporting conditions developed. Rogers has formulated these latter conditions in his analysis of the therapist-client relationship—trustworthiness, empathy, caring, and others.[34] Maslow has worked out a similar idea in his analysis of the hierarchy of needs in persons.[35] If lower needs are met, higher need-meeting actions will take place. McGregor[36] has formulated the ways in which existing organizations operate to fixate persons in lower levels of motivation and has sought to envision an organization designed to release and support the growth of persons in fulfilling their higher motivations as they function within the organizations.

Various intervention methods have been designed to help people discover themselves as persons and commit themselves to continuing personal growth in the various relationships of their lives.

1. One early effort to install personal counseling widely and strategically in an organization has been reported by Roethlisberger and Dickson.[37]

2. Training groups designed to facilitate personal confrontation and growth of members in an open, trusting, and accepting atmosphere have been conducted for individuals from various back-home situations and for persons from the same back-home setting. The processes of

these groups have sometimes been described as "therapy for normals."[38]

3. Groups and laboratories designed to stimulate and support personal growth have been designed to utilize the resources of nonverbal exchange and communication among members along with verbal dialogue in inducing personal confrontation, discovery, and commitment to continuing growth.

4. Many psychotherapists, building on the work of Freud and Adler, have come to use groups, as well as two-person situations, as media of personal reeducation and growth. Such efforts are prominent in mental health approaches to changing and have been conducted in educational, religious, community, industrial, and hospital settings. While these efforts focus primarily upon helping individuals to change themselves toward greater self-clarity and fuller self-actualization, they are frequently designed and conducted in the hope that personal changes will lead to changes in organizations, institutions, and communities as well.

We have presented the two variants of normative-reeducative approaches to changing in a way to emphasize their differences. Actually, there are many similarities between them as well, which justify placing both under the same general heading. We have already mentioned one of these similarities. Both frequently use temporary systems—a residential laboratory or workshop, a temporary group with special resources built in, an ongoing system which incorporates a change agent (trainer, consultant, counselor, or therapist) temporarily—as an aid to growth in the system and/or in its members.

More fundamentally, both approaches emphasize experience-based learning as an ingredient of all enduring changes in human systems. Yet both accept the principle that people must learn to learn from their experiences if self-directed change is to be maintained and continued. Frequently, people have learned to defend against the potential lessons of experience when these threaten existing equilibria, whether in the person or in the social system. How can these defenses be lowered to let the data of experience get into processes of perceiving the situation, of constructing new and better ways to define it, of inventing new and more appropriate ways of responding to the situation as redefined, of becoming more fully aware of the consequences of actions, of rearticulating value orientations which sanction more responsible ways of managing the consequences of actions, and so forth? Learning to learn from ongoing experience is a major objective in both approaches to changing. Neither denies the relevance or importance of the noncognitive determinants of behavior—feelings, attitudes, norms, and relationships—along with cognitive-perceptual determinants, in effecting behavioral change. The problem-solving approaches emphasize the cognitive determinants more than personal growth approaches do. But exponents of the former do not accept the rationalistic biases of the rational-empirical family of change strategies, already discussed. Since exponents of both problem-solving and personal growth approaches are committed to reeducation of persons as integral to effective change in human systems, both emphasize norms of openness of communication, trust between persons, lowering of status barriers between parts of the system, and mutuality between parts as necessary conditions of the reeducative process.

Great emphasis has been placed recently upon the releasing of creativity in persons, groups, and organizations as requisite to coping adaptively with accelerated changes in the conditions of modern living. We have already stressed the emphasis which personal growth approaches put upon the release of creative responses in persons being reeducated. Problem-solving approaches also value creativity, though they focus more upon the group and organizational conditions which increase the probability of creative responses by persons functioning within those conditions than upon persons directly. The approaches do differ in their strategies for releasing creative responses within human systems. But both believe that creative adaptations to changing conditions may arise *within* human systems and do not have to be imported from *outside* them as in innovation-diffusion approaches already discussed and the power-compliance models still to be dealt with.

One developing variant of normative-reeducative approaches to changing, not already noted, focuses on effective conflict management. It is, of course, common knowledge that differences within a society which demand interaccommodation often manifest themselves as conflicts. In the process of managing such conflicts, changes in the norms, policies, and relationships of the society occur. Can conflict management be brought into the ambit of planned change as defined in this volume? Stemming from the work of the Sherifs in creating intergroup conflict and seeking to resolve it in a field-laboratory situation,[39] training in intergroup conflict and conflict resolution found its way into training laboratories through the efforts of Blake and others. Since that time, laboratories for conflict management have been developed under NTL and other auspices and methodologies for conflict resolution and management, in keeping with the values of planned change, have been devised. Blake's and Walton's work represents some of the findings from these pioneering efforts.[40]

Thus, without denying their differences in assumption and strategy, we believe that the differing approaches discussed in this section can be seen together within the framework of normative-reeducative approaches to changing. Two efforts to conceptualize planned change in a way to reveal the similarities in assumptions about changing and in value orientations toward change underlying these variant approaches are those by Lippitt, Watson, and Westley and by Bennis, Benne, and Chin.[41]

Another aspect of changing in human organizations is represented by efforts to conceive human organization in forms that go beyond the bureaucratic form which captured the imagination and fixed the contours of thinking and practice of

organizational theorists and practitioners from the latter part of the 19th through the early part of the 20th century. The bureaucratic form of organization was conceptualized by Max Weber and carried into American thinking by such students of administration as Urwick.[42] On this view, effective organization of human effort followed the lines of effective division of labor and effective establishment of lines of reporting, control, and supervision from the mass base of the organization up through various levels of control to the top of the pyramidal organization from which legitimate authority and responsibility stemmed.

The work of industrial sociologists like Mayo threw doubt upon the adequacy of such a model of formal organization to deal with the realities of organizational life by revealing the informal organization which grows up within the formal structure to satisfy personal and interpersonal needs not encompassed by or integrated into the goals of the formal organization. Chester Barnard may be seen as a transitional figure who, in discussing the functions of the organizational executive, gave equal emphasis to his responsibilities for task effectiveness and organizational efficiency (optimally meeting the human needs of persons in the organization).[43] Much of the development of subsequent organizational theory and practice has centered on problems of integrating the actualities, criteria, and concepts of organizational effectiveness and of organizational efficiency.

A growing group of thinkers and researchers have sought to move beyond the bureaucratic model toward some new model of organization which might set directions and limits for change efforts in organizational life. Out of many thinkers, we choose four who have theorized out of an orientation consistent with what we have called a normative-reeducative approach to changing.

Rensis Likert has presented an intergroup model of organization. Each working unit strives to develop and function as a group. The group's efforts are linked to other units of the organization by the overlapping membership of supervisors or managers in vertically or horizontally adjacent groups. This view of organization throws problems of delegation, supervision, and internal communication into a new light and emphasizes the importance of linking persons as targets of change and reeducation in processes of organizational development.[44]

We have already stressed McGregor's efforts to conceive a form of organization more in keeping with new and more valid views of human nature and motivation (Theory Y) than the limited and false views of human nature and motivation (Theory X) upon which traditional bureaucratic organization has rested. In his work he sought to move thinking and practice relevant to organization and organizational change beyond the limits of traditional forms. "The essential task of management is to arrange organizational conditions and methods of operation so that people can achieve their own goals best by directing their own efforts toward organizational objectives."[45]

Bennis has consciously sought to move beyond bureaucracy in tracing the contours of the organizations of the future.[46] And Shepard has described an organizational form consistent with support for continual changing and self-renewal, rather than with a primary mission of maintenance and control.[47]

Power-Coercive Approaches to Effective Change

It is not the use of power, in the sense of influence by one person upon another or by one group upon another, which distinguishes this family of strategies from those already discussed. Power is an ingredient of all human action. The differences lie rather in the ingredients of power on which the strategies of changing depend and the ways in which power is generated and applied in processes of effecting change. Thus what we have called rational-empirical approaches depend on knowledge as a major ingredient of power. In this view, men of knowledge are legitimate sources of power and the desirable flow of influence or power is from men who know to men who don't know through processes of education and of dissemination of valid information.

Normative-reeducative strategies of changing do not deny the importance of knowledge as a source of power, especially in the form of knowledge-based technology. Exponents of this approach to changing are committed to redressing the imbalance between the limited use of behavioral knowledge and people technologies and the widespread use of physical-biological knowledge and related thing technologies in effecting changes in human affairs. In addition, exponents of normative-reeducative approaches recognize the importance of noncognitive determinants of behavior as resistances or supports to changing—values, attitudes, and feelings at the personal level and norms and relationships at the social level. Influence must extend to these noncognitive determinants of behavior if voluntary commitments and reliance on social intelligence are to be maintained and extended in our changing society. Influence of noncognitive determinants of behavior must be exercised in mutual processes of persuasion within collaborative relationships. These strategies are oriented against coercive and nonreciprocal influence, both on moral and on pragmatic grounds.

What ingredients of power do power-coercive strategies emphasize? In general, emphasis is upon political and economic sanctions in the exercise of power. But other coercive strategies emphasize the utilization of moral power, playing upon sentiments of guilt and shame. Political power carries with it legitimacy and the sanctions which accrue to those who break the law. Thus getting a law passed against racial imbalance in the schools brings legitimate coercive power behind efforts to desegregate the schools, threatening those who resist with sanctions under the law and reducing the resistance of others who are morally oriented against breaking the law. Economic power exerts coercive influence over the decisions of those to whom it is applied. Thus federal appropriations granting funds to local schools for increased emphasis upon science instruction tend to exercise coercive influence over the decisions of local school officials concerning the emphasis of the school curriculum. In general, power-coercive strategies of changing seek to mass political and economic power behind the change goals which the strategists of change have decided are desirable. Those who oppose these goals, if they adopt the same strategy, seek to mass political and economic power in opposition. The strategy thus tends to divide the society when there is anything like a division of opinion and of power in that society.

When a person or group is entrenched in power in a social system, in command of political legitimacy and of political and economic sanctions, that person or group can use power-coercive strategies in effecting changes which they consider desirable, without much awareness on the part of those out of power in the system that such strategies are being employed. A power-coercive way of making decisions is accepted as in the nature of things. The use of such strategies by those in legitimate control of various social systems in our society is much more widespread than most of us might at first be willing or able to admit. This is true in educational systems as well as in other social systems.

When any part of a social system becomes aware that its interests are not being served by those in control of the system, the coercive power of those in control can be challenged. If the minority is committed to power-coercive strategies, or is aware of no alternatives to such strategies, how can they make headway against existing power relations within the system? They may organize discontent against the present controls of the system and achieve power outside the legitimate channels of authority in the system. Thus teachers' unions may develop power against coercive controls by the central administrative group and the school board in a school system. They may threaten concerted resistance to or disregard of administrative rulings and board policies or they may threaten work stoppage or a strike. Those in control may get legislation against

teachers' strikes. If the political power of organized teachers grows, they may get legislation requiring collective bargaining between organized teachers and the school board on some range of educational issues. The power struggle then shifts to the negotiation table, and compromise between competing interests may become the expected goal of the intergroup exchange. Whether the augmented power of new, relevant knowledge or the generation of common power through joint collaboration and deliberation are lost in the process will depend on the degree of commitment by all parties to the conflict and to a continuation and maintenance of power-coercive strategies for effecting change.

What general varieties of power-coercive strategies, to be exercised either by those in control as they seek to maintain their power or to be used by those now outside a position of control and seeking to enlarge their power, can be identified?

Strategies of Nonviolence

Mahatma Gandhi may be seen as the most prominent recent theorist and practitioner of nonviolent strategies for effecting change, although the strategies did not originate with him in the history of mankind, either in idea or in practice. Gandhi spoke of Thoreau's *Essay on Civil Disobedience* as one important influence in his own approach to nonviolent coercive action. Martin Luther King was perhaps America's most distinguished exponent of nonviolent coercion in effecting social change. A minority (or majority) confronted with what they see as an unfair, unjust, or cruel system of coercive social control may dramatize their rejection of the system by publicly and nonviolently witnessing and demonstrating against it. Part of the ingredients of the power of the civilly disobedient is in the guilt which their demonstration of injustice, unfairness, or cruelty of the existing system of control arouses in those exercising control or in others previously committed to the present system of control. The opposition to the disobedient group may be demoralized and may waver in their exercise of control, if they profess the moral values to which the dissidents are appealing.

Weakening or dividing the opposition through moral coercion may be combined with economic sanctions—like Gandhi's refusal to buy salt and other British manufactured commodities in India or like the desegregationists' economic boycott of the products of racially discriminating factories and businesses.

The use of nonviolent strategies for opening up conflicts in values and demonstrating against injustices or inequities in existing patterns of social control has become familiar to educational leaders in the demonstrations and sit-ins of college students in various universities and in the demonstrations of desegregationists against de facto segregation of schools. And the widened use of such strategies may be confidently predicted. Whether such strategies will be used to extend collaborative ways of developing policies and normative-reeducative strategies of changing, or whether they will be used to augment power struggles as the only practical way of settling conflicts, will depend in some large part upon the strategy commitments of those now in positions of power in education systems.

Use of Political Institutions to Achieve Change

Political power has traditionally played an important part in achieving changes in our institutional life. And political power will continue to play an important part in shaping and reshaping our institutions of education as well as other institutions. Changes enforced by political coercion need not be oppressive if the quality of our democratic processes can be maintained and improved.

Changes in policies with respect to education have come from various departments of government. By far the most of these have come through legislation on the state level. Under legislation, school administrators have various degrees of discretionary powers, and policy and program changes are frequently put into effect by administrative rulings. Judicial decisions have played an important part in shaping educational policies, none more dramatically than the Supreme Court decision declaring laws and policies supporting school segregation illegal. And the federal courts have played a central part in seeking to implement and enforce this decision.

Some of the difficulty with the use of political institutions to effect changes arises from an overestimation by change agents of the capability of political action to effect changes in practice. When the law is passed, the administrative ruling announced, or the judicial decision handed down legitimizing some new policy or program or illegitimizing some traditional practice, change agents who have worked hard for the law, ruling, or decision frequently assume that the desired change has been made.

Actually, all that has been done is to bring the force of legitimacy behind some envisioned change. The processes of reeducation of persons who are to conduct themselves in new ways still have to be carried out. And the new conduct often requires new knowledge, new skills, new attitudes, and new value orientations. And, on the social level, new conduct may require changes in the norms, the roles, and the relationship structures of the institutions involved. This is not to discount the importance of political actions in legitimizing changed policies and practices in educational institutions and in other institutions as well. It is rather to emphasize that normative-reeducative strategies must be combined with political coercion, both before and after the political action, if the public is to be adequately informed and desirable and commonly acceptable changes in practice are to be achieved.

Changing through the Recomposition and Manipulation of Power Elites

The idea or practice of a ruling class or of a power elite in social control was by no means original with Karl Marx. What was original with him was his way of relating these concepts to a process and strategy of fundamental social change. The composition of the ruling class was, of course, for

Marx those who owned and controlled the means and processes of production of goods and services in a society. Since, for Marx, the ideology of the ruling class set limits to the thinking of most intellectuals and of those in charge of educational processes and of communicating, rationales for the existing state of affairs, including its concentration of political and economic power, is provided and disseminated by intellectuals and educators and communicators within the system.

Since Marx was morally committed to a classless society in which political coercion would disappear because there would be no vested private interests to rationalize and defend, he looked for a counterforce in society to challenge and eventually to overcome the power of the ruling class. And this he found in the economically dispossessed and alienated workers of hand and brain. As this new class gained consciousness of its historic mission and its power increased, the class struggle could be effectively joined. The outcome of this struggle was victory for those best able to organize and maximize the productive power of the instruments of production—for Marx this victory belonged to the now dispossessed workers.

Many of Marx's values would have put him behind what we have called normative-reeducative strategies of changing. And he recognized that such strategies would have to be used after the accession of the workers to state power in order to usher in the classless society. He doubted if the ruling class could be reeducated, since reeducation would mean loss of their privileges and coercive power in society. He recognized that the power elite could, within limits, accommodate new interests as these gained articulation and power. But these accommodations must fall short of a radical transfer of power to a class more capable of wielding it. Meanwhile, he remained committed to a power-coercive strategy of changing until the revolutionary transfer of power had been effected.

Marxian concepts have affected the thinking of contemporary men about social change both inside and outside nations in which Marxism has

become the official orientation. His concepts have tended to bolster assumptions of the necessity of power-coercive strategies in achieving fundamental redistributions of socio-economic power or in recomposing or manipulating power elites in a society. Democratic, reeducative methods of changing have a place only after such changes in power allocation have been achieved by power-coercive methods. Non-Marxians as well as Marxians are often committed to this Marxian dictum.

In contemporary America, C. Wright Mills has identified a power elite, essentially composed of industrial, military, and governmental leaders, who direct and limit processes of social change and accommodation in our society. And President Eisenhower warned of the dangerous concentration of power in substantially the same groups in his farewell message to the American people. Educators committed to democratic values should not be blinded to the limitations to advancement of those values, which are set by the less than democratic ideology of our power elites. And normative-reeducative strategists of changing must include power elites among their targets of changing as they seek to diffuse their ways of progress within contemporary society. And they must take seriously Marx's questions about the reeducability of members of the power elites, as they deal with problems and projects of social change.

The operation of a power elite in social units smaller than a nation was revealed in Floyd Hunter's study of decision making in an American city. Hunter's small group of deciders, with their satellite groups of intellectuals, front men, and implementers, is in a real sense a power elite. The most common reaction of educational leaders to Hunter's "discovery" has been to seek ways in which to persuade and manipulate the deciders toward support of educational ends which educational leaders consider desirable—whether bond issues, building programs, or anything else. This is non-Marxian in its acceptance of power relations in a city or community as fixed. It would be Marxian if it sought to build counter power to offset and reduce the power of the presently deciding group where this power interfered with the achievement of desirable educational goals. This latter strategy, though not usually Marxian inspired in the propaganda sense of that term, has been more characteristic of organized teacher effort in pressing for collective bargaining or of some student demonstrations and sit-ins. In the poverty program, the federal government in its insistence on participation of the poor in making policies for the program has at least played with a strategy of building countervailing power to offset the existing concentration of power in people not identified with the interests of the poor in reducing their poverty.

Those committed to the advancement of normative-reeducative strategies of changing must take account of present actual concentrations of power wherever they work. This does *not* mean that they must develop a commitment to power-coercive strategies to change the distribution of power except when these may be necessary to effect the spread of their own democratically and scientifically oriented methods of changing within society.

FIGURE 1   **Strategies of Deliberate Changing**

A. RATIONAL–EMPIRICAL
Views of the enlightenment and classical liberalism

B. NORMATIVE—
Views of therapists,

FIGURE 1   *(concluded)*

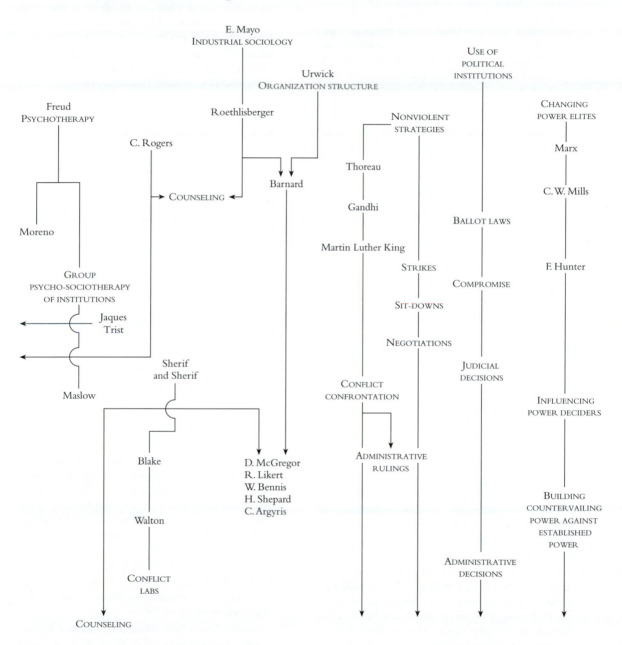

RE-EDUCATIVE
trainers, and situation changers

C. POWER-COERCIVE

Endnotes

1. Throughout our discussion of strategies and procedures, we will not differentiate these according to the size of the target of change. We assume that there are similarities in processes of changing, whether the change affects an individual, a small group, an organization, a community, or a culture. In addition, we are not attending to differences among the aspects of a system, let us say an educational system, which is being changed—curriculum, audiovisual methods, team teaching, pupil grouping, and so on. Furthermore, because many changes in communities or organizations start with an individual or some small membership group, our general focus will be upon those strategies which lead to and involve individual changes.

   We will sidestep the issue of defining change in this paper. As further conceptual work progresses in the study of planned change, we shall eventually have to examine how different definitions of change relate to strategies and procedures for effecting change. But we are not dealing with these issues here.

2. We have indicated the main roots of ideas and idea systems underlying the principal strategies of changing and their subvariants on a chart which appears as Figure 1 at the end of this essay. It may be useful in seeing both the distinctions and the relationships between various strategies of changing in time perspective. We have emphasized developments of the past 25 years more than earlier developments. This makes for historical foreshortening. We hope this is a pardonable distortion, considering our present limited purpose.

3. Jean Hills, "Social Science, Ideology and the Purposes of Educational Administration," *Education Administration Quarterly,* Autumn 1965, pp. 23–40.

4. Garth Jones, "Planned Organizational Change, a Set of Working Documents," Center for Research in Public Organization, School of Public Administration (Los Angeles: University of Southern California, 1964).

5. For a review, see Ronald G. Havelock and Kenneth D. Benne, "An Exploratory Study of Knowledge Utilization," in *The Planning of Change,* 2nd ed. Warren G. Bennis, Kenneth D. Benne, and Robert Chin (New York: Holt, Rinehart & Winston, 1969), chap. 3, p. 124.

6. Paul R. Mort and Donald R. Ross, *Principles of School Administration* (New York: McGraw-Hill, 1957). Paul R. Mort and Francis G. Cornell, *American Schools in Transition: How Our Schools Adapt Their Practices to Changing Needs* (New York: Bureau of Publications, Teachers College, Columbia University Press, 1941).

7. Robert Chin, "Research Approaches to the Problem of Civic Training," in *The Adolescent Citizen,* ed. F. Patterson (New York: Free Press, 1980).

8. Matthew B. Miles, *Some Propositions in Research Utilization in Education* (March 1965), in press. Kenneth Wiles, paper for seminar on Strategies for Curriculum Change (Columbus: Ohio State University, 1965). Charles Jung and Ronald Lippitt, "Utilization of Scientific Knowledge for Change in Education," in *Concepts for Social Change* (Washington, D.C.: National Educational Association, National Training Laboratories, 1967). Havelock and Benne, "Exploratory Study of Knowledge Utilization," in Bennis et al., *Planning of Change,* chap. 3, p. 124. David Clark and Egon Guba, "An Examination of Potential Change Roles in Education," seminar on Innovation in Planning School Curricula (Columbus: Ohio State University, 1965).

9. David Clark, "Educational Research and Development: The Next Decade," in *Implications for Education of Prospective Changes in Society,* a publication of "Designing Education for the Future—an Eight State Project" (Denver, Colo., 1967).

10. Elihu Katz, "The Social Itinerary of Technical Change: Two Studies on the Diffusion of Innovation," in Bennis et al., *Planning of Change,* chap. 5, p. 230. Richard Carlson, "Some Needed Research on the Diffusion of Innovations" (paper at the Washington Conference on Educational Change, Columbus, Ohio, Ohio State University). Everett Rogers, "What Are Innovators Like?" in *Change Process in the Public Schools,* Center for the Advanced Study of Educational Administration (Eugene: University of Oregon, 1965). Everett Rogers, *Diffusion of Innovations* (New York: Free Press, 1962).

11. Carl Hovland, Irving Janis, and Harold Kelley, *Communication and Persuasion* (New Haven, Conn.: Yale University Press, 1953).

12. Raymond Bauer, "The Obstinate Audience: The Influence Process from the Point of View of Social

Communication," in Bennis et al., *Planning of Change,* chap. 9, p. 507.

13. B. F. Skinner, *Walden Two* (New York: Crowell-Collier and Macmillan, 1948).

14. "Designing Education for the Future—an Eight State Project" (Denver, Colo., 1967).

15. Karl Mannheim, *Ideology and Utopia* (New York: Harcourt Brace Jovanovich, 1946).

16. Alfred Korzybski, *Science and Sanity,* 3rd ed. (International Non-Aristotelian Library Publishing Company, 1948). S. I. Hayakawa, *Language in Thought and Action* (New York: Harcourt Brace Jovanovich, 1941).

17. John Dewey, *Philosophy, Psychology and Social Practice,* ed. Joseph Ratner (New York: Capricorn Books, 1967).

18. Kurt Lewin, *Resolving Social Conflicts* (New York: Harper & Row, 1948). Kurt Lewin, *Field Theory in Social Science* (New York: Harper & Row, 1951).

19. For Freud, an interesting summary is contained in Otto Fenichel, *Problems of Psychoanalytic Technique* (Albany: NT Psychoanalytic Quarterly, 1941).

20. W. Bennis, K. Benne, and R. Chin, *The Planning of Change,* 1st ed. (New York: Holt, Rinehart & Winston, 1961). R. Lippitt, J. Watson, and B. Westley, *The Dynamics of Planned Change* (New York: Harcourt Brace Jovanovich, 1958). W. Bennis, *Changing Organizations* (New York: McGraw-Hill, 1966).

21. Raup, Benne, Smith, and Axtelle, *The Discipline of Practical Judgment in a Democratic Society,* Yearbook No. 28 of the National Society of College Teachers of Education (Chicago: University of Chicago Press, 1943).

22. Mary Follett, *Creative Experience and Dynamic Administration* (New York: David McKay, 1924).

23. Karl Mannheim, *Man and Society in an Age of Reconstruction* (New York: Harcourt Brace Jovanovich, 1940).

24. Elliot Jaques, *The Changing Culture of a Factory* (New York: Holt, Rinehart & Winston, 1952).

25. William J. Dickson and F. J. Roethlisberger, *Personal Counseling in an Organization: A Sequel to the Hawthorne Researchers* (Boston: Harvard Business School, 1966).

26. Elton Mayo, *The Social Problems of an Industrial Civilization* (Cambridge, Mass.: Harvard University Press, 1945).

27. Leland Bradford, Jack R. Gibb, and Kenneth D. Benne, *T-Group Theory and Laboratory Methods* (New York: John Wiley & Sons, 1964).

28. Matthew B. Miles, "On Temporary Systems," in *Innovation in Education,* ed. M. B. Miles (New York: Bureau of Publications, Teachers College, Columbia University Press, 1964), pp. 437–92.

29. Robert R. Blake and Jane S. Mouton, *The Managerial Grid* (Houston: Gulf Publishing, 1961).

30. Jay W. Lorsch and Paul Lawrence, "The Diagnosis of Organizational Problems," in Bennis et al., *Planning of Change,* chap. 8, p. 468.

31. Stephen M. Corey, *Action Research to Improve School Practices* (New York: Bureau of Publications, Teachers College, Columbia University Press, 1953).

32. See contributions by Miles et al., "Data Feedback and Organizational Change in a School System," in Bennis et al., *Planning of Change,* chap. 8, p. 457; and Lorsch and Lawrence, "Diagnosis of Organizational Problems," in Bennis et al. *Planning of Change,* chap. 8, p. 468.

33. C. Argyris, "Explorations in Consulting-Client Relationships," in Bennis et al., *Planning of Change,* chap. 8, p. 434. See also Richard Beckhard, "The Confrontation Meeting," in Bennis et al., *Planning of Change,* chap. 8, p. 478.

34. Carl Rogers, "The Characteristics of a Helping Relationship," in Bennis et al. *Planning of Change,* chap. 4, p. 153.

35. Abraham Maslow, *Motivation and Personality* (New York: Harper & Row, 1954).

36. Douglas M. McGregor, "The Human Side of Enterprise," in W. Bennis et al., *The Planning of Change,* 1st ed. (New York: Holt, Rinehart & Winston, 1961), pp. 422–31.

37. Dickson and Roethlisberger, *Personal Counseling in an Organization.*

38. James V. Clark "A Healthy Organization," in Bennis et al., *Planning of Change,* chap. 6, p. 282. Irving Weschler, Fred Massarik, and Robert Tannenbaum, "The Self in Process: A Sensitivity Training Emphasis," in *Issues in Training,* ed. I. R. Weschler and E. Schein. Selected Reading Series No. 5 (Washington, D.C.: National Training Laboratories).

39. Muzafer and Carolyn Sherif, *Groups in Harmony and Tension* (New York: Harper & Row, 1953).

40. Robert Blake et al., "The Union Management Inter-Group Laboratory," in Bennis et al., *Planning of Change,* chap. 4, p. 176. Richard Walton, "Two Strategies of Social Change and Their Dilemmas," in Bennis et al., *Planning of Change,* chap. 4, p. 167.

41. Lippitt et al., *Dynamics of Planned Change.* Bennis et al., *Planning of Change,* 1st ed.

42. Lyndall Urwick, *The Pattern of Management* (Minneapolis: University of Minnesota Press, 1956).

43. Chester I. Barnard, *The Functions of the Executive* (Cambridge, Mass.: Harvard University Press, 1938).

44. Rensis Likert, *New Patterns of Management* (New York: McGraw-Hill, 1961).

45. McGregor, "Human Side of Enterprise," pp. 422–31.

46. W. G. Bennis, "Changing Organizations," in Bennis et al., *Planning of Change,* chap. 10, p. 568.

47. H. A. Shepard, "Innovation-Resisting and Innovation-Producing Organizations," in Bennis et al., *Planning of Change,* chap. 9, p. 519.

Reading 4

Toward Third-Wave Managing and Consulting

Marvin R. Weisbord

The results of this generalized speedup of the corporate metabolism are multiple: shorter product life cycles, more leasing and renting, more frequent buying and selling, more ephemeral consumption patterns, more fads, more training time for workers (who must continually adjust to new procedures), more frequent changes in contracts, more negotiations and legal work, more pricing changes, more job turnover, more dependence on data, more ad hoc organization. . . . Under these escalating pressures, it is easy to see why so many businessmen, bankers, and corporate executives wonder what exactly they are doing and why. Brought up with Second-Wave certainties, they see the world they knew tearing apart under the impact of an accelerating wave of change.

Alvin Toffler
The Third Wave, 1980

We live in the midst of a historic global revolution—from physical to knowledge work, mechanical to process technologies, manufacturing to service economies, cultural sameness to greater diversity. Future-thinker Alvin Toffler calls this sea change "the third wave" to differentiate it from the agricultural and industrial revolutions of centuries past. Above all, it is a social revolution. Quality of working life (QWL)—meaning quality of products, services, and work itself—has become a worldwide aspiration. QWL is also an umbrella for every sort of "change" program—from quality circles, organization development, statistical quality control, sociotechnical systems design, and cultural transformation.

In this article I want to suggest another "bottom line" for the widespread interest in QWL. I see a hunger everywhere for community among people alienated from work and each other by new technologies and global economics. *Community,* as I use it here, means a workplace where people pro-

Source: Reprinted from *Organizational Dynamics,* Winter 1987. Copyright © 1987 Marvin R. Weisbord. Reprinted by permission of American Management Association International, New York, NY. All rights reserved. http://www.amanet.org.

duce goods or services for a living. A productive community is one where people find dignity, meaning, and security in contributing to the whole.

My purpose is as old as the industrial revolution. More than 40 years ago, Elton Mayo, founder of industrial human relations, noted how "science and industry put an end to the individual's feeling of identification with his group, of satisfaction in his work." We still seek constructive responses to Mayo's diagnosis. Consider the historic 1986 agreement between the United Steelworkers of America and National Steel Corporation. Management, despite economic hard times, promised employment security. The union offered greater job flexibility to increase output. That deal marked a radical break with adversarial traditions. Both parties will be a long time, however, learning to make it work. Yet it exactly embodies the spirit of productive community.

A Practice Theory for Managers and Consultants

Here I offer some spadework toward a "third-wave" practice theory of managing and consulting grounded in these values. My ideas apply to what I know best—reorganizations and work re-design to improve output, quality, and customer focus. They synthesize my work as manager and consultant for more than 25 years with my observations of the uneasy relationship between engineering and psychology in this century. I seek a coherent way of reorganizing under what management professor Peter Vaill calls conditions of "permanent white water."

I want to shift my gaze away from "problems" like cost control *or* interpersonal conflict, that are symptomatic of needs, toward productive community—based on purposes, missions, strategies, and structures worthy of our aspirations, cooperation, and sweat. What can we do today—right now—to make work more secure and improve quality? If you had only a few hours or a few weeks, how would you use your time?

The need to build workplace communities, I'm convinced, is closely tied to preserving democratic values as global economic pressures mount and new hardware, software, and robots pump into the workplace at a furious rate. These developments encompass at once the best and the scariest aspects of American individualism. We revere entrepreneurial behavior and self-actualization. We always have been ambivalent about commitments to each other across levels, functions, lines of status, ethnicity, and class.

"We insist, perhaps more than ever before, on finding our true selves independent of any cultural or social influence," Robert Bellah and partners write in *Habits of the Heart.* "Yet we spend much of our time navigating through immense bureaucratic structures—multiversities, corporations, government agencies—manipulating and being manipulated by others."

We want things every which way. We demand freedom, equal opportunity, and the right to run our own lives, making good Jefferson's Declaration of Independence for "life, liberty, and the pursuit of happiness." We also covet personal security, dignity, support—as promised in the Constitution and Bill of Rights. In the workplace this sometimes plays out as a demand that management "give" people these qualities, when, in fact,

all management has the power to do is join in searching for ways to preserve them.

We are driven together again out of necessity. Work methods change so fast now they cannot be controlled by traditional management systems. Social scientists Fred Emery and Eric Trist observed in the 1960s that firms were in increasingly "turbulent fields"—making prediction and control impossible. In *Beyond the Stable State* (1971), Donald Schon saw technology disrupting all "anchors for personal identity." Now the top is spinning faster. Companies, agencies, institutions that used to reorganize every five years now rearrange themselves annually. Many change work sites, job content, titles, and product and service concepts in a perpetual redirection of technologies and markets. How shall we manage these chaotic transactions among economics, technology, and people in the workplace? I suggest that the only steady beacons in such stormy seas are aspirations for dignity and meaning—the wellsprings of motivation—in work.

Invoking Science

For more than 100 years the image of science has been invoked as the key to human motivation. This holy grail was pursued by Frederick Taylor, "the father of scientific management," long before management became a profession. It was pursued with equal intensity by social psychologist Kurt Lewin, "the practical theorist" who invented "force field analysis," discovered participative management, and laid the intellectual groundwork for organization development (OD) in the 1940s.

Taylor, a self-taught engineer, realized that managers awash in the "the second wave" could not motivate factory workers. In 1893 he invented a new profession, "consulting engineer," linking cost accounting, time study, wage incentives, and planning into a system that today influences nearly every workplace in the industrial world. Taylor sought to squeeze human discretion from work. He raised wages dramatically if people would do things "the one best way" specified by his engineers.

Taylor today is reviled for his rigid methods. His values, lost in the mists, were quite contemporary. A pacifist as a child, he hated conflict. He wanted to increase labor-management cooperation, cut out authoritarian supervision, reduce job stress, give people more equitable pay for jobs challenging their highest abilities. Taylor made industrial engineers third-party arbiters between labor and management. They devised the "correct" methods for cooperation and conflict resolution. Both organization development and sociotechnical systems design (STS), guided by Kurt Lewin's action research theories, adopted similar purposes. OD managers became the industrial engineers of group development, prescribing self-awareness and interpersonal skills and/or self-managing work teams instead of time and motion study for taking the arbitrariness out of work.

Taylor fell from grace when his descendants divorced his values and married his techniques. Similarly, many OD practitioners, seduced by social technologies, lost sight of Lewin's values—the spirit of inquiry, cooperation, and democratic principles. They were mesmerized by an innovative bag of tricks for diagnosis and intervention—survey feedback, team building, inter-group problem solving, experiential training. Like time study, these could be shoehorned into organizations without dignity, meaning, or worker commitment. In the ultimate absurdity, people were sent wholesale to learn free choice and commitment—whether they wanted to or not.

A Trip through the Forests of Change Theory

To appreciate why I want to redefine the playing field, I would like you to join me on a trip through the thickets of organizational change theory. OD case studies for 25 years have reflected two *different* theories of improvements, coexisting uneasily. One was a theory of "process" diagnosis based on the expert's data-collecting abilities, what I call "snap-shooting." Another was Lewin's brilliant theory of participative change-oriented action—

"movie-making" in my lingo, but very different from Hollywood's. Most practitioners know that the two theories are really one—that how we take the snapshot determines the quality of the movie. Yet all of us have one foot in what Eric Trist, the originator of sociotechnical thinking, calls the "old paradigm"—Taylor's cause-effect reasoning.

Diagnosis and Action

All consultants advocate expert diagnosis and action-taking. Engineers and behavioral scientists alike have diagnoses of organizational conflict and prescriptions for solving it. *Diagnosis* is medical jargon for the gap between sickness and health. As biology exploded in the late 19th century, the human body, like the workplace, was divided into manageable components, too. Doctors became the industrial engineers of the human physique. Their claim to expertise was based on their ability to factor in every relevant "variable" and thus heal the sick.

It is no surprise that early psychologists thought the same way about mental processes. Indeed, until the biologist Ludwig von Bertalanffy proposed a general systems theory, people educated in Western industrial nations could hardly think any other way. Diagnosis, conceived as identifying and closing gaps between how things are and how they should be, used all the tools of science and technology. It was the ultimate expression of the industrial revolution.

Lewin added a new dimension to the medical model. He highlighted processes unseen through 19th-century eyes because nobody had a conceptual lens powerful enough. Lewin's force fields allowed the taking of "process" snapshots—the feelings, motives, intentions, and other intangibles accompanying "results." Lewin portrayed diagnostic gaps in dynamic terms, as an interaction of social forces—personal, group, company-wide, societal. Who are the gatekeepers, asked Lewin, whose behavior must change to assure constructive action? What forces prevent or accelerate their involvement? Answers could be found through "action research"—a collaboration between activist scholars and social institutions to bring about constructive personal change.

Two Core Concepts

From Lewin I inherited two core concepts that made my consulting practice possible. Human systems, Lewin believed, were almost, but not quite, static and resistant to change. The consulting goal was to help organizations "unfreeze," "move," and "refreeze." Like all OD consultants, I learned to take diagnostic pictures that would make people want to act—to melt the ice of indifference, ignorance, or uncertainty and unfreeze the system. Once melted, it would follow more natural channels until cooled enough to refreeze in more functional patterns. All OD case studies fit that framework. At the heart of this diagnostic act was a confrontation: The client must "own" the incongruity between what is said and what is done—the demon to be exorcised before healing could begin. It was not necessary to assume sickness to use Lewin's model. However, it was not easy to avoid it either for those of us socialized to view life as one long medical model.

A second concept goes by the name of the "task/process" relationship—the subtle chicken/egg interplay between ends and means, methods and goals. A task is something concrete, observable, and thing-oriented. It can be converted into criteria, measurements, targets, and deadlines—just the way Taylor did. A task—group dynamics people were fond of saying—refers to *what* is to be done.

Process refers to *how.* It reflects perceptions, attitudes, reasoning. Process diagnosticians ask, "Why aren't we making progress?" Or, "Who feels committed to this?" They don't ask when, where, and how many but why, how, and whether. Task/process thinking can be likened to the famous visual paradox of the Old Woman/Young Woman, reproduced below. Do you see a young beauty with her head turned or a wizened crone in profile?

You can't see both at once. By some mental gyration, you can learn to shift between them. Does one picture "cause" the other? Cause-effect thinking that gave rise both to Taylorism and the medical model led to a relentless propensity to see one form of task only as *the* "task." Western industrial managers developed an exquisite "left-brain"—linear, rational, A causes B, three steps, nine phases, finish by Tuesday, get to the bottom line. Diagnosis, even of "processes," requires structure and precision. Whether your categories are "hard" or "soft," listing and prioritizing puts the left brain into high gear.

Action, on the other hand, reflects pure process. We guide it largely on automatic pilot, fueled by little explosions of energy in the right brain—of creativity, insight, synthesis—that can't be quantified or specified as "targets." Lewin ingeniously expanded left-brain thinking. He shifted the diagnostician's viewpoint to the other picture—*processes* always present and not previously visible because nobody was looking for them. From his work came my simple practice theory: "Process" issues *always* block work on "tasks."

Through trained observation, you can diagnose ingenious linkages between task and process. When work stalls, for example, determine what is *not* being talked about—the gap between word and deed, the all-too-human shortfall between aspiration and action. You must shift attention the way a pilot scans instruments—from compass to altimeter to air speed indicator—to keep task and process synchronized. That requires skills few of us learn in school.

Musings on Getting "Whole Systems" in a Room

1. I don't like one-shot events. School boards and town councils meet repeatedly. A one-shot conference is not adequate to the tasks of productive community in a workplace, either.

2. In planning workshops, I seek to *reduce* dynamic tensions. A decision to work with groups of 12 is a decision to train group leaders or facilitators—a step away from self-management. Subteams of three or four work well for many tasks, in which mode 100 people can easily work in one room on their own. I suggest that people make time for small groups to review each other's work and for whole system reviews—so all task forces or departments find out what the others are up to.

3. I contract to manage time boundaries and task structures. In self-managed conferences, I suggest that people monitor their own processes and be responsible for output.

4. I do better organizing the search than "the data." I don't withhold my observations, perspectives, or knowledge. But I don't want to make them the center of the action, either. I like to see "task structures"—worksheets, lists, hints, glossaries, exercises, bibliographies, handouts, overheads— devised with client help. I wish to keep them simple and use them sparingly. I aspire to give people information when they can use it, or call

for it, not all at once. This does not square with what some people want from consultants. I am unable to help people who are convinced there's a lot more.

5. I aspire to keep the task front and center, directed toward output, and to shift focus to "process" only to get the task back on track. I am not against struggle, anxiety, or bewilderment. We have to go through Confusion to get to Renewal. I tend to become more involved if asked and/or when I see people running away from the task or fighting with each other. I do not always know what to do. Fortunately, someone else usually does.

6. I want to help set norms for productive learning. I reduce my involvement as people get past initial anxiety and take over the work. I have found Merrelyn Emery's advice to avoid attaching to a particular subgroup and becoming its (informal) leader a useful discipline for managing large group events.

7. I like rooms with windows and plenty of light. Hotel "dungeon rooms" depress groups and make productive community very difficult.

8. None of these practices are "the" answer to anything—except how one consultant and ex-manager seeks meaning in work.

Unfortunately, left-brain diagnostic thinking— perfected by scientists for more than 100 years— leads people to pay attention to the compass and to consider the altimeter a frill. The diagnoser is assumed to stand outside, impartial, "objective," and aloof from what is observed. If you add to this our propensity to defer to authority—parents, bosses, experts—you have a setup for disappointment. For the authority/dependency relationship *itself* becomes a "process" issue, especially when the person invested with magical abilities lacks satisfactory "answers." Group dynamics' great contribution to management was its relentless gaze at the process picture as inseparable from the task, the diagnoser inseparable from the diagnosis, a leader's effectiveness inseparable from follower contributions.

Unfreezing, Etc.

Now, let us visit the connection between the task/process interplay and "unfreezing, moving, and refreezing." This linkage made the OD profession possible. Unresolved "process" issues accumulate in organizations like junk in an attic. People "freeze" in dysfunctional patterns— nobody listens, appreciates, communicates. Output and quality suffer. Reacting to crises drives out planning. Lewin sought to "unfreeze" this self-perpetuating ice storm over corporate headquarters with action research.

If the stored-up stuff could be got out in the open, if "undiscussable" topics could be talked about, energy would be released. People would become aware of their own contributions to their problems. New behavior would emerge, accelerated by explicit skill training. Unfrozen people could evolve strategy, policy, procedure, systems, relationships, and norms more to their liking. Implementing new action plans would refreeze the system into more functional patterns. Shifting your gaze between task and process could become a "way of life." Results could be feedback loops. When you had new dilemmas, you would realize how your own assumptions contributed. You would be more inclined, for example, to involve others previously left out. This is called "learning how to learn"—studying a situation in which you assume responsibility by taking account of "data" previously ignored.

Consulting Skills and Cultural Change

In the 1950s, people began working out a new form of third-party behavior, "consulting skills," to encourage this form of learning. Technical experts diagnosed and prescribed without involving others in their analyses. Behavioral science consultants made a different deal. They proposed a "scientific" method of data collection, arrangement, and discussion derived from Lewin's insights that people are more likely to act on solutions they have helped develop. It included a minor fiction—that questions, methods of inquiry, data presentation, analysis, and action steps would be jointly planned. I say "fiction" because the methods inevitably belonged to the consultants, and so did the theories of task/process, unfreezing, etc. The "feedback meeting" became a pivotal point of social change—the payoff for action research. There the data was "owned," the system melted, and movement initiated. Those were the OD change assumptions so far as the "movie" was concerned.

As for the "snapshot," the OD consultant may have been an open-systems dreamer, but the practice did not reflect the aspiration. It was too attached to feelings, perceptions, and communications, too separated from technology, economics, and structural relations. "Social researchers," wrote William H. Whyte in *Learning from the Field,* "tended to concentrate almost exclusively on human relations. We gave lip service to the importance of technology but tended to treat it as a constant instead of as a variable, which could be changed along with changes in human relations."

However, many "sociotechnical systems" practitioners who saw technology and people as one system lost sight of the participatory process. They prescribed complex methods of analysis and change that only trained consultants could apply. They evolved analytical tools that belied the movie's basic simplicity. Yet STS was not an "expert" invention. In 1949 Eric Trist found a British coal mine where union workers and a mine manager, driven by a change in roof-control technology, had worked out a system of self-managing teams.

Trist and Emery worked out some simple procedures embodying what they had learned—about redundant skills, managing boundaries, and full participation. In no time their successors had added checklists, analytical tools, exercises, procedures, steps, principles, team building, and other "have tos" enough to deter even the most dedicated clients. Thus we have the central paradox of the changeover from industrial to postindustrial societies—how to encourage people to solve their own problems when every simple new idea can be elaborated endlessly by specialists. What becomes of dignity, community, and meaning in work if you can't reorganize yourself without three years of full-time study? Traditional science has no answers for that paradox.

Yet second-wave ODers thought they had found one. They added up the three stages—unfreezing by third parties, movement by principals and third parties together, refreezing by the principals—that made up a "cultural change strategy." Science could be mobilized to beat back authoritarianism and bureaucracy. What made this different from Taylorism were the psychological content and participative techniques—learning to do things with others, not to them or for them.

The Snapshot Sets Up the Movie

For decades OD diagnoses were based on what might be called Lewin's law. The "snapshot" focused attention on discrepancies and pinpointed ways to close gaps. In *Productive Communities,* I recount four OD projects from 1969 to 1980 based on Lewinian action research methods. Two involved surveys and feedback of structured data and two interviews, group diagnosis, and problem-solving task forces. One project led to a reduction in employee turnover in food service cafeterias, another to a more focused research and development effort in a chemical firm, the third to production improvements in a pill factory, the fourth to strategic redirection in a solar energy company.

In all four, the consultants—with client acceptance—supplied the methods, collected and summarized data, prepared reports, created situation "maps," facilitated discussions. Eventually client groups took over, planned, and implemented changes with consulting help. Reviewing these now, I detect a subtle shift in my practice—from classical action research, based on consultant-centered problem diagnosis, toward much greater client involvement in looking at the whole system regardless of the problem. Why diagnostic technologies for systems change? The reason is not far to seek. We have assumed since Lewin that only accurate "data" and thorough analyses will "unfreeze" structures, procedures, relationships, and norms. Anything less would be unprofessional and unscientific. That is precisely what Taylor assumed about lathes and drillpresses.

Rethinking Lewin

I find my old-practice theory unsatisfying from two perspectives now. First, global markets, technologies, and worker expectations change so fast

that a frozen workplace is a temporary phenomenon. Today, change goes more like a bullet train than a melting iceberg. The rate of change has accelerated since Kurt Lewin died in 1947. It occurs too fast for experts to pin down, even the "process" kind. Conventional diagnoses may serve many useful functions, but "unfreezing" systems is not one of them.

Second, we change our behavior when we are ready to do it, not because of a force field (or any) analysis. The first law of techniques is: Everything works; nothing works. Nobody is skilled enough to push the river. That is supported by consulting experiences clear back to Frederick Taylor. The best a consultant can do is create opportunities for people to discover and do what they want to do anyway. When we apply the "bag of tricks" in a linear way, without informed cooperation and self-control, *only* the content differs from Taylor's. The process comes out uncomfortably the same.

If you accept that proposition, you will see why I worry more about responding to needs for dignity and meaning in work—which means *solving your own problems*—than about supplying "right" answers. There is considerable anxiety and confusion everywhere. I think it is wrong to assume our mutual dilemmas mean "sickness," as if only the diagnostician is whole and in control. Nothing holds still long enough to be diagnosed and "changed" anyway. So consultant-centered diagnostic activities intended to unfreeze systems, even when welcomed by clients willing to defer to authority, may inadvertently distract people from taking charge of their own lives.

Building on Lewin

To honor Lewin now, we must go beyond him. But how? We need new processes for managing and consulting that I do not fully understand. I'm conscious of profound paradoxes. I have at my fingertips diagnostic techniques for every "issue" in the cosmos. On my bookshelf I find more models for fixing things than there are stars in the galaxy. Yet I am strangely undernourished by this intellectual cornucopia. My objective, I keep reminding myself, is not to diagnose and heal "sickness," but to help people manage their work lives better—to enact productive community.

The consultants' dilemma is that we always arrive in the middle of somebody else's movie and leave before the end. It usually has many subplots and informal directors. The consultant negotiates a role—sometimes major, sometimes minor—but always limited by the willingness of others to play along. My view of the consultant's role has turned upside down from what I once thought it was. I imagine it now as helping people discover a more whole view of what they are doing than any one "discipline" or perspective can provide, *including mine.*

I find that proposition fraught with uncertainty. Is it "doable"? To the extent that I can help people integrate worthy values and tasks, I make an important contribution. Yet that means being at some level an "expert" and accepting people's projections of authority, even when I don't act the authoritarian. None of us knows, exactly, how to be both an expert and just one of the gang—when we are dedicated more to collaboration and mutual learning than to being "right." There is no substitute for learning. That any of us can teach others to "learn how to learn" is, in my opinion, a theory full of iffiness.

Toward Assessing Possibilities

We come at last to the heart of it: It is not always practical or desirable to negotiate a consulting role that, at its simplest, is helping people do what they are going to do anyway. The consultant's task in the movie is to see confusion and anxiety through to energy for constructive action and to learn along with everybody else. That has an odd ring to somebody, like me, who grew up in the "second wave." I find myself thinking that assessing conditions under which such an unusual client/consultant partnership is feasible should be the first task of consultation. I wouldn't be deciding how to help, but whether to even make the of-

fer. That means a different kind of snapshot from the "unfreezing" variety.

Diagnosis, the gap between sickness and health, is not the right word for what I mean. The third wave of change is not a sickness, although some consequences can be. Anxiety is not a sickness. It is a sign of learning and potential energy. We need another term. Maybe *assessment* will do. Third-wave mangers need simple ways for assessing the potential for action, unifying themes to focus attention, methods to help people learn together about the whole contraption. That is quite different from having a consultant build a "problem list" and prioritize it. I am not against expertise—only the assumption that the specialist (or boss, or consultant) knows *everything* required to resolve the situation defined by his or her expertise or authority without having to do anything new or risky. This is especially true in the complex activity called "reorganizing." That's a developmental task—a great deal of it governed by the right brain and not amenable, except in small details, to ordinary problem solving.

Moreover, we should not mistake "human resources management" for third-wave practices. A major limitation on action is the belief that a human resources department on the 8th floor, just like the strategic planning department on the 14th, somehow makes us immune from reductionistic, linear, rigid solutions. Staff-centered activity is not necessarily conducive to productive community, whether named "participative management," or "dynamic synergistic wholistic transformation." It doesn't matter what you call it. If people don't join in the process of planning their own work, it's old Fred Taylor all over again, only with sociopsychological window dressing instead of his time-and-motion study.

Whose Movie Is It?

It is terribly important to grasp this point if you wish to enact a productive community. An effective snapshot, seen as a dual image—task/process—portrays the whole system in relation to a worthy purpose. It can only do that accurately when the whole system, to the extent possible, takes it, appears in it, and looks it over together. When the whole system is in perpetual motion, every relationship changing, it's impossible for one person to take a coherent picture. As soon as people start making a collective self-portrait, it is no longer a snapshot. *Voilà,* it's part of the ongoing movie, a form of *cinéma vérité,* as messy as life itself.

Only those most involved can make such a movie. The best role a consultant can hope for is stage manager. Kurt Lewin showed that during World War II when he discovered participative management by having Iowa housewives decide whether to change their food habits. Nobody has improved on the principle—that the wisest decisions, given as much information as we can get, are the ones we make for ourselves. People benefit most, I'm convinced, from talking with each other and deciding what to do. I'm for any consulting methods that enhance the dialog.

Thoughts on Stage Managing Third-Wave Movies

To be part of a good movie—to influence committed action—we need a practice theory that (1) respects the past, (2) enhances productive community, and (3) is responsive to the sea change of the third wave. Such a theory requires imagining under what conditions people will work together, which is the manager's dilemma, and under what conditions a consultant can help. "Ninety percent of living," comedian Woody Allen once said, "is just showing up." Just making it possible for the right people to show up may also be 90 percent of consultation. The other 10 percent is helping people focus on worthy purposes they identify for themselves.

My task as consultant is to do the minimum needed to accomplish those objectives. I want to use my data-collecting skills to identify *essential starting conditions* rather than to codify problems. I want to move away from discrepancies between words and deeds—an act of verbal abstraction which, in my view, has very little moti-

vating power—and focus on people's willingness to be responsible for doing important tasks together. In short, I'm more interested in figuring out whether I can make a contribution to this movie than I am in being seen as a brilliant snapshooter. I am not saying that this is the best consultation, only that I find it compatible with my faith in the metaphor of productive community.

Four Useful Practices

In reviewing my projects over 25 years, I find recurring patterns—related to leadership, energizing situations, and energizing people—under which I do better work. The leaders I have learned most from seem to me to have certain knacks. They *focus attention* on worthy aspirations; they *mobilize energy* by involving others; they seem *willing to face the unknown* without "answers."

My leadership observation underlies the first of four "useful practices" I have been experimenting with in evolving a third-wave practice theory. The other three depend on the outcome of the first. I consider these practices plausible (though far from trouble free) alternatives to more traditional consultation for reorganizing large companies and restructuring work. The four practices are to (1) assess the potential for action, (2) get the whole system into the room, (3) focus on the future, and (4) structure tasks that people can do for themselves. They focus on enacting productive community as the backdrop for finding appropriate solutions in "permanent white water." They seem to be well-known among current practitioners, though not well articulated.

Many of us—we can hardly avoid it—continue to mix them indiscriminately with "second-wave" procedures. I believe that as we use these and similar practices more confidently we will enable "third-wave" reorganizations and work redesigns in the spirit of productive community. Yet moving away from traditional uses of expertise and authority takes us down paths riddled with potholes and pitfalls, for which there are no easy "how tos." Perhaps an explanation of each of the four third-wave practices along with examples will make things easier.

Useful Practice 1: Assess the Potential for Action

Instead of diagnosing "gaps," I find myself asking under what conditions I could make a contribution. That leads me away from problem lists toward an assessment of leadership, business opportunities, and sources of energy.

Condition 1: committed leadership. Does the person authorized to hire me have itches he or she wants to scratch badly enough to put his or her own rear end on the line? Consultants make better contributions when a person in authority says, "I think this is so important that I'm willing to take a risk, too." I'm wary of requests to fix somebody else or to supply unilateral "expert" answers.

Condition 2: good business opportunities. Good business opportunities come in packages labeled economics and technology—the glue of productive community. So I listen sympathetically to the "people problem" list, but I don't focus on it. Rather, I focus on the opportunities for cooperative action—chances to innovate products/services and/or ways of making/delivering them. These occur most dependably in mergers, acquisitions, reorganizations, declining markets, overhead crises, structures that don't function, new technologies, the need to save jobs.

The Medical Products Division of Atomic Energy of Canada, Ltd., for example, in 1985 rescued itself from economic disaster and mass layoffs by assuring jobs for a year and employing much of its workforce in market studies, work redesign, and new employment opportunities. The payoff was a viable, $30-million-a-year business, managed participatively by employees.

These two conditions—a leader and a promising dilemma—can't be "behavioral-scienced" in, nor "engineered." Frederick Taylor understood their importance in 1900. He did not know as much as we do, though, about commitment and support. Taylor assumed that only the expert's diagnosis and prescription counted. Thanks to action research, we know a great deal more about

commitment and support than our grandparents did. We have many choices about how we focus attention and mobilize energy. We know that every task needs a viable process, that every process exists only in relation to a worthy task. We also know that task and process cannot be integrated *for* people. Thus underlying theory—pure Lewin—is that involving those most affected leads to better solutions and quicker actions. Yet participative techniques, or economic ones for that matter, are useless in the absence of leadership and purposeful goals.

Condition 3: energized people. The third dimension is a little trickier. We all drag our feet some days and burst with energy on others. What can a consultant do about this? Ches Janssen, a Swedish social psychologist, has devised a simple tool for visualizing potential energy. Each person, group, department, company, says Janssen, lives in a "four-room apartment."

We move from room to room, depending on perceptions, feelings, and aspirations triggered by external events. The rooms represent cyclical phases, not unlike the process of death and dying. Indeed, change represents a "little death," a letting go of the past to actualize a desired future. We change rooms as we grow. However, it's not an ever upward spiral where things only get better. It's a circle game. Our feelings and behavior go up and down as outside pressures impinge on our own "life space." How much energy we have for support and commitment depends upon which room we're in.

In Contentment, we like the status quo. When that changes—through merger, reorganization, new leader, new system, market crisis, job threat—we move into Denial. We stay there until we own up to fear or anxiety. That moves us through the door into Confusion. Mucking about in Confusion, sorting out bits and pieces, opens the door to Renewal. The passage to Renewal leads from Denial through Confusion. You can't get there from Contentment by any other route.

Anxiety, in Gestalt terminology "blocked excitement," is the emotional décor of the Confusion room. Far from a state to be avoided, it signifies readiness to learn. Anxiety is the place we store energy while deciding whether to invest it. Every new project, course correction, major change requires optimal anxiety. If there's too much, we are paralyzed; too little, unmotivated.

In every Confusion room there are people already taking constructive action. It is they who will carry the movie forward—if they can be brought together to learn how their initiatives integrate with the whole. So I seek to assess which room people live in right now, and how they are acting there. That helps me decide how I can act constructively in the situation. (See Figure 1.)

People in Contentment or Denial are not "frozen." Events will move them soon enough. Little can be done to hasten the day, though rational problem solving can certainly delay it. We can make our presence felt and accepted by acting appropriately with people in those rooms—supporting their right to stay there as long as they wish. To mobilize energy, we need to be with people in Confusion or Renewal. I believe if someone were to revisit OD cases from this perspective, they would see that "failure" correlates closely with action-research methods foisted onto people living in Contentment or Denial. The seeds of success are sown in Confusion and sprout in Renewal. Those are the rooms where people welcome flip charts, models, and OD techniques.

Even that is too simple. Any task—at some point—may shake people into Denial when the going gets rough. When that happens I don't know what to do except keep talking and wait it out. They won't be ready to work toward any changes until they have moved from the Denial room to Confusion or Renewal.

The urge to hold on—to old habits, familiar patterns, relationships, and structures (whether they satisfy or not)—is as old as human history. Robert Tannenbaum and Robert Hanna have pointed out the powerful losses change represents for each of us—of identity, of certainty, of meaning itself. Under these conditions no "unfreezing" techniques are likely to help. According to

FIGURE 1   **Action-Taking in the Four-Room Apartment**

Contentment Room	Renewal Room
What clients say: "I like it just the way it is."	*What clients say:* "We've got more possibilities than we can ever use. I don't know what to do first."
What a consultant should do: Leave people alone, unless you think the building's on fire.	*What a consultant should do:* Offer assistance through simple, mutually arranged tasks.
Denial Room	**Confusion Room**
What clients say: "What, me worry?! Everything's fine—I think. . . ."	*What clients say:* "This is the damnedest mess I ever saw. Helllppp!"
What a consultant should do: Ask questions. Give support. Heighten awareness. Do *not* offer advice.	*What a consultant should do:* Structure tasks. Focus on the future. Get people together. Ask for/offer help.

Tannenbaum and Hanna, "Realistic patience and a sense of an appropriate time scale must underlie and guide the change process itself." We can help by giving people a chance to come together, to experience their mutual dilemmas more fully, to make their own choices about when and how to move.

Hooking together many activities requires only a little linear planning. If we provide the right container, people will fill it with the right elixir. This happens spontaneously as the other practices—getting the system in the room, focusing on the future, constructing doable tasks—are applied. I think it is more likely to happen when we work on important tasks, mutually defined, that improve our chances for survival and self-control.

"Should We/Shouldn't We" Discussions

The activities I like best—because they involve whole systems—are joint planning of business strategy (external focus), work redesign (internal focus), and reorganizations that embody both strategy and structure. In each mode the people most affected help devise and test various structural models, using consulting help. I don't mean to make this sound easy as pie. I usually find myself in long "should we/shouldn't we" dialogs—hours or days of hashing out the pros and cons of opening the action to many others, whether there's time to do it all, whether short-term results will suffer, what good alternatives exist. Above all, each of us uses the dialogs to decide whether to become personally involved.

So I look for a leader, a business opportunity, and a "should we/shouldn't we" discussion. If we decide to team up, I help people plan how to raise a crowd, structure a task, and provide some (left brain) methods for getting started. As right brains are activated, they take care of what can't be planned in advance.

Useful Practice 2: Get the "Whole System" in the Room

There are many ways to get a "whole system" together. A system can be there, for example, in your head—a conceptual rather than logistical feat that most people can master. Try the "All-Purpose Viewing Lens" in Figure 2, and see how fast you can become a "systems" thinker.

However, knowing what's going on is not the same as enacting productive community. People need shared perceptions to make their contributions. That means getting together to *live* the open system. How many functions, levels, managers, operators, staff, lines can be mustered to work on their own organization all at once? Could customers and suppliers be involved? My inclination is to push for "more" and let others say what's "realistic." I confess I don't know how to involve a cast of thousands all at once. Yet keeping that as a benchmark helps me remember what I set out to do. Systems get better when the members cooperate on joint tasks. When people from top and bottom meet across lines of status, function, sex, race, and hierarchy, and when "problems" can be seen as systemic rather than

FIGURE 2   **An All-Purpose Viewing Lens**

	Inside Picture	**Outside Picture**
Economics	Are costs up or down?	Is revenue up or down?
Technology	Do systems work as intended?	How are products/services being improved?
People	How do people feel about their work?	How do customers feel about the company?

Note: Each question can be followed by a "why," and each person who answers these questions will provide a new slant.

discrete, wonderful new (and unpredictable) things happen. These can't be "planned" except in the sense of making them more probable. Such happenings lead to more creative and committed actions, more secure and engaging work. Let's look at some examples.

In the merger that created Sovran Bank, the largest financial services institution in Virginia, the operations departments used an interlocking chain of team-development conferences, starting with three top executives from each bank, cascading to the next two levels, culminating in a mass meeting of several hundred people. People planned their own roles and divided up work—an exercise many believed was impossible.

Bethlehem Steel's Sparrows Point plate mill reorganized during a two-week training marathon attended by 80 people—managers, supervisors, and staff—who specified, in advance, which problems they wished to manage better. Together they studied every aspect of the mill—its internal dynamics, the marketplace, corporate connections, and relationships across levels and functions. They visited "suppliers" in steel-making and customers in distant cities. As workshop "inputs" linked to their own experience, they quickly changed mill practices to serve customers better. They could do this because of an unusual business opportunity—the annual maintenance shutdown. The key new management behavior: paying people to come in and learn instead of taking a two-week vacation.

A fast-growing software development company, McCormack & Dodge, lacked the structure to implement a new strategic plan. Top management convened four conferences for 50 people representing all levels and functions. Design teams organized by product line analyzed the system and created new organization designs. They included in the "design specs" a 1990 strategy, their own values about employees and customers, and their analysis of how to close information gaps, improve career paths and develop more accountability and self-control. Then came the unpredictable part: Twenty-four hours into the first meeting they began making changes to existing

practices as information gaps were discovered. Long before a design was "finalized" people were already acting in ways neither planned for nor diagnosed in advance. As a design emerged, the 50 talked over implementation issues with 1,000 other employees.

There is a further benefit to having a whole system present. New patterns of action that are achieved in the room are often carried outside of it *because* all the relevant parties enacted them together. There is less "sell" needed when three or four levels are able to come to the same conclusion at the same time.

Useful Practice 3: Focus on the Future

This practice derives from work by the late Ronald Lippitt, the coiner, with Kurt Lewin, of the term *group dynamics* 40 years ago. In 1949 Lippitt began tape-recording planning meetings. The tapes revealed that people's voices grew softer, more stressed, depressed, as problems were listed and prioritized. You could hear the energy drain away as the lists grew longer.

In the 1950s Lippitt started using "images of potential," rather than gripes, as springboards for change. In the 1970s he created new workshops merging group dynamics with future thinking. He has people visualize *preferred futures* in rich detail—as they wish things to be two, three, and even five years into the future. This simple concept has enormous power. While untangling present problems leads to depression, imagining scenarios energizes common values. Taking a stand for a desired future provides purposeful guidance for goal setting, planning, and skill building. Successful entrepreneurs, notes Charles Garfield in *Peak Performers,* are uniquely skilled at projecting alternative futures. They get "feedforward" from their imagination, which is a qualitatively different experience from feedback on past behavior.

This concept—"visioning" is one name for it—is so attractive that most people want to go out and run a group through a visioning training session. This technique *will not work* in the absence of committed leadership, a business opportunity, and some energized people. But don't take my word for it. Try it anyway.

Useful Practice 4: Structure Tasks That People Can Do for Themselves

What structures make it possible for people to learn, focus on the future, and action plan for themselves (when leadership, opportunity, and energy exist)? A conference series designed by clients and consultants together is one way to bring the productive community alive. These are task-focused, working conferences to reorganize work or refocus effort; they shouldn't serve as add-ons or data dumps.

For consultants to manage such events, they need, first of all, sanction from credible parties. If that can be got, then any plausible "bag of tricks" will do. It is here—at the very last—we get to OD (or any) techniques. If the other signals say "go," then we need few of what Richard Hackman in *Work Design* calls "task performance strategies." One example (out of hundreds) is "responsibility charting," which is a simple way of symbolizing whether people are expected to be active or passive vis-à-vis a decision. Other examples include simple worksheets—which are derived from sociotechnical analysis—to help people with the process of analyzing and redesigning their own work.

Merrelyn Emery, a leading advocate of this perspective, points out that the purpose of consulting technique is to create a learning climate, not solutions. This is a subtle and important distinction. It is essential that we do nothing that would reinforce the idea—both undemocratic and unscientific—"that people cannot make sense of their own experience." Creating a learning climate, points out Emery, results in "an almost immediate increase in energy, common sense, and goodwill."

Summary Observations

Working in these ways, I find myself doing things which don't "come naturally." I have had to shift my focus—a real mental wrench—away from "content" diagnoses and problem lists, even of "process issues." I need to *understand* what a company is up against in the marketplace, what it takes to create committed customers. But I help more and faster when I can assess the potential for action rather than dictate the solution required. So I look for a leader, a business opportunity, some energized employees—conditions no consultant should leave home without. When they exist, I have faith that I can make a contribution to the most complicated reorganizations, despite my concerns that I always do too little or too much.

I have stopped fantasizing that one or two "experts"—even the process kind—are smart enough to figure out on their own the right learning structures. That's 1950s thinking. Anybody who offers to sell you an exemption from the clarifying experience of muddling through to renewal is a charlatan. The more we experts know about our own specialty, the less likely we are to see our favorite solution's impact on a system. When the "whole system" gets into one room, when people have valued tasks to accomplish, I believe the right diagnoses and action steps occur in "real time." Designing somebody else's work is not in any way, shape, or form an expert task.

Nor do I imagine that I can take away, by any known magical mystery trick, technique, system, jargon, book, speaker, or dog-and-pony show, the travail, confusion, chaos, and anxiety that are as natural to our species as breathing. These conditions fertilize growth, excitement, creativity, joy, energy, and commitment. As a consultant I am often invested with the power to grant people exemptions from states of denial and confusion. Alas, like the Wizard of Oz (who knew he was a fraud pretending that his technologies "worked"), I can't do it.

Instead, I seek to reduce anxiety (my own and others') through simple procedures that allow people to sort through and use their own experience. I help those who wish to design their own futures. I hate to hear anxious people labeled "change resisters," as if the natural cycle of human experience is an evil legion to be defeated by superior methodological firepower on the force fields of organizational strife. Resistance is as natural as eating. I am learning to accept my own resistance, too, especially to client expectations I cannot meet.

In sum, I believe that elaborate, consultant-centered diagnoses are unnecessary to reorganize workplaces flooded by tides of change. As the author of a widely used "six-box" diagnostic model, I expect some fans will be startled by my statement. That model served its function for me long ago—translating process language into managerial tasks. I'm delighted that so many still modify and use it, for it shows that they own it—and this is a development consistent with my theory.

With or without a model, I have learned to expect frustration and anxiety, not smooth sailing, in every white-water voyage. I greet them as familiar traveling companions. I try to rejoin them each time with good humor and to forgive myself when I can't. I recall Rudyard Kipling's poem about keeping your head "when others all about you are losing theirs and blaming it on you." The productive community for me is an anchor point for dignity and meaning in democratic societies. We need to preserve, enhance, and extend it for reasons at once pragmatic, moral, humanistic, ethical, economic, technical, and social.

QWL—far from "cultural change"—can be seen as a serious effort to conserve our culture's deepest values against erosion by narrow economic and technocratic thinking. That for me is the song and dance of restructuring workplaces. I am interested in preserving economic stability beyond quarterly dividends because I believe that democratic societies depend on creating employment. Moreover, I would like to find new ways to help people manage economic and technical innovation so that all of us, myself included, find dignity and meaning in work.

In 1900, Taylor had experts solve problems for people—"scientific management." In 1950, Lewin's descendants started "everybody" solving their own problems—participative management. About 1960, experts discovered "systems" thinking—and began improving whole systems *for* other people. Now, we are learning how to get "everybody" improving whole systems. The most

successful third-wave managers and consultants will be those who learn to do that soonest.

References

The "generalized speedup of the corporate metabolism" has been documented with increasing frequency since World War II. Donald A. Schon celebrated it in *Beyond the Stable State* (Random House, 1971). Alvin Toffler describes it as a historic global shift in human consciousness in *The Third Wave* (Bantam Books, 1980), detailing the impact of new technologies on families, work, lifestyles, and human societies. Toffler's conclusion—more direct democracy is an imperative for survival in a high-tech age—will come as no surprise to this journal's readers.

The negative impact of technology on human aspirations for dignity, meaning, and community has been observed repeatedly from the dawn of history as an antidote to paeans of progress. Elton Mayo's *The Social Problems of an Industrial Civilization* (Harvard University Division of Research, 1945) remains a vivid statement of our own primacy over machines—although why we need to keep asserting this when people devised the contraptions to begin with troubles me. My quote is from Chapter 1, "The Seamy Side of Progress." Donald A. Schon makes the same point in *Beyond the Stable State* (Random House, 1971), adding that organizations and people have to become "learning systems" if they wish to prosper.

The tension between individualism and community in American life predates industrialization. Alexis de Tocqueville, the awed French critic of U.S. democracy, fingered this issue more than 150 years ago. For a contemporary update on his observation see *Habits of the Heart: Individualism and Commitment in American Life* (University of California, 1985) by Robert N. Bellah, Richard Madsen, William M. Sullivan, Anne Swidler, and Steven M. Tipton. This is "must reading" for anybody who cares about the future of interdependence on a shrinking planet, an old-fashioned sociology of real people above statistics in a scholarly genre I haven't seen for 20 years.

Frederick W. Taylor's values have resurfaced in a powerful way in the 1980s, even while we bury his methods for good. *The Principles of Scientific Management,* first published in 1911, is still available in paperback (W. W. Norton, 1967). It's as readable as your newspaper and just as contemporary—perhaps the earliest treatise on collaborative techniques of human resources management. If you ever believed it was anything else, you should read it for yourself—as a reminder that "participation," "commitment," and "excellence" are just as liable to "taylorization" as time-and-motion study.

For evidence of that, look what happened to Kurt Lewin's change concepts. Lewin started with a startling observation—that you can't understand a person's behavior without knowing more about the present situation he or she is in, and vice versa, embodied in "field theory." He talked "psychological ecology" before such a term was fashionable. He believed (not unlike Taylor) that an exact science could be made of human behavior. His original writings are full of obscure mathematical formulae (he used topological geometry to map social-psychological problems). It was only a short jump for appliers of his thinking to imagine (old paradigm) that "unfreezing" techniques could be divined to accelerate human development. I recommend Alfred Marrow's *The Practical Theorist* (Basic Books, 1969), an admiring, intimate, readable account of Lewin's life. In *Productive Communities,* I show Lewin's vast influence on management and the similarity of his interests to Taylor's. I think his most readable work is in *Resolving Social Conflicts: Selected Papers on Group Dynamics* (Harper & Row, 1948) edited by Gertrud Weiss Lewin.

The clearest-eyed antidote I know to megalomania about change techniques is the work of Robert Tannenbaum and Robert Hanna, accessible in "Holding On, Letting Go, and Moving On: Understanding a Neglected Perspective on Change," Chapter 6 in *Human Systems Development,* by Robert Tannenbaum, Newton Margulies, Fred Massarik and Associates (Jossey-Bass,

1985). They make the point that we can't purport to change organizations if we don't appreciate the importance of the human need to hold onto certainty, even the unpleasant kind. Their practice theory supports my belief that Douglas McGregor's Theories X and Y are not so much opposing assumptions about human nature as they are an internal dialog in each of us between our need for control and our wish to be free—a major theme of *Productive Communities.*

For consulting skills—in all areas of experience—I know of no better guide than Peter Block's *Flawless Consulting* (Learning Concepts, 1981). Block's readable follow-up, *The Empowered Manager* (Jossey-Bass, 1986) describes the choices available to those who would take initiative and risk to make their organizations great—a beacon for those who would "let go" of old assumptions and create their own futures.

There is no way to overstate the contributions of Fred Emery, Eric Trist, and colleagues to the revamping of the work world—a history I take up in my book. The best overview I know is Trist's *The Evolution of Socio-Technical Systems: A Conceptual Framework and an Action Research Program* (Ontario Quality of Working Life Centre, June 1981). These concepts will one day be seen as the most revolutionary in human history. That they are not better known now is partly a function of their dense vocabulary (e.g., "causal texture," "turbulent social field") and partly our slowness to recognize how the "new paradigm"—of necessity—is replacing the old in the same way that autos replaced buggies. To extend the analogy, our 1986 understanding of sociotechnical design in the workplace corresponds now to 1917 in the development of the car. Many people have heard of it, far fewer have seen it in action, relatively few have one, not everybody is sure they want one, and those who own one find it cranky, unpredictable, and needing constant maintenance. Eventually everybody will take new paradigm practices for granted.

The "future-oriented" book that has most influenced my practice of workplace improvements is *Building the Collaborative Community: Mobilizing Citizens for Action* (University of California Extension, 1980), by Eva Schindler-Rainman and the late Ronald Lippitt. It describes the methods used to get whole systems in the room to focus on the future and do the job for themselves in 88 community conferences for cities and states all over North America—involving thousands from all walks of life. This book is so diffident its title does not appear on the spine, making it hard to pick off a bookshelf. It deals with voluntary community action, not business firms. It shows more concretely than any work I know that what people can imagine, people can do.

Reading 5

Organization Development and Transformation

Jerry I. Porras
Robert C. Silvers

Introduction

Rapidly changing environments demand that organizations generate equally fast responses in order to survive and prosper. Planned change that makes organizations more responsive to environmental shifts should be guided by generally accepted and unified theories of organizations and organizational change—neither of which currently exists. Yet despite this absence of clear conceptual underpinnings, the field continues to evolve and grow.

In this chapter, we review recent research that improves our understanding of planned change theory and practice. We begin by proposing a new model of the change process rooted in a conception of organizations presented by Porras (1987) and Porras et al. (1990). This change model organizes our understanding of the field and guides the discussion of research presented in the second half of the chapter.[1]

A Model of Planned Change

Organizational change is typically triggered by a relevant environmental shift that, once sensed by the organization, leads to an intentionally generated response. This intentional response is "planned organizational change" and consists of four identifi-

Source: Jerry Porras and Robert Silvers, "Organization Development and Transformation," *Annual Review of Psychology* 42 (1991), pp. 51–78. With permission, from the *Annual Review of Psychology*, Volume 42, © 1991, by Annual Reviews.

able, interrelated components: *(a)* a change intervention that alters *(b)* key organizational target variables that then impact *(c)* individual organizational members and their on-the-job behaviors resulting in changes in *(d)* organizational outcomes. These broad components of planned change are shown at the top of Figure 1. The lower part of the figure adds more detail to each component and graphically summarizes our Planned Process Model;[2] we discuss each component below.

Change Interventions

Planned change interventions can be divided into two general types. The first comprises the more traditional approach. Organization Development (OD), which until recently was synonymous with the term *planned change*. The second, Organization Transformation (OT), is the cutting edge of planned change and may be called "second-generation OD." At present, OD is relatively well defined and circumscribed in terms of its technologies, theory, and research. OT, on the other hand, is emerging, ill-defined, highly experimental, and itself rapidly changing.[3]

Organization Development. Organization development is defined as:

1. A set of behavioral science theories, values, strategies, and techniques

2. aimed at the planned change of organizational work settings

3. with the intention of generating alpha, beta, and/or gamma (A) cognition change in individual organizational members, leading to behavioral change and thus

FIGURE 1

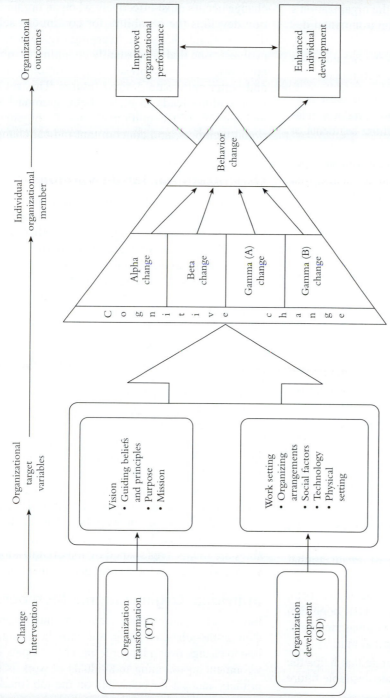

4. creating a better fit between the organization's capabilities and its current environmental demands, or

5. promoting changes that help the organization to better fit predicted future environments.

OD often occurs in response to modest mismatches with the environment and produces relatively moderate adjustments in those segments of the organization not congruent with the environment. This form of OD results in individuals experiencing only alpha and beta cognition change, with a correspondingly limited change in behaviors.

Additionally, OD is triggered not only by current environmental mismatches but also by an organization's desire to fit into future desirable environmental niches. This results in the creation of new modes of functioning and impacts substantial segments of the organization. This second type of OD leads to alpha, beta, and gamma (A) cognition change in organizational members, and behavioral changes are broader.[4]

In summary, then, OD concentrates on work-setting changes that either help an organization better adapt to its current environment or improve its fit into expected future environments. This approach to planned change produces appreciable, not radical, change in individual employees' cognitions as well as behaviors.

Organization Transformation. Organization transformation is:

1. A set of behavioral science theories, values, strategies, and techniques

2. aimed at the planned change of organizational vision and work settings

3. with the intention of generating alpha, beta, gamma (A) and/or gamma (B) cognition change in individual organizational members, leading to behavioral change and thus

4. promoting paradigmatic change that helps the organization better fit or create desirable future environments.

OT is also planned and primarily directed at creating a new vision for the organization. Vision change occurs most effectively when an organization develops the capability for continuous self-diagnosis and change; a "learning organization" evolves—one that is constantly changing to more appropriately fit the present organizational state and better anticipate desired futures. This set of interventions leads to alpha, beta, gamma (A), and gamma (B) cognition change in organizational members, and concomitant radical change in their behaviors.

Organizational Target Variables

Planned change interventions impact two major types of organizational variables: organizational vision and the work setting. Taken together, these create the internal organizational environment in which individual employees function.

Vision consists of three main factors: *(a)* the guiding beliefs and principles of the organization; *(b)* the enduring organizational purpose that grows out of these beliefs; and *(c)* a catalyzing mission that is consistent with organizational purpose and, at the same time, moves the organization toward the achievement of that purpose (Collins & Porras, 1989).

The work setting consists of many dimensions and, as such, requires a parsimonious framework to organize our understanding of it. From our perspective, the organizational work setting can be subdivided into four major streams of variables: *(a)* organizing arrangements, *(b)* social factors, *(c)* technology, and *(d)* physical setting (Porras, 1987). Table 1 lists the subvariables that constitute each of these streams. These four streams of variables are themselves shaped by the organization's vision, which gives them coherence and direction.

Individual Organizational Members

Individual organizational members must change their on-the-job behaviors in order for the organization to change over a longer term. The complex environment surrounding individuals at work is the primary catalyst for behaviors on the job (moderated, as discussed below, by cognitive change). Organizational behaviors are generated by individuals behaving in response to the signals received directly

TABLE 1 **Organizational Components in the Stream Organizational Model**

Organizing Arrangements (OA)	Social Factors (SF)	Technology (T)	Physical Setting (PS)
A. goals	A. culture	A. tools, equipment, & machinery	A. space configuration
B. strategies	1. basic assumptions	B. technical expertise	1. size
C. formal structure	2. values	C. job design	2. shape
D. administrative policies & procedures	3. norms	D. work flow design	3. relative locations
E. administrative systems	4. language & design	E. technical policies & procedures	B. physical ambiance
F. formal reward systems	5. rituals	F. technical systems	1. light
1. evaluation system	6. history		2. heat
2. pay systems	7. stories		3. noise
3. benefits packages	8. myths		4. air quality
G. ownership	9. symbols		5. cleanliness
	B. interaction processes		C. interior design
	1. interpersonal		1. decorations
	2. group		2. furniture
	3. intergroup		3. window coverings
	C. social patterns & networks		4. floor coverings
	1. communication		5. colors
	2. problem solving/ decision making		a. floors
	3. influence		b. walls
	4. status		c. ceilings
	D. individual attributes		D. architectural design
	1. attitudes & beliefs		
	2. behavioral skills		
	3. feelings		
	E. management style		

Source: Adapted from Porras, J. I. 1987. *Stream Analysis.* Reading, Mass.: Addison-Wesley: p. 52, Table 3–1.

from their work setting and indirectly from organizational vision. Therefore, successful planned change efforts must alter these two components of the internal organizational environment such that new signals influence individuals to produce new behaviors. Employees consciously process work setting cues and modify their behavior as a result.

Individual Cognition and Planned Change. The types of individual cognitive change that occur as a result of planned change activities have been discussed in the management and organization literature for over four decades (e.g. Lindblom, 1959; Vickers, 1965; Greiner, 1972; Sheldon, 1980). For our purposes, the most useful conceptualization appeared in the OD literature 15 years ago when Golembiewski and his colleagues proposed alpha, beta, and gamma change as the three possible measurable outcomes of OD interventions (Golembiewski et al., 1976):

1. "Alpha change involves a variation in the level of some existential state, given a constantly calibrated measuring instrument related to a constant conceptual domain" (p. 134).

2. "Beta change involves a variation in the level of some existential state complicated by the fact that some intervals of the measurement continuum associated with a constant conceptual domain have been recalibrated" (p. 135).

3. "Gamma change involves a redefinition or reconceptualization of some domain, a major change in the perspective or frame of reference within which phenomena are perceived and classified, in what is taken to be some relevant slice of reality" (p. 135).

This perspective is primarily oriented toward framing change in the context of measurement issues, but it highlights some important principles. Alpha change is a perceived change in objective circumstances, while beta change is that type of change coupled with changing standards of individual interpretation. Gamma change is a radical shift in an individual's assumptions about causal relationships, the values attached to various dimensions of reality, and the interpretive frameworks that describe reality. In other words, gamma change describes a "paradigm shift" in organizational members' mental constructs (Kuhn, 1970).

The notion of paradigm is useful for conceptualizing the change process. An organizational paradigm may be defined as:

> a prevailing world-view or collective belief system. The fundamental set of beliefs or organizing principles which are unquestioned and unexamined assumptions about the nature of reality (Adams, 1984, p. 278).[5]

Integrating the construct of organizational paradigm with the notions of alpha, beta, and gamma change is a useful way to develop a new typology that conceptualizes individual cognitive change processes. The focus here is not on measurement but on broad categories of individual cognitive change. This leads to the following four types:

1. Alpha change: change in the perceived levels of variables within a paradigm without altering their configuration (e.g. a perceived improvement in skills).
2. Beta change: change in people's view about the meaning of the value of any variable within an existing paradigm without altering their configuration (e.g. change in standards).
3. Gamma (A) change: change in the configuration of an existing paradigm without the addition of new variables (e.g. changing the central value of a "production-driven" paradigm from "cost containment" to "total quality focus"; this results in the reconfiguration of all variables within this paradigm).

4. Gamma (B) change: the replacement of one paradigm with another that contains some or all new variables (e.g. replacing a "production-driven" paradigm with a "customer-responsive" paradigm).

Each of these cognitive changes leads to corresponding changes in behavior. As an illustration, a change in standards (the example given above for beta change) causes behavior to change in order to meet these new standards. As another example, a paradigm shift from "production-driven" to "customer-responsive" alters existing behaviors, creates new behaviors, and gives individual employees a totally new way of viewing their work. The level and depth of behavior change will therefore correspond to the shift in individual cognitions.

Organizational Outcomes

Two kinds of organizational outcomes are central to our model. The first is organizational performance, captured in such factors as productivity, profitability, efficiency, effectiveness, quality, and so on. The second is individual development, an actualization of the self that occurs as individuals alter their world views, expand their repertoire of behaviors, and/or improve their skills and abilities.

Summary

The Change Process Model identifies the key components of a change process and organizes them in a way that improves one's understanding of the field as a whole. We use this model to categorize our review of recent research by analyzing articles according to the intervention approach used, the variables targeted for change, the type of individual cognitive change that occurs, and the organizational outcomes derived from the intervention activity. Unfortunately, much of the research does not give enough detail to fully analyze work by the last two above-mentioned categories, so we categorize articles primarily by intervention approach and target variables.

Research Findings

This review examines articles concerning OD and OT that were published between 1985 and 1989 in journals with an organizational behavior and/or organization development focus (e.g., the *Journal of Applied Behavioral Science, Human Relations, Group and Organizational Studies, Journal of Applied Psychology, Academy of Management Journal, Academy of Management Review, Organizational Dynamics,* and more). Because little literature on OT was found in these sources, we reviewed books and other journals that do contain work on OT (e.g., Levy & Merry, 1986; Adams, 1984).

Organization Development

We first focus our discussion on OD research and structure our comments using the change targets (i.e., organizing arrangements, social factors, technology, and physical space) as subcategories in our review. Articles that do not fit these categories are reviewed at the end of this section.

Organizing Arrangements. Research on a variety of interventions focuses on this stream of target variables. Quality circles (QCs), gainsharing interventions, and other forms of employee involvement are the topics most prevalent in the period reviewed. Some research also focused on other OA dimensions, such as alternative work schedules, new design tools, and new design options. We review the key articles that further our understanding of these various interventions and/or discuss innovative practices and ideas.[6]

Quality circles. Generally, the literature on QCs lacks empirical and statistical rigor. One important cause of this appears to be the absence of a clear theoretical foundation to guide research. Initial attempts at theory have been made that primarily classified QCs as focusing on work technology, with productivity as its end target (Steel & Shane, 1986). Later attempts to strengthen QC theory provided a more detailed model of the QC process, focusing on both structural and proces-

sual variables. However, the empirical evidence supporting these models has been mixed (Steel & Lloyd, 1988).

Other additions to QC theory emphasize the conditions leading to failure in QC implementation. One approach views disappointments with QCs as due to flawed assumptions (e.g., that groups always outperform individuals) and a lack of understanding regarding the cultural differences between the United States and Japan (Ferris & Wagner, 1985). Another proposes that a myriad of organizational factors hamper QC success, such as supervisory resistance, lack of volunteers, departmental transfer of employees (leading to less QC continuity), unskilled meeting facilitation, et cetera (Meyer & Stott, 1985). A third suggests that QCs are an employee-involvement strategy leading to minimal changes in organizational power and should be used primarily when conditions are not favorable for more extensive employee involvement (Lawler & Mohrman, 1987; Lawler, 1988). These perspectives all imply that changes in both structure and process are necessary to improve QC success rates.

Additional empirical research investigating QC efficacy has focused on assessing the impact of QC interventions on a variety of attitudinal and perceptual variables. QC membership significantly affects attitudes specific to QC functioning, such as communication, participation (Marks et al., 1986), and influence (Rafaeli, 1985); changes in more general attitudes, such as satisfaction and commitment, have also been found (Griffin, 1988).[7]

Findings on the effects of QCs on task perceptions have been contradictory. Rafaeli (1985) showed significant effects from QC membership on task perceptions while, in a similar study, Head et al. (1986) did not. Overall, the evidence regarding QCs is most positive for attitudinal and behavioral impacts directly related to QC functioning; the evidence is contradictory about QC impact on task perceptions.

Gainsharing. Theory and research on gainsharing has emphasized its motivational effects on performance. Although the theory base for this approach is relatively weak, there have been recent attempts at strengthening it. For example, Florkowski (1987) proposed a theoretical model explaining the connection between profit sharing and behavioral and attitudinal outcomes. Drawing on expectancy theory and labor relations theory, he hypothesizes that profit sharing is a motivator for individual employees to the extent that it is a salient and important part of earnings and/or based on subunit performance.

Empirical investigations of this motivation dimension have not yielded highly positive findings. For example, Pearce et al. (1985) found that merit pay for federal agency managers had no effect on improved performance in the manager's units. Jordan (1986) examined the effects of performance-contingent rewards and found that this type of pay for social service workers decreased intrinsic motivation and did not affect satisfaction with pay. However, positive effects were reported in a study of a manufacturing firm that had employed the Scanlon Plan for approximately a decade. Miller & Schuster (1987) found that the plan had statistically significant effects on employment stability along with positive effects on productivity and labor-management cooperation.

The negative empirical findings regarding gain-sharing theory appear to be derived from change projects of more limited scope and duration. On the other hand, much more positive findings seem to obtain when gainsharing is part of a long-term, broad-based program (i.e., the Scanlon Plan study). It appears that gainsharing has the greatest effect when it is part of a larger-scale and more extensive change process.

Employee ownership. Research on employee ownership is expanding and developing a stronger theory base. Some of the most substantial work in this arena was done by Klein (1987), who tested three competing models relating employee stock ownership to employee attitudes. She found that the financial benefits and influence opportunities of ownership most strongly impacted attitudes. This evidence supported extrinsic and instrumental models of ownership, but not an intrinsic model where ownership is satisfying in and of itself.

Regarding the influence effects of employee ownership, some research contradicts the "expected" link between employee ownership and desire for influence in organizational policies. For example, French (1987) characterized employees as investors who only seek influence when it is in their best financial interests to do so. As a consequence, he concludes that ownership may not be a solution for increasing power equalization within the firm.

In summary, research on employee ownership has grown and illustrates a promising and innovative approach to organizing in this country. However, it still lacks a strong theory base, one that is much needed to guide both practice and research.

Alternative work schedules. Researchers here have primarily investigated the impact of alternative work schedules on attitudes and productivity. Attitude changes about the schedule and free time have been found to be a primary effect of work schedule changes, with smaller impacts on general attitudes and effectiveness (Dunham et al., 1987). The process used to implement alternative work schedules is also important. As would be expected, the greater the participation in the implementation process, the more favorable the attitudes toward the change (Latack & Foster, 1985).[8] Regarding only the relationship between alternative work schedules and productivity, positive effects of flextime on productivity occur when resources are scarce and productivity is measured at the group level (Ralston et al., 1985).

In summary, although this approach to organizational improvement has existed for over a decade, there has been little research on it. Alternative schedules appear to improve attitudes and performance, but more research is needed to determine the conditions under which these effects extend beyond variables specific to the intervention.

Organizational structure. Changes in organizational structure have been discussed in the literature from a variety of perspectives. One approach has focused on the development of new structural options. Ackoff (1989) proposed the "circular organization," where each manager reports to a "board of directors" consisting of his or her immediate superiors, subordinates, and important peers or outsiders. These boards are responsible for planning and coordination with other units, and, in some cases, for evaluating managerial performance. This approach to organization structure highlights one way that democracy and responsiveness need not conflict in modern organizations.

A second perspective focuses on new tools for design, rather than the final design itself. Two such tools have been proposed by McDaniel et al. (1987) and Nelson (1988). The former examined the usefulness of decision analysis for interventions involving organizational design. They found this tool helped participants to identify problems and resolve them productively. The latter discussed the uses of "blockmodeling" (a form of network analysis found primarily in sociology) for structural diagnosis, coalition identification, and intergroup relations analysis. Network analysis uncovers groupings and patterns not easily identified by traditional OD diagnostic methods. These two approaches to the problem of organization design are creative and should set the stage for additional (and much needed) development in this area.[9]

Summary. While it is encouraging to see more theory related to organization-level issues and structural interventions, most of the above research consists of "little studies." Although these further knowledge of a specific intervention and its particular effects, no attempt is made to explore multifaceted interventions and systemic outcomes. Intervention research in this and other areas would be more profitable if it explored broader and more complex system change and its outcomes (e.g., the effects of gainsharing on social factors variables, such as culture). In addition, research needs to expand its focus from direct effects to more pervasive and indirect impacts in order to assess the overall effectiveness of organizing arrangement interventions.

Social Factors. The social factors (SF) variables have historically been the most frequent targets of OD in organizations, but research in this area has decreased somewhat in recent years. In addition, the particular dimensions of interest have shifted; team interventions and group variables (which used to be the primary focus of this area) do not dominate the more current literature.

We begin our discussion with interventions oriented toward the alteration of individual attributes, next review research on group change, and then treat work focusing on culture change.

Personality theory. An exciting development in the SF area is the increased integration of personality theory with OD. Personality theory research reported in the period reviewed has been applied to all levels of analysis: to the individual employee, the manager, the small group, and the overall organization.

At the individual level, personality theory has been applied to identifying traits that might moderate the acceptance and effects of planned change. One that has been identified is the employee's "focus of attention" (Gardner et al., 1987). Employees may either focus on the job, the work unit, or off the job; each focus leads to different effects from various interventions. It was hypothesized that job design interventions would positively affect individuals focused on their jobs, with similar types of predictions made for the other foci. Empirical evidence indicated that job focus and job change impacted hard measures, whereas work unit focus and job change impacted soft measures. Off-the-job focus impacted both types of measures negatively.

An important application of personality theory to the understanding of manager behavior has been made by Fisher et al. (1987), who drew on developmental psychology to create a four-stage model of the managerial life cycle. Their research showed that few managers have reached the final two stages (which emphasize a tolerance for ambiguity and "transformational" leadership); therefore, problems in the organization may indicate a mismatch between organizational needs and managers' development. This framework could be useful as a diagnostic tool to identify dysfunctional matches.

Krantz (1985) used a Tavistock Institute approach to explore how unconscious group processes, such as defenses against anxiety, serve to create a specific organizational structure and culture. Examples of organizational decline were used to elucidate this process. This analysis provides an innovative method for understanding resistance to change and implementing effective organizational designs.

These three articles further our understanding of the impact of individual differences on intervention efficacy. They also highlight the link between organizational form and individual personality. However, this area (like many others) needs substantially more attention than it has been given. Other personality factors should be explored, and a more comprehensive model of personality related to OD should be developed.

Team building. We found relatively few studies of team building. Those we identified were clustered into three broad groups: one that investigated the effects of team building on group process variables, a second that explored the impact of team building on the productivity or performance of the group, and a third that presented new perspectives on team building dynamics and appropriate research methods.

The impact of team building interventions on process measures was explored in two studies by Eden (1985, 1986a). Working with Israel Defense Forces (IDF) officers, Eden found that team building significantly affected self-perceptions of the efficacy of the intervention but did not effect actual changes (as rated by subordinates). A follow-up study (Eden, 1986a) showed significant effects on teamwork, conflict handling, and information about plans but not on other variables less directly related to the intervention itself (such as challenge, officer support, and so on). These studies provide only mixed evidence for the efficacy of the team building intervention.

The impact of team building on performance measures was examined in three different investigations. Bottger & Yetton (1987) studied the impact of individual training in problem solving on group performance and found significantly positive effects. Mitchell (1986) showed that revealing one's "internal frame of reference" leads to improved task accomplishment. However, these re-

sults were not significantly better than a traditional team building intervention. Research by Buller & Bell (1986) examined a team building/goal setting intervention with miners and found only marginally significant effects on outcomes such as productivity. It appears that narrowly focused team building interventions have a positive effect on performance. This suggests that the creative combination of some of these more narrowly focused intervention techniques could produce a substantially greater impact.

Contributions to the theory base of team building were made by Buller (1986), who utilized concepts from force-field analysis and participative decision making to develop a more precise definition of team building. He proposed that the effect of "team building–problem solving" on task performance occurs due to a variety of individual, group, task, and organizational factors. Finally, Buller suggests that team building research can be substantially improved through the development of clear operational definitions of variables, clear conceptualization of causal mechanisms, increased use of experimental designs, and the development of objective performance measures. We agree with these recommendations, except for the use of experimental designs. The reality of field research often precludes the use of true experiments; in addition, there are strong arguments against the use of these types of designs in OD (Bullock & Svyantek, 1987).

Multilevel issues. Social factor interventions that attempt to affect more complex organizational problems or arenas were reported in two studies. The first (Evans, 1989) dealt with multinational corporate development, where there has been a shift from structural to processual approaches. This is because the major challenge faced today by multinational corporations is to couple global integration with local responsiveness. For OD to be relevant in this arena, it must focus more on macro/substantive issues and become more culturally sensitive.

In contrast to the multinational setting, Golembiewski et al. (1987) discussed an intervention within a large company where the human resources staff was experiencing high levels of burnout. Both the sources and solutions to the situation were multilevel and required that a complex set of actions be undertaken. Active intervention into the culture, processes, and structure of the unit not only reduced the incidence of burnout but also improved working conditions.

New tools. An interesting new tool in OD demonstrates the time-honored principle that the sounder the theory base, the more potent any tool derived from it will be. Bernstein & Burke (1989) began with a theory of meaning systems in organizations; an implication of this theory is that belief systems must change in order to produce behavioral change in organizations. The authors used survey data and multivariate methods to uncover basic belief structures held by individuals and groups within organizations, and stated that making beliefs explicit allows for their conscious change. We encourage the use of new tools in OD, especially when these tools are derived from a sound theoretical base.

Technology. Research focusing on interventions in the technology area has utilized primarily sociotechnical systems (STS) and quality of work life (QWL) approaches. These approaches have, over time, been more broadly applied to change of entire organizations or major subsystems. A more recent variant of these two approaches uses parallel organizations (POs) as a key mechanism to implement change. We begin our discussion by focusing on studies where POs were used.

Parallel organizations. Research on POs focuses on the contingencies and outcomes associated with their success or failure. Scholars such as Herrick (1985) view POs as a "metapractice" of STS theory. If successful, POs serve as models leading to the implementation of STS concepts across the whole organization. Bushe (1987) studied a QWL intervention involving POs and found that they were more effective when a permanent middle-management problem-solving group was also created; these groups led to greater feelings of empowerment and security for the managers, who were then less threatened by

changes in employees' power. Shani & Eberhardt (1987) examined the implementation of the PO in a hospital, and employees who were a part of the PO became highly involved with organizational issues and suggestions for change. Ironically, this very interest proved threatening to top management, and this aspect of POs must be carefully managed in order to ensure their effective use. Bushe (1988), in a later study, examined the implementation of five QWL projects within a large organization and showed that QWL projects utilizing POs outperformed projects involving QCs.[10]

Quality of work life. Bocialetti (1987) examined a QWL intervention in a unionized metals processing plant and found younger workers more satisfied with the intervention because it allowed them to circumvent both the seniority system and the adversarial relations between management and older workers. Ondrack & Evans (1987) examined the effects of QWL in both greenfield and redesigned plants in the petrochemical industry in Canada. No differences were found in either job enrichment or satisfaction between traditional and QWL plants. Sorenson et al. (1985) examined the effects of QWL on a small organization and found positive changes in attitudes and performance over a four-year period. These results suggest that QWL interventions frequently have positive effects on attitudes but that performance effects are somewhat more mixed.

Sociotechnical systems. Two studies explored theoretical issues about STS interventions. Kolody & Stjernberg (1986) drew upon case studies to develop a model of the STS process that highlights specific organizational subsytems as important to design efforts in plant settings. Susman & Chase (1986) explored the technical and social challenges that computer-integrated manufacturing poses for traditional STS plant design. The authors suggest changes in the STS process that will result in more successful implementation. Unfortunately, no subsequent research appears to be guided by either approach.

Other research explored STS interventions in a variety of settings. Pasmore et al. (1986) found that negative results from an STS intervention in a health care setting were due to the consultants' lack of sensitivity to the unique dynamics of this setting. Wall et al. (1986) instituted an autonomous workgroup design in a greenfield plant site and found positive effects only for intrinsic job satisfaction. Other individual-level measures showed no positive and/or lasting effects. Conversely, Taylor (1986) created an STS intervention in a computer operations department that did not involve semiautonomous work groups (a mainstay of typical STS interventions). Positive effects on turnover and production were demonstrated.

Reviewing the technology interventions as a whole, we are heartened that, by and large, they increasingly focus on whole-system issues and change. At the same time, the mixed success of these interventions means that their theoretical base still needs more refinement. Questions regarding the appropriateness of STS to different settings as well as the efficacy of QWL arrangements in creating both satisfaction and productivity are prime targets for further examination.

Physical Setting. Although planned change interventions focusing on physical settings have been part of the OD literature for over 15 years (e.g., Steele, 1973), we located only two more recent studies that focused on this intervention strategy. Oldham, one of the more active researchers in this area, investigated the effects of changing from a normal open office plan to either a more spacious open office plan or partitioned cubicles (Oldham, 1988). Both approaches resulted in positive effects on variables specific to the change (such as privacy satisfaction); individual differences in privacy needs and stimulus screening were significant moderators of these relations. In a somewhat similar study, Zalesny & Farace (1987) examined the effects of moving from closed offices to an open office plan for governmental employees. Symbolic theory (i.e., that work environments communicate information symbolically) best explained the results because those with higher positions were less

satisfied (i.e., managers felt losing their offices indicated a loss of position).

Other Areas of Interest. A substantial amount of theory and research in OD focuses on general processes and issues.

New settings for OD. Gray & Hay (1986) extended political analysis to interorganizational domains to explicate the necessary conditions and actions for successful interventions in this arena. For interventions to be successful, powerful and legitimate stakeholders must participate in domain definition and action. Key environmental forces must also be successfully managed. Some have focused on how well OD might fit with other cultures. Boss & Mariono (1987) examined the history and practice of OD in Italy and showed that it has primarily occurred in large organizations that train their own professionals. Italian work culture appears to be oriented more toward role-oriented and structural interventions than does the United States. Jaeger (1986) drew upon Hofstede's work (1980) on national values to determine the fit of OD with various cultures. He concluded that some areas, such as Scandinavia, have values very consonant with OD; while others, such as Latin America, do not.[11] The author suggests that the success of OD in other nations will be determined by its adaptation to the dominant local values.

The applicability of OD to settings other than traditional corporate ones has also been examined. Leitko & Szczerbacki (1987) found that applying traditional OD strategies in professional bureaucracies (such as found in human service organizations) often fails. Traditional OD typically uses interpersonal interventions that loosen the constraints imposed by the "machine" bureaucracies found in industry. However, as the authors note, professional bureaucracies are often loosely integrated, and interventions that create more bounded systems are more appropriate here. Shamir & Salomon (1985) investigated telecommuting (i.e., work at home employing computer technology) and concluded that home work is not a panacea for the problems of modern organization. Thus research needs to consider carefully both the problems and benefits of home work before it is suggested as a desirable alternative. These studies explore the role of OD in situations that require the development of new concepts and new techniques for intervention.

Research methods. Methodology issues in OD have also been researched. One controversy in this area concerns the appropriateness of different measurement approaches. Bullock & Svyantek (1987) argued persuasively that evaluating OD interventions using random strategies fundamentally contradicts the need for collaboration and participation found in effective OD. Therefore the authors suggest the use of more appropriate research methods such as case meta-analysis (discussed below). Eden (1986b) suggested that rigorous research designed to eliminate "expectation effects" associated with interventions is misguided. He argues that these effects are an important part of OD's success and should be studied and clarified, rather than removed from research. Woodman (1989) takes the position that research should be useful to both practitioners and academics, and therefore should require both "thick" description and generalizable propositions. He proposes a "combined paradigm" approach (using both qualitative and quantitative methods), with stream analysis (Porras, 1987) and appreciative inquiry (Cooperrider & Srivasta, 1987) as possible examples for this.

Appreciative inquiry is an exciting new method of inquiry that deserves mention. Cooperrider & Srivasta view action research as impotent in generating alternative forms for organizing that can lead to social betterment. They propose appreciative inquiry as a revitalization of action research that both improves practice and generates theory. It does this by highlighting areas where an organization "works" and, using collaborative inquiry processes, determines directions for growth and renewal. This approach is distinct from the organizational pathology model implicit in most OD.

Stream analysis is also an important new intervention method. Porras (1987) has developed a graphical tool that maps organizational problems into the four streams (OA, SF, T, and PS), and then diagrams the links between them. By doing this, core problems are identified and targeted for change. A stream diagram is then developed mapping out the intervention's time-line and targets. This approach is a simple yet powerful way to diagnose and intervene in organizational issues.

Research in this period has also focused on better measurement of the Golembiewski et al. (1976) typology. Millsap & Hartog (1988) propose a methodology based on factorial structures within a structural equation framework to determine whether either gamma or beta change has occurred. Van de Vliert et al. (1985) propose a method to distinguish between alpha and beta change in which, once gamma change is ruled out (by examining the construct validity of pre- and post-test measures), dynamic correlations are used to separate alpha and beta change.

An exciting innovation in OD research is the use of both quantitative and case meta-analysis to combine results across many different studies. Case meta-analysis (Bullock & Tubbs, 1987) integrates OD case studies (still the most prevalent form of OD research) by coding study variables and then performing correlational analysis on them. Quantitative meta-analysis uses the statistics provided in more quantitative research and determines "effect sizes" due to interventions on outcome variables.

Guzzo et al. (1985) performed a meta-analysis that examined the effects of psychologically based interventions on "hard" measures. Interventions such as team building showed strong effects on productivity (in contrast to the team building research cited above) but not on withdrawal or disruption (e.g., absenteeism, grievances, et cetera). Beekun (1989) conducted a meta-analysis of STS interventions and demonstrated generally positive effects on productivity and withdrawal behaviors. Several moderator variables were also important to STS success but, interestingly enough, workgroup autonomy was not one of them. This again indicates the need for some rethinking of STS theory. Finally, Newman et al. (1989) conducted a meta-analysis of OD interventions on attitudinal outcomes. The authors find the primary effects on attitudes to be due to human processual, not technostructural interventions.

Some authors have investigated measures to improve OD research. Porras & Hoffer (1986) conducted a survey of leading OD professionals and found substantial agreement among them on a set of nine behaviors that correlate with successful interventions. Hoffer (1986) operationalized the behaviors into a questionnaire that she then used to explore the relationship between them and hard measures of organizational performance. Her results showed a highly significant relationship between an index representing the entire set of behaviors and various hard measures of organizational performance, such as sales levels, market share, costs, profits, et cetera. This indicates that these behaviors hold promise for providing a common base upon which to aggregate findings from disparate change studies.

Nicholas & Katz (1985) also focused on the same "aggregation" issue. They reviewed OD research from 1948 to 1982 and suggested a set of reporting standards to make cross-study comparison much more effective. It is clear that one of the challenges facing OD research is to find ways to aggregate the research findings of the field. In turn, this aggregation process will help to improve the quality of theory found in OD.

The generation of theory and new methodology in OD should be encouraged. At the same time, much of this research is fragmented and does not build on work done by other authors laboring in a similar arena. More effort should be directed at the development of a paradigm for OD, and thus researchers must build more consciously on each other's work.

Organization Transformation

OT has emerged over the last decade as a distinct form of planned change. It is an advancement over OD owing to its focus on precipitating more profound change in organizations. This occurs because the variables targeted by OT approaches (organizational beliefs, purpose, and mission, the components of organizational vision) affect a "deeper" level in the organization than those traditionally targeted for change by OD (i.e., work-setting variables).

First we examine interventions focused on organizational vision. We then discuss the practice of industrial democracy in Norway. This type of intervention has not usually been considered part of OT, but recent developments indicate that the types of change pursued here are transformational. Finally, we survey other areas of interest in the OT field. The literature on OT was quite limited, reflecting the newness of this area.

Organizational Vision

Organizational-level views of vision examine the processes through which organizations are able to change and learn. Individual-level perspectives assume that organizational transformation is dependent upon individual workers radically shifting their typical ways of thinking and doing.

Levy & Merry (1986) identify two distinct approaches to individual consciousness change: reframing (which draws from theory in family therapy—e.g., Watzlawick et al., 1974) and consciousness raising (which has many roots—e.g., Harrison, 1984). Reframing consists of organizational interventions that change an organization member's perceptions of reality. Reframing does not change current organizational reality; instead, it alters the way individuals view the world. This new worldview leads to corresponding changes in attitudes and behaviors, and organizational transformation follows.

Consciousness raising, on the other hand, makes the processes of transformation visible to organization members. Thought is viewed as the source of both existing circumstances and potential change; therefore, individuals with more awareness of transformative processes are better able to guide them. Theory here has been primarily adapted from transpersonal psychology (e.g., Walsh & Vaughan, 1980). Techniques such as meditation and creativity exercises are suggested as practice interventions in this approach.

Other work on organizational transformation focuses on creating organizations that understand how (and when) to initiate radical change and have strategies and structures in place to produce this change. Beer (1987) examined three cases of organizational transformation where successful change included the concurrent development of a vision of the future and a heightened dissatisfaction with the status quo throughout the whole organization. These factors, coupled with a well-managed change process, led to successful transformation. Nadler & Tushman (1989) developed a model of the transformation process similar to Beer's; however, these authors also stressed diagnosis and provided more detail regarding implementation steps. For example, they stress the need for a "magic leader," who serves as a focus for the change effort, followed by a diffusion of energy for change throughout the organization.

Bartunek & Moch (1987) and Levy & Merry (1986) examined transformation caused by changing the organizational "paradigm." Transformation is accomplished here by increasing the system's ability to analyze and change current paradigms, as well as to envision desirable future paradigms. Lundberg (1989) discussed organizational learning in OD and proposed a cyclical process of learning occurring at three successively deeper levels: organizational change, development, and transformation. His model provides a useful set of analytical tools for implementing transformative processes.

The differences between the micro and macro approaches to organizational vision reflect a "top-down" versus "bottom-up" orientation. Organizational-level approaches typically view top management as the catalyst for changes in organizational vision; these changes then spread throughout the whole organization. Individual-level approaches view vision change as decentralized; when enough organizational members change their consciousness, organizational change occurs. We believe that whether an intervention focuses on the macro or micro level matters less than how effective it is at producing change; it is also likely that interventions combining both strategies will have the greatest impact.

Industrial Democracy

The theory and practice of industrial democracy developed outside the United States and has not been generally considered part of either OD or OT. However, the change processes initiated by this approach result in paradigm shifts. The techniques that constitute the industrial democracy change strategy all relate to the shifting of power in the organization toward the end goal of democratizing the work setting. The intervention techniques used in this approach have their roots in STS and QWL concepts and technology but have evolved to the point where they focus primarily on gamma (A) and gamma (B) change.

Perhaps the most interesting and innovative work in this area has occurred in Norway and increasingly centers on "local theory" (Gustavsen & Engelstad, 1986). Local theory evolved when change projects based on general OD, STS, and QWL theory were not successful. This led to the realization that theories of democracy not generated by employees themselves are, in some sense, not democratic. Thus generative capacity (i.e., the ability of people to develop solutions to their own organizational problems) is most important, and interventions should be designed to increase this capacity. Gustavsen & Engelstad view "the conference" (an off-site meeting involving managers and employees from several companies) as an ideal setting for the practice of industrial democracy. Successes at such conferences can then be translated into practices appropriate for individuals' home organizations.

Elden (1986), in a very insightful piece, discussed how these ideas have become a part of public policy in Norway. Empowering participation is the key phrase in the Norwegian efforts; workers shape the actual conditions of their work through participatory STS activity. Participation is seen as second-order [gamma (A) and gamma (B)] change in this new framework. In this way, the change thrust has moved from empowerment through structure (e.g., instituting autonomous work groups) to empowerment through process (workers making local-level decisions about appropriate work practices). Some necessary conditions for empowering participation include institutional and political support at higher levels, participatory research, researchers as co-learners, empowering the less powerful, and rejecting conventional OD and STS.

Other Areas of Interest

An interesting area of OT research examines disequilibrium models, where transformation is the rule, rather than the exception. Gemmill & Smith (1985) developed a dissipative structure model of transformation, where turbulent conditions prevent organizations from damping change and reaching equilibrium. When this happens, old forms of organizing break down and experimentation with many new forms occurs. Eventually, the most successful experiment reorganizes the system at a higher functional level. Leifer (1989) also proposed a dissipative structure model but stressed that a vision of the future is needed to mobilize the energy for experimentation. The premise of these articles is that organizations move from transformation to transformation, with only brief periods of stability (characterized by efficiency concerns) in between.

Several other authors have proposed intervention methods appropriate for OT work. Argyris et al. (1985) described "action science," an approach that attempts to catalyze double-loop learning [roughly equivalent to gamma (B) change] in individuals and organizations. The theoretical underpinning of this work parallels work discussed above on individual consciousness change and paradigm shifts. Pava (1986) proposed the concept of "normative incrementalism," an intervention method appropriate when both high complexity and high conflict exist in organizations (a condition ripe for transformation). These conditions only allow for interventions that are incremental and not threatening to current interests. This intervention therefore introduces some general theme (such as "quality of working life")

without specifying how this translates into day-to-day organizational practice. However, this theme triggers employees to engage in activities that begin to clarify it retrospectively. This is a dialectic process that leads to the reformulation of values and ultimately to major organizational change.

After reviewing the breadth of ideas in OT, it is apparent how much vitality exists in this emerging approach to planned change. Although the broad outlines of the field may be sketched (e.g., focus on vision, consciousness change, et cetera), there is still considerable diversity in this area and consequently many different directions for future development. It is therefore difficult to predict where the field will be in 10 years, but we are certain that it will still be generating excitement and interest for both scholars and practitioners.

Summary

There was much research on OD in the period reviewed, while relatively little published literature exists in the area of OT. OD is still vigorous, as judged by the number of publications in this area, but the field has moved (since the late 1960s) from an energetic adolescence to a somewhat sedate maturity. In categorizing OD intervention approaches and target variables, we noticed two interesting patterns (noted only regarding the OA and SF streams). First of all, SF interventions dominated OD in the 1960s and early 1970s. However, in the period reviewed there had been a definite shift in emphasis from interventions emphasizing individual and group processes to interventions focusing on structural arrangements and reward systems (i.e., a shift from SF to OA research). OD research has, over time, increasingly emphasized organizational-level factors, and this is reflected by the increased volume of work on OA interventions.

The second pattern we noted concerned the target variables of research. OA research, although examining newer types of interventions in OD, typically focuses on "traditional" variables. These include participation (e.g., Marks et al.,

1986), motivation (e.g., Jordan, 1986), task perceptions (e.g., Rafaeli, 1985), etc. In addition, OA research typically investigates the connection between these variables and outcomes such as productivity (e.g. Ralston et. al., 1985). In contrast, SF research has focused on a more innovative set of variables. These include internal frames of reference (Mitchell, 1986), managerial life cycles (Fisher et al, 1987), organizational embodiments of ego defenses (Krantz, 1985), et cetera. OA research seems to "lag" SF research in its choice of variables, and we suggest more integration of organizational-level intervention research with newer variables. At the same time, SF research can be criticized for not more explicitly theorizing and researching the link between innovative target variables and organizational outcomes (Buller's 1986 study was an exception).

Although there are some innovative areas of OD research in the period reviewed, no fundamental new paradigms have been developed and embraced by the field, and major new insights are rare. OT, on the other hand, is exciting precisely because it involves dramatically new premises for planned change. OT draws on more recent developments in psychology, transpersonal psychology, and systems theory, and often challenges traditional concepts in OD regarding models and methods. However, since this area is so underdeveloped, it is our hope that an increasing amount of rigorous theory development and research will appear in the near future.

Future Directions in Planned Change

Our analysis of the last five years of organizational change research has led us to a series of conclusions about where the field should head.

An important arena for future research concerns organizational paradigms. Paradigms are a key concept in OT work, but no clear conceptualization or research strategy for them has been developed. Specifying the mechanisms and boundaries of paradigm change is also important.

Organizational vision is another crucial area where research could improve OT theory and practice. Collins & Porras (1989) discuss vision and its component parts (guiding beliefs, purpose, mission) in detail, but more work needs to be done. The role of vision in maintaining organizational coherence should be explored, as should the dynamics of vision change in organizational change.

Concepts from Asian philosophy underlie some types of OT practice (e.g., the use of meditation as a tool for consciousness change). However, these concepts are not rigorously integrated into OT theory, and more theory development exploring Eastern conceptions of individual and group change should be done.

Planned change theory in general also needs much more development. The Change Process Model is one attempt to improve this area, but we encourage other attempts at developing theoretical models of change. In addition to general models of change, research should focus on how interventions impact important organizational variables and how change in these variables cascades throughout the organizational system.

The dynamics and effects of new organizational forms need much more research. Exploring Ackoff's (1989) circular organization, parallel organizations, and other innovations will increase the knowledge bases of both OD and OT. Another important area of research concerns changes in ownership, rather than in governance. More employee ownership research on ESOPs and their outcomes is needed, as well as research on organizations that are fully employee owned.

Finally, as mentioned above, more research is needed on the direct effects of physical-setting change. Beyond that, exploring the interrelationship of physical setting and other organizational factors (such as structure and culture) has important implications for change theory and practice. Research should investigate the contingencies that make different types of physical setting optimal under different conditions.

There are also some important directions in which research methods and measures should head. Of course theory building that results in testable models is a key to improving research. Such models are the best guides for research, and can lead to more productive exploration of OD and OT issues.

In addition to better theory, developing a common set of variables upon which to aggregate findings is important. Meta-analysis provides the analytical tools for cross-study comparison, but meaningful comparisons can only be made when common measures are employed. We believe that the behaviors of individual organizational members are a useful and easily measured set of variables that could serve this function. The set of behaviors proposed by Porras & Hoffer (1986) are an example of this.

The Golembiewski et al. (1976) typology of alpha, beta, and gamma change would be another way to develop a common set of measures. Given the amount of interest generated by this typology in the last 15 years, it was shocking to find no studies in our review that used these measures. One reason may be that methodologists are still exploring the optimal way to measure these types of change (e.g. Millsap & Hartog 1988); however, several such measures already exist, and this typology provides another common metric for more integration of research. Better reporting standards (Nicholas & Katz 1985) also would aid in promoting cross-study comparison. All in all, better theory coupled with more integration of findings would immeasurably improve the effectiveness of planned change interventions.

Endnotes

1. The six previous major reviews of the field (Friedlander & Brown, 1974; Beer, 1976; Alderfer, 1977; Faucheux et al., 1982; Beer & Walton, 1987; Porras et al., 1990) each used different frameworks to organize their discussions—frameworks based on change targets, strategies, functions, or theories. None, however, was based on a model of the change process itself. We hope our attempt to model the change process will interest others in doing the same. The field sorely needs a clear model of change to guide research and action.

2. This perspective is rooted in the Stream Organization Model, a model of organizations proposed by Porras (1987) and Porras et al. (1990) as a conceptual base for planned change work. Its key assumptions include these: that individual behavior is central to producing organizational outcomes; that individual work behavior is mostly driven by the context (work setting) of individual employees; that organizational vision provides the basic rationale for the design of the work setting; and that two major outcomes, organizational performance and individual development, derive from collective behaviors.

3. Each of these two intervention approaches will be defined in terms of subsequent sections of the Change Process Model. As such, these definitions may not be completely clear to the reader at this point. We ask the reader to bear with us until all components are discussed.

4. While this type of change is primarily caused by OD, some OT interventions focus on the work setting and also produce this pattern of change.

5. Kuhn (1970) defined a knowledge paradigm as "the collection of ideas within the confines of which scientific inquiry takes place, the assumed definition of what are legitimate problems and methods, the accepted practice and point of view with which the student prepares for membership in the scientific community, the criteria for choosing problems to attack, the rules and standards of scientific practice" (p. 11). This definition of paradigm, which is widely cited in both the natural and social sciences, is consistent with Adam's definition, which focuses specifically on organizations.

6. This same criteria will be applied to each of the following sections.

7. It should be noted, however, that these findings were reported for the second and third years of a longitudinal study. By the fourth year, the measures of these indicators did not differ from the first year.

8. Latack & Foster (1985) also propose an interesting unanticipated consequence of altering work schedules—that if they are compressed schedules they will tend to lead to job enrichment, since workers on duty at any one time will have to perform more tasks.

9. It is useful to note that, irrespective of the technique used to design organizational structures, their implementation is strongly enhanced through the use of employee involvement and process consultation work. Stebbins & Shani (1989) reviewed four major

approaches to organizational design (Galbraith's Information Processing Model; MacKenzie's ABCE model and OA&A process; Kilmann's MAPS technology; and Sociotechnical Systems consulting) and found that while all four methods varied in their foci and key variables, they all incorporated process consultation and employee involvement principles in their implementation process.

10. Bushe also found the evidence mixed regarding the usefulness of traditional QWL theory and proposed intergroup theory as a better way to understand QWL.

11. Faucheux et al. (1982), in their review of OD, also emphasized the substantial differences in change approaches between Latin and Anglo-Saxon countries.

References

Ackoff, R. L. 1989, "The Circular Organization: An Update." *Acad. Mange. Exec.* 3:11–16.

Adams, J. D., ed. 1984. *Transforming Work: A Collection of Organizational Transformation Readings.* Alexandria, VA: Miles River Press.

Alderfer, C. P. 1977. "Organization Development." *Annu. Rev. Psychol.* 28:197–223.

Argyris, C.; Putnam, R.; Smith, D. M. 1985. *Action Science.* San Francisco: Jossey-Bass.

Bartunek, J. M.; Moch, M. K. 1987. "First-Order, Second-Order, and Third-Order Change and Organization Development Interventions: A Cognitive Approach." *J. Appl. Behav. Sci.* 23:483–500.

Beekun, R. I. 1989. "Assessing the Effectiveness of Sociotechnical Intervention: Antidote or Fad?" *Hum. Relat.* 42:877–97.

Beer, M. 1976. "The Technology of Organization Development." In *Handbook of Industrial and Organizational Psychology,* ed. M. Dunnette. Chicago: Rand McNally College Publishing.

Beer, M. 1987. "Revitalizing Organizations: Change Process and Emergent Model." *Acad. Manage. Exec.* 1:51–55.

Beer, M., Walton, A. E. 1987. "Organization Change and Development." *Annu. Rev. Psychol.* 38:339–67.

Bernstein, W. M.; Burke, W. W. 1989. "Modeling Organizational Meaning Systems." See Woodman & Pasmore, 1989, pp. 117–59.

Bocialetti, G. 1987. "Quality of Work Life: Some Unintended Effects on the Seniority Tradition of an Industrial Union." *Group Organ. Stud.* 12:386–410.

Boss, R. W., Mariono, M. V. 1987. "Organization Development in Italy." *Group Organ. Stud.* 12:245–56.

Bottger, P. C., Yetton, P. W. 1987. "Improving Group Performance by Training in Individual Problem Solving." *J. Appl. Psychol.* 72:651–57.

Buller, P. F. 1986. "The Team Building-Task Performance Relation: Some Conceptual and Methodological Refinements." *Group Organ. Stud.* 11:147–68.

Buller, P. F., Bell, C. H., Jr. 1986. "Effects of Team Building and Goal Setting on Productivity: A Field Experiment." *Acad. Manage. J.* 29:305–28.

Bullock, R. J., Svyantek, D. J. 1987. "The Impossibility of Using Random Strategies to Study the Organization Development Process." *J. Appl. Behav. Sci.* 23:255–62.

Bullock, R. J., Tubbs, M. E. 1987. "The Case Meta-Analysis Method for OD." See Woodman & Pasmore, 1987, pp. 171–228.

Bushe, G. R. 1987. "Temporary or Permanent Middle-Management Groups? Correlates with Attitudes in QWL Change Projects." *Group Organ. Stud.* 12:23–37.

Bushe, G. R. 1988. "Developing Cooperative Labor-Management Relations in Unionized Factories: A Multiple Case Study of Quality Circles and Parallel Organizations within Joint Quality of Work Life Projects," *J. Appl. Behav. Sci.* 24:129–50.

Collins, J. C., Porras, J. I. 1989. "Making Impossible Dreams Come True." *Stanford Bus. Sch. Mag.* 57:12–19.

Cooperrider, D. L., Srivasta, S. 1987. "Appreciative Inquiry in Organizational Life." See Woodman & Pasmore, 1987, pp. 129–69.

Dunham, R. B.; Pierce, J. L.; Castaneda, M. B. 1987. "Alternative Work Schedules: Two Field Experiments." *Personnel Psychol.* 40:215–41.

Eden, D. 1985. "Team Development: A True Field Experiment at Three Levels of Rigor." *J. Appl. Psychol.* 70:94–100.

Eden, D. 1986a. "Team Development: Quasi-Experimental Confirmation among Combat Companies." *Group Organ. Stud.* 11:133–46.

Eden, D. 1986b. "OD and Self-Fulfilling Prophecy: Boosting Productivity by Raising Expectations." *J. Appl. Behav. Sci.* 22:1–13.

Elden, M. 1986. "Sociotechnical Systems Ideas as Public Policy in Norway: Empowering Participation through Worker-Managed Change," *J. Appl. Behav. Sci.* 22:239–55.

Evans, P. A. L. 1989. "Organizational Development in the Transnational Enterprise." See Woodman & Pasmore, 1989, pp. 1–39.

Faucheux, C., Amado, G., Laurent, A. 1982. "Organizational Development and Change." *Annu. Rev. Psychol.* 33:343–70.

Ferris, G. R., Wagner, J. A. III. 1985. "Quality Circles in the United States: A Conceptual Reevaluation." *J. Appl. Behav. Sci.* 21:155–67.

Fisher, D.; Merron, K.; Torbert, W. R. 1987. "Human Development and Managerial Effectiveness." *Group Organ. Stud.* 12:257–73.

Florkowski, G. W. 1987. "The Organizational Impact of Profit Sharing." *Acad. Manage. Rev.* 12:622–36.

French, J. L. 1987. "Employee Perspectives on Stock Ownership: Financial Investment or Mechanism of Control?" *Acad. Manage. Rev.* 12:427–35.

Friedlander, F., Brown, L. D. 1974. "Organization Development." *Annu. Rev. Psychol.* 25:313–41.

Gardner, D. G.; Dunham, R. B.; Cummings, L. L.; Pierce, J. L. 1987. "Employee Focus of Attention and Reactions to Organizational Change." *J. Appl. Behav. Sci.* 23:351–70.

Gemmill, G., Smith, C. 1985. "A Dissipative Structure Model of Organizational Transformation." *Hum. Relat.* 38:751–66.

Golembiewski, R. T.; Billingsley, K.; Yeager, S. 1976. "Measuring Change and Persistence in Human Affairs: Type of Change Generated by OD Designs." *J. Appl. Behav. Sci.* 12:133–57.

Golembiewski, R. T.; Hilles, R.; Daly, R. 1987. "Some Effects of Multiple OD Interventions on Burnout and Work Site Features." *J. Appl. Behav. Sci.* 23: 295–313.

Gray, B., Hay, T. M. 1986. "Political Limits to Interorganizational Consensus and Change." *J. Appl. Behav. Sci.* 22:95–112.

Greiner, L. 1972. "Evolution and Revolution as Organizations Grow." *Harv. Bus. Rev.* 50:39–46.

Griffin, R. W. 1988. "Consequences of Quality Circles in an Industrial Setting: A Longitudinal Assessment." *Acad. Manage. J.* 31:388–58.

Gustavsen, B., Engelstad, P. H. 1986. "The Design of Conferences and the Evolving Role of Democratic Dialogue in Changing Work Life." *Hum. Relat.* 39:101–16.

Guzzo. R. A.; Jette, R. D.; Katzell, R. A. 1985. "The Effects of Psychologically Based Intervention Programs on Worker Productivity: A Meta-Analysis." *Personnel Psychol.* 38:275–91.

Harrison, R. 1984. "Leadership and Strategy for a New Age." In *Transforming Work,* ed. J. Adams. Alexandria, VA: Miles River Press.

Head, T. C.; Molleston, J. L.; Sorenson, P. F., Jr.; Gargano, J. 1986. "The Impact of Implementing a Quality Circle Intervention on Employee Task Perceptions." *Group Organ. Stud.* 11:360–73.

Herrick, N. Q. 1985. "Parallel Organizations in Unionized Settings: Implications for Organizational Research." *Hum. Relat.* 38:963–81.

Hoffer, S. J. 1986. *Behavior and Organizational Performance: An Empirical Study."* PhD thesis. Stanford Univ. Grad. Sch. Educ.

Hofstede, G. 1980. *Culture's Consequences: International Differences in Work Related Values.* Beverly Hills, CA: Sage.

Jaeger, A. M. 1986. "Organization Development and National Culture: Where's the Fit?" *Acad. Manage. Rev.* 11:178–90.

Jordan, P. C. 1986. "Effects of an Extrinsic Reward on Intrinsic Motivation: A Field Experiment." *Acad. Manage. J.* 29:405–12.

Klein, K. J. 1987. "Employee Stock Ownership and Employee Attitudes: A Test of Three Models." *J. Appl. Psychol.* 72:319–32.

Kolodny, H.; Stjernberg, T. 1986. "The Change Process of Innovative Work Designs: New Design and Redesign in Sweden, Canada, and the U.S." *J. Appl. Behav. Sci.* 22:287–301.

Krantz, J. 1985. "Group Processes under Conditions of Organizational Decline." *J. Appl. Behav. Sci.* 21: 1–17.

Kuhn, T. 1970. *The Structure of Scientific Revolution.* Chicago: Univ. Chicago Press. 2nd ed.

Latack, J. C.; Ooster, L. W. 1985. "Implementation of Compressed Work Schedules: Participation and Job Redesign as Critical Factors for Employee Acceptance." *Personnel Psychol.* 38:75–92.

Lawler, E. E. III. 1988. "Choosing an Involvement Strategy." *Acad. Manage. Exec.* 2:197–204.

Lawler, E. E. III; Mohrman, S. A. 1987. "Quality Circles: After the Honeymoon." *Organ. Dyn.* 15:42–54.

Leifer, R. 1989. "Understanding Organizational Transformation Using a Dissipative Structure Model." *Hum. Relat.* 42:899–916.

Leitko, T. A.; Szczerback, D. 1987. "Why Traditional OD Strategies Fail in Professional Bureaucracies." *Organ. Dyn.* 15:52–65.

Levy, A.; Merry, U. 1986. *Organizational Transformation.* New York: Praeger.

Lindblom, C. 1959. "The Science of Muddling Through." *Public Admin. Rev.* 21:78–88.

Lundberg, C. C. 1989. "On Organizational Learning: Implications and Opportunities for Expanding Organizational Development." See Woodman & Pasmore, 1989, pp. 61–82.

Marks, M. L.; Mirvis, P. H.; Hackett, E. J.; Grady, J. F. Jr. 1986. "Employee Participation in a Quality Circle Program: Impact on Quality of Work Life, Productivity, and Absenteeism." *J. Appl. Psychol.* 71:61–69.

McDaniel, R. R. Jr.; Thomas, J. B.; Ashmos, D. P.; Smith, J. P. 1987. "The Use of Decision Analysis for Organizational Design: Reorganizing a Community Hospital." *J. Appl. Behav. Sci.* 23:337–50.

Meyer, G. W., Stoff, R. G. 1985. "Quality Circles: Panacea or Pandora's Box?" *Organ. Dyn.* 13:34–50.

Miller, C. S., Schuster, M. 1987. "A Decade's Experience with the Scanlon Plan: A Case Study." *J. Occup. Behav.* 8:167–74.

Millsap, R. E.; Hartog, S. B. 1988. "Alpha, Beta, and Gamma Change in Evaluation Research: A Structural Equation Approach." *J. Appl. Psychol.* 73:574–84.

Mitchell, R. 1986. "Team Building by Disclosure of Internal Frame of Reference." *J. Appl. Behav. Sci.* 22:15–28.

Nadler, D. A.; Tushman, M. L. 1989. "Organizational Frame Bending: Principles for Managing Reorientation." *Acad. Manage. Exec.* 3:194–204.

Nelson, R. E. 1988. "Social Network Analysis as an Intervention Tool: Examples from the Field." *Group Organ. Stud.* 13:39–58.

Neuman, G. A.; Edwards, J. E.; Raju, N. S. 1989. "Organization Development Interventions: A Meta-Analysis of Their Effects on Satisfaction and Other Attitudes." *Personnel Psychol.* 42:461–89.

Nicholas, J. M.; Katz, M. 1985. "Research Methods and Reporting Practices in Organization Development: A Review and Some Guidelines." *Acad. Manage. Rev.* 10:737–49.

Oldham, G. R. 1988. "Effects of Changes in Workspace Partitions and Spatial Density on Employee Reactions: A Quasi-Experiment." *J. Appl. Psychol.* 73:253–58.

Ondrack, D. A.; Evans, M. G. 1987. "Job Enrichment and Job Satisfaction in Greenfield and Redesign QWL Sites." *Group Organ. Stud.* 12:5–22.

Pasmore, W.; Petee, J.; Bastian, R. 1986. "Sociotechnical Systems in Health Care: A Field Experiment." *J. Appl. Behav. Sci.* 22:329–39.

Pava, C. 1986. "New Strategies of Systems Change: Reclaiming Nonsynoptic Methods." *Hum. Relat.* 39:615–33.

Pearce, J. L.; Stevenson, W. B.; Perry, J. L. 1985. "Managerial Compensation Based on Organizational Performance: A Time Series Analysis of the Effects of Merit Pay." *Acad. Manage. J.* 28:261–78.

Porras, J. I., 1987. *Stream Analysis: A Powerful New Way to Diagnose and Manage Change.* Reading, MA: Addison-Wesley.

Porras, J. I.; Hoffer, S. J. 1986. "Common Behavior Changes in Successful Organization Development Efforts." *J. Appl. Behav. Sci.* 22:477–94.

Porras, J. I.; Robertson, P.; Goldman, L. 1990. "Organization Development." In *Handbook of Industrial and Organizational Psychology,* ed. M. Dunnette. Palo Alto, CA: Psychological Press.

Rafaeli, A. 1985. "Quality Circles and Employee Attitudes." *Personnel Psychol.* 38:603–15.

Ralston, D. A.; Anthony, W. P.; Gustafson, D. J. 1985. "Employees May Love Flextime, But What Does It Do to the Organization's Productivity?" *J. Appl. Psychol.* 70:272–79.

Shamir, B.: Salomon, I. 1985. "Work-at-Home and the Quality of Working Life." *Acad. Manage. Rev.* 10:455–64.

Shani, A. B.; Eberhardt, B. J. 1987. "Parallel Organization in a Health Care Institution." *Group Organ. Stud.* 12:147–73.

Sheldon, A. 1980. "Organizational Paradigms: A Theory of Organizational Change." *Organ. Dyn.* 8:61–80.

Sorenson, P. F. Jr.; Head, T. C.; Stotz, D. 1985. "Quality of Work Life and the Small Organization: A Four-Year Case Study." *Group Organ. Stud.* 10:320–39.

Stebbins, M. W.; Shani, A. B. 1989. "Organization Design: Beyond the Mafia Model." *Organ. Dyn.* 17:18–30.

Steel, R. P.; Lloyd, R. F. 1988. "Cognitive, Affective, and Behavioral Outcomes of Participation in Quality Circles: Conceptual and Empirical Findings." *J. Appl. Behav. Sci.* 24:1–17.

Steel, R. P.; Shane, G. S. 1986. "Evaluation Research on Quality Circles: Technical and Analytical Implications." *Hum. Relat.* 39:449–68.

Steele, F. I. 1973. *Physical Settings and Organization Development.* Reading, MA: Addison-Wesley.

Susman, G. I.; Chase, R. B. 1986. "A Sociotechnical Analysis of the Integrated Factory." *J. Appl. Behav. Sci.* 22:257–70.

Taylor, J. C. 1986. "Long-Term Sociotechnical Systems Change in a Computer Operations Department." *J. Appl. Behav. Sci.* 22:303–13.

Van de Vliert, E.; Huismans, S. E.; Stok, J. J. L. 1985. "The Criterion Approach to Unraveling Beta and Alpha Change." *Acad. Manage. Rev.* 10:269–74.

Vickers, G. 1965. *The Art of Judgment.* New York: Basic Books.

Wall, T. D.; Kemp, N. J.; Jackson, P. R.; Clegg, C. W. 1986. "Outcomes of Autonomous Workgroups: A Long-Term Field Experiment." *Acad. Manage. J.* 29:280–304.

Walsh, R. N.; Vaughan, F. 1980. *Beyond Ego: Transpersonal Dimensions in Psychology.* Los Angeles: J. P. Tarcher.

Watzlawick, P.; Weakland, J; Fisch, R. 1974. *Change.* New York: W. W. Norton.

Woodman, R. W. 1989. "Evaluation Research on Organizational Change: Arguments for a 'Combined Paradigm' Approach." See Woodman & Pasmore, 1989, pp. 161–80.

Woodman, R. W.; Pasmore, W. A., eds. 1987. *Research in Organizational Change and Development,* vol. 1. Greenwich, CT: JAI Press.

Woodman, R. W.; Pasmore, W. A., eds. 1989. *Research in Organizational Change and Development,* vol. 3. Greenwich, CT: JAI Press.

Zalesny, M. E.: Farace, R. V. 1987. "Traditional versus Open Offices: A Comparison of Sociotechnical, Social Relations, and Symbolic Meaning Perspectives." *Acad. Manage. J.* 30:240–59.

Reading 6

Most Influential Management Books of the 20th Century

Arthur G. Bedeian
Daniel A. Wren

As we turn the last page of the century, it is time to take a step back from the mundane and reflect on the path that management discipline has followed. In the best tradition of management scholarship, we may thus continue to learn from the past as it informs the present and, perhaps, discern where our discipline ought to be going. To this end, a list of the Twentieth Century's most influential management books offers a compelling basis for understanding the heritage from which we will build our common future.

Authors' Note:

The authors wish to express appreciation to Stephen J. Carroll, W. Jack Duncan, Paul J. Gordon, John B. Miner, Dennis W. Organ, and George Strauss for serving as shadow consultants and to those Fellows of the Academy of Management who assisted in data collection. The assistance of Cynthia E. Kisling in data coding and survey preparation is also gratefully acknowledged.

Correspondence concerning this manuscript should be addressed to Arthur G. Bedeian, Department of Management, Louisiana State University, Baton Rouge, LA 70803-6312, USA. E-mail address: *abede@lsu.edu.*

Arthur G. Bedeian is a Boyd Professor at Louisiana State University, where he specializes in the study of workplace behavior. He is a former president of the Academy of Management and past dean of its Fellows Group.

Daniel A. Wren is the David Ross Boyd Professor of Management-Emeritus, and curator of the Harry W. Bass Business History Collection at the University of Oklahoma. He is a fellow of the Academy of Management and a Founding Fellow of the Southern Management Association.

Source: Arthur G. Bedeian and Daniel A. Wren, "Most Influential Management Books of the 20th Century," *Organizational Dynamics,* Winter 2001, Vol. 29, No. 3, pp. 221–225. Reprinted by permission.

By "influential," we mean those books that had a major impact on management thinking at the time of their publication. Some influential books of the past are rarely mentioned today, but at the time they were published had a profound influence on the management discipline as a whole. Nonetheless, their ideas, unlike their authors, live on and on in the received knowledge of contemporary thinking. In a very real sense, the identification of such "influential books" forces us to go beyond the obvious and consider the illumination these books offered their original readers. The exercise likewise serves to challenge what C. S. Lewis called the "snobbery of chronology"—the belief that because we live after those who went before us, we must be wiser, better, and different. Moreover, as heirs to an inherited intellectual legacy, it is good to remember, in the words of Sir Issac Newton, "If we have seen a little farther it is by standing on the shoulders of the giants who have gone before us."

The preparation of a "most influential" list is thus a challenge of our contemporary assumptions and selection skills. To assist in this task, we initially sought the advice of a panel of consultants from various subject areas. They were asked to review a "starter" list we had prepared and then to nominate additional books they believed merited further consideration. We then polled the 137 members of the Fellows Group of the Academy of Management, asking them to judge 50 titles and vote for the books they believed were "the 25 most influential books of the 20th century." Respondents were also invited to identify any additional titles they believed we might have failed to consider. Every system has a bias. This system tilts toward the judgments of an admittedly more established group of scholars. Yet, it does tap the insights of a group formally recognized for its outstanding contributions to the management profession and who have collectively witnessed and contributed to the epoch's tremendous growth in management knowledge.

Prominent on the "most influential" lists are numerous volumes of extraordinary insight and reflection. We expect that some of the titles will provoke ire and others agreement. More important, we hope that the following list brings its readers years of pleasure, illumination, and, even, revelation. "Some books are to be tasted, others are to be swallowed," observed philosopher Sir Francis Bacon, and "some few are to be chewed and digested." So, go taste, chew, and digest!

The 25 Most Influential Management Books of the 20th Century

1. Frederick W. Taylor, *The Principles of Scientific Management* (1911)

The most influential book on management ever published. Although Taylor remains the favorite bogeyman of the popular press, the fundamental principle of Taylor's philosophy—the rule of knowledge as opposed to tradition and personal opinion—is as valid today as it was in his time.

2. Chester I. Barnard, *The Functions of the Executive* (1938)

Celebrated as the first "paradigmatic" statement of the management discipline. Written by a former American Telephone and Telegraph executive, this book yet inspires succeeding generations of both scholars and practitioners, remaining a wellspring for contemporary thinking.

3. Peter F. Drucker, *The Practice of Management* (1954)

Written by perhaps the most influential and widely read authority on modern organizations,

this book is a seminal contribution, full of ideas that remain fresh and provocative decades after first appearing in print.

4. Douglas M. McGregor, *The Human Side of Enterprise* (1960)

Popularized the idea that managerial assumptions about human nature and human behavior are all-important in determining managers' styles of operating. McGregor's Theory X and Theory Y remain an indelible part of contemporary management thinking.

5. Herbert A. Simon, *Administrative Behavior: A Study of Decision-Making Processes in Administrative Organizations* (1947)

A groundbreaking work in which Simon applied his pioneering theory of human choice to administrative decision-making. One of the most referenced works in the social sciences.

6. Paul R. Lawrence and Jay W. Lorsch, *Organization and Environment: Managing Differentiation and Integration* (1967)

Questioned the existence of regularities in organizational characteristics as described by classical management theory, making the argument that there is no one best way to organize. Implanted the term "contingency theory" in the vocabulary of all those studying the nature of organizations.

7. James G. March and Herbert A. Simon (with the assistance of Harold Guetzkow), *Organizations* (1958)

Draws on contemporary empirical research to develop a theory of formal organizations replete with a series of propositions about organizational behavior. The *summa* of modern organization theory.

8. Abraham H. Maslow, *Motivation and Personality* (1954)

Presents a general theory of human motivation whose influence remains enduring in management education and theory. Maslow's hierarchy of needs remains a "classic among classics."

9. Michael E. Porter, *Competitive Strategy: Techniques for Analyzing Industries and Competitors* (1980)

A defining work that presents an overview of competitive industry analysis following Porter's Five-Force Model. Transformed the theory, practice, and teaching of business strategy.

10. Fritz J. Roethlisberger and William J. Dickson (with the assistance of Harold A. Wright), *Management and the Worker* (1939)

The official account of the Hawthorne Studies conducted at the Western Electric Company in Cicero, IL; the most famous, but also the most criticized, studies in the history of management. Gave credence to the then nascent human-relations movement that persists today with the contemporary study of organizational behavior.

11. Alfred D. Chandler, Jr., *Strategy and Structure: Chapters in the History of American Enterprise* (1962)

A tour de force of U.S. business history that explains how production advances in the later half of the nineteenth century led to the growth of large corporations. Its main deduction is that keeping structure in tune with strategy plays a vital role not only in corporate effectiveness, but also in corporate survival and growth.

12. Richard M. Cyert and James G. March, *A Behavioral Theory of the Firm* (1963)

Delivered a major blow to the accepted economic fiction of the "theory of profit-maximizing firms" by presenting a positivist theory of the behavior of individual businesses. A harbinger of the behavioral revolution in economic thought that dominates today.

13. Max Weber, *The Theory of Social and Economic Organization* (1922)

The most complete general statement of Weber's sociological theory of economic and social order, outlining the systematic requirements of rational (i.e., bureaucratic) organization.

14. Daniel Katz and Robert L. Kahn, *The Social Psychology of Organizations* (1966)

Applies open-systems theory to the study of organizations and champions the use of social psychological principles for understanding all forms of collective action. Known as the "bible" of organizational psychology.

15. Chris Argyris, *Personality and Organization: The Conflict between System and the Individual* (1957)

Argues that a basic incongruency exists between the needs of healthy, mature individuals and those of formal organizations. Unless harmony between these sets of needs can be achieved, the predictable and inevitable results will be high turnover and absenteeism, together with low productivity and organizational commitment.

16. Henri Fayol, *General and Industrial Management* (1916)

An extraordinary little book that offers the first theory of general management and statement of management principles. Fayol's ideas so permeate modern management thinking that they have become an unquestioned part of today's received knowledge on how organizations should be designed.

17. Rensis Likert, *New Patterns of Management* (1961)

One of the century's most distinguished social scientists draws on an impressive array of studies, many conducted during his tenure as director of the University of Michigan Institute of Social Research, to establish the benefits of participative management as a means for developing a system that integrates the interests of organizations and their employees.

18. Joan Woodward, *Industrial Organization: Theory and Practice* (1965)

The first major attempt to view organization structure from a technological perspective. Although many of Woodward's ideas have been subsequently qualified, they are still cornerstones in our knowledge of organizations.

19. Elton Mayo, *The Human Problems of an Industrial Civilization* (1933)

A thoughtful exposition on the role of emotional factors in determining employee behavior, contending that the most powerful influence on productive efficiency is the degree to which employees receive social satisfaction in the workplace.

20. Tom Burns and George M. Stalker, *The Management of Innovation* (1961)

The first major attempt to deal with the nature of organization-environment relations and identify the types of organizational structure and managerial practices that are appropriate for different environmental conditions. Introduced the mechanistic-organic polarity (never a dichotomy) to the management lexicon.

21. W. Edwards Deming, *Quality, Productivity and Competitive Position* (1982)

Introduced the "Deming Management Method," featuring his now famous 14 imperatives for improving quality and their use as a competitive weapon; a biting critique of contemporary American management practices.

22. James D. Thompson, *Organizations in Action* (1967)

A masterpiece on the behavior of organizations, incorporating an open-systems perspective to explore the influence of technology on the manner in which work systems are structured for task accomplishment.

23. George C. Homans, *The Human Group* (1950)

An intellectual inquiry into the nature of small groups, this work develops a broad model that strives to understand the inter-workings of social entities by analyzing the interaction between forces that impinge upon groups from outside, and those that operate inside a group's boundaries.

24. David C. McClelland, *The Achieving Society* (1961)

Identifies achievement motivation as an important psychological foundation for economic development and explains how the motivation needed for entrepreneurial success can be promoted in underdeveloped nations.

25. Frederick Herzberg, Bernard Mausner, and Barbara B. Snyderman, *The Motivation to Work* (1959)

Revealed for the first time how employee satisfaction comes primarily from such factors as achievement, recognition for accomplishment, challenging work, increased job responsibility, and opportunities for growth and development. Set the stage for the ensuing job redesign movement and quality-of-working-life revolution.

. . .And the Rest of the Best

Other books receiving a significant number of votes include: Philip Selznick, *Leadership and Administration* (1957), Victor H. Vroom, *Work and Motivation* (1964), Karl E. Weick, *The Social Psychology of Organizing* (1969), and Geert Hofstede, *Culture's Consequences* (1980).

Foundations of Organization Development and Transformation

Part 2

The field of organization development emerged as advances were made in understanding the nature of change and the nature of organizational dynamics. Organization development uses knowledge from the basic and applied behavioral sciences to design action programs to solve problems, correct deficiencies, and seize opportunities in ongoing organizations. In the broadest and most general sense, the objective of OD programs is to increase short-term and long-term organizational effectiveness.

Operationally this means the client system (organization) must learn to solve current problems and must build the capacity to adapt to changing conditions, demands, and exigencies. Leaders and members of organizations today are required to have problem-solving skills, action-taking skills, and self-renewal skills. The role of the OD practitioner is to help organization members obtain these skills.

At least four kinds of knowledge are required of OD practitioners and leaders who desire to create problem-solving, self-renewing organizations: knowledge of how organizations work; knowledge of how change occurs; knowledge of how to intervene in organizations to produce desired changes; and knowledge of how to diagnose and solve problems.

The knowledge of how organizations work comes mainly from basic behavioral science research and theory. It entails an understanding of the dynamics of individuals, groups, and goal-oriented social systems. Knowledge of how change occurs involves understanding the processes of change and changing. In the case of organization development, gaining this knowledge is difficult because the phenomena are so complex and are themselves changing as they are being studied. Knowledge of how to intervene in organizations relates to change, but goes beyond it to investigate the processes of consultation and "helping." What constitutes effective intervention? What are the ingredients of effective client-consultant relationships?

When is help helpful? Other applied disciplines, such as education, psychotherapy, social work, and management, provided insights that are used in OD.

Knowledge of diagnosis and problem solving comes from many sources but culminates in the ability to answer the questions: What is wrong? What made it wrong? What must be done to correct the situation? Competent problem solving and action taking require being able to do two things: classify problem and opportunity situations accurately, and select appropriate remedies. This competence in turns rests on the prior existence of two bodies of knowledge: valid diagnostic categories (having a good classification scheme for differentiating between different types of problems or opportunities), and a set of efficacious remedial treatments (having an array of different solutions or actions that will solve different problems or achieve particular desired results). In relatively advanced applied sciences, such as medicine, great progress has been made in refining diagnostic categories and discovering appropriate treatments. Organization development classification schemes are not as advanced as those in medicine, but substantial progress has been made.

It is not possible to explore all the foundations of organization development and transformation in this section. Instead, we will look briefly at the nature of planned change and the nature of organizational dynamics.

The Nature of Planned Change

The action arena of OD is organizations. The name of the game is planned change. Organization improvement programs require an understanding of change processes and knowledge of the nature of organizations.

Kurt Lewin was the great practical theorist whose action and research programs provided much of the early foundation for understanding change processes in social situations.[1] Lewin (1890–1947) was a personality theorist, a social psychologist, and a man who wanted to improve the lot of humankind through behavioral science knowledge and application. To improve things means to change them; to change them requires knowledge of the structure and dynamics of change. Lewin's work had a significant impact on group dynamics, intergroup relations, and applied social psychology. Lewin once said, "If you want to understand a phenomenon, try to change it." And he devoted a considerable part of his career trying to understand processes of change.

Two concepts proposed by Kurt Lewin are especially useful in thinking about change. The first idea suggests that what is occurring at any point in time is the result of a field of opposing forces. Thus, for example, the production level of a manufacturing plant or the level of morale in a work group should be thought of as *equilibrium points* in a field of forces, some forces pushing toward higher and some pushing toward lower levels of production or morale. In order to understand a problematic situation the investigator must know what major forces are operating in that particular instance. A technique called the force field analysis can be used to diagram the field of forces and show how to develop action plans for moving the equilibrium point in one direction or another. This is a useful model for understanding what is going on in complex situations.

The second idea proposed by Lewin analyzes what must occur for permanent change to take place. He conceptualized change as a three-stage process: *unfreezing* the old behavior, *moving* to a new level of behavior, and *freezing* the behavior at the new level. This is a useful model for knowing how to move an equilibrium point to a new, desired level and *keep it there*. These two simple ideas undergird the theories of change of most OD practitioners.

Ronald Lippitt, Jeanne Watson, and Bruce Westley later refined Lewin's three phases into a seven-phase model of the change process as follows:

Phase 1. The development of a need for change. This phase corresponds to Lewin's *unfreezing* phase.
Phase 2. The establishment of a change relationship. This is a crucial phase in which a client system in need of help and a "change agent" from outside the system establish a working relationship with each other.
Phase 3. The clarification or diagnosis of the client system's problem.
Phase 4. The examination of alternative routes and goals; establishing goals and intentions of action.
Phase 5. The transformation of intentions into actual change efforts. Phase 3, 4, and 5 correspond to Lewin's *moving* phase.
Phase 6. The generalization and stabilization of change. This corresponds to Lewin's *freezing* phase.
Phase 7. Achieving a terminal relationship.[2]

The models of change developed by Lewin and by Lippitt, Watson, and Westley advanced both theory and practice in organization development. They are foundations of the discipline. Promoting change in organizations presents additional challenges, however. In an article entitled "Change Does Not Need to Be Haphazard," Kenneth Benne and Max Birnbaum suggest additional principles for effecting organizational change. Their principles are as follows:

1. To change a subsystem or any part of a subsystem, relevant aspects of the environment must also be changed.
2. To change behavior on any one level of a hierarchical organization, it is necessary to achieve complementary and reinforcing changes in organization levels above and below that level.
3. The place to begin change is at those points in the system where some stress and strain exist. Stress may give rise to dissatisfaction with the status quo and thus become a motivating factor for change in the system.
4. If thoroughgoing changes in a hierarchical structure are desirable or necessary, change should ordinarily start with the policy-making body.

5. Both the formal and the informal organization of an institution must be considered in planning any process of change.

6. The effectiveness of a planned change is often directly related to the degree to which members at all levels of an institutional hierarchy take part in the fact-finding and the diagnosing of needed changes and in the formulating and reality testing of goals and programs of change.[3]

More recently, authors have focused on the nature of change using the terms *incremental/continuous change* and *radical/discontinuous change.* Incremental change requires modifications, adjustments, and adaptations, but the nature of the organization and its tasks stay relatively the same. Radical or discontinuous change requires massive, systemwide, paradigm-shifting changes in the organization and its tasks.

For example, in Reading 21, Robert A. Zawacki and Carol A. Norman state,

> Over the last 50 years, it appears that the nature of organizational change has changed. . . . Beginning with the 1950s and 1960s, change was incremental; people adapted and were rewarded for their new behaviors. Then, during the 1960s and 1970s change became more rapid and individual contributors responded by working harder and smarter. . . . The 1980s and 1990s brought even more rapid and random change. Change nowadays seems to lack predictability.

In order to cope with rapid, radical, and unpredictable change, organizations must *transform* themselves. This was a major impetus for developing organization transformation theory and practice. The "self-directed teams" described by Zawacki and Norman represent a fundamental shift in the way people and work are organized and are thus an example of organization transformation.

Warner Burke and George Litwin developed a model to show how *first-order* (incremental, transactional) change and *second-order* (radical, transformational) change occur in organizations.[4] The premise of the Burke-Litwin model is this: OD interventions directed toward organizational structures, management practices, and systems (policies and procedures) will result in first-order change; interventions directed toward the organization's mission and strategy, leadership, and culture will result in second-order change. Thus, if organizations need to be transformed, practitioners and leaders should focus on mission, strategy, leadership philosophy and practice, and culture.

In summary, advances in understanding the nature of change led to improvements in intervention techniques, which resulted in OD programs becoming more effective.

The Nature of Organizational Dynamics

Organization development efforts are directed toward social systems called organizations. Organizations exist to accomplish specific purposes or goals—a mission, task, products, or services. In most organizations the decision to belong is a voluntary choice made by the individual. There is division of labor and responsibility in organizations, with the consequence that a social structure of roles, duties, and offices is created. Individuals perform role behaviors; they are expected to do some things and not others by virtue of the positions they hold. One cannot know how organizations function simply by knowing how individuals function and then summing across individuals, because organizations have unique characteristics of their own.

One characteristic of organizations is that much of the work gets done by teams consisting of bosses and subordinates. Work teams are the basic building blocks of organizations. If teams function well, it is more likely that the organization as a whole will function well. Advances in understanding the dynamics of groups served as a foundation for the development of OD. Insights, theories, and techniques concerning group processes formed a large part of the basic toolkit of early OD practitioners.

Relations between groups in organizations are often problematic and dysfunctional. Another characteristic of organizations is that these relations are very important for organizational performance. As knowledge about intergroup dynamics was developed, it was incorporated into organization development.

A fundamental tenet of OD is that organizations are open systems. Russell Ackoff defines a system as "a set of interrelated elements. Thus a system is an entity which is composed of at least two elements and a relation that holds between each of its elements and at least one other element in the set. Each of a system's elements is connected to every other element, directly or indirectly."[5] Systems (and organizations) must be treated from a holistic point of view, because certain properties derive from the *relationships* between the parts of the system and cannot be discovered from an analysis of the components themselves. In addition, organizations are open systems—they are in interaction with and in exchange with their environments. Organizations are impacted by and have an impact on their environments. As Katz and Kahn state,

> Organizations as a special class of open systems have properties of their own, but they share other properties in common with all open systems. These include the importation of energy from the environment, the throughput or transformation of the imported energy into some product form that is characteristic of the system, the exporting of that product into the environment, and the reenergizing of the system from sources in the environment.[6]

The organization development practitioner must understand the nature of the client systems in which he or she works. That is a basic prerequisite. The selections in this section contribute to that end.

Readings in Part 2

The readings in this part are classic statements that improve with age and with each reading.

The first selection is an excerpt from Kurt Lewin's highly influential book, *Field Theory in Social Science.* Lewin's field theory approach postulates that any phenomenon is the resultant in a field of opposing forces—a model that has proved very useful for organizational change. A technique called the force field analysis allows one to map the field of forces and build action plans to change the field of forces. The brief piece by Carl Rogers looks at the dynamics of two-person conflict. He describes four elements that will almost always be found in such situations. Becoming aware of these elements is the first step in resolving interpersonal disputes.

Chris Argyris has made significant contributions to the field of organization development and transformation. This reading is from a very influential book published in 1970. OD practitioners intervene in ongoing organizations to help produce positive results. But the intervention process itself was mainly based on rules of thumb and principles derived from experience until Argyris formulated a systematic statement of intervention theory and method. Argyris sees three primary tasks of the interventionist: to help the client system generate valid information; to help ensure that client system members act on the basis of free and informed choice; and to help ensure internal commitment to the choices made. What is the practitioner trying to do? What theory is available to guide behavior and give overall direction? The reading by Argyris addresses these issues.

Intergroup relations are especially important phenomena in organizations. Just as individuals may be interdependently related on a work team for task accomplishment, entire teams are interdependently related to other teams for task accomplishment. The ways groups work together can either help or hinder organizational performance. The selection by Edgar Schein summarizes much of the literature on cooperation and competition between groups. Schein has packaged a wealth of empirical research, much of it conducted by Muzafer Sherif and Robert Blake and Jane Syrgley Mouton, in such a way that the OD practitioner and the manager alike can gain insights into this important area.

The article on organizational culture is also by Edgar Schein, who has written extensively on the subject. OD practitioners have recognized the importance of culture since the early days of the field, but it was not until the 1980s that serious and systematic attention was given to this important determinant of behavior. The reading by Schein defines organizational culture, shows how to analyze culture, and describes how to think about culture change.

In the final selection, William Fox describes the foundation of sociotechnical systems theory by examining its principles and guidelines. Sociotechnical systems theory (STS) postulates that organizations consist of two interdependently related systems (a social system and a technical system) that must be jointly optimized if the organization is to achieve effective performance. Thus, STS professionals are deeply involved in job design, job redesign, systems design, and organization design programs. Many of the leading ideas for designing high-performance work systems come from STS consultants. Sociotechnical systems theory is an important foundation of both OD and OT.

Endnotes

1. Alfred J. Marrow, *The Practical Theorist: The Life and Work of Kurt Lewin* (New York: Basic Books, 1969).

2. Ronald Lippitt, Jeanne Watson, and Bruce Westley, *The Dynamics of Planned Change* (New York: Harcourt Brace Jovanovich, 1958). See chapter 6 for a discussion.

3. Kenneth D. Benne and Max Birnbaum, "Change Does Not Need to Be Haphazard," *Notebook for Summer Participants,* NTL Institute for Applied Behavioral Science.

4. W. Warner Burke, *Organization Development: A Process of Learning and Changing* (Reading, MA: Addison-Wesley Publishing Company, 1994), chap. 7.

5. Russell L. Ackoff, "Toward a System of Systems Concepts," *Management Science,* July 1971, p. 662.

6. Daniel Katz and Robert L. Kahn, *The Social Psychology of Organizations,* 2nd ed. (New York: John Wiley & Sons, 1978), p. 33.

Reading 7

The Field Approach: Culture and Group Life as Quasi-Stationary Processes

Kurt Lewin

This question of planned change or of any "social engineering" is identical with the question: What "conditions" have to be changed to bring about a given result and how can one change these conditions with the means at hand?

One should view the present situation—the status quo—as being maintained by certain conditions or forces. A culture—for instance, the food habits of a certain group at a given time—is not a static affair but a live process like a river which moves but still keeps a recognizable form. In other words, we have to deal, in group life as in individual life, with what is known in physics as "quasi-stationary" processes.[1]

Food habits do not occur in empty space. They are part and parcel of the daily rhythm of being awake and asleep; of being alone and in a group; of earning a living and playing; of being a member of a town, a family, a social class, a religious group, a nation; of living in a hot or a cool climate, in a rural area or a city, in a district with good groceries and restaurants, or in an area of poor and irregular food supply. Somehow all of these factors affect food habits at any given time. They determine the food habits of a group every day anew just as the amount of water supply and the nature of the river bed determine from day to day the flow of the river, its constancy, or its change.[2]

Food habits of a group, as well as such phenomena as the speed of production in a factory, are the result of a multitude of forces. Some

forces support each other, some oppose each other. Some are driving forces, others restraining forces. Like the velocity of a river, the actual conduct of a group depends upon the level (for instance, the speed of production) at which these conflicting forces reach a state of equilibrium. To speak of a certain culture pattern—for instance, the food habits of a group—implies that the constellation of these forces remains the same for a period or at least that they find their state of equilibrium at a constant level during that period.

Neither group "habits" nor individual "habits" can be understood sufficiently by a theory which limits its consideration to the processes themselves and conceives of the "habit" as a kind of frozen linkage, an "association" between these processes. Instead, habits will have to be conceived of as a result of forces in the organism *and* its life space, in the group *and* its setting. The structure of the organism, of the group, of the setting, or whatever name the field might have in the given case, has to be represented and the forces in the various parts of the field have to be analyzed if the processes (which might be either constant "habits" or changes) are to be understood scientifically. The process is but the epi-phenomenon, the real object of study is the constellation of forces.

Therefore, to predict which changes in conditions will have what result we have to conceive of the life of the group as a result of specific constellations of forces within a larger setting. In other words, scientific predictions or advice for methods of change should be based on any analysis of the "field as a whole," including both its psychological and nonpsychological aspects.

Source: Kurt Lewin, *Field Theory in Social Science* (New York: Harper & Row, 1951), pp. 172–174.

Endnotes

1. For the general characteristics of quasi-stationary processes see Wolfgang Koehler, *Dynamics in Psychology* (New York: Liveright Publishing, 1940).

2. The type of forces, of course, is different; there is nothing equivalent to "cognitive structure" or "psychological past" or "psychological future" in the field determining the river.

Two-Person Disputes

Carl Rogers

When persons are in serious discord, whether we are speaking of a discordant marital relationship, friction between an employer and an employee, a formal and icy dispute between two diplomats, or tension growing out of some other base, we tend to find certain very common elements:

1. In such a dispute there is no doubt at all but that I am right and you are wrong. I am on the side of the angels, and you belong with the forces of darkness.

2. There is a breakdown of communication. You do not hear what I say, in any understanding way; and I am unwilling and unable to hear what you are really saying.

3. There are distortions in perception. The evidence which is taken in by my senses—your words, your actions, your responses to my words and actions—is trimmed and shaped by my needs to fit the views of you which I already hold. Evidence which is clearly and openly contradictory to my rigidly held views is conveniently ignored or made acceptable by being grossly distorted. Thus, a real gesture toward reconciliation on your part can be perceived by me as only another deceitful trick.

4. Implicit in all this is the element of distrust. While whatever *I* do is obviously done with honorable intent, whatever *you* do is equally obviously done with an underlying evil intent, no matter how sweetly reasonable it may appear on the surface. Hence, from the perspective of each opponent, the whole relationship is shot through with suspicion and mistrust.

I believe I am correct in saying that in any serious two-person dispute, these four elements are invariably present and often make the situation appear hopeless. Yet there are knowledge and skill available which can be applied to such a situation. If there is to be progress in reducing this kind of tension, we have learned that the first necessity is a facilitative listener—a person who will listen empathetically and will understand the attitudes of each disputant.

Source: Carl Rogers, "Dealing with Psychological Tensions," in *Journal of Applied Behavioral Science* (1, no. 1) pp. 12–13, copyright © 1965 by NTL Institute for Applied Behavioral Science. Reprinted by permission of Sage Publications, Inc.

Reading 9

Intervention Theory and Method

Chris Argyris

A Definition of Intervention

To intervene is to enter into an ongoing system of relationship, to come between or among persons, groups or objects for the purpose of helping them. There is an important implicit assumption in the definition that should be made explicit: the system exists independently of the intervenor. There are many reasons one might wish to intervene. These reasons may range from helping the clients make their own decisions about the kind of help they need to coercing the clients to do what the intervenor wishes them to do.

Our view acknowledges interdependencies between the intervenor and the client system but focuses on how to maintain, or increase, the client system's autonomy; how to differentiate even more clearly the boundaries between the client system and the intervenor; and how to conceptualize and define the client system's health independently of the intervenor's. This view values the client system as an ongoing, self-responsible unity that has the obligation to be in control over its own destiny. An intervenor, in this view, assists a system to become more effective in problem solving, decision making, and decision implementation in such a way that the system can continue to be increasingly effective in these activities and have a decreasing need for the intervenor.

Source: Chris Argyris, *Intervention Theory and Methods: A Behavioral Science View* (Reading, Mass.: Addison-Wesley Publishing, 1970), pp. 15–20. © 1970, Addison-Wesley. Reprinted with permission.

Basic Requirements for Intervention Activity

Are there any basic or necessary processes that must be fulfilled regardless of the substantive issues involved, if intervention activity is to be helpful with any level of client (individual, group, or organizational)? One condition that seems so basic as to be defined axiomatic is the generation of *valid information*. Without valid information, it would be difficult for the client to learn and for the interventionist to help.

A second condition almost as basic flows from our assumption that intervention activity, no matter what its substantive interests and objectives, should be so designed and executed that the client system maintains its discreteness and autonomy. Thus, *free, informed choice* is also a necessary process in effective intervention activity.

Finally, if the client system is assumed to be ongoing (that is, existing over time), the clients require strengthening to maintain their autonomy not only vis-à-vis the interventionist but also vis-à-vis other systems. This means that their commitment to learning and change has to be more than temporary. It has to be so strong that it can be transferred to relationships other than those with the interventionist and can do so (eventually) without the help of the interventionist. The third basic process for any intervention activity is therefore the client's *internal commitment* to the choices made.

In summary, valid information, free choice, and internal commitment are considered integral parts of any intervention activity, no matter what the substantive objectives are (for example, developing a management performance evaluation scheme, reducing intergroup rivalries, increasing the degree of trust among individuals, redesigning budgetary systems, or redesigning work). These three processes are called the primary intervention tasks.

Primary Tasks of an Interventionist

Why is it necessary to hypothesize that, in order for an interventionist to behave effectively and in order that the integrity of the client system be maintained, the interventionist has to focus on three primary tasks, regardless of the substantive problems that the client system may be experiencing?

Valid and Useful Information

First, it has been accepted as axiomatic that valid and useful information is the foundation for effective intervention. Valid information is that which describes the factors, plus their interrelationships, that create the problem for the client system. There are several tests for checking the validity of the information. In increasing degrees of power they are public verifiability, valid prediction, and control over the phenomena. The first is having several independent diagnoses suggest the same picture. Second is generating predictions from the diagnosis that are subsequently confirmed (they occurred under the conditions that were specified). Third is altering the factors systematically and predicting the effects upon the system as a whole. All these tests, if they are to be valid, must be carried out in such a way that the participants cannot, at will, make them come true. This would be a self-fulfilling prophecy and not a confirmation of a prediction. The difficulty with a self-fulfilling prophecy is its indication of more about the degree of power an individual (or subset of individuals) can muster to alter the system than about the nature of the system when the participants are behaving without knowledge of the diagnosis. For example, if an executive learns that the interventionist predicts his subordinates will behave (*a*) if he behaves (*b*), he might alter (*b*) in order not to lead to (*a*). Such an alteration indicates the executive's power but does not test the validity of the diagnosis that if (*a*), then (*b*).

The tests for valid information have important implications for effective intervention activity. First, the interventionist's diagnoses must strive to represent the total client system and not the point of view of any subgroup or individual. Otherwise, the interventionist could not be seen only as being under the control of a particular individual or subgroup, but also his predictions would be based upon inaccurate information and thus might not be confirmed.

This does not mean that an interventionist may not begin with, or may not limit his relationship to, a subpart of the total system. It is totally possible, for example, for the interventionist to help management, blacks, trade union leaders, etc. With whatever subgroup he works he simply should not agree to limit his diagnosis to its wishes.

It is conceivable that a client system may be helped even though valid information is not generated. Sometimes changes occur in a positive direction without the interventionist having played any important role. These changes, although helpful in that specific instance, lack the attribute of helping the organization to learn to gain control over its problem-solving capability.

The importance of information that the clients can use to control their destiny points up the requirement that the information must not only be valid, it must be useful. Valid information that cannot be used by the clients to alter their system is equivalent to valid information about cancer that cannot be used to cure cancer eventually. An interventionist's diagnosis should include variables that are manipulable by the clients and are complete enough so that if they are manipulated, effective change will follow.

Free Choice

In order to have free choice, the client has to have a cognitive map of what he wishes to do. The objectives of his action are known at the moment of decision. Free choice implies voluntary as opposed to automatic; proactive rather than reactive.

The act of selection is rarely accomplished by maximizing or optimizing. Free and informed choice entails what Simon has called "satisficing"; that is, selecting the alternative with the highest probability of succeeding, given some specified cost constraints. Free choice places the locus of decision making in the client system. Free choice makes it possible for the clients to remain responsible for their destiny. Through free choice the clients can maintain the autonomy of their system.

It may be possible that clients prefer to give up their responsibility and their autonomy, especially if they are feeling a sense of failure. They may prefer, as we shall see in several examples, to turn over their free choice to the interventionist. They may insist that he make recommendations and tell them what to do. The interventionist resists these pressures because, if he does not, the clients will lose their free choice and he will lose his own free choice, also. He will be controlled by the anxieties of the clients.

The requirement of free choice is especially important for those helping activities where the processes of help are as important as the actual help. For example, a medical doctor does not require that a patient with a bullet wound participate in the process by defining the kind of help he needs. However, the same doctor may have to pay much more attention to the processes he uses to help patients when he is attempting to diagnose blood pressure or cure a high cholesterol. If the doctor behaves in ways that upset the patient, the latter's blood pressure may well be distorted. Or, the patient can develop a dependent relationship if the doctor cuts down his cholesterol—increasing habits only under constant pressure from the doctor—and the moment the relationship is broken off, the count goes up.

Effective intervention in the human and social sphere requires that the processes of help be congruent with the outcome desired. Free choice is important because there are so many unknowns, and the interventionist wants the client to have as much willingness and motivation as possible to work on the problem. With high client motivation and commitment, several different methods for change can succeed.

A choice is free to the extent the members can make their selection for a course of action with minimal internal defensiveness; can define the path (or paths) by which the intended consequence is to be achieved; can relate the choice to their central needs; and can build into their choices a realistic and challenging level of aspiration. Free choice therefore implies that the members are able to explore as many alternatives as they consider significant and select those that are central to their needs.

Why must the choice be related to the central needs and why must the level of aspiration be realistic and challenging? May people not choose freely unrealistic or unchallenging objectives? Yes, they may do so in the short run, but not for long if they still want to have free and informed choice. A freely chosen course of action means that the action must be based on an accurate analysis of the situation and not on the biases or defenses of the decision makers. We know, from the level of aspiration studies, that choices which are too high or too low, which are too difficult or not difficult enough will tend to lead to psychological failure. Psychological failure will lead to increased defensiveness, increased failure, and decreased self-acceptance on the part of the members experiencing the failure. These conditions, in turn, will tend to lead to distorted perceptions by the members making the choices. Moreover, the defensive members may unintentionally create a climate where the members of surrounding and interrelated systems will tend to provide carefully censored information. Choices made under these conditions are neither informed nor free.

Turning to the question of centrality of needs, a similar logic applies. The degree of commitment to the processes of generating valid information, scanning, and choosing may significantly vary according to the centrality of the choice to the needs of the clients. The more central the choice, the more the system will strive to do its best in developing valid information and making free and informed choices. If the research from perceptual psychology is valid, the very perception of the clients is altered by the needs involved. Individuals tend to scan more, ask for more information, and be more careful in their choices when they are making decisions that are central to them. High involvement may produce perceptual distortions, as does low involvement. The interventionist, however, may have a greater probability of helping the clients explore possible distortion when the choice they are making is a critical one.

Internal Commitment

Internal commitment means that course of action or choice that has been internalized by each member so that he experiences a high degree of ownership and has a feeling of responsibility about the choice and its implications. Internal commitment means that the individual has reached the point where he is acting on the choice because it fulfills his own needs and sense of responsibility, as well as those of the system.

The individual who is internally committed is acting primarily under the influence of his own forces and not induced forces. The individual (or any unity) feels a minimal degree of dependence upon others for the action. It implies that he has obtained and processed valid information and that he has made an informed and free choice. Under these conditions, there is a high probability that the individual's commitment will remain strong over time (even with reduction of external rewards) or under stress, or when the course of action is challenged by others. It also implies that the individual is continually open to reexamination of his position because he believes in taking action based upon valid information.

Reading 10

Intergroup Problems in Organizations

Edgar H. Schein

The first major problem of groups in organizations is how to make them effective in fulfilling both organizational goals and the needs of their members. The second major problem is how to establish conditions between groups which will enhance the productivity of each without destroying intergroup relations and coordination. This problem exists because as groups become more committed to their own goals and norms, they are likely to become competitive with one another and seek to undermine their rivals' activities, thereby becoming a liability to the organization as a whole. The overall problem, then, is how to establish collaborative intergroup relations *in those situations where task interdependence or the need for unity makes collaboration a necessary prerequisite for organizational effectiveness.*

Some Consequences of Intergroup Competition

The consequences of intergroup competition were first studied systematically by Sherif in an ingeniously designed setting (Sherif, Harvey, White, Hood, & Sherif, 1961). He organized a boys' camp in such a way that two groups would form and would gradually become competitive. Sherif then studied the effects of the competition and tried various devices for reestablishing collaborative relationships between the groups. Since his original experiments, there have been many replications with adult groups; the phenomena are so

Source: Edgar H. Schein, *Organizational Psychology,* 3rd ed., 1980, pp. 172–80. Reprinted by permission of Prentice Hall, Inc., Englewood Cliffs, NJ.

constant that it has been possible to make a demonstration exercise out of the experiment (Blake & Mouton, 1961). The effects can be described in terms of the following categories:

A. What happens *within* each competing group?

1. Each group becomes more closely knit and elicits greater loyalty from its members; members close ranks and bury some of their internal differences.

2. The group climate changes from informal, casual, playful to work and task oriented; concern for members' psychological needs declines while concern for task accomplishment increases.

3. Leadership patterns tend to change from more democratic toward more autocratic; the group becomes more willing to tolerate autocratic leadership.

4. Each group becomes more highly structured and organized.

5. Each group demands more loyalty and conformity from its members in order to be able to present a "solid front."

B. What happens *between* competing groups?

1. Each group begins to see the other group as the enemy, rather than merely a neutral object.

2. Each group begins to experience distortions of perception—it tends to perceive only the best parts of itself, denying its weaknesses, and tends to perceive only the worst parts of the other group, denying its strengths; each group is likely to develop a negative stereotype of the other ("they don't play fair like we do").

3. Hostility toward the other group increases while interaction and communication with the

other group decreases; thus it becomes easier to maintain the negative stereotype and more difficult to correct perceptual distortions.

4. If the groups are forced into interaction—for example, if they are forced to listen to representatives plead their own and the others' cause in reference to some task—each group is likely to listen more closely to their own representative and not to listen to the representative of the other group, except to find fault with his or her presentation; in other words, group members tend to listen only for that which supports their own position and stereotype.

Thus far, we have listed some consequences of the competition itself, without reference to the consequences if one group actually wins out over the other. Before listing those effects, I would like to draw attention to the generality of the above reactions. Whether one is talking about sports teams, interfraternity competition, labor-management disputes, or interdepartmental competition as between sales and production in an industrial organization—or about international relations and the competition between the Soviet Union and the United States—the same phenomena tend to occur. These responses can be very useful to the group, by making it more highly motivated in task accomplishment, but they also open the door to group thinking. Furthermore, the same factors which improve intragroup effectiveness may have negative consequences for intergroup effectiveness. For example, as we have often seen in labor-management disputes or international conflicts, if the groups perceive themselves as competitors, they find it more difficult to resolve their differences, and eventually both become losers in a long-term strike or even a war.

Let us next look at the consequences of winning and losing, as in a situation where several groups are bidding to have their proposal accepted for a contract or as a solution to some problem. Many intraorganizational situations become win-or-lose affairs, hence it is of particular importance to examine their consequences.

C. What happens to the *winner*?

1. Winner retains its cohesion and may become even more cohesive.

2. Winner tends to release tension, lose its fighting spirit, become complacent, casual, and playful (the condition of being "fat and happy").

3. Winner tends toward high intragroup cooperation and concern for members' needs, and low concern for work and task accomplishment.

4. Winner tends to be complacent and to feel that the positive outcome has confirmed its favorable stereotype of itself and the negative stereotype of the "enemy" group; there is little motivation for reevaluating perceptions or reexamining group operations in order to learn how to improve them, hence the winner does not learn much about itself.

D. What happens to the *loser*?

1. If the outcome is not entirely clear-cut and permits a degree of interpretation (say, if judges have rendered it or if the game was close), there is a strong tendency for the loser to *deny or distort the reality of losing;* instead, the loser will find psychological escapes like "the judges were biased," "the judges didn't really understand our solution," "the rules of the game were not clearly explained to us," "if luck had not been against us at the one key point, we would have won," and so on. In effect, the loser's first response is to say "we didn't really lose!"

2. If the loss is psychologically accepted, the losing group tends to seek someone or something to blame; strong forces toward scapegoating are set up; if no outsider can be blamed, the group turns on itself, splinters, surfaces previously unresolved conflicts, fights within itself, all in the effort to find a cause for the loss.

3. Loser is more tense, ready to work harder, and desperate (the condition of being "lean and hungry").

4. Loser tends toward low intragroup cooperation, low concern for members' needs, and high concern for recouping by working harder in order to win the next round of the competition.

5. Loser tends to learn a lot about itself as a group because its positive stereotype of itself and its negative stereotype of the other group are disconfirmed by the loss, forcing a reevaluation of perceptions; as a consequence, the loser is likely to reorganize and become more cohesive and effective once the loss has been accepted realistically.

The net effect of the win-lose situation is often that the losers refuse psychologically to accept their loss, and that intergroup tension is higher than before the competition began.

Intergroup problems of the sort we have just described arise not only out of direct competition between clearly defined groups but are, to a degree, intrinsic in any complex society because of the many bases on which a society is stratified. Thus we can have potential intergroup problems between men and women, between older and younger generations, between higher and lower ranking people, between blacks and whites, between people in power and people not in power, and so on (Alderfer, 1977). Any occupational or social group will develop "ingroup" feelings and define itself in terms of members of an "outgroup," toward whom intergroup feelings are likely to arise. Differences between nationalities or ethnic groups are especially strong, particularly if there has been any conflict between the groups in the past.

For intergroup feelings to arise we need not belong to a psychological group. It is enough to feel oneself a member of what has been called a "reference group"; that is, a group with which one identifies and compares oneself or to which one aspires. Thus, aspirants to a higher socioeconomic level take that level as their reference group and attempt to behave according to the values they perceive in that group. Similarly, members of an occupational group uphold the values and standards they perceive that occupation to embody. It is only by positing the existence of reference groups that one can explain how some individuals can continue to behave in a deviant fashion in a group situation. If such individuals strongly iden-

tify with a group that has different norms they will behave in a way that attempts to uphold those norms. For example, in Communist prison camps some soldiers from elite military units resisted their captors much longer than draftees who had weak identification with their military units. In order for the Communists to elicit compliant behavior from these strongly identified prisoners, they had to first weaken the attachment to the elite unit—that is, destroy the reference group—by attacking the group's image or convincing the prisoner that it was not a group worth belonging to (Schein, 1961). Intergroup problems arise wherever there are any status differences and are, therefore, intrinsic to all organizations and to society itself.

Reducing the Negative Consequences of Intergroup Competition

The gains of intergroup competition may, under some conditions, outweigh the negative consequences. It may be desirable to have work groups pitted against one another or to have departments become cohesive loyal units, even if interdepartmental coordination suffers. Often, however, the negative consequences outweigh the gains, and management seeks ways of reducing intergroup tension. Many of the techniques proposed to accomplish this come from the basic researches of Sherif, Blake, Alderfer, and others; they have been tested and found to be successful. The chief stumbling block remains not so much being unable to think of ways for reducing intergroup conflict as being *unable to implement some of the most effective ways.*

Destructive intergroup competition results basically from a conflict of goals and the breakdown of interaction and communication between the groups. This breakdown in turn permits and stimulates perceptual distortion and mutual negative stereotyping. The basic strategy of reducing conflict, therefore, is to locate goals which the competing groups can agree on and to reestablish valid communication between the groups. Each of the tactical devices that follows can be used singly or in combination.

Locating a Common Enemy

For example, the competing teams in a league can compose an all-star team to play another league, or conflicts between sales and production can be reduced if both can harness their efforts to helping their company successfully compete against another company. The conflict here is merely shifted to a higher level.

Bringing Leaders or Subgroups of the Competing Groups into Interaction

An isolated group representative cannot abandon his or her group position, but a powerful leader or a subgroup that has been delegated power not only can permit itself to be influenced by its counterpart negotiation team, but also will have the strength to influence the remainder of its home group if negotiation produces common agreements. This is the basis for "summit meetings" in international relations.

Locating a Superordinate Goal

Such a goal can be a brand-new task which requires the cooperative effort of the previously competing groups, or it can be a task like analyzing and reducing the intergroup conflict itself. For example, the previously competing sales and production departments can be given the task of developing a new product line that will be both cheap to produce and in great customer demand; or, with the help of an outside consultant, the competent groups can be invited to examine their own behavior and reevaluate the gains and losses from competition (Walton, 1969).

Experiential Intergroup Training

The procedure of having the conflicting parties examine their own behavior has been tried by a number of psychologists, notably Blake and Mouton (1962), with considerable success. Assuming the organization recognizes that it has a problem,

and assuming it is ready to expose this problem to an outside consultant, the experiential workshop approach to reducing conflict might proceed with the following steps:

1. The competing groups are both brought into a training setting and the common goals are stated to be an exploration of mutual perceptions and mutual relations.

2. The two groups are then separated and each group is invited to discuss and make a list of its perceptions of itself and the other group.

3. In the presence of both groups, representatives publicly share the perceptions of self and others which the groups have generated, while the groups are obligated to remain silent (the objective is simply to report to the other group as accurately as possible the images that each group has developed in private).

4. Before any exchange has taken place, the groups return to private sessions to digest and analyze what they have heard; there is a great likelihood that the representatives' reports have revealed discrepancies to each group between its self-image and the image that the other group holds of it; the private session is partly devoted to an analysis of the reasons for these discrepancies, which forces each group to review its actual behavior toward the other group and the possible consequences of that behavior, regardless of its intentions.

5. In public session, again working through representatives, each group shares with the other what discrepancies it has uncovered and the possible reasons for them, focusing on actual, observable behavior.

6. Following this mutual exposure, a more open exploration is then permitted between the two groups on the *now-shared goal* of identifying further reasons for perceptual distortions.

7. A joint exploration is then conducted of how to manage future relations in such a way as to minimize a recurrence of the conflict.

Interspersed with these steps are short lectures and reading assignments on the psychology of intergroup conflict, the bases for perceptual distortion, psychological defense mechanisms, and so on. The goal is to bring the psychological dynamics of the solution into conscious awareness and to refocus the groups on the common goal of exploring jointly the problem they share. In order to do this, they must have valid data about each other, which is provided through the artifice of the representative reports.

Blake's model deals with the entire group. Various other approaches begin by breaking down group prejudices on an individual basis. For example, groups A and B, each proposing an alternative product (idea), can be divided into pairs composed of an A and a B member. Each pair can be given the assignment of developing a joint product that combines the best ideas from the A product and the B product. Or, in each pair, members may be asked to argue for the product of the opposing group. It has been shown in a number of experiments that one way of changing attitudes is to ask a person to play the role of an advocate of the new attitude to be learned (Janis & King, 1954). The very act of arguing for another product, even if it is purely an exercise, makes the person aware of some of its virtues which he or she can now no longer deny. A practical application of these points might be to have some members of the sales department spend time in the production department and be asked to represent the production point of view to some third party, or to have some production people join sales teams to learn the sales point of view.

Most of the approaches cited depend on *recognition* of some problem by the organization and a *willingness* on the part of the competing groups to participate in some program to reduce negative consequences. The reality, however, is that most organizations neither recognize the problem nor are willing to invest time and energy in resolving it. Some of the unwillingness also arises from each competing group's recognition that in becoming more cooperative it may lose some of its own identity and integrity as a group. Rather than risk this loss, the group may prefer to continue the competition. This may well be the reason why, in

international relations, nations refuse to engage in what may seem like perfectly simple ways of resolving their differences. They resist partly in order to protect their integrity—that is, save face. For all these reasons, the *implementation* of strategies and tactics for reducing the negative consequences of intergroup competition is often a greater problem than the initial development of such strategies and tactics.

Preventing Intergroup Conflict

Because of the great difficulties of reducing intergroup conflict once it has developed, it may be desirable to prevent its occurrence in the first place. How can this be done? Paradoxically, a strategy of prevention challenges the fundamental premise upon which organization through division of labor rests. Once it has been decided by a superordinate authority to divide up functions among different departments or groups, a bias has already been introduced toward intergroup competition; for in doing its own job well, each group must, to some degree, compete for scarce resources and rewards from the superordinate authority. The very concept of division of labor implies a reduction of communication and interaction between groups, thus making it possible for perceptual distortions to occur.

The organization planner who wishes to avoid intergroup competition need not abandon the concept of division of labor, but should follow some of the steps listed below in creating and handling the different functional groups.

1. Relatively greater *emphasis should be given to total organizational effectiveness* and the role of departments in contributing to it; departments should be measured and rewarded on the basis of their contributions to the total effort, rather than their individual effectiveness.

2. *High interaction and frequent communication* should be stimulated between groups to work on problems of intergroup coordination and help; organization rewards should be given partly on the basis of help rendered to other groups.

3. *Frequent rotation of members* among groups or departments should be encouraged to stimulate a high degree of mutual understanding and empathy for one another's problems.

4. *Win-lose situations should be avoided* and groups should never be put into the position of competing for some scarce organizational reward; emphasis should always be placed on pooling resources to maximize organizational effectiveness; rewards should be shared equally with all the groups or departments.

Most managers find the fourth point particularly difficult to accept because of the strong belief that performance can be improved by pitting people or groups against one another in a competitive situation. This may indeed be true in the short run, and may even on occasion work in the long run, but the negative consequences described above are undeniably the product of the win-lose situation. Thus, if managers wish to prevent such consequences, they must face the possibility that they may have to abandon competitive relationships altogether and seek to substitute intergroup collaboration toward organizational goals. The more *interdependent* the various units are, the more important it is to stimulate collaborative problem solving.

Implementing a preventive strategy is often more difficult, partly because most people are inexperienced in stimulating and managing collaborative relationships. Yet observations of organizations using the Scanlon Plan not only reveal that it is possible to establish collaborative relationships, even between labor and management, but also that when this has been done, organizational and group effectiveness have been as high as or higher than under competitive conditions. Training in how to set up collaborative relations may be a prerequisite for any such program to succeed, especially for those managers who have themselves grown up in a highly competitive environment.

References

Alderfer, C. P. (1977). Group and Intergroup Relations. In J. R. Hackman & J. L. Suttle (eds). *Improving Life at Work.* Santa Monica, CA: Goodyear.

Blake, R. R., & Mouton, J. S. (1961). "Reactions to Intergroup Competition under Win-Lose Conditions." *Management Science* 7, 420–35.

Blake, R. R., & Mouton, J. S. (1962). "Headquarters-Field Team Training for Organizational Improvements." *Journal of the American Society of Training Directors* 16.

Janis, I. L., & King, B. T. (1954). The Influence of Role Playing on Opinion Change. *Journal of Abnormal and Social Psychology* 69, 211–18.

Schein, E. H. (1961). Management Development as a Process of Influence. *Industrial Management Review* 2, 59–77.

Sherif, M., & Harvey, O. J., White, B. J., Hood, W. R. and Sherif, C. (1961). *Intergroup Conflict and Cooperation: The Robbers' Cave Experiment.* Norman, OK: University Book Exchange.

Walton, R. E. (1969). *Interpersonal Peacemaking: Confrontations and Third Party Consultation.* Reading, MA: Addison-Wesley.

Reading 11
Organizational Culture

Edgar H. Schein

To write a review article about the concept of organizational culture poses a dilemma because there is presently little agreement on what the concept does and should mean, how it should be observed and measured, how it relates to more traditional industrial and organizational psychology theories, and how it should be used in our efforts to help organizations. The popular use of the concept has further muddied the waters by hanging the label of "culture" on everything from common behavioral patterns to espoused new corporate values that senior management wishes to inculcate (e.g., Deal & Kennedy, 1982; Peters & Waterman, 1982).

Serious students of organizational culture point out that each culture researcher develops explicit or implicit paradigms that bias not only the definitions of key concepts but the whole approach to the study of the phenomenon (Barley, Meyer, & Gash, 1988; Martin & Meyerson, 1988; Ott, 1989; Smircich & Calas, 1987; Van Maanen, 1988). One probable reason for this diversity of approaches is that culture, like role, lies at the intersection of several social sciences and reflects some of the biases of each—specifically, those of anthropology, sociology, social psychology, and organizational behavior.

A complete review of the various paradigms and their implications is far beyond the scope of

this article. Instead, I will provide a brief historical overview leading to the major approaches currently in use and then describe in greater detail one paradigm, firmly anchored in social psychology and anthropology, that is somewhat integrative in that it allows one to position other paradigms in a common conceptual space.

This line of thinking will push us conceptually into territory left insufficiently explored by such concepts as "climate," "norm," and "attitude." Many of the research methods of industrial/organizational psychology have weaknesses when applied to the concept of culture. If we are to take culture seriously, we must first adopt a more clinical and ethnographic approach to identify clearly the kinds of dimensions and variables that can usefully lend themselves to more precise empirical measurement and hypothesis testing. Though there have been many efforts to be empirically precise about cultural phenomena, there is still insufficient linkage of theory with observed data. We are still operating in the context of discovery and are seeking hypotheses, rather than testing specific theoretical formulations.

A Historical Note

Organizational culture as a concept has a fairly recent origin. Although the concepts of "group norms" and "climate" have been used by psychologists for a long time (e.g., Lewin, Lippitt, & White, 1939), the concept of "culture" has been explicitly used only in the last few decades. Katz and Kahn (1978), in their second edition of *The Social Psychology of Organizations,* referred to roles, norms, and values but presented neither climate nor culture as explicit concepts.

Source: Edgar H. Schein, "Organizational Culture," *American Psychologist* 45, no. 2 (February 1990), pp. 109–19. Copyright 1990 by the American Psychological Association. Reprinted by permission. Table 1 and Table 2 originally appeared in E. H. Schein's *Organizational Culture and Leadership: A Dynamic View,* pp. 52, 86. Copyright ©1985 by Jossey-Bass, Inc., Publishers. Reprinted by permission.

Organizational "climate," by virtue of being a more salient cultural phenomenon, lent itself to direct observation and measurement and thus has had a longer research tradition (Hellriegel & Slocum, 1974; A. P. Jones & James, 1979; Litwin & Stringer, 1968; Schneider, 1975; Schneider & Reichers, 1983; Tagiuri & Litwin, 1968). But climate is only a surface manifestation of culture, and thus research on climate has not enabled us to delve into the deeper causal aspects of how organizations function. We need explanations for variations in climate and norms, and it is this need that ultimately drives us to "deeper" concepts such as culture.

In the late 1940s social psychologists interested in Lewinian "action research" and leadership training freely used the concept of "cultural island" to indicate that the training setting was in some fundamental way different from the trainees' "back home" setting. We knew from the leadership training studies of the 1940s and 1950s that foremen who changed significantly during training would revert to their former attitudes once they were back at work in a different setting (Bradford, Gibb, & Benne, 1964; Fleishman, 1953, 1973; Lewin, 1952; Schein & Bennis, 1965). But the concept of "group norms," heavily documented in the Hawthorne studies of the 1920s, seemed sufficient to explain this phenomenon (Homans, 1950; Roethlisberger & Dickson, 1939).

In the 1950s and 1960s, the field of organizational psychology began to differentiate itself from industrial psychology by focusing on units larger than individuals (Bass, 1965; Schein, 1965). With a growing emphasis on work groups and whole organizations came a greater need for concepts such as "system" that could describe what could be thought of as a *pattern* of norms and attitudes that cut across a whole social unit. The researchers and clinicians at the Tavistock Institute developed the concept of "socio-technical systems" (Jaques, 1951; Rice, 1963; Trist, Higgin, Murray, & Pollock, 1963), and Likert (1961, 1967) developed his "Systems 1 through 4" to describe integrated sets of organizational norms and attitudes. Katz and Kahn (1966) built their entire analysis of organizations around systems theory and systems dynamics, thus laying the most important theoretical foundation for later culture studies.

The field of organizational psychology grew with the growth of business and management schools. As concerns with understanding organizations and interorganizational relationships grew, concepts from sociology and anthropology began to influence the field. Cross-cultural psychology had, of course, existed for a long time (Werner, 1940), but the application of the concept of culture to organizations *within* a given society came only recently as more investigators interested in organizational phenomena found themselves needing the concept to explain (*a*) variations in patterns of organizational behavior, and (*b*) levels of stability in group and organizational behavior that had not previously been highlighted (e.g., Ouchi, 1981).

What has really thrust the concept into the forefront is the recent emphasis on trying to explain why U.S. companies do not perform as well as some of their counterpart companies in other societies, notably Japan. In observing the differences, it has been noted that national culture is not a sufficient explanation (Ouchi, 1981; Pascale & Athos, 1981). One needs concepts that permit one to differentiate between organizations within a society, especially in relation to different levels of effectiveness, and the concept of organizational culture has served this purpose well (e.g., O'Toole, 1979; Pettigrew, 1979; Wilkins & Ouchi, 1983).

As more investigators and theoreticians have begun to examine organizational culture, the normative thrust has been balanced by more descriptive and clinical research (Barley, 1983; Frost, Moore, Louis, Lundberg, & Martin, 1985; Louis, 1981, 1983; Martin, 1982; Martin & Powers, 1983; Martin & Siehl, 1983; Schein, 1985a; Van Maanen & Barley, 1984). We need to find out what is actually going on in organizations before we rush in to tell managers what to do about their culture.

I will summarize this quick historical overview by identifying several different research streams that today influence how we perceive the concept of organizational culture.

Survey Research

From this perspective, culture has been viewed as a property of groups that can be measured by questionnaires leading to Likert-type profiles (Hofstede, 1980; Hofstede & Bond, 1988; Kilmann, 1984; Likert, 1967). The problem with this approach is that it assumes knowledge of the relevant dimensions to be studied. Even if these are statistically derived from large samples of items, it is not clear whether the initial item set is broad enough or relevant enough to capture what may for any given organization be its critical cultural themes. Furthermore, it is not clear whether something as abstract as culture can be measured with survey instruments at all.

Analytical Descriptive

In this type of research, culture is viewed as a concept for which empirical measures must be developed, even if that means breaking down the concept into smaller units so that it can be analyzed and measured (e.g., Harris & Sutton, 1986; Martin & Siehl, 1983; Schall, 1983; Trice & Beyer, 1984; Wilkins, 1983). Thus organizational stories, rituals and rites, symbolic manifestations, and other cultural elements come to be taken as valid surrogates for the cultural whole. The problem with this approach is that it fractionates a concept whose primary theoretical utility is in drawing attention to the holistic aspect of group and organizational phenomena.

Ethnographic

In this approach, concepts and methods developed in sociology and anthropology are applied to the study of organizations in order to illuminate descriptively, and thus provide a richer understanding of certain organizational phenomena that had previously not been documented fully enough (Barley, 1983; Van Maanen, 1988; Van Maanen & Barley, 1984). This approach helps to build better theory but is time consuming and ex-

pensive. A great many more cases are needed before generalizations can be made across various types of organizations.

Historical

Though historians have rarely applied the concept of culture in their work, it is clearly viewed as a legitimate aspect of an organization to be analyzed along with other factors (Chandler, 1977; Dyer, 1986; Pettigrew, 1979; Westney, 1987). The weaknesses of the historical method are similar to those pointed out for the ethnographic approach, but these are often offset by the insights that historical and longitudinal analyses can provide.

Clinical Descriptive

With the growth of organizational consulting has come the opportunity to observe in areas from which researchers have traditionally been barred, such as the higher levels of management where policies originate and where reward and control systems are formulated. When consultants observe organizational phenomena as a byproduct of their services for clients, we can think of this as "clinical" research even though the client is defining the domain of observation (Schein, 1987a). Such work is increasingly being done by consultants with groups and organizations, and it allows consultants to observe some of the systemic effects of interventions over time. This approach has been of how members of the organization react. We can see and feel that one company is much more formal and bureaucratic than another, but that does not tell us anything about why this is so or what meaning it has to the members.

For example, one of the flaws of studying organizational symbols, stories, myths, and other such artifacts is that we may make incorrect inferences from them if we do not know how they connect to underlying assumptions (Pondy, Boland, & Thomas, 1988; Pondy, Frost, Morgan, & Dandridge, 1983; Wilkins, 1983). Organizational stories are especially problematic in this regard because the "lesson" of the story is not clear if one does not understand the underlying assumptions behind it.

Through interviews, questionnaires, or survey instruments one can study a culture's espoused and documented *values,* norms, ideologies, charters, and philosophies. This is comparable to the ethnographer's asking special "informants" why certain observed phenomena happen the way they do. Open-ended interviews can be very useful in getting at this level of how people feel and think; but questionnaires and survey instruments are generally less useful, because they prejudge the dimensions to be studied. There is no way of knowing whether the dimensions one is asking about are relevant or salient in that culture until one has examined the deeper levels of the culture.

Through more intensive observation, through more focused questions, and through involving motivated members of the group in intensive self-analysis, one can seek out and decipher the taken-for-granted, underlying, and usually unconscious *assumptions* that determine perceptions, thought processes, feelings, and behavior. Once one understands some of these assumptions, it becomes much easier to decipher the meanings implicit in the various behavioral and artifactual phenomena one observes. Furthermore, once one understands the underlying taken-for-granted assumptions, one can better understand how cultures can seem to be ambiguous or even self-contradictory (Martin & Meyerson, 1988).

As two case examples I present later will show, it is quite possible for a group to hold conflicting values that manifest themselves in inconsistent behavior while having complete consensus on underlying assumptions. It is equally possible for a group to reach consensus on the level of values and behavior and yet develop serious conflict later because there was no consensus on critical underlying assumptions.

This latter phenomenon is frequently observed in mergers or acquisitions where initial synergy is gradually replaced by conflict, leading ultimately to divestitures. When one analyzes these examples historically, one often finds that there was insufficient agreement on certain basic assumptions, or, in our terms, that the cultures were basically in conflict with each other.

Deeply held assumptions often start out historically as values but, as they stand the test of time, gradually come to be taken for granted and then take on the character of assumptions. They are no longer questioned and they become less and less open to discussion. Such avoidance behavior occurs particularly if the learning was based on traumatic experiences in the organization's history, which leads to the group counterpart of what would be repression in the individual. If one understands culture in this way, it becomes obvious why it is so difficult to change culture.

Deciphering the "Content" of Culture

Culture is ubiquitous. It covers all areas of group life. A simplifying typology is always dangerous because one may not have the right variables in it; but if one distills from small group theory the dimensions that recur in group studies, one can identify a set of major external and internal tasks that all groups face and with which they must learn to cope (Ancona, 1988; Bales, 1950; Bales & Cohen, 1979; Benne & Sheats, 1948; Bennis & Shepard, 1956; Bion, 1959; Schein, 1988). The group's culture can then be seen as the learned response to each of these tasks (see Table 1).

Another approach to understanding the "content" of a culture is to draw on anthropological typologies of universal issues faced by all societies. Again, there is a danger of overgeneralizing these dimensions (see Table 2), but the comparative studies of Kluckhohn and Strodtbeck (1961) are a reasonable start in this dimension.

If one wants to decipher what is really going on in a particular organization, one has to start more inductively to find out which of these dimensions is the most pertinent on the basis of that organization's history. If one has access to the organization, one will note its *artifacts* readily but will not really know what they mean. Of most value in this process will be noting *anomalies* and things that seem different, upsetting, or difficult to understand.

TABLE 1 **The External and Internal Tasks Facing All Groups**

External Adaption Tasks	Internal Integration Tasks
Developing consensus on:	Developing consensus on:
1. The core mission, functions, and primary tasks of the organization vis-à-vis its environments.	1. The common language and conceptual system to be used, including basic concepts of time and space.
2. The specific goals to be pursued by the organization.	2. The group boundaries and criteria for inclusion.
3. The basic means to be used in accomplishing the goals.	3. The criteria for the allocation of status, power, and authority.
4. The criteria to be used for measuring results.	4. The criteria for intimacy, friendship, and love in different work and family settings.
5. The remedial or repair strategies if goals are not achieved.	5. The criteria for the allocation of rewards and punishments.
	6. Concepts for managing the unmanageable—ideology and religion.

Note: Adapted from *Organizational Culture and Leadership* (pp. 52, 56) by E. H. Schein, 1985, San Francisco: Jossey-Bass. Copyright 1985 by Jossey-Bass. Adapted by permission.

TABLE 2 **Some Underlying Dimensions of Organizational Culture**

Dimension	Questions to Be Answered
1. The organization's relationship to its environment	Does the organization perceive itself to be dominant, submissive, harmonizing, searching out a niche?
2. The nature of human activity	Is the "correct" way for humans to behave to be dominant/pro-active, harmonizing, or passive/fatalistic?
3. The nature of reality and truth	How do we define what is true and what is not true; and how is truth ultimately determined both in the physical and social word? By pragmatic test, reliance on wisdom, or social consensus?
4. The nature of time	What is our basic orientation in terms of past, present, and future, and what kinds of time units are most relevant for the conduct of daily affairs?
5. The nature of human nature	Are humans basically good, neutral, or evil, and is human nature perfectible or fixed?
6. The nature of human relationships	What is the "correct" way for people to relate to each other, to distribute power and affection? Is life competitive or cooperative? Is the best way to organize society on the basis of individualism or groupism? Is the best authority system autocratic/paternalistic or collegial/participative?
7. Homogeneity vs. diversity	Is the group best off if it is highly diverse or if it is highly homogeneous, and should individuals in a group be encouraged to innovate or conform?

Note: Adapted from *Organizational Culture and Leadership* (p. 86) by E. H. Schein, 1985, San Francisco: Jossey-Bass. Copyright 1985 by Jossey-Bass. Adapted by permission.

If one has access to members of the organization, one can interview them about the issues in Table 1 and thereby get a good roadmap of what is going on. Such an interview will begin to reveal *espoused values,* and, as these surface, the investigator will begin to notice inconsistencies between what is claimed and what has been observed. These inconsistencies and the anomalies observed or felt now form the basis for the next layer of investigation.

Pushing past the layer of espoused values into underlying *assumptions* can be done by the ethnographer once trust has been established or by the clinician if the organizational client wishes to be helped. Working with motivated insiders is essential, because only they can bring to the surface their own underlying assumptions and articulate how they basically perceive the world around them.

To summarize, if we combine insider knowledge with outsider questions, assumptions can be brought to the surface; but the process of inquiry has to be interactive, with the outsider continuing to probe until assumptions have really been teased out and have led to a feeling of greater understanding on the part of both the outsider and the insiders.

Two Case Examples

It is not possible to provide complete cultural descriptions in a short article, but some extracts from cases can be summarized to illustrate particularly the distinctions between artifacts, values, and assumptions. The "Action Company" is a rapidly growing high-technology manufacturing concern still managed by its founder roughly 30 years after its founding. Because of its low turnover and intense history, one would expect to find an overall organizational culture as well as functional and geographic subcultures.

A visitor to the company would note the open office landscape architecture; a high degree of informality; frenetic activity all around; a high degree of confrontation, conflict, and fighting in meetings; an obvious lack of status symbols, such

as parking spaces or executive dining rooms; and a sense of high energy and emotional involvement of people staying late and expressing excitement about the importance of their work.

If one asks about these various behaviors, one is told that the company is in a rapidly growing high-technology field where hard work, innovation, and rapid solutions to things are important and where it is essential for everyone to contribute at their maximum capacity. New employees are carefully screened; and when an employee fails, he or she is simply assigned to another task, not fired or punished in any personal way.

If one discusses this further and pushes to the level of assumptions, one elicits a pattern or paradigm such as that shown in Figure 1. Because of the kind of technology the company manufactures, and because of the strongly held beliefs and values of its founder, the company operates on several critical and coordinated assumptions: (*a*) Individuals are assumed to be the source of all innovation and productivity. (*b*) It is assumed that truth can only be determined by pitting fully involved individuals against each other to debate ideas until only one idea survives; and it is further assumed that ideas will not be implemented unless everyone involved in implementation has been convinced through the debate of the validity of the idea. (*c*) Paradoxically, it is also assumed that every individual must think for himself or herself

FIGURE 1
The Action Company Paradigm

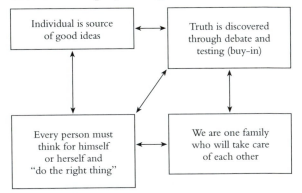

and "do the right thing" even if that means dis-obeying one's boss or violating a policy. (*d*) What makes it possible for people to live in this high-conflict environment is the assumption that the company members are one big family who will take care of each other and protect each other even if some members make mistakes or have bad ideas.

Once one understands this paradigm, one can understand all of the different observed artifacts, such as the ability of the organization to tolerate extremely high degrees of conflict without seem-ing to destroy or even demotivate its employees. The value of the cultural analysis is that it pro-vides insight, understanding, and a roadmap for future action. For example, as this company grows, the decision process may prove to be too slow, the individual autonomy that members are expected to exercise may become destructive and have to be replaced by more disciplined behavior, and the notion of a family may break down be-cause too many people no longer know each other personally. The cultural analysis thus permits one to focus on those areas in which the organization will experience stresses and strains as it continues to grow and in which cultural evolution and change will occur.

By way of contrast, in the "Multi Company," a 100-year-old multidivisional, multinational chem-ical firm, one finds at the artifact level a high de-gree of formality; an architecture that puts great emphasis on privacy; a proliferation of status symbols and deference rituals, such as addressing people by their titles; a high degree of politeness in group meetings; an emphasis on carefully thinking things out and then implementing them firmly through the hierarchy; a formal code of dress; and an emphasis on working hours, punctu-ality, and so on. One also finds a total absence of cross-divisional or cross-functional meetings and an almost total lack of lateral communication. Memos left in one department by an outside con-sultant with instructions to be given to others are almost never delivered.

The paradigm that surfaces, if one works with insiders to try to decipher what is going on, can best be depicted by the assumptions shown in Fig-ure 2. The company is science based and has al-ways derived its success from its research and development activities. Whereas "truth" in the Action Company is derived through debate and conflict and employees down the line are ex-pected to think for themselves, in the Multi Com-pany truth is derived from senior, wiser heads and employees are expected to go along like good sol-diers once a decision is reached.

The Multi Company also sees itself as a fam-ily, but its concept of a family is completely dif-ferent. Whereas in the Action Company, the family is a kind of safety net and an assurance of

FIGURE 2
The Multi Company Paradigm

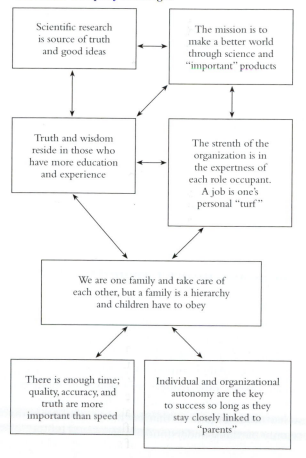

Scientific research is source of truth and good ideas

The mission is to make a better world through science and "important" products

Truth and wisdom reside in those who have more education and experience

The strenth of the organization is in the expertness of each role occupant. A job is one's personal "turf"

We are one family and take care of each other, but a family is a hierarchy and children have to obey

There is enough time; quality, accuracy, and truth are more important than speed

Individual and organizational autonomy are the key to success so long as they stay closely linked to "parents" membership, in the Multi Company it is an authoritarian/paternalistic system of eliciting loyalty and compliance in exchange for economic security. The paradoxical absence of lateral communication is explained by the deeply held assumption that a job is a person's private turf and that the unsolicited providing of information to that person is an invasion of privacy and a potential threat to his or her self-esteem. Multi Company managers are very much on top of their jobs and pride themselves on that fact. If they ask for information they get it, but it is rarely volunteered by peers.

This cultural analysis highlights what is for the Multi Company a potential problem. Its future success may depend much more on its ability to become effective in marketing and manufacturing, yet it still treats research and development as a sacred cow and assumes that new products will be the key to its future success. Increasingly, the company finds itself in a world that requires rapid decision making, yet its systems and procedures are slow and cumbersome. To be more innovative in marketing it needs to share ideas more, yet it undermines lateral communication.

Both companies reflect the larger cultures within which they exist, in that the Action Company is an American firm whereas the Multi Company is European; but each also is different from its competitors within the same country, thus highlighting the importance of understanding *organizational* culture.

Cultural Dynamics: How Is Culture Created?

Culture is learned; hence learning models should help us to understand culture creation. Unfortunately, there are not many good models of how groups learn—how norms, beliefs, and assumptions are created initially. Once these exist, we can see clearly how leaders and powerful members embed them in group activity, but the process of learning something that becomes shared is still only partially understood.

Norm Formation around Critical Incidents

One line of analysis comes from the study of training groups (Bennis & Shepard, 1956; Bion, 1959; Schein, 1985a). One can see in such groups how norms and beliefs arise around the way members respond to critical incidents. Something emotionally charged or anxiety producing may happen, such as an attack by a member on the leader. Because everyone witnesses it and because tension is high when the attack occurs, the immediate next set of behaviors tends to create a norm.

Suppose, for example, that the leader counterattacks, that the group members "concur" with silence or approval, and that the offending member indicates with an apology that he or she accepts his or her "mistake." In those few moments a bit of culture has begun to be created—the norm that "we do not attack the leader in this group; authority is sacred." The norm may eventually become a belief and then an assumption if the same pattern recurs. If the leader and the group consistently respond differently to attacks, a different norm will arise. By reconstructing the history of critical incidents in the group and how members dealt with them, one can get a good indication of the important cultural elements in that group.

Identification with Leaders

A second mechanism of culture creation is the modeling by leader figures that permits group members to identify with them and internalize their values and assumptions. When groups or organizations first form, there are usually dominant figures or "founders" whose own beliefs, values, and assumptions provide a visible and articulated model for how the group should be structured and how it should function (Schein, 1983). As these beliefs are put into practice, some work out and some do not. The group then learns from its own experience what parts of the "founder's" belief system work for the group as a whole. The joint learning then gradually creates shared assumptions.

Founders and subsequent leaders continue to attempt to embed their own assumptions; but increasingly they find that other parts of the organization have their own experiences to draw on and, thus, cannot be changed. Increasingly the learning process is shared, and the resulting cultural assumptions reflect the total group's experience, not only the leader's initial assumptions. But leaders continue to try to embed their own views of how things should be, and, if they are powerful enough, they will continue to have a dominant effect on the emerging culture.

Primary embedding mechanisms are (*a*) what leaders pay attention to, measure, and control; (*b*) how leaders react to critical incidents and organizational crises; (*c*) deliberate role modeling and coaching; (*d*) operational criteria for the allocation of rewards and status; and (*e*) operational criteria for recruitment, selection, promotion, retirement, and excommunication. *Secondary articulation and reinforcement mechanisms* are (*a*) the organization's design and structure; (*b*) organizational systems and procedures; (*c*) the design of physical space, facades, and buildings; (*d*) stories, legends, myths, and symbols; and (*e*) formal statements of organizational philosophy, creeds, and charters.

One can hypothesize that, as cultures evolve and grow, two processes will occur simultaneously: a process of differentiation into various kinds of subcultures that will create diversity, and a process of integration, or a tendency for the various deeper elements of the culture to become congruent with each other because of the human need for consistency.

Cultural Dynamics: Preservation through Socialization

Culture perpetuates and reproduces itself through the socialization of new members entering the group. The socialization process really begins with recruitment and selection in that the organization is likely to look for new members who already have the "right" set of assumptions, beliefs, and values. If the organization can find such presocialized members, it needs to do less formal socialization. More typically, however, new members do not "know the ropes" well enough to be able to take and enact their organizational roles, and thus they need to be trained and "acculturated" (Feldman, 1988; Ritti & Funkhouser, 1987; Schein, 1968, 1978; Van Maanen, 1976, 1977).

The socialization process has been analyzed from a variety of perspectives and can best be conceptualized in terms of a set of dimensions that highlight variations in how different organizations approach the process (Van Maanen, 1978; Van Maanen & Schein, 1979). Van Maanen identified seven dimensions along which socialization processes can vary:

1. *Group versus individual:* the degree to which the organization processes recruits in batches, as in boot camp, or individually, as in professional offices.

2. *Formal versus informal:* the degree to which the process is formalized, as in set training programs, or is handled informally through apprenticeships, individual coaching by the immediate superior, or the like.

3. *Self-destructive and reconstructing versus self-enhancing:* the degree to which the process destroys aspects of the self and replaces them, as in boot camp, or enhances aspects of the self, as in professional development programs.

4. *Serial versus random:* the degree to which role models are provided, as in apprenticeship or mentoring programs, or are deliberately withheld, as in sink-or-swim kinds of initiations in which the recruit is expected to figure out his or her own solutions.

5. *Sequential versus disjunctive:* the degree to which the process consists of guiding the recruit through a series of discrete steps and roles versus being open-ended and never letting the recruit predict what organizational role will come next.

6. *Fixed versus variable:* the degree to which stages of the training process have fixed

timetables for each stage, as in military acade-mies, boot camps, or rotational training pro-grams, or are open-ended, as in typical promotional systems where one is not ad-vanced to the next stage until one is "ready."

7. *Tournament versus contest:* the degree to which each stage is an "elimination tourna-ment" where one is out of the organization if one fails or a "contest" in which one builds up a track record and batting average.

Socialization Consequences

Though the goal of socialization is to perpetuate the culture, it is clear that the process does not have uniform effects. Individuals respond differ-ently to the same treatment, and, even more im-portant, different combinations of socialization tactics can be hypothesized to produce somewhat different outcomes for the organization (Van Maanen & Schein, 1979).

For example, from the point of view of the or-ganization, one can specify three kinds of out-comes: (*a*) a *custodial orientation,* or total conformity to all norms and complete learning of all assumptions; (*b*) *creative individualism,* which implies that the trainee learns all of the central and pivotal assumptions of the culture but rejects all peripheral ones, thus permitting the individual to be creative both with respect to the organization's tasks and in how the organization performs them (role motivation); and (*c*) *rebellion,* or the total re-jection of all assumptions. If the rebellious indi-vidual is constrained by external circumstances from leaving the organization, he or she will sub-vert, sabotage, and ultimately foment revolution.

We can hypothesize that the combination of socialization techniques most likely to produce a custodial orientation is (1) formal, (2) self-reconstructing, (3) serial, (4) sequential, (5) vari-able, and (6) tournament-like. Hence if one wants new members to be more creative in the use of their talents, one should use socialization tech-niques that are informal, self-enhancing, random, disjunctive, fixed in terms of timetables, and contest-like.

The individual versus group dimension can go in either direction in that group socialization methods can produce loyal custodially oriented cohorts or can produce disloyal rebels if counter-cultural norms are formed during the social-ization process. Similarly, in the individual apprenticeship the direction of socialization will depend on the orientation of the mentor or coach.

Efforts to measure these socialization dimen-sions have been made, and some preliminary support for the above hypotheses has been forthcoming (Feldman, 1976, 1988; G. R. Jones, 1986). Insofar as cultural evolution is a function of innovative and creative efforts on the part of new members, this line of investigation is espe-cially important.

Cultural Dynamics: Natural Evolution

Every group and organization is an open system that exists in multiple environments. Changes in the environment will produce stresses and strains inside the group, forcing new learning and adap-tation. At the same time, new members coming into the group will bring new beliefs and assump-tions that will influence currently held assump-tions. To some degree, then, there is constant pressure on any given culture to evolve and grow. But just as individuals do not easily give up the elements of their identity or their defense mecha-nisms, so groups do not easily give up some of their basic underlying assumptions merely be-cause external events or new members disconfirm them.

An illustration of "forced" evolution can be seen in the case of the aerospace company that prided itself on its high level of trust in its em-ployees, which was reflected in flexible working hours, systems of self-monitoring and self-control, and the absence of time clocks. When a number of other companies in the industry were discovered to have overcharged their government clients, the government legislated a system of controls for *all* of its contractors, forcing this company to install time clocks and other control mechanisms that undermined the climate of trust that had been built up over 30 years. It remains to be seen whether the company's basic assumption that people can be trusted will gradually change or whether the company will find a way to discount the effects of an artifact that is in fundamental conflict with one of its basic assumptions.

Differentiation

As organizations grow and evolve they divide the labor and form functional, geographical, and other kinds of units, each of which exists in its own specific environment. Thus organizations begin to build their own subcultures. A natural evolutionary mechanism, therefore, is the differentiation that inevitably occurs with age and size. Once a group has many subcultures, its total culture increasingly becomes a negotiated outcome of the interaction of its subgroups. Organizations then evolve either by special efforts to impose their overall culture or by allowing dominant subcultures that may be better adapted to changing environmental circumstances to become more influential.

Cultural Dynamics: Guided Evolution and Managed Change

One of the major roles of the field of organization development has been to help organizations guide the direction of their evolution; that is, to enhance cultural elements that are viewed as critical to maintaining identity and to promote the "unlearning" of cultural elements that are viewed as increasingly dysfunctional (Argyris, Putnam, & Smith, 1985; Argyris & Schon, 1978; Beckhard & Harris, 1987; Hanna, 1988; Lippitt, 1982; Walton, 1987). This process in organizations is analogous to the process of therapy in individuals although the actual tactics are more complicated when multiple clients are involved and when some of the clients are groups and subsystems.

Leaders of organizations sometimes are able to overcome their own cultural biases and to perceive that elements of an organization's culture are dysfunctional for survival and growth in a changing environment. They may feel either that they do not have the time to let evolution occur naturally or that evolution is heading the organization in the wrong direction. In such a situation one can observe leaders doing a number of different things, usually in combination, to produce the desired cultural changes.

1. Leaders may unfreeze the present system by highlighting the threats to the organization if no change occurs, and, at the same time, encourage the organization to believe that change is possible and desirable.
2. They may articulate a new direction and a new set of assumptions, thus providing a clear and new role model.
3. Key positions in the organization may be filled with new incumbents who hold the new assumptions because they are either hybrids, mutants, or brought in from the outside.
4. Leaders systematically may reward the adoption of new directions and punish adherence to the old direction.
5. Organization members may be seduced or coerced into adopting new behaviors that are more consistent with new assumptions.
6. Visible scandals may be created to discredit sacred cows, to explode myths that preserve dysfunctional traditions, and to destroy symbolically the artifacts associated with them.
7. Leaders may create new emotionally charged rituals and develop new symbols and artifacts around the new assumptions to be embraced, using the embedding mechanisms described earlier.

Such cultural change efforts are generally more characteristic of "midlife" organizations that have become complacent and ill adapted to rapidly changing environmental conditions (Schein, 1985a). The fact that such organizations have strong subcultures aids the change process, in that one can draw the new leaders from those subcultures that most represent the direction in which the organization needs to go.

In cases where organizations become extremely maladapted, one sees more severe change efforts. These may take the form of destroying the group that is the primary cultural carrier and reconstructing it around new people, thereby allowing a new learning process to occur and a new culture to form. When organizations go bankrupt or are turned over to "turnaround managers," one often sees such extreme measures. What is important to note about such cases is that they invariably involve the replacement of large numbers of people, because the members who have grown up in the organization find it difficult to change their basic assumptions.

Mergers and Acquisitions

One of the most obvious forces toward culture change is the bringing together of two or more cultures. Unfortunately, in many mergers and acquisitions, the culture compatibility issue is not raised until after the deal has been consummated, which leads, in many cases, to cultural "indigestion" and the eventual divestiture of units that cannot become culturally integrated.

To avoid such problems, organizations must either engage in more premerger diagnosis to determine cultural compatibility or conduct training and integration workshops to help the meshing process. Such workshops have to take into account the deeper assumption layers of culture to avoid the trap of reaching consensus at the level of artifacts and values while remaining in conflict at the level of underlying assumptions.

The Role of the Organizational Psychologist

Culture will become an increasingly important concept for organizational psychology. Without such a concept we cannot really understand change or resistance to change. The more we get involved with helping organizations to design their fundamental strategies, particularly in the human resources area, the more important it will be to be able to help organizations decipher their own cultures.

All of the activities that revolve around recruitment, selection, training, socialization, the design of reward systems, the design and description of jobs, and broader issues of organization design require an understanding of how organizational culture influences present functioning. Many organizational change programs that failed probably did so because they ignored cultural forces in the organizations in which they were to be installed.

Inasmuch as culture is a dynamic process within organizations, it is probably studied best by action research methods, that is, methods that get "insiders" involved in the research and that work through attempts to "intervene" (Argyris et al., 1985; French & Bell, 1984; Lewin, 1952; Schein, 1987b). Until we have a better understanding of how culture works, it is probably best to work with qualitative research approaches that combine field work methods from ethnography with interview and observation methods from clinical and consulting work (Schein, 1987a).

I do not see a unique role for the traditional industrial/organizational psychologist, but I see great potential for the psychologist to work as a team member with colleagues who are more ethnographically oriented. The particular skill that will be needed on the part of the psychologist will be knowledge of organizations and of how to work with them, especially in a consulting relationship. Organizational culture is a complex phenomenon, and we should not rush to measure things until we understand better what we are measuring.

References

Ancona, D. G. (1988). "Groups in Organizations: Extending Laboratory Models." In C. Hendrick (ed.), *Annual Review of Personality and Social Psychology: Group and Intergroup Processes.* Beverly Hills, CA: Sage.

Argyris, C.; Putnam, R.; & Smith, D. M. (1985). *Action Science.* San Francisco: Jossey-Bass.

Argyris, C.; & Schon, D. A. (1978). *Organizational Learning: A Theory of Action Perspective.* Reading, MA: Addison-Wesley.

Bales, R. F. (1950). *Interaction Process Analysis.* Chicago, University of Chicago Press.

Bales, R. F.; & Cohen, S.P. (1979). *SYMLOG: A System for the Multiple Level Observation of Groups.* New York: Free Press.

Barley, S. R. (1983). "Semiotics and the Study of Occupational and Organizational Cultures." *Administrative Science Quarterly,* 28, 393–413.

Barley, S. R.; Meyer, C. W.; & Gash, D. C. (1988). "Culture of Cultures: Academics, Practitioners and the Pragmatics of Normative Control." *Administrative Science Quarterly* 33, 24–60.

Bass, B. M. (1965). *Organizational Psychology.* Boston: Allyn & Bacon.

Beckhard, R. (1969). *Organization Development: Strategies and Models.* Reading, MA: Addison-Wesley.

Beckhard, R.; & Harris, R. T. (1977). *Organizational Transitions: Managing Complex Change.* Reading, MA: Addison-Wesley.

Beckhard, R.; & Harris, R. T. (1987). *Organizational Transitions: Managing Complex Change* (2nd ed.). Reading, MA: Addison-Wesley.

Benne, K.; & Sheats, P. (1948). "Functional Roles of Group Members." *Journal of Social Issues* 2, 42–47.

Bennis, W. G. (1966). *Changing Organizations.* New York: McGraw-Hill.

Bennis, W. G. (1969). *Organization Development: Its Nature, Origins and Prospects.* Reading, MA: Addison-Wesley.

Bennis, W. G.; & Shepard, H. A. (1956). "A Theory of Group Development." *Human Relations* 9, 415–37.

Bion, W. R. (1959). *Experiences in Groups.* London: Tavistock.

Bradford, L. P.; Gibb, J. R.; & Benne, K. D. (eds.). (1964). *T-Group Theory and Laboratory Method.* New York: John Wiley & Sons.

Chandler, A.P. (1977). *The Visible Hand.* Cambridge, MA: Harvard University Press.

Deal, T. W.; & Kennedy, A. A. (1982). *Corporate Cultures.* Reading, MA: Addison-Wesley.

Durkin, J. E. (ed.). (1981). *Living Groups: Group Psychotherapy and General Systems Theory.* New York: Brunner/Mazel.

Dyer, W. G., Jr. (1986). *Cultural Change in Family Firms.* San Francisco: Jossey-Bass.

Feldman, D. C. (1976). "A Contingency Theory of Socialization." *Administration Science Quarterly* 21, 433–52.

Feldman, D. C. (1988). *Managing Careers in Organizations.* Glenview, IL: Scott, Foresman.

Festinger, L. (1957). *A Theory of Cognitive Dissonance.* New York: Harper & Row.

Fleishman, E. A. (1953). "Leadership Climate, Human Relations Training, and Supervisory Behavior." *Personnel Psychology* 6, 205–22.

Fleishman, E. A. (1973). "Twenty Years of Consideration and Structure." In E. A. Fleishman & J. G. Hunt (eds.), *Current Developments in the Study of Leadership* (pp. 1–39). Carbondale: Southern Illinois University Press.

French, W. L.; & Bell, C. H. (1984). *Organization Development* (3rd ed.). Englewood Cliffs, NJ: Prentice Hall.

Frost, P. J.; Moore, L. F.; Louis, M. R.; Lundberg, C. C.; & Martin, J. (eds.). (1985). *Organizational Culture.* Beverly Hills, CA: Sage.

Hanna, D. P. (1988). *Designing Organizations for High Performance.* Reading, MA: Addison-Wesley.

Harris, S. G.; & Sutton, R. I. (1986). "Functions of Parting Ceremonies in Dying Organizations." *Academy of Management Journal* 29, 5–30.

Hebb, D. (1954). "The Social Significance of Animal Studies." In G. Lindzey (ed.), *Handbook of Social Psychology,* Vol. 2, pp. 532–61. Reading, MA: Addison-Wesley.

Heider, F. (1958). *The Psychology of Interpersonal Relations.* New York: John Wiley & Sons.

Hellriegel, D.; & Slocum, J. W., Jr. (1974). "Organizational Climate: Measures, Research, and Contingencies." *Academy of Management Journal,* 17, 255–80.

Hirschhorn, L. (1987). *The Workplace Within.* Cambridge, MA: MIT Press.

Hofstede, G. (1980). *Culture's Consequences.* Beverly Hills, CA: Sage.

Hofstede, G.; & Bond, M. H. (1988). "The Confucius Connection: From Cultural Roots to Economic Growth." *Organizational Dynamics* 16(4), 4–21.

Homans, G. (1950). *The Human Group.* New York: Harcourt Brace Jovanovich.

Jaques, E. (1951). *The Changing Culture of a Factory.* London: Tavistock.

Jones, A. P.; & James, E. R. (1979). "Psychological Climate: Dimensions and Relationships of Individual and Aggregated Work Environment Perceptions." *Organizational Behavior and Human Performance* 23, 201–50.

Jones, G. R. (1986). "Socialization Tactics, Self-Efficacy, and New-Comers' Adjustments to Organizations." *Academy of Management Journal* 29, 262–79.

Katz, D.; & Kahn, R. L. (1966). *The Social Psychology of Organizations.* New York: John Wiley & Sons.

Katz, D.; & Kahn, R. L. (1978). *The Social Psychology of Organizations* (2nd ed.). New York: John Wiley & Sons.

Kets de Vries, M. F. R.; & Miller, D. (1984). *The Neurotic Organization.* San Francisco: Jossey-Bass.

Kets de Vries, M. F. R.; & Miller, D. (1986). "Personality, Culture, and Organization." *Academy of Management Review* 11, 266–79.

Kilmann, R. H. (1984). *Beyond the Quick Fix.* San Francisco: Jossey-Bass.

Kluckhohn, F. R.; & Strodtbeck, F. L. (1961). *Variations in Value Orientations.* New York: Harper & Row.

Lewin, K. (1952). "Group Decision and Social Change." In G. E. Swanson, T. N. Newcomb, & E. L. Hartley (eds.), *Readings in Social Psychology* (rev. ed., pp. 459–73). New York: Holt, Rinehart & Winston.

Lewin, K; Lippitt, R.; & White, R. K. (1939). "Patterns of Aggressive Behavior in Experimentally Created 'Social Climates.'" *Journal of Social Psychology* 10, 271–99.

Likert, R. (1961). *New Patterns of Management.* New York: McGraw-Hill.

Likert, R. (1967). *The Human Organization.* New York: McGraw-Hill.

Lippitt, G. (1982). *Organizational Renewal* (2nd ed.). Englewood Cliffs, NJ: Prentice Hall.

Litwin, G. H.; & Stringer, R. A. (1968). *Motivation and Organizational Climate.* Boston: Harvard Business School, Division of Research.

Louis, M. R. (1981). "A Cultural Perspective on Organizations." *Human Systems Management* 2, 246–58.

Louis, M. R. (1983). "Organizations as Culture Bearing Milieux." In L. R. Pondy, P. J. Frost, G. Morgan, & T. C. Dandridge (eds.), *Organizational Symbolism* (pp. 39–54). Greenwich, CT: JAI Press.

Martin, J. (1982). "Stories and Scripts in Organizational Settings." In A. Hastorf & A. Isen (eds.), *Cognitive Social Psychology.* New York: Elsevier.

Martin, J.; Feldman, M. S.; Hatch, M. J.; & Sitkin, S. (1983). "The Uniqueness Paradox in Organizational Stories." *Administrative Science Quarterly* 28, 438–54.

Martin, J.; & Meyerson, D. (1988). "Organizational Cultures and the Denial, Channeling, and Acknowledgement of Ambiguity." In L. R. Pondy, R. J. Boland, & H. Thomas (eds.), *Managing Ambiguity and Change.* New York: John Wiley & Sons.

Martin, J.; & Powers, M. E. (1983). "Truth or Corporate Propaganda: The Value of a Good War Story." In L. R. Pondy, P. J. Frost, G. Morgan, & T. C. Dan-

dridge (eds.), *Organizational Symbolism* (pp. 93–108). Greenwich, CT: JAI Press.

Martin, J.; & Siehl, C. (1983). "Organizational Culture and Counter-Culture: An Uneasy Symbiosis." *Organizational Dynamics* 12, 52–64.

Menzies, I. E. P. (1960). "A Case Study in the Functioning of Social Systems as a Defense Against Anxiety." *Human Relations,* 13, 95–121.

O'Toole, J. J. (1979). "Corporate and Managerial Cultures." In C. L. Cooper (ed.), *Behavioral Problems in Organizations.* Englewood Cliffs, NJ: Prentice Hall.

Ott, J. S. (1989). *The Organizational Culture Perspective.* Chicago: Dorsey Press.

Ouchi, W. G. (1981). *Theory Z.* Reading, MA: Addison-Wesley.

Pascale, R. T.; & Athos, A.G. (1981). *The Art of Japanese Management.* New York: Simon & Schuster.

Peters, T. J.; & Waterman, R. H., Jr. (1982). *In Search of Excellence.* New York: Harper & Row.

Pettigrew, A. M. (1979). "On Studying Organizational Cultures." *Administrative Science Quarterly,* 24, 570–81.

Pondy, L. R.; Boland, R. J.; & Thomas, H. (1988). *Managing Ambiguity and Change.* New York: John Wiley & Sons.

Pondy, L. R.; Frost, P. J.; Morgan, G.; & Dandridge, T. C. (eds.). (1983). *Organizational Symbolism.* Greenwich, CT: JAI Press.

Rice, A.K. (1963). *The Enterprise and its Environment.* London: Tavistock.

Ritti, R. R.; & Funkhouser, G. R. (1987). *The Ropes to Skip and the Ropes to Know* (3rd ed.). New York: John Wiley & Sons.

Roethlisberger, F. J.; & Dickson, W. J. (1939). *Management and the Worker.* Cambridge, MA: Harvard University Press.

Schall, M. S. (1983). "A Communication-Rules Approach to Organizational Culture." *Administrative Science Quarterly,* 28, 557–81.

Schein, E. H. (1965). *Organizational Psychology.* Englewood Cliffs, NJ: Prentice Hall.

Schein, E. H. (1968). "Organizational Socialization and the Profession of Management." *Industrial Management Review (MIT)* 9, 1–15.

Schein, E. H. (1969). *Process Consultation.* Reading, MA: Addison-Wesley.

Schein, E. H. (1978). *Career Dynamics.* Reading, MA: Addison-Wesley.

Schein, E. H. (1983). "The Role of the Founder in Creating Organizational Culture." *Organizational Dynamics* 12, 13–28.

Schein, E. H. (1985a). *Organizational Culture and Leadership.* San Francisco: Jossey-Bass.

Schein, E. H. (1985b). "Organizational Culture: Skill, Defense Mechanism or Addiction?" In F. R. Brush & J. B. Overmier (eds.), *Affect, Conditioning, and Cognition* (pp. 315–23). Hillsdale, NJ: Erlbaum.

Schein, E. H. (1987a). *The Clinical Perspective in Fieldwork.* Beverly Hills, CA: Sage.

Schein, E. H. (1987b). *Process Consultation* (Vol. 2). Reading, MA: Addison-Wesley.

Schein, E. H. (1988). *Process Consultation* (rev. ed.). Reading, MA: Addison-Wesley.

Schein, E. H.; & Bennis, W. G. (1965). *Personal and Organizational Change through Group Methods.* New York: John Wiley & Sons.

Schneider, B. (1975). "Organizational Climate: An Essay." *Personnel Psychology* 28, 447–79.

Schneider, B.; & Reichers, A. E. (1983). "On the Etiology of Climates." *Personnel Psychology* 36, 19–40.

Smircich, L.; & Calas, M. B. (1987). "Organizational Culture: A Critical Assessment." In F. M. Jablin, L. L. Putnam, K. H. Roberts, & L. W. Porter (eds.), *Handbook of Organizational Communication* (pp. 228–63). Beverly Hills, CA: Sage.

Tagiuri, R.; & Litwin, G. H. (eds.). (1968). *Organizational Climate: Exploration of a Concept.* Boston: Harvard Business School, Division of Research.

Trice, H.; & Beyer, J. (1984). "Studying Organizational Cultures through Rites and Ceremonials." *Academy of Management Review* 9, 653–69.

Trist, E. L.; Higgin, G. W.; Murray, H.; & Pollock, A. B. (1963). *Organizational Choice.* London: Tavistock.

Van Maanen, J. (1976). "Breaking in: Socialization to Work." In R. Dubin (ed.), *Handbook of Work, Organization and Society* (pp. 67–130). Chicago: Rand McNally.

Van Maanen, J. (1977). "Experiencing Organizations." In J. Van Maanen (ed.), *Organizational Careers: Some New Perspectives* (pp. 15–45). New York: John Wiley & Sons.

Van Maanen, J. (1978). "People Processing: Strategies of Organizational Socialization." *Organizational Dynamics,* 7, 18–36.

Van Maanen, J. (1984). "Occupational Communities: Culture and Control in Organizations." In B. M. Staw & L. L. Cummings (eds.), *Research in Organizational Behavior* (Vol. 6). Greenwich, CT: JAI Press.

Van Maanen, J. (1988). *Tales of the Field.* Chicago: University of Chicago Press.

Van Maanen, J.; & Schein, E. H. (1979). "Toward a Theory of Organizational Socializations." In B. M. Staw & L. L. Cummings (eds.), *Research in Organizational Behavior* (Vol. 1, pp. 204–64). Greenwich, CT: JAI Press.

Walton, R. (1987). *Innovating to Compete.* San Francisco: Jossey-Bass.

Werner, H. (1940). *Comparative Psychology of Mental Development.* New York: Follett.

Westney, D. E. (1987). *Imitation and Innovation.* Cambridge, MA: Harvard University Press.

Wilkins, A. L. (1983). "Organizational Stories as Symbols Which Control the Organizations." In L. R. Pondy, P. J. Frost, G. Morgan, & T. C. Dandridge (eds.), *Organizational Symbolism* (pp. 81–91). Greenwich, CT: JAI Press.

Wilkins, A. L.; & Ouchi, W. G. (1983). "Efficient Cultures: Exploring the Relationship between Culture and Organizational Performance." *Administrative Science Quarterly* 28, 468–81.

Sociotechnical System Principles and Guidelines: Past and Present

William M. Fox

The sociotechnical systems (STS) approach is devoted to the effective blending of both the technical and social systems of an organization. These two aspects must be considered interdependently, because arrangements that are optimal for one may not be optimal for the other and trade-offs are often required. Thus, for effective organization design, there is need for both dual focus and joint optimization. This article traces the development of STS from the presentation of its first principles by Eric Trist, its leading founder, who was guided by earlier systems thinking, research on participation, and the action research work of Kurt Lewin, to the present, including discussion of adaptations and refinements that have enhanced its applicability to nonmanufacturing organizations. The approach has more relevance today than ever before, as organizational personnel seek more fruitful means of empowerment and as their organizations strive for greater productivity and viability in increasingly turbulent environments.

In 1946, the newly nationalized British coal industry was doing poorly. Productivity had not increased sufficiently to compensate for increases in costly mechanization; labor disputes were frequent and absenteeism was running at about 20%, despite improvements in working conditions.

Ken Bamforth, a postgraduate Tavistock Institute Fellow and former coal miner, gained ready access for himself and one of the Institute's founders, Eric Trist, to observe a highly successful departure from current mining practice: The use of relatively autonomous work groups that interchanged roles and shifts and managed themselves with a minimum of supervision. They found that, in effect, the miners had "rediscovered" a successful, small-group approach that had been used before the advent of mechanization.

Further investigation suggested that most of the industry's problems had resulted from the introduction of significant changes in the technical aspects of production *without* adequate attention to their appropriateness for a particular physical environment or their impact on social structure and needs. Inadvertently, this type of oversight had been encouraged by the post-World War II human relations movement through its emphasis on personal and group development practices that largely shunned the technical aspects of work systems.

These findings provided a revelation for Trist; one that occurs rarely in a lifetime. He suddenly visualized a new paradigm of work: one that would effectively blend the requirements of *both* the technical and social systems. He then set about formulating the sociotechnical systems concept and approach, guided by earlier systems thinking, Lewin's ideas, and his own research. He first presented the new paradigm in 1950 to the British Psychological Society via a paper titled "The Relations of Social and Technical Systems in Coal-Mining" (Trist, 1981; E. L. Trist, personal communication, March 1988).[1]

Source: William M. Fox, "Sociotechnical System Principles and Guidelines: Past and Present" in *Journal of Applied Behavioral Science* (vol. 31, no. 1) pp. 91–105, copyright © 1995 by NTL Institute for Applied Behavioral Science. Reprinted by permission of Sage Publications, Inc.

In addition to Trist's continuing efforts, many others contributed to the subsequent development and refinement of sociotechnical theory and practice. Among them, Trist regards Fred Emery as his most noteworthy co-pioneer. He also cites Louis Davis, Philip Herbst, Cal Pava, A. K. Rice, Gerald Susman, Einar Thorsrud, Hans van Beinum, Richard Walton, and Marvin Weisbord as significant contributors (E. L. Trist, personal communication, March 1988).

Although there is no single, unequivocal set of sociotechnical principles and practices, I will consider those that most knowledgeable researchers and practitioners today agree are highly relevant to the approach. In addition, I will look at various ways in which this approach is being adapted to nonmanufacturing work environments.

Analysis Guidelines

Dual Focus on Two, Interdependent, Open Systems

The term *sociotechnical systems* (STS) reflects the goal of integrating the social requirements of people doing the work with the technical requirements needed to keep the work systems viable with regard to their environments. These two aspects must be considered interdependently, because arrangements that are optimal for one may not be optimal for the other, and trade-offs are often required. Thus there is a need for both *dual focus* and *joint optimization*.

To the extent that an organization is effective and efficient in creating and distributing products or services, it justifies the human, material, and informational resources that the environment provides. In order for it to survive and develop, the systems involved must remain open to, and interact constructively with, their environments.

The Technological System

This system comprises the materials, machines, territory, and processes used to convert inputs to outputs. It not only sets limits to what can be done, it creates demands that must be accommodated by the internal organization and by end objectives.

At any time, the technological system may be subject to stresses that arise in the external environment. The extent to which it can tolerate required input and output variations is largely a function of its flexibility. In turn, the quality of this flexibility is an important determiner of the self-regulating properties of the organization (Emery, 1959, pp. 4–5).

Among the important features of the technological system (based on Emery, 1959, pp. 9–15) are the following:

- The characteristics of the material being processed in terms of encouraging or discouraging uncontrollable variation in the labor requirements of the production process.

- The immediate physical work setting in terms of such factors as temperature, light, noise, dust or dirt, and orderliness. Does the setting create over- or understimulation? Are dysfunctional conditions reasonably avoidable?

- The spatio-temporal distribution of machines, workers, and processes. Are operations performed simultaneously or sequentially? On one shift or across several shifts? How are machines and workers physically dispersed? These factors will influence the ease with which interdependent activities can be supplied, informed, coordinated, and maintained.

- The level of mechanization or automation; that is, the contribution made by machines relative to workers in processing inputs into outputs. Changes in this dimension of technology will frequently negate other dimensions or enhance their criticalness.

- The grouping of unit operations (those that transform the material or product) into *production phases* to facilitate the identification of needed changes in coordination and in knowledge and skill demands.

- The identification of necessary as opposed to optional operations and the extent to which these operations demand attention, effort, and/or special skill.

• The nature and placement of repair and maintenance operations that will most economically reduce downtime.

• The nature of supply operations that can maintain planned rates of production in the face of unplanned variations in the transfer of materials from and to the external environment.

The Social System

The social structure—comprising occupational roles—has, to a large extent, been created and institutionalized by the operation of the technological system (Trist & Bamforth, 1951, p. 5).

Among the important features of the social system (based on Emery, 1959, pp. 16, 19–21; Trist, 1971; Trist, 1981, p. 23; Trist & Bamforth, 1951, pp. 14–15) are the following:

• Whether work roles are organized so that workers are cooperative rather than competitive with each other.

• Whether work roles are organized so that workers view an end result as their responsibility or as someone else's responsibility.

• Whether workers are made jointly responsible for how supportive services and implements are delivered or are provided separately and unilaterally to each worker.

• The extent to which *key variances* (those that significantly affect the quantity or quality or operating cost or social cost of production) are imported or exported across the social system boundary rather than being controlled by the workers, supervisors, and managers directly concerned.

• The possibilities for complex and simultaneous interdependencies among the workers to provide for task accomplishment in less time and for continuity in the face of individual failure.

• How each worker's role is experienced; not only in terms of its inherent attractiveness but also in terms of perceptions of dependence, pay equity, subordination, self worth, trust, constraining factors, and isolation with regard to others.

• The extent to which task interdependencies are coordinated in terms of the social relations that are required by the task rather than in terms of social relations that develop for other reasons (such as friendship).

• The presence of personal worker goals and task interdependencies that are threatened by, or are not adequately handled by, formal organizational provisions. The presence of formal overspecification as well as underspecification.

Emery (1987) observes that the critical dimensions of work organization have to do with control and coordination:

> In any work setting, regardless of the technology, the requirements for control and coordination can be determined and then there is, in practically every instance, a choice open to management about how much of that control and coordination is left to the people actually performing the activities. . . . In 1974 we were able to demonstrate in some detail that this same "organizational choice" exists even in the design of maximum security prisons. (p. 4)

With regard to this choice, Emery describes experimentation with an unusual form of worker participation: The owner-manager of a plant in Melbourne, Australia, invited some 40 employees to manage the plant. The workers (for the most part, highly skilled machinists) decided to rotate service on a managing committee by periodically drawing names from a hat, rather than by election. Subsequently, two other Australian plants tried this idea of rotating membership on joint labor-management planning committees through the drawing of lots.

Apparently, these three "experiments" were quite successful. Both management and the workers decided that this was the most effective way to sensitize all workers to the problems and dynamics of running the plants (Emery, 1987, p. 6).

As noted by Trist (1981),

The technical and social systems are *independent* of each other in the sense that the former follows the laws of the natural sciences while the latter follows the laws of the human sciences and is a purposeful system. Yet they are *correlative* in that one requires the other for the *transformation* of an input into an output, which comprises the functional task of a work system (p. 24)

In some organizations, such as regulative ones, the sociotechnical aspects have secondary instrumentality: They are primarily concerned with instilling, changing, or maintaining values. Those aspects that are primarily sociotechnical are directly dependent on material means for their outputs.

The technical and social systems may spontaneously reorganize to become more or less heterogeneous and complex and achieve a steady state at an operable level. They possess the characteristic of *equi-finality:* the ability to achieve a steady state from different initial conditions and in different ways. This is a concept from systems theory. Typically, these systems grow by processes of internal elaboration. Because both are open systems that interact with external environments, management is confronted with managing both internal systems and external environments (see Bertalanffy, 1950; Emery, 1959, pp. 3, 6; Herbst, 1954; Trist, 1981, pp. 11–12).

Three Levels of Analysis

Drawing further from systems theory, sociotechnical systems design activity is based on three levels of analysis (Trist, 1981, pp. 6, 11).

The Primary Work System

This system is associated with a whole and meaningful piece of work; a set of activities that make up a functioning whole in an identifiable and bounded subsystem of an organization. It may comprise one or several face-to-face groups, along with support, specialist, and management-representative personnel and relevant equipment and resources. The system can provide reliable information to the group as to the adequacy of performance.

The most satisfying and efficient primary work system comprises the smallest number of people that can perform a whole task while satisfying the social and psychological needs of system members as well as the performance requirements of the organization (see Hackman & Oldham, 1980, pp. 171–172; Rice, 1958, p. 36; Trist, 1981, p. 24).

The Whole Organization System

This system comprises plants or equivalent, self-standing workplaces; an entire corporation or public agency.

The Macrosocial System

This system comprises multiple organizational systems in community and industrial sectors; it could be an institution operating at the overall level of a society.

The target system, and the adjoining systems, should be considered in the context of the organization's *general management system* with regard to the impact of policies or development plans. A key reason for the failure of a primary, new-design work group is lack of support in the surrounding organizational milieu.

At the organization level, the social system is considered in terms of the functions of governing as well as those of production and servicing. Relations among top managers provide the strategic solidarity for the organization.

It is at this level that goals must be set that appropriately reflect organizational capabilities in conjunction with the demands of the external environment. And only at this level do managers have the potential power for aligning the organization's structural arrangements and values.

As a corollary of this, the success of human resources management as an integrating function is dependent on top-management solidarity.

The solidarity of both workers and management is prerequisite to a high level of solidarity in the organization as a whole. The communication of purpose, knowledge, requests, and values among organizational members plays a critical role in the development of shared objectives, norms, and feelings of belonging that underlie loyalty and commitment to common cause (based on Ancona, 1989; O'Reilly & Flatt, 1989; Rice & Trist, 1952; Trist, 1981, p. 35; Tushman, Virany, & Romanelli, 1989; Wilson, 1957).

With regard to the macrosocial system, Trist asserts that a different larger environment has evolved: "The new environment is called *the turbulent field* in which large competing organizations, all acting independently in diverse directions, produce unanticipated and dissonant consequences" (1981, p. 39).

He suggests that organizations can best adapt to this environmental turbulence by identifying shared ideals to guide them in fashioning new objectives and their related goals.

Other Principles and Practices

- The design of a work system should use an *action research* approach, an approach that was contributed to systems theory by Kurt Lewin. It entails collaborative analysis, design, and implementation by those directly concerned— workers, supervisors, and specialists—in seeking the *dual optimization* of the needs of the technological and the social systems (see Trist, 1981, p. 10).

Trist underscores the importance of this never-ending design objective of dual optimization:

> Attempts to optimize for either the technical or social system alone will result in the suboptimization of the socio-technical whole. . . . The distinctive characteristics of each must be respected else their *contradictions* will intrude and their *complementarities* will remain unrealized. (1981, p. 24)

With regard to Trist's concern about contradictions, Campion and Thayer (1985) found that satisfaction of *only* the motivational aspects of the social system (as embodied in the Hackman and Oldham Job Characteristics Theory, 1980) can significantly decrease efficiency and reliability

while providing an expected increase in worker satisfaction.

- In designing a work system, comply with the principle of *redundancy of functions* (proliferation of functions within the work group— multiskilling the individual) rather than the traditional principle of *redundancy of parts* (proliferation of individuals performing the same specific function) to provide for flexibility, innovative potential, adaptation to rapid change, and enhanced worker satisfaction (based on Emery, 1967).

- There should be adherence to the principle of minimum critical specifications: Give the design team for a lower level sociotechnical system only the larger system requirements (boundary conditions) that they must work within, leaving as many design decisions as possible to those closest to the work (based on Herbst, 1974).

- An important consideration is the optimal length of the work cycle (one study suggests a range of 1 to 1½ hours) (see Trist, 1981, p. 31).

- Work roles associated with interdependent tasks should be defined so as to enhance mutual support. The tasks should be so organized or rewarded so as to facilitate the identification of part-tasks with the whole.

- In a stable sociotechnical system, knowledge that is relevant to cooperative performance under varying circumstances should be incorporated in the role system. Then, knowledge of the role system can inform a worker of what to expect of others and of what will be expected of him or her.

- Knowledge of the role system and prevention of harmful misperceptions are facilitated by role rotation, and role rotation is facilitated by the use of a multiskill/skill-based pay system.

- A self-managing group that has some scope for setting standards and ongoing goals, has some responsibility for auxiliary and preparatory tasks, and is characterized by a wide sharing of the skills needed for its tasks is more likely than a traditional group to

—provide group members with optimal arousal and feelings of "being in control"

—induce group members to set goals and to strive toward group objectives

—produce superior results and group-member satisfaction (as the result of more key variances being controlled by the group)

—adapt well to unexpected conditions and provide a higher degree of continuity in performance (such a group being a learning system that extends its "decision space" as its capabilities increase) (based on Emery, 1959, pp. 24–26, 50; Trist, 1981, p. 34).

In view of the developmental dynamics embodied in the material presented above, the organization must provide opportunities for individual advancement and employment security (so that workers do not perceive that they are being "dead-ended" or that they are being invited to work themselves out of a job). We see, also, that the *sharing of power* is a generic feature of sociotechnical systems.

In this regard, Trist feels that, at some point, *gainsharing*—sharing the added material fruits made possible by the developing partnership between workers and managers—is necessary to prevent perceptions of inequity on the part of the workers. He regards this as one of the requirements of sound, sociotechnical systems design (E. L. Trist, personal communication, March 1988).

In some installations, an elected team leader who works alongside his or her teammates is given responsibility for facilitating group self-management, training group members, and procuring needed materials, equipment, and support services.

In addition, a coordinator may be appointed by management to assist the group (or groups) and provide liaison with other groups. Based on their field study, Manz and Sims (1987) report that the coordinator's most important contribution to the group resides in encouraging the following: self-reinforcement, self-observation/evaluation, self-

expectation, rehearsal, and goal setting (see also Trist, 1981, p. 31; Weisbord, 1987, p. 334).

When only one supervisory position is used, there must be a shift away from traditional management to a greater focus on the management of boundary relationships and the provision of coaching and support to the group toward the enhancement of its self-management.

The following table provides a dramatic contrast of sociotechnical concepts with traditional concepts.

Steps in Data Collection and Analysis

Taylor, Gustavson, and Carter (1986) observe that much of the success of the sociotechnical model is due to its reliance upon a structured process, as outlined below, for analyzing and implementing operational improvements.

Systems Scan

The first phase of a *systems scan* is grounded in the following types of questions: What is the organization's mission (What values does it create and distribute to justify itself)? What managerial philosophy and organizational values underlie this mission? What relationships does the organization have with various stakeholders and the larger environment?

The next phase relates to reconciling agreement about what is and what is likely to be with agreement about what is most desired by organizational stakeholders and at the same time is viable with regard to the outside environment.

The *search conference* provides a useful means for implementing these phases of a systems scan. It was originated by Trist and Emery in 1959 (Weisbord, 1987, p. 282; see also Morley & Trist, 1981). Meaningful mission and philosophy statements are products of this activity.

The next phase of the systems scan has to do with determining existing inputs, outputs, and system boundaries—both physical and technological. The purpose is to identify problems, needs, and opportunities for improvement.

TABLE 1   **Comparison of the Sociotechnical Model with the Traditional Model**

Old	New
Technology first	Joint optimization of social-technical systems
People as extensions of machines	People as complements to machines
People as expendable spare parts	People as a resource to be developed
Maximum task breakdown, simple, narrow skills	Optimal task grouping, multiple, broad skills
External controls: procedures, supervisors, specialist staffs	Internal controls: self-regulating subsystems
More organization levels, autocratic style: unilateral goal setting, assignment of workers	Fewer levels, participative style: bilateral goal setting, selection of workers
Competitive gamesmanship	Collaboration, collegiality
Organization's purposes only (often with poor understanding/acceptance at lower levels)	Members' and society's purposes also (with good understanding/acceptance at lower levels): shared vision and philosophy
Frequent alienation: "It's only a job"	Commitment: "It's *my* job, group, and organization"
Tendency toward low risk taking, maladaptation	Tendency toward innovation, adaptation
Less individual development opportunity and employment security	More individual development opportunity and employment security

Based on Trist (1981).

Technical Analysis

Sociotechnical analysis defines technology in terms of inputs and outputs, rather than by tools, processes, or techniques. When input and output boundaries are defined, unit operations can be determined (the output of each unit operation being the physical or informational transformation of input).

This approach assures that technical systems will be analyzed apart from the jobs and work of people, and apart from supervisory systems and other control systems. A *unit-operations flow chart* is a product of this activity, and one of the issues explored is a possible reduction in the number of unit operations.

Next, all product variances—other than those representing human error or breakdowns in the technical process itself—are recorded for each unit operation. The *key variances*—those that have an impact most importantly on quantity, quality, or costs—are identified through the construction of a *key-variance matrix table*.

Then, through the preparation of a *table of variance control,* key variances are examined to determine the manner in which they are controlled—by whom, through what actions, and with what information. Are they controlled where they arise, by appropriate personnel, and in a timely, effective, and efficient manner?

Social Analysis

A foremost concern of social analysis is called *focal-role analysis:* determination of the role expectations and work-related interactions of those in positions most involved with the control of key variances. This kind of analysis entails mapping patterns of cooperation and coordination among those with focal roles and others within and outside the work process.

Another aspect of social analysis involves examination of the relationships among the work-related interactions of focal persons and four "survival criteria:" sound key-variance control, adaptation to the external environment, integration of in-system people activities, and long-term development.

This examination is aided by construction of a *grid of social relations*. Then, with data from this social grid, focal-role interactions can be mapped in a *focal-role network* that indicates their frequency, direction of contact, and function served.

Quality-of-Working-Life Considerations

Through the use of action research, organizational members and other stakeholders influence design solutions through their participation in the analyses described above about organizational mission, management philosophy, organizational values, and the design (or redesign) of work systems. As far as is feasible, their preferences are accommodated. In addition, the nature and rate of transitional activities to implement a new design reflect both individual and group training and development needs.

Ideally, the sociotechnical systems design process should be iterative or never ending. The question "How can we improve upon the way we operate?" should always remain open. To a large extent, maintenance of this *action-research-based process* is more important than any given design solution.[2]

Limitations and New Directions

The STS concepts presented above have ably guided improvements in the design and redesign of many work systems, both here and abroad. However, most of this successful experience has been with well-defined linear systems rather than with the growing number of ill-defined, nonlinear systems that are characterized by entwined (and often-iterative) multiple-conversion processes.

Well-defined linear systems are characterized by programmed tasks that adhere to a sequential conversion process of "input" to "output." The absence of this property in nonlinear systems makes it difficult to separate different conversion flows into well-bounded entities through the use of such tools as the variance matrix (Pava, 1986, pp. 204–205).

Another property of some nonlinear systems is the absence of an explicit input point. Taylor (1990) describes this aspect with regard to professional work in a nonroutine system: "The throughput is accumulated knowledge and persuasive argument. This throughput has no concrete starting point . . . in contrast to other intangible delivery systems, such as service systems, which have requests as inputs" (p. 11).

In addition to this qualification about the use of the matrix, another is presented by Sitter and Hertog (1990). They point out that redesign should not be based on *current* matrix data, but rather upon insight about the quantity and quality of variance in a future approach that takes into account emergent opportunities for improved variance control.

> The designers' goal should be to design an architecture of structure sustaining and reinforcing the development of interactive relationships which support and reinforce each other with respect to all functional requirements such as flexibility, delivery time, throughput time, product quality, innovative capacity, pollution control, quality of work and industrial relations. (p. 8)

On the other hand, Pava (1986, p. 205) discusses how charting independencies in a variance matrix can reveal whether there will be a sufficiently distinct clustering of variances to guide the partitioning of the work system. When used this way, the variance matrix serves as a diagnostic tool for determining the extent of the nonlinear nature of the system.

In addition to Pava (1986), others—such as Sitter and Hertog (1990), and Taylor (1986)—stress the need for increased research to broaden the applicability of STS design concepts. They decry the tendency of some STS consultants who treat the use of self-managing or autonomous groups as a "standard solution" for all occasions rather than as a carefully arrived at design choice based on an organization's special characteristics.

In addressing this standard solution mistake, Pava (1986) notes:

> Many professionals doing nonroutine tasks are extensively trained specialists . . . all their expectations about work activities, career advancement, and reward emphasize individual contributions. . . . Because specialization is extreme and not highly transferable, shared skills are less likely to be a source of cohesion, making autonomous work groups an impractical solution (pp. 205–206).

New Approaches to Technical/Social Analysis

For complex, nonlinear situations, Pava (1986, pp. 206–208) suggests an additional type of analysis: determination of the quality of interpersonal and group "deliberations" (encounters, meetings, personal reflections) about problematic issues facing the organization. He conceptualizes "discretionary coalitions" of people associated with the various deliberations, and the determination of a "role network" of persons for each issue. Such analysis includes determining the incidence and locus of informed trade-offs—as well as barriers to such trade-offs—and the absence of ritual posturing and arbitrary battles.

Pava sees the technique of "blockmodeling" as a promising analytical tool for guiding these determinations (see 1986, pp. 206–208). He points out that such analysis can set the stage for change agents to

> acknowledge and charter major deliberations . . . delineate responsibility within each coalition . . . and identify technical enhancements . . . that assist discretionary coalitions engaged in major deliberations. . . . In linear work systems, this emergent configuration has been designated the autonomous work group organization. In nonlinear work systems, this new template is a *recticular organization,* which is characterized by a fluid distribution of information and authority that shifts as required (Pava, 1986, pp. 208–209).

Another innovation, the integration of *cause maps* and *social network analysis* to produce a *juxtaposition matrix,* has been developed by Nelson and Mathews (1991). They point out that the former two are useful for operationalizing the concepts of organizational complexity and structure in a concrete, practical manner and that the latter matrix can identify where we may expect interdependence in an organization to be highest. Also, they point out that the matrix should be useful for estimating new-design effects.

To increase efficiency and effectiveness, Sitter and Hertog (1990) discuss the design strategy of *reducing required variation* (while increasing op-

tions for process variations through such means as flexible automation, integrated tasks, and multiskilled personnel). As a means for doing this, they propose *deconcentrating structure* by a first step they call *parallelization:* splitting the production system into subsystems. This causes an exponential reduction in the input complexity of a system and thus a reduction in the amplifying effects of variations in the system.

The next step they propose is the selective clustering of performance operations in these parallel flows or subsystems into segments with a minimum of interfaces, to reduce internal variation further. They call this step *segmentation.* The performance functions to be clustered are those with a maximum of mutual interdependence.

As the above measures reduce variety, they reduce the need for control, because it is variety that creates this need. This is why the design of production structures should precede the design of control structures and should be done top down, and the allocation of control activity should be done bottom up. In summary, "debureaucratization" involves moving from complex structures comprising simple tasks to simple structures comprising complex tasks (Sitter & Hertog, 1990, pp. 12–16, 19).

Last, in their report on contemporary STS design modeling in the Netherlands, van Eijnatten, Hoevenaars, and Rutte (1992) discuss a multilevel method of integrating task design and organization design.

Current Research Sites

Research on the adaptation and further development of STS concepts and practices is being pursued by various organizations and research centers. Among the organizations in North America are Alcan, the American Productivity Center in Houston, AT&T, Best Foods, Clark Equipment, Cummins Engine, Digital Equipment Company, Exxon, Ford, General Foods, General Motors, Harman International, Hewlett Packard, Inland Steel, LTV Steel, Mead Paper, Proctor and Gamble, Shell Oil, Sherwin-Williams, Tektronix, TRW, Weyerhaeuser, the Work in America Institute in New York, Xerox, Zilog, and various U.S. and Canadian government agencies, such as the Total Quality Management program of the U.S. Defense Department.

Among the organizations abroad that are conducting research are the Dutch Maastricht Economic Research Institute on Innovation and Technology (MERIT), the more than 100 companies and public institutions that are involved in the Swedish Work Environment Fund's LOM program, and the Work Research Institute in Oslo, Norway.

Campus researchers are now active at Case Western Reserve University, Cornell, the Fielding Institute, and the University of Toronto, as well as Pennsylvania State University's Harrisburg campus Center for Managing Technology and Organizational Change, Sonoma State University's Center for Studies on Human Dignity in Organizations, Texas Technological University's Center for Productivity and QWL, the University of California at Los Angeles's Center for Quality of Working Life, the University of Indiana's Center for Quality and Productivity Improvement, the University of Michigan's National Quality of Work Center, and the University of Southern California's Center for Effective Organizations (Cummings & Huse, 1989, pp. 264–270; Engelstad, 1990, p. 8; Sitter & Hertog, 1990, p. 5; Taylor, 1990, pp. 4–12; J. C. Taylor, personal communication, November 1990).

Conclusion

Initially, sociotechnical principles and practices were developed for, and were applied to, routine, linear work systems. Consequently, they were less useful for dealing with the nonroutine office work of managers and professionals.

For example, the absence of an explicit input point, and/or the absence of a clear-cut input to output conversion system, makes it difficult to separate different conversion flows into well-bounded entities through the use of the *variance matrix*. However, as Pava points out, the matrix can still be a useful diagnostic tool for determining the nonlinear nature of the system.

In addition, Pava (1986, pp. 205–206) qualifies the use of the sociotech principle of redundancy of functions (the multiskilling of individuals). He points out that it is less applicable to professional personnel in that their in-depth areas of specialization are not readily diffused in a group. In fact, at times the traditional principle of redundancy of parts (proliferation of individuals) may be preferable as a means of enhancing an organization's innovative potential.

Also, the creation of a recticular organization (characterized by a fluid distribution of information and authority that changes as required) may be more appropriate than the use of the STS autonomous work group in some nonlinear work systems. Still, Cohen and Ledford (1994) and Teram (1991) report that self-managing groups are more effective than traditionally managed groups in a variety of nonmanufacturing work settings.

Clearly, a major revolution is not required to broaden the applicability of STS principles. Pava (1986) observes that

> modifying the practices employed in STS design to include nonlinear work systems is consistent with the essential precepts of STS design: open systems analysis, a best match of social and technical subsystems, redundant function over redundant parts, systemic interrelationships between design factors, self-design, and minimum critical specifications. (p. 211)

In fact, such broadening has already occurred. Taylor (1990, pp. 10, 13) reports more than 28 currently operative STS designs or redesigns in the United States for noncontinuous process technologies such as dimensional manufacturing work, transaction processing work, service work, nonroutine work, and professional work.

Today, as organizational personnel seek more fruitful means of empowerment and their organizations strive for greater productivity and viability in increasingly turbulent environments, we may well conclude that the STS movement—given its fundamental strengths and demonstrated adaptability—has more relevance than ever before.

Endnotes

1. As a matter of interest, the validity of STS principles for coal mining was reaffirmed by Winterton (1994).
2. This whole section on data collection and analysis has drawn heavily upon the presentation by Taylor, Gustavson, and Carter (1986, pp. 158–163).

References

Ancona, D. G. (1989, August 13–16). *Top management teams: Preparing for the revolution.* Paper presented at the annual meetings of the Academy of Management, Washington, DC.

Bertalanffy, L. (1950). The theory of open systems in physics and biology. *Science, 3,* 23–29.

Campion, M. A., & Thayer, P.W. (1985). Development and field evaluation of an interdisciplinary measure of job design. *Journal of Applied Psychology, 70,* 29–43.

Cohen, S.G., & Ledford, G. E., Jr. (1994). The effectiveness of self-managing teams: A quasi-experiment. *Human Relations, 47,* 13–43.

Cummings, T. G., & Huse, E. F. (1989). *Organizational development and change.* New York: West.

Emery, F. E. (1959). *Characteristics of socio-technical systems* (Document No. 527). London: Tavistock Institute of Human Relations.

Emery, F. E. (1967). The next thirty years: Concepts, methods and anticipations. *Human Relations, 20,* 199–237.

Emery, F. E. (1987, June 15–19). *Paper No. 24.* Paper presented at Einar Thorsrud memorial symposium and workshop: Strategies for work and learning—1999. Work Research Institute, Oslo, Norway.

Engelstad, P. H. (1990, August 12–15). *The evolution of network strategies in action research supported socio-technical redesign programs in Scandinavia.* Symposium presentation at Academy of Management meetings, San Francisco.

Hackman, J. R. & Oldham, G. R. (1980). *Work redesign.* Menlo Park, CA: Addison-Wesley.

Herbst, P. G. (1954). The analyses of social flow systems. *Human Relations, 7,* 327–336.

Herbst, P. G. (1974). *Socio-technical design.* London: Tavistock Institute of Human Relations.

Manz, C. C., & Sims, H. P. (1987). Leading workers to lead themselves: The external leadership of self-managing work teams. *Administrative Science Quarterly, 32,* 106–128.

Morley, D., & Trist, E. (1981). *Children: Our number one resource, a report on the Saskatchewan search conference on day care.* Unpublished manuscript, York University, Faculty of Environmental Studies, Toronto.

Nelson, R. E., & Mathews, K. M. (1991). Cause maps and social network analysis in organizational diagnosis. *Journal of Applied Behavioral Science, 27,* 379–397.

O'Reilly, C. A., & Flatt S. (1989, August 13–16). *Executive team demography, organizational innovation, and firm performance.* Paper presented at the annual meetings of the Academy of Management, Washington, DC.

Pava, C. (1986). Redesigning sociotechnical systems design: Concepts and methods for the 1990s. *Journal of Applied Behavioral Science, 22,* 201–221.

Rice, A. K. (1958). *Productivity and social organization: The Ahmedabad experiment.* London: Tavistock Institute of Human Relations.

Rice, A. K., & Trist, E. L. (1952). Institutional and subinstitutional determinants of change in labour turnover. *Human Relations, 5,* 347–372.

Sitter, L. U. de, & Hertog, J. F. de. (1990, August 12–15). *Simple organizations, complex jobs: The Dutch sociotechnical approach.* Paper presented at the annual meetings of the Academy of Management, San Francisco.

Taylor, J. C. (1986). Long-term sociotechnical systems change in a computer operations department. *Journal of Applied Behavioral Science, 22,* 303–313.

Taylor, J. C. (1990, August 12–15). *Two decades of sociotechnical systems in North America.* Symposium paper presented at the annual meetings of the Academy of Management, San Francisco.

Taylor, J. C., Gustavson, P., & Carter, W. (1986). Integrating the social and technical systems of organizations. In D. D. Davis and Associates (Eds.), *Managing technological innovation* (pp. 154–186). San Francisco: Jossey-Bass.

Teram, E. (1991). Interdisciplinary teams and the control of clients: A sociotechnical perspective. *Human Relations, 44,* 343–356.

Trist, E. L. (1971). Critique of scientific management in terms of socio-technical theory. *Prakseologia, 39–40,* 159–174.

Trist, E. L. (1981). *The evolution of socio-technical systems: A conceptual framework and action research program* (Occasional paper No. 2). Ontario, Canada: Ontario Quality of Working Life Centre.

Trist, E. L. & Bamforth, K. (1951). Social and psychological consequences of longwall coal mining. *Human Relations, 4,* 3–38.

Tushman, M. L., Virany, B., & Romanelli, E. (1989, August 13–16). *Effects of CEO and executive team succession on subsequent organization performance.* Paper presented at the annual meetings of the Academy of Management, Washington, DC.

van Eijnatten, F. M., Hoevenaars, A. M., & Rutte, C. G. (1992). Holistic and participative (re)design: Contemporary STSD modeling in the Netherlands. In Dian M. Hosking & N. Anderson (Eds.), *Organiza-tional change and innovation: Psychological perspectives and practices in Europe* (pp. 187–207). London: Routledge.

Weisbord, M. R. (1987). *Productive workplaces: Organizing for dignity, meaning, and community.* San Francisco: Jossey-Bass.

Wilson, A. T. (1957). *General management and the personnel function: Research report to Unilever, Ltd.* London: Tavistock Institute of Human Relations.

Winterton, J. (1994). Social and technological characteristics of coal face work: A temporal and spatial analysis. *Human Relations, 47,* 89–118.

Fundamental Interventions

Part 3 is central to this volume because it includes fairly detailed descriptions of many interventions that tend to be widely used in contemporary OD practice. Techniques for use in team building, intergroup activities, survey feedback, and other interventions are described. Although diagnostic activities underlie all of these interventions, diagnosis is so fundamental that additional attention is paid to it.

The introduction to Part 3 first defines intervention, then looks at different ways of classifying interventions, and then looks at diagnosis as a special, but pervasive, kind of intervention in OD. A brief comment on each of the essays then follows.

A Definition of *Intervention*

Argyris defines *intervention* as follows: "To intervene is to enter into an ongoing system of relationship, to come between or among persons, groups, or objects for the purpose of helping them."[1] More specifically related to OD, the term OD *interventions* refers to the range of planned, programmatic activities clients and consultants participate in during the course of an organization development program. Largely these are diagnostic and problem-solving activities that ordinarily occur with the assistance of a consultant who is not a regular member of the particular system or subsystem culture. However, many of the activities typically become absorbed by the client system as the process unfolds.

Classifications of OD Interventions

There are a number of ways of classifying OD interventions, depending on the dimensions one wishes to emphasize.[2] Several classification methods are based on the *type of causal mechanism* hypothesized to underlie the particular technique used.

For example, feedback, which refers to receiving new data about oneself, others, or group dynamics, is assumed to have potential for constructive change if it is not too threatening. Techniques for providing more *awareness of changing organizational norms* are assumed to result in modification of behavior, attitudes, and values. *Increased interaction* and communication may effect changes in attitudes and behavior. Homans, for example, suggests that increased interaction leads to positive sentiments,[3] and Murphy refers to "tunnel vision" or "autism," which develops in individuals and groups in isolation.[4] *Confrontation,* a surfacing and addressing of differences in perceptions, values, attitudes, feelings, or norms, is assumed to help remove obstacles to effective interaction if handled in constructive ways. *Education* is designed to upgrade (1) knowledge and concepts, (2) out-moded beliefs and attitudes, or (3) skills and has long been accepted as a change mechanism.

Depth of intervention is another useful dimension for classifying interventions. In an essay by Roger Harrison that appears in Part 5, interventions can be distinguished in terms of the accessibility of the data and the degree of individuality or self-exposure involved. For example, we see a family T-group involving a work group and formal leader ("family" group) as a deeper intervention than a task-oriented team-building (problem-solving) workshop with such a group. The use of collages describing where team members see their unit going may be a deeper intervention than an interview that includes general questions about how things are going in the unit.

A different approach to classifying OD interventions is provided by Robert Blake and Jane Mouton when they list the major interventions in terms of their underlying causal mechanisms.[5] They describe the following kinds of interventions: (1) a *discrepancy intervention,* which calls attention to a contradiction in action or attitudes that then leads to exploration; (2) a *theory intervention,* in which behavioral science knowledge and theory are used to explain present behavior and assumptions underlying the behavior; (3) a *procedural intervention,* which represents a critiquing of how something is being done to determine whether the best methods are being used; (4) a *relationship intervention,* which focuses attention on interpersonal relations (particularly ones where there are strong negative feelings) and surfaces the issues for exploration and possible resolution; (5) an *experimentation intervention,* in which two different action plans are tested for their consequences before final decision on one is made; (6) a *dilemma intervention,* in which an imposed or emergent dilemma is used to force close examination of the possible choices involved and the assumptions underlying them; (7) a *perspective intervention,* which draws attention away from immediate actions and demands and allows a look at historical background, context, and future objectives in order to assess whether or not the actions are still on target; (8) an *organization structure intervention,* which calls for examination and evaluation of structural causes for organizational ineffectiveness; and (9) a *cultural intervention,* which examines traditions, precedents, and practices—the fabric of the organization's culture—in a direct, focused approach.

These are largely process consultation interventions, and they tend to occur within the context of a broader intervention, such as team building or in intergroup activities.

The *time and comprehensiveness* involved in the intervention can be another way of distinguishing between interventions. Some interventions, such as the use of a simple questionnaire, may take only minutes; others, such as the role analysis process (called "Operation KPE" in the Dayal and Thomas article) may take two hours relative to one job incumbent. Team building of different varieties may be an intervention taking place over one to three or more days and will include within it a variety of brief interventions. It should be added that successful interventions will probably always have a broader context; even the simplest of interventions needs to occur in the setting of some prework, which serves to make the intervention acceptable to the client, and needs follow-up to maximize the odds of success.

Another way of classifying OD interventions might be in terms of the emphasis on *task* versus *process*. Some team-building activities, for example, may have a high focus on interpersonal and group processes, such as the quality of communications or the dynamics of informal leadership and influence processes occurring in the group. Other activities might have a more task-related orientation, such as goal setting or the reallocating of responsibilities. This dichotomy of task and process can be somewhat misleading, however, because they are highly interrelated.

Finally, another way of classifying OD interventions is in terms of the *size and complexity of the client group*. For example, the client group may consist of *(a) individuals, (b) dyads or triads, (c) a self-managed team, (d) an intact work team,* including the formal leader, *(e) intergroup configurations* (two or more interfacing units), *(f) all of the managers of an organization,* or *(g) everybody in the total organization.* As we move from interventions with individuals, to dyads, to groups, to intergroups and then to the total organization, the interdependencies and the number of dimensions to be concerned about obviously increases. For example, an intervention that is successful in dealing with two groups in conflict must also successfully deal with the intragroup communications problems and conflict that become manifest. That is one reason it is usually a wise step to help teams deal with internal problems and increase their interpersonal and group skills before undertaking intergroup activities.

A simple classification scheme based on the size and complexity of the client group is shown in Figure 1. Some interventions appear in more than one category because they have utility with more than one type of client group. What the figure does not show are the many mini-interventions used by OD consultants within the context of broader interventions like team building or even within techniques used in team building (e.g., the role analysis technique)—that is, there are interventions within interventions within interventions. For example, this typology says nothing about the consultant's ability to point out a discrepancy, to provide support, to clarify,

FIGURE 1 Typology of Interventions Based on the Size and Complexity of the Client Group

Source: Modified from Wendell L. French and Cecil H. Bell, Jr., *Organization Development: Behavioral Science Interventions for Organization Improvement*, 6th ed. (Englewood Cliffs, NJ: Prentice Hall, 1999), chap. 8.

Client Group	Types of Interventions
Interventions designed to improve the effectiveness of *individuals* (although most are conducted in group settings).	Life and career-planning activities. Role analysis technique. Coaching and counseling. T-group (sensitivity training). Training to increase technical skills, relationship skills, group process skills, or decision-making, problem-solving, planning, goal-setting skills. Grid OD phase 1.* Transactional analysis. Behavior modeling.
Interventions designed to improve the effectiveness of *dyads/triads*.	Process consultation. Third-party peacemaking. Transactional analysis.
Interventions designed to improve the effectiveness of *teams and groups*.	Interviews or questionnaires. Team building. Responsibility charting. Survey feedback. Process consultation. Appreciations and concerns exercise. Role negotiation. Role analysis technique. Collages. Gestalt OD. "Start-up" team-building activities. Training in decision making, problem solving, planning, goal setting in group settings. Grid OD phase 2. Appreciative inquiry. Visioning.
Interventions designed to improve the effectiveness of *intergroup relations*.	Interviews or questionnaires. Intergroup activities. Organizational mirroring (three or more groups). Process consultation. Third-party peacemaking at group level. Grid OD phase 3. Survey feedback.
Interventions designed to improve the effectiveness of the *total organization*.	Interviews or questionnaires. Sensing. "Confrontation" meetings (Beckhard). Team building at all levels. Appreciative inquiry. Strategic planning activities. Grid OD phases 4, 5, 6. Survey feedback. OD strategy planning. Quality of work life programs. Total quality management programs. Future search conferences. Large scale system change interventions.

*For a discussion of the Managerial Grid® approach to OD, see Robert R. Blake and Jane Srygley Mouton, *Consultation* (Reading, MA: Addison-Wesley Publishing, 1976), chap. 27.

to use subgroups, or to have data made visible on newsprint, or, for that matter, to know when to use various interventions. (A number of these professional skills are discussed in Part 5.)

This classification scheme generally underlies the organization of Part 3. The first several essays are largely on team interventions. Part 3 then moves to intergroup interventions and then to more comprehensive interventions, such as the use of parallel learning structures and survey feedback.

Notes on Diagnosis

As will be evident in the essays that follow, diagnostic activities are pervasive aspects of the participant action research model that underlies most organization development interventions. Basically, to diagnose is to identify the underlying forces or conditions giving rise to the present state of affairs. Diagnosis may pertain broadly to the present state of a system, including the many positive forces giving rise to desirable outcomes; or it may be narrower in the sense of focusing on the dysfunctional forces that are producing undesirable outcomes, or it may focus on changes in the state of the system over time.

Three Types of Theories

As Ronald Lippitt has stated, "Every consultant has a cluster of ideas, or a set of concepts, which guide his perception of 'what exists' and 'what is going on' when he or she comes in contact with a particular group or organization." This *descriptive-analytic theory,* to whatever degree of refinement, assists the consultant in understanding and interpreting the complexities of group or organization functioning. Lippitt goes on to say that every consultant has, in addition, some form of *diagnostic theory* that assists in identifying symptoms of disturbances in the system and what some of the probable causes might be. A diagnostic theory, to Lippitt then, is a set of notions that relate more to the dysfunctional or anomalous aspects of organizational life than does descriptive analytic theory.[6] We might add that OD consultants also need some form of *change theory* that assists in understanding the consequences of the interaction of various forces over time. This would be congruent with Lippitt's ideas. Thus organizational diagnosis stems from some theoretical base, however partially or completely formulated.

An illustration of a descriptive analytic theory (perhaps combined with a diagnostic theory) is the theory underlying the "Survey of Organizations" questionnaire developed by the Institute for Social Research at the University of Michigan. The survey is based, as Taylor and Bowers describe, on a "metatheory of organizational system functioning" as presented by Rensis Likert and others in various writings. Part of the theory is represented by a model, which includes the notions of causal variables, intervening variables, and end-result variables. Questionnaire categories and items are related to these broader concepts and to the underlying theory.[7]

Dimensions to Consider in Diagnosis

In addition to the importance of the consultant having descriptive, analytic, and diagnostic theories, a number of other dimensions of diagnosis are important for the consultant to consider. A description of seven such dimensions follows.

Timing of the diagnostic activities is a significant dimension. For example, it is one thing to collect and analyze organizational climate data and then to develop a strategy for how to use it, but quite another to gather data about the perceived usefulness and timeliness of doing a climate survey in the first place. Much time, and therefore many resources, can be wasted if organizational participants are not prepared to work with the data.

Extent of participation is a key aspect of diagnosis. Who, in a preliminary way, decided that diagnosis should take place? Who decided how it should be done? Which people were systematically involved in supplying data, and further in analyzing and describing the dynamics revealed by the data? One person? Two people? The top team? The top team plus others? One or more people in conjunction with a consultant? All of the members of the system or subsystem? Customers of the system? One of the underlying assumptions in OD is the efficacy of participative problem identification and diagnosis in contrast to unilateral problem identification and diagnosis.

The dimension of *confidentiality,* or individual-anonymous versus group surfacing of data, has important facets. In the early stages of an OD effort, when trust between group members may be low and their feedback skills inadequate, the situation may call for individual interviews, with responses kept anonymous and only reported to the group in terms of themes. As trust is earned and grows, people can become more open in terms of surfacing attitudes, feelings, and perceptions about organizational dynamics in group settings.

The degree to which there *was preselection of variables versus an emergent selection of variables* to be considered is another important dimension. The University of Michigan version of survey feedback utilizes the Survey of Organizations questionnaire, which taps some 19 dimensions subsumed under three broad categories: leadership, organizational climate, and satisfaction. Another approach, Grid OD, depends heavily in early phases on an analysis of leadership style using a questionnaire called the "Managerial Grid." This analysis focuses on two dimensions: concern for people and concern for production. On the other hand, data gathering can be more emergent with less structuring of questions. Some OD consultants will use interviews that are structured only to the extent that two or three general questions are asked at the outset, such as: What things are going well in the organization? What problems do you see? Follow-up probes are then used to pursue important issues uncovered. Positive and problem themes are then distilled from these data.

The extent to which data gathering and analysis are isolated events in contrast to being part of a long-range strategy is also important. One usual assumption in OD efforts is that diagnostic activities should be part of an overall plan. Diagnostic activities lead to action programs that in turn call for diagnostic activities—this is the action research model. Diagnostic activities that are not part of any such plan or that are prompted by someone's whim to know "what they are thinking" may produce resentment and resistance and can seriously hinder attempts to get valid data from system members.

The nature of the target population in both preliminary and later systematic data gathering and analysis is also a key dimension. The size and nature of the target group can affect the acceptability of the diagnostic process, what kinds of inter-dependencies can be examined, and what kinds of issues can be worked successfully. The data-providing group can be different from the data-analyzing group, of course, but in OD, suppliers of the information usually work with their own data in intact work teams.

And finally, *the type of technique used* obviously has a number of important ramifications. By type we mean questionnaire-versus-interview techniques, individual-versus-group surfacing of data, or other categories of techniques that can be differentiated in major ways. We have already discussed how the type of instrument, such as the Survey of Organizations, can structure the responses. As another example of the importance of technique selection, an interview can be used for trust building as well as collecting data; a face-to-face conversation is a better vehicle for building a relationship than sending someone a questionnaire. Concerns can be expressed and responded to, questions can be answered, assurances can be provided as to how the data will be used, and so on. As another example of the importance of the type of technique selected, giving diagnostic assignments to subgroups in a workshop setting can be a powerful diagnostic technique. But the way these groups are constituted—for example, heterogeneous versus homogeneous in terms of rank, position, or aggressiveness-reticence—can be crucial to the amount and candor of the data generated.

Readings in Part 3

The readings in this part describe widely used basic OD and OT interventions. The interventions vary from methods of finding out what is going on to more complex interventions such as creating parallel structures.

Jack Fordyce and Raymond Weil's "Methods for Finding out What's Going On" presents seven methods for collecting information in order of their degree of confrontation. The second, interviewing, is probably the most fundamental intervention in OD. Each method is discussed in terms of uses, benefits, limitations, and operating hints.

Ishwar Dayal and John Thomas's "Operation KPE" describes an intervention that we call role analysis technique or role analysis process,[8] in which a job incumbent listens to what extent colleague expectations are being met relative to the incumbent's performance and is provided an opportunity to respond.

In "When Power Conflicts Trigger Team Spirit," Roger Harrison describes a role negotiation technique that can be used in small or large groups, although he recommends that groups of over eight or ten be subdivided. Underlying the technique is the assumption that "most people prefer a fair negotiated settlement to a state of unresolved conflict." Harrison states that he has used the technique with such diverse groups as top management teams and husband and wife pairs.

Robert Blake, Herbert Shepard, and Jane Mouton's "Strategies for Improving Headquarters-Field Relations" is an early, classic essay describing a process for managing intergroup confrontation and conflict resolution. Personal correspondence with Blake and Mouton reveals that they saw no fundamental improvements in the design over a 25-year span after its invention.

In Reading 17 French and Bell describe the organization mirror as a set of activities for giving and receiving feedback in the host organization. This is a powerful intervention for discovering how the people in various organizational units feel about the host organization or headquarters. This is a "quick" method to improve relations between work-related task groups.

Richard Beckhard's "Confrontation Meeting" describes an intervention design that allows the total management group "to take a quick reading on its own health, and—*within a matter of hours*—to set action plans for improving it."

Bushe and Shani describe a technostructural intervention to help bureaucratic organizations become more innovative and adaptable to rapid and even random change. This intervention is designed to improve and advance the entire sociotechnical system of the organization. The authors further go on to explain that the term "sociotechnical system" was coined by the Tavistock Institute in England and highlighted the relationship between the technical and social systems. They further state that much of the past work in OD concentrated on the social system. Parallel learning structure interventions balance the intervention between the technical and social systems.

The essay "Survey-Guided Development" by David Bowers and Jerome Franklin describes the nature of and rationale for a powerful intervention strategy that includes the administration of a comprehensive questionnaire; feedback of the results to intact work groups, including the formal leader; problem solving based on the data; and planning for feedback to successively lower levels of the organization. The questionnaire design and the survey feedback process are based on many years of research.

Endnotes

1. Chris Argyris, *Intervention Theory and Method: A Behavioral Science View* (Reading, MA: Addison-Wesley Publishing, 1970), p. 15.
2. For a more detailed discussion of several of these dimensions, see Wendell French and Cecil Bell, *Organization Development: Behavioral Science Interventions for Organization Improvement,* 6th ed. (Englewood Cliffs, NJ: Prentice Hall, 1999), chap. 8.
3. George C. Homans, *The Human Group* (New York: Harcourt Brace Jovanovich, 1950).
4. G. Murphy, "The Freeing of Intelligence," *Psychological Bulletin* 42 (1945), pp. 1–19.

5. Robert R. Blake and Jane Srygley Mouton, *The Managerial Grid* (Houston: Gulf Publishing, 1964), pp. 282–83.

6. Ronald Lippitt, "Dimensions of the Consultant's Job," in *The Planning of Change,* 1st ed., ed. Warren G. Bennis, Kenneth D. Benne, and Robert Chin (New York: Holt, Rinehart & Winston, 1961), p. 157.

7. James C. Taylor and David G. Bowers, *Survey of Organizations* (Ann Arbor: Institute for Social Research, University of Michigan, 1972), pp. 1–6.

8. Wendell L. French and Cecil H. Bell, Jr. *Organization Development: Behavioral Science Interventions for Organization Improvement,* 5th ed. (Englewood Cliffs, NJ: Prentice Hall, 1995), p. 181.

Reading 13

Methods for Finding out What's Going On

Jack K. Fordyce
Raymond Weil

This section contains seven basic methods for collecting information. They include:

- Questionnaires and Instruments.
- Interviewing.
- Sensing.
- Polling.
- Collages.
- Drawings.
- Physical Representation of Organizations.

The methods are ranked in order of degree of confrontation. Thus Questionnaires are generally relatively impersonal because the source of the information is not publicly revealed, while Physical Representations (in which, for example, participants literally position themselves according to degree of influence) are highly confronting.

As a rule of thumb, the more confronting the method, the richer the response and the stronger the impulse to change. But groups vary considerably in their readiness to work with intimate methods.

Another important method for collecting information is Subgrouping. However, Subgrouping has more general uses and consequently it is described in the section on Methods for Better Meetings.

1. Questionnaires and Instruments

Questionnaires are an old standby for detecting opinion and sentiment. We send out questionnaires to customers, production workers, the pro-

Source: Jack K. Fordyce and Raymond Weil, *Managing WITH People,* 2nd ed., (pp. 143–158). © 1979 Jack K. Fordyce and Raymond Weil. Reprinted by permission of Addison-Wesley Longman.

fessional staff, constituents, television and movie viewers, lower levels of management, people who sojourn at motels and ride in planes, and others.

Unfortunately, traditional questionnaires have often been disappointing as a means of bringing about significant change within organizations. They do not create the kind of personal involvement and discussion that is so valuable in changing hearts and minds. The information garnered by questionnaires tends to be canned, anonymous, ambiguous, and detached—cool data rather than hot. The replies may be interesting but they lack punch. It is too easy to hold them at arm's length, put them off until another day, or take token action. And the questionnaire asks the person only what *we* want to know, not what he or she thinks we should know. You might say a filled-out questionnaire amounts to half a conversation. The employee opinion questionnaire is regarded by many as a device that some managements use to avoid coming to grips with strong opinions and sentiments.

Nevertheless, to our mind the questionnaire can be useful when it is developed jointly by the manager and representatives of the population to be canvassed.

The *instrument* as used in organization development is similar to the questionnaire, with the important addition that it is constructed around a theory of management in such manner as to help the respondent understand the theory and rate himself or herself or the organization in terms of that theory. Thus in "Grid Organization Development," the manager answers questions which help to place himself or herself in the grid model of management styles. Others in the group rate the manager, too. In this manner, instruments are a means by which a group can collect information from itself about itself. This information then provides the starting point for feedback and confrontation within the group.

Uses

As a primary vehicle for learning in one complete system of organization development (Grid Organization Development).

To collect information as part of a specific, planned strategy of change, preferably jointly managed.

Instruments may be used by a group to collect information quickly about itself, as part of a diagnostic or team-building meeting. In this use, the instrument is the same as Polling except that the instrument is predesigned and may incorporate criteria for evaluation.

Benefits

Questionnaires and instruments are economical means for gathering information from a large population.

They lend themselves readily to legitimate statistical use.

Instruments are valuable for self-confrontation, for learning, and as stepping stones to interpersonal confrontations.

You can more readily afford to spend time and money on the quality of the questionnaires or instruments because the unit cost is low.

There is wide acceptance of these methods.

They reduce reliance on expert third parties.

Anonymity may bring to light previously undisclosed strong sentiment.

Limitations

Questionnaires and instruments produce findings which seem canned, a quality which is mitigated if they are used, as in Grid Organization Development, as a stepping stone to confrontation. The hazard is that the parties involved may merely imitate the motions of engaging with one another—shadowbox, so to speak.

One becomes too readily dependent on the questionnaire, pressing upon it (and thrusting away from oneself) a load it can't carry: direct human communication.

Operating Hints

Unless the objective is purely personal learning, be sure the questionnaire or instrument leads to real engagement among people. Make sure that those involved are really hearing one another well enough—both heart-to-heart and head-to-head—so that their communication may have consequences in constructive action.

2. Interviewing

Before a team-building or similar meeting, it is common practice to interview the participants. The interviewer is generally a third party. The purpose of the interview is to explore ways in which the group can be more effective. The interviews uncover both positive and negative opinions and sentiments about a wide range of subjects—for example, clarity of individual and group goals, impact of the manager's style, and personal concerns that have never been aired.

The question should help the interviewee to express whatever is on his or her mind about life in the organization. Examples of general opening questions:

"How are things going around here?"

"What changes would you like to see?"

"How do you think this organization could be more effective? What do you feel it does best? Does poorly?"

The interviewer may also ask about management:

"How would you describe the management style of X? How do you think he or she could be more effective?"

Questions may also be asked about relationships within the organization:

"Whom do you like to work with most? Least?"

"Who is most influential in your organization?"

"Are you kept informed of what goes on?"

And about relationships with other organizations:

"When there are problems with other organizations, what can you do about them?"

"Can you give examples of unresolved issues with other organizations?"

"Do you think you could give them advice that would help them do a better job?"

Information from the interviews is fed back to the total group, usually at the beginning of the meeting.

Uses

Interviewing is a way to get private views and feeling on the table. The information collected often furnishes the principal basis for the meeting agenda.

Benefits

The interview is an excellent way to probe for the problems and opportunities of the organization. Interviewing has the virtue of facilitating private expression. A sensitive interviewer can also invite ideas and emotions that the subject has not previously formulated in any conscious way. Interviewing also furnishes an occasion to develop trust between the third party and members of the organization; such trust is valuable in later work.

Limitations

A good interview often takes one to two hours. For a large organization, interviewing can therefore consume a lot of time.

Skillful interviewing runs the risk of turning up more information of a personal and perhaps threatening nature than the group is ready to deal with. When confronted with the interview findings, the group may close up, reject the information, and attack the interviewers.

If the interviewer is clumsy or is not trusted as impartial, interviewing may worsen matters. Under these circumstances, it is best to gather information by open group process. (See methods 3–7 in this section.)

Operating Hints

There should be an understanding between the interviewer, the manager, and members of the team as to how the information will be used, especially with respect to protecting the privacy of sources. Normally, interviewees are promised that the information will be presented anonymously. The interviewer must keep that promise. The information can be presented verbatim or thematically. The former has greater impact but does not protect privacy as well, and some data may be too hot for the group to handle. Thematically presented material has the opposite virtues: it's cooler, protects privacy better, has a softer impact. It is usually easily summarized, and hence easier to grasp.

One variation in reporting is to present themes and to back them up with supporting verbatim quotes.

If the findings are highly critical of the manager or another member of the group, it is advisable for the interviewer to disclose enough of the information to the manager in advance of the group meeting so that he or she will not feel ambushed.

Interviews may be carried out on an individual or subgroup basis, the latter having the obvious advantage of saving time. Interviewing of subgroups does not confer the same advantages of privacy and sensitivity, but the information disclosed tends to be of a character that the group is ready and willing to deal with. Moreover, the person who volunteers data in a subgroup interview normally feels committed to confirm it in a larger meeting. A way to disseminate the interview findings is to type and distribute copies to all members of the group. Summary statements and corroborative information can then be posted on chart pads.

3. Sensing

Sensing is an organized method by which a manager can learn about the issues, concerns, needs, and resources of persons in any suborganization with which he or she has limited personal contact. It takes the form of an unstructured group interview and is usually tape-recorded. The recording may be then used to educate others.

Example

The general manager of an organization which employs 2,000 wants to make an annual report to employees highly pertinent to their interests. To discover what subjects most concern them, the personnel manager schedules a series of meetings with a sampling of employees.

The personnel manager schedules four meetings, each two hours in length and each with a different group of 12 employees. To help the general manager get a "feel" for people in all parts of the organization, the personnel manager selects the attendees as follows:

Group I—Nonsupervisory, shop and service, and technical and office employees.
Group II—Professional employees and staff specialists.
Group III—Supervisors.
Group IV—A diagonal cross section (i.e., one person from each organizational level; no one of the persons selected reports to any other).

Before scheduling the meetings, the personnel manager contacts the supervisor of each prospective participant. He or she explains the purpose of the meeting and the intention that no direct actions will ensue which might affect the supervisor or people who report to the supervisor.

Each meeting begins with a statement from the personnel manager who says that the general manager will arrive in half an hour. The personnel manager explains the general manager's purpose for the meeting and the hope that the conversation will be open and informal. The per-

sonnel manager suggests: "Suppose you board an airplane to Europe and you happen to find yourself sitting next to the general manager. What would you say?" The personnel manager also tells the group that, unless they object, to ease the burden of notetaking, the meeting will be tape-recorded. The general manager may also later use the tape as an aid to memory or to present illustrative excerpts to the division's top staff. If any member of the group prefers, the recorder will be promptly turned off now or at any time during the conversation.

During the meeting, the general manager spends most of the time listening, sometimes asking clarifying questions. The general manager also expresses his or her own thoughts and intentions regarding the various topics introduced.

Another Example

A manager has been hearing from outsiders that recently hired engineers in the organization are dissatisfied. To better understand the nature of their complaints, the manager asks the personnel manager to rearrange sensing sessions with several groups of engineers and a group of engineering supervisors.

Another Example

A third party uses the sensing procedure to make a quick assessment of the health of a company. He or she meets with four representative small groups from different parts of the organization, asking each group to discuss what is going well in the company and what needs to be changed. To avoid inhibiting the discussion, the third party does not record it but periodically stops the conversation and, in front of the group, dictates into the tape recorder a digest of what they have said. Then, with the recorder still running, he or she asks if they have been heard correctly and records their response. In a day's time, a 15-minute tape can summarize the four discussions. This tape is given to the top-management group of the company.

If the consultant were collecting information for a team-building meeting, he or she might use a different question, such as: "The general manager and the division directors are going to hold an off-site meeting to work on improving their performance as a management team. What issues do you think they should take up?"

Uses

To collect information as part of a general diagnosis of the organization.

To learn the desires and agonies of a group that seems to be dissatisfied.

To learn how organization objectives are understood by diverse people within an organization.

To test a proposed course of action for its effect on various groups of people.

To collect information for a team-building meeting.

Benefits

The interaction of the group often produces rich information and ideas.

More economical than individual interviews.

May provide a quick glimpse of what's going on.

Allows for communication of impressions and feelings as well as opinions and ideas.

Provides a check on conventional and more formal communication channels.

Admits the rumble of humanity into the ivory tower.

Tapes from sensing sessions communicate more vividly to later listeners than second-hand transmission, written reports, or questionnaires.

Limitations

Won't work well unless the relations at various levels in the organization are basically trusting.

Is not as statistically rigorous or as economical as a questionnaire.

May be suspected as "snooping."

Success of the meeting is highly dependent on the manager's ability to listen effectively and on a willingness to engage with the members of the group in a personal way.

The meeting may fail to get at the attendees' real concerns because for one reason or another they are not willing to reveal them.

Operating Hints

Make sure that all intermediate supervisors understand the objectives and possible outcomes of the meeting so that they will not feel "spied on." Be clear and explicit about the objectives of the meeting and what is to become of the information.

Notetaking may interfere with easy, informal discussion while the tape recorder is less likely to. But tape-record the session only if the group is willing. Be explicit about how the tape will be used and make a commitment to control its use.

Don't try to use sensing as a substitute for maintaining effective communication channels throughout the organization, or to "get the boss's message across," or to reprimand or judge.

Allow about two hours (enough time for a comfortable discussion).

Provide some warm-up time with a third party, especially for people who have never seen the big boss.

Convene the session in a comfortable setting and one that is not strange or intimidating to the group. (Don't meet in the boss's office.)

Establish a single and limited objective for a given sensing session. Don't try to cover too much at once. Start the meeting in an open-ended way. This will permit individuals to express their view points (e.g., "How does it feel to work around here?" or "I'm interested in how things are going," rather than, "Do you like the company benefits plan?").

If the manager doing the sensing is a poor listener, include a third party who, by prearrangement, can intervene if the manager seems to be blocking the group's efforts to express itself.

Don't do a lot of sensing unless the groups sensed can see positive results coming from it.

Overuse of sensing can be as bad as overuse of questionnaires. Sensing may be conducted by persons other than a key manager; for example, by a third party or someone from the personnel department.

4. Polling

Sometimes a group becomes uneasy with itself. The members may feel anxious, bored, or in some way out of tune with one another. Such conduct is a common symptom of a buried issue. The way out is to move the discussion to the unspoken agenda item. Polling is a way to reveal it. Or, in a more positive way, a group may wish to evaluate its current state as a prelude to action.

One approach is to poll the group on a question that calls attention to its present condition. The third party might float a tentative question and, with the help of the group, modify the question so that it becomes one that the group wants to deal with. The participants must also decide upon the procedure for conducting the poll.

Example

The group has been planning goals for improvement. At this time, the discussion is agreeable but lethargic. The third party suggests polling the group members on their optimism about whether they can agree upon and later achieve a goal involving significant change. The group consents. He or she suggests a procedure and draws on the chalkboard a scale of optimism:

```
0              5              10
|--+--+--+--+--+--+--+--+--+--|
None        Moderate      Complete
```

Each member is asked to assign a number to his or her degree of optimism. The third party will mark each response on the scale.

The responses cluster around 2½. Now the group members begin to comment on their pes-

simism, on their history of past failures at meeting their goals. They begin to analyze weaknesses in their methods of planning and execution of change. More than one member acknowledges a feeling of guilt at not having been able to subscribe to the manager's wishes, having done instead what seemed fitting and necessary.

The truth begins to sink in. As a group, they have a way to travel before they can plan realistic goals to which they will feel strongly committed.

Another Example

One person remarks that participation in the meeting has been uneven. Some have said little or nothing. Others have made important comments to which there was no response; perhaps they have not been heard. One or two have dominated the conversation.

The group determines to poll itself on this concern. The members will score one another (from 1 to 5) on two questions:

- Amount of participation?
- Quality of participation?

Each member writes a self-rating and a rating of the others with respect to the two questions. The results are presented to the group on grids, one grid for each question (see Figure 1). Following the poll, the group members agree on the need to police themselves better. They also decide to rotate the responsibility for calling attention to weaknesses in future meetings.

FIGURE 1

		Raters					
		John	Betty	Ted	Sam	Frances	Fred
Subjects	John	②	1	1	1	2	1
	Betty	5	⑤	5	5	5	5
	Ted	4	5	③	4	4	5
	Sam	2	1	2	①	2	2
	Frances	1	2	1	1	③	1
	Fred	1	1	1	1	1	②

Circled numbers are self-ratings

FIGURE 2

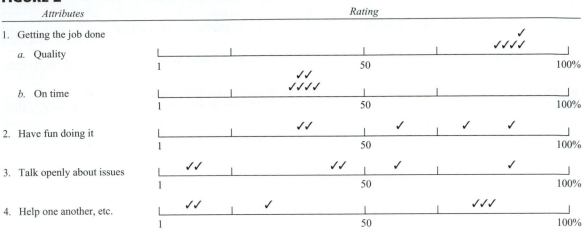

Attributes					Rating		

1. Getting the job done
   a. Quality

   1   50   100%

   b. On time

   1   50   100%

2. Have fun doing it

   1   50   100%

3. Talk openly about issues

   1   50   100%

4. Help one another, etc.

   1   50   100%

Another Example

One member wonders aloud how effective the group is as a team. The third party suggests that the members first decide upon the attributes of an effective team (in their situation) and then rate themselves on each attribute. The group now *develops its own* questionnaire, which is posted. Each member now marks his or her ratings (see Figure 2). Now the group members reflect on why the ratings came out as they did. They become specific about what they do well and what they do poorly as a team.

Another Example

The third party asks on what questions would the members like to know the position of the others. The group arrives at a set of questions:

• Should we do something about our relationship with organization X?
• Am I able to influence what goes on in this organization?
• Do I plan to leave this organization in the next two years?

Each members jots down a yes or no reply to each question, and then predicts the number of yes and no answers for the total group. The results are tab-ulated and posted on the wall (see Figure 3). The range of the *predictions* is an indicator of common understanding. The *actual count* starts the group working on some real problems.

Another Example

After an effort lasting some period of time, the group has reached a fairly high level of trust and mutual helpfulness. However, one member is troubled by certain relationships among members, and feels the group has been avoiding the subject.

The third party invites each group member to pursue two questions:

• Which two persons in the group do I *like* working with the *most*?
• Which two persons in the group do I *like* working with the *least*?

FIGURE 3

Question	Actual Counts		Predicted Count (range)	
	Yes	No	Yes	No
1. Organization X	5	5	3–8	2–7
2. Influence	3	7	1–4	6–9
3. Leaving, etc.	4	6	2–5	5–8

FIGURE 4

		Choosers				
	Jane	Frank	Nan	Mary	Ken	Mark
Jane		✓		✗	✗	✗
Frank	✓		✓			✓
Nan	✓	✓		✓	✓	✓
Mary	✗		✓		✓	
Ken		✗	✗	✓		✗
Mark	✗	✗	✗	✗	✗	

Chosen (vertical label on left)

✓ = Most   ✗ = Least

The responses are collected on signed slips of paper and tabulated on a grid (see Figure 4). In the ensuing discussion, the group deals with the intensity of the choices, the reasons for them, and perhaps what sort of conduct can improve the relationships.

Uses

Polling is a quick way of bringing buried issues to light. Such issues may be of two types:

• Those which are interfering with the progress of a meeting.

• Chronic problems in the organization.

Benefits

Polling is fast, interesting, and simple.

Anyone can devise his or her own questions and polling procedure.

The whole group takes part in the process and feels greater commitment to the results. It is an easy way to get issues out into the open, and a good way to move from general, inconclusive discussions to specifics that can be dealt with. It is a highly flexible method that can be improvised to suit the needs of the moment.

Limitations

The questions aren't as carefully thought out as those on professionally developed questionnaires, and they don't lend themselves to large groups. They are most useful in groups of 5 to 30.

Operating Hints

Don't rush into polling at your next meeting to suit *your* interests. The questions and the procedure must make sense to the group. If not, the responses won't be very useful, and other members will start wondering about *you*.

Group involvement is important for another reason. As the examples show, polls can touch people where they are quite sensitive. The group's OK to go ahead is the only evidence that they feel up to it.

If sensitive relationships are to be taken up, it's wise to have a competent third party present.

Be cautious about secretive methods of collecting information. An occasional secret ballot may be all right, but beware of raising issues which the group is unwilling to confront openly.

Once the questions have been answered, move the discussion to specifics as soon as possible. General discussions leave a lot of fog in the atmosphere.

5. Collages

Individuals, subgroups, or groups may be asked to prepare collages around a theme (e.g., "How do you feel about this team?," "How do you feel about yourself in this organization, and this organization in the company?," "What is happening to this organization and the team?"). Materials for the collage include large sheets of paper, magazines from which pictures and words may be clipped, crayons, felt pens, glue, scissors, and so on. Each finished collage is then described for the total group by the individual or subgroup preparing it. If a single, large collage is prepared by the total group, it becomes the focal point for a total group discussion.

Uses

As an instrument for tracing the cultural and emotional topography of a group. The collage allows the members to express themselves to one another on a fairly deep, personal level. Common themes from collages tend to find their way onto group agendas.

Benefits

Collages can be quite effective in breaking the ice. Afterward, the group may be more willing to deal with personal and interpersonal issues. Besides, they are fun to do.

When the group produces a large single collage, the members are apt to be proud of their accomplishment. The experience is unifying.

Limitations

Groups that are formal in behavior may resist what first appears to be a children's game.

As noted, collages are highly expressive. On the other hand, they may reveal little that is hard and specific.

Operating Hints

Lead boldly into the assignment to help the group overcome its resistance to this "child's play."

If they want, let the participants suggest the theme for the collage. Provide plenty of magazines and ample space, and be prepared to wind up with a cluttered room. Suggest to the participants that they cut out any pictures or words which "ring a bell" without giving much thought to why they do so.

The time for preparing the collages should be approximately one-half hour to an hour and a half. Judge the time by whether the participants seem productively employed, but apply deadline pressure to discourage excessive deliberation.

Don't let the responses to the presentation turn into a game of interpretation. The object is to understand the presenter without putting words into his or her mouth and without awakening defensiveness.

The boss's collage should be presented last so as not to set the tone for others.

6. Drawings

One member of the group (or some, or all members) is asked to make a drawing about an aspect of the individual's life, or something about the nature of the organization. The drawings are made on large sheets of paper posted on the walls. The authors are then asked to discuss their drawings in the presence of the group. Members of the group may ask questions to clarify the author's intent. Common themes and problems, or significant differences of opinion, are then culled from the drawings and posted on chart pads. Here is an example of an instruction given to all members of a group:

Draw a circle for each person in the group, including your boss and your boss's boss. Make the circle proportionately larger for those individuals who seem to have greater influence over the way the group does its work.

Place the circles near or far apart, depending on how closely you feel those individuals must work together to get their job done. Label the circles with the names of the people.

With a blue line, connect those people who are personally close to one another. Connect with a red line those people who are far apart (i.e., individuals who communicate very little with one another or between whom you feel there is friction).

Other Examples

Draw a picture of how it feels to be in your organization.

Draw a picture of your organization today and another picture of what you would like it to be in five years.

The drawings may vary in style from conventional organizational charts to imaginative symbolic representations.

Uses

Drawings of the sort suggested can be a powerful way of unearthing for the group issues that have been buried alive—for example, the presence of cliques, inappropriate competition, or personal influence contrary to organizational goals. While they may be used to describe a current situation, drawings can also display what people want and hope for in place of what they have now.

Drawings can be used for building an agenda for team-building or similar meetings.

Benefits

Pictures are often rich compressions of meaning. Moreover, they are inherently stimulating to work with. Drawings may also afford an easy entry into discussion of tender subjects.

Limitations

Drawings are an expressive medium. But they are difficult for some to enter into unless the directions are quite literal and easy to follow.

Operating Hints

Don't attempt to cover too many subjects in a single drawing or it will become difficult to understand.

Spend enough time on the instructions so that the members understand the *objectives* of the activity. Don't discourage people from departing from your rules; they may do better in their own fashion.

When a person presents a drawing to the group, encourage clarifying questions. *Discourage* general discussion, debate, or clever interpretation of the drawing by other members of the group.

Keep in readiness large sheets of paper, colored markers, and tape.

Some groups need more guidance than others. A group that is esthetically inclined is apt to respond swiftly to the assignment. Others may want more specific instruction.

7. Physical Representation of Organization

Members of a group are asked to arrange themselves physically in the room according to some group characteristic they are troubled about. For example, if the participants are apparently concerned about cliques, they may be asked to position themselves in the room so that each stands nearest to those he or she feels warmest about and farthest from those he or she feels coolest about. Or, if inappropriate influence is an issue, they may be asked to arrange themselves closer or farther from the boss according to the amount of influence they feel they have. Usually, the manager takes a position in the middle of the room as a starting point. Members are asked to call attention to any aspect of the deployment which they believe to be inaccurate. Usually no further instructions are given. Discussion normally occurs spontaneously.

Uses

For bringing into the open relationship issues which are bothering the group. These may include cliques, feelings about being "in" or "out" of the group, influence, competitiveness, communication channels, and the like.

Benefits

A good, rapid, and dramatic diagnostic tool for disclosing interpersonal issues that are hindering a group.

Creates strong motivation to improve the situation.

Limitations

Many groups find this sort of thing too "far out," so the method isn't useful to them and may do more harm than good.

Operating Hints

You will need a qualified third party.

Reading 14

Operation KPE: Developing a New Organization

Ishwar Dayal
John M. Thomas

It was . . . decided that analysis of each role in the organization might be facilitated if, as a group, we could strive for an atmosphere in these sessions where individuals could express disagreement with the manner in which a particular role was being defined or currently being performed by the focal role incumbent, particularly in terms of how this performance either failed to meet expectations from others or convey obligations to others. Analysis of the role system could best be accomplished alongside some critical analysis of current role performance, with a view toward helping individuals understand how they might alter their characteristic styles of working with others. Our hope here was to be able to assist the group in developing a climate where it could begin to undertake analysis of the interpersonal sphere in conjunction with analysis of its task interdependencies: in other words, how the group might begin to share and work together on these concerns about interpersonal needs discussed with us in individual counseling sessions. In addition to ideas of one's own role, it would be valuable for each other member of the group to think about the role under discussion in terms of its specific linkages with his role.

As a model for role analysis in the group we attempted to integrate the Glacier formulations of *prescribed* and *discretionary* components of roles

(Brown, 1960) with that of Kahn, et al. (1964). This included discussion of the following:

1. Analysis of why a particular role is needed and what purpose in the organization it would serve. This point has relevance to the expressed individual problem of identity.
2. The expectations and obligations of related roles in relation to a focal role (Kahn, et al., 1964).

Thus each role analysis consisted of three parts: discussion of purpose of the role, its prescribed and discretionary components, and its linkages with other roles.

Beginning with the GM as the first focal role, the phase aimed at developing what we have termed interdependence was launched. To date, each member of the management group has taken sessions in which he has been a focal role under discussion. The live format evolved for these discussions came to include the following steps:

The focal role individual initiates discussion and the group begins an analysis of the purpose of the role in the organization, how it fits into the overall objectives of the company, and its rationale.

The focal role individual lists on the blackboard the activities which he feels constitute his role; other members discuss this and ask for clarification; additions and subtractions are often made to this list. The group agrees upon the prescribed elements of the role and helps the role incumbent analyze its discretionary elements. Often this enables the individual to clarify the responsibility he must take on himself for decisions, the choices open to him for alternative courses of action, and new competencies he must develop in

Source: Ishwar Dayal and John M. Thomas, "Operation KPE: Developing a New Organization," in *The Journal of Applied Behavioral Science* (vol. 4, no. 4), pp. 443–505, copyright © 1968 by NTL Institute for Applied Behavioral Science. Reprinted by permission of Sage Publications, Inc.

his assigned role. For example, during discussion of the role of the sales manager, he thought that the GM should initiate contact with major customers because he was more likely to influence them by virtue of his social contacts with top management in those companies. In contrast, the consultants suggested that the sales manager might, for various reasons, be taking "flight" from this responsibility and wondered whether he had any feelings about this matter that he could explore with the group. This led to an intensive, useful clarification of the relationship of the general manager with customers and with the sales manager. Similar issues came to center stage while discussing the roles of the purchasing and personnel officers. These discussions also helped the GM and the members of the management team visualize what kind of support they would have to give to one another in this activity. For example, the sales and purchasing role incumbents discussed the development of a formal system for effective exchange of information about customers and suppliers.

The focal role individual then lists his expectations from each of those other roles in the group which he feels most directly affect his own role performance. Often a lively dialogue ensues at this point between the focal role incumbent and the role sender under discussion. They may disagree over expectations and obligations. Other group members enter in to help clarify by adding their own perceptions of that role relationship. In the end a workable formula is evolved describing mutual expectations and obligations.

Each role sender then presents his list of expectations from the focal role. This consists of their views of his obligations to them in role performance, and much the same process as in the previous step is repeated.

Upon concluding an individual role analysis, the focal role incumbent is held responsible for writing up the major points evolved during the group discussion. This consists of *(a)* a set of activities classified as to the prescribed and discre-

tionary elements of the role, *(b)* the obligations of the role to each role in its set, and *(c)* the expectations of this role from others in its set. Viewed in toto, this provides a comprehensive understanding of each individual's "role space." In addition, note is made of procedures and suggestions which may have been brought out as to how the role incumbent might more effectively implement his role activities. This write-up is done with the aid of the consultants and is circulated to all group members.

Briefly, at the next meeting, before another focal role is taken up, the previous role write-up is discussed and points are clarified. This statement is then accepted as a picture of the responsibilities and activities of that position in the organization. Unlike the traditional job description, however, this statement has been evolved live and entirely in the context of the *interaction* of that role with others. It expresses the group's views of how that role fits into the internal structure of the organization.

References

Argyris, C. *Interpersonal Competence and Organizational Effectiveness.* Homewood, IL: Irwin-Dorsey, 1962.

Bamforth, K. "Some Experiences of the Use of T-Groups and Structured Groups with a Company." *Working paper no. 3.* University of Leeds, U.K.: Industrial Management Division, 1963.

Benne, K. "Deliberate Changing as the Facilitation of Growth." In Bennis, W. G., Benne, K., & Chin, R., eds. *The Planning of Change.* New York: Holt, Rinehart & Winston, 1961.

Bennis, W. G. *Changing Organizations.* New York: McGraw-Hill, 1966.

Brown, W. *Explorations in Management.* London: Heinemann, 1960.

Burns, T., & Stalker, G. *The Management of Innovation.* London: Tavistock, 1961.

Dayal, I. "Organization of Work." In Baumgartel, H., Bennis, W., & De, N., eds. *Readings in Group Development for Managers and Trainers.* Bombay: Asia Publishing House, 1967.

Deutsch, M. "Cooperation and Trust: Some Theoretical Notes." In Bennis, W., Schein, E., Berlew, D., & Steele, F., eds. *Interpersonal Dynamics.* Homewood, IL: Dorsey Press, 1964.

Jaques, E., & Brown, W. *The Glacier Project Papers.* London: Heinemann, 1965.

Kahn, R., & Rosenthal, R. *Organizational Stress,* New York: John Wiley & Sons, 1964.

Lorsch, J., & Lawrence, P. "Organizing for Product Innovations." *Harvard Business Review* 43, no. 1 (1965), pp. 109–22.

Rogers, C., & Roethlisberger, F. J. "Barriers and Gateways to Communication." *Harvard Business Review* 30, no. 4 (1952), pp. 46–52.

Schultz, W. *FIRO—B.* New York: Holt, Rinehart & Winston, 1958.

Selznick, P. *Leadership in Administration.* New York: Harper & Row, 1957.

Shepard, H., & Blake, R. "Changing Behavior through Cognitive Change." *Human Organization* 21, no. 2 (1962), pp. 88–96.

Walker, C. *Modern Civilization and Technology.* New York: McGraw-Hill, 1958.

Reading 15

When Power Conflicts Trigger Team Spirit

Roger Harrison

Getting people to work together in harmony is no easy task. Modern management techniques abound with new approaches to improving the working relationship between employees. In the United States, sensitivity training has had quite a vogue, and various techniques such as the T-group or the managerial grid have been brought forth to encourage managers to abandon their competitiveness and to create mutual trust and egalitarian approaches to decision making.

Or managers have been urged to change their motivations from reliance upon monetary reward or punishment to more internal motivation based on intrinsic interest in the job and personal commitment to meeting work objectives: for example, in Management by Objectives and programs of job enrichment. Still other practitioners have developed purely rational approaches to group problem solving: for example, Kepner Tregoe in the United States, and Coverdale in Britain.

Running through these approaches is the tendency to ignore or explain away competition, conflict and the struggle for power and influence. They assume people will be cooperative and productive if they are taught how, or if the barriers to their so being are removed. These approaches may be called *tender minded,* in that they see power struggles as a symptom of a managerial *mistake,* rather than a basic and ubiquitous process in organizations.

The problem of organizational change is seen as one of *releasing* human potential for collaboration and productivity, rather than as one of controlling or checking competition for advantage and position.

Source: Roger Harrison, *European Business,* Spring 1972, pp. 57–65.

However, consider the case of the production and engineering managers of a plant who had frequent disagreements over the work that was done by the latter for the former. The production manager complained that the engineering manager set maintenance priorities to meet his own convenience and reduce his own costs, rather than to make sure production targets were met. The engineering manager maintained that the production manager gave insufficient notice of jobs which could be anticipated, and the production operators caused unnecessary breakdowns by failure to carry out preventive maintenance procedures faithfully. The two men aired their dissatisfaction with one another's performance from time to time; but, according to both parties, no significant change has occurred.

Or take the case of the scientist in a development department, who complains of overly close supervision by his section manager. According to the scientist, the manager intervenes to change the priorities he assigns to work, or to interfere with his development of promising lines of enquiry, and to check up with insulting frequency to see whether the scientist is carrying out the manager's instructions.

The scientist is actively trying to get a transfer to another section, because he feels he cannot do a proper job with so much hampering interference from above.

On the other hand, the section manager says the scientist does competent work but is secretive and unwilling to heed advice. He fails to let the manager know what he is doing and deviates without discussion from agreements the manager thought they had reached about how the work should be carried out. The manager feels he has to spend far too much time checking up on the scientist and is beginning to wonder whether his otherwise good work is worth the trouble required to manage him.

In both of these examples, the men are concerned with either gaining increased control over the actions of the other, reducing control by the other or both. And they know it. A consultant talking to them about communication problems or target setting would no doubt be listened to politely, but in their hearts, these men would still feel it was a question of who was going to have the final say, who was going to be boss.

And, in a way, they are more intuitively right than any outside consultant could be. They know where the power and influence lie, whether people are on their side or against them. They are aware of those with whom they can be open and honest and those who will use information against them. And these concerns are much more accurate and real than an outsider's suggestions for openness and collaboration.

Knowing Where the Power and Coercion Lie

Does this mean that most behavioral science approaches to business are too optimistic? What is certain is that they fail to take into account the forces of power, competitiveness, and coercion. In this article, I shall propose a method that does work directly with these issues, a method that gets tough with the team spirit.

This program is based on role negotiation. This technique describes the process that involves changing through *negotiation* with other interested parties the *role* that an individual or group performs in the organization. By an individual's or a group's *role,* I mean what activities he is supposed to perform, what decisions he can make, to whom he reports and about what and how often, who can legitimately tell him what to do and under what circumstances, and so on. Some people would say that a man's *job* is the same as what I have called his *role,* and I would partially agree with this. But what I mean by *role* includes not only the formal job description but also all the in-

formal understandings, agreements, expectations, and arrangements with others which determine the way one person's or group's work affects or fits in with another's.

Role negotiation intervenes directly in the relationships of power, authority, and influence within the group. The change effort is directed at the work relationships among members. It avoids probing into the likes and dislikes of members for one another. In this it is more consonant with the task-oriented norms of business than are most other behavioral approaches.

The Fear of Touchy Emotional Confrontations

When I first developed the technique, I tried it out on a client group which was proving particularly hard to work with. They were suspicious and mistrustful of me and of each other, and said quite openly that talking about their relationships was both "irrelevant to our work problems" and "dangerous—it could split the group apart." When I introduced them to role negotiation, they saw ways they could deal with issues that were bothering them without getting into touchy emotional confrontations they could not handle. They dropped their resistance dramatically and turned to work with a will that surprised and delighted me.

I have used role negotiation successfully with top management groups, project teams, even between husbands and wives. The technique can be used with very small or quite large groups— although groups of over 8 or 10 should be broken down.

The technique makes one basic assumption: *most people prefer a fair negotiated settlement to a state of unresolved conflict,* and they are willing to invest some time and make some concessions in order to achieve a solution. To operate the program a modest but significant risk is called for from the participants: they must be open about the changes in behavior, authority, responsibility, and so on they wish to obtain from others in the situation.

If the participants are willing to specify concretely the changes they desire from others, then significant changes in work effectiveness can usually be obtained.

How does this program work in reality? First of all, the consultant must have the participants' sufficient confidence in his motives and competence so that they are willing at his behest to try something new and a bit strange. It also stands to reason that the consultant should know enough about the people, their work system, and their relationship problems to satisfy himself that the members of the group are ready to make a real effort towards improvement. No technique will work if the clients don't trust the consultant enough to give it a fair try or if the members of the group (particularly the high-influence members) devote most of their effort to maintaining the status quo. In the description that follows I am assuming that this confidence and readiness to work have been established. Although this is a rather large assumption, these problems are universal in consulting and not peculiar to role negotiation. If anything, I have found that role negotiation requires somewhat less preparation than other team development techniques I have used.

Let us say we are working with a group of five to seven people, including a manager and his subordinates, two levels in the formal organization. Once basic assumptions of trust are established, I try to get at least a day with the group away from the job location to start the role negotiation process going. A two-day session with a commitment to follow up in three to four weeks is best. If the group is not felt to be quite prepared to undertake serious work, the session may be made longer with some trust building and diagnostic activities in the beginning, working into the role negotiation when and if the group is ready for it.

No Probing into People's Feelings

The first step in the actual role negotiation is *contract setting*. Its purpose is to make it clear between the group and the consultant what each may expect from the other. This is a critical step in the change process. It controls and channels everything that happens afterwards.

My contract is usually based on the following provisions, which should be written down, if only as a first practice step in the formal way of working which I try to establish.

It is not legitimate for the consultant to press or probe anyone's *feelings*. We are concerned about work: who does what, how, and with whom. How people *feel* about their work or about others in the group is their own business, to be introduced or not according to their own judgment and desire. The expression or nonexpression of feelings is not part of the contract.

Openness and honesty about behavior are expected and essential for achieving results. The consultant will insist that people be specific and concrete in expressing their expectations and demands for the behavior of others. Each team member is expected to be open and specific about what he wants others to *do more* or *do better* or *do less* or *maintain unchanged*.

No expectation or demand is adequately communicated until it has been *written down* and is clearly understood by both sender and receiver, nor will any change process be engaged in until this has been done.

The full sharing of expectations and demands does not constitute a completed change process. It is only the precondition for change to be agreed through negotiation. It is unreasonable for anyone in the group, manager or subordinate, to expect that any change will take place merely as a result of communicating a demand or expectation. Unless a team member is willing to change his own behavior in order to get what he wants from the other(s), he is likely to waste his and the group's time talking about the issue. When a member makes a request or demand for changed behavior on the part of another, the consultant will always ask what quid pro quo (something for something) he is willing to give in order to get what he wants. This goes for the manager as well as for the subordinates. If the former can get what he wants simply by issuing orders or clarifying expectations from his position of authority, he probably does not need a consultant or a change process.

The change process is essentially one of bargaining and negotiation in which two or more members each agree to change behavior in exchange for some desired change on the part of the other. This process is not complete until the agreement can be *written down* in terms which include the agreed changes in behavior and make clear what each party is expected to give in return.

Threats and pressures are neither illegitimate nor excluded from the negotiation process. However, group members should realize that overreliance on threats and punishment usually results in defensiveness, concealment, decreased communication and retaliation, and may lead to breakdown of the negotiation. The consultant will do his best to help members accomplish their aims with positive incentives wherever possible.

The Secret Game of Influence Bargaining

Each member has power and influence in the group, both positively to reward and collaborate with others, and negatively to resist, block or punish. Each uses his power and influence to create a desirable and satisfying work situation for himself. Most of the time this process is gone about secretly. People use a lot of time and energy trying to figure out how to influence another person's behavior covertly; but since they rarely are aware of others' wants and needs, their attempts fail.

Although in stable organizations, employees can learn what works on others just through trial and error over long periods of time, nowadays the fast personnel turnover makes this primitive process obsolete.

Role negotiation tries to replace this old process with a more efficient one. If one person knows because it has been made public what another's wants or intentions are, he is bound to be more effective in trying to influence that person. In addition, when someone tries to influence him, the quid pro quo put forward is more likely to be one he really wants or needs. I try to show my clients that, by sharing the information about desires and attempts, *role negotiation increases the total amount of influence group members have on one another.*

The next stage is *issue diagnosis*. Each member spends some time thinking about the way business is conducted between himself and the others in the group. What would he change if he could? What would he like to keep as is? Who and what would have to change in order to improve things? I ask the participants to focus especially on the things which might be changed to improve their *own effectiveness,* since these are the items to be discussed and negotiated.

After he has spent 20 minutes or so thinking about these matters and perhaps making a few notes, each member fills out one Issue Diagnosis Form (like the one in Figure 1) for each other member, listing those things he would like to see the other person:

1. Do more or do better.
2. Do less or stop doing.
3. Keep on doing, maintain unchanged.

FIGURE 1
Issue Diagnosis Form

Messages from   *Jim Farrell*
           to   *David Sills*

1. If you were to do the following things *more* or *better,* it would help me to increase my own effectiveness:
   —*Being more receptive to improvement suggestions from the process engineers.*
   —*Give help on cost control (see 2).*
   —*Fight harder with the G.M. to get our plans improved.*

2. If you were to do the following things *less,* or were to *stop* doing them, it would help me to increase my own effectiveness:
   —*Acting as judge and jury on cost control.*
   —*Checking up frequently on small details of the work.*
   —*Asking for so many detailed progress reports.*

3. The following things which you have been doing help to increase my own effectiveness, and I hope you will continue to do them:
   —*Passing on full information in our weekly meetings.*
   —*Being available when I need to talk to you.*

All of these messages are based on the sender's increasing his own effectiveness in his job.

These lists are exchanged so that each person has all the lists pertaining to his work behavior. Each member makes a master list for himself on a large piece of paper itemizing the behavior which each other person desires him to do *more* or *better, less,* or *continue unchanged* (Figure 2). These are posted so that the entire group can peruse and refer to each list. Each member is allowed to question the others who have sent messages about his behavior, querying the what, why, and how of their requests; *but no one is allowed a rebuttal, defense or even a yes or no reply to the messages he has received.* The consultant must assure that only clarification is taking place; argument, discussion, and decision making about issues must be engaged in at a later stage.

Defensiveness Just to Save Face

The purpose of the consultant's rather rigid and formal control on communication is to prevent the group from having a negative problem-solving experience, and members from becoming polarized on issues or taking up extreme positions which they will feel impelled to defend just to save face. Communication is controlled to prevent escalation of actual or potential conflicts. Channeling the energy released by the sharing of demands and expectations into successful problem solving and mutual influence is behind this strategy of control.

The consultant intervenes to inhibit hostile and destructive expression at this point and later to facilitate constructive bargaining and negotiation of mutually beneficial agreements.

This initial sharing of desires and change goals among group members leads to a point at which the team development process is most vulnerable. If sufficient anger and defensiveness are generated by the problem sharing, the consultant will not be able to hold the negative processes in check long enough for the development of the positive problem-solving spiral on which the process depends for its effectiveness. It is true that such an uncontrollable breakthrough of hostility has not yet occurred in my experience with the method. Nevertheless, concern over the negative possibilities is in part responsible for my slow, deliberate, and rather formal development of the confrontation of issues within the group.

FIGURE 2
Summary of Messages to James Farrell from Other Group Members

More or Better:	Less or Stop:	Continue as Now:
Give information on project progress (completion date slippage)—Bill, Tony, David.	Let people go to other good job opportunities—stop hanging on to your good engineers—Tony, Bill.	Training operators on preventive maintenance—Henry.
Send progress reports on Sortair project—Bill.	Missing weekly planning meetings frequently—Jack, Henry, David.	Good suggestions in meetings—Tony, Henry.
Make engineers more readily available when help needed—Jack, Henry.	Ignoring memos and reports re cost control—David	Asking the difficult and awkward questions—Tony, Jack.
Keep better informed re plans and activities—David.	Setting aside my priorities on engineering work—Henry, Jack.	Willingness to help on design problems—Bill, Jack.
Enforce safety rules on engineers when in production area—Henry.	Charging time on Sortair to other accounts—David.	Good quality project work—Bill, Henry, David, Jack.
Push harder on the Sensiter project—David, Henry, Tony, Jack.	Overrunning agreed project budget without discussing beforehand—David.	

The Influence Trade

After each member had had an opportunity to clarify the messages he has received, the group selects the issues for negotiation. The consultant begins this phase by reemphasizing that, unless a quid pro quo can be offered in return for a desired behavior change, there is little point in having a discussion about it: *unless behavior changes on both sides the most likely prediction is that the status quo will continue.*

If behavior changes merely as the result of an exchange of views between men of good will, all the better. However, one cannot count on it.

Each participant is asked to choose one or more issues on which he particularly wants to get some changes on the part of another. He is also asked to select one or more issues on which he feels it may be possible for him to move in the direction desired by others. He does this by marking his own flip chart and those of the other members. In effect, *each person indicates the issues upon which he most wants to exert influence and those on which he is most willing to accept influence.* With the help of the consultant, the group then goes through the list to select the most negotiable issues, those where there is a combination of a high desire for change on the part of an initiator and a willingness to negotiate on the part of the person whose behavior is the target of the change attempt. The consultant asks for a group of two or more persons who are involved in one such issue to volunteer for a negotiation demonstration before the rest of the group.

The negotiation process consists of the parties making contingent offers to one another such as "If you do X, I will do Y." The negotiation ends when all parties are satisfied that they will receive a reasonable return for whatever they are agreeing to give. The consultant asks that the agreement be formalized by writing down specifically and concretely what each party is going to give and receive in the bargain (Figure 3). He also asks the participants to discuss openly what sanctions can be applied in the case of nonfulfillment of the bargain by one or another party. Often this involves no more than reversion of the status quo,

FIGURE 3
Final Agreement between James Farrell and David Sills

Jim agrees to let David know as soon as agreed completion dates and cost projections look as though they won't be met, and also to discuss each project's progress fully with David on a bi-weekly basis.

In return, David agrees not to raise questions about cost details and completion dates, pending a trial of this agreement to see if it provides sufficient information soon enough to deal with questions from above.

but it may involve the application of pressures and penalties as well.

After the negotiation demonstration, the members are asked to select other issues they wish to work on. A number of negotiations may go on simultaneously, the consultant being involved at the request of any party to any negotiation. All agreements are published to the entire group, however, and questioned by the consultant and the other members to test the good faith and reality orientation of the parties in making them. Where agreement proves impossible, the consultant and other group members try to help the parties find further incentives (positive or, less desirably, coercive) which they may bring to bear to encourage agreement.

This process is, of course, not as simple as it sounds. All kinds of difficulties can occur, from bargaining in bad faith, to refusal to bargain at all, to escalation of conflict. In my experience, however, group members tend to be rather wise about the issues they can and cannot deal with, and I refrain from pushing them to negotiate issues they feel are unresolvable. My aim is to light the sparks of team development with a successful experience which group members can look on as a fruitful way of improving their effectiveness and satisfaction.

The Consultant Withers Away

The cycle ends here. Each group must then try living with their agreements. There is always, of course, the occasion to meet later with the consultant to work out new agreements or renegotiate old ones.

Ideally, the group should learn this process so thoroughly that the consultant's role withers away. To do this, though, they must be so fully aware of the dangers and pitfalls involved in the negotiation process that a third party's arbitration is no longer needed.

So far this has not occurred in my experience. The positive results are expressed mostly in terms of less backsliding between visits than has occurred in groups where I have applied more interpersonal behavior-change methods. Role negotiation agreements have more teeth in them.

What are the advantages of role negotiation? First of all, participants seem more at home with problems of power and influence than other interpersonal issues. They feel more competent and less dependent on the consultant in dealing with the problems and so they are ready to work sooner and harder.

Furthermore, the consultant's or referee's amount of skill and professional training which is required to conduct role negotiation is less than for more sensitive approaches.

That does not mean that role negotiation poses no threat to organization members. The consultant asks participants to be open about matters that are often kept secret in everyday life. This requires more than the normal amount of trust and confidence. If not, these matters would have been talked about before the group ever got to the role negotiation.

There also seems to be some additional discomfort involved in *writing down* the changes one would like to see another make in his work behavior. Several times participants have questioned the necessity of doing this, because one feels so *exposed* when his concerns are written out for all to see, and there is the fear that others will think them silly, childish or odd (though this never seems to happen). If the matter comes up, I point out that one need not write down *all* the concerns he has, but only those he would like to work on with others at this time.

Of course, role negotiation, like any other process that changes relationships, does pose a threat to the participants. The members are never sure they will personally be better off after the change than before. In the case of role negotiation, most of these fears arise around losing power and influence, or losing freedom and becoming more controlled by others. Particular resistance to talking openly about issues occurs when someone is trying to manipulate another person to his own advantage, or when he feels that he might want to do this in the future. I think this is the main reason participants in role negotiation so often try to avoid the step of writing down their agreements. If things aren't down in black and white, they feel, it will be easier to ignore the agreement later on if it becomes inconvenient. Also, writing down agreements seems to dispel the aura of trust and good fellowship which some groups like to create on the surface and below which they engage in quite a lot of cutthroat competition.

Role negotiation is of course no panacea for power problems in groups and between people. People may bargain in bad faith; agreements once reached may be broken; circumstances and personnel may change so that the work done becomes irrelevant. Of course, these problems can exist in any group or organization. What role negotiation *does* is try to deal with the problems directly and to identify and use constructively those areas of *mutual* advantage where both sides can benefit from discussion and agreement. These areas are almost always larger than people think they are, and when they find that they can achieve something *for* themselves by open negotiation which they could not achieve by covert competition, then the more constructive process can begin to grow.

Avoiding the Consultant's High Fees

One other likely advantage of role negotiation is the ease and economy with which it can be introduced into the firm.

One disadvantage of most behavioral approaches to team development is that the consultant's level of skill and experience must be very high indeed. Managers themselves are not confident in dealing with these issues, and because they feel uneasy in this area they reasonably want to have as much safety and skill as money can buy. This demand for skilled consultants on interpersonal and group processes has created a shortage and a meteoric rise in consulting fees. It seems unlikely that the supply will soon catch up with the demand.

The shortage of highly skilled workers in team development argues for deskilling the requirements for effective consultant performance. I see role negotiation as a way of reducing the skill requirements for team development consultation. Preliminary results by internal consultants using the approach have been promising.

For example, one management development manager teamed up with a colleague to conduct a successful role negotiation with his own top management. He reported that his main problem was getting up enough confidence to take on the job. The team development session itself went smoothly. Although I cannot say whether this experience was typical (I suspect it was not), it does lead me to hope that role negotiation will prove to be practical for use by internal consultants without professional training in the behavioral sciences.

What then are the main points about role negotiation? First, role negotiation focuses on work relationships: what people do, and how they facilitate and inhibit one another in the performance of their jobs. It encourages participants to work with problems using words and concepts they are used to using in business. It avoids probing to the deeper levels of their feelings about one another unless this comes out naturally in the process.

Second, it deals directly with problems of power and influence which may be neglected by other behavioral approaches. It does not attempt to dethrone the authority in the group, but other members are helped to explore realistically the sources of power and influence available to them.

Also, unlike some other behavioral approaches to team development, role negotiation is highly action-oriented. Its aim is not just the exposing and understanding of issues as such, but achieving changed ways of working through mutually negotiated agreements. Changes brought about through role negotiation thus tend to be more stable and lasting than where such negotiated commitments are lacking.

In addition, all the procedures of role negotiation are clear and simple if a bit mechanical, and can be described to participants in advance so they know what they are getting into. There is nothing mysterious about the technique, and this reduces participants' feelings of dependency upon the special skill of the consultant.

Furthermore, role negotiation actually requires less skill from the consultant than some other behavioral approaches. Internal consultants can suitably use the technique without lengthy special training in the behavioral sciences. It can therefore be a moderate cost approach to organization change.

It's important to understand that role negotiation does not necessarily replace other "soft" behavioral approaches to organization change. Work groups can be effective and achievement-oriented and at the same time allow open and deeply satisfying interpersonal relationships.

However, resolving conflict successfully at the interpersonal level can only be done by first attacking the ever-present issues of power and influence among members. Role negotiation does this and provides a sound and effective base on which to build more satisfying relationships.

If role negotiation is an effective first or "basic" approach to team development, it goes without saying that employee growth means moving beyond this stage into a deeper exploration of integrating work and relationships.

Reading 16

Strategies for Improving Headquarters–Field Relations

Robert Blake
Herbert A. Shepard
Jane S. Mouton

Organizations whose operations extend over great distances encounter complex problems in maintaining effective integration between the headquarters facility and field installations.[1] Geographical distance makes communications difficult. Differences in regional experience are hard for the person at a distance to comprehend. Psychological distance develops to enhance the mechanical difficulties created by geography.

In all other parts of an organization, subordinate groups are joined to subordinate groups by a common member (i.e., the leader of a subordinate group is himself a subordinate in the group consisting of himself, his peers, and his boss).[2] The linkpin between groups of unequal power, while more responsive to those above than below, nonetheless has a powerful mediating effect. He is placed in personal conflict and stress if the two groups in which he has membership are in conflict. The stresses on the foreman are so great that in many organizations he loses membership in both groups; that is, he has little influence up or down. Clearly, there is no linkpin between union and management, and, through unionization and legislative supports, union and management are approximately equal in power.

Most headquarters-field relationships lack this cement, and it is not uncommon for negative attitudes to develop between the parties. In formal theory, field units are subordinate to headquarters, but field units can acquire great informal power. This is particularly true if one field organization is very much larger than other field divisions and accounts for a majority, or at least a large portion, of the company's business. In such cases, the head of the field division may be given formal membership in the top corporate group, thus providing the missing cement. But if, as is more often the case, there are several large or many small field units, headquarters maintains its power by placing them in competition with one another. Building good relations and a good record with headquarters can lead to promotion for key executives in a field unit and to a favored position when headquarters contemplates new investment.

Field groups can develop resentment toward headquarters for many reasons. For example, each field unit is, in most companies, treated as a profit center. However, the profitability of the whole corporation may sometimes require that a given field unit do something which reduces its own profitability. Similarly, new investment by headquarters in one field unit can arouse feelings of injustice in others.

Such problems were causing severe deterioration of relationships between headquarters and a large division in the Tennex Corporation. The following pages describe the problem-solving procedures employed to bring about adequate working relationships. The design was, of course, adapted to the particular set of problems being experienced by Tennex. A different design would be used, for example, if the object were to build better team relations among several field units, and between them and headquarters.

Source: Robert Blake, Herbert A. Shepard, and Jane S. Mouton, *Managing Intergroup Conflict in Industry* (Houston: Gulf Publishing, 1964), pp. 114–21.

The Scofield Case

The following example illustrates an approach to the improvement of working relationships between headquarters and field. The Scofield Division is one of several subsidiaries of the Tennex Corporation. The Tennex Corporation is a highly diversified organization, moderately decentralized.

Since World War II, Tennex has grown quite rapidly, partly by acquisition. Corporate efforts to develop strategies in marketing and production which took advantage of its diverse resources brought many changes which affected Scofield, one of the divisions. Over a period of years, a number of points of friction had developed between the division's management and the top corporate management.

Headquarters personnel felt the division managers were "secretive" and "unresponsive." The division was looked upon as unwilling to provide information that headquarters felt it needed. In turn, Scofield Division management saw the headquarters management as "prying" and "arbitrary." For example, headquarters was critical of the labor relations practices of the division. The division management resented the criticism, regarding it as prejudiced and ill-informed. Again, headquarters felt that Scofield managers had been "dragging their feet" in implementing corporate marketing policies. Scofield felt that headquarters' demands in the area were unrealistic and that the corporate marketing group was behaving "unilaterally," and so on.

The behavioral science consultants called in to help first acquainted themselves with key management in both locations and were exposed to the patterns of action and reaction, frustration, and negative stereotypes, which characterize a deteriorating intergroup working relationship. Some of the headquarters executives were considering replacing certain Scofield managers. The latter, in their turn, were attempting to influence other top corporate officers in Scofield's behalf.

Gaining Perspective on Intergroup and Intragroup Dynamics

In separate three-day conferences with each group, the consultants provided intragroup (or "team") and intergroup training experiences and theory. The intergroup training had two effects. First, managers were able to see the headquarters-field problem in sufficient perspective to analyze the destructive consequences of the win-lose trap which had been dictating their actions. Second, an intergroup experiment and its analysis created a degree of openness within each group of managers that enabled them to review their own intragroup relationships and to develop greater mutual understanding and acceptance. This teamwork training is an important prelude to intergroup confrontation, because friction, "politics," or inability to level within each team clouds and confuses intergroup communication when the two groups are brought together.

The Headquarters-Field Laboratory

As a next step after the separate three-day conferences, the two teams met together, again for a three-day period. It will be convenient to describe their work as a sequence of phases.

Phase I: Listing Issues Requiring Joint Problem Solving

The laboratory opened with a joint session in which members discussed those issues they felt the group should debate. These were then listed in order of priority to provide an overview of the work to be accomplished over the three-day period.

Phase II: Preparation of Group Self-Images and Images of the Other Group

Each group met separately to prepare a description of itself as viewed by its members. The issues listed in Phase I provided a basis for elaborating and giving substance to the self-image descriptions.

Next, each group constructed a verbal image of the other group. Scofield's "secretiveness" as experienced by headquarters and headquarters' "prying" as experienced by Scofield could thus be brought into open communication.

Finally, each group built a description of the relationship between Tennex headquarters and the Scofield Division.

These images were developed to provide a background statement of existing attitudes, feelings, and difficulties which needed to be examined, understood, and overcome.

Phase III: Exchange of Images

During this phase, each group in turn exposed its own image of itself, and in turn listened to the image as perceived by the other group. The process of bringing these images into the open created a background of understanding and brought a new atmosphere of mutual acceptance into the discussion.

Finally, a review was undertaken of relationship problems with respect to the issues that had been listed at the beginning of the conference. Since most of these were related to specific functions and activities, they provided the basis for moving to the subgroup meetings of Phase IV.

Phase IV: Subgroup Meetings Based on Similarity of Function in Field and Headquarters

During Phase IV, members from the headquarters staff with functional responsibilities at the corporate level met with Scofield managers who had responsibility for the corresponding function in the plant.

The purpose of these discussions was akin to the "team development" of the earlier three-day conferences: to explore relationship problems between individuals whose responsibilities make them interdependent. Once interpersonal relationship issues had been explored and sources of difficulty had been cleared out of the way, it was possible to discuss functional problems in a climate conducive to understanding and collaboration.

The latter part of Phase III and beginning of Phase IV brought out dramatically how confused and inadequate communication between Scofield and headquarters had been in many areas. The headquarters group seized on the relationship-image exchange as an excellent opportunity to "explain" to Scofield things that they believed Scofield did not understand. As the discussion proceeded, however, the tables were turned. When the field group presented its view of the relationship it began to "get through" to headquarters. By the end of Phase IV, headquarters staff members were really able to understand operational difficulties from a field point of view. They were also able to see more clearly how they might serve as consultants in the field, rather than as persons who attempt to "control" field operations.

Phase V: Review and Planning

In this phase the two groups met to prepare an overall summary of problems that had been identified and defined. This led to a joint discussion of the kinds of changes required to bring about improvements. Some of the problems implied changes in the behavior of only one of the groups, but most required joint implementation by functional subgroups.

The most significant product of this phase was that it provided a new concept of the way to bring about change and innovation. For instance, prior to the headquarters-field conference, it was accepted that "headquarters formulates policy; the field implements it." The inappropriateness of this concept for policies which had long been in force was evident to both parties. Reports from the field told headquarters whether the policy was being implemented adequately and enabled the headquarters to take special action where departures from policy were detected.

Conference discussions clearly disclosed that this control was woefully inadequate during a period of policy changing, policymaking, or during implementation of new or changed policies. Communication distortions and breakdowns, areas of mutual frustration with the accompanying charges of "foot-dragging" and "arbitrariness," were seen to be the result of those methods which had been used in developing and implementing new policies.

Both sides came to see clearly that making and implementing new or changed policy is a complex process requiring continuous feedback among those involved. Efforts to implement a change are experiments, the results of which need to be quickly available to the organization. They are reality tests which may lead to policy modification, and they are explorations to find sufficient methods of implementation. The policy-making-and-implementing process was thus seen as an innovation phase requiring open communication and collaboration among members of the leadership groups.

Phase VI: Followup

By the end of Phase V, much had been accomplished in the areas of mutual trust, respect, and understanding. Moreover, the groups had made a number of commitments to new ways of working and had reached a number of agreements in defining certain problems and the courses of action to be taken in solving them.

Realizing that planning is insufficient to bring about desired results, the groups established some means for operational follow-up. The groups also agreed to reconvene for review and evaluation after a period of implementation. The purpose of this meeting would be to insure that they could find ways to handle possible difficulties in carrying out the plans of Phase V, and in "checking on the health" of the relationship. Thus, if new sources of friction were to arise for which no problem-solving procedure was available, they could be dealt with appropriately.

Summary

The normal day-by-day arrangements between the headquarters facilities and field units often generate many problem areas. Some of the problems tend to become chronic. As a rule, formal communication and decision-making arrangements are insufficient for correcting these chronic difficulties.

Headquarters-field training situations as described in this article are useful devices for exploring and improving organizational interrelationships, including: headquarters interrelations and operations, field interrelations and operations, problems at the general level between headquarters and the field, and functional and concrete operational difficulties within those segments of the organization which are responsible for smooth working arrangements between headquarters and field.

Appendix: Postscript for "Strategies for Improving Headquarters-Field Relations"

This article represented one of the series of spin-off applications of the basic intergroup confrontation and resolution design that we pioneered in the mid-50s. We see no revisions, based on our experience with it over 25 years, that constitute fundamental improvements. However, consultants using this design implement it in short-cut ways that may fail to solve problems underlying headquarters-field tensions. Limitations such as this in using the design are most likely to derive from the consultant's failure to sense the depth of intergroup tensions, and therefore to prompt premature informality in a way that is not present in the design itself. This is likely to lead to mutual accusations and defensive retaliations, rather than to constructive efforts to resolve the underlying problems.[3]

Endnotes

1. R. R. Blake and J. S. Mouton, "Headquarters-Field Team Training for Organizational Improvement." *ASTD* J. 16, no. 3 (1962), pp. 3–11.

2. R. R. Blake and J. S. Mouton, *The Managerial Grid* (Houston: Gulf Publishing, 1964); and R. Likert, *New Patterns of Management* (New York: McGraw-Hill, 1961).

3. Robert Blake and Jane Mouton, personal correspondence.

Reading 17

Organization Mirror Interventions

Wendell L. French
Cecil H. Bell, Jr.

The *organization mirror* is a set of activities in which a particular organizational group, the host group, gets feedback from representatives from several other organizational groups about how it is perceived and regarded. This intervention is designed to improve the relationships between groups and increase the intergroup work effectiveness. It is different from the intergroup team-building intervention in that three or more groups are involved, representatives of other work-related groups typically participate rather than the full membership, and the focus is to assist the host unit that requested the meeting.[1]

The flow of events is as follows: an organizational unit that is experiencing difficulties with units to which its work is related may ask key people from those other units to come to a meeting to provide feedback on how they see the host unit. The consultant often interviews the people attending the meeting before the meeting takes place in order to get a sense of the problems and their magnitude, to prepare the participants, and to answer any questions that the participants may have.

After opening remarks by the manager of the host group, in which he or she sets the climate by stating that the host group genuinely wants to hear how the unit is perceived, the consultant feeds back to the total group information from the interviews. The outsiders "fishbowl" to discuss and explore the data presented by the consultant. (A fishbowl is a group seating and talking configuration in which there is an inner circle of chairs for people who talk and an outside circle of observers and noninteractors.) The fishbowl allows the invited participants to talk about the host unit in a natural, uninterrupted way while the host group members listen and learn. Following this, the host group members fishbowl and talk about what they have heard, ask for any clarification, and generally seek to understand the information they have heard. At this point, a general discussion can ensure that everyone understands what is being said, but at this time the participants do not start to work on the problems that have been uncovered.

For actually working on the problems, subgroups composed of both host group members and invited participants are formed. The subgroups are asked to identify the most important changes that need to be made to improve the host unit's effectiveness. After the small groups have identified the key problems, the total group convenes to make a master list to work out specific action plans for bringing about the changes deemed most important. The total group hears a summary report from each subgroup. Action plans are firmed up, people are assigned to tasks, and target dates for completion are agreed upon. This last group of activities concludes the organization mirror intervention, but a follow-up meeting to assess progress and to review action steps is strongly recommended.

Source: Wendell L. French and Cecil H. Bell Jr., *Organization Development: Behavioral Science Interventions for Organization Improvement,* 1999, page 186, copyrighted by Prentice Hall. Reprinted by permission of Prentice Hall.

In a short period of time an organizational unit can get the feedback it needs to improve its relations with significant work-related groups. The organization mirror intervention provides this feedback effectively. It is imperative that following the meeting the host group in fact implement the action plans that were developed in the meeting.

Endnote

1. Fordyce and Weil, in *Managing WITH People,* discuss this intervention in detail, pp. 101–105.

Reading 18

The Confrontation Meeting

Richard Beckhard

One of the continuing problems facing the top-management team of any organization in times of stress or major change is how to assess accurately the state of the organization's health. How are people reacting to the change? How committed are subordinate managers to the new conditions? Where are the most pressing organization problems?

In the period following a major change—such as that brought about by a change in leadership or organization structure, a merger, or the introduction of a new technology—there tends to be much confusion and an expenditure of dysfunctional energy that negatively affects both productivity and morale.

At such times, the top-management group usually spends many hours together working on the business problems and finding ways of coping with the new conditions. Frequently, the process of working together under this pressure also has the effect of making the top team more cohesive.

Concurrently, these same managers tend to spend less and less time with their subordinates and with the rest of the organization. Communications decrease between the top and middle levels of management. People at the lower levels often complain that they are less in touch with what is going on than they were before the change. They feel left out. They report having less influence than before, being more unsure of their own decision-making authority, and feeling less sense of ownership in the organization. As a result

of this, they tend to make fewer decisions, take few risks, and wait until the "smoke clears."

When this unrest comes to the attention of top management, the response is usually to take some action such as:

Having each member of the top team hold team meetings with his subordinates to communicate the state of affairs, and following this procedure down through the organization.

Holding some general communication improvement meetings.

Conducting an attitude survey to determine priority problems.

Any of these actions will probably be helpful, but each requires a considerable investment of time, which is competitive with the time needed to work on the change problem itself.

Action Plans

Recently I have experimented with an activity that allows a total management group, drawn from all levels of the organization, to take a quick reading on its own health, and—*within a matter of hours*—to set action plans for improving it. I call this a "confrontation meeting."

The activity is based on my previous experience with an action-oriented method of planned change in which information on problems and attitudes is collected and fed back to those who produced it, and steps are taken to start action plans for improvement of the condition.

Sometimes, following situations of organizational stress, the elapsed time in moving from identification of the problem to collaborative action planning must be extremely brief. The confrontation meeting can be carried out in 4½ to

Source: Reprinted by permission of *Harvard Business Review*. "The Confrontation Meeting" by Richard Beckhard, March–April 1967, pp. 159–65. Copyright © 1967 by the President and Fellows of Harvard College, all rights reserved.

5 hours' working time, and it is designed to include the entire management of a large system in a joint action planning program.

I have found this approach to be particularly practical in organization situations where there are large numbers in the management group and/or where it is difficult to take the entire group off the job for any length of time. The activity has been conducted several times with one evening and one morning session—taking only 2½ hours out of a regular working day.

The confrontation meeting discussed in this article has been used in a number of different organization situations. Experience shows that it is appropriate where:

There is a need for the total management group to examine its own workings.

Very limited time is available for the activity.

Top management wishes to improve the conditions quickly.

There is enough cohesion in the top team to ensure follow-up.

There is real commitment to resolving the issues on the part of top management.

The organization is experiencing, or has recently experienced, some major change.

In order to show how this technique can speed the process of getting the information and acting on it, let us first look at three actual company situations where this approach has been successfully applied. Then we will examine both the positive results and the possible problems that could occur through the use and misuse of this technique. Finally, after a brief summary there are appendixes for the reader interested in a more elaborate description of the phasing and scheduling of such a meeting.

Case Example A

The initial application of the confrontation meeting technique occurred in 1965 in a large food products company. Into this long-time family-owned and closely controlled company, there was introduced for the first time a nonfamily profes-

sional general manager. He had been promoted from the ranks of the group that had previously reported to the family-member general manager.

This change in the "management culture," which had been carefully and thoroughly prepared by the family executives, was carried out with a minimum number of problems. The new general manager and his operating heads spent many hours together and developed a quite open problem-solving climate and an effective, cohesive team. Day-to-day operations were left pretty much in the hands of their immediate subordinates, while the top group focused on planning.

A few months after the change, however, the general manager began getting some information that indicated all was not well further down in the organization. On investigation, he discovered that many middle-level managers were feeling isolated from what was going on. Many were unclear about the authority and functions of the "management committee" (his top team); some were finding it very difficult to see and consult with their bosses (his operating heads); others were not being informed of decisions made at his management committee meetings; still others were apprehensive that a new power elite was developing which in many ways was much worse than the former family managers.

In discussing this feedback information with his operating heads, the general manager found one or two who felt these issues required immediate management committee attention. But most of the members of the top team tended to minimize the information as "the usual griping," or "people needing too many decisions made for them," or "everybody always wanting to be in on everything."

The general manager than began searching for some way to:

Bring the whole matter into the open.

Determine the magnitude and potency of the total problem.

Give his management committee and himself a true picture of the state of the organization's attitudes and concerns.

Collect information on employee needs, problems, and frustrations in some organized way so that corrective actions could be taken in priority order.

Get his management committee members in better tune with their subordinates' feelings and attitudes, and put some pressure on the team members for continued two-way communication within their own special areas.

Make clear to the total organization that he—the top manager—was personally concerned.

Set up mechanisms by which all members of the total management group could feel that their individual needs were noticed.

Provide additional mechanisms for supervisors to influence the whole organization.

The confrontation meeting was created to satisfy these objectives and to minimize the time in which a large number of people would have to be away from the job.

Some 70 managers, representing the total management group, were brought together for a confrontation meeting starting at 9:00 in the morning and ending at 4:30 in the afternoon. The specific "design" for the day, which is broken down into a more detailed description in Appendix A, had the following components:

1. Climate setting—establishing willingness to participate.
2. Information collecting—getting the attitudes and feelings out in the open.
3. Information sharing—making total information available to all.
4. Priority setting and group action planning—holding work-unit sessions to set priority actions and to make timetable commitments.
5. Organization action planning—getting commitment by top management to the working of these priorities.
6. Immediate follow-up by the top management committee—planning first actions and commitments.

During the daylong affair, the group identified some 80 problems that were of concern to people throughout the organization; they selected priorities from among them; they began working on these priority issues in functional work units, and each unit produced action recommendations with timetables and targets; and they got a commitment from top management of actions on priorities that would be attended to. The top-management team met immediately after the confrontation meeting to pin down the action steps and commitments.

(In subsequent applications of the confrontation meeting approach, a seventh component—a progress review—has been added, since experience has shown that it is important to reconvene the total group four to six weeks later for a progress review both from the functional units and from the top-management team.)

Case Example B

A small company which makes products for the military had been operating at a stable sales volume of $3 million to $4 million. The invention of a new process and the advent of the war in Vietnam suddenly produced an explosion of business. Volume rose to the level of $6 million within six months and promised to redouble within another year.

Top management was desperately trying to (a) keep raw materials flowing through the line, (b) get material processed, (c) find people to hire, (d) discover quicker ways of job training, and (e) maintain quality under the enormously increased pressure.

There was constant interaction among the five members of the top-management team. They were aware of the tension and fatigue that existed on the production line, but they were only vaguely aware of the unrest, fatigue, concern, and loneliness of the middle manager and foreman groups. However, enough signals *had* filtered up to the top team to cause concern and a decision that something needed to be done right away. But, because of the pressures of work, finding the time to tackle the problems was as difficult as the issues themselves.

The entire management group agreed to give up one night and one morning; the confrontation meeting was conducted according to the six component phases described earlier, with phases 1, 2, and 3 being held in the evening and phases 4, 5, and 6 taking place the following morning.

Case Example C

A management organization took over the operation of a hotel, which was in a sorry state of affairs. Under previous absentee ownership, the property had been allowed to run down; individual departments were independent empires; many people in management positions were nonprofessional hotel people (i.e., friends of the owners); and there was very low competence in the top management team.

The general manager saw as his priority missions the need to:

Stop the downhill trend.

Overcome a poor public image.

Clean up the property.

Weed out the low-potential (old friends) management.

Bring in professional managers in key spots.

Build a management team.

Build effective operating teams, with the members of the top-management team as links.

He followed his plan with considerable success. In a period of one year he had significantly cleaned up the property, improved the service, built a new dining room, produced an enviable food quality, and begun to build confidence in key buyers, such as convention managers. He had acquired and developed a very fine, professional, young management team that was both competent and highly motivated. This group had been working as a cohesive team on all the hotel's improvement goals; differences between them and their areas seemed to have been largely worked through.

At the level below the top group, the department and section heads, many of whom were also new, had been working under tremendous pressure for over a year to bring about improvements in the property and in the hotel's services. They felt very unappreciated by the top managers, who were described as "always being in meetings and unavailable," or "never rewarding us for good work," or "requiring approval on all decisions but we can't get to see them," or "developing a fine top-management club but keeping the pressure on us and we're doing the work."

The problem finally was brought to the attention of the top managers by some of the department heads. Immediate action was indicated, and a confrontation meeting was decided on. It took place in two periods, an afternoon and the following morning. There was an immediate follow-up by the top-management team in which many of the issues between departments and functions were identified as stemming back to the modus operandi of the top team. These issues were openly discussed and were worked through. Also in this application, a follow-up report and review session was scheduled for five weeks after the confrontation meeting.

Positive Results

The experience of the foregoing case examples, as well as that of other organizations in which the confrontation meeting technique has been applied, demonstrates that positive results—particularly, improved operational procedures and improved organization health—frequently occur.

Operational Advantages

One of the outstanding plus factors is that procedures which have been confused are clarified. In addition, practices which have been nonexistent are initiated. Typical of these kinds of operational improvement, for example, are the reporting of financial information of operating units, the handling of the reservation system at a hotel, and the inspection procedures and responsibilities in a changing manufacturing process.

Another advantage is that task forces, and/or temporary systems, are set up as needed. These may be in the form of special teams to study the overlap in responsibilities between two departments and to write new statements and descriptions, or to work out a new system for handling order processing from sales to production planning, or to examine the kinds of information that should flow regularly from the management committee to middle management.

Still another improvement is in providing guidance to top management as to specific areas needing priority attention. For example, "the overtime policy set under other conditions is really impeding the achievement of organization requirements," or "the food in the employee's cafeteria is really creating morale problems," or "the lack of understanding of where the organization is going and what top management's goals are is producing apathy," or "what goes on in top management meetings does not get communicated to the middle managers."

Organization Health

In reviewing the experiences of companies where the confrontation meeting approach has been instituted, I have perceived a number of positive results in the area of organization health:

A high degree of open communication between various departments and organization levels is achieved very quickly. Because people are assigned to functional units and produce data together, it is possible to express the real feeling of one level or group toward another, particularly if the middle echelon believes the top wants to hear it.

The information collected is current, correct, and "checkable."

A real dialogue can exist between the top management team and the rest of the management organization, which personalizes the top manager to the total group.

Larger numbers of people get "ownership" of the problem, since everyone has some influence through his unit's guidance to the top-management team; thus people feel they have made a real contribution. Even more, the requirement that each functional unit take personal responsibility for resolving some of the issues broadens the base of ownership.

Collaborative goal setting at several levels is demonstrated and practiced. The mechanism provides requirements for joint goal setting within each functional unit and between top and middle managers. People report that this helps them to understand "management by objectives" more clearly than before.

The top team can take corrective actions based on valid information. By making real commitments and establishing check or review points, there is a quick building of trust in management's intentions on the part of lower level managers.

There tends to be an increase in trust and confidence both toward the top-management team and toward colleagues. A frequently appearing agenda item is the "need for better understanding of the job problems of other departments," and the output of these meetings is often the commitment to some "mechanism for systematic interdepartmental communication." People also report a change in their stereotypes of people in other areas.

This activity tends to be a "success experience" and thus increases total morale. The process itself, which requires interaction, contribution, and joint work on the problems and which rewards constructive criticism, tends to produce a high degree of enthusiasm and commitment. Because of this, the follow-up activities are crucial in ensuring continuation of this enthusiasm.

Potential Problems

The confrontation meeting technique produces, in a very short time, a great deal of commitment and desire for results on the part of a lot of people. Feelings tend to be more intense than in some other settings because of the concentration of time and manpower. As a result, problems can develop through misuse of the techniques.

If the top-management team does not really use the information from its subordinates, or if there are great promises and little follow-up action, more harm can be caused to the organization's health than if the events were never held.

If the confrontation meeting is used as a manipulative device to give people the "feeling of participation," the act can boomerang. They will soon figure out management's intentions, and the reaction can be severe.

Another possible difficulty is that the functional units, full of enthusiasm at the meeting, set unrealistic or impractical goals and commitments. The behavior of the keyman in each unit—usually a department manager or division head—is crucial in keeping suggestions in balance.

One more possible problem may appear when the functional units select a few priority issues to report out. While these issues may be the most *urgent*, they are not necessarily the most *important*. Mechanisms for working *all* of the information need to be developed within each functional unit. In one of the case examples cited earlier, the groups worked the few problems they identified very thoroughly and never touched the others. This necessitated a "replay" six months later.

In Summary

In periods of stress following major organization changes, there tends to be much confusion and energy expended that negatively affects productivity and organization health.

The top-management team needs quick, efficient ways of sensing the state of the organization's attitudes and feelings in order to plan appropriate actions and to devote its energy to the most important problems.

The usual methods of attitude surveys, extended staff meetings, and so forth demand extensive time and require a delay between getting the information and acting on it.

A short micromechanism called a "confrontation meeting" can provide the total management group with:

An accurate reading on the organization's health.

The opportunity for work units to set priorities for improvement.

The opportunity for top management to make appropriate action decisions based on appropriate information from the organization.

An increased involvement in the organization's goals.

A real commitment to action on the part of subgroups.

A basis for determining other mechanisms for communication between levels and groups, appropriate location of decisions, problem solving within subunits, as well as the machinery for upward influence.

Appendix A: Confrontation Meeting

Here is a detailed description of the seven components which make up the specific "design" for the day-long confrontation meeting.

Phase 1. Climate Setting (45 minutes to one hour)

At the outset, the top manager needs to communicate to the total management group his goals for the meeting, and his concern for and interest in free discussion and issue facing. He also has to assure his people that there is no punishment for open confrontation.

It is also helpful to have some form of information session or lecture by the top manager or a consultant. Appropriate subjects might deal with the problems of communication, the need for understanding, the assumptions and the goals of the total organization, the concept of shared responsibility for the future of the organization, and the opportunity for and responsibility of influencing the organization.

Phase 2. Information Collecting (one hour)

The total group is divided into small heterogeneous units of seven or eight people. If there is a top-management team that has been holding sessions regularly, it meets as a separate unit. The rest of the participants are assigned to units with a "diagonal slice" of the organization used as a basis for composition—that is, no boss and subordinate are together, and each unit contains members from every functional area.

The assignment given to each of these units is along these lines:

> Think of yourself as an individual with needs and goals. Also think as a person concerned about the total organization. What are the obstacles, "demotivators," poor procedures or policies, unclear goals, or poor attitudes that exist today? What different conditions, if any, would make the organization more effective and make life in the organization better?

Each unit is instructed to select a reporter to present its results at a general information-collecting session to be held one hour later.

Phase 3. Information Sharing (one hour)

Each reporter writes his unit's complete findings on newsprint, which is tacked up around the room.

The meeting leader suggests some categories under which all the data from all the sheets can be located. In other words, if there are 75 items, the likelihood is that these can be grouped into six or seven major categories—say, by type of problem, such as "communications difficulties"; or by type of relationship, such as "problems with top management"; or by type of area involved, such as "problems in the mechanical department."

Then the meeting breaks, either for lunch or, if it happens to be an evening session, until the next morning.

During the break all the data sheets are duplicated for general distribution.

Phase 4. Priority Setting and Group Action Planning (one hour and 15 minutes)

The total group reconvenes for a 15-minute general session. With the meeting leader, they go through the raw data on the duplicated sheets and put category numbers by each piece of data.

People are now assigned to their functional, natural work units for a one-hour session. Manu-

facturing people at all levels go to one unit, everybody in sales to another, and so forth. These units are headed by a department manager or division head of that function. This means that some units may have as few as 3 people and some as many as 25. Each unit is charged to perform three specific tasks:

1. Discuss the problems and issues which affect its area. Decide on the priorities and early actions to which the group is prepared to commit itself. (They should be prepared to share this commitment with their colleagues at the general session.)
2. Identify the issues and/or problems to which the top-management team should give its priority attention.
3. Decide how to communicate the results of the session to their subordinates.

Phase 5. Organization Action Planning (one to two hours)

The total management group reconvenes in a general session, where:

1. Each functional unit reports its commitment and plans to the total group.
2. Each unit reports and lists the items that its members believe the management team should deal with first.
3. The top manager reacts to this list and makes commitments (through setting targets or assigning task forces or timetables, and so on) for action where required.
4. Each unit shares briefly its plans for communicating the results of the confrontation meeting to all subordinates.

Phase 6. Immediate Follow-Up by Top Team (one to three hours)

The top-management team meets immediately after the confrontation meeting ends to plan first follow-up actions, which should then be reported back to the total management group within a few days.

Phase 7. Progress Review (two hours)

Follow-up with total management group four to six weeks later.

Appendix B: Sample Schedule

9:00 A.M. Opening Remarks, by general manager.

Background, goals, outcomes.

Norms of openness and "leveling."

Personal commitment to follow-up.

9:10 General Session.

Communications Problems in Organizations, by general manager (or consultant).

The communications process.

Communications breakdowns in organizations and individuals.

Dilemmas to be resolved.

Conditions for more openness.

10:00 Coffee.

10:15 Data Production Unit Session.

Sharing feelings and attitudes.

Identifying problems and concerns.

Collecting data.

11:15 General Session.

Sharing findings from each unit (on newsprint).

Developing categories on problem issues.

12:15 P.M Lunch.

2:00 General Session.

Reviewing list of items in categories.

Instructing functional units.

2:15 Functional Unit Session.

Listing priority actions to be taken.

Preparing recommendations for top team.

Planning for presentation of results at general meeting.

3:15 General Session.

Sharing recommendations of functional units.

Listing priorities for top team action.

Planning for communicating results of meeting to others.

4:15 Closing Remarks, by general manager.

4:30 Adjournment.

Reading 19

Parallel Learning Structures

Gervase R. Bushe
A. B. (Rami) Shani

A nonunionized semiconductor manufacturer wants to increase the amount of innovation in, and overall effectiveness of, its operations. It creates a structure for employees to propose ideas, gather resources, meet in small groups on company time, and support implementation of new ideas that gather support.

A bank decides to improve its responsiveness to the environment and its ability to take advantage of opportunities. It creates a structure for employees to propose areas in need of attention, generate small groups to work on these areas, and implement solutions that emerge.

A unionized automotive manufacturer tries to improve its adaptability, its effectiveness, and the quality of work life. In partnership with the local union, it creates a structure for employees to meet regularly to identify and solve problems, gather necessary resources to solve those problems, and increase cooperation between all levels of the plant.

A hospital wants to explore alternative ways of providing service. It creates a structure for employees to propose ideas, meet in small groups to further refine those ideas, and provide support and resources for implementing those ideas.

A Department of Education in a university wishes to improve the quality of education in a county school system with fifteen districts. A structure is created that integrates the various school districts, state bodies, and universities as a vehicle for comprehensive educational reform.

A manufacturing organization attempts to implement new quality control technologies. The techniques are quite simple, but their use directly violates a number of political and cultural norms within the organization. They create a structure of overlapping groups from the plant manager on down to the shop floor. The senior management steering committee sanctions groups that want to try applying these new techniques and ensures that the groups have the resources and support they need. As they learn from their success and failures, changes in the basic design of the organization are made to help institutionalize the use of these quality techniques.

Each of these vignettes briefly describes the use of a technostructural intervention to aid a bureaucratic organization in becoming more innovative and adaptable and/or to attain some complex organizational purpose. We call these interventions "parallel learning structures." They are one of the most important innovations in organizational development (OD) technology developed during the 1980s. In this book we will look at the theory and practice of parallel learning structure interventions in different types of bureaucratic organization. To begin with, let's briefly look at what we mean by the term "technostructural intervention."

Technostructural Intervention

A technostructural intervention is a change in the technology and/or structure of an organization with the purpose of improving or stabilizing the

Source: Gervase R. Bushe and A. B. (Rami) Shani, *Parallel Learning Structures,* pp. 1–4, 9–12. Copyright 1991 Addison-Wesley Publishing Company. Used with permission from Addison-Wesley.

entire sociotechnical system in that organization. "Sociotechnical system" is a term coined at the Tavistock Institute in England to highlight the fact that all organizations are composed of a technical system (the technology, formal structure, rules and regulations) and a social system (informal groups, cliques, patterns of interaction) nested in an environment. Historically, most OD work has focused on the social system. In the past decade, more attention has been paid to both the technical system and the environment. Sociotechnical systems theory[1] has been the guiding force in such technostructural innovations as autonomous workgroups and technical design based on variance analysis. Work redesign is another example of a widely used technostructural intervention. Quality circles are a more recent technostructural intervention being used by some OD practitioners.

Some of the early theory that greatly influenced OD focused on technostructural issues. Chris Argyris's early work showed how the structure of bureaucratic organizations was in conflict with adult development. Rensis Likert's System 4 involved the use of a specific type of organizing structure. The matrix form of organizational structure emerged out of pioneering OD work in the aerospace and electronics industries.

A technostructural intervention could be the primary intervention or a supporting intervention in a planned change process. Like any change process, it can be used for first-order change (i.e., a change that helps to maintain the basic character of the system, like a tune-up) or second-order change (i.e., a change that affects the fundamental character of the system, like putting jet engines in a car). Some people view structural change with suspicion. These are people who have lived through one or more "reorganizations" where a lot of time and energy was spent but "nothing really changed." In these cases, we are probably dealing with a first-order change—the boxes on the organization chart were moved around, but the underlying logic of the boxes remained the same. A technostructural intervention will not result in second-order change unless there is a real change in the basic elements of structure, and even then, there are no guarantees.

Structure is the division and coordination of labor. Organizations exist because there is something to do that requires more than one person; therefore, the work is divided up among several employees. Once the work is divided up, some way has to be found to coordinate the efforts of these individuals to ensure that the final product or service comes together. Structures are environments that affect how people behave. They channel effort and energy in a particular direction. When they are well designed, they support employees in accomplishing their tasks; when they are poorly designed, they can get in the way. Since they channel effort, changes in structure can lead to changes in how people behave at work.

Take, for example, the number of employees a person has to supervise. Direct supervision is one way of coordinating employees. The number of employees a person supervises is a result of the division of labor. Imagine a person who has three people to supervise, and little else to do. We are likely to find that this person is constantly peering over the shoulder of his or her subordinates, getting involved in all their decisions, and rarely calling group meetings, preferring instead to deal with each one individually. In fact, we would probably find that this supervisor behaves like McGregor's "theory X" manager.[2] We might attribute this behavior to the manager's personality, attitudes, or values. Give the same supervisor forty people to supervise, and we're likely to find that he or she is now delegating decision making, permitting subordinates to make their own choices, using group meetings for departmental coordination, and, in general, acting more like a "theory Y" manager. In our experience, people tend to attribute poor supervision to personality flaws, warped values, and/or lack of training, but we often find that poor supervision is a result of poor structure. There is something in the organization that makes it seem to be in a person's best interest to act in a less than optimal way. No amount of training, process consultation, or therapy is going to change anything while the structure stays the same. Therefore, we think of technostructural interventions as attempts to sculpt environments to support a particular set of behaviors.

One of the causes of OD failure is the attempt to develop a new set of behaviors within a structure that supported old behaviors. Sometimes this can get ridiculous. Take, for example, the attempt to increase worker participation in factories through training managers in participative management. The vast majority of factories coordinate worker labor through the standardization of work processes. In practice, this means that the actual work people do is designed by engineers in some corporate office who have little contact with either the workers or their supervisors. Each task is designed to fit with all the others. Few people outside of the engineering staff will actually understand how all the various operations fit together. What coordinates people's labor is the work itself, the standardization built into the design. But what decisions are these workers going to participate in when neither they nor their supervisors have any say over their work and don't really know how their part fits into the whole? Discussions about fairly minor matters, such as housekeeping, parking lots, tool cribs, and machine maintenance are possible, but they wear thin after a year or two. In the long run, real employee involvement in decision making in factories requires change in the way the typical factory is structured.

More than other types of OD interventions, structural interventions have to be actively supported by the top of the organization. Over a decade ago Barry Oshry pointed out what many current writers on "transformational leadership" are now saying, that the basic ways in which those at the top influence an organization are through (a) providing compelling visions that capture employee energy and commitment, and (b) providing structures that channel that energy toward that vision.[3] In most cases, a structural intervention is going to affect everyone in the organization and will have to be sanctioned by the person who sits at the very top of the organization. Therefore,

technostructural interventions are strategic interventions. They require a vision of what the change is about, expounded by senior management. They are not the sort of thing that a manager or OD consultant can pull out of his or her pocket in a pinch. They generally require a lot of up-front planning with senior management, a fairly long-term perspective, and trained internal resource people to aid in implementation.

Parallel learning structures are used in bureaucratic organizations.

Defining Parallel Learning Structures

One of the reasons that parallel learning structure interventions are not widely discussed in OD textbooks at this time is that they have been given so many different names.[4] Problems of interpretation have been compounded because sometimes the same name is used to describe very different interventions and other times different names are used to label the same thing. We are not too concerned about the name, and we don't believe there is any one best way to structure the intervention. We offer the term "parallel learning structure" as a generic label to cover interventions where: (a) a "structure" (that is, a specific division and coordination of labor) is created that (b) operates "parallel" (that is, in tandem or side-by-side) with the formal hierarchy and structure and (c) has the purpose of increasing an organization's "learning" (that is, the creation and/or implementation of new thoughts and behaviors by employees).

We have also found that the term "parallel structure" is the one that seems to stay with people most easily and evokes a fairly accurate image of the intervention. Throughout the book we'll use the terms "parallel learning structure" and "parallel structure" interchangeably.

We will describe parallel learning structures in greater detail throughout the book. At this point, let's just note that in its most basic form, a parallel learning structure consists of a steering committee that provides overall direction and authority and a number of small groups with norms and operating procedures that promote a climate conducive to innovation, learning, and group problem solving. Members of the parallel learning structure are also members of the formal organization, though within the parallel learning structure their relationships are not limited by the formal chain of command. Some parallel learning structures are set up on a temporary basis, while others are intended to be permanent.

The key thing about parallel structures is that they create a bounded space and time for thinking, talking, deciding, and acting differently than normally takes place at work. If you don't implement different norms and procedures, you don't have a parallel structure. The most important and difficult task for the people creating the parallel learning structure is to create a different culture within it.

It isn't the supplemental structure that's important. What's important is that people act in a way that promotes learning and adaptation. Most of us are not so evolved that we can operate in ambiguity and flexibly change styles to fit the occasion. This is the Achilles' heel of many of the new organizational designs that create loose roles and ambiguous responsibilities. Some people thrive in loosely structured organizations, but most don't. The designs that work in the long run, without regressing to more authoritarian forms, seem to have much clearer role definitions and procedures—they pay attention to the content of people's jobs as well as the process. People operating in tightly designed bureaucracies cannot be expected to know how and when it is appropriate to follow procedures and when to question them. So to reduce ambiguity and confusion, bureaucracies discourage deviance. The problem is that in systems where procedures are never questioned, managers develop an oversimplified, insular, distorted and, eventually, self-destructive view of their organization. Questioning, puzzlement, and doubt are needed for learning and adaptation to take place.

The parallel learning structure provides a time and place where organizational inquiry is legitimate. Its existence tells people this is where it is okay to question, to express doubts and reservations. When you're in the parallel structure, your role is to question the organization and promote change. When you're in the formal organization, your role is to comply with the organization and maintain its stability. This simple bounding of time, space, and role increases the possibility that some people might actually summon the courage to speak up and say the unsayable, question the unquestionable, and bring to light what the system has been trying so hard to not see. Of course, simply setting up a parallel structure will not, in and of itself, make people more courageous. But establishing clear boundaries and role expectations that build legitimacy for such behaviors surely increases the possibility that people will risk a different way of behaving at work.

To further clarify what we are dealing with in this book, the following are *not* parallel learning structure interventions:

Task Forces and Teams. The key feature distinguishing parallel learning structures from a set of task forces is the emphasis on creating the kinds of norms and procedures that facilitate learning and innovation. Unless specific interventions are made, task forces mirror the norms and procedures of the formal organization. In addition, task forces tend to be set up by a manager. Parallel learning structures always involve a steering committee.

Matrix and Project-Management Structures. Parallel learning structures do not have dual authority or reporting relations and the composition of groups is not based solely on functional expertise.

Semiautonomous Work Teams. This is a way to design the formal organization of manufacturing. Such teams do not operate in parallel, and are mainly concerned with producing goods (not learning).

Industrial Democracy. Joint determination generally involves setting up some form of works council, but these are oriented more toward defining organizational policy than generating innovation. In addition, norms and procedures tend to be highly formalized and oriented more toward maintaining order and equity than supporting group problem solving.

Endnotes

1. Trist (1981), Pasmore (1988).
2. McGregor (1960).
3. Oshry, B. (1977).
4. For example. *collateral organization* (Zand, 1974, 1981; Nadler, 1977; Susman, 1981; Kilmann, 1982; Rubinstein and Woodman, 1984), *parallel organization* (Carlson in Miller, 1978; Stein and Kanter, 1980; Bushe, Danko, and Long, 1984; Moore, 1986; Moore and Miners, 1988), *parallel structures* (Shani and Bushe, 1987), *dualistic structures* (Goldstein, 1978, 1985), *shadow structures* (Schein and Greiner, 1977), *action research systems* (Shani and Pasmore, 1985), *circular organizations* (Ackoff, 1981), *parallel learning structures* (Bushe and Shani, 1990), and *vertical linking* (Hawley, 1984). In addition, a number of reports of change projects implicitly describe the use of such supplemental structures without labeling them (e.g., Brekelmans and Jonsson, 1976; Emery and Thorsrud, 1976; Drexler and Lawler, 1977; Adizes, 1979; Pasmore and Friedlander, 1982; Greenbaum, Holden, and Spataro, 1983; Shea, 1986).

References

Ackoff, R. L. 1981. *Creating the corporate Future.* New York: Wiley.

Adizes, I. 1979. Organizational Passages: Diagnosing and treating lifecycle problems of organizations. *Organizational Dynamics* (Summer): 3–25.

Brekelmans, W., and Jonsson, B. 1976. The diffusion of work design changes in Volvo. *Columbia Journal of World Business* (Summer): 96–99.

Bushe, G. R., Danko, D., and Long, K. J. 1984. A structure for successful worker problem-solving groups. In *Matrix Management Systems Handbook,* ed. D. Cleland, pp. 714–31. New York: Von Nostrand Reinhold, 714–31.

Bushe, G. R., and Shani, A. B. 1990. Parallel learning structure interventions in bureaucratic organizations. In *Research in Organizational Change and Development, Volume 4,* eds. R. W. Woodman and W. A. Pasmore, pp. 193–220. Greenwich, CT: JAI Press.

Drexler, J. A., and Lawler, E E. 1977. A union-management cooperative project to improve the quality of work life. *Journal of Applied Behavioral Science* 13:373–87.

Emery, F. E., and Thorsrud, E. 1976. *Democracy at Work.* Leiden, Neth.: Martinus Nijhoff.

Goldstein, S. G. 1985. Organizational dualism and quality circles. *Academy of Management Review* 10:504–17.

———. 1978. A structure for change. *Human Relations* 31:957–83.

Greenbaum, H. H., Holden, E. J., and Spataro, L. 1983. Organizational structure and communication processes: A study of change. *Group and Organization Studies* 8:61–82.

Hawley, J. A. 1984. Transforming organizations through vertical linking. *Organizational Dynamics* (Winter): 68–80.

Kilmann, R. H. 1982. Designing collateral organizations. *Human Systems Management* 3:66–76.

McGregor, D. 1960. *The Human Side of Enterprise.* New York: McGraw-Hill.

Miller, E. C. 1978. The parallel organization structure at General Motors . . . An interview with Howard C. Carlson. *Personnel* (Sept.–Oct.): 64–69.

Moore, M. L., Designing parallel organizations to support organizational productivity programs. In *Handbook of Human Resources Administration,* ed. J. Famularo, pp. 4.1–4.18. New York: McGraw-Hill.

Moore, M. L., and Miners, I. A. 1988. Hidden consequences in combining OD interventions with policy and technology approaches to absence control: Implications for consultants. *Consultation* 7:86–111.

Nadler, D. A. 1977. *Feedback and Organizational Development.* Reading, MA: Addison-Wesley.

Oshry, B. 1977. *Power and Position.* Boston: Power & Systems, Inc.

Pasmore, W. A. 1988. *Designing Effective Organizations: The Sociotechnical Systems Perspective.* New York: Wiley.

Pasmore, W. A., and Friedlander, F. 1982. An action research program for increasing employee involvement in problem solving. *Administrative Science Quarterly* 27:343–62.

Rubinstein, D., and Woodman, R. W. 1984. Spiderman and the Burma raiders: Collateral organization theory in action. *Journal of Applied Behavioral Science* 20:1–21.

Schein, V. E., and Greiner, L. E. 1977. Can organization development be fine tuned to bureaucracies? *Organizational Dynamics* (Winter): 48–61.

Shani, A. B., and Bushe, G. R. 1987. Visionary action research: A consultation process perspective. *Consultation* 6:3–19.

Shani, A. B., and Pasmore, W. A. 1985. Organization inquiry: Towards a new paradigm of the action research process. In *Contemporary Organization Development,* ed. D. Warrick, pp. 438–48. Glenview, IL: Scott, Foresman.

Shea, G. P. 1986. Quality circles: The danger of bottled change. *Sloan Management Review* (Spring): 3–46.

Stein, B. A. and Kanter, R. M. 1980. Building the parallel organization: Creating mechanisms for permanent quality of work life. *Journal of Applied Behavioral Science* 16:371–88.

Susman, G. I. 1981. Planned change: Prospects for the 1980's. *Management Science* 27:139–54.

Trist, E. L. 1981. *The Evolution of Sociotechnical Systems.* Toronto, Ontario: Ontario Quality of Work Life Centre.

Zand, D. E. 1974. Collateral organization: A new change strategy. *Journal of Applied Behavioral Science* 10:63–89.

——— 1981. *Information, Organization and Power.* New York: McGraw-Hill.

Reading 20

Survey-Guided Development: Using Human Resources Measurement in Organizational Change

David G. Bowers
Jerome L. Franklin

As it exists today, organizational development (OD) in various forms and practices includes many common values and goals. However, there is also a considerable degree of difference in the various concepts, procedures, and assumptions that are identified within this field. The common elements reflect to some extent the fact that those engaged in the field share some aspects of their backgrounds. The differences reflect different evolutionary streams from which the practice of OD has emerged. Much of what is currently considered within the realm of OD can be traced to the fields of adult education, personnel training, industrial consultation, and clinical psychology. Organizational development now represents a crystallization of the experiences of practitioners from these fields. Examples of the techniques and procedures that have evolved in this way include sensitivity training, human relations training, team development training, process consultation, and role-playing.

Some portion of what presently may be considered organizational development came into existence through a different route, which is perhaps best described as a concern for the utilization of scientific knowledge. This data-based type of development and, specifically, the survey feedback technique, originated not from the search by practitioners for more effective helping tools, but from

Source: David G. Bowers and Jerome L. Franklin, "Survey-Guided Development: Using Human Resources Measurement in Organizational Change," *Journal of Contemporary Business* 1, no. 3 (Summer 1972), pp. 43–55. School of Business Administration, University of Washington, DJ-10, Seattle. Reprinted with permission.

the concern of organizational management researchers for better ways of moving new scientific findings from the producers (researchers) to the consumers (organizational managers).

This view is clearly spelled out in the prospectus which launched the organizational behavior research program at the Institute for Social Research over 25 years ago:

> The general objective of this research program will be to discover the underlying principles applicable to the problems of organizing and managing human activity. *A second important objective of the project will be to discover how to train persons to understand and skillfully use these principles* [9, p. 2].

> The major emphasis during the last four years of the project will be on the experimental verification of the results and *especially on learning how to make effective use of them in everyday situations.* . . . Each experiment will be analyzed in terms of measures made before and after the experiment, and often a series of measures will be made during the experiment [9, p. 10].

> The entire progress of our society depends upon our skill in organizing our activity. Insofar as we can achieve efficiently through systematic research new understandings and skills instead of relying on trial and error behavior, we can speed the development of a society capable of using constructively the resources of an atomic age. Unless we achieve this understanding rapidly and intelligently, we may destroy ourselves in trial and error bungling. Understanding individual behavior is not enough, nor is an understanding of the principles governing the behavior of men in small groups. We need generalizations and principles

which will point the way to organizing human activity on the scale now required [9, p. 12].

This same prospectus also stated that the basic measurement tool to be used in the proposed studies would be the sample survey, employing procedures that the proposers had developed during their years with the Program Surveys Division of the Department of Agriculture. It was also stated that the study design would be generally like that employed by Rensis Likert in the Agency Management Study [7].

Thus the stage was set for an organizational development emphasis that first engaged in scientific search for principles of organizational management, and then, once such principles were established, set forth to identify effective implementation strategies for them. This plan was provided impetus by real-life circumstances. Researchers rapidly discovered that the generation of sound findings regarding organizational management was one thing and their implementation quite another. Two factors seriously diminished the effective use of early findings. First, although survey items referred to work-world events, there was often no readily accepted "map" tying what was measured to operating realities in ways that were readily understood. Second, because there was a lack of implementation procedures geared to the data, presentation of findings normally involved a narrative report. As a result of both these factors, there was a great propensity either to file the report away, to pass it along to lower levels accompanied by vague directives to "use it," or simply to seize selectively upon bits which reinforced managers' existing biases [3].

The Nature of Survey Feedback

In an effort to solve this problem, Floyd Mann and his colleagues at the Institute for Social Research developed the *survey feedback* procedure as an implementation tool. No authoritative volume has as yet been written about this development tool. Partially as a result of this absence of detailed description, many persons mistakenly believe that survey feedback consists of a rather superficial handing back of tabulated numbers and percentages, but little else. On the contrary, where the survey feedback is employed with skill and experience, it becomes a sophisticated tool for using the data as a springboard to development. Data are typically tabulated for each and every work group in an organization, as well as for each combination of groups that represents an area of responsibility, including the total organization.

Each supervisor and manager receives a tabulation of this sort, containing data based on the responses of *his own* immediate subordinates, together with documents describing their interpretation and use. A resource person, sometimes from an outside (consulting) agency and at other times from the client system's own staff, usually counsels privately with the supervisor-recipient about the contents of the package and then arranges a suitable time when the supervisor can meet with his subordinates to discuss the findings and their implications. The resource person attends that meeting to provide help to the participants, both in the technical aspects of the tabulations and in the process aspects of the discussion.

Procedures by which the feedback process progresses through an organization may vary from site to site. In certain instances a "waterfall" pattern is adhered to, in which the process substantially is completed at high-level groups before moving down to subordinate groups. In other instances, feedback is more or less simultaneous to all groups and echelons.

By whichever route it takes, an effective survey feedback operation depicts the organization's groups as moving, by a discussion process, from the tabulated perceptions, through a cataloging of their implications, to commitment for solutions to the problems that the discussion has identified and defined.

The Necessity of Differential Diagnosis

From these general and specific concerns there has emerged a viewpoint, largely identified with persons associated with the Institute for Social

Research, that constructive change is measurement-centered, beginning with a quantitative reading of the state of the organization and direction of movement. Even more than this, change is, throughout, a rational process that makes use of information, pilot demonstrations, and the persuasive power of evidence and hard fact.

A successful change effort begins with rigorous measurement of the way in which the organization presently is functioning. These measurements provide the material for a diagnosis, and the diagnosis forms the basis for the design of a program of change activities. Likert has stated this quite pointedly in an early publication:

> One approach that can be used to apply the findings of human relations research to your own operation can be described briefly. Your medical departments did not order all of your supervisors nor all of your employees to take penicillin when it became available, even though it is a very effective antibiotic. They have, however, administered it to many of your employees. But note the process of deciding when it should be administered. The individual was given certain tests and measurements obtained—temperature, blood analysis, etc. The results of these measurements were compared with known facts about diseases, infections, etc., and the penicillin was prescribed when the condition was one that was known or believed to be one that would respond to this antibiotic.
>
> We believe the same approach should be used in dealing with the human problems of any organization. This suggests that human relations supervisory training programs should not automatically be prescribed for all supervisory and management personnel. Nor should other good remedies or methods for improvement be applied on a blanket basis to an entire organization hoping it will yield improved results [5, p. 35].

One of the reasons for the importance of the diagnostic step early in the life of a change program is stated explicitly in the preceding quotation: it will increase the probability of focusing upon the right, not the wrong, problems, and it will add to the likelihood of the right, not the wrong, course of treatments being prescribed. A clear statement of the problems, courses of action, and change objectives, based on sound measurements allied to the best possible conceptualization from research and theory, will maximize the likelihood that true causal conditions, rather than mere symptoms, will be dealt with [2].

The Rationale for Survey-Guided Development

The preceding sections have pointed to the existence of two somewhat different approaches to organization development. One, growing out of applied practice, is identified more obviously with the laboratory approach to education. It uses the *immediate* behavior (verbal and nonverbal) of the participants as the source material around which development forms. It focuses much more on the "here-and-now" than on the "there-and-then" and emphasizes experience-based learnings. It focuses more sharply on issues related to interpersonal processes than those less observable issues of role and structure.

The other approach, which we propose to elaborate on in greater detail, is related more obviously to an information-systems approach to adaptation. This approach uses participants' summarized perceptions of behavior and situation as the source material around which development is focused. It focuses on the there-and-then at least as much as on the here-and-now, attaches considerably more importance to cognitive understanding than does the other approach, and is concerned with such issues as role and structure, at least as much as with those of interpersonal process.

These brief identifications are more descriptive than explanatory. A true understanding of the survey-guided approach requires that we look more closely at the assumptions which it appears to make and the operating propositions which it derives from those assumptions.

Like most organization development techniques, survey feedback is only one aspect of a measurement-guided approach to change. As a tool or procedure, it emerged as a response to a practical need to see research findings implemented. It did not emerge as the logical conclusion of a formal body of scientific thought, and it remains for us presently to search, after the fact, for a rationale about how and why it works.

In this vein, two bodies of scientific thought seem relevant. One comes from the research done in the area of perception and involves the fundamental concept that a difference between perceptions is motivating—an idea originally and most clearly stated by Peak [8]. This is perhaps illustrated by the following example: if I perceive, on the one hand, that I cannot complete a particular piece of work by the end of the normal workday and perceive, on the other hand, that that work must be complete by the start of office hours in the morning, I am motivated to work late or to take home a work-loaded briefcase.

According to this view, the perceptions must be associated (i.e., they must be seen as belonging to the same "domain"). I may perceive that I do not play the piano as well as Arthur Rubenstein, but this discrepancy is hardly motivating, because I do not consider myself to be a professional concert pianist. Although associated, the perceptions must be different, yet not so different as to destroy their association. The perceptions may be related to emotion-laden or "feelings" issues, or they may consist of different perceptions of conditions in the external world. Peak illustrates the process by drawing an analogy:

> Think of a thermostat. Here there are two events. One is the temperature setting (an expected state if you will). The other event or term in the system is the height of the mercury in the tube, representing the present state of affairs (room temperature). These are analogous then to the two events in our motive construct, and disparity exists between them when there is a difference in the setting and in the temperature reading. Now, the second feature of our motive construct, which is called contact or association, is provided by the structure of the thermostat and is not modifiable in this system as it is in the motive system. In other words, the two terms (or events) remain in association. Only disparity can vary, and when there is disparity there is "motivation" and action;

> i.e., the furnace starts to run. The results of this action are fed back to produce change in one of the terms of the disparity relation (the mercury level). When the disparity disappears through rise in temperature or resetting of the thermostat, action ceases. . . . But since the thermostat lacks the capacity to stop action through isolation, and in the simple design we have described, cannot select different actions, the model must be regarded merely as illustrative . . .
> [8, pp. 172–73].

Another closely related set of ideas comes from engineering psychology and begins with the observation that human behavior is goal-seeking or goal-oriented. As such, behavior is characterized by a search for processes by which the human being controls his environment (i.e., means by which he reshapes it toward more constructive or productive ends).

Oversimplifying the control process greatly, at least four elements are involved: (1) a model, (2) a goal, (3) an activity, and (4) feedback. The *model* is a mental picture of the surrounding world, including not only structural properties, but cause-and-effect relations. It is built by the person(s) from past accumulations of information, stored in memory. From the workings of the model and from the modeling process which he employs, alternative possible future states are generated, of which one is selected as a *goal*. At this point what is called the "goal selection system" ends and what is known as the "control system" per se begins. *Activities* are initiated to attain the goal, and *feedback,* which comes by some route from the person's environment, is used to compare, confirm, adjust, and correct responses by signaling departures from what was expected.

The process as just described is beguilingly simple. However, in actual life it is often extremely complex. The thermostat example, although embodied in a marvelous and valuable piece of equipment, is basically a simple instance of an adaptive system. Others are much more complicated, such as that contained in the role of a Mississippi river boat pilot. The shifting character of currents and channels makes this adaptive task quite complex. Therefore the difficulty in this as in other complex systems stems from not having learned how to predict system performance under various conditions. As one of the foremost human factors writers has described it, "The ability to predict system performance is in major respects the same as the ability to control the system" [4, p. 42].

The human organization reflects the same type of a complex, difficult control system, in part for these same reasons. Activity is only as good as the model which leads to it, yet human organizations are often managed according to grossly imperfect models (models which ignore much of what is known from research about organizational structure and functioning). Predictability is enhanced, in human systems as elsewhere, by quantification, yet many of the relationships are often not quantified, if, indeed, they are recognized at all.

In the absence of a sound model, what is expected varies with immediate experience. It is for this reason that objective feedback on organizational functioning is absolutely essential in organizational development. In its absence, true deviations are unknown because expectations constantly adjust to incurred performance.

From this very condensed discussion, it is apparent that, when organizational change is viewed as a problem in optimal control or adaptation (which it inherently is) several things are required:

1. An adequate model—one which is a valid representation of that external reality known as "the organization," including both structural properties, knowledge of cause-effect relations, and predictive capability.
2. A goal—a preferred potential future state, generated by the model.
3. An activity—selected as instrumental to attaining that goal.
4. Objective feedback—about deviations from what the model would lead us to expect.

These two sets of concepts—the one drawn from basic work in the area of perception, the other taken from the human factors work of engineering psychology—provide jointly a plausible rationale for survey-guided development. As in the human factors area, feedback of information about the actual state of functioning provides key input to selecting development goals and making mid-course corrections. It tells the developing system what needs to be done. The power source, which in human factors descriptions is shown as an external input, is in survey-guided development provided by the sort of discrepancy described by Peak. Survey feedback, by pointing to the existence of differences between what is actually going on and what the model indicates one wants and needs, provides the energy (motivation) to undertake change activities.

In detail, as in general, organizational development (as the survey-guided approach envisions) may be seen as an analog of adaptation as described by human factors theorists. What they have termed the "goal selection system" is, in survey-based development, the *diagnostic* process. What they have referred to as the "control system" is the *therapeutic* process.

To serve its function within the diagnostic process, the work group draws inputs from the same sorts of areas drawn upon by all adaptive systems:

From higher-level systems: from the larger organization, its top management, and from society in general in the form of performance trends, top-management evaluations, labor relations trends, changes in laws or regulations, and so on.

From its own information about the model which they have thus far accepted, as well as information concerning past experiences and results.

From a reading of how things actually are: from the survey; through what we have described as survey feedback, which deals largely with intragroup behavior, attitudes, and relationships; and from a more formal *diagnosis* (an analytic report prepared by persons skilled in the survey data area), which deals with intergroup and systemic properties.

From the environment: in many forms, but particularly from the "change agent," the organizational development scientist-consultant who helps to catalyze the overall change process.

Each of these input sources has potential impact by virtue of its presence or comparative absence, its kind, and its quality. For example, the higher-level system inputs ordinarily create some degree of felt urgency. Often, discrepancy generated by this input motivates the initial search and culminates in serious consideration of organizational development as a possible course of action. The extent to which these inputs encourage the development efforts of the client entity is also critical. Many of the development failures occur in instances in which higher-level system inputs are either lacking, which indicates acquiescence, or instead, are signaling outright disapproval of organizational development. A general example of such an instance might involve a supervisor who verbally acquiesces to an organizational development effort for his subordinates but behaves and rewards his subordinates for behaving in ways which are incongruent with the values, assumptions, and goals that are emphasized in organizational development. Efforts that proceed in the face of such higher-level system inputs run a great risk of death by neglect.

From the group's own information storage comes the model of organizational functioning already held by group members. This includes information regarding past organizational practices (behaviors, interaction patterns, managerial styles) as well as outcomes at various levels of finality (absenteeism, turnover, profit, production efficiency, growth, et cetera).

The survey provides a means by which multiple perceptions of behaviors and organizational conditions related to effectiveness can be gathered, compiled, and compared. As has been indicated above, one must consider not one, but two, separate input streams from the survey. One of these input streams consists of the survey feedback process itself, in which tabulations of the group's *own data,* especially concerning its inter-

nal functioning, is used as a springboard to the identification, understanding, and solving of problems. The other consists of a more formal diagnosis, prepared by persons skilled in multivariate analysis, and focuses on those problem streams which occur in the system as a whole and which can be seen only by careful comparison of the tabulated data of many groups.

The Change Agent's Role

The change agent, as an adjunct person, seems to have no exact counterpart in *manual* control problems. The reason for his presence in organizational development is that a model of organizational functioning and human behavior is not as simple or programmable as that involved in manual control. Reading and digesting survey data are not the same as reading a gauge. Accomplishing an organizational "correction" is much more complicated than pushing a button or turning a wheel a certain number of degrees. In most instances the controller in organizational change—the client group—must be shown what the "gauge" says and how to read it, and must be guided through the operations of making the desired changes. The survey discrepancy, properly digested with the aid of the change agent, both builds the *motivation* to make the change and indicates *what* changes in functioning must occur. However, the change agent helps the client group learn *how* to make the necessary changes.

The primary role of the change agent in survey-guided development is that of a transducer (i.e., an energy link between scientific knowledge regarding principles of organizational functioning and the particular organization or group with which he is working). As such, the change agent enters into both the diagnostic and therapeutic phases of the development effort. During the diagnostic phase, the model that the change agent presents must be reasonably complete, predictive, and adequate to provide the client with useful information. If the model lacks any of these characteristics, the change agent will be supplying the system with little more than noise.

In addition to having these characteristics, the model must be presented to the members of the group or organization accurately and adequately. The issue of acceptance is critical: the best model loses its value unless it is understood in useful ways by members of the system. The model and evidence in its support must be presented in such a manner that acceptance is based upon rational evaluations of the evidence as well as the experiences and insights of those involved in the organization. During this activity, the change agent must have the model clearly in mind, must be able to present the model and its evidence clearly, and must also be able to call upon his group process and related skills to facilitate understanding and acceptance.

As in any other situation in which the talents and knowledge of one man are to be made available to assist another, the manner in which that occurs is, of course, important. In the area of human organizational development, of all places, it is important that the knowledge be made available in a supportive, not a demeaning, fashion; it is not to be "laid on," ordered into place, or delivered as some form of speech from a pretentious throne. Skill in patient explanation, in aiding understanding, and in helping the client entities themselves to come to grips with reality—in short, the whole array of interpersonal skills—are extremely important. But the change agent must have the knowledge of what must be explained, the grasp of what must be understood, and the comprehension of what that reality is.

In this vein, the change agent facilitates the understanding and digesting of diagnostically useful information. In the survey-guided approach, this role involves helping members of the system to understand better the survey feedback information. It also may involve a range of activities, from a detailed explanation of the meaning and relevance of certain content areas to helping group members understand information from the survey in terms of the here-and-now of the feedback meeting process. In addition, he aids the client group members in setting goals and formulating action plans for the development effort. In this activity, as in the others, the change agent may serve both as a source of information (e.g., suggesting potential actions to be undertaken or considered) and as a facilitator who focuses upon the group's processes.

The change agent also serves as a transducer in the therapeutic phase of survey-guided organizational development. Once a diagnosis has pointed to problem areas in organizational functioning, the change agent provides a link between scientific knowledge regarding effective methods of correcting specific problems and the problems exhibited in the immediate situation. A variety of activities may be undertaken during this phase. Each has, as its ultimate goal, movement toward the model of organizational functioning held (after its initial establishment) by both change agent and clients.

In part, the specific type of activity undertaken depends on the stage in the therapeutic phase. In the early stages, the change agent is likely to be involved largely with supplying informational inputs regarding specific possible activities, helping organizational members cope with attitudinal shifts, and handling defensive reactions. The motivation to change created by a discrepancy between the ideal model and the actual state of the organization is alone not sufficient to produce change. Methods of actually accomplishing the change must also be evident to organizational members. In this respect, the change agent in part fulfills his transducer role by informing members of the client system of the available alternatives.

In later stages, the change agent is often involved with skill acquisition and perfection by group members. The range and variety of potentially necessary skills is large. Problem solving, giving and receiving personal feedback, listening, general leadership, goal-setting, resolving conflict, and diagnosing group processes are but a few of those which might be cited. The change agent must not only know which skills are needed but also must be competent in guiding their acquisition. It is a result of this acquisition and perfection of skill that organizational members come to rely less on the change agent and more on themselves in movement toward the goal.

In addition to the emphasis on skills, the change agent provides and facilitates informal intermediate-phase feedback during the therapeutic phase. For example, he may provide the group with feedback in the form of process comments inserted during or after key intragroup interactions. He may also facilitate attempts by the members themselves to gather and understand information regarding their progress toward accepted goals.

A Recapitulation

As the preceding pages have indicated, the survey-guided approach suggests several general propositions regarding: (1) certain basic assumptions of organizational development; (2) change processes; and (3) the change agent's role.

Basic Assumptions of OD

There are systemic properties (i.e., characteristics of the organization as a total system) not definable by the simple sum of individual and/or group behaviors.

A *model* of organizational functioning, which includes these systemic properties, reflecting available evidence and testable by quantifiable and scientific means, should be used as a basis for development efforts.

Systemic properties in particular can improve only as a result of *carefully sequenced planned interventions.*

Valid information about the state of group and organizational functioning (objectives and useful reflections of reality) is best obtained from summarized, quantified longitudinal perceptions. (There-and-then data are at least as useful as here-and-now data.)

A *diagnosis* based upon a quantitative comparison with the model and prepared by competent professionals should be used to evaluate the organization on both intragroup and systemic levels.

Prescription of intervention activities should be *diagnostically based.*

Change Processes

Motivation is created by the realization that the actual state differs from the accepted model (i.e., a discrepancy exists between that which is desired and that which exists).

The discrepancies exist in terms of both *intragroup* and *systemic* processes and properties.

Change involves a *sequence of events,* including: informational inputs; formation of a model; selection of a goal; assessment of the situation; formation of a diagnosis; feedback; adjustment; and reevaluation.

Change Agent's Role and Activities

The change agent acts as *transducer* between scientific knowledge regarding organizational functioning and change processes, on the one hand, and the particular situation, on the other.

He has a *model* of organizational functioning and *works toward* its realization.

Except in those rare instances which require a nondirective stance, the change agent is an *active advocate of goal-oriented behavior.* He evaluates and helps the client group to *evaluate progress toward the goals,* but he is not punitive.

He must have a *wide range of knowledge and skills* and not be bound to one or two particular techniques.

These general propositions of survey-guided development are illustrated as a flow of events in Figure 1.

Perspective and Prologue

We conclude by offering an apology to the reader who anticipated a less-labored description. What has been written has been, in many ways, a rather technical document. It reflects our strong belief that organizational development rightfully is becoming more a science than an art. This view was expressed several years ago by one of the authors:

> By science I mean discernible in replicatable terms—objective, understandable (rather than "mystique"), verifiable, and predictive. Should these conditions for organizational development

FIGURE 1 Survey-Guided Development

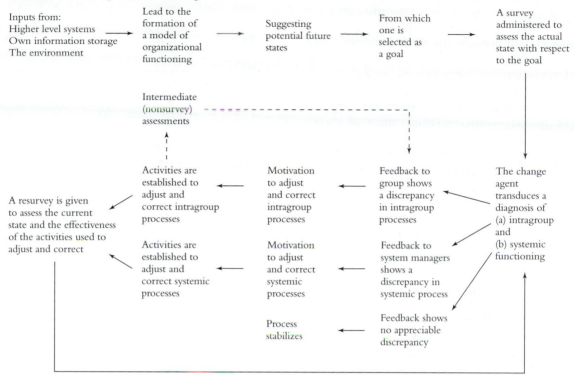

fail to be met, it will go the way of the Great Auk and the "Group Talking Technique." In short, organizational development will die, having been remembered as one more fad.

Organizational development cannot survive on the goodwill of top management persons who are already sold on its potential and effectiveness. It can survive only if it proves its method and its contribution beyond reasonable doubt to the hardheaded skeptics. Organizational development must prove with hard, rigorous evidence that it can beneficially affect: *(a)* the volume of work done by the organization, *(b)* the cost per unit of doing the organization's work, and *(c)* the quality of work done [1, p. 62].

The same article described barriers which, up to that time, had impeded the progress of organizational development as a science:

The lack of a "critical mass" of knowledge in the field.

The tendency for organizational development to take the form of a single general practitioner, operating on an isolated island.

The absence of an adequate measuring instrument, geared to an adequate model of organizational functioning, for use in organizational development efforts.

Within the last decade, considerable progress has been made on each of these fronts. Books and articles, describing and integrating findings in this field, have appeared in increasing numbers and richness. This present journal issue is a case in point.

To the extent that our own experience is typical, opportunities for researchers and change agents to collaborate in multifaceted, large system development efforts have emerged.

Efforts have similarly been undertaken by a number of persons to develop procedures and instruments for rigorous description of change agent interventions and their immediate effects.

Finally, we feel that survey-guided development has pressed, from its own necessity, the construction of reliable, valid, standardized instruments for assessing organizational functioning.

The availability of such instruments, together with the accumulating critical mass of knowledge, leads us to considerable optimism concerning the future of organizational development in general and concerning the survey-guided approach, in particular.

References

1. Bowers, D. G. "The Scientific Data-Based Approach to Organization Development," Part 2, in A. L. Hite, ed. *Organizational Development: The State of the Art.* Ann Arbor, MI: Foundation for Research on Human Behavior, 1971.

2. Bowers, D. G. *System 4: The Ideas of Rensis Likert.* New York: Basic Books, 1972.

3. Katz, Daniel, and Kahn, Robert L. *The Social Psychology of Organizations.* New York: John Wiley & Sons, 1966.

4. Kelly, C. R. *Manual and Automatic Control.* New York: John Wiley & Sons, 1968.

5. Likert, R. "Findings on Research on Management and Leadership." *Proceedings,* 43, Pacific Coast Gas Assn., 1952.

6. Likert, R. *The Human Organization.* New York: McGraw-Hill, 1967.

7. Likert, R., and Willets, J. M. *Morale and Agency Management.* Hartford, CT: Life Insurance Agency Management Association, 1940, 4 vols.

8. Peak, H. "Attitude and Motivation," in M. R. Jones, ed., *Nebraska Symposium on Motivation.* Lincoln, NE: University of Nebraska Press, 1955.

9. Survey Research Center. *A Program of Research on the Fundamental Problems of Organizing Human Behavior.* Ann Arbor: University of Michigan, 1947.

10. Taylor, J. C., and Bowers, D. G. *The Survey of Organizations: A Machine-Scored, Standardized Questionnaire Instrument.* Ann Arbor: Institute for Social Research, 1972.

Part 4

Cutting-Edge Change Strategies

This part includes seven articles that address what we call cutting-edge strategies because they describe organization development and transformation (OD & T) interventions that are relatively new or are in the process of development and refinement. All have a strong foundation of "systems" thinking. Some are relatively abstract and difficult to explain, for example, "appreciative inquiry" and "the learning organization," but all can be translated into specific interventions. All are difficult to implement successfully.

Because some of these interventions are nontraditional and may not be easily recognized as organization development and transformation, it might be useful to review what kind of intervention we include in a book on OD & T. Table 1 attempts to summarize the characteristics of intervention strategies we call OD & T and, conversely, what characteristics would suggest that a particular intervention or set of interventions falls outside that domain. Reengineering, for example, is not included because most descriptions of reengineering pay little attention to the social system or human-social-psychological processes of organizations.

The article by Robert A. Zawacki and Carol A. Norman, "Successful Self-Directed Teams and Planned Change: A Lot in Common," begins with an overview of the transition from first-generation planned change (OD) to second-generation planned change (OT). They then go on to assert that self-directed teams (SDTs) are part of this second-generation OT and are rapidly growing in popularity. They go on to say that the utilization of SDTs has resulted in significant increases in productivity when implemented effectively. They also discuss the law as it relates to SDTs and end their essay with guidelines for successful implementation.

In Reading 22 the authors start with the bold assertion that "appreciative inquiry is the new frontier of OD." They further state that Ai reflects the core values of OD practice and theory as developed over the last 50 years. The article contains an excellent overview of Ai historical roots and basic principles such as "action

TABLE 1   Organizational Improvement Strategies

	Organization Development (OD)	Non-OD (examples)
Target of intervention	Work-related groups.	Individuals, or noninterdependent persons in a group or audience setting.
Consultant model used	Collaborative equal power (change agent model).	Expert or "purchase" model.
Task or structure versus process orientation	Focuses largely on processes such as group interaction, norms, leadership, decision making; outcomes may be task/structural changes.	Focuses largely on changing tasks or structure.
Depth of culture managed	Attempt to manage culture in depth; both formal aspects and informal (e.g., cognizance of attitudes, perceptions, feelings).	Primary focus on one selected aspect of formal system (e.g., structure, technology, tasks, or goals).
Time perspective	Two to three years and beyond.	Ad hoc, short-range orientation.
Systems perspective	High systems orientation (i.e., high cognizance of interdependencies).	Narrow attention to functional organizational subsystem or problem.

research," "appreciation" and "social constructionism." They conclude their overview of Ai with the essential Ai process and very detailed organizational applications. This reading is a "must read" for students of OD and large-scale system wide change programs.

Marvin Weisbord and Sandra Janoff describe Future Search in Reading 23. They explain that Future Search is an OD intervention that brings large-scale system change to life. This method provides the organizational participants with a structure that permits them to act systemically by uniting various teams that are in each other's territory. After describing specific uses of the intervention, they continue with the process and economic benefits. They conclude with some provocative statements on the differences between OD and Future Search.

Gary Jusela's essay, "Meeting the Global Competitive Challenge: Building Systems That Learn on a Large Scale," was written especially for an earlier edition of this book. Jusela describes "getting the whole system in the room," an intervention used successfully at the Ford Motor Company and at Boeing Aerospace and Electronics Division. The total process at Boeing included three major phases. Phase I was a two-day working session with the Aerospace and Electronics Division manager and 15 of the top executives. Phase II was expanded to include the top 170 managers of the division who met for three days and then two more days 13 weeks later. Phase III, a series of three-day sessions, brought a total of some 3,000 managers into the strategic planning process in groups of 180 to 330 managers per session.

In "Centers of Excellence," Steven Lyle and Robert A. Zawacki describe a form of organization that has these characteristics: "a logical grouping of related skills or disciplines," "an administrative entity focused on the well-being and development of people," and "a place where individuals learn skills and share knowledge across functional boundaries." The COE is headed by a "coach" who has responsibilities in training and development, mentoring, "facilitating and enabling the exchange and sharing of ideas and information," recruitment and assignment of individuals, and salary administration and administrative support. COE members are sourced out to vertically organized project teams across the organization.

David Garvin, in his essay "Building a Learning Organization," adds some clarity to the concept of the "learning organization" or the "knowledge-creating companies," a topic that he says "in large part remains murky, confused, and difficult to penetrate." His definition: *"A learning organization is an organization skilled at creating, acquiring, and transferring knowledge, and at modifying its behavior to reflect new knowledge and insights."* He cites Honda, Corning, and General Electric as passing this definitional test and gives illustrations from Xerox, Chaparral Steel, General Food's Topeka plant, GM's Saturn Division, and the Copeland Corporation. At Xerox, for example, employees are trained in "family groups" and learn a six-step process for problem solving and such skills as brainstorming, interviewing, and surveying.

We believe that one of the key drivers of change is "time to market (fast cycle time)." Almost all of the accepted definitions of OD/OT define one of the characteristics as a long range planned change strategy. It is our experience that with reduced time to market for new products, many organizational leaders believe they do not have the time or luxury for a sustained long term system wide OD/OT effort. Thus, we believe this Reading 27 by Merrill C. Anderson begins the process of forcing OD practitioners/consultants to think about fast cycle OD/OT. With the current and future emphasis on faster, more cost effective and even better customer service, this article is a key read for the future OD person.

Successful Self-Directed Teams and Planned Change: A Lot in Common

Robert A. Zawacki
Carol A. Norman

Over the last 50 years, it appears that the nature of organizational change has changed. In the past, change flowed along a reasonably predictable course and individual contributors in the organization adjusted by working harder and smarter to stay ahead of the changes (Morland, 1984). Recently, however, organizations are facing high-speed change that is frequently transforming the direction and behavior of individual contributors.

This notion of rapid and random change is further discussed in Argyris (1991). He claims that the very behavior that has been reinforced by yesterday's performance can become a liability in the organization of the future. A brief example illustrates this point. The computer giant, IBM, built its success delivering mainframe computers. However, when the pace of change quickened, this computer giant was not flexible enough to perform effectively. In fact, the very behaviors that made it successful in the first few decades have now become a handicap.

Figure 1 illustrates this shift. Beginning with the 1950s and 1960s, change was incremental; people adapted and were rewarded for their new behaviors. Then, during the 1960s and 1970s change became more rapid and individual contributors responded by working harder and smarter. Leaders and managers in organizations helped people stay ahead of the increasing rate of change by introducing more and improved tech-

nologies such as personal computers and networks, and demonstrated some general movement toward empowering employees. The 1980s and 1990s brought even more rapid and random change. Change nowadays seems to lack predictability.

Interestingly, it was during the early decades of adaptive change that Organization Development as a response was born. The first generation of change agents, the OD practitioners, helped organizations respond to change over the long term. Numerous change initiatives were planned and delivered over a period of several years.

Now, however, as we move increasingly toward rapid and random change, business leaders do not have the luxury of time. It is out of this extreme need for more timely change that a second generation of OD is being born. Some in the profession call it Organization Transformation (OT), with its experimental feel and self-designing emphasis (Porras & Silvers, 1991). Whatever you call it, there is a shift in the approach organizations and OD practitioners are taking to respond to random change, and that is the use of teams. Organizations no longer rely on individual contributors to wade their way through change. Self-directed teams (SDTs), total quality circles, and employee empowerment are just a few of the team-oriented technologies designed to cope with fast-paced, random change.

The purpose of this article is to help organizations of the future improve their ability to adapt to random change, yet maintain some degree of order, stability, and internal equity through the successful use of self-directed teams.

Source: Reprinted by permission of the Organization Development Network, 71 Valley Street, Suite 301, South Orange, NJ 07079-2825. (973) 763-7337—voice, (973) 763-7488—fax, http://www.odnet.org.

FIGURE 1   **The Changing Nature of Organizational Change**

Source: This is a modification of D. Verne Morland, "Lear's Fool: Coping With Change Beyond Future Shock" (1984).

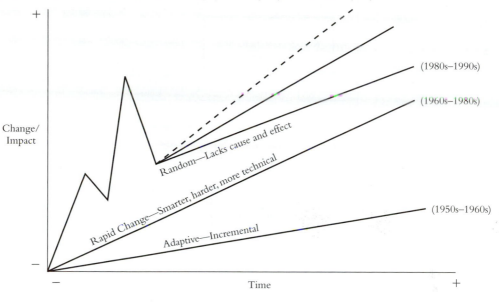

The History of Self-Directed Teams

The concept of self-directed teams came from the early research of Kurt Lewin at the Research Center for Group Dynamics and of the Tavistock Institute of Human Relations, whose members conceptualized sociotechnical systems theory as an approach to designing organizations (Lewin, 1951).

The Research Center at MIT (the initial group dynamics effort founded in 1945 under Lewin's direction, which later evolved into the National Training Laboratory in Group Development) introduced the idea of feedback to group members and the effect of feedback on individual and group behavior (French & Bell, 1984). At about the same time, the Tavistock group began to look at the interdependence between technology and people. "A concrete outcome of this theoretical perspective was the development of self-regulating work groups," according to Cummings (1978). Various authors have named these groups:

autonomous, self-managed, self-regulating, composite, self-directed, or work teams. Yet the common denominator across the initiatives was the goal of transferring the control of work process over time from the manager to members in the work unit.

It is our experience that many managers, coaches, and OD consultants view SDTs as binary: You either have them or you don't. However, recent research indicates that the key to successful SDTs is that the transfer of control must be planned and implemented over time with managers who have the ability to make the transition into coaches.

In fact, successful SDTs evolve through five stages. Figure 2 depicts the evolution from a control model to a self-directed model and the corresponding organizational structure. Stage 1 reflects the typical hierarchical organization; Stage 2 introduces the group manager whose role is to make the transition into team coordinator/coach; in Stage 3 the group manager provides a structure

FIGURE 2 The Evolution of a Self-Directed Team

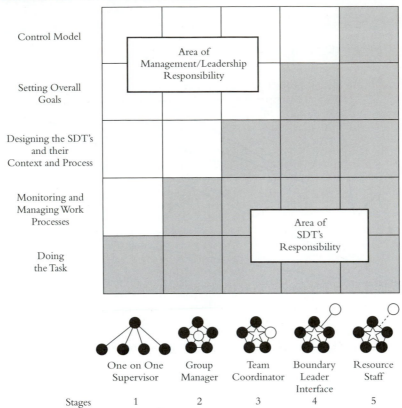

for the necessary training for SDT members to take on more leadership tasks; in Stage 4 the team assumes most of the duties of the previous manager, who now becomes a boundary interface; and finally, in Stage 5, the manager is a resource for the SDT. A typical organization will have SDTs in all five stages at various times. Furthermore, any SDT can revert back to an earlier stage as team members of the SDT leave or new members enter the group.

Cummings (1978) adds to our understanding of SDTs. He states, ". . . the design of self-regulating work groups depends on at least three conditions that enhance technically required co-operation and employees' capacity to control variances from goal attainment: task differentiation, boundary control, and task control."

Task differentiation refers to the autonomous nature of the team's work. This permits the SDT to develop an identity whereby technical specialists emerge within the team to solve technical problems.

Boundary control is defined as the ability of the team members to control quality decisions, staffing and performance appraisal issues rather than relying on outside resources. Also, a well-defined work area increases the boundary control of the SDT.

Task control is the degree of control that the team members have over how they change inputs into a completed product or service.

Based on our research and experience with successful SDTs, we will add a fourth condition to Cummings's list. The fourth condition is the ability of the control manager to make the transition into a coach.

Why SDTs Succeed or Fail

For the last six years we have experimented with SDTs in organizations from small manufacturing firms to large service companies. Our experience is that SDTs can succeed or fail, regardless of the core technology, for several reasons.

Many organizations that profess to having SDTs in fact do not. A further examination of their teams reveals that they typically violated one or usually all four of the conditions mentioned above. Thus, what some organizations claim are SDTs are really only people going to staff meetings. Many organizations are chasing the quick fix and do not plan properly or even understand the dimensions of successful SDTs.

Additionally, only about 50 percent of managers can make the transition from controller to coach because of the need to unlearn old behaviors and learn new helping, negotiation, and conflict resolution skills.

Combined with this lack of understanding of the dimensions of successful SDTs is the impatience of top management. Top management is generally looking for the next quick fix because they usually are rewarded on a quarterly basis and are unwilling to "stay the course" for a long-term planned change program such as SDTs.

The key is to have people who believe they are valued and empowered, managers who can make the transition into coaches over time, and a well-designed plan. Cummings recognized the need to plan for SDTs and implement them over time. He refers to this process as "developmental system design," which came out of the early Tavistock research.

Developmental System Design

There is a group of leadership competencies that must be performed within an SDT; the key to becoming a successful SDT is to transfer these competencies from leader to team members with a

plan over time. Although rare to find, there are managers who have the ability to sense the timing and training required before team members share in some of the leadership tasks. Figure 3 illustrates this transfer of competencies.

The critical activities are transferred from the leader to the team members over a period of 30 months, which our experience suggests is an optimum goal. OD consultants should experiment with reducing this time even more if they are to be perceived in the 1990s as adding value to the organization. With a good plan and checklist you can load the experiment for success!

Establish a Steering Committee

The first activity we recommend is to establish a steering committee to help the SDT, the primary purpose of which is to demonstrate top-level support but also to provide linkages to other parts of the organization. The steering committee should be a 12-member team consisting of senior executives, middle managers, technical people, and the individual contributors who report directly to the president or CEO. Their primary activity is to meet every three to six months with the SDT to check progress and provide needed support. In some organizations, the steering committee even becomes an SDT because it functions as a role model for the rest of the organization.

Provide Training for the SDT

Although each activity on the checklist is extremely important, training is critical to successful SDTs and will be discussed briefly. Many leaders of technical organizations attempt to save money by not committing to sufficient training before and during the evolution of SDTs. One leader, who attempted to save money up front, stated later, "If only I would have listened to you and approved of the training before we started SDTs. Now we are playing 'catch up' as the team grew without any planned way to deal with conflict."

At the outset. After the formation of an SDT, the first skill set needed by the group is a course on problem solving, since decision making in the group becomes the primary function. Additionally,

FIGURE 3   The Transfer of Competencies to SDTs

Activity	Before Design/ Implementation	Months					
		3	6	12	18	24	30
1. Steering committee	X	X	X	X	X	X	X
2. Leadership's/coach's responsibilities	X						
3. Team members' responsibilities	X						
4. Goals	X						
5. Assumptions (about SDTs and people)	X						
6a. Technical and quality training		X					
6b. People skills training:							
Problem solving		X					
Team building			X	X	X	X	X
Conducting meetings			X				
Presentation skills			X				
Conflict resolution				X			
Change skills				X			X
6c. Management skills training							
Interviewing				X			
Feedback and coaching				X			
Performance appraisal		X					
Group rewards		X			X		
Budgets							X
7a. Internal measurement		X	X	X	X		
7b. Customer service measurement				X		X	
8. Feedback—Team and other SDTs		X	X	X	X	X	X

the SDT will need training in team building, followed by courses on *facilitating meetings* and *making presentations.*

After 12 months. As the group matures, interviewing and hiring decisions transfer from the leader to the SDT. However, the transfer must not happen until the team members have been trained in *interviewing skills, performance appraisal,* and *giving constructive feedback.*

After 18 months. In most traditional hierarchical organizations, managers tend to resist performance appraisal and are usually late doing the performance appraisals of their subordinates. One typically hears employees report that they do not receive sufficient feedback. Norman & Zawacki (1991) describe the process for a peer evaluation system within SDTs. Our early findings indicate that although the leader/coach may be threatened

or at best hesitant to turn this process over to the team, once the new process is in place, the leader/coach becomes a strong advocate because it relieves him/her of a burden—getting those performance appraisals into personnel on time. However, transferring the performance appraisal process from the leader/coach to the team members should occur only after adequate training has taken place.

Tracking SDT Performance

Internal and external measures of performance are critical to the success of SDTs. Those things that get measured get done! If the leaders of an organization support a pilot SDT, invariably someone will ask for measures of effectiveness or value added. There are many good measures of customer service that should be administered every six months. Furthermore, the measures should be simple and quick so the customer is not burdened with bureaucracy. Internal measures of team satisfaction usually are administered every week during the early stages of the SDT. As the SDT matures, the team should measure and feed back the results to the team every two weeks. After the sixth month, the SDT can move back to a three- or four-month cycle.

Teams and the Law

On December 16, 1992 the National Labor Relations Board issued a decision in Electromation, Inc., 309 NLRB No. 163 (1992), which raised the issue of whether employee committees are labor organizations as defined in the 1935 National Labor Relations Act. The decision of the NLRB was that Electromation violated the 1935 act against setting up a company union by establishing and dominating five employee representation committees. Unfortunately, the NLRB's decision is a setback for organizations looking to teams to increase motivation and productivity. However, the decision will continue to be challenged in the courts or addressed by Congress because the NLRB's decision ". . . was narrowly focused on the particular facts of the case, which was a disappointment to many who had hoped the Board would provide general guidelines for lawfully creating and maintaining employee involvement committees" (Frum, 1993).

The problem is that the National Labor Relations Act of 1935 is a statute ". . . largely written in the days of wrenches and blast furnaces, [and] can be read as outlawing these groups" (Frum, 1993). OD consultants should continue to help organizations design SDTs; however, they must be aware of this outdated law and use every opportunity to communicate with their representatives in Congress the need for a change in it.

Our advice to change agents is to watch the OD and human resource journals for further comment on this extremely serious development regarding teams. For example, the NLRB is likely to rule on a similar case at DuPont.

Guidelines for Implementing Successful SDTs

Successful SDTs have a lot in common with processes firmly rooted in the realm of OD. For example, both have elements of the definition of OD by French and Bell (1984), such as long-range effort, top management support, improved problem-solving, emphasis on teams, the assistance of a facilitator, and the use of theory to guide the change agents.

To stack your SDT for success requires:

- Setting up a steering committee with top management support and planning a long-range effort with a pilot SDT.

- Making certain that the pilot SDT is congruent with organizational values and goals. Recognize that designing and implementing SDTs is a Theory Y philosophy and this may be a cultural shift for the organization.

- Selecting a natural work group whose members are committed to employee empowerment and are involved in a technology/product/service with task interdependencies.

- Establishing base-line customer measures of internal team satisfaction and customer service to inform all members of the organization on the progress of the pilot and future SDTs. Consider having SDT members brief top leaders on their progress. Feedback permits the program to adjust, grow, and remain viable over time (Goodman & Dean, 1981).

- Visiting other organizations with SDTs to determine "best practices."

- Recognizing that many managers are threatened by the mere mention of SDTs. No longer the expert, managers must now become coaches and problem solvers or facilitators. It is our experience that only about one-half of existing managers can make the transition even after training in the new competencies. Organization leaders need to clearly state expectations up front that good managers who cannot make the transition to coaches will be retrained as individual contributors as long as they add value to the bottom line.

- Revamping the reward system to allow for greater employee participation in reward decisions and designing gain-sharing plans or profit-sharing schemes that encourage cross-functional cooperation. At about the 18-month point, consider changing the reward from individual to part group/individual. Consider a bonus for the volunteers in the first pilot SDT.

- Being patient. There is an actual drop in productivity during the early stages of an SDT because the team members are learning new skills, conducting staff meetings, and so on. But as the team grows and as the individual members feel they are truly empowered, the gains are greater productivity, lower costs, higher quality products, greater customer service, and more adaptability. It may be 18–24 months before the organization begins to see the positive results of the change program.

References

Argyris, C. (1991). "Teaching Smart People How to Learn," *Harvard Business Review,* May–June: 99–109.

Cummings, T. G. (1978). "Self-Regulating Work Groups: A Socio-Technical Synthesis," *Academy of Management Review,* No. 3, July: 625–634.

French, W. L. and Bell, C. H. Jr. (1984). "A History of Organization Development," in *Organization Development: Behavioral Science Interventions for Organization Development,* 3rd ed. Englewood Cliffs, NJ: Prentice Hall.

Frum, D. (1993). "Electromation Appeals NLRB Ruling," *Human Resources Management,* No. 293, January 20:9.

Goodman, P. S. and Dean, J. W. Jr. (1981). "Why Productivity Efforts Fail." Paper presented at the American Psychological Association, August 1981.

Morland, D. V. (1984). "Lear's Fool: Coping with Change Beyond Future Shock," *New Management,* 2(2).

Norman, C. A. and Zawacki, R. A. (1991). "Team Appraisals-Team Approach," *Personnel Journal,* September: 101–104.

Overman, S. (1993). "NLRB Ruling on Teams Fails to End Dispute," *HR News,* January, p. A3. See also "Manager's Newsfront," *Personnel Journal,* February 1993:20.

Porras, J. I. and Silvers, R. C. (1991). "Organization Development and Transformation," *Annual Review of Psychology,* 42: 51–78.

Trist, E. L. and Bamforth, K. W. (1951). "Some Social and Psychological Consequences of the Longwall Method of Coal Getting," *Human Relations,* 4:3–38.

Reading 22

Appreciative Inquiry: *The New Frontier*

Stephen P. Fitzgerald
Kenneth L. Murrell
H. Lynn Newman

Appreciative inquiry (Ai) is the new frontier! What a provocative and bold assertion. So what is this appreciative approach, and what's new about it? Is it a current fad or truly something new in organization development? Many people have called Ai "ground-breaking." Certainly, as conceived of and described in some of the foundational work of David Cooperrider and colleagues at Case Western Reserve University, in the doctoral program in organizational behavior created in 1960 by Herb Shephard, and at the Taos Institute, Ai reflects the core values of organization development (OD) practice and theory developed over the past half-century. At a minimum, it encourages us to rethink and enlarge how OD professionals approach this work, possibly leading to a reinventing of OD itself.

Cooperrider and Whitney (1999) offer the following practice-oriented definition of Ai:

> Appreciative Inquiry is the cooperative search for the best in people, their organizations, and the world around them. It involves systematic discovery of what gives a system "life" when it is most effective and capable in economic, ecological, and human terms. Ai involves the art and practice of asking questions that strengthen a system's capacity to heighten positive potential. It mobilizes inquiry through crafting an "unconditional positive

Note: We thank David Cooperrider for his feedback on this chapter and helpful additions to it.

Source: "Appreciative Inquiry: The New Frontier," by Stephen P. Fitzgerald, Kenneth L. Murrell, and H. Lynn Newman. From *Organization Development: A Data-Driven Approach to Organization Change,* Janine Waclawski and Allan H. Church, editors, San Francisco: Jossey-Bass, Inc., a Wiley Company, 2002, used with permission.

question" often involving hundreds or sometimes thousands of people [p. 10].

Ai is not a technique or method, although there is a basic Ai approach that has been articulated in the literature and practiced in various settings. Most important, Ai is an affirmative worldview that shapes what we look for in organizational inquiry. It involves a conscious value choice to seek the most affirmative, valuing, and generative information available. The intention is to discover and build on the strength and vitality of human systems as experienced and reported by their members.

Ai is a novel approach to organizational change work. The affirmative value choice is what distinguishes it from other forms of OD. It influences every aspect of Ai, from the design of topics and questions to explore, to data analyses and feedback. As a strategy of change, Ai inspires collaborative action that engages and serves the whole system.

Ai's Historical Roots and Basic Principles

Ai is relationally linked to contemporary forms of action research. It is rooted in radical social constructionism, appreciation, and the generative power of positive imagery. These historical roots are the bases of Ai's five basic principles (constructionist, simultaneity, poetic, anticipatory, and positive). In addition, there are complementary innovations in other fields that are co-constructing a similarly affirmative worldview (for example, solution-focused therapy in counseling psychology; De Shazer et al., 1986).

Action Research

Action research underlies most current OD approaches for studying and simultaneously changing social systems. . . . Lewin (1946) introduced this scientific process as a way of generating knowledge about a social system while simultaneously attempting to change it. He initially described action research as a "spiral of steps, each of which is composed of a circle of planning, action, and fact-finding about the result of the action" (pp. 34–35).

Cooperrider and Srivastva (1987) first articulated the idea and coined the term *appreciative inquiry* as they reenvisioned the possibility of action research. They noted that action research had not "achieved its potential for advancing social knowledge of consequence and [had] not, therefore, achieved its potential as a vehicle for human development and social-organizational transformation" (p. 130). They claimed that this was due to the problem-oriented view of organizing that pervaded the approaches to action research that were current when they wrote. Their argument was essentially that action research had become too focused on the client and the solving of the client's problem, to the exclusion of the theory-generating aspects so critical to the definition of action research that Lewin had outlined. It remains true to this day that practitioners too often focus exclusively on linear problem solving of immediate organizational issues, which is what clients most readily understand and expect.

Other contemporary forms of action research have also emerged, among them participatory action research, action science, and action learning. All of the contemporary approaches, including Ai, emphasize full client-consultant partnership, collaborative learning throughout the action research process, the importance of local tacit knowledge, a willingness to examine assumptions in the system, and organizational transformation. These newer approaches might be viewed as extending an action research continuum that ranges from more traditional, consultant-directed, linear applications toward increasingly collaborative,

systemic, transformational change processes (Newman & Fitzgerald, 2000).

Appreciation

Beyond sharing these characteristics of contemporary action research, Ai selectively values appreciation. The work of Sir Geoffrey Vickers, published in the late 1950s and early 1960s in the United Kingdom and United States, offered what was for many a completely new understanding of the concept of appreciation. For Vickers, appreciation is a process of developing a full and penetrating understanding of a particular world, as well as a focus on what one wants to make of it. His concept of appreciated worlds provided the impetus to go deeply into the meaning of the ideas or events one is trying to assist in changing. He encouraged us to focus on what is right and not just what is lacking. Today the Ai practice of creating dialogue helps to bring out what a fuller and deeper appreciation means.

Social Constructionism

Social constructionism is a fundamental underpinning of Ai. This philosophy of science (Berger & Luckmann, 1966) suggests that we have considerable influence over the nature of the realities that we perceive and experience, and to a great extent we actually create our realities through collective symbolic and mental processes.

Cooperrider's initial inspiration for Ai rose from the more radical forms of social constructionism (Gergen, 1982), out of which Ai emerged as a theory-building process. The notion of generative theory is central to this in that it "has the capacity to challenge the guiding assumptions of the culture, to raise fundamental questions regarding contemporary life, to foster reconsideration of that which is taken for granted, and thereby furnish new alternatives for social action" (Cooperrider, 1999, p. 1, citing Gergen, 1982).

Reflecting on Ai's early history, Cooperrider (1999) wrote, "It was later, partly because of social constructionism's relational view of knowledge that [we] began doing 'theory building' with organizations . . . literally creating the theory and propositions with the organizations we were working with . . . making the theory-building totally collaborative. We invited people to challenge the status quo, to stretch, to provoke new ways of thinking and talking about the future" (p. 1).

Five basic principles have been described as central to Ai's theory base of change (Cooperrider, Barrett, & Srivastva, 1995; Cooperrider & Srivastva, 1987; Cooperrider & Whitney, 1999). Social constructionism serves as the primary theoretical foundation for at least three of those five principles: the constructionist principle, the principle of simultaneity, and the poetic principle. The constructionist principle holds that human knowledge and organizational destiny are intricately interwoven. To be effective as executives, leaders, and change agents, we must be adept in the art of understanding, reading, and analyzing organizations as living, human constructions. Knowing (organizations) stands at the center of any and virtually every attempt at change. Thus, the way we know is fateful.

Because organizations are living human constructions, inquiry and change cannot be separated; they occur simultaneously. This is the principle of simultaneity. The seeds of change—the things that we think and talk about, discover and learn together, and that inform our dialogue and inspire our images of the future—are implicit in the very first questions we ask. Those questions set the stage for what we find, and what we discover (the data) becomes the linguistic material, the stories out of which the future is conceived, conversed about, and constructed.

Thus, human organizations are a lot more like an open book than, say, a machine. An organization's story is constantly being coauthored. Moreover, pasts, presents, and futures are endless sources of learning, inspiration, and interpretation—much like the endless interpretive possibilities in a good piece of poetry or literature. This is the essence of Ai's poetic principle. The important implication is that we can study virtually any topic related to human experience in any human system or organization. We can inquire into the nature of alienation or joy, enthusiasm or low morale, efficiency or ex-

cess. There is not a single topic related to organization life that we could not study.

The Power and Role of Image

The Ai approach is based on the formidable power of cognitive image to create action. Consider two different settings: anticipating what we expect may be a conflictual meeting with a friend versus anticipating sharing a favorite activity with a friend. Each of these images creates different expectations and feelings in us that are likely to result in different behaviors. Anticipation is a potent, generative force. It is the basis for Ai's fourth principle.

One of the basic theorems of this anticipatory principle is that the image of the future guides what might be called the current behavior of any organism or organization. Much like a movie projector on a screen, human systems are forever projecting ahead of themselves a horizon of expectation (in their talk in the hallways, in the metaphors and language they use) that brings the future powerfully into the present as a mobilizing agent. To inquire in ways that refashion anticipatory reality, especially through the artful creation of positive imagery on a collective basis, may be the most productive thing any inquiry can do.

Furthermore, research from diverse fields substantiates the power of positive imagery to generate positive action (see Cooperrider, 1990, for a thorough treatment of these concepts). For example, in medicine, the well-documented placebo effect results from people's positive expectancy about the healing potential of medication that they are given, even when, without their knowledge, it contains only sugar.

Classic research in the field of education found that a so-called Pygmalion effect occurred when teachers were told that some of their students had high potential when in fact they were no different from other students. In study after study, the supposedly high-potential students significantly outperformed their classmates. This positive expectancy effect has been demonstrated in the workplace as well as in the world of sports. It is the basis for Ai's fifth principle.

This positive principle grows out of years of experience with Ai. Building and sustaining momentum for change requires large amounts of positive affect and social bonding—things like hope, excitement, inspiration, caring, camaraderie, sense of urgent purpose, and sheer joy in creating something meaningful together. We have found that it does not help to begin inquiries from the standpoint of the world as a problem to be solved. Instead, we have seen that the more positive the questions are that we ask in our work and the longer we can retain the spirit of inquiry of the everlasting beginner, the more long-lasting and successful are our change efforts. The thing that makes the most difference is to craft and seed, in better and more catalytic ways, the unconditional positive question. Changes never thought possible are suddenly and democratically mobilized.

In sum, Ai is relationally linked to contemporary forms of action research. It is rooted in radical social constructionism, appreciation, and the generative power of positive imagery. These historical roots are the bases of Ai's five basic principles. In addition, there are complementary innovations in other fields that are coconstructing a similarly affirmative worldview (for example, solution-focused therapy in counseling psychology; see De Shazer et al., 1986).

The Essential Ai Process

Ai's five underlying principles (constructionist, simultaneity, poetic, anticipatory, and positive) come to life through the design of the basic Ai process, which is typically presented as a cycle of four phases known the *4-D cycle* (Cooperrider, 1996):

Phase 1: Discovery of people's experiences of their group, organization, or community at its most vital and alive and what made those experiences possible

Phase 2: Dreaming together to envision a future in which those exceptional experiences form the bases for organizing

Phase 3: Designing appreciative systems and structures to support the manifestation of the co-created dreams

Phase 4: Destiny or delivery, which involves implementation of those systems and structures in an ever-expanding positive-feedback loop of appreciative learning

Ai practitioners have developed several variations on the 4-D cycle involving additional phases for use in a variety of settings. One addition that had always been considered the cycle's precursor is an initial defining phase in which three to five topics are collaboratively selected to focus the inquiry. Key practitioner guidelines on each of these five phases are described below.

Phase 1: Define

Based on Ai's underlying principles, the most powerful tools at our disposal are our capacity to inquire together and focus the nature of the inquiry. Hammond (1996) notes that "what we focus on becomes our reality" (p. 20). Therefore, defining the topics for an appreciative inquiry is perhaps the most critical phase of the process.

To ensure broad-based support and whole system impact, include representatives of all stakeholder groups in defining the topics for the inquiry. For large applications, topic definition may require a preliminary two-day Ai retreat or systemwide Ai interviews. During this process, value-rich, locally meaningful topics are collaboratively developed—for example, "transform leadership development into open, just, and inclusive leadership" (Newman & Fitzgerald, 2000, p. 7). As a general rule of thumb, three to five broad topics are the maximum for an Ai process. Ai interview questions are then developed out of the chosen topics.

Phase 2: Discover

The discovery phase typically begins with paired appreciative interviews exploring participants' peak experiences of each topic and what made those experiences possible. The interview questions and process are designed to elicit and revitalize the positive affect associated with participants' stories, which nurtures intrinsic motivation.

The highlights and most "quotable quotes" from participants' stories are then shared in small and large groups. This essentially builds a live, collective database of organizational excellence that includes metaphor, imagery, and affect, in addition to concrete examples. Capturing these elements graphically on large surfaces in addition to or instead of expressing them in verbal and written words greatly amplifies their impact throughout the process.

Phase 3: Dream

During the dream phase, the best of the past is amplified into collectively envisioned and desired futures. Working together in groups, participants review the images, metaphors, hopes, and dreams that were generated in the discovery phase. (Paired appreciative interviews typically conclude with questions that elicit individuals' hopes and dreams regarding the Ai topics.) Participants are then encouraged to expand, stretch, and elaborate their collective dreams and to embody them creatively through skits, art, songs, and other forms, which are then shared with the entire group.

Phase 4: Design

During the design phase, participants identify key facets of organizational systems and structures that will be needed to support the realization of their collectively generated dreams. The facilitator may introduce a model of organizational structure for participants to work with or may support participants in generating their own models.

Working again in groups, participants craft bold, affirmative possibility statements, also known as *provocative propositions* (PPs), that express their expansive dreams as already realized in the present tense. Language, imagery, and examples from the discovery and dream phases are incorporated into these design statements, each crafted around a facet of the organizational structure. The finished PPs are then visually displayed and shared with the entire group. Together, the

PPs form the basis for developing vision-guided action plans.

Phase 5: Deliver

This fifth phase may begin prior to the conclusion of an Ai summit . . . , but it extends into the ongoing life of the group, organization, and community. Participants self-select into task groups according to the design statements that they feel most strongly drawn to. They then work together to ground those design statements in action steps. Action plans may be shared with the entire group. Participants then self-select projects or tasks that they would like to work on or otherwise support. Actions are implemented over time in an iterative, appreciative learning journey.

Organizational Applications

Ai processes have been successfully implemented in a wide variety of organizational settings in the business, government, and non-profit sectors. Ai applications have ranged from appreciative human resource practices, team development, diversity initiatives, and strategic planning, to the transformation of global corporate cultures and social change organizations (Hammond & Royal, 1998; Head, 2000; Mohr, Smith, & Watkins, 2000; Newman & Fitzgerald, 2000; Whitney & Cooperrider, 1998; Williams, 1996). The diversity of these applications continues to increase as practitioners explore Ai approaches in a wide variety of organizational settings.

Given the breadth and diversity of Ai applications, some may protest that Ai is being hailed as a magic bullet that works in all situations. Yet to make this same claim for the highly accepted problem-solving orientation is not that unusual. The problem-identification-analysis-solution approach is so firmly grounded in our culture of critique that it is seldom questioned as to the overall effect it has on the way we characterize the world as a problem to be solved.

There are at least four reasons for choosing Ai for large-scale applications: (1) high levels of participation and cooperation are required, (2) the change process needs to be accelerated, (3) the work requires innovation among diverse groups in a high-stakes environment, or (4) multiple change initiatives need to be synthesized (Whitney & Cooperrider, 1998). Even when these conditions are met, however, Ai may not be appropriate if sufficient resources are unavailable for adequate implementation or leadership does not support affirmative approaches or full system participation. Some successful organizational applications are briefly described.

Large-Scale System Change

In its fullest expression, Ai is an approach to large-scale system change. Whole system Ai transformation is the ideal because it affects the mind-set and culture of the entire enterprise, influencing every facet of organizational life. Thus, Ai is approached not as an intervention or event but as a continual, systemic, self-reinforcing learning journey.

A cornerstone of large-scale Ai system change is the Appreciative Inquiry Summit, which integrates the best of current large group change processes . . . into an appreciative framework. (Whitney & Cooperrider, 1998) It is typically a four-day event that includes the entire organization and its customers, suppliers, and other community stakeholders. An Ai Summit incorporates the full 4-D cycle. It also provides unstructured time for informal relationship building, which is crucial to the effectiveness of any significant change initiative.

Ai Summits have proven to be effective in a wide variety of organizational settings—for example, "launching a union-management partnership throughout GTE; strategic planning for the entire company, Nutramental; for culture change in numerous organizations in health care, government, and consulting services; for economic development in a region of the country; for citywide community development and for drafting a charter for a newly emerging global organization" (Whitney & Cooperrider, 1998, p. 21).

Team-Based Applications

Whole system, large-scale Ai implementation may be ideal, but applications with teams can also be successful. Furthermore, Ai success with one or more teams can lead to wider organizational implementation.

That is exactly what happened in the case of an Ai strategic planning session with the executive team of a 120-person nonprofit health care facility (Newman & Fitzgerald, 2000). A large-scale organizational change effort had been in process at the clinic since 1996. Traditional action research approaches (for example, customized survey to identify organizational issues, and executive coaching) were used in the first years. A trusting relationship between the executive director and lead consultant developed over time, allowing for the implementation of increasingly collaborative action research processes.

By the third year, the executive team wanted to increase creativity in its problem solving and strategic planning. An Ai design was incorporated into the executive retreat. The interview questions focused on the topic of "open, just, and inclusive leadership" so as to address issues that had been identified in that year's employee survey.

Results far exceeded expectations. Team members generated a powerful vision of inclusive leadership. They created fundamental structural changes that addressed key organizational issues from a place of vision expressed through their PPs.

Ai has also been used effectively with teams experiencing significant conflict. In one case, an engineering design team was six weeks behind schedule at the eleventh month of a strategically critical twenty-month project. At that point, Ai was employed in a team retreat. As a result, the team finished a month ahead of schedule and "delivered a product that performed significantly above specifications for less than the expected cost" (Brittain, 1998, p. 228). As a result of the team's success, Ai was implemented for all product design teams throughout the organization.

A recent empirical study (Head, 2000) substantiates the efficacy of Ai in fostering the development of heterogonous teams. Three interventions—Ai, team building, and a control group—were divided among eighteen new management teams in the U.S. Postal Service. The Ai teams exhibited the largest decline in self-directed behaviors and greatest increase in team-related behaviors on the Group Style Instrument, the best results (although not statistically significant) on external measures of team performance, and significantly more positive imagery regarding their future interactions and performance. Furthermore, a statistically significant, strongly positive correlation ($r(34) = .74$, $p < .001$) was observed between group image and performance, indicating that the more positive a team's image of itself, the better is its performance. "The results lend support to the theory that Ai aids in assisting groups to improve their image of the future and that allows groups to more quickly develop and perform" (Head, 2000, p. 66).

Program Evaluation

Program evaluation has traditionally been approached as a past-focused critique. However, Mohr et al. (2000) collaborated to develop a vital, appreciative program valuation for the R&D division of SmithKline Beecham. Over a six-week period, they conducted 109 appreciative interviews with research scientists in two countries who had participated in an innovative simulation-based training program. To their surprise, they found that the scientists were very receptive to the appreciative approach, the process "increasingly became a forward-focused intervention in its own right, rather than the backward look of a typical evaluation study" (p. 39), and "not only were these traditional evaluation questions effectively met with this approach, but the corporation benefited from both the learning reinforcement that occurred and the richness of data which would not have been captured in a normal evaluation process" (p. 49).

In another example, an appreciative approach was used in a follow-up evaluation for the Acad-

emy of Management's Theme-Summit, from the design of the survey instrument to the analysis, display, and discussion of the data (Fitzgerald, 1999).

Human Resource Practices

Many traditional human resource practices have been redesigned from an appreciative framework. For example, Bosch (1998) describes her experiments in approaching exit interviews with "an appreciative eye." Based on learning derived from her experience, she provides detailed ideas for improving Ai-based exit interviews.

In addition, many innovative Ai applications such as using multi-source feedback processes . . . have not yet found their way into books or journals. The Ai listserv and newsletter are prime sources for current information on the development of Ai theory and applications around the world.

Deliverables

Traditionally, OD consultants contract with their clients to produce specific tangible products, known as *deliverables*. Examples are customized surveys and data analysis reports. Consistent with the positivist worldview, these deliverables are generally prepared independently by the consultant serving as a neutral observer of the client system. As in any other OD consultation, clarifying Ai deliverables is a vital, integral part of the contracting process.

Ai deliverables are dependent on the nature of the particular consultation. Consistent with more participatory forms of action research, the consultant may support the client in producing deliverables in order to promote ownership and organizational learning or may co-create them in full partnership with the client (Mohr et al., 2000). In either case, the Ai practitioner serves as a participant with client co-participants rather than as a neutral observer.

Ai deliverables may be tangible or intangible. Potential tangibles include a compendium of best practices and stories, visual displays, customized appreciative interview protocols or surveys, organizational design and action plan statements, train-the-trainer plans and meetings, skill-building activities for client personnel, customized Ai workshop curricula, meeting designs, and special events such as a whole system meeting.

Intangible deliverables may range from process consultation . . . and appreciative data analysis approaches to culture change and organizational transformation. In his detailed rendering of an Ai proposal for large-scale organizational change, Cooperrider (1996b) provides vivid, real-life examples of intangible deliverables (which he calls *objectives*)—for example, "to build an affirmative atmosphere of hope and confidence necessary to sustain, over the next several years, the largest whole-system transformation in the company's history" (p. 25).

Slaying Ai's Mythical Dragons

As the affirmative "knight in shining armor" of OD, Ai has surfaced its share of mythical dragons that appear as fearsome threats to its validity and applicability.

Warm-Fuzzy Dragon

This most formidable dragon labors under the unfortunate misconception that while Ai excels at facilitating warm and fuzzy "group hugs," it has no basis in or use for hard data. In fact, Ai is as data driven as any other OD application. However, the nature of the data, and how they are collected and analyzed, is different.

Ai thrives on rich, qualitative data, but quantitative data are often incorporated as well. As in traditional OD applications, qualitative data from interviews and focus groups may be used to support the development of a quantitative survey instrument for wider organizational implementation. . . . Williams (1996) illustrates the efficacy of such an approach using an Ai framework in transforming a serious crisis situation (significant loan losses leading to a 10 percent downsizing, hostile takeover attempt) in an $11 billion

regional commercial banking institution with eight thousand personnel.

Scaredy-Cat Dragon

This dragon's fire is fueled by the illusion that Ai cowers behind a security blanket of positive thinking and therefore cannot, and should not, be used to address difficult organizational challenges. That dragon evaporates in the light of the banking institution (Williams, 1996) and product design team (Brittain, 1998) cases already described and others. Furthermore, Ai differs from positive thinking in that meaning is collectively and continually co-created, whereas positive thinking is an individual practice that strives to maintain affirmative thought patterns and hold fast to particular affirmative images.

Wildly Imbalanced Dragon

This dragon thunders that Ai is dangerously lopsided in its unwavering devotion to the affirmative and that so-called problem-solving OD approaches have always balanced a search for problems with a search for strengths (Golembiewski, 2000). Three points may help to tame this dragon.

First, although many traditional OD applications include a search for strengths, scant attention is given to discovering the factors that make the strengths possible and how they might be profitably amplified. Furthermore, as a by-product of the pervasiveness of our deficit-elimination continuous improvement culture, negative data automatically and unconsciously steal focus, no matter how positive the overall results may be.

Second, the rationale for a balanced design may be predicated on the underlying assumption of a normal bell curve. That assumption may fuel the unconscious co-construction of a purposefully normative organizational reality that strives to reduce or eliminate behavioral variations to the mean. Such a homogenization process substantially subdues the human spirit so vital to effective organizations.

Third, Ai is grounded in at least three legitimate forms of qualitative sampling: a search for the extreme or exceptional, in which learning de-

Practice Tips

1. Begin with yourself. Practice being appreciative of yourself and others. Catch people doing something right, and acknowledge them for it.

2. Experience Ai, and get more Ai training. Take an Ai workshop. Partner with a seasoned Ai practitioner.

3. Read everything you can about Ai and its foundations and applications.

4. Practice crafting appreciative questions.

5. Try some Ai interviews with your coworkers and family.

6. Begin meetings with appreciative questions like, "Describe something that you did really well this week, something that made you excited and proud of your work. What made that possible? What can we learn from this?"

7. If you do not have access to the top of the organization, start where you are; it may lead to the top.

8. Always educate clients on Ai's basic assumptions and research foundations. Make sure you include enough time in your contract and design for this.

9. Make sure your clients are on board philosophically and that they are fully committed to including the voices of all stakeholders.

10. Encourage your clients' (and your own) sense of adventure and innovation. Make sure they understand that no one really knows precisely where this (or any other real change process) will lead.

11. Let your light shine, and share your enthusiasm. Participate fully. Act consistently with Ai principles.

12. Codesign an iterative, ongoing Ai learning journey rather than a one-time event.

13. Establish a mutual learning partnership with your clients rather than contracting to serve as an Ai expert or vendor.

14. Pay careful attention to facilitation of the design phase, which is a challenging exercise in social construction. Allow ample time for this when designing an Ai process.

15. Avoid the following: mixing Ai with problem-solving approaches, pressing forward in an inhospitable environment (for example, with autocratic leadership, lack of support for inclusion of all stakeholders, or inadequate resources), and analyzing Ai data or finalizing the provocative propositions on behalf of the client without their direct participation and ownership.

---

rives from "highly unusual manifestations of the phenomenon of interest" (Miles & Huberman, 1994, p. 28); a dedication to maximizing the diversity of the positive exceptions discovered in the inquiry, a form of "maximum variation sampling" (p. 28); and a delight in "taking advantage of the unexpected," that is, "opportunistic" sampling (p. 28).

Conclusion

Clearly, Ai is a powerful new OD approach. Yet it is not a disembodied miracle worker. As with all other OD work, results are dependent on the practitioner's experience with the approach, at-

tunement with self and others, and his or her overall physical, spiritual, mental, and emotional well-being. Furthermore, effective Ai practice is built on living a solid foundation of traditional OD values like inclusiveness, integrity, developing trusting relationships, challenging the status quo, collaboration, and contracting effectively. . . .

True to its philosophy, Ai is in a constant state of experimentation, learning, and self-reflective appreciation for innovation. Creating and exploring this new frontier can be an exciting and challenging evolution for OD practitioners. It requires continual change, development, and renewal within both ourselves and our field.

References

Berger, P., & Luckmann, T. (1966). *The social construction of reality.* New York: Doubleday.

Bosch, L. (1998). Exit interviews with an "appreciative eye." In S. A. Hammond & C. Royal (Eds.), *Lessons from the field: Applying appreciative inquiry* (pp. 230–244). Plano, TX: Practical Press.

Brittain, J. (1998). Do we really mean it? In S. A. Hammond & C. Royal (Eds.), *Lessons from the field: Applying appreciative inquiry* (pp. 216–229). Plano, TX: Practical Press.

Cooperrider, D. L. (1990). Positive image, positive action: The affirmative basis of organizing. In S. Srivasta & D. L. Cooperrider (Eds.), *Appreciative management and leadership: The power of positive thought and action in organizations* (pp. 91–125). San Francisco: Jossey-Bass.

Cooperrider, D. L. (1996a). The "child" as agent of inquiry. *OD Practitioner, 28,* 5–11.

Cooperrider, D. L. (1996b). Resources for getting appreciative inquiry started: An example OD proposal. *OD Practitioner, 28,* 23–33.

Cooperrider, D. L. (1999, Mar. 31). "Re: Provocative Propositions." In Appreciative Inquiry listserv. Available at: appreciative-inqry@utdallas.edu.

Cooperrider, D. L. Barrett, F., & Srivastva, S. (1995). Social construction and appreciative inquiry: A journey in organizational theory. In D. Hosking, P. Dachler, & K. J. Gergen (Eds.), *Management and organization: Relational alternatives to individualism* (pp. 157–200). Aldershot, England: Avebury Press.

Cooperrider, D. L., & Srivastva, S. (1987). Appreciative inquiry in organizational life. In R. W. Woodman & W. A. Pasmore (Eds.), *Research in organizational change and development* (Vol. 1, pp. 129–169). Greenwich, CT: JAI Press Inc.

Cooperrider, D. L., & Whitney, D. (1999). Appreciative inquiry: A positive revolution in change. In P. Holman & T. Devane (Eds.), *The change handbook* (pp. 245–263). San Francisco: Berrett-Koehler.

Cooperrider, D. L., & Whitney, D. (2000). A positive revolution in change: Appreciative inquiry. In D. L. Cooperrider, P. F. Sorensen Jr., D. Whitney, & T. F. Yaeger (Eds.), *Appreciative inquiry: Rethinking human organization toward a positive theory of change* (pp. 3–27). Champaign, IL: Stipes.

De Shazer, S., Berg, I. K., Lipchik, E., Nunnally, E., Molnar, A., Gingerich, W., & Weiner-Davis, M. (1986). Brief therapy: Focused solution development. *Family Process, 25,* 207–222.

Fitzgerald, S. P. (1999, Aug.). *Academy of Management ThemeSummit '99: A pluralistic program evaluation.* Paper presented at the annual meeting of the Academy of Management, Chicago.

Gergen, K. J. (1982). *Toward transformation in social knowledge.* New York: Springer.

Golembiewski, R. T. (2000). Three perspectives on appreciative inquiry. *OD Practitioner, 32,* 53–58.

Hammond, S. A. (1996). *The thin book of appreciative inquiry.* Plano, TX: Practical Press.

Hammond, S. A., & Royal, C. (Eds.). (1998). *Lessons from the field: Applying appreciative inquiry.* Plano, TX: Practical Press.

Head, R. L. (2000). Appreciative inquiry as a team-development intervention for newly formed heterogeneous groups. *OD Practitioner, 32,* 59–66.

Lewin, K. (1946). Action research and minority problems. *Journal of Social Issues, 2,* 34–46.

Miles, M. B., & Huberman, A. M. (1994). *Qualitative data analysis* (2nd ed.). Thousand Oaks, CA: Sage.

Mohr, B. J., Smith, E., & Watkins, J. M. (2000). Appreciative inquiry and learning assessment: An embedded evaluation process in a transnational pharmaceutical company. *OD Practitioner, 32,* 36–52.

Newman, H. L., & Fitzgerald, S. P. (2000, July). *Appreciative inquiry with an executive team: Moving along the action research continuum.* Paper presented at the Seventh International Conference on Advances in Management, Colorado Springs, CO.

Whitney, D., & Cooperrider, D. L. (1998, Summer). The appreciative inquiry summit: Overview and applications. *Employment Relations Today, 25,* 17–28.

Williams, R. F. (1996). Survey guided appreciative inquiry: A case study. *OD Practitioner, 28,* 43–51.

Reading 23

Future Search: Acting on Common Ground in Organizations and Communities[1]

Marvin Weisbord
Sandra Janoff

> *Nobody can force change on anyone else. It has to be experienced. Unless we invent ways where paradigm shifts can be experienced by large numbers of people, then change will remain a myth.*

—Eric Trist

Historical Account

Whole Foods Market CEO John Mackey wanted a shared vision, strategic direction, and set of action plans for his company. The year was 1988. Whole Foods consisted of eight natural foods supermarkets, mostly in Texas; 600 employees; and $45 million in revenues. He organized a future search called "Where We Be in '93" that included team members, team leaders, vendors, suppliers, board members, management, and customers from each store. Participants envisioned a fivefold growth in the business as central to their mission of providing healthy food to people (24 stores and $223 million in sales). They committed to using local organic producers, to setting aside a percentage of profits for environmental causes, and to engaging the community in healthy lifestyle education.

Five years later, having exceeded its growth, revenue, and social goals (32 stores, $240 million in sales, community action budgets in every store), Whole Foods held another future search called "We Be Great in '98." Present were the same stakeholder groups, including people from three newly acquired natural foods chains. The challenge, they said, would be in learning from

Source: *Future Search: An Action Guide to Finding Common Ground in Organizations and Communities,* by Marvin R. Weisbord and Sandra Janoff, Berrett-Koehler Publishers, 1995, pp. 1–13. Reprinted by permission of the publisher.

each other, preserving the local identity of various stores, and building a corporate culture that reflected the best of all members and made the corporate values of customer and community service, knowledgeable team members, and a commitment to healthy food and healthy living cornerstones for the future that were not to be compromised by rapid growth.

In October 1998, 140 people from 87 stores around the United States gathered in Estes Park, Colorado. The company now has 16,000 employees, $1.5 billion in revenues, and regional offices in most parts of the country. Many of its top executives had been there from the start. Once again they addressed the issues of growth, high quality, and their mission, now framed as "Whole Foods, Whole People, and Whole Planet." Their conference—"What We See for 2003"—addressed the many dilemmas of customer service, team development, and succession planning in a giant company growing 25 percent a year. In particular, they focused on how to maintain the core values that had made them successful—including support for organic farming, food safety, and nutritional and health education—while responding to the pressures for growth and globalization of the business.

In a recent CEO's conference, John Mackey was asked how his fast-growing company, which had defined a new niche in the supermarket industry, pulled together strategic planning and gained commitment in such a far-flung, decentralized business. "We hold a future search conference every five years," he said.

People in businesses, communities, and non-profits all over the world use future search to transform their capability for action. They do it in a few days by involving a "whole system" in the same room working together on a task chosen in advance by a planning committee. Diverse groups explore their past, present, and future; confirm shared values; and commit to action plans. Everybody participates and shares leadership. The most significant changes occur in planning, when people agree to a set of unfamiliar meeting conditions. The key to the success of the method is matching the overall purpose with the right people needed to ensure action.

The Basics

Why future search? As a society we have painted ourselves into a technological corner. We have more ways to do things than ever before. Yet a lot of what matters to us is not getting done, despite the large sums we spend. We experience high walls between haves and have-nots, experts and amateurs, leaders and followers. In future search meetings we take down the walls. We take control of our own futures. We take back responsibility for ourselves. We discover that we can learn from and work with people from many walks of life.

In a future search we become more secure knowing firsthand where other people stand. We discover resources in ourselves and others that we didn't know were there. We begin to accept our differences—in background, viewpoints, and values—as realities to be lived with, not problems to be solved. We are more likely to let go of stereotypes. New relationships emerge. Surprising projects become possible. Future search is a simple way of meeting that has profound implications for organizations and communities everywhere.

Future search brings systems thinking to life. The method provides people a way of acting systematically. By uniting diverse parties who are each other's "environment," we enable people to experience themselves connected to a larger whole rather than talk about it as something "out there." When people all talk about the same elephant, putting together their perceptions of the head, tail, trunk, legs, and tusks, they enable actions that none of them previously thought possible.

Too Good to Be True? Data Suggest an Emphatic No!

Now, it is against common sense that much implementation would flow from one short planning meeting among people who have not met before. Yet this unusual, ongoing action, often on intractable issues, has been documented worldwide following future searches. We believe that this could not be happening unless future search enabled people to use skills they already have—skills always there and rarely accessible in more familiar structures.

We have found that extraordinary results happen when groups assemble and follow just a few key principles, namely,

- have the right people in the room—that is, a cross section of the whole system;
- create conditions where participants experience the whole "elephant" before acting on any part of it;
- seek and build upon common ground;
- take responsibility for learning and action.

Uses of Future Search

Future search has been used to help diverse groups find common ground and develop plans based on that common ground. Here are some examples:

TABLE 1   **Examples**

Groups Searching for Common Ground	Specific Use of the Future Search
Bay State Skills Corporation technical assistance program, small and medium-size manufacturers, public and private service providers, and state government	Participants developed plans to create a centralized extension service to help small and medium-size manufacturers become more competitive. Their plans for coordinated services sparked political action that resulted in a $1 million state grant and a $10 million federal grant.
Inuit people of the Arctic region, land claims organizations, territorial and federal governments, banks, business firms, a mining company, aboriginal funding organizations, and other aboriginal groups	Participants developed an economic-development framework and action plan for education and training, social development, preservation of culture and language, development of small business and industry, investments, organizational development, transportation and infrastructure, renewable resource development, and protection of the environment.
Teachers, students, school administrators, citizens, commissioners, police, firefighters, highway officials, town department heads, and business leaders of Hopkinton, Massachusetts	Participants developed a plan for "Hopkinton 2000 A.D.," which addressed thorny issues such as the town's doubling in size between 1977 and 1992, a tax-limiting referendum that left education and other budgets level-funded for three years, and a 6 percent-a-year inflation rate that eliminated contractual raises for school employees. Within a year of the conference, residents raised the school budget 12 percent, and a local business firm partnered with the high school and donated $350,000 worth of computers, technology, and teacher training and pledged $300,000 for the next two years. A 1998 follow-up reports that the town maintains double-digit increases to the school budget and has an ongoing partnership with local businesses, which continues to provide approximately $150,000 a year to the system in support of libraries, technology, and teacher training. Henry Fredette, superintendent of the Water Department at the time of the future search, now on the Board of Selectmen, said, "We have succeeded in doing everything we set out to do." The most recent approvals include a $34.7 million high school and a master plan to preserve open space and scenic roads.
The Alliance for Employee Growth and Development (a nonprofit venture of the Communications Workers of America, the International Brotherhood of Electrical Workers, and AT&T)	The Alliance empowers AT&T workers displaced by technology to develop new skills and build their careers. The board—senior executives from the three partners—now conducts board meetings around the country based on future search principles. In these meetings the board convenes local employers and representatives from government, education, and social services in order to help them develop action plans for the mutual benefit of all.
Union officials and senior management from 3M Company's St. Paul Area Plant Engineering organization	Participants helped forward the common purpose of union and management to improve the quality of work life, productivity, and management practice. The groups defined the concept of "Unity through Partnership" by working together in a future search. They produced a joint vision of a workplace redesigned around customer needs and devised processes for including people who did not attend. Plant Engineering subsequently moved into a large-scale redesign effort, with union and management working together, that included hundreds of employees.

(continued)

TABLE 1   Examples (continued)

Groups Searching for Common Ground	Specific Use of the Future Search
Kansas City, Missouri, community members interested in youth empowerment, services integration, funding, regional collaboration, technology, and volunteer youth programs	Participants implemented the community consensus reached earlier in Kansas City to become "The Child Opportunity Capital." Some key outcomes: Children's Mercy Hospital put young people on boards dealing with oversight and procedures; a local Junior League chose youth empowerment as its next four-year community commitment, offering 90 volunteers and a $200,000 activities grant including an annual future search involving young people.

The Process

Our conferences typically involve 60 to 80 people. We consider 64 an optimum number—eight groups of eight. Our purpose is always joint action toward a desired future for X—that is, a community, organization, or issue.

We do five tasks in the approximate timeframes shown below.

Day 1 Afternoon
    Task 1—Focus on the Past
    Task 2—Focus on the Present, External Trends
Day 2 Morning
    Task 2 Continued—Stakeholder Response to External Trends
    Task 2 Continued—Focus on the Present, Owning Our Actions
Day 2 Afternoon
    Task 3—Ideal Future Scenarios
    Task 4—Identify Common Ground
Day 3 Morning
    Task 4 Continued—Confirm Common Ground
    Task 5—Action Planning

The Focus on the Past, Ideal Future Scenarios, and Confirm Common Ground tasks are done in mixed groups, each a cross section of the whole. The Focus on the Present task is done by "stakeholder" groups whose members have a shared perspective. The Identify Common Ground task is the business of the whole conference. Action Planning employs both existing and voluntary groups. Every task includes a total group dialogue.

The task sequence and group composition are not optional. These set up powerful dynamics that can lead to constructive outcomes. We experience the conference's peaks and valleys as an emotional roller-coaster ride, swooping down into the morass of global trends, soaring to idealistic heights in an ideal future. Uncertainty, anxiety, and confusion are necessary by-products. So are fun, energy, creativity, and achievement. Future search relies on a counterpoint between hope and despair. We believe good contact with our ups and downs leads to realistic choices. In a future search we live with the inevitability of differences, the recognition that no meeting design can reconcile them, and the acknowledgment that people are capable of riding the roller coaster to important new action plans without "more data" or "more dialogue" if they agree to keep working together.

Economic Benefits

In the business world there is no way to calculate the benefits of future search in economic terms. Indeed, these conferences make possible levels of integration not achievable by other means at any cost. In the Hayworth Inc. future search, employees, customers, and suppliers in dialogue with company members discovered and solved a waste-disposal packaging problem that could have taken months in task forces and that may be worth millions of dollars at many levels of the economy. They reduced both cost and environmental impact in a few hours. However, this was only one of dozens of key issues addressed in the future search. When people discover new forms of cooperation, then time, energy, and resources are used profitably.

In addition, these conferences generate dollars that were not previously available. Examples include Bay State Skills; Hopkinton, Massachusetts; and Kansas City, Missouri, cited in the cases above. Many times we have seen money flow from haves to have-nots in an eye blink once people join in making realistic commitments. In one California conference a major foundation executive offered substantial financial support for an action plan that he said would not have been considered if it had come through regular channels. In an eastern city a deputy from the mayor's office offered a community $2 million in public funds, which, she said, had sat idle for lack of any practical plans for its use—until now. These examples are the tip of a very large iceberg that could, if fully understood, turn our assumptions about how to assure wise use of money, public and private, in constructive new directions.

Getting Started

In a future search we seek to take the first important step by

- getting the "whole system" in the room,
- creating a learning environment for participants to experience the whole system,
- searching for common ground from which to build action plans,
- asking individuals to take responsibility to act on the common ground articulated.

The change begins in the planning. Future search requires no training, inputs, data collection, or diagnoses. People face each other rather than concepts, expert advice, or assumptions about what they lack and should do. The method involves comparing notes and listening, sometimes to a mishmash of assumptions, misinformation, stereotypes, and judgments rattling around

in all of us. Amazingly, it is *not* necessary to straighten all this out to succeed. Commitment builds as we encounter chaos together, hang on despite our anxiety, and come out the other side with some good ideas, people we can trust, and faith in our ability to work together. In short, we uncover buried potential that already exists.

Roles and Responsibilities

The table below describes the key roles and their responsibilities before, during, and after the future search:

Shifts in Organizational Power and Authority

During the future search conference, participants work as peers as they build the information base, communicate what they learn, make decisions and prepare action plans. After the conference there may or may not be formal changes in power and authority throughout the organization or community. Such changes would depend on the future search action plans and their subsequent implementation.

Conditions for Success

Our conference design embodies a set of mutually reinforcing practices:

- getting the "whole system" in the room,
- all looking at the same "elephant" before working on any part of it (e.g., thinking globally before acting locally),
- exploring current reality and common futures, not problems and conflicts,
- self-managing your own groups and action plans,
- attending the whole meeting,
- meeting under healthy conditions,
- working across three days (i.e., "sleeping twice"),
- taking responsibility publicly for follow-up.

TABLE 2 Roles and Responsibilities

	Before	During	After
Sponsor	• Become clear about the risks and benefits • Decide what you hope to accomplish and how future search applies • Provide support and assurance that you believe in what people are doing	• Be a participant. Share your learnings • Empower people to act	• Have periodic review meetings that bring together stakeholders from the original conference and other interested parties
Designer/Facilitator	• Help people decide if future search will serve their needs • Help sponsors gather the necessary information, courage, and resources to proceed	• Manage tasks and time • Keep purpose front and center • Encourage self-management and responsibility • Allow the uncertainty until people decide what they will and will not do together • Help people resolve the struggle between old patterns and new paths	• Facilitate a review meeting six months after the conference
Steering Committee	• Frame the conference task • Get the right people in the conference • Set the planning time horizons		
Participants		• Take ownership of your past, present, and future • Confirm mutual values • Search for common ground • Develop independent or joint action plans based on the established common ground • Share leadership	• Take responsibility and follow through with your plans

If we want to help people act boldly and creatively, we have to get out of the way. So we do not strive to reduce complexity to a few manageable issues, to resolve disagreements, or to solve long-standing problems, Nor do we give people management models for organizing their varied perceptions. Instead, participants engage in a series of open dialogues on where they've been, where they are, and what they want to do. Future searches often include total strangers or people with a history of conflict who come with confusing and contradictory information. As they experience each other's diverse agendas, they realize that change means accepting each other where they are if they are to go forward together. Those who stay the course find that quick action is inevitable.

What We Can't Do with Future Search

Shore Up Ineffective Leaders

We cannot make up for weak leadership with a future search. A worldwide religious service organization's lawyer wanted to head off a drive to unionize by disgruntled central staff. A reluctant CEO went along with the "legal" advice to sponsor a future search that would enable people to devise the workplace they wanted. People welcomed a chance to make their own plans. They were not surprised, though, when the boss acted on none of them. Nor was their attorney surprised when the staff voted in a union to fill the leadership vacuum.

Convince Skeptics to Go Forward

We have had no success "selling" future search to people paralyzed by worry about losing control. One troubled corporate giant planned to put thousands of people through a training event staged by a prestigious business institute. To the staff's proposal that the company substitute future searches—on the theory that people could get the company out of the box if given a chance—top management turned a deaf ear. Nobody could imagine anything useful happening that wasn't prescribed by experts. They opted for expert training. But nothing new happened. Having two years to "transform the culture or die," they gave up on training their way out of trouble after a year. Several separate departments ran successful future searches, but the company as a whole continued its downward slide.

Reconcile Values Differences

We don't know how to reconcile intractable values differences through future search. When people disagree about deep-seated religious, ethical, or political beliefs that they hold sacred, a future search is unlikely to help them reconcile their beliefs. In a school conference, people brought up highly charged feelings about sex education. The differences between those who did and did not want a particular curriculum were fierce, deeply felt, and long-standing. The parties believe each other to be wrong. At the same time, they agreed on a host of other goals, such as better use of school facilities and more involvement of parents in learning and teaching. They found that they were not going to work out their moral values in this forum but that they had a priceless chance to make progress on matters of benefit to all if they cooperated.

Change Team Dynamics

We can create new dynamics quickly only if we bring together a *new* group and give it a *new* task. Systems expert Russell Ackoff pointed out long ago that systems change only in relation to the larger systems of which they are a part. That explains why peer-only events—training, T-groups, team meetings—have little effect on the larger system. This seems to be true even when the narrow group does a broad task, such as "scanning the environment." So our guiding principle is always the "whole system" in the room.

Using future search work sheets, for example, a consultant ran a single department through its past, present, and future. To make sure everybody "got it," she included a trust questionnaire and data feedback. "Same old stuff" was the word after the conference from the participants, who neither trusted nor distrusted each other more, although they had learned to trust consultants less. Same people + new inputs = same interactions.

Theoretical Basis

Future search is based on solid, proven theories about how people can best develop plans in groups. While practitioners of future search continue to enhance the conduct of the process, the process is based on just a few simple, but high-leverage principles.

Historical Roots

Our main sources of inspiration come from parallel innovations on both side of the Atlantic. One is Ronald Lippitt and Eva Schindler-Rainman's large-scale community futures conferences in North America during the 1970s. Another is the pioneering work of Eric Trist, an Englishman, and Fred Emery, an Australian, in developing the Search Conference (hence the name future search). From Lippitt and Schindler-Rainman we learned to get the whole system in the room and focus on the future, not on problems and conflicts. From Trist and Emery we learned the importance of thinking globally before acting locally and of having people manage their own planning. We share with all of them a commitment to democratic ideals and their embodiment of the "action research" tradition of the famed social psychologist Kurt Lewin.

People, Whole Systems, and Planning

We see future search as a learning laboratory for "getting everybody to improve whole systems."[2] It is not the complete answer to anything. Yet the dynamics apply to many kinds of meetings and change strategies. To experience this method in a single meeting is to open many new doors for future action. We have chosen to stay with lowercase letters to emphasize that future search is not a "thing" carved in stone but a set of principles and opportunities for learning and action. Our society has hardly begun to explore what we can do with diverse parties working on the same task despite their differences.

Future searches enable us to experience and accept polarities. They help us learn how to bridge barriers of culture, class, age, gender, ethnicity, power, status, and hierarchy by working as peers on tasks of mutual concern. The future search process interrupts our tendency to repeat old patterns—fighting, running away, complaining, blaming, or waiting for others to fix problems. And it gives us a chance to express our highest ideals.

Instead of trying to change the world or each other, we change the conditions under which we interact. *That* much we can control, and changing the conditions leads to surprising outcomes.

In future search, major systemic changes occur in the planning process. A diverse group of 6 to 10 people meets from a few days to a few months. They agree on a task and invite a spectrum of stakeholders. They also agree to a novel set of conditions, e.g., meeting for 16 hours over three days, skipping speakers and expert input, putting off action until near the end, and working interactively. In a meeting structured this way, people discover new capabilities no matter what agendas come up. This opens the door to new, unpredictable, highly desired, and long-lived cooperative action that is a high order of systems change.

We don't work to improve relationships among people or functions. Rather, we set up conditions under which people can choose new ways of relating. We don't abstract out social issues (e.g., diversity, trust, communications, collaboration) from economic and technical issues. We are unlikely to run a conference on "the future of diversity in X." Rather, we'd propose that a diverse group of people explore together what kind of X they want to live and work in. Whatever people's skills, education, or experience, they already have what they need to engage in this process. As facilitators, our main job is to maintain boundaries of time and task and to make sure that all points of view are supported.

Sharing the Work

Ours is an encounter with the whole—self, community, organization. But we do not provide an expert systems analysis. Instead, we set up a situation that involves the whole person on many levels. People experience themselves in action as part of a larger whole. They talk over issues they have not raised before with people they have never met. They take responsibility for matters previously avoided or ignored. They dramatize ideal futures as if they have actually happened, thus anchoring them in their bodies. They identify what they *really* want. They voluntarily commit to actions made possible only because of the other people in the room.

Our procedures evolved while working mainly with people who can read and write. However, the underlying principles do not depend on literacy. We believe this work could be done entirely with spoken and/or symbolic communication. The results have been repeated in many cultures and culturally diverse groups. Indeed, *any* techniques that help people explore their whole system, experience their common stakes, share their ideals, internalize the experience, and take responsibility for what happens are worth applying.

A Learning Laboratory

We believe conferences designed according to the principles we have adopted lead to (1) more participants taking personal responsibility, (2) faster implementation of action plans, and (3) longer-lasting relationships across key boundaries. For now this is a tantalizing hypothesis—an unproved theory. The only way to test it is to find out what participants do afterward that they couldn't do before. Enough good stories abound to keep us going on this path. So for us, future search is a learning laboratory.

How Future Search Differs from Organizational Development

We see many differences between future search and traditional organization development (OD) meetings. First, OD was conceived not as a single meeting but rather as strategy for large-scale systemic change. Future search describes a process for one meeting lasting fewer than three days. Second, where OD depended on many people accepting the "need for change," future search depends on 64 people accepting an invitation to spend a few days together.

Third, OD was based on diagnostic gaps between what is and what ought to be. Consultants applied a diagnostic framework, did interviews or surveys, and used the information to create dissonance between what people did and what they said. This was intended to "unfreeze" a system, leading people to reorder their ways of working.

Consultants prescribed action steps to close the gaps. Nearly always these involved training, based on the theory that people did not know how to do what they said they wanted to do.

A final difference from OD concerns our neutral assessment of "current reality." What might be seen through an OD lens as deficiencies to be remedied, we consider part of current reality. We don't judge information as good or bad, complete or sketchy, useful or futile, appropriate or redundant. Whatever people do or say—their words, their behavior, their wishes, and their reactions—belongs to them. Whatever happens is an expression of the stakeholders, for better or worse. We are witnessing in action the best that this system is capable of. We don't expect dramatic individual change, only a change in the action potential within the system. For example, people will not suddenly give up authority/dependency needs because they spent a few days as peers. But they may learn more about their ability to work together with more shared authority.

Sustaining the Results

The single most worrisome aspect of planning is implementation. No process, however comprehensive, guarantees action. Still, we have seen more plans implemented from future searching than any method either of us has used in 30 years. People act quite apart from whether they had a good time, liked the facilitators, collected handouts, resolved their differences, or felt that they had finished. Nor is success a function of how complete an action-planning format is. People find ways to carry out their plans if they have clear goals, the right people are in the room, and they take the whole ride together. Action requires people who understand and believe in their plans and trust each other enough to join in new steps. We think future search fosters understanding, belief, and commitment.

So, while there are no guarantees, what factors contribute to sustainable results? We believe periodic review meetings that bring together stakeholders from the original conference and other interested parties is a simple, congruent way to keep action planning fresh, connected, and relevant for all. What happens after a future search depends largely on what people sign up to do. No sign-up, no action. The fact is, nobody knows how to get other people to do things they don't want to do. Future search theory holds that we get more implementation when we attend to each stage of the process, giving people ample opportunity to engage each other, create an umbrella of shared values, commit to action steps they believe in, and get together regularly to share what they are doing.

Some Final Comments

We see future search as a building block of theory and practice for a house that will never be finished. Practitioners are infusing future search principles into everything they do and enriching this process with many other perspectives. We cannot compare or contrast what we do with other processes because we believe that all large-group processes are independently valuable. Ours are not the only techniques for accomplishing our goals. They are simply the techniques we know best. The roller-coaster ride is inevitable in human affairs. Conceptual schemes and meeting designs come and go. The business of muddling through life's ups and downs together strikes us as a universal process. We believe future searches are good for us and good for society. We hope this work enables thousands of constructive action projects everywhere.

Endnotes

1. Adapted from *Future Search: An Action Guide to Finding Common Ground in Organizations and Communities,* by Marvin R. Weisbord and Sandra Janoff, Ph.D. (Berrett-Koehler, 1995).

2. Weisbord, Marvin R. *Productive Workplaces: Organizing and Managing for Dignity, Meaning, and Community.* San Francisco: Jossey-Bass, 1987, pp. 237–252.

Reading 24

Meeting the Global Competitive Challenge: Building Systems That Learn on a Large Scale

Gary E. Jusela

Introduction

Global competition, corporate downsizing, industrial renaissance, economic dislocation, these are the new watchwords of American business. Through the Cold War era the American public viewed the principal external threat to the United States as the military and political force of the Soviet Union and its allies. With the dissolution of the former Soviet Union and the Eastern Bloc this threat has nearly evaporated, while an economic threat from Japan has emerged as the more serious perceived challenge to the future of the United States.[1] Postman (1985, as cited in Mitroff, 1987) argues that the United States is organized to fight the wrong enemy, specifically the Soviet Union, when the more serious enemy, the root of our non-competitiveness, is contained within our own borders.[2]

While we have shored up our military strength, our economic vitality has atrophied at an alarming rate. The United States world market share has dropped more than 50 percent in 20 years in 20 major industries.[3] Where in 1972 9 of the 10 largest banks in the world, as ranked by total assets, were American, today the top 8 and 15 of the top 25 belong to Japan.[4] Our standard of living has declined significantly in the last two decades; our rate of productivity growth from 1950 to 1985 (2.5 percent) lags far behind that of Japan (8.4 percent), Germany (5.5 percent), Italy (5.5 percent), and France (5.3 percent); and economists estimate that as many as 30 million people within the

United States have been dislocated in their working careers by the "restructuring" in manufacturing during the last decade.[5] So what has happened, and what is industrial America to do about it?

This paper will examine some of the organizing assumptions and models that have contributed to the competitive decline within U.S. industry and explore one approach to addressing this decline that has been applied within the Ford Motor Company beginning in 1981 and within the Boeing Company beginning in 1988. The approach is called "large-scale systems change" and represents an evolutionary application of many elements of planned change and team development. The large-scale systems change methodology will be described as it has been applied in cultural change and in strategic planning efforts. The paper will further explore some of the outcomes of the large-scale process, internal political prerequisites for applying the methodology, and how the approach may be expected to evolve further.

Organizing Paradigms

While recognizing that industrial competitiveness is rooted in an array of factors broader than within-firm behavior (see, for example, Porter, 1990), the present discussion will be kept principally at the intrafirm level, with some attention given to changes in market expectations and external competitive conditions. The premise of this exploration, and of the intervention work on which it is based, is that many aspects of competitiveness can be addressed and resolved by rethinking and reorienting internal management practices. The chairman of Toyota Motors has

Source: Written especially for this volume.

been quoted as saying that "competitiveness is a microeconomic issue."[6] While this may be viewed by many as an oversimplification, there are beginning to be enough examples of individual firms turning around declining fortunes to assert that microeconomic factors are, at a minimum, an important dimension of competitive success.[7]

Peters (1988) argues that what is required are new models of industrial organization. Ackoff (1981) has laid out two contrasting organizing paradigms, the machine bureaucracy and the organization as system, that reflect respectively the dominant model for industrial organization for the past hundred years and the evolving model being adopted by the world's most successful firms. The large-scale systems change methodology is aimed at enabling large complex enterprises built around the machine model to adapt to changing external circumstances and move toward the systems model of organization. Before exploring the methodology, we will look first at these contrasting views of the organization.

The Machine Bureaucracy

The machine bureaucracy model of organization evolved out of early industrial engineering and scientific management concepts and Weberian concepts of hierarchical control (see Figure 1).[8] As described by Ackoff (1981), the machine model is based on analysis and reductionism. The underlying assumption is that, for the organization as a whole to work most effectively, each of its parts must be designed and honed to achieve a local optimum of performance. Within the machine bureaucracy, problems are solved by breaking them into their component parts, fixing the parts, and then reaggregating the whole. Authority is clearly defined by organizational level and work is neatly subdivided between functions. As the machine bureaucracy evolves (or devolves), the boundaries between levels and functions may become very severely drawn, limiting local coordination and the flow of people, of ideas, and of resources between units and placing a large responsibility for regulation and control on senior levels of management. In this case the organiza-

tion may be characterized as "overbounded" or "arthritic" (see Alderfer, 1976; Dannemiller, 1985). Under conditions in which the owner of the firm has enormous power over his or her employees, the skill requirements of jobs and educational level of employees is low, and the external environment of the organization is relatively stable, this model of industrial organization may be extraordinarily effective. In fact, the rise of the U.S. economy through the first seven decades of this century bears witness to the success of this dominant paradigm.

The Systems Model

Where the machine model is founded on analysis or taking things apart, systems thinking is built on synthesis or putting things together (Ackoff, 1981). Ackoff defines a system as a set of two or more elements that satisfies the following three conditions:

1. The behavior of each element has an effect on the behavior of the whole.
2. The behavior of the elements and their effects on the whole are interdependent.
3. However subgroups of the elements are formed, each has an effect on the behavior of the whole and none has an independent effect on it (p.15).

Ackoff describes further that:

> The essential properties of a system taken as a whole derive from the interactions of its parts, not their actions taken separately. Therefore, when a system is taken apart it loses its essential properties. Because of this—and this is the critical point—a system is a whole that cannot be understood by analysis (p. 16).

Under the systems way of thinking, problems are solved not by taking things apart but rather by (1) identifying the larger whole containing the element to be explained, (2) explaining the behavior or properties of the containing whole, and then (3) explaining the behavior or characteristics of the element in question in terms of the role or function it serves within the larger context. Per-

FIGURE 1
The Machine
Bureaucracy

Authority is allocated according to hierarchial level.

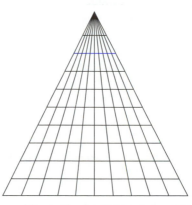

Responsibilities are delineated by clear divisions between functional groups
(e.g., engineering, manufacturing, finance, sales, and human resources).

Over time, and with increasing specificity of rules, procedures, and organization
charters, the organization becomes overbounded or "arthritic" in its joints and
information flow and coordination across subunit boundaries is impeded.

haps the most significant implication of this paradigm for organizational effectiveness is that, to the extent each part of the system is considered independently and is made to operate as efficiently as possible, the system as a whole will not operate to its potential. The logic of this paradigm suggests that the optimal performance of the system as a whole requires suboptimization at the unit level.

For an organization to function effectively as a whole system, boundary permeability between an organization and its environment and among subunits within the organization must be maintained at an optimal level (Alderfer, 1976). Under conditions of either overboundedness or underboundedness, effective internal regulation or adaptation to a changing external environment breaks down. The extreme form of the machine bureaucracy, where boundaries are hardened to near impermeable states, may be considered, in these terms, a highly overbounded system.

The contrast between the machine and the system paradigms parallels Mitroff's (1987) characterization of old organizing assumptions and new organizing assumptions in the design of jobs and organizations (based on Mills and Lovell, 1985) and Imai's (1986) comparison of Western innovation-oriented management with the Japanese kaizen or continuous improvement philosophy. Two of the core concepts that appear repeatedly in recent discussions of new organizing paradigms are an emphasis on continual learning and the involvement of everyone in the continuous improvement of the system as a whole (see, for example, Hayes, Wheelwright and Clark, 1988; Imai, 1986, Keichel, 1990; Mitroff, 1987; and Stata, 1989). In fact, one of the common targeted objectives of the new paradigm models is that of creating organizations that learn within the context of dynamic boundary relations internally and externally.

Given the objective of moving large complex bureaucracies from old organizing paradigms to new systems perspectives, what are the implications for the practice of organization development and planned change? The answer to this can be found in tracing the roots of organization devel-

opment and integrating historical group or team-oriented practice with systems-level thinking.

Beyond Teambuilding: Large-Scale Systems Change as a Vehicle for Shifting Culture

Teambuilding

The practice of organization development has grown in large part out of the early research on group dynamics by Lewin, Lippitt, Bradford, and Benne and the experiential learning processes pioneered by the National Training Laboratories beginning in 1947.[9] This origin is reflected in a predominant focus on group behavior and team development by organization development practitioners. Describing characteristics of successful organization development efforts, Beckhard (1969) suggests that they entail a planned program involving the whole system, and that they usually rely on some form of experience-based learning activities. Yet he says they also work primarily with groups. In practice, this has tended to mean relatively small groups.

Today throughout much of industry, one finds cadres of internal facilitators providing consultative support to quality circles and problem-solving teams with 8 to 10 members. Teambuilding has probably been the most common intervention of organization development practitioners in the past 30 years. While the core tenets of early T-group theory parallel systems thinking, the field of organization development seemed to lock onto small-group technology. Teambuilding can have many positive contributions to an organization's vitality or effectiveness. Teams and the individuals within them can develop process skills for handling conflict, making decisions, and setting direction. Yet, when teambuilding is conducted at a subunit level within a complex organization, large system level phenomena, if addressed at all, are typically addressed in only an oblique way (see Figure 2).

Teambuilding, as a vehicle for organization development, can be an instrument for reinforcing

FIGURE 2 Teambuilding

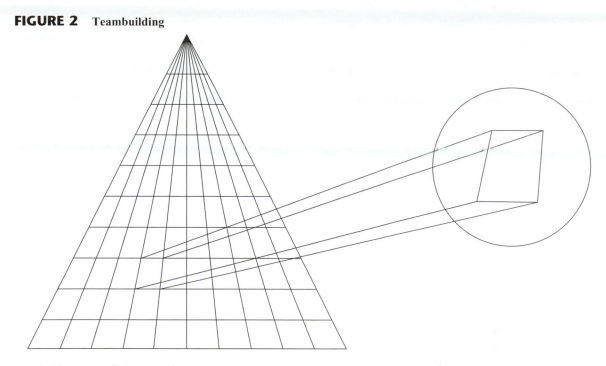

Teambuilding is typically conducted by extracting a single subunit from the larger system, developing the group's skills and capabilities, and then returning the subunit to the larger system, the elements of which often exert pressure to return to the original status quo.

the machine bureaucracy and for tightening, rather than opening, the boundaries between groups. Within-group cohesion may be increased at the expense of between-group or systemic integration. Each group being built separately is likely to work with its own unique dataset and shape its objectives in a way that optimizes subunit performance, rather than the performance of the system as a whole. This is a natural consequence not simply of an inherent bias toward self interest but of the fact that the whole system is not present or represented in the room. In the absence of relevant stakeholders influencing the discussion, groups will tend to focus on their own parochial needs.

Getting the Whole System in the Room

Weisbord (1987a) describes an evolution in the practice of management consulting and organization development starting in the early 1900s with

Frederick Taylor's scientific management up to the present. The evolution process begins with experts solving problems for others. The second stage, which Weisbord dates from the 1950s to the middle 1960s, has everyone getting involved in the problem-solving process. Stage three is characterized by experts working to improve whole systems. The final stage, which Weisbord sees as the next evolution in organization development, entails getting everyone involved in improving whole systems.

Drawing on the community development and futuring research and practice of Lippitt and Schindler-Rainman (1980), Weisbord (1987a, 1987b) describes four useful practices he feels characterize this next or "third wave" of managing and consulting. The first is an assessment of the potential for action by determining the presence of three prerequisite conditions: committed leadership, a good business opportunity (i.e., a critical business need that must be addressed, such as merger, acquisition, reorganization, business strategy planning, overhead crises, or new technologies), and energized people. Before proceeding, Weisbord advocates a thorough "should we/shouldn't we" discussion with the key stakeholders. The second useful practice is to "get the whole system in the room." The third is to focus on the future, and the fourth is to structure tasks that people can do for themselves. Weisbord's description of these four practices as the next phase of organization development practice matches closely with the large-scale systems change methodology that was initiated within the Ford Motor Company in 1982 and which is the subject of the present discussion.

Large-Scale Systems Change at Ford Motor Company

Ford Motor Company in 1981 was in the depths of a competitive crisis. The economy was in a cyclical downturn, new and stronger competitors were challenging the market, and customer expectations about automotive quality and performance were shifting dramatically. The company lost nearly 10 percentage points of U.S. market share, and, between 1980 and 1983, recorded losses of $3.3 billion and a North American workforce reduction of approximately 100,000 employees. Chrysler had recently gone to the U.S. government for a bailout, and Ford appeared to be not far behind. With the company hemorrhaging in the newly competitive global environment, in what Peter Vaill (1986) calls the "permanent whitewater" of present day environmental turbulence, small-scale quick fixes aimed at repairing the boxes of the organization would not produce the required cultural and competitive adjustment or the capacity for continual renewal. Out of these circumstances was born the earliest iteration of the large-scale systems change methodology applied within a large corporate setting.

Ford Motor Company and the United Auto Workers signed an agreement on Employee Involvement as part of their contract negotiations in 1979. This agreement resulted in the initiation of extensive problem solving and quality circle group activities at the shop floor level of the company. As a result of these activities, the company culture in the manufacturing plants began to shift from the highly authoritarian model of the past to a more participative model that engaged the employees' minds as well as their hands. By 1980, as business performance was beginning to collapse severely, the senior management of the company began a process of personal study and education on quality improvement under the tutelage of Dr. W. Edwards Deming. At this time, Ford launched its "Quality is Job #1" campaign, internally as well as externally. The pressure for change within Ford was becoming enormous as the company's competitive position continued to slip, and with these new initiatives, Employee Involvement and "Quality is Job #1," change was beginning nearly simultaneously at the bottom and at the top.

By 1981, the pressure for change had become particularly acute within the Diversified Products Operations (DPO) of the Ford Motor Company. This unit consisted of approximately 70,000 employees within 10 operating divisions, most of which supplied component parts or materials for the automotive business (e.g., steel, castings, climate control, electronics, glass, plastics, paint, and vinyl). These divisions were under especially acute pressure, given that alternative sources for many or most of their products were available outside the company. Their customer divisions were beginning to demand that they meet or beat the external competition in quality, cost, and delivery. This provided the impetus for Tom Page, then executive vice president in charge of DPO, to seek a means to bring about a cultural change rapidly within his entire 70,000 person organization.

Page could see the beginning of positive momentum at the top with the new focus on quality and at the bottom with the emphasis on Employee Involvement. These initiatives, however, left a large gap in the middle, that vast domain containing the roughly 20 layers of hierarchy between his office and the shop floor. Not only had this large bulk of employees not been brought into the fold of the new quality and employee involvement initiatives, but they had been schooled in and continued to practice the best of the old paradigm, machine bureaucracy model of management. Authorities and perquisites were carefully allocated among the vertical layers, and functions were tightly segmented into what were referred to as the "chimneys" (including such organizations as engineering, finance, labor relations, manufacturing, research, and sales). Small-scale initiatives, such as training or teambuilding with groups of 20 to 25, would not reach a critical mass of people quickly enough, nor would they get at the root of the organizational arthritis that had crept into the organization latticework.

To address the competitive crisis and the necessity for large-scale change, a group of external consultants was invited to collaborate with Page and his management team.[10] The consultants came from Ann Arbor, Michigan, where several of them had each been influenced by the research and practice of Ron Lippitt. Page asked the group to develop a strategy to shift the mass of his organization from an old authoritarian management style to the participative management style he was seeking. The external consultants collaborated with Page's manager for employee involvement and training to develop a methodology they believed could accomplish the needed magnitude and speed of change.[11] What they proposed to Tom Page in 1981 is precisely what Weisbord (1987a, 1987b) describes as the next phase of organization development. The consultants came back to Page with a proposal to work with each of his 10 divisions by developing and conducting what would be division-specific participative management seminars using a large-scale systems change methodology.

The proposed seminars were to be conducted with the division general manager and his top five layers of management as an intact group, which included anywhere from 60 to 150 people (see Figure 3). The intent of the sessions was to create a highly interactive learning environment where participative management would be the medium and a real-time, real-life case analysis of the division's business conducted by the program participants would be the content. Participants were to work together in a series of small group and large group configurations that would bring people together across the hierarchical and functional barriers that had traditionally kept them apart. What the seminar proposed to do, consistent with Weisbord's prescription, was to get the whole system into the room, to focus on the future (and also on the past and present), and to design tasks that people could do for themselves. The participants would provide the vast majority of the content within a context that was designed to promote interactive individual, group, and organizational learning across the whole system. Tom Page was eager to bring about a rapid transformation and saw no better alternative for getting there. Therefore, in an act reflecting what Kanter (1983) describes as the paradox of initiation, Page decreed that each of his general managers should launch the large-scale participative management seminar process within their respective divisions.

The participative management seminar was designed as a five-day event, beginning with an initial three-day meeting followed six to eight weeks later with a two-day follow-up. The sessions were held off-site and brought the top five layers of division management together into what might be called an "organization quality circle." In many cases, this was the first time the entire management group had been in one room at the same time. The seminar was intended to both build participative skills in the management team and to help managers find new ways of working together vertically and horizontally within the system. Managers worked in different teams during the five days; they were grouped variously in maximum-mix teams (microcosm groups consisting of multiple levels and functions), functional teams, natural work teams, Myers-Briggs-personality-type teams, and, finally, as a team of the whole, planning, voting, and coming to consensus around a shared vision for the future.

Within each of the 10 divisions, the seminars were designed using a five-step process:

1. The creation of a consultant/client division collaborative design team to plan the event.

FIGURE 3 **Large-Scale Systems Change**

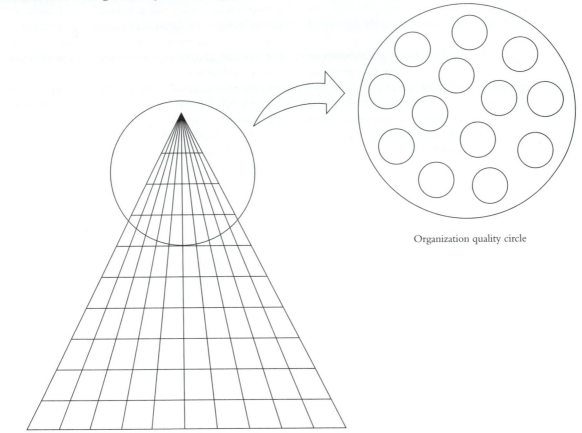

Organization quality circle

The large-scale systems change methodology employed in the Ford participative management seminars took the top five layers of an operating division off-site as an intact group. Participants worked in a variety of small group and large group configurations, beginning with maximum-mix teams that mixed people by level and function into microcosms of the whole.

2. The collection of data from key stakeholders within the system.

3. The development of a clear statement of purpose.

4. The development of a detailed process plan for the flow of each day in the five-day design.

5. The continual evaluation of the plan against the purpose and the data and the evaluation of the events themselves at the end of each day.

Using this approach, each seminar could be custom-tailored to meet the unique and specific requirements of a given division. The design process itself became a vehicle for learning, renewal, and the building of ownership for the large-scale methodology by the microcosm group participating in the planning.

Part of the internal architecture for the seminar was provided by the Gleicher formula for organizational change described by Beckhard and Harris (1977). The formula was adapted for mnemonic purposes as follows:

$C = D \times V \times F > R$

C = Change

D = Dissatisfaction with the status quo

V = Vision of the future

F = First steps

R = Resistance to change

This equation suggests that in order to bring about change in a large system there must be a sufficient degree of dissatisfaction with the status quo (D), a vision of the future that is clear, compelling, and different from the present (V), and practical first steps to move toward the vision (F). Multiplied together these three variables must be greater than the resistance to change, which is assumed to always have a value greater than zero. If any of the three variables D, V, or F is equal to zero the total product will be equal to zero, and resistance to change will win out.

Building from this change formula, the participative management seminar was designed in its various division specific iterations to build a shared systemwide understanding (a common database) of D, V, and F. The participants were invited to identify (through a series of interactive processes working with self-facilitated table teams) what was working and not working within the division and in the division's relationship with key external stakeholders. Second, they were asked to build preferred future visions for the whole system and for their natural work teams. Finally, they were given the opportunity to work together both cross-functionally and in natural teams to begin to develop the first steps and action plans that would move the division toward the shared vision.

One of the significant outcomes of the participative management seminars was that the participants left the sessions better connected with one another across system boundaries (functional and hierarchical) that had historically kept them apart. They left with more understanding of the interdependencies that would determine the future success of the enterprise. The seminars not only addressed Page's concerns about creating the right environment for participative management and quality improvement but, by breaking people out of narrow arthritic boxes, helped move each division from the machine model into the systems age.

While the large-scale change process in each division was initiated with the top five management layers, there was soon demand to diffuse the process through the rest of the organization in order to expand and accelerate the change process through all of the layers. Diffusion seminars were created to accommodate this need. These diffusion seminars were built in a similar fashion to the original participative management seminar, with the difference that those who were at the lowest levels in the initial event became the senior levels of the next event and so on through the system. This linking pin and cascading process provided an opportunity for many layers of management to demonstrate their leadership capabilities and for the system as a whole to build a broad and shared understanding around the key elements of the change formula. The sense of shared understanding and participation in creating a new vision for quality, participation, and teamwork became refined and enriched by each level as the process moved down through the entirety of the Diversified Products divisions.

The process of large-scale systems change came to be viewed positively within the leadership hierarchy at Ford as a vehicle for effecting cultural change and organization learning. The Diversified Products divisions were able, for the most part, to make significant quantifiable gains in their quality performance and were able to hold onto their business base in a highly competitive environment. The internal manager of employee involvement and training within DPO, with the support of Tom Page and then Ford chairman Donald Petersen, was promoted and given responsibility to create the Ford Executive Development Center for the top managers in the company worldwide. The methodology employed in the large-scale systems change process was integrated as a part of the core technology in the new executive university.

This large-scale change methodology was developed initially to address the need to change management style and build new skills in a management team that was fighting for its competitive life. Thus the initial application was designed to address two (style and skills) of what Pascale and Athos (1980) refer to as the "soft S's" in their seven S model of organization effectiveness. Next we will look at how the large-scale approach has been applied to one of the "hard S's," strategy, within a different context, the Boeing Company in Seattle, Washington.[12]

Large-Scale Strategic Planning

A Vehicle for Building Alignment

Getting the whole system in the room helps to build an internal community within the organization and to break down barriers between individuals, between groups, and between different functions and hierarchical levels. One potential advantage that was not clearly anticipated at the outset was that of gaining organization alignment around a common strategic direction. In the box-by-box teambuilding approach to organization development there is the opportunity to help subteams within the organization establish clarity of mission, goals, and objectives. Unfortunately this is often conducted without a systems view, and the various subunits aim themselves in different and incompatible directions. Some groups head off to the northeast, while others decide a westerly direction makes more sense. This leads to a lack of coordination internally, confusion for external stakeholders (including customers), and a diminished capacity for a rapid and effective response to a changing business environment. The large-scale systems change process provides a methodology for getting all of the functions and multiple layers of management aligned in one direction simultaneously.

A story from Waterman (1987) based on a consulting project with the Sanwa Bank in Japan illustrates this point nicely. Waterman describes how the broad involvement of multiple layers and functions within the bank led to the successful turnaround of market share losses in record time.

The application of the large-scale systems change methodology to the strategic planning process is a vehicle for creating the type of simultaneity in planning and implementation that

Waterman describes. Designed properly, the process of planning can have at least as much influence on organizational outcomes as the specifics of the plan itself.[13] Large-scale strategic planning was launched within Boeing Computer Services in March of 1989 and within Boeing Aerospace and Electronics in September of 1989. The present discussion of the process will focus on the work with the Aerospace and Electronics Division, since this represents the most advanced evolution of the approach. The discussion of outcomes, however, will address observations from each of these Boeing Company divisions.

Boeing Aerospace and Electronics

The circumstances under which large-scale strategic planning was launched at Boeing Aerospace and Electronics Division were not as dire as those confronting the Diversified Products Operations of Ford Motor Company in 1981. However, early warning signs were apparent to the senior division leadership that the organization was headed for trouble. The division was on its way to its first-ever net loss year, with several key programs running behind schedule and over cost and a number of historically loyal customers beginning to question the division's capabilities. The impetus for initiating the process came from Art Hitsman, the executive vice president responsible for the 27,000 person Boeing Aerospace and Electronics Division.[14] In his new role, Hitsman was seeking to both build bridges among the many units making up his division and to establish a strategic alignment from top to bottom.

One of Hitsman's customer divisions within Boeing had begun experimenting with the Japanese concept of hoshin planning, modeled after Hewlett-Packard's application of the same concept. Under this hoshin planning philosophy, the organization as a whole established clear measurable goals for the year and communicated these to all employees. Each successive layer of the organization from the top on down was responsible for taking the division goals and translating those into unit specific actions that would enable the division to achieve its annual targets. Hitsman was impressed with what he saw in the other division. In his own division, Hitsman hoped to both break down the traditional barriers among functions and hierarchical levels and to achieve a strategic flow-down that would enable each employee to understand how he or she fit into the larger picture. A joint consultant/client design team was created to develop a process that would address the needs for both cultural change and strategic alignment.

The Strategic Planning Model

Following a development process consistent with that used in creating the participative management seminars at Ford, the design team began its work by conducting diagnostic interviews with key members of the division management team. The data from the interviews were shared openly in the design sessions, as were the views of the design team members on the state of the organization. These data and a simple model for strate-

gic planning (see Figure 4) were used to shape the purpose and process for the intervention.

Applying Ackoff's (1981) concept of systems thinking, the strategic planning model starts by looking at the larger containing whole within which the focal subsystem (in this case Boeing Aerospace and Electronics Division) is contained. Before agreeing on the division level strategic focus, the organization members first develop a clear understanding of their key stakeholders and trends within their industry. Therefore, step one in the strategic planning process is to create the means for bringing the relevant data about the operating environment into the room. This includes information about customers, industry trends, and corporate management expectations, as well as internal management and employee perceptions of organizational performance and the quality of work life. The next step is to take that understanding of the environment and come to an agreement

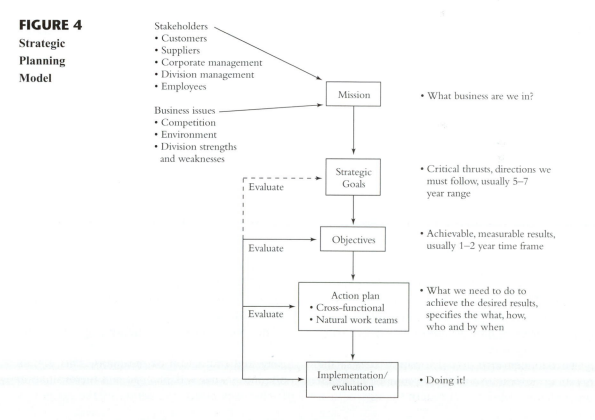

FIGURE 4

Strategic Planning Model

Stakeholders
• Customers
• Suppliers
• Corporate management
• Division management
• Employees

Business issues
• Competition
• Environment
• Division strengths and weaknesses

Mission — • What business are we in?

Strategic Goals — • Critical thrusts, directions we must follow, usually 5–7 year range

Objectives — • Achievable, measurable results, usually 1–2 year time frame

Action plan
• Cross-functional
• Natural work teams
— • What we need to do to achieve the desired results, specifies the what, how, who and by when

Implementation/ evaluation — • Doing it!

Evaluate

on the specific business mission of the organization. In this case, "mission" is understood to mean the definition of the division's business or reason for being.

Next, based on the agreed statement of mission, and the opportunities and challenges identified in the environmental assessment, strategic goals are established. Strategic goals are defined as the critical thrusts or directions the organization should pursue or on which it should focus its energies in the next five to seven years if it is to be successful in achieving its mission.[15] By looking five to seven years out, the participants in the process have the opportunity to define a preferred future for the organization; they can create a picture of what they want to see happen, rather than simply planning from where they are and extending themselves inchbug style into the future. In this model, the strategic goals are not developed by building best case and worst case scenarios. Rather, they are built in a manner consistent with what Ackoff (1981) describes as interactive planning. Ackoff's interactive planning begins with what he calls the "formulation of the mess"—that is understanding the system's threats and opportunities. From that understanding, Ackoff's model moves to the definition of the desirable future state or what he calls "ends planning." The goal planning stage identified in Figure 4 is analogous to this idea of ends planning or to what Lindeman and Lippitt (1979) describe as preferred futuring. Rather than predicting the future and then planning according to the prediction (what Ackoff calls "preactive planning"), the preferred futuring approach works from the premise that the organization members can define a realistic and desirable future state for themselves and then build their plans accordingly. Lippitt (1983), moreover, finds that groups working on preferred futures, as contrasted with those addressing past or present problems, have higher energy and greater ownership for the plans they develop and that their solutions are more creative.

This longer-term goal formation step in the planning process also addresses another common organization dilemma, the activity bias. Often, out of a keen bias for action, organizations, groups, or individuals will jump directly from an environmental squeaky wheel directly to an action to stop the squeak. While this may be effective for addressing near-term problems, this approach can be highly destructive in the long run. In the absence of a coherent set of strategic goals, organization members are left to respond to whatever squeaky wheels they may happen to see and hear, and, as a result, the organization strategy becomes a random assortment of independent actions. These actions over time can work at cross purposes and lead to the dissipation of the organization's energy. This is an example of the optimization of parts of the system at the expense of the whole. In contrast, the strategic planning process organizes a myriad of internal and external squeaky wheels, first into a coherent environmental analysis, and second, into a clear statement of mission and a preferred set of priority goals. This strategic planning process then can reduce the tyranny of a reactive management style and bring alignment and discipline to near-term actions.

While the strategic goals provide a general sense of direction, the objectives specify achievable and measurable results that must be realized within one or two years if the organization is to make progress toward its desired future state. The objectives are developed with the idea of moving from the abstract to the concrete. The objectives begin to translate the vision implied in the goals to the practical first steps the organization must take to achieve them. The process gets even more specific in the action planning stage. In this phase, action plans—identifying what needs to happen, who needs to be involved, and by when—are developed for each of the organization objectives. This type of action planning is done both on a cross-functional total organization basis and at the natural work team level.

The final element of the strategic planning model is the implementation and continual monitoring and evaluation of the plans. This entails both doing what was planned and the evaluation of what was done. Evaluation of the actions in this case should be done not only in relation to the action plans (did we do what we said we were going to do?) but in relation to the objectives (by doing what we agreed to do, did we achieve the results we expected?) and in relation to the goals (by doing what we agreed to and achieving or not achieving the results we expected, did we move ourselves any closer toward the destination we agreed was desirable?). This model, together with the Gleicher formula for organization change, provided the framework for the strategic planning process.

Involving the Organization in Three Phases

Using a top-down and bottom-up approach, the strategic planning process was designed in three phases, each phase building towards and being enriched by the next (see Figure 5). Phase I was designed as a two-day working session for the division general manager and 14 of his top execu-tives representing the major functional organizations and the four major product units (Electronics Systems, Missile Systems, Space Systems, and the Huntsville Division) which make up the division. Following the path laid out in the strategic planning model, this executive group spent most of the first day building a common understanding of the corporation's mission, goals, and objectives, and of how the Aerospace and Electronics Division was viewed by several key stakeholders, including senior corporate management, customers, suppliers, and employees. The group also analyzed the strengths and weaknesses of their key competitors, assessed the existing business environment within the defense and space industry, and evaluated the current capabilities of their organization by examining each of their respective organizations against the Malcom Baldrige National Quality Award criteria.

This environmental analysis provided the basis for the top-management group to develop a

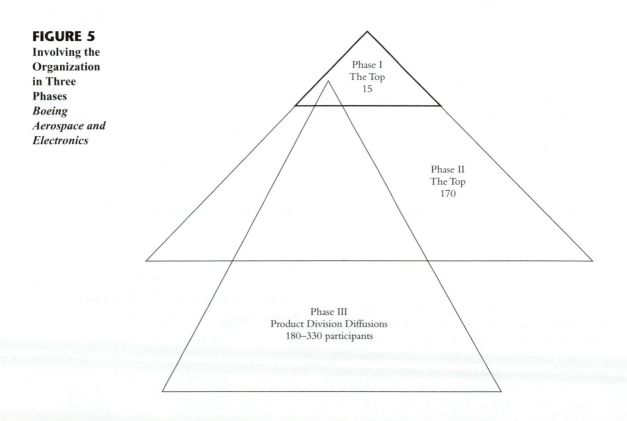

FIGURE 5
Involving the Organization in Three Phases
Boeing Aerospace and Electronics

Phase I
The Top
15

Phase II
The Top
170

Phase III
Product Division Diffusions
180–330 participants

first-draft statement of mission, goals, and objectives for the Aerospace and Electronics Division. The objective of this two-day session was to both strengthen the division leadership group (they were referred to as the Division Quality Council) as a team and to develop a preliminary strategic plan that could be used as the basis for further evolution in phase II.

Phase II occurred four weeks after phase I. This phase expanded the planning circle from the top 15 to the top 170 managers in the division. Phase II was designed as a five-day intervention, with the first three days separated from the last two days by a 13-week interim period (see Figure 6). The phase II event began in a similar way to phase I, starting with an assessment of the key stakeholders, several of whom participated in the meeting, and of the existing business environment.

Once they had the opportunity to build a broader understanding of the business environment, the 155 participants below the top 15 were asked to critique and recommend changes to the draft mission, goals, and objectives proposed by the leadership team. The output from phase I thus became input for phase II. The leadership group took all of the feedback from the 155 on the evening of day two and, working late into the night, integrated their comments into a final statement of mission, goals, and objectives. This was reviewed with the 155 the next morning and became the basis for subsequent systemwide and work unit level action planning on day three and in the postinterim session on days four and five. With the overnight turnaround on recommendations for changes to the mission, goals, and objectives, the ownership for the strategy underwent a major shift from the top 15 to the entire group of 170. Many saw their specific words and concerns incorporated and reflected in the revised document.

Phase III was designed as a series of three-day diffusion events to bring the other 3,000 managers within the division into the strategic planning process. These meetings involved between 180 and 330 managers at a time and each was organized with a focus on one of the four product units. These sessions began with the Corporate and Aerospace and Electronics Division mission, goals, and objectives as givens. The product unit manager and his top leadership team (approximately 15 people in each case) were the principal clients for each of these events. They played the same role that the division general manager and his leadership team had in the phase II events.

As in the phase II process, the product unit leadership team developed a draft statement of mission, goals, and objectives for its organization before the session began. This draft strategy then became the material for debate, critique, and modification by the next tiers of the hierarchy across the functional spectrum in the phase III events. The product units were large organizations in their own right, ranging from 2,000 to 8,000 employees each.

In the product program events, the overall product unit strategy was taken as a given. The results of these sessions included stronger bonds among the participants and an agreed-to set of action priorities and plans at the program level. These priorities and plans were targeted at serving the identified needs of both external and internal customers and at supporting the overall strategic direction of the product unit, the Aerospace and Electronics Division, and ultimately the corporation as a whole.

Phase III was a vehicle for greatly broadening the involvement base in the planning process and for knitting together, through a series of overlapping and interlocking events, the many management layers, functional organizations, product units, and program groups that made up the division. Subsequently, the involvement and team-building process was cascaded through the nonmanagement ranks of the organization.

Systems Theory in the Context of Planning

Ackoff (1981) outlines three operating principles for carrying out his model of interactive planning: the participative principle, the holistic principle,

FIGURE 6 *Boeing Aerospace and Electronics*
Large-Scale Systems Change, Phase II, October 23–25, 1989, and January 16–17, 1990

Purpose: To come together as leaders of Boeing Aerospace and Electronics to:

- Build a shared understanding of our business environment.
- Agree on our BA&E Mission, Goals, and Objectives.
- Identify what we need to do individually and together to lead BA&E successfully into the future with a sense of urgency and strategic intent.

Agenda

Day 1

7:30	Continental Breakfast
8:00	Opening and Welcome—Art Hitsman
8:10	Purpose, Agenda, and Norms
8:30	Telling Your Story
9:15	Break
9:30	View from the Corporate Bridge—Frank Shrontz, Boeing Company Chairman and CEO
10:30	View from the BA&E Bridge—Dan Pinick, President, Boeing Defense and Space Group, and Art Hitsman, Executive Vice President, Boeing Aerospace and Electronics
12:10	Lunch
1:10	Celebrating Diversity (Myers-Briggs)
3:20	Organization Diagnosis: Glads and Sads
4:50	Evaluation
5:00	Adjourn

Day 2

7:30	Continental Breakfast
8:00	Feedback on Evaluations and Agenda for the Day
8:10	Industry Assessment
9:45	Break
10:00	Voice of the Customer
11:40	Lunch
12:30	Interorganization Conflict
3:20	Break
3:35	Revisit Mission, Strategic Goals, and Objectives
3:55	Critique of Mission, Strategic Goals, and Objectives
4:40	Feedback to Quality Council
5:10	Evaluation of the Day
5:15	Adjourn
5:20	Quality Council (Leadership Team) and Design Team remain to read evaluations and integrate feedback to achieve new consensus on Mission, Strategic Goals, and Objectives

Day 3

7:30	Continental Breakfast
8:00	Feedback on Evaluations and Agenda for the Day
8:10	Quality Council Response to Critique of Mission, Strategic Goals, and Objectives
9:15	Participants Self-select to Work on Objectives
9:25	BA&E Objective Strategy Groups
	• Preferred Futuring on Objectives
	• Systemwide Action Recommendations
12:00	Lunch
1:00	BA&E Objective Strategy Groups (continued)
1:30	Roomwide Post, Read, and Vote

(continued)

FIGURE 6   (*concluded*)

2:00   Quality Council Summarizes and Reports Voting Results
2:30   Break
2:45   Back Home Groups: Planning for the Interim
3:45   Headline Reports
4:15   Quality Council Commitments for the Interim
4:30   Wrap-up and Next Steps
4:45   Evaluation of the Three Days
5:00   Social Hour

A 13-week interim period separated days three and four.

Day 4

7:30   Continental Breakfast
8:00   Welcome—Art Hitsman
8:10   Purpose, Agenda, and Logistics
8:20   Look Back: Learnings from the Interim
9:50   Break
10:05   Introductions in New Maximum-mix Teams
10:10   Executive Vice President's Commentary on Reports from the Interim
10:15   Motorola Story: What Motorola Learned from Pursuing the Malcolm Baldrige National Quality Award—
        William Smith, Corporate Senior Executive for Quality, Motorola
11:45   Lunch
12:30   Assessment of BA&E Against the Malcolm Baldrige Criteria
2:45   Break
3:00   View from the BA&E Leadership Bridge—Programs in the News
4:55   Evaluation of the Day
5:00   Adjourn

Day 5

7:30   Continental Breakfast
8:00   Feedback on Evaluations and Agenda for the Day
8:10   Global View—Dr. William J. Taylor, Vice President, International Security Programs, Center for Strategic
        International Studies
9:45   Strategic Objective Analysis—Assessment of Progress on Objectives Plans Since Day 3 and Identification of
        Show Stoppers
11:45   Lunch—Show-stopper lists posted in main room for reading and voting for show-stoppers with the most
        leverage under each objective
1:00   Show-stopper Action Planning
2:45   Break
3:00   Show-stopper Reports
3:35   Back Home Planning
4:35   Headline Reports
5:05   Closing Comments—Art Hitsman
5:15   Evaluation of the Two Days
5:20   Social Hour

and the principle of continuity. The participative principle, as Ackoff describes, implies that:

> no one can plan effectively for someone else. It is better to plan for oneself, no matter how badly, than to be planned for by others, no matter how

well. The reason for this derives from the meaning of development: an increase in one's desire and ability to satisfy one's own desires and those of others. This ability and desire are not increased by being planned for by others, but by planning for oneself (p. 66).

The three phases of planning outlined here were not designed to simply inform the 3,000 members of management what their leaders had decided, but to involve them actively and simultaneously in both strategy formulation and implementation.

The holistic principle applies Ackoff's systems model of the organization within the planning context and argues for the criticality of building coordination and integration into the process:

> Problems, no matter where they appear, should be attacked simultaneously and cooperatively from as many points of view as possible (p. 73).

and:

> planning done independently at any level of a system cannot be as effective as planning carried out interdependently at all levels (p. 73).

Combining these concepts of coordination and integration, Ackoff maintains that:

> the more parts of a system and levels of it that plan simultaneously and interdependently the better. This concept of all-over-at-once planning stands in opposition to sequential planning, either top-down or bottom-up (p. 74).

In his principle of continuity, Ackoff simply cautions that planning should not be done as a discontinuous or static process, but rather should be continuous and dynamic. In the process of moving toward a destination, new information is gained. Plans therefore need to have the flexibility built in to accommodate new data and to allow the setting of new and more appropriate courses.

The process outlined in the present discussion is an attempt to address in particular Ackoff's principles of participation and holism. The effective application of these two principles is likely to build within the organization the adaptive and renewing capabilities addressed by the principle of continuity. While many have argued for the need to address broad participation and holistic thinking in the planning process, little has been written on how to effectively bring this about. What

seems to have been missing is a process model for working with large groups. It is in this domain that the work at Ford and Boeing has provided an especially unique opportunity for learning.

Getting the Whole System in the Room Sounds Good in Theory, but What Do You Do When They Actually Show Up?

Conceptually, getting the whole system in the room—what Weisbord (1987) describes as the next phase in the evolution of organization development—makes sense. For all the reasons stated above, about the limitations of the machine model in contrast to the systems perspective, we need to find ways to plan and manage organizations as a whole and not simply on a box-by-box basis. But in reality, how do you do it? What do you do when the whole system decides to show up?

Large-Scale Application of Small Group Principles

What I have learned, first as a participant observer of the large-scale methodology and subsequently as a process designer, is that the same principles that hold true for managing process effectively at the small group level also apply when larger numbers are brought into the room. Schutz (1984) identifies inclusion, control, and openness as critical elements of effectiveness in a small group's life. When one brings into the room 30 groups of eight people each, the same principles apply. Issues of inclusion, control, and openness must be addressed at the table group level and at the level of the whole room.

In the large-scale systems change methodology, inclusion mechanisms range from the simple—such as having name tags and clear table assignments when people arrive (participants are assigned to cross-level, cross-functional microcosm groups called "maximum-mix teams")—to the more substantial, such as having each participant share his or her personal story about life in the organization with the others at his or her table. Throughout the process of a multiday large group event, the design encourages a maximum of individual involvement and a minimum of passive one-way listening. In each of the series of structured subgroup activities that make up the three days of a phase III event, the subteams are asked to designate members of their group to serve as group facilitator, flipchart recorder, and group spokesperson. Guidelines and coaching for effective performance in these roles are provided by the conference facilitation team. The groups are expected to rotate these roles among their members in successive rounds. This approach is inclusive and places responsibility for control squarely in the groups' hands. In other parts of the design, individuals are given the opportunity to use post-it notes to generate ideas on a roomwide basis under specific strategic issues or to vote with stick-on dots (green for "go for it," red for "don't even think of it") on action plans generated by their own and other subteams. Each element of the design is attentive to both the adult learning principle of active engagement and the individual level needs for inclusion.

Issues of control are also addressed throughout the process, with the objective of keeping the locus of control internal to the participants to the maximum extent possible. Starting with the involvement of the multilevel, cross-functional client/consultant team in the design of each event, participants are involved in shaping the process. The consultants provide an organizing framework for the process, including such concepts as the change formula, the strategic planning model, and the principles of effective group process. The client representatives on the design team and the session participants during the events identify the issues that must be addressed and bring the content specifics to the mission, goals, objectives, and action plans. Both before and during the events, the participants are kept informed of the purpose, agenda, and the underlying theoretical models. Selective prereadings are assigned to prepare the participants to contribute effectively.

Assessment of the process is sought systemically at the end of each day through written participant evaluations. The design team gathers after each session to read the participant evaluations and, based on the feedback, to make any required changes in the subsequent day's agenda. The evaluations are also summarized in extensive detail overnight and fed back to the group as a whole the next morning. The evaluation feedback helps to create a common database of perception on the process and allows the participants to self-correct their behaviors. In this way, the entire process is managed as an open system, with real-time ongoing feedback and adjustment of the design in accordance with the needs of the participants.

Openness is fostered in several ways. Through much of the design, participants are seated in microcosm groups that, by design, exclude their immediate bosses and their direct subordinates. The sessions themselves are conducted in off-site settings and the participants are asked to dress in casual attire. The elements of the design invite the subgroups to diagnose aspects of system performance that under normal circumstances might be considered undiscussable (Argyris, 1986). However, given that the diagnosis is allowed to be carried out and reported as a group product, no individual is required to risk his or her career or reputation in raising difficult questions or in identifying troublesome problems. Diagnostic data, images of the future, and action plans are generated in teams and shared openly across the room through table team reports, either verbal or written. The sessions are designed to both (1) build a common understanding among the participants of how their management peers view the organization and (2) model an environment of openness that may be continued back in the workplace. The transfer of openness back to the work setting may be expected to be enhanced (when contrasted with learning designs involving only a few individuals or a single unit within the organization) by the fact that a large mass of the system is sharing in the opening process simultaneously.

Designing Simultaneously for the Individual, Group, Intergroup, and the Whole System

The Tavistock model (Bion, 1961; Miller and Rice, 1967) views organization life simultaneously through multiple windows, analyzing behavior at the levels of the individual, the group, intergroup relations, and the organization as a whole system. Similarly, the large-scale systems change methodology is designed to address all four of these levels of behavior.

At the individual level, participants in the large-scale process have the opportunity to simply be students of their own organization and of the organization's stakeholders. The top leader of the subject organization will usually gain insights into how he or she is perceived by others in the system. Each of the participants has the opportunity to gain insights into each's behavioral and leadership style through a self-assessment and group discussion with like-type peers applying the Myers-Briggs Type Indicator. Each participant is also encouraged throughout to take the learnings from the broad view and apply them to his or her product or functional perspective.

Group level phenomena are addressed in a variety of configurations. During the three days of a phase III event, participants work in several team formats: maximum-mix, Myers-Briggs type, functional, self-select around strategic issues, and back home work group. Many of these are artificially created temporary task teams with a life span limited to a portion of the conference. For the participants, however, these temporary task teams provide opportunities to try out and practice new group roles (e.g., leader, follower, arbitrator, facilitator, recorder, or spokesperson) and to make connections and form relationships with counterparts from other work units. Some of the temporary task teams continue to meet back in the workplace. Natural or back home work teams provide the most obvious transfer device for learnings from the session back into the organization. In some sessions, opportunity is provided for natural work teams to meet for the purpose of assessing, discussing, and improving how they work together. In all of the sessions, the natural work teams serve as the focal points for taking systemwide strategies and action plans and translating them into specific follow-up actions with clear timelines and accountability. The probability of effective follow up is enhanced by virtue of the fact that the entire natural work team experiences the process together.

Intergroup relations are addressed most directly through a process called "organizational valentines."[16] For this activity, participants are seated in functional groups and are asked to work as a team to prepare and send valentines to every other functional group. In this case, a valentine is a response to the statement "these are the things you do as a part of your job that make it more difficult for us to get our job done." Each team receives a blank valentine to send to each of the other functional teams and is asked to work quickly to generate intergroup feedback that is as behaviorally specific as possible. The teams are also asked to sign each valentine with the name of their function. At the conclusion of the writing period, all of the valentines are posted in the main meeting room under headers with the different function names. Again, operating as an open system process, all of the participants are invited to read as many of the valentines as they wish in the time allowed. In this way, individuals can compare the feedback to their own groups with that sent to others.

The functional teams are then sent back to breakout rooms with their valentines and asked to go through a four-step assignment: (1) react and ventilate, (2) listen to and understand what the data are saying, (3) summarize the major themes, and (4) prepare a nondefensive response to the feedback. At the conclusion, the teams return to the main room to report their summaries and responses. All of the participants are asked to hiss softly if they detect defensiveness in a given report. The hissing, humorously and gently, provides feedback on how a group's response to conflict data is perceived by the others in the room. The valentines process not only helps to create part of the database for effective planning but identifies many specific issues on which the functional teams can follow up.

Intergroup relations are also addressed subtly through the relationship building in various sub-team configurations and explicitly in the back home action planning where teams are invited to make requests for assistance from other teams.

Systemwide considerations are built into every facet of the design at a large-scale systems change meeting. The organizational valentines process expands intergroup conflict resolution to a whole system level. Each maximum-mix working team provides its members the opportunity to view the organization from other functional or hierarchical perspectives. The mission, goals, and objectives are the product of hundreds of inputs from the many points of view represented; and action planning is designed with at least two phases—a cross-functional systemwide look and the view from within natural back home work teams. By bringing five layers and all of the functions of the organization together at one time, the large-scale systems change methodology provides the opportunity for creating new circuits of connection within the system as a whole. Systems thinking is at the core of the process.

A Dynamic Environment for Learning

Meetings within Boeing (and many other organizational environments) have historically been designed as a process in which one or a few presenters share information in a show-and-tell format. These sessions usually make use of overhead projectors and are managed in a way that minimizes interaction among members of the audience. The interactions that occur are usually limited to questions or commentary from individuals in the audience to the presenters. In this way, the complexity of group interaction is kept to a minimum, control of meetings is relatively easily maintained, and the audience has relatively little input to the shaping of ideas or decisions and lit-

tle accountability for follow-on action. Meetings, in many cases, have been conducted in a manner analogous to read only memory in a computer, as a one-way information sharing exercise. This has been a virtually absolute norm for meetings with over 20 participants and fairly typical even of much smaller gatherings.

The large-scale systems change approach represents a major departure from the historical meeting paradigm. At one level, what we are attempting to accomplish is to teach the participants a new process model. We have designed a way of coming together with other organizational members, whether in small groups or large, that encourages openness, dialogue, participation, and complex multilayer and multifunctional communication. By giving the table groups guidelines on facilitation and recording and asking them to select and rotate members to serve in these roles, we are both setting an expectation of and providing practice in effective meeting management. In instances where the agenda calls for presentations by key stakeholders, such as customers, suppliers, senior management, or industry experts, we give the presenters very specific guidelines on the issues we want them to address. Further, we ask that they limit their remarks to a narrow prescribed time, and that they use no slides or viewgraphs. We have found that this approach minimizes audience passivity and maximizes the energy and spontaneity in the presenter's delivery. Such presentations are then immediately followed by time for table discussions, where the participants are asked to share with each other what they heard and their reactions and to generate, as a group, the questions of clarification or understanding they need to ask of the given stakeholder to better comprehend the stakeholder's point of view. The question-generation process then leads to an extended open forum give and take, where table groups are called on to ask their questions of the presenter. In this way, the participants are given the opportunity to shape the agenda with each stakeholder, and important information is shared through a dynamic exchange. Both the presenters and the session participants have responded enthusiastically to this process.

The other elements of the design, as described earlier, involve even more audience participation as subteams are called on to diagnose the effectiveness of existing management systems and practices, critique the draft mission, goals, and objectives, and develop the action plan to move the organization toward the desired future state. So, when the whole system actually does arrive in the room, what we do is provide a framework, including a statement of purpose and process design, that allows the participants maximum opportunity to create their own database, their own vision for the future, and their own plan to get there. The framework, designed effectively, allows a complex array of inputs to be organized into a coherent plan that is both understood and owned by the people responsible for implementation.

Outcomes

Improved organizational performance is the most significant outcome sought through the large-scale systems change methodology. The precise causal linkage between the large-systems approach and performance factors, such as quality, profitability, and customer and employee satisfaction, is difficult to establish, because, in the circumstances in which the methodology has been applied, other management and organization development initiatives have been underway simultaneously. Within the Ford Motor Company, the large-scale systems change methodology was used in concert with a major joint effort between the union and the company to promote employee involvement and an extensive companywide focus on quality improvement and cost-cutting. Each of these interventions is likely to have contributed to the major improvements the company realized in product quality, profitability, and employee satisfaction between the early 1980s and late 1980s. However, one indication of the perceived value of large-scale change process at Ford was the fact that several of the division general managers in-

stituted the methodology as a regular part of their annual business planning activity—bringing together their top 160 managers each year to create a systemwide business plan. Feedback from program participants as well as qualitative assessments within the organization suggested that many of the intervention objectives (e.g., promotion of cross-functional teamwork, increased awareness of the business environment and the need for change, and a shift toward participative management) were achieved. Thompson (1989) documents both business and cultural outcomes associated with the large-scale change applications at Ford.

At Boeing, the large-scale strategic planning methodology was implemented both within the Aerospace and Electronics Division and Boeing Computer Services. Common observations of the organization leaders, as well as other stakeholders, pertain to increased teamwork across functional boundaries and with suppliers and customers, accelerated implementation of major systems and programs, a broader awareness of the needs of customers both internal and external, and much more extensive understanding of business goals and objectives within the organizations. The president of Boeing Computer Services, when asked by the company chairman for his assessment of the process, identified two significant changes. First, he noted that his calendar was much more open than before, because people below him were assuming greater responsibility for running the business, thus freeing him to devote more time to customer relations and strategic issues. Second, he felt his division had achieved unprecedented penetration of awareness even to the nonmanagement ranks regarding the organization's mission, goals, and objectives. One manager within the division remarked that he had accomplished the implementation of an interorganizational network system within six months, which previously would have taken two to three years, given the history of turf battles among the organizations involved. An outside computing hardware vendor noted a significant improvement in internal communications that increased both the efficiency and the effectiveness of his work with the division.

In other cases, organizations within Boeing Computer Services became much more proactive in forming teaming relationships with their customers. Several have created their own large-scale systems change meetings with the customer to focus on their working relationship. In one such meeting, where the historical customer-supplier relationship had been fractious, the principals from the two interfacing organizations enacted their historical conflict by simultaneously dousing one another with lemon meringue pies. As they did so, over 100 of their respective subordinates cheered them on and celebrated the cathartic parody of their past. Then they got down to work and forged a new partnership.

Employees and managers who have participated in the events (both within Boeing Computer Services and Boeing Aerospace and Electronics) have responded in an overwhelmingly positive manner to the experience, based on the data from postsession evaluations and later anecdotal evidence. Several have indicated that the meetings were the most productive they had seen in their careers with the company. Others have been observed explaining, to skeptical nonparticipants from other organizations, the power of seeing their own words incorporated into the substance of the division strategic plan.

In both of the Boeing divisions engaging in this process, significant initiatives were launched to address the strategic goals and objectives developed through the large-scale meetings. However, not all of the goals or objectives received equal attention nor was every subunit within the two organizations equally vigilant in pursuing their actions plans. The long-term impact and implementation depends, as with most organizational initiatives, on the quality of the strategy and plan that is developed as well as on individual responsibility, on division and sub-unit leadership, on the ongoing measurement and tracking of performance, and on the linkage of performance to pay and other incentives. The preliminary qualitative evidence of positive impact within Boeing is

encouraging. The ultimate measure will be based on how much more effectively the organizations are able to serve the needs of their customers as well as their own employees.

Next Steps

Participation in an initial round of large-scale strategic planning does not deliver an organization wholesale from the machine model into the systems age. The intent of the intervention approach described here is to launch and accelerate the cultural transformation process. Much more remains to be done. Most immediately will be a continuation of the large-scale meeting process to encompass the managers and nonmanagers alike who have not yet been involved. At the same time, the development of internal consulting resources to support the substantial demand for follow-on activity within and between subunits is a practical necessity. Some of the internal resources have been developed already through participation in large-scale system change design and implementation teams. Yet, further skill building for these and other resources will be important to equip the organization to extend the process independently. For the leadership teams that have been through one or two rounds of the process, periodic large-scale sessions will help prevent the reinstitution of organizational arthritis and maintain a whole system perspective.

In the longer term, career development philosophies, information systems, and organization structures will need to be adapted to develop and reinforce systemic thinking and behavior. Increased cross-functional career rotation could go a long way toward bridging the differences among disciplines. Information systems designed with broad access can shorten the communication paths among hierarchical layers and among functional organizations. Finally, new organization structures (e.g., Ackoff's, 1981, 1989 circular organization) can bring different organization elements into closer proximity and easier and more fluid relationships. All of these approaches will need to be pursued in assisting old-line corporate hierarchies in the evolution toward whole system integration.

Getting Started: Internal Political Considerations

The approach to cultural and systems change described represents a substantial investment of both financial and human resources. Such an approach can only be undertaken in an environment where the senior leadership is convinced of the necessity for change and has confidence that the large-scale systems change methodology can help. The divisions within Ford and within Boeing where the process was launched were the parts of the respective systems experiencing the most pressure for change. This pressure, coupled in each case with a top leader willing to take a risk, made the large-scale systems change interventions possible. Without a compelling need to change, the intervention would probably appear too complex or too expensive, or both. Without the willingness to take a risk, the leaders would most likely settle for a more conservative and perhaps less demanding approach. The willingness to trust the process at Ford was based both on the criticality of the presenting crisis and pure faith that the consultants were competent. By the time the process was proposed at Boeing, there were already six years of experience with the approach at Ford on which to draw.

I was hired into Boeing in September of 1987 as corporate manager for organization development, with the explicit objective of initiating the type of cultural change approach with which I had been involved at Ford. My position was announced broadly in the organization and came with a good amount of corporate endorsement. The impact of this endorsement and the early footing it provided should not be underestimated. At a minimum, this positioning opened the door to several of what Weisbord (1987) calls "should we/shouldn't we" conversations about the large-scale systems change methodology. Moreover, it may have given the respective leaders confidence that the methodology itself had the blessing and

support of corporate management and was thus less of a political risk than it might otherwise have been.

Beyond these considerations, the respective leaders also needed to be convinced purely on their own terms that the approach had merit. In the first year of my tenure with Boeing, I made numerous presentations on the evolution of organization theory from the machine bureaucracy to the systems model and on the experience with large-scale systems change at Ford. The presentations became the basis for planting seeds that might lead to further in-depth conversations with key organization leaders.

In both of the divisions within Boeing, as well as in the Diversified Products Operations within Ford where the process was begun, the senior leader made a decision to proceed with the approach with minimal or no input from his staff. While the approach was greeted initially by the staffs with skepticism, as they became involved their skepticism tended to fade. Symbolically, the large-scale events have sent a message of a willingness to open the company's systems and processes for broad scrutiny. The method has proved valuable for engaging a wide range of employees in the process of change and for taking the first steps toward organizational alignment.

There are also many organizations within Boeing that so far have not been involved. The process is best expanded on a pull basis, drawing on the internal motivation of organization leaders to select themselves for involvement in the approach. Further diffusion of the methodology into Boeing may be easier, because of growing awareness in the organization of the approach and the potential it represents. On the other hand, further diffusion may be more difficult. Other organizations may not experience as much urgency for change as those that went first; or, because of a not-invented-here bias, a general skepticism about the methodology, or an intracompany rivalry, these organizations may opt out.

At the moment, considerable energy and a raft of folklore have been unleashed as a result of the large-scale interventions. How the process continues to unfold within the company as a whole cannot be easily predicted. Boeing has embarked on a significant cultural shift. The large-scale systems change methodology is one vehicle for effecting the shift.

Reprise on Global Competitiveness

The large-scale systems change methodology was developed as a vehicle to accelerate change within overbounded, arthritic corporate hierarchies buffeted by global competition. Building new organizations with effective practices from the ground up certainly presents many unique challenges. Undoing the past and beginning anew with an existing workforce and infrastructure presents quite another set of dilemmas. The large-scale approach was created within this latter context. Neither of the companies described have the luxury of simply shutting down and building afresh with a new workforce and an entirely new set of resources. The challenges they face are not dissimilar to the challenge faced by many other corporations across the United States and throughout the world: that of building their capacity for learning and for adaptation in an increasingly competitive environment.

De Geus (1988) suggests that the only sustainable competitive advantage any firm enjoys is the ability to learn faster than its competitors. Whether one started with a new or an existing workforce, the necessity to build in a continuous learning capability would be the same. None of our large industrial enterprises can afford for long to close themselves off from new learning or to self-righteously cling to a comfortable status quo. There is much renewal to be done in the enterprises that make up our economy, and for many the time available to accomplish this before succumbing to outside competition is growing frightfully short (Dertouzos, Lester, and Solow, 1989; Grayson and O'Dell, 1988). If we are to be successful in turning around our large enterprises and the millions of people they employ, we must find new models of management and people involvement strategies that will greatly accelerate the rate at which these new models are learned and absorbed into the fiber of the organization. Preliminary evidence indicates that the large-scale systems change methodology represents a promising avenue for both accelerated learning and the accelerated involvement of the workforce in the process of change.

Endnotes

1. "Rethinking Japan." *Business Week,* August 7, 1989, pp. 44–52.

2. Postman argues that the seeds of our national decline may be found in the trivialization of issues and the neutering of substantive debate brought about through the medium of television. While this is not my contention in this paper, I am in agreement with Postman that much of the explanation for our relative decline can be found in factors internal to our society. However, rather than focusing on causality at the macrosocietal level, I will restrict my focus to the firm level.

3. *United Nations International Trade Statistics Yearbook.* New York: United Nations Publications, 1989. The assessment of market share loss was conducted by Colin Fox, managing director, Deltapoint Corporation, Bellevue, WA.

4. "The 100 Largest Commercial Banking Companies." *Fortune,* August 24, 1992, pp. 213–14. Grayson, C. J., and O'Dell, C. *American Business: A Two Minute Warning.* New York: Free Press, 1988. The 1972 banking statistic was provided by Colin Fox, managing director, Deltapoint Corporation, Bellevue, WA.

5. Peters, T. *Thriving on Chaos.* New York: Alfred A. Knopf, 1987, pp. 4–5.

6. Peters, T. "Restoring American Competitiveness: Looking for New Models of Organizations." *Academy of Management Executive,* May 1988, pp. 103–09.

7. The United States business landscape is dotted with companies having made significant turnarounds in quality, profitability, and customer and employee satisfaction. Some of those most commonly referenced include Ford Motor Company, Harley David-

son, Hewlett-Packard, Milliken, Motorola, and Xerox.

8. Kathleen Dannemiller provided the original illustration of the arthritic organization. See Jusela, G. E.; Ball, R. A.; Tyson, C. E.; and Dannemiller, D. K. "Work Innovations at Ford Motor." In Shetty, Y. K., and Buehler, V. M. *Quality, Productivity and Innovation.* New York: Elsevier, 1987.

9. See Chin, R., and Benne, K. D. "General Strategies for Effecting Changes in Human Systems." In Bennis, W. G.; Benne, K. D.; and Chin, R. *The Planning of Change.* 2nd ed. New York: Holt, Rinehart & Winston, 1969.

10. The consultants included Kathleen Dannemiller, Alan Davenport, Bruce Gibb, Chuck Tyson, and Jeff Walsh, each of whom had been working independently until they were called together to collaborate on this project.

11. The consulting team was managed and coordinated by Nancy Badore, manager of employee involvement and training for DPO. I joined Ford as an internal organization development consultant in June of 1983 and began to collaborate with the Ann Arbor consultants on further iterations of the large-scale systems change methodology over the next few years.

12. I left the Ford Motor Company in August 1987 to assume the position of corporate manager for organization development with the Boeing Company.

13. See De Geus, A. P. "Planning as Learning." *Harvard Business Review,* March–April 1988, pp. 70–74. See also Stata, R. "Organizational Learning—The Key to Management Innovation." *Sloan Management Review,* Spring 1989, pp. 63–74.

14. The Boeing Electronics Division and its 5,000 employees were subsequently merged with the Aerospace Division, and Hitsman was given responsibility for the entire combined division.

15. The time frame for the look at strategic goals is influenced both by the size of the organization and the magnitude of change required. A smaller organization than Boeing Aerospace and Electronics seeking less substantial changes might use a narrower time horizon.

16. The organizational valentines process was developed by the original large-scale design team at Ford Motor Company as an element of the participative management seminar.

References

Ackoff, R. L. *Creating the Corporate Future.* New York: John Wiley & Sons, 1981.

Ackoff, R. L. "The Circular Organization: An Update." *Academy of Management Executive,* February 1989, pp. 11–16.

Alderfer, C. P. "Boundary Relations in Organizational Diagnosis." In H. Meltzer, and F. R. Wicker, (eds.), *Humanizing Organizational Behavior.* Springfield, IL: Thomas, 1976.

Argyris, C. "Skilled Incompetence." *Harvard Business Review,* September–October 1986, pp. 74–79.

Beckhard, R. *Organization Development: Strategies and Models.* Reading, MA: Addison-Wesley, 1969.

Beckhard, R., and Harris, R. T. *Organizational Transitions.* Reading, MA: Addison-Wesley, 1977.

Bion, W. R. *Experiences in Groups.* London: Turistock, 1961.

Dannemiller, K. D. "Teambuilding at a Macro Level or Ben Gay for Arthritic Organizations." Arlington, VA: NTL Publications, 1985.

De Geus, A. P. "Planning as Learning." *Harvard Business Review,* March–April 1988, pp. 70–74.

Dertouzos, M. L.; Lester, R. K.; and Solow, R. M. *Made in America: Regaining the Productive Edge.* Cambridge, MA: MIT Press, 1989.

Grayson, C. J., Jr., and O'Dell, C. *American Business: A Two-Minute Warning.* New York: Free Press, 1988.

Hayes, R. H.; Wheelwright, S. C.; and Clark, R. B. *Dynamic Manufacturing: Creating the Learning Organization.* New York: Free Press, 1988.

Imai, M. *Kaizen: The Key to Japan's Competitive Success.* New York: Random House, 1986.

Kanter, R. M. *The Change Masters.* New York: Simon & Schuster, 1983.

Keichel, W., III. "The Organization That Learns." *Fortune,* March 12, 1990, pp. 133–36.

Lindaman, E. B., and Lippitt, R. O. *Choosing the Future You Prefer.* Washington, DC: Development Publications, 1979.

Lippitt, R. "Future before You Plan." In *NTL Managers' Handbook.* Arlington, VA: NTL Institute, 1982.

Miller, E. J., and Rice, A. K. *Systems of Organization.* London: Tavistock, 1967.

Mills, D. Q., and Lovell, M. R., Jr. "Enhancing Competitiveness: The Contribution of Employee Relations."

In B. R. Scott and G. C. Lodge (eds.), *U.S. Competitiveness in the World Economy.* Boston: Harvard Business School Press, 1985, pp. 455–78.

Mitroff, I. I. *Business Not as Usual.* San Francisco: Jossey-Bass Publishers, 1987.

Pascale, R., and Athos, A. *The Art of Japanese Management.* New York: Simon & Schuster, 1980.

Peters, T. *Thriving on Chaos.* New York: Alfred A. Knopf, 1987.

Peters, T. "Restoring American Competitiveness: Looking for New Models of Organizations." *Academy of Management Executive,* May 1988, pp. 103–9.

Porter, M. E. "The Competitive Advantage of Nations." *Harvard Business Review,* March–April, 1990, pp. 73–93.

Postman, N. *Amusing Ourselves to Death: Public Discourse in the Age of Show Business.* New York: Viking Penguin, 1985.

"Rethinking Japan." *Business Week,* August 7, 1989, pp. 44–52.

Schindler-Rainman, E., and Lippitt, R. O. *Collaborative Community: Mobilizing Citizens for Action.* Riverside: University of California, 1980.

Schutz, W. *The Truth Option.* Berkeley, CA: Ten Speed Press, 1984.

Stata, R. "Organizational Learning—The Key to Management Innovation." *Sloan Management Review,* Spring 1989, pp. 63–74.

Thompson, G. "Large-System Change at the Executive Level in a Traditional Maufacturing Industry." Pepperdine University, unpublished master's thesis, 1989.

United Nations International Trade Statistics Yearbook. New York: United Nations Publication, 1989.

Vaill, P. B. "Seven Process Frontiers for Organization Development." George Washington University, 1986, prepublication draft.

Waterman, R. H., Jr. *The Renewal Factor.* Toronto: Bantam Books, 1987.

Weisbord, M. R. *Productive Workplaces.* San Francisco: Jossey-Bass, 1987a.

Weisbord, M. R. "Toward Third-Wave Managing and Consulting." *Organizational Dynamics,* Winter 1987b, pp. 4–24.

Reading 25

Centers of Excellence: Empowering People to Manage Change

Steven W. Lyle
Robert A. Zawacki

Problems Addressed

Historically, organizations have bounced from centralized organizational structures to decentralized structures and back again. The cycle of restructuring has been endless; only the specific forms of redesign have changed.

Against this backdrop, today's information technology (IT) managers attempt to add value to the bottom line of their business units. While facing reductions in staff, they are challenged to maintain or even increase customer satisfaction and productivity.

IT managers look to structural change as the answer to the multiple challenges they face. The efforts of many managers to apply the latest quick-fix or management tenets often fail, however, because they aim to implement changes designed for the organizations of the 1950s, not the 1990s.

In the past, change flowed along a reasonably predictable course. Individual contributors in the IT organization adjusted to change by working harder and smarter, and by introducing technology that helped them stay ahead of change. Today's organizations, however, are facing high-speed random change that affects the direction, focus, strategy, and behaviors of the organization and its members.[1]

Several similar organizational structures have been designed to facilitate random change: the learning organization, the horizontal organization, the shamrock organization, the STAR (i.e., strategic goals in a constant state of transition and renewal) organization, and the high-velocity organization. One additional, evolving design is the center of excellence (COE). This article describes the center of excellence and reports on Texas Instruments' experience with it.

Conceptual Model of the Center of Excellence

Organizational design and restructuring have traditionally involved the transfer of control—the control of people. Yet organizational redesign is not about controlling people. It is about providing a strategy and structure that facilitates the growth of people by giving them the opportunity to do their best work. True organizational restructuring enables people to use their unique talents and abilities to the best interest of the business or institution—in other words, it empowers them.

The concept of a center of excellence is designed to prevent businesses from repeating past mistakes and stop the constant transfer of control over people. However, effective implementation of a center of excellence can only be accomplished by change agents who have abandoned the mindset of the 1950s.

The COE model concentrates on the acquisition and development of the skill sets that foster the distinctive competencies the organization needs to remain competitive. Two mutually dependent imperatives are key to the success of today's organization:

1. An organizational structure must be implemented that ensures fast mobilization and

Source: Reprinted by permission from *Information Management: Strategy, Systems, and Technologies* (1-03-35), pp. 1–7, 1996. Copyright CRC Press, Boca Raton, Florida.

development of intellectual property (i.e., time-based competition).

2. The organization must engage and keep the customer's attention (i.e., customer satisfaction).

Most organizations have focused more on the second imperative than on the first—that is, they focus on the execution of projects (i.e., engagement of customers) rather than on investing in the development of their people. This pattern is not the result of a lack of desire to invest in people or poor management per se; rather, it stems from a lack of focus. Organizational leaders and managers are human, and they can only focus their attention on a limited number of tasks.

Lack of focus on the development of people has caused many organizations to perform poorly in their ability to engage customers. The end result is that they not only lose customers, they lose their people too. Many companies never recover from this costly spiral.

Characteristics of a Center of Excellence

The COE model provides a framework for creating an environment that allows organizations to address the imperatives for success in the 1990s and gain competitive advantage. The mission of a COE is to place people resources where they are needed most by the business and to ensure that people are trained appropriately and have the necessary experiences and background to succeed on projects.

A COE is defined by the following characteristics:

• It is a logical grouping of related skills or disciplines.

• It is an administrative entity focused on the well-being and development of people.

• It is a place where individuals learn skills and share knowledge across functional boundaries.

• It is a physical organizational unit in which members are all together or a virtual unit that

is only a learning and communications vehicle.

• It matches resources to demand.

Appropriate placement, training, and development of human resources necessitates that the COE be staffed with a forward-thinking coach who is able to stay ahead of the need curve. To ensure that there is an equal emphasis on the two organizational imperatives to success—time-based competition and user satisfaction—the responsibilities of the coach must be separate from those of the organization leader or project leader. Separating the coach's responsibilities not only helps achieve this equality of emphasis, it promotes the cultural change process by sending a clear signal to the organization that management is serious about valuing its people resources. When people feel valued, they add value to the customer. The COE is about valuing people.

IT Transformation at Texas Instruments

Like many IT organizations around the world, the IT organization at Dallas-based Texas Instruments is faced with increased pressure to perform and deliver at greatly reduced cycle times. To meet the challenge, the IT organization commissioned a project to reengineer information technology at Texas Instruments. The project is known by the acronym RITTI.

The IT leadership team recognized that a transformation of the IT environment requires a concurrent engineering approach involving several elements:

• Organization.

• People.

• Business processes.

• Technology.

The team realized that each of these elements alone would not guarantee successful business leadership for the IT organization or its customers. Considering these elements together, however, could achieve major improvements.

Three major strategies address the elements:

1. A process strategy necessitates that the team map, understand, and address entire business processes versus piecemeal patch work.
2. An architecture strategy based on Texas Instruments' component-based applications development methodology and object-modeling techniques separates the presentation level, the data level, and the logic (i.e., business rules) level. The methodology is facilitated by Composer and Arranger, two business products of Texas Instruments Software, as well as by repository technology currently being jointly developed by Texas Instruments Software and Microsoft Corp.
3. An organization and people strategy promotes the ability to develop, deploy, and retain the critical skills needed to compete.

Texas Instruments has successfully implemented the center of excellence concept to achieve an equality of focus between the development of human resources and the engagement of customers and to allow the IT team to develop the talent needed to refine and execute the three transformation strategies. Unlike many organizational leadership bodies whose members assert that people are their most valued resource, the leadership team at Texas Instruments wanted to back its words with actions.

Horizontal Skills-Centered Units

Texas Instruments' IT organization went from a vertical functional-department structure to a horizontal skills-centered COE structure that sources people to vertical project teams across the organization. The COE structure separates the traditional elements of control between two distinct roles: a COE coach and a project or organization leader.

To ensure that everyone understands the roles and the accountability within the COE structure,

the IT organization rewrote organizational processes to reflect the new roles. The processes were published and then explained during open discussion meetings. Some of the major processes rewritten for the IT organization at Texas Instruments include:

- The performance-evaluation process.
- The development planning process.
- The compensation planning process.
- The staffing and assignment process.
- The knowledge-capture process.
- The cost-management and labor-tracking process.

Originally published in October 1994 by an implementation team, the processes were refined in June 1995. Each process is currently owned by a COE coach who is responsible for leading any further refinement activity. Both the coach and project or organization leader work with COE members to ensure that each individual understands—from both a project standpoint and a self-development standpoint—the requirements of success within the organization and the market.

Responsibilities of the COE Coach

The COE coach has no responsibilities outside the center of excellence. The responsibilities of the coach include:

- Training, developing, and assessing COE members in support of projects.
- Mentoring COE members in their areas of expertise or discipline.
- Facilitating and enabling the exchange and sharing of ideas and information.
- Recruiting and facilitating the assignment of individuals to projects.
- Managing the base salaries of COE members.
- Providing administrative support to COE members.
- Managing costs within the COE.

Responsibilities of the Project or Organization Leader

The project or organization leader/manager has the following responsibilities:

- Attaining performance objectives for all project milestones.
- Forecasting time-phased and skills-based resource requirements.
- Providing technical project direction and setting task-level priorities.
- Validating COE core competencies and future skills development.
- Providing coaches with feedback from team members' performance evaluations in support of the performance-evaluation feedback process and the promotion and base-salary adjustment process.
- Initiating and participating in the corrective-action process regarding performance issues.
- Managing and distributing variable compensation to project members.

Human Resource and Other Support Programs

The center of excellence at Texas Instruments is supported by three human-resource-related processes that are of great importance to the individual and the organization. These are:

- The staffing and assignment process.
- The performance-evaluation process.
- The compensation planning process.

The following sections summarize the significant characteristics of these processes.

The Staffing and Assignment Process

Under the staffing and assignment process, administrative responsibilities for individuals reside with only one COE. Individuals are encouraged to remain with their project assignment until completion of a major phase or milestone. They are also encouraged to participate in a wide range of assignments that provide exposure across the IT environment.

An open process for communication of assignment opportunities helps individuals achieve maximum exposure across the organization. Assignment changes are discussed with all involved parties (i.e., the individual, the project or organization leader, and the coach) before they occur.

The Performance-Evaluation Process

Performance review sessions are held with the coach when individuals change assignments, or at least annually. They are initiated by individuals and based on feedback the coach obtains from various project or organization leaders. In addition, individuals are expected to collect 360-degree feedback throughout the year. As much as possible, performance review sessions are separate from the compensation review process.

The Compensation Planning Process

COE coaches manage the base pay (i.e., salary) of COE members. Base pay is determined according to the individual's competency level within the skill set/ discipline, customer results, skills acquisition, teamwork, and knowledge sharing. Project and organization leaders manage variable compensation based on superb execution of tasks that map back to a key customer or organizational success criterion. All leaders are compensated based on attainment of performance objectives and staff development, not organization size.

Recommended Course of Action

Many IT organizations are limited in their ability to enable the type of business change required by their customers. These organizations must take care not to repeat the historical change pattern of centralization and decentralization.

Random change warrants implementation of a learning organization that is based on the center of excellence model. Successful implementation of a center of excellence depends on several factors.

CSFs for Implementing a Center of Excellence

A successful implementation has the following:

- Leaders who are visibly committed to the change in focus.
- A clearly articulated vision.
- Benchmarking activity that facilitates learning.
- Clear communication of the reason for and benefits of the change.
- Involvement of as many organizational members as possible.
- Thorough communications planning throughout the transition.

A center of excellence implemented along these lines provides the flexibility organizations need to meet the two imperatives of success:

- It engages the customer.
- It provides continuity to an individual's career and development while adding value to the bottom line of the customer in a timely fashion.

Organizations should not waste their and their peoples' time with repeated reorganizations. An organizational design that is flexible, responsive to random change, and customer-focused will outlive the next technology wave. The center of excellence model offers a fix, not another management fad.

Endnote

1. Robert A. Zawacki et al; *Transforming the Mature Information Technology Organization* (Colorado Springs, CO: EagleStar Publishing, 1995), pp. 22–23.

Reading 26

Building a Learning Organization

David A. Garvin

Continuous improvement programs are sprouting up all over as organizations strive to better themselves and gain an edge. The topic list is long and varied, and sometimes it seems as though a program a month is needed just to keep up. Unfortunately, failed programs far outnumber successes, and improvement rates remain distressingly low. Why? Because most companies have failed to grasp a basic truth. Continuous improvement requires a commitment to learning.

How, after all, can an organization improve without first learning something new? Solving a problem, introducing a product, and reengineering a process all require seeing the world in a new light and acting accordingly. In the absence of learning, companies—and individuals—simply repeat old practices. Change remains cosmetic, and improvements are either fortuitous or short-lived.

A few farsighted executives—Ray Stata of Analog Devices, Gordon Forward of Chaparral Steel, Paul Allaire of Xerox—have recognized the link between learning and continuous improvement and have begun to refocus their companies around it. Scholars too have jumped on the bandwagon, beating the drum for "learning organizations" and "knowledge-creating companies." In rapidly changing businesses like semiconductors and consumer electronics, these ideas are fast taking hold. Yet despite the encouraging signs, the topic in large part remains murky, confused, and difficult to penetrate.

Source: Reprinted by permission of *Harvard Business Review*. From "Building a Learning Organization," by David A. Garvin, July–August 1993, pp. 76–91. Copyright © 1993 by the President and Fellows of Harvard College. All rights reserved.

Meaning, Management, and Measurement

Scholars are partly to blame. Their discussions of learning organizations have often been reverential and utopian, filled with near mystical terminology. Paradise, they would have you believe, is just around the corner. Peter Senge, who popularized learning organizations in his book *The Fifth Discipline,* described them as places "where people continually expand their capacity to create the results they truly desire, where new and expansive patterns of thinking are nurtured, where collective aspiration is set free, and where people are continually learning how to learn together."[1] To achieve these ends, Senge suggested the use of five "component technologies": systems thinking, personal mastery, mental models, shared vision, and team learning. In a similar spirit, Ikujiro Nonaka characterized knowledge-creating companies as places where "inventing new knowledge is not a specialized activity . . . it is a way of behaving, indeed, a way of being, in which everyone is a knowledge worker."[2] Nonaka suggested that companies use metaphors and organizational redundancy to focus thinking, encourage dialogue, and make tacit, instinctively understood ideas explicit.

Sound idyllic? Absolutely. Desirable? Without question. But does it provide a framework for action? Hardly. The recommendations are far too abstract, and too many questions remain unanswered. How, for example, will managers know when their companies have become learning organizations? What concrete changes in behavior are required? What policies and programs must be in place? How do you get from here to there?

Most discussions of learning organizations finesse these issues. Their focus is high philosophy and grand themes, sweeping metaphors rather than the gritty details of practice. Three critical issues are left unresolved; yet each is essential for effective implementation. First is the question of *meaning.* We need a plausible, well-grounded definition of learning organizations; it must be actionable and easy to apply. Second is the question of *management.* We need clearer guidelines for practice, filled with operational advice rather than high aspirations. And third is the question of *measurement.* We need better tools for assessing an organization's rate and level of learning to ensure that gains have in fact been made.

Once these "three Ms" are addressed, managers will have a firmer foundation for launching learning organizations. Without this groundwork, progress is unlikely, and for the simplest of reasons. For learning to become a meaningful corporate goal, it must first be understood.

What Is a Learning Organization?

Surprisingly, a clear definition of learning has proved to be elusive over the years. Organizational theorists have studied learning for a long time; the accompanying quotations suggest that there is still considerable disagreement (see the insert "Definitions of Organizational Learning"). Most scholars view organizational learning as a process that unfolds over time and link it with knowledge acquisition and improved performance. But they differ on other important matters.

Some, for example, believe that behavioral change is required for learning; others insist that new ways of thinking are enough. Some cite information processing as the mechanism through which learning takes place; others propose shared insights, organizational routines, even memory. And some think that organizational learning is common, while others believe that flawed, self-serving interpretations are the norm.

Definitions of Organizational Learning

Scholars have proposed a variety of definitions of organizational learning. Here is a small sample:

> Organizational learning means the process of improving actions through better knowledge and understanding.
> C. Marlene Fiol and Marjorie A. Lyles, "Organizational Learning," *Academy of Management Review,* October 1985.

> An entity learns if, through its processing of information, the range of its potential behaviors is changed.
> George P. Huber, "Organizational Learning: The Contributing Processes and the Literatures," *Organization Science,* February 1991.

> Organizations are seen as learning by encoding inferences from history into routines that guide behavior.

Barbara Levitt and James G. March, "Organizational Learning," *American Review of Sociology,* Vol. 14, 1988.

> Organizational learning is a process of detecting and correcting error.
> Chris Argyris, "Double Loop Learning in Organizations," *Harvard Business Review,* September–October 1977.

> Organizational learning occurs through shared insights, knowledge, and mental models . . . [and] builds on past knowledge and experience—that is, on memory.
> Ray Stata, "Organizational Learning—The Key to Management Innovation," *Sloan Management Review,* Spring 1989.

How can we discern among this cacophony of voices yet build on earlier insights? As a first step, consider the following definition:

> A learning organization is an organization skilled at creating, acquiring, and transferring knowledge, and at modifying its behavior to reflect new knowledge and insights.

This definition begins with a simple truth: new ideas are essential if learning is to take place. Sometimes they are created de novo, through flashes of insight or creativity; at other times they arrive from outside the organization or are communicated by knowledgeable insiders. Whatever their source, these ideas are the trigger for organizational improvement. But they cannot by themselves create a learning organization. *Without accompanying changes in the way that work gets done, only the potential for improvement exists.*

This is a surprisingly stringent test for it rules out a number of obvious candidates for learning organizations. Many universities fail to qualify, as do many consulting firms. Even General Motors, despite its recent efforts to improve performance, is found wanting. All of these organizations have been effective at creating or acquiring new knowledge but notably less successful in applying that knowledge to their own activities. Total quality management, for example, is now taught at many business schools, yet the number using it to guide their own decision making is very small. Organizational consultants advise clients on social dynamics and small-group behavior but are notorious for their own infighting and factionalism. And GM, with a few exceptions (like Saturn and NUMMI), has had little success in revamping its manufacturing practices, even though its managers are experts on lean manufacturing, JIT production, and the requirements for improved quality of work life.

Organizations that do pass the definitional test—Honda, Corning, and General Electric come quickly to mind—have, by contrast, become adept at translating new knowledge into new ways of behaving. These companies actively manage the learning process to ensure that it occurs by design rather than by chance. Distinctive policies and practices are responsible for their success; they form the building blocks of learning organizations.

Building Blocks

Learning organizations are skilled at five main activities: systematic problem solving, experimentation with new approaches, learning from their own experience and past history, learning from the experiences and best practices of others, and transferring knowledge quickly and efficiently throughout the organization. Each is accompanied by a distinctive mind-set, tool kit, and pattern of behavior. Many companies practice these activities to some degree. But few are consistently successful because they rely largely on happenstance and isolated examples. By creating systems and processes that support these activities and integrate them into the fabric of daily operations, companies can manage their learning more effectively.

1. Systematic problem solving. This first activity rests heavily on the philosophy and methods of the quality movement. Its underlying ideas, now widely accepted, include:

- Relying on the scientific method, rather than guesswork, for diagnosing problems (what Deming calls the "Plan, Do, Check, Act" cycle, and others refer to as "hypothesis-generating, hypothesis-testing" techniques).

- Insisting on data, rather than assumptions, as background for decision making (what quality practitioners call "fact-based management").

- Using simple statistical tools (histograms, Pareto charts, correlations, cause-and-effect diagrams) to organize data and draw inferences.

Most training programs focus primarily on problem-solving techniques, using exercises and practical examples. These tools are relatively straightforward and easily communicated; the necessary mind-set, however, is more difficult to

Xerox's Problem-Solving Process

Step	Question to Be Answered	Expansion/ Divergence	Contraction/ Convergence	What's Needed to Go to the Next Step
1. Identify and select problem	What do we want to change?	Lots of problems for consideration	One problem statement, one "desired state" agreed upon	Identification of the gap "Desired state" described in observable terms
2. Analyze problem	What's preventing us from reaching the "desired state"?	Lots of potential causes identified	Key cause(s) identified and verified	Key cause(s) documented and ranked
3. Generate potential solutions	How *could* we make the change?	Lots of ideas on how to solve the problem	Potential solutions clarified	Solution list
4. Select and plan the solution	What's the *best* way to do it?	Lots of criteria for evaluating potential solutions Lots of ideas on how to implement and evaluate the selected solution	Criteria to use for evaluating solution agreed upon Implementation and evaluation plans agreed upon	Plan for making and monitoring the change Measurement criteria to evaluate solution effectiveness
5. Implement the solution	Are we following the plan?		Implementation of agreed-on contingency plans (if necessary)	Solution in place
6. Evaluate the solution	How well did it work?		Effectiveness of solution agreed upon Continuing problems (if any) identified	Verification that the problem is solved, or Agreement to address continuing problems

establish. Accuracy and precision are essential for learning. Employees must therefore become more disciplined in their thinking and more attentive to details. They must continually ask, "How do we know that's true?", recognizing that close enough is not good enough if real learning is to take place. They must push beyond obvious symptoms to assess underlying causes, often collecting evidence when conventional wisdom says it is unnecessary. Otherwise, the organization will remain a prisoner of "gut facts" and sloppy reasoning, and learning will be stifled.

Xerox has mastered this approach on a companywide scale. In 1983, senior managers launched the company's Leadership Through Quality initiative; since then, all employees have been trained in small-group activities and problem-solving techniques. Today a six-step process is used for virtually all decisions (see the insert "Xerox's Problem-Solving Process"). Employees are provided with tools in four areas: generating ideas and collecting information (brainstorming, interviewing, surveying); reaching consensus (list reduction, rating forms, weighted voting); analyzing and displaying data (cause-and-effect diagrams, force-field analysis); and planning actions (flow charts, Gantt charts). They then practice these tools during training sessions that last several days. Training is presented in "family groups," members of the same department or business-unit team, and the tools are applied to real problems facing the group. The result of this process has been a common vocabulary and a consistent, companywide approach to problem solving. Once employees have been trained, they are expected to use the techniques at all meetings, and no topic is off-limits. When a high-level group was formed to review Xerox's organizational structure and suggest alternatives, it employed the very same process and tools.[3]

2. Experimentation. This activity involves the systematic searching for and testing of new knowledge. Using the scientific method is essential, and there are obvious parallels to systematic problem solving. But unlike problem solving, experimentation is usually motivated by opportunity and expanding horizons, not by current difficulties. It takes two main forms: ongoing programs and one-of-a-kind demonstration projects.

Ongoing programs normally involve a continuing series of small experiments, designed to produce incremental gains in knowledge. They are the mainstay of most continuous improvement programs and are especially common on the shop floor. Corning, for example, experiments continually with diverse raw materials and new formulations to increase yields and provide better grades of glass. Allegheny Ludlum, a specialty steelmaker, regularly examines new rolling methods and improved technologies to raise productivity and reduce costs.

Successful ongoing programs share several characteristics. First, they work hard to ensure a steady flow of new ideas, even if they must be imported from outside the organization. Chaparral Steel sends its first-line supervisors on sabbaticals around the globe, where they visit academic and industry leaders, develop an understanding of new work practices and technologies, then bring what they've learned back to the company and apply it to daily operations. In large part as a result of these initiatives, Chaparral is one of the five lowest cost steel plants in the world. GE's Impact Program originally sent manufacturing managers to Japan to study factory innovations, such as quality circles and kanban cards, and then apply them in their own organizations; today Europe is the destination, and productivity improvement practices the target. The program is one reason GE has recorded productivity gains averaging nearly 5 percent over the last four years.

Successful ongoing programs also require an incentive system that favors risk taking. Employees must feel that the benefits of experimentation exceed the costs; otherwise, they will not participate. This creates a difficult challenge for managers, who are trapped between two perilous extremes. They must maintain accountability and control over experiments without stifling creativity by unduly penalizing employees for failures. Allegheny Ludlum has perfected this juggling act: it keeps expensive, high-impact experiments off the scorecard used to evaluate managers but requires prior approvals from four senior vice presidents. The result has been a history of productivity improvements annually averaging 7 percent to 8 percent.

Finally, ongoing programs need managers and employees who are trained in the skills required to perform and evaluate experiments. These skills are seldom intuitive and must usually be learned. They cover a broad sweep: statistical methods, like design of experiments, that efficiently compare a large number of alternatives; graphical techniques, like process analysis, that are essential for redesigning work flows; and creativity techniques, like storyboarding and role playing that keep novel ideas flowing. The most effective training programs are tightly focused and feature a small set of techniques tailored to employees' needs. Training in design of experiments, for example, is useful for manufacturing engineers, while creativity techniques are well suited to development groups.

Demonstration projects are usually larger and more complex than ongoing experiments. They involve holistic, systemwide changes, introduced at a single site, and are often undertaken with the goal of developing new organizational capabilities. Because these projects represent a sharp break from the past, they are usually designed from scratch, using a "clean slate" approach. General Foods's Topeka plant, one of the first high-commitment work systems in this country, was a pioneering demonstration project initiated to introduce the idea of self-managing teams and high levels of worker autonomy; a more recent example, designed to rethink small-car development, manufacturing, and sales, is GM's Saturn Division.

Demonstration projects share a number of distinctive characteristics:

- They are usually the first projects to embody principles and approaches that the organization hopes to adopt later on a larger scale. For this reason, they are more transitional efforts than endpoints and involve considerable "learning by doing." Mid-course corrections are common.
- They implicitly establish policy guidelines and decision rules for later projects. Managers must therefore be sensitive to the precedents they are setting and must send strong signals if they expect to establish new norms.
- They often encounter severe tests of commitment from employees who wish to see whether the rules have, in fact, changed.
- They are normally developed by strong multifunctional teams reporting directly to senior management. (For projects targeting employee involvement or quality of work life, teams should be multilevel as well.)
- They tend to have only limited impact on the rest of the organization if they are not accompanied by explicit strategies for transferring learning.

All of these characteristics appeared in a demonstration project launched by Copeland Corporation, a highly successful compressor manufacturer, in the mid-1970s. Matt Diggs, then the new CEO, wanted to transform the company's approach to manufacturing. Previously, Copeland had machined and assembled all products in a single facility. Costs were high, and quality was marginal. The problem, Diggs felt, was too much complexity.

At the outset, Diggs assigned a small, multifunctional team the task of designing a "focused factory" dedicated to a narrow, newly developed product line. The team reported directly to Diggs and took three years to complete its work. Initially, the project budget was $10 million to $12 million; that figure was repeatedly revised as the team found, through experience and with Diggs's prodding, that it could achieve dramatic improvements. The final investment, a total of $30 million, yielded unanticipated breakthroughs in reliability testing, automatic tool adjustment, and programmable control. All were achieved through learning by doing.

The team set additional precedents during the plant's start-up and early operations. To dramatize the importance of quality, for example, the quality manager was appointed second-in-command, a significant move upward. The same reporting relationship was used at all subsequent plants. In addition, Diggs urged the plant manager to ramp up slowly to full production and resist all efforts to proliferate products. These instructions were unusual at Copeland, where the marketing department normally ruled. Both directives were quickly tested; management held firm, and the implications were felt throughout the organization. Manufacturing's stature improved, and the company as a whole recognized its competitive contribution. One observer commented, "Marketing had always run the company, so they couldn't believe it. The change was visible at the highest levels, and it went down hard."

Once the first focused factory was running smoothly—it seized 25 percent of the market in two years and held its edge in reliability for over a decade—Copeland built four more factories in quick succession. Diggs assigned members of the initial project to each factory's design team to ensure that early learnings were not lost; these people later rotated into operating assignments. Today focused factories remain the cornerstone of Copeland's manufacturing strategy and a continuing source of its cost and quality advantages.

Whether they are demonstration projects like Copeland's or ongoing programs like Allegheny Ludlum's, all forms of experimentation seek the same end: moving from superficial knowledge to

Stages of Knowledge

Scholars have suggested that production and operating knowledge can be classified systematically by level or stage of understanding. At the lowest levels of manufacturing knowledge, little is known other than the characteristics of a good product. Production remains an art, and there are few clearly articulated standards or rules. An example would be Stradivarius violins. Experts agree that they produce vastly superior sound, but no one can specify precisely how they were manufactured because skilled artisans were responsible. By contrast, at the highest levels of manufacturing knowledge, all aspects of production are known and understood. All materials and processing variations are articulated and accounted for, with rules and procedures for every contingency. Here an example would be a "lights out," fully automated factory that operates for many hours without any human intervention.

In total, this framework specifies eight stages of knowledge. From lowest to highest, they are:

1. Recognizing prototypes (what is a good product?).
2. Recognizing attributes within prototypes (ability to define some conditions under which process gives good output).

3. Discriminating among attributes (which attributes are important? Experts may differ about relevance of patterns; new operators are often trained through apprenticeships).

4. Measuring attributes (some key attributes are measured; measures may be qualitative and relative).

5. Locally controlling attributes (repeatable performance; process designed by expert, but technicians can perform it).

6. Recognizing and discriminating between contingencies (production process can be mechanized and monitored manually).

7. Controlling contingencies (process can be automated).

8. Understanding procedures and controlling contingencies (process is completely understood).

Source: Adapted from work by Ramchandran Jaikumar and Roger Bohn, "The Development of Intelligent Systems for Industrial Use: A Conceptual Framework," *Research on Technological Innovation, Management and Policy,* Vol. 3 (1986), pp. 182–188.

deep understanding. At its simplest, the distinction is between knowing how things are done and knowing why they occur. Knowing how is partial knowledge; it is rooted in norms of behavior, standards of practice, and settings of equipment. Knowing why is more fundamental: it captures underlying cause-and-effect relationships and accommodates exceptions, adaptations, and unforeseen events. The ability to control temperatures and pressures to align grains of silicon and form silicon steel is an example of knowing how; understanding the chemical and physical process that produces the alignment is knowing why.

Further distinctions are possible, as the insert "Stages of Knowledge" suggests. Operating knowledge can be arrayed in a hierarchy, moving from limited understanding and the ability to

make few distinctions to more complete understanding in which all contingencies are anticipated and controlled. In this context, experimentation and problem solving foster learning by pushing organizations up the hierarchy, from lower to higher stages of knowledge.

3. Learning from past experience. Companies must review their successes and failures, assess them systematically, and record the lessons in a form that employees find open and accessible. One expert has called this process the "Santayana Review," citing the famous philosopher George Santayana, who coined the phrase "Those who cannot remember the past are condemned to repeat it." Unfortunately, too many managers today are indifferent, even hostile, to the past, and by failing to reflect on it, they let valuable knowledge escape.

A study of more than 150 new products concluded that "the knowledge gained from failures [is] often instrumental in achieving subsequent successes. . . . In the simplest terms, failure is the ultimate teacher."[4] IBM's 360 computer series, for example, one of the most popular and profitable ever built, was based on the technology of the failed Stretch computer that preceded it. In this case, as in many others, learning occurred by chance rather than by careful planning. A few companies, however, have established processes that require their managers to periodically think about the past and learn from their mistakes.

Boeing did so immediately after its difficulties with the 737 and 747 plane programs. Both planes were introduced with much fanfare and also with serious problems. To ensure that the problems were not repeated, senior managers commissioned a high-level employee group, called Project Homework, to compare the development processes of the 737 and 747 with those of the 707 and 727, two of the company's most profitable planes. The group was asked to develop a set of "lessons learned" that could be used on future projects. After working for three years, they produced hundreds of recommendations and an inch-thick booklet. Several members of the team were then transferred to the 757 and 767 start-ups, and guided by experience, they produced the most successful, error-free launches in Boeing's history.

Other companies have used a similar retrospective approach. Like Boeing, Xerox studied its product development process, examining three troubled products in an effort to understand why the company's new business initiatives failed so often. Arthur D. Little, the consulting company, focused on its past successes. Senior management invited ADL consultants from around the world to a two-day "jamboree," featuring booths and presentations documenting a wide range of the company's most successful practices, publications, and techniques. British Petroleum went even further and established the post-project appraisal unit to review major investment projects, write up case studies, and derive lessons for planners that were then incorporated into revisions of the company's planning guidelines. A five-person unit reported to the board of directors and reviewed six projects annually. The bulk of the time was spent in the field interviewing managers.[5] This type of review is now conducted regularly at the project level.

At the heart of this approach, one expert has observed, "is a mind-set that . . . enables companies to recognize the value of productive failure as contrasted with unproductive success. A productive failure is one that leads to insight, understanding, and thus an addition to the commonly held wisdom of the organization. An unproductive success occurs when something goes well, but nobody knows how or why."[6] IBM's legendary founder, Thomas Watson, Sr., apparently understood the distinction well. Company lore has it that a young manager, after losing $10 million in a risky venture, was called into Watson's office. The young man, thoroughly intimidated, began by saying, "I guess you want my resignation." Watson replied, "You can't be serious. We just spent $10 million educating you."

Fortunately, the learning process need not be so expensive. Case studies and post-project reviews like those of Xerox and British Petroleum can be performed with little cost other than managers' time. Companies can also enlist the help of faculty and students at local colleges or universities; they bring fresh perspectives and view internships and case studies as opportunities to gain experience and increase their own learning. A few companies have established computerized data banks to speed up the learning process. At Paul Revere Life Insurance, management requires all problem-solving teams to complete short registration forms describing their proposed projects if they hope to qualify for the company's award program. The company then enters the forms into its computer system and can immediately retrieve a listing of other groups of people who have worked or are working on the topic, along with a contact person. Relevant experience is then just a telephone call away.

4. *Learning from others.* Of course, not all learning comes from reflection and self-analysis.

Sometimes the most powerful insights come from looking outside one's immediate environment to gain a new perspective. Enlightened managers know that even companies in completely different businesses can be fertile sources of ideas and catalysts for creative thinking. At these organizations, enthusiastic borrowing is replacing the "not invented here" syndrome. Milliken calls the process SIS, for "Steal Ideas Shamelessly"; the broader term for it is benchmarking.

According to one expert, "benchmarking is an ongoing investigation and learning experience that ensures that best industry practices are uncovered, analyzed, adopted, and implemented."[7] The greatest benefits come from studying *practices,* the way that work gets done, rather than results, and from involving line managers in the process. Almost anything can be benchmarked. Xerox, the concept's creator, has applied it to billing, warehousing, and automated manufacturing. Milliken has been even more creative: in an inspired moment, it benchmarked Xerox's approach to benchmarking.

Unfortunately, there is still considerable confusion about the requirements for successful benchmarking. Benchmarking is not "industrial tourism," a series of ad hoc visits to companies that have received favorable publicity or won quality awards. Rather, it is a disciplined process that begins with a thorough search to identify best-practice organizations, continues with careful study of one's own practices and performance, progresses through systematic site visits and interviews, and concludes with an analysis of results, development of recommendations, and implementation. While time-consuming, the process need not be terribly expensive. AT&T's Benchmarking Group estimates that a moderate-sized project takes four to six months and incurs out-of-pocket costs of $20,000 (when personnel costs are included, the figure is three to four times higher).

Benchmarking is one way of gaining an outside perspective; another, equally fertile source of ideas is customers. Conversations with customers invariably stimulate learning; they are, after all, experts in what they do. Customers can provide up-to-date product information, competitive comparisons, insights into changing preferences, and immediate feedback about service and patterns of use. And companies need these insights at all levels, from the executive suite to the shop floor. At Motorola, members of the Operating and Policy Committee, including the CEO, meet personally and on a regular basis with customers. At Worthington Steel, all machine operators make periodic, unescorted trips to customers' factories to discuss their needs.

Sometimes customers can't articulate their needs or remember even the most recent problems they have had with a product or service. If that's the case, managers must observe them in action. Xerox employs a number of anthropologists at its Palo Alto Research Center to observe users of new document products in their offices. Digital Equipment has developed an interactive process called "contextual inquiry" that is used by software engineers to observe users of new technologies as they go about their work. Milliken has created "first-delivery teams" that accompany the first shipment of all products; team members follow the product through the customer's production process to see how it is used and then develop ideas for further improvement.

Whatever the source of outside ideas, learning will only occur in a receptive environment. Managers can't be defensive and must be open to criticism or bad news. This is a difficult challenge, but it is essential for success. Companies that approach customers assuming that "we must be right, they have to be wrong" or visit other organizations certain that "they can't teach us anything" seldom learn very much. Learning organizations, by contrast, cultivate the art of open, attentive listening.

5. Transferring knowledge. For learning to be more than a local affair, knowledge must be spread quickly and efficiently throughout the organization. Ideas carry maximum impact when they are shared broadly rather than held in a few hands. A variety of mechanisms spur this process, including written, oral, and visual reports, site

visits and tours, personnel rotation programs, education and training programs, and standardization programs. Each has distinctive strengths and weaknesses.

Reports and tours are by far the most popular mediums. Reports serve many purposes: they summarize findings, provide checklists of dos and don'ts, and describe important processes and events. They cover a multitude of topics, from benchmarking studies to accounting conventions to newly discovered marketing techniques. Today written reports are often supplemented by videotapes, which offer greater immediacy and fidelity.

Tours are an equally popular means of transferring knowledge, especially for large, multidivisional organizations with multiple sites. The most effective tours are tailored to different audiences and needs. To introduce its managers to the distinctive manufacturing practices of New United Motor Manufacturing Inc. (NUMMI), its joint venture with Toyota, General Motors developed a series of specialized tours. Some were geared to upper and middle managers, while others were aimed at lower ranks. Each tour described the policies, practices, and systems that were most relevant to that level of management.

Despite their popularity, reports and tours are relatively cumbersome ways of transferring knowledge. The gritty details that lie behind complex management concepts are difficult to communicate secondhand. Absorbing facts by reading them or seeing them demonstrated is one thing; experiencing them personally is quite another. As a leading cognitive scientist has observed, "It is very difficult to become knowledgeable in a passive way. Actively experiencing something is considerably more valuable than having it described."[8] For this reason, personnel rotation programs are one of the most powerful methods of transferring knowledge.

In many organizations, expertise is held locally: in a particularly skilled computer technician, perhaps, a savvy global brand manager, or a division head with a track record of successful joint ventures. Those in daily contact with these experts benefit enormously from their skills, but their field of influence is relatively narrow. Transferring them to different parts of the organization helps share the wealth. Transfers may be from division to division, department to department, or facility to facility; they may involve senior, middle, or first-level managers. A supervisor experienced in just-in-time production, for example, might move to another factory to apply the methods there, or a successful division manager might transfer to a lagging division to invigorate it with already proven ideas. The CEO of Time Life used the latter approach when he shifted the president of the company's music division, who had orchestrated several years of rapid growth and high profits through innovative marketing, to the presidency of the book division, where profits were flat because of continued reliance on traditional marketing concepts.

Line to staff transfers are another option. These are most effective when they allow experienced managers to distill what they have learned and diffuse it across the company in the form of new standards, policies, or training programs. Consider how PPG used just such a transfer to advance its human resource practices around the concept of high-commitment work systems. In 1986, PPG constructed a new float-glass plant in Chehalis, Washington; it employed a radically new technology as well as innovations in human resource management that were developed by the plant manager and his staff. All workers were organized into small, self-managing teams with responsibility for work assignments, scheduling, problem solving and improvement, and peer review. After several years running the factory, the plant manager was promoted to director of human resources for the entire glass group. Drawing on his experiences at Chehalis, he developed a training program geared toward first-level supervisors that taught the behaviors needed to manage employees in a participative, self-managing environment.

As the PPG example suggests, education and training programs are powerful tools for transferring knowledge. But for maximum effectiveness, they must be linked explicitly to implementation.

All too often, trainers assume that new knowledge will be applied without taking concrete steps to ensure that trainees actually follow through. Seldom do trainers provide opportunities for practice, and few programs consciously promote the application of their teachings after employees have returned to their jobs.

Xerox and GTE are exceptions. As noted earlier, when Xerox introduced problem-solving techniques to its employees in the 1980s, everyone, from the top to the bottom of the organization, was taught in small departmental or divisional groups led by their immediate superior. After an introduction to concepts and techniques, each group applied what they learned to a real-life work problem. In a similar spirit, GTE's Quality: The Competitive Edge program was offered to teams of business-unit presidents and the managers reporting to them. At the beginning of the 3-day course, each team received a request from a company officer to prepare a complete quality plan for their unit, based on the course concepts, within 60 days. Discussion periods of two to three hours were set aside during the program so that teams could begin working on their plans. After the teams submitted their reports, the company officers studied them, and then the teams implemented them. This GTE program produced dramatic improvements in quality, including a recent semifinalist spot in the Baldrige Awards.

The GTE example suggests another important guideline: knowledge is more likely to be transferred effectively when the right incentives are in place. If employees know that their plans will be evaluated and implemented—in other words, that their learning will be applied—progress is far more likely. At most companies, the status quo is well entrenched; only if managers and employees see new ideas as being in their own best interest will they accept them gracefully. AT&T has developed a creative approach that combines strong incentives with information sharing. Called The Chairman's Quality Award (CQA), it is an internal quality competition modeled on the Baldrige prize but with an important twist: awards are given not only for absolute performance (using

the same 1,000-point scoring system as Baldrige) but also for improvements in scoring from the previous year. Gold, silver, and bronze Improvement Awards are given to units that have improved their scores 200, 150, and 100 points, respectively. These awards provide the incentive for change. An accompanying Pockets of Excellence program simplifies knowledge transfer. Every year, it identifies every unit within the company that has scored at least 60 percent of the possible points in each award category and then publicizes the names of these units using written reports and electronic mail.

Measuring Learning

Managers have long known that "if you can't measure it, you can't manage it." This maxim is as true of learning as it is of any other corporate objective. Traditionally, the solution has been "learning curves" and "manufacturing process functions." Both concepts date back to the discovery, during the 1920s and 1930s, that the costs of airframe manufacturing fell predictably with increases in cumulative volume. These increases were viewed as proxies for greater manufacturing knowledge, and most early studies examined their impact on the costs of direct labor. Later studies expanded the focus, looking at total manufacturing costs and the impact of experience in other industries, including shipbuilding, oil refining, and consumer electronics. Typically, learning rates were in the 80 percent to 85 percent range (meaning that with a doubling of cumulative production, costs fell to 80 percent to 85 percent of their previous level), although there was wide variation.

Firms like the Boston Consulting Group raised these ideas to a higher level in the 1970s. Drawing on the logic of learning curves, they argued that industries as a whole faced "experience curves," costs and prices that fell by predictable amounts as industries grew and their total production increased. With this observation, consultants suggested, came an iron law of competition. To enjoy the benefits of experience, companies would have to rapidly increase their production ahead of competitors to lower prices and gain market share.

Both learning and experience curves are still widely used, especially in the aerospace, defense, and electronics industries. Boeing, for instance, has established learning curves for every work station in its assembly plant; they assist in monitoring productivity, determining work flows and staffing levels, and setting prices and profit margins on new airplanes. Experience curves are common in semiconductors and consumer electronics, where they are used to forecast industry costs and prices.

For companies hoping to become learning organizations, however, these measures are incomplete. They focus on only a single measure of output (cost or price) and ignore learning that affects other competitive variables, like quality, delivery, or new product introductions. They suggest only one possible learning driver (total production volumes) and ignore both the possibility of learning in mature industries, where output is flat, and the possibility that learning might be driven by other sources, such as new technology or the challenge posed by competing products. Perhaps most important, they tell us little about the sources of learning or the levers of change.

Another measure has emerged in response to these concerns. Called the "half-life" curve, it was originally developed by Analog Devices, a leading semiconductor manufacturer, as a way of comparing internal improvement rates. A half-life curve measures the time it takes to achieve a 50 percent improvement in a specified performance measure. When represented graphically, the performance measure (defect rates, on-time delivery, time to market) is plotted on the vertical axis, using a logarithmic scale, and the time scale (days, months, years) is plotted horizontally. Steeper slopes then represent faster learning (see the insert "The Half-Life Curve" for an illustration).

The logic is straightforward. Companies, division, or departments that take less time to improve must be learning faster than their peers. In the long run, their short learning cycles will translate into superior performance. The 50 percent target is a measure of convenience; it was derived empirically from studies of successful improvement processes at a wide range of companies. Half-life curves are also flexible. Unlike learning and experience curves, they work on any output measure, and they are not confined to costs or prices. In addition, they are easy to operationalize, they provide a simple measuring stick, and they allow for ready comparison among groups.

Yet even half-life curves have an important weakness: they focus solely on results. Some types of knowledge take years to digest, with few visible changes in performance for long periods. Creating a total quality culture, for instance, or developing new approaches to product development are difficult systemic changes. Because of their long gestation periods, half-life curves or any other measures focused solely on results are unlikely to capture any short-run learning that has occurred. A more comprehensive framework is needed to track progress.

Organizational learning can usually be traced through three overlapping stages. The first step is cognitive. Members of the organization are exposed to new ideas, expand their knowledge, and begin to think differently. The second step is behavioral. Employees begin to internalize new insights and alter their behavior. And the third step is performance improvement, with changes in behavior leading to measurable improvements in results: superior quality, better delivery, increased market share, or other tangible gains. Because cognitive and behavioral changes typically precede improvements in performance, a complete learning audit must include all three.

Surveys, questionnaires, and interviews are useful for this purpose. At the cognitive level, they would focus on attitudes and depth of understanding. Have employees truly understood the meaning of self-direction and teamwork, or are the terms still unclear? At PPG, a team of human resource experts periodically audits every manufacturing plant, including extensive interviews with shop-floor employees, to ensure that the concepts are well understood. Have new approaches to customer service been fully accepted? At its

The Half-Life Curve

Analog Devices has used half-life curves to compare the performance of its divisions. Here monthly data on customer service are graphed for seven divisions. Division C is the clear winner: even though it started with a high proportion of late deliveries, its rapid learning rate led eventually to the best absolute performance. Divisions D, E, and G have been far less successful, with little or no improvement in on-time service over the period.

On-Time Customer Service Performance—Monthly Data (August 1987–July 1988)

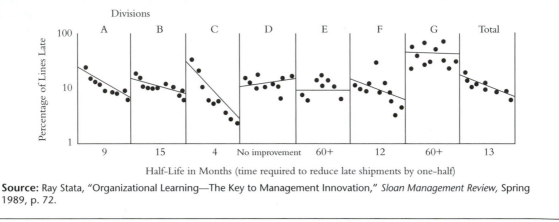

Half-Life in Months (time required to reduce late shipments by one-half)

Source: Ray Stata, "Organizational Learning—The Key to Management Innovation," *Sloan Management Review,* Spring 1989, p. 72.

1989 Worldwide Marketing Managers' Meeting, Ford presented participants with a series of hypothetical situations in which customer complaints were in conflict with short-term dealer or company profit goals and asked how they would respond. Surveys like these are the first step toward identifying changed attitudes and new ways of thinking.

To assess behavioral changes, surveys and questionnaires must be supplemented by direct observation. Here the proof is in the doing, and there is no substitute for seeing employees in action. Domino's Pizza uses "mystery shoppers" to assess managers' commitment to customer service at its individual stores; L. L. Bean places telephone orders with its own operators to assess service levels. Other companies invite outside consultants to visit, attend meetings, observe employees in action, and then report what they have learned. In many ways, this approach mirrors that

of examiners for the Baldrige Award, who make several-day site visits to semifinalists to see whether the companies' deeds match the words on their applications.

Finally, a comprehensive learning audit also measures performance. Half-life curves or other performance measures are essential for ensuring that cognitive and behavioral changes have actually produced results. Without them, companies would lack a rationale for investing in learning and the assurance that learning was serving the organization's ends.

First Steps

Learning organizations are not built overnight. Most successful examples are the products of carefully cultivated attitudes, commitments, and management processes that have accrued slowly and steadily over time. Still, some changes can be made immediately. Any company that wishes to become a learning organization can begin by taking a few simple steps.

The first step is to foster an environment that is conducive to learning. There must be time for reflection and analysis, to think about strategic plans, dissect customer needs, assess current work systems, and invent new products. Learning is difficult when employees are harried or rushed; it tends to be driven out by the pressures of the moment. Only if top management explicitly frees up employees' time for the purpose does learning occur with any frequency. That time will be doubly productive if employees possess the skills to use it wisely. Training in brainstorming, problem solving, evaluating experiments, and other core learning skills is therefore essential.

Another powerful lever is to open up boundaries and stimulate the exchange of ideas. Boundaries inhibit the flow of information; they keep individuals and groups isolated and reinforce preconceptions. Opening up boundaries, with conferences, meetings, and project teams, which either cross organizational levels or link the company and its customers and suppliers, ensures a fresh flow of ideas and the chance to consider competing perspectives. General Electric CEO Jack Welch considers this to be such a powerful stimulant of change that he has made "boundarylessness" a cornerstone of the company's strategy for the 1990s.

Once managers have established a more supportive, open environment, they can create learning forums. These are programs or events designed with explicit learning goals in mind, and they can take a variety of forms: strategic reviews, which examine the changing competitive environment and the company's product portfolio, technology, and market positioning; systems audits, which review the health of large, cross-functional processes and delivery systems; internal benchmarking reports, which identify and compare best-in-class activities within the organization; study missions, which are dispatched to leading organizations around the world to better understand their performance and distinctive skills; and jamborees or symposiums, which bring together customers, suppliers, outside experts, or internal groups to share ideas and learn from one another. Each of these activities fosters learning by requiring employees to wrestle with new knowledge and consider its implications. Each can also be tailored to business needs. A consumer goods company, for example, might sponsor a study mission to Europe to learn more about distribution methods within the newly unified Common Market, while a high-technology company might launch a systems audit to review its new product development process.

Together these efforts help to eliminate barriers that impede learning and begin to move learning higher on the organizational agenda. They also suggest a subtle shift in focus, away from continuous improvement and toward a commitment to learning. Coupled with a better understanding of the "three Ms," the meaning, management, and measurement of learning, this shift provides a solid foundation for building learning organizations.

Endnotes

1. Peter M. Senge, *The Fifth Discipline* (New York: Doubleday, 1990), p. 1.

2. Ikujiro Nonaka, "The Knowledge-Creating Company," *Harvard Business Review,* November–December 1991, p. 97.

3. Robert Howard, "The CEO as Organizational Architect: An Interview with Xerox's Paul Allaire," *Harvard Business Review,* September–October 1992, p. 106.

4. Modesto A. Maidique and Billie Jo Zirger, "The New Product Learning Cycle," *Research Policy,* Vol. 14, No. 6 (1985), pp. 299, 309.

5. Frank R. Gulliver, "Post-Project Appraisals Pay," *Harvard Business Review,* March–April 1987, p. 128.

6. David Nadler, "Even Failures Can Be Productive," *New York Times,* April 23, 1989, Sec. 3, p. 3.

7. Robert C. Camp, *Benchmarking: The Search for Industry Best Practices That Lead to Superior Performance* (Milwaukee: ASQC Quality Press, 1989), p. 12.

8. Roger Schank, with Peter Childers, *The Creative Attitude* (New York: Macmillan, 1988), p. 9.

Fast Cycle OD: "Faster, Better, Cheaper" Catches up to Organization Development

Merrill C. Anderson

In recent years business organizations have faced unprecedented challenges to grow revenue, reduce operating costs, and invest in new product development and new market opportunities. Global competition is fierce. Speed of execution is paramount. Business organizations do not have the luxury of time to set a strategic direction and engage all employees in achieving strategic business goals. As a result, businesses have reduced cycle time in many aspects of their operations with innovations such as simultaneous engineering, lean manufacturing, and just-in-time inventory. The mantra of "faster, better, cheaper" guides many decisions to improve business operations.

Organization development practitioners have been designing and implementing organization change for the past fifty years. They have created a body of knowledge and skills that have proven to be invaluable to business leaders who have needed to implement organizational change. The OD value cycle—diagnose, design, deploy, evaluate, and enhance—represents proven methodology to implement change. However, OD does not operate in a vacuum, and the pressures that are operating on other aspects of the business are also impacting the practice of OD in business settings. Organizations have fewer people with less time to be engaged in organizational change. It is now time to reduce the cycle time of designing and implementing organizational change.

Fast Cycle OD represents a recognition of the global business reality that organizations face as well as a body of new interventions that are faster,

better, and cheaper than more traditional OD interventions: *faster* in the sense that the steps of the OD value cycle are being collapsed and performed simultaneously and not in a serial fashion; *better* in the sense that these newer OD interventions deliver greater business value with a clearer line of sight to strategy; *cheaper* in the sense that less time to execute translates to greater return on investment.

The purpose of this chapter is to explore the concept of Fast Cycle Organization Development. Three trends accelerating how OD is practiced will be described and implications discussed for how these trends impact OD value creation for clients. The term "OD practitioner" refers to anyone whose primary role is implementing organizational change. Ideally, line business managers would also have OD competencies in planning and deploying organizational change. This book is intended to share some OD tools, concepts, and business applications that exemplify fast cycle OD to a wide audience of OD practitioners and business leaders.

Three Trends Accelerating the Cycle of OD Interventions

There are at least three major trends that are accelerating the pace at which OD creates value for business clients: First, the pace of business change is accelerating; second, OD interventions are increasingly engaging the *whole* client organization system; and third, OD is taking on an increasingly strategic focus. These three trends are depicted in Figure 1 as arrows accelerating the OD value cycle.

Source: *Fast Cycle Organization Development,* by Merrill C. Anderson, South-Western Publishing Company, 2000, pp. 3–12. Reprinted by permission of the publisher.

FIGURE 1
The
**Organization
Development
Value Cycle**

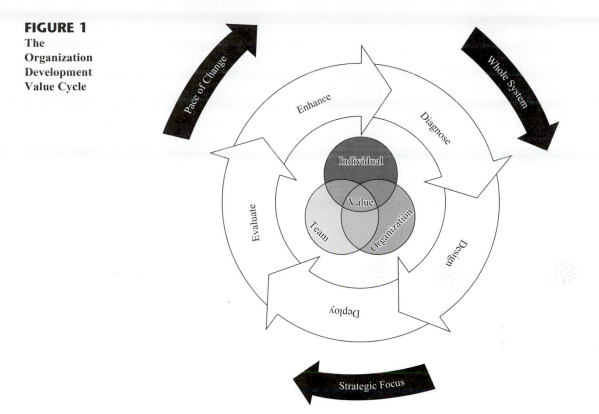

Pace of Business Change

Businesses operating in a globally integrated and highly complex economy have embraced *speed* as a key differentiator. Indeed, it is the sheer complexity of the emerging global economy that has placed even more emphasis on execution. The difference between winning and losing does not so much depend on who has the right strategy but rather who can execute the quickest. To paraphrase Jack Welsh, Chairman and CEO of General Electric, there are two kinds of people: those who try to predict the future and those who know they can't. Organizations that deal more effectively with present business realities will gain advantage in the market place. Organizations that refrain from taking action until the future can be accurately predicted and the right strategy can be formulated will inevitably lose.

While knowing the future is not humanly possible, *preparing* the organization to meet future global challenges is possible. Organization development plays a critical role in changing or even transforming organizations so that these organizations are better prepared to meet global challenges. OD practitioners are discovering that playing this critical change role has required them to reinvent and reduce the cycle time of their change interventions. The mantra of "faster, better, cheaper" seems to have caught up with the practice of OD. Many business clients now expect OD practitioners to accomplish organization change objectives more quickly and more effectively with less investment of the organization's resources.

Whole System Interventions

OD change efforts are increasingly dealing with the *whole* client organization system rather than solely working on subsystem parts. OD practitioners and business leaders are approaching the organization as a complex, adaptive, and dynamic system composed of interrelated and interdependent elements: strategy, process, structure, people, reward mechanisms, culture, and other elements. Organizational change efforts now routinely include reengineering business processes, redesigning the organization structure, and aligning people and reward processes, to fully support these organizational changes. Large system interventions, for example, organize hundreds of representatives from each unit of the client organization system into a highly integrated event. These interventions ensure that representatives from the whole organization interact in one (often very large) work space to bring the strategy and vision to life, explore organization design issues and alternatives, and align peoples' actions to achieve shared objectives.

Strategic Focus

The practice of OD is also becoming more strategic in nature. This trend also seems to reflect the increasing strategic focus of human resource management. Clients are expecting OD consultants to engage the entire client system and find more effective ways to execute strategy. Many business leaders cite their inability to effectively *execute* strategy as their biggest obstacle to success. OD is increasingly looked upon to help business leaders overcome this obstacle. Organizations are being viewed as complex and highly adaptive systems. Whole systems interventions, such as search conferences, reinforce a systems perspective and engage every constituency in an organization to co-create their future. Chapter 3 explores search conferencing as a strategic tool in detail. OD professionals can develop overarching change architectures that build the organization's capabilities to execute business strategy and better prepare the organization to successfully meet global competitive pressures.

The practice of formulating and communicating business strategy has in recent years become much more participative and open to people of all levels of the organization. No longer is strategy the exclusive preserve of senior executives gathering in corporate cloisters. The shelf life of business strategies has shortened. Strategies not quickly executed are of little value. The challenge is to *quickly* engage the hearts and minds of people in the organization to align their action to the strategy and to do so as quickly as possible. Highly participative approaches to strategy development effectively merge strategy formulation, communication, and commitment activities. These approaches quickly create a foundation for strategy understanding and commitment, and therefore reduce the cycle time for overall strategy execution.

As strategy professionals become more concerned with engaging a diverse set of people in the organization to share in strategy formulation and as OD professionals become more focused on strategy execution, a natural and positive relationship between strategists and OD professionals is possible. In fact, not only is it possible, but each group's success—and business success—mutually depends upon their active collaboration. Strategists work with business leaders to make strategic choices about markets, technologies, products, assets, and so forth. OD practitioners craft and deploy interventions that engage all constituencies in the organization to digest these strategic choices and co-create their future. People develop ownership for the strategy they help create and more readily align their actions to the strategic direction of the business.

Implications for OD Practitioner Competencies

There are three major sets of competencies that OD practitioners must have in order to be effective in strategy execution consulting. First, OD practitioners must speak the language of business and do so fluently. A basic understanding of finance and the theory and logic of financial decision-making is required. Second, OD practitioners must have a solid understanding of strategic formulation tools and conceptual models. Third, it is important for every OD consultant to do his or her business homework before beginning any client engagement: understand industry trends and issues, learn about the client company's history, explore the backgrounds of the leaders, and be able to articulate, at a minimum, the company's strategic intent, core competencies, competitive pressures, and market challenges. These represent some of the major "content" areas that OD practitioners are increasingly being called upon to create business value.

Another consequence of the pressure on OD to deliver the goods more quickly is that clients increasingly expect substantial *content* knowledge, not just process expertise, from their OD practitioner. It is no longer adequate to merely offer clients process facilitation services and eschew content. "Where's the beef?" is a commonly heard refrain. When an OD consultant is called upon to develop an executive team, for example, clients now expect the OD consultant to provide specific content regarding critical leadership competencies, offer industry knowledge on strategic leadership issues, and provide specific case study examples for benchmark comparisons with other companies. OD consultants are expected to be astute business professionals and offer astute business-related content knowledge.

There is a potential danger here of course. An OD consultant who offers too much in the way of content knowledge risks supplanting valuable client deliberations about what is important to the client's organization and strategy. These deliberations provide clients the opportunity to challenge their assumptions about the business, reframe their strategic issues, and develop creative new business approaches. Strategic deliberations offer a wealth of learning. Content knowledge should be introduced to stimulate learning and not supplant it.

Value Creation

"Value" may be defined in this context as the creation of positive and lasting change that enables individuals, teams, and organizations to realize their full potentials and contribute to the success of the business enterprise. Enabling the execution of strategy and learning about how to improve the business are two primary ways that OD creates lasting value for business clients. The OD practitioner, the business clients, and many others work collaboratively to design and deploy a series of OD interventions. Each of these interventions must be linked to business strategy and explicitly identify at which level these interventions are primarily intended to impact: organization, team, or individual. Value creation for the business is accelerated by utilizing many interventions that address change at all three levels.

Transformative change requires change interventions to be simultaneously addressed at the individual, team, and organizational levels. Individuals in an organization, for example, may greatly expand their own learning, but if the work teams of which they are members do not fundamentally change the way they work together, then the "transformed" individual will quickly be reshaped and brought back into the corporate fold. Team norms exert tremendous influence. The team setting will actively discourage individuals who try to shake things up and try to perform new behaviors that they have learned. Team-building interventions that fundamentally shift team norms would additionally be required in this situation to embrace the new perspectives and new behaviors of the newly transformed individual.

Similarly, a work team that has learned to transform itself will not be able to sustain its new performance for long unless the organization's work process, power structure, HR policies, and other elements fully support the team's new perspectives and work habits. Organizational interventions would need to be conducted to allow all work teams to share in the same learnings and adopt the same practices as the newly transformed team. For example, strategic search conferences could be conducted that would engage all teams and constituencies in embracing new learnings and creating a new compelling vision of the future.

This book has organized some of the newest and most powerful OD interventions according to the primary level at which these interventions are addressed. Change at the organization level is addressed in Chapters 3 (search conferences) and 4 (organization redesign). Change at the team level is exemplified by Chapters 5 (Kaizen) and 6 (fostering team spirit). Change at the individual level is explored in Chapters 7 (fast cycle learning) and 8 (coaching). Chapter 9 presents a case study illustrating how an integrated approach featuring interventions directed at all three levels can achieve strategic change and outstanding business results. Chapter 10 discusses the role of leadership in times of tumultuous change.

The OD Value Cycle

OD professionals create positive and lasting value for their clients by following the five basic process steps outlined in the OD value cycle (see Figure 1). Most OD interventions include these five basic process steps. Of course, these basic steps may be taken in various sequences or compressed or combined in unique and creative ways. The point here is that successful OD interventions will feature each of these process steps. The essence of fast cycle OD is to accelerate how these steps are enacted by finding ways to reduce cycle time and by enacting these steps in parallel rather than tacitly following them in a sequential fashion. Briefly reviewing each of the steps in the OD value cycle will clarify how OD interventions are conducted, as well as to provide some insights into how OD professionals are reducing their cycle time to create lasting value for client organizations.

Diagnosis

Diagnosis of individuals, teams, and the organization is the first step. The intention for this diagnosis is to enable people to learn about themselves,

their teams, and their organizations. OD practitioners will engage representatives from many (if not all) of the relevant constituencies and stakeholders to conduct a series of analyses. All relevant and available data will be reviewed, such as organizational surveys, investor reports, annual reports, strategy documents, and other information. Internal best practices can be discovered and documented at this point. Customized surveys, focus groups, executive interviews, and other probes can be developed and fielded as necessary. The end result of the analysis is to understand the organization (its strategy, processes, structure, and so forth), its business context (markets and competition), and major improvement opportunities (e.g., improving the business sales process, reducing fixed costs associated with support work, and the like). Also, these analyses are conducted and results communicated in such a way that the entire organization understands and buys into the rationale and the context for change.

Communication is a key ingredient. A foundation for understanding, acceptance and ownership of the proposed organization change must be established as early as possible. Key messages must be crafted and shared with all organization constituencies. Measures must also be taken to ensure *comprehension* and not just communication. Often, messages must be communicated several times in several ways to ensure full comprehension by all constituencies.

Design

The next step in the value cycle is to work with the client organization to design an appropriate series of interventions. These interventions address the improvement opportunities—or at least provide some direction as to how these improvement opportunities will be addressed. OD consultants and clients agree on the change outcomes and objectives, resource requirements, project deliverables, and their respective responsibilities in the change effort. Very often a Gantt chart and project approach will be developed that will help manage the change effort. The project approach will outline each intervention, its scope, sequencing, timing, and resource requirements. The design of the change effort will be flexible to allow ample midcourse corrections.

Deployment

Deployment refers to the OD consultant and client co-implementing the agreed upon interventions. Very often a joint consultant/client change team is formed. This team leverages the skills, knowledge, and abilities of the consultant while also facilitating transfer of thought leadership from the consultant to the client organization. The progress of deployment is reviewed on a regular basis by the joint change team and by the client leadership team(s). Successes are celebrated and problems are discussed and corrected in real time.

Evaluation

The deployment of change interventions is formally evaluated. Internal best practices are highlighted and documented. Various client groups are formed to determine what worked well and what lessons were learned in the process of change. Surveys, focus groups, interviews, and other methods of data collection that were fielded in the diagnosis phase can be refielded to provide a pre-post trend analysis.

Another critical aspect of evaluation is to determine the business impact and the return on the investment that the business leaders made in the change effort. Business impact refers to the measurement of the impact that the change interventions had on operational performance. For example, a change effort designed to improve inventory management would presumably impact inventory turns and return-on-asset measurements. Return on investment is expressed as a ratio of financial benefits that the client realized as a direct result of the change intervention to the amount of money that the client had to invest in order to produce these financial benefits. . . .

It is also essential at this point for the change team to reflect upon their role in the change process. Change team members are engaged in dialogue to better understand how their mental models shape their perceptions, influence their actions, and contribute to determining project outcomes. This represents key learning for OD practitioners to help them improve and hone their skills and incorporate new knowledge and new learnings into their practice of OD. This is an essential step for building personal mastery.

Lines of inquiry that can be utilized to gain further insight into the change process include: What was learned about the process of change? What did the clients learn about themselves? How well were the learnings harvested and shared across organizational boundaries? The insight gained from answering these questions may be utilized to enhance not only the effectiveness of the implementation effort but also the effectiveness of the change intervention methodology.

Enhance

The critical evaluation of the change effort provides a foundation for continuous improvement of the business organization as well as improving how change is conceived and executed. Best demonstrated practices can be expanded throughout the organization. Lessons learned can be translated into change management practices. New opportunities for operational improvements can be acted upon. The OD value cycle then repeats as new change initiatives are designed and launched. This is how new ways of creating value are discovered and the learning process continues.

Value is created for clients at each step of the value cycle. Diagnosis enables clients to develop new insights into their business. Designing a *change architecture* provides clients with a sense of the "big picture" and how each business unit contributes to the whole enterprise. Deployment of the change creates lasting improvements in the business organization and also builds strategy execution skills, leadership abilities, and organizational knowledge of those who are involved in the change. Evaluating what went well and what went poorly opens up opportunities for reward, recognition and learning valuable lessons. Enhancing the learning capability of the organization may be the greatest gift of all. Ideally, enacting and accelerating the OD value cycle becomes a continuous and natural way that the organization operates. People continue to learn, the organization continues to grow, and business results become even more spectacular.

The Practice of Fast Cycle OD

In today's global business environment business leaders must accelerate strategy execution, and OD practitioners must accelerate how they add value in the eyes of business leaders. Ways must be found to accelerate the OD value cycle. Conducting two or more of the five cycle steps simultaneously, rather than sequentially, is a powerful way to accelerate change. This reduces the cycle time. Multigeneration organization design . . . blends design and deployment to accelerate change. Kaizen . . . rapidly accelerates the entire cycle. Fast cycle learning . . . utilizes ethnographic analysis to improve diagnosis and design of learning interventions.

The authors hope that readers will utilize this book to gain greater clarity and insight into executing organizational change and apply the concepts, tools, and methodologies to their own work. Each chapter offers a unique theoretical perspective or an innovative methodology (or both) that elaborates on the concept of Fast Cycle OD. While there is no cookbook on how to practice OD, the final two chapters attempt to provide some sense of how all of the pieces can be fit together to successfully execute strategic change. It is hoped that readers will find some helpful ways of thinking about their work and find some useful tools and methodologies to bring added value to their business clients.

Suggested Readings

To better understand the evolving practice of OD:

Anderson, M. C., August, J., & London, J. (1995). Insights from OD best practices pilot survey: guiding the start-up of an internal OD team. *Organization Development Journal* 13(3), 57–65.

Bunker, B., & Alban, B. (1996). *Large Group Interventions,* San Francisco: Jossey-Bass.

Lawler, E. E., & Galbraith, J. R. (1993). New roles for staff: strategic support and services. In J. R. Galbraith & E. E. Lawler (Eds.), *Organizing for the Future.* San Francisco: Jossey-Bass.

McMahan, G. C., & Woodman, R. W. (1992). The current practice of organization development within the firm: a survey of the 500 largest industries. *Group and Organization Management* 17, 117–134.

Mohrman, A. M., & Lawler, E. E. (1993). Human resource management: Building a strategic partnership. In J. R. Galbraith & E. E. Lawler (Eds.), *Organizing for the Future,* San Francisco: Jossey-Bass.

To better understand the foundations of strategic thinking and the latest trends in the practice of strategy formulation:

Byrne, D. (1996). Strategic planning. *Business Week,* August 26.

Galagan, P. A. (1997). Strategic planning is back. *Training and Development Journal,* April.

Hamel, G., & Prahalad, C. K. (1994). *Competing for the future,* Boston: Harvard Business School.

Porter, M. E. (1980). *Competitive strategy,* New York: The Free Press.

Part 5

Implementation Guidelines and Issues

Successful OD and OT programs depend on many things: sound theory regarding the nature of change and the nature of organizations, solid and robust interventions appropriately chosen for the tasks at hand, and effective implementation and execution. This section examines guidelines and issues for effective implementation.

A sizable body of knowledge exists to guide leaders' and practitioners' implementation efforts. One aspect of implementation relates to the overall flow of events, what Warner Burke calls the *phases* of OD programs.[1] These are:

1. Entry
2. Contracting
3. Diagnosis
4. Feedback
5. Planning change
6. Intervention
7. Evaluation

Entry represents the initial contact between consultant and client; this includes exploring the situation that led the client to seek a consultant and determining whether there is a good match between the client, the consultant, and the problematic situation. *Contracting* involves establishing mutual expectations; reaching agreement on expenditures of time, money, and resources; and generally clarifying what each party expects to get and give to the other. *Diagnosis* is the fact-finding phase, which produces a picture of the situation through interviews, observations, questionnaires, examination of organization documents, and the like. This phase has two steps: collecting information and analyzing it. *Feedback* represents returning the analyzed information to the client system. In this phase, the clients explore the information for understanding, clarification, and accuracy; they own the data as their picture of the situation and their problems and opportunities. *Planning change* involves the clients' deciding what actions to take on the basis of information they have just learned. Alternatives are explored and critiqued; action plans are selected and developed. *Intervention* involves implementing sets of actions designed to correct the problems or seize the opportunities. *Evaluation* represents assessing the effects of the program: What changes occurred? Are we satisfied with the results?

One very important aspect of this sequence of steps is that each phase builds the foundation for subsequent phases; therefore, each phase must be executed with care and precision. For example, if expectations are not clear in the contracting phase, this mismatch will surface later in unmet expectations and dissatisfaction. Or, if the analysis of the data during the diagnostic phase is incorrect, interventions may not be appropriate. Thus, understanding the phases and attending to the details of each phase are critical for success.

Cummings and Worley also explore implementation issues.[2] They identify five sets of activities required for effective management of OD and OT programs: (1) motivating change, (2) creating a vision, (3) developing political support, (4) managing the transition, and (5) sustaining momentum. These activities include specific steps for the consultant to take to ensure effective implementation. For example, *motivating change* involves creating readiness for change and overcoming resistance to change. *Creating a vision* involves providing a picture of the future and showing how individuals and groups will fit into that future, as well as providing a road map and interim goals. *Developing political support* involves obtaining the support of key individuals and groups and influencing key stakeholders to move the change effort forward. *Managing the transition* means planning the needed transition activities, getting commitments of people and resources, and creating necessary structures and milestones to help people locomote from "where we are" to "where we want to be." *Sustaining momentum* involves providing resources for the change effort, helping people develop new competencies and skills, and reinforcing the desired new behaviors. These are the details consultants and leaders must attend to when implementing organization development and transformation programs.

There are other issues as well, such as trust, the consultant's expertise, making competent diagnoses, choosing appropriate interventions, dealing with power and politics, treating confidential information with integrity, and the like. Learning the craft of facilitating organizational change involves both art and science.

Readings in Part 5

The articles in this section cover a range of topics related to managing OD and OT programs for success. The first selection, by Achilles Armenakis, Stanley Harris, and Kevin Mossholder, deals with the issue of creating readiness for change. This is a practical piece written by change agents for change agents. A major ingredient of success in change programs is creating readiness for change in the client system. The authors present good insights and sound advice for leaders and practitioners alike.

Larry Greiner and Virginia Schein's selection deals with power, a troublesome topic for many OD practitioners. The authors evaluate three models of how organizations work and argue for the validity and usefulness of a "pluralistic/political" model. The pluralistic/political model assumes that organizations contain self-interested groups seeking their own goals. This selection is from their book *Power and Organization Development: Mobilizing Power to Implement Change,* a must read for organization development practitioners.

The next selection goes all the way back to the early days of the T-group movement. It deals with leadership and group (team) effectiveness. Kenneth Benne and Paul Sheats identify important group member roles that increase group effectiveness, along with a number of individual roles that can block effective group functioning. In later years, OD consultants and T-group trainers have been more likely to refer to these roles as behaviors. Training group members to be effective in the use of these behaviors can be very important for team building and other organization development and transformation activities.

Roger Harrison looks at OD interventions in terms of their impact and intrusiveness on individuals, and asks the question, How deeply should we be intruding into people's private lives? Or, put another way, What is the appropriate depth of OD interventions?

This is clearly an important issue for practitioners and laypersons. Harrison suggests two criteria to answer these questions: *"first, to intervene at a level no deeper than that required to produce enduring solutions to the problems at hand;* and second, *to intervene at a level no deeper than that at which the energy and resources of the client can be committed to problem solving and to change."* Practitioners need to think seriously about these issues.

The next selection, by Herbert Shepard, is a classic, insightful essay that presents some rules of thumb for intervening in organizations. Issues of survival, initial entry, and building support are examined. Shepard uses a model of organizational change that includes notions about complexity and interdependency in organizations, about the use of power, and about helping relationships (i.e., the need for empathy, participation, and patience).

The selection by John Malone introduces the ideas of "coaching," self-efficacy, and social cognitive theory. Coaching is a proven technique for enhancing individual skill development and performance. Coaching skills are an important part of the OD practitioner's repertoire. Malone places coaching in the context of organizational change, shows the relationship between self-efficacy and behavior, and credits Albert Bandura's social cognitive theory[3] as the major foundation for this "emerging discipline."

Endnotes

1. W. Warner Burke, *Organization Development: A Process of Learning and Changing* (Reading, MA: Addison-Wesley Longman, Inc., 1994), chap. 4.

2. T. G. Cummings and C. G. Worley, *Organization Development and Change* (St. Paul, MN: West Publishing Company, 1993), chap. 8.

3. Albert Bandura, *Social Foundations of Thought & Action: A Social Cognitive Theory* (Englewood Cliffs, N.J.: Prentice-Hall, Inc., 1986).

Reading 28

Creating Readiness for Organizational Change

Achilles A. Armenakis
Stanley G. Harris
Kevin W. Mossholder

Introduction

Because of increasingly dynamic environments, organizations are continually confronted with the need to implement changes in strategy, structure, process, and culture. Many factors contribute to the effectiveness with which such organizational changes are implemented. One such factor is readiness for change. Readiness, which is similar to Lewin's (1951) concept of unfreezing, is reflected in organizational members' beliefs, attitudes, and intentions regarding the extent to which changes are needed and the organization's capacity to successfully make those changes. Readiness is the cognitive precursor to the *behaviors of* either resistance to, or support for, a change effort. Schein (1979) has argued "the reason so many change efforts run into resistance or outright failure is usually directly traceable to their not providing for an effective unfreezing process before attempting a change induction" (p. 144). Although some researchers have discussed the importance of readiness (cf. Beckhard & Harris, 1987; Beer & Walton, 1987; Turner, 1982), it has seldom been recognized as being distinct from resistance (cf. Coch & French, 1948; Kotter & Schlesinger, 1979; Lawrence, 1954). Specifically, creating readiness has been most often explained in conjunction with prescriptions for reducing resistance. For example, Kotter and Schlesinger (1979)

Source: Achilles A. Armenakis, Stanley G. Harris, and Kevin W. Mossholder, "Creating Readiness for Organizational Change," *Human Relations,* vol. 46, no. 6, June 1993, pp. 681–703. Reprinted by permission of Plenum Publishing Corporation.

discuss several strategies in dealing with resistance (e.g., education and communication, participation and involvement, facilitation and support, negotiation and agreement). Such prescriptions are effective in reducing resistance to the extent that they first create readiness. In essence, readiness for change may act to preempt the likelihood of resistance to change, increasing the potential for change efforts to be more effective.

Making an explicit distinction between readiness and resistance helps refine discussions of the implementation of change efforts and captures the spirit of the proactive change agent (cf. Armenakis, Mossholder, & Harris, 1990; Kanter, 1983; Kissler, 1991). Framing a change project in terms of readiness seems more congruent with the image of proactive managers who play the roles of coaches and champions of change, rather than those whose role is to reactively monitor the workplace for signs of resistance.

The purpose of this article is to clarify the readiness concept and examine how change agents can influence organizational members' readiness for change. Because the energy, inspiration, and support necessary to create readiness must come from within the organization, this article focuses primarily on the activities of internal change agents (i.e., organizational leaders, managers, etc.). Clearly, external change agents can also benefit from a heightened sensitivity to the creation of readiness. In addition to playing a role in providing information important to readiness creation, external change agents are often in a position to educate internal change agents regarding the importance of readiness.

As a means of fulfilling the article's purpose, the theoretical underpinnings of the readiness concept and the strategies used in creating readiness will be described and an integrative model offered. To enrich this discussion, the actual efforts of one organization to create readiness for a large-scale change are highlighted.

A Readiness Model

Theoretical Basis

A classic study by Coch and French (1948), traditionally described as an experiment in reducing resistance to change, demonstrated the value of allowing organization members to participate in change efforts. Four research groups were formed to represent varying degrees of participation including no participation (the comparison group), participation via representation, and total participation. The researchers found that the productivity of the experimental groups exceeded that of the comparison group and concluded that participation reduced resistance to organizational change. Interestingly, Bartlem and Locke (1981) and Gardner (1977) have subsequently identified differing readiness-creating procedures used by Coch and French with the four groups as an overlooked factor in the original research design. The comparison group was told that competitive conditions required a higher productivity standard. The new standard was explained and questions were answered. In contrast, for each of the experimental groups, a meeting was called during which the need for the change was presented in stark fashion. For example, as part of this presentation, the presence of fierce price competition was dramatized by showing two identical garments produced in the factory. One was produced in 1946 and had sold for 100 percent more than its match, produced in 1947. When asked to do so, the group could not identify the cheaper garment. This dramatization effectively communicated that cost reduction was a very real necessity (Coch & French, 1948).

As exemplified in the Coch and French experiment, creating readiness involves proactive attempts by a change agent to influence the beliefs, attitudes, intentions, and ultimately the behavior of a change target. At its core, the creation of readiness for change involves changing individual cognitions across a set of employees. The dynamics concerned with bringing about such changes in individuals has been explored at length in the cognitive change literature (see, e.g., Bandura, 1982; Fishbein & Azjen, 1975). It is important to note, however, that the creation of readiness for organizational change must extend beyond individual cognitions since it involves social phenomena as well. As social-information processing models suggest (cf. Griffin, 1987), any individual's readiness may also be shaped by the readiness of others. Factors relevant in creating readiness for change are summarized in Figure 1. Drawing on the individual-level cognitive change, collective behavior, social-information processing, mass communications, and organizational change literatures, each aspect of this model is addressed in more detail below.

The Message

The primary mechanism for creating readiness for change among members of an organization is the message for change. In general, the readiness message should incorporate two issues: (*a*) the need for change, that is, the discrepancy between the desired end-state (which must be appropriate for the organization) and the present state; and, (*b*) the individual and collective efficacy (i.e., the perceived ability to change) of parties affected by the change effort.

Discrepancy. The discrepancy aspect of the message communicates information about the need for change and should be consistent with relevant contextual factors (e.g., increased competition, changes in governmental regulations, depressed economic conditions). Creating the belief that change is needed requires showing how the current performance of the organization differs from some

FIGURE 1 Creating Readiness for Change

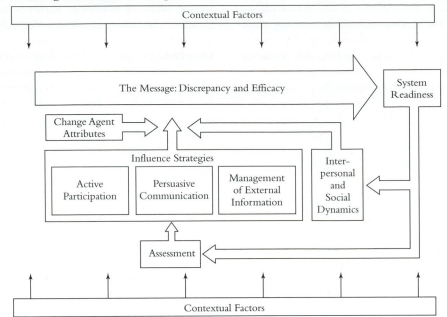

desired end-state (Katz & Kahn, 1978). Pettigrew (1987) emphasizes the importance of changes in external contextual factors (namely, social, economic, political, and competitive environments) in justifying the need for organizational change. He argues that the legitimacy for organizational change can be established by interpreting the effect of external contextual factors on an organization's performance. In the Coch and French experiment, the pricing discrepancy between the garments implied that the productivity standard was too low (relative to the competition) and that the challenge was to increase productivity to facilitate competitive pricing.

Others have discussed the importance of creating the awareness of a discrepancy concept, using different phraseology. For example, Nadler and Tushman (1989) refer to creating intellectual pain, the realization that something is awry. Spector (1989) advocates diffusing dissatisfaction throughout the organization to make appropriate discrepancies self-evident. Bandura (1982) frames this in

terms of unfavorable personal consequences, the organizational analog of which would be the threat of a complete failure of the organization. In essence, intellectual pain, diffused dissatisfaction, and organizational failure may be used to suggest aspects of a discrepancy between the present state and some apparent or implied desired end-state.

While the appropriateness of certain end-states, such as survival, is rarely questioned, the appropriateness of others may be. For example, successfully convincing members of an organization that changes are necessary to become *No. 1* in the industry on some measure rests on their acceptance of being *No. 1* as an appropriate end-state. Much of the recent literature on leadership vision emphasizes the importance of clarifying and gaining commitment to the end-state against which the organization is judging its present condition and justifying the need for change (cf. Bennis & Nanus, 1985). Therefore, the discrepancy message involves communicating where the organization is currently, where it wants to be, and why that end-state is appropriate.

Efficacy. While the realization that a discrepancy exists can be a powerful motivator for change, other reactions are also possible. For example, Nadler and Tushman (1989) discuss the possibility that awareness of discrepancy can result in counterproductive energy. They warn that negative information can result in defensive reactions, like denial, flight, or withdrawal.

To minimize the possibility of a counterproductive reaction, a change agent should build the target's confidence that it has the capability to correct the discrepancy. This confidence has been referred to as efficacy (Bandura, 1982, 1986) and may be viewed as the perceived capability to overcome the discrepancy. Efficacy has been consistently found to influence thought patterns, actions, and emotional arousal. Bandura (1982) reports that individuals will avoid activities believed to exceed their coping capabilities, but will undertake and perform those which they judge themselves to be capable of. Thus, in creating readiness, one must not only communicate a salient discrepancy, but must also bolster the efficacy of organizational members regarding the proposed changes to reduce the discrepancy.

Interpersonal and Social Dynamics

Because a readiness effort involves convincing a collection of socially-interacting individuals to change their beliefs, attitudes, and intentions in accordance with the discrepancy and efficacy aspects of the message, a change agent must understand the distinction between individual and collective readiness, as well as what influences the collective interpretation of the readiness message. This understanding can be facilitated by an integration of the literature on collective behavior (cf. Smelser, 1963), social information processing (cf. Griffin, 1987), and mass communications (cf. DeFleur & Ball-Rokeach, 1989).

Interventions to create readiness for change are attempts to mobilize collective support by building and shaping awareness across organizational members regarding the existence of, the sources of, and solutions to the organization's problems (cf. Smelser, 1963). Through the dynamics of social information processing, an organization's collective readiness is constantly being influenced by the readiness of the individuals comprising it. System members look to one another for clues regarding the meaning of events and circumstances facing the organization. Any readiness-building activities must take this social exchange into account. It is important to consider that the change agent is not the sole source of discrepancy and efficacy information. The impact of any message generated by the change agent will be shaped by the *social* interpretation of that message.

From the mass communications literature, three theories offer insight into various social dynamics that could operate in readiness interventions—the individual differences, social differentiation, and social relationships theories (DeFleur & Ball-Rokeach, 1989).

Individual differences theory argues that the response of one individual may diverge from that of another because of differing cognitive structures. One example of this can be found in research by Kirton (1980) on the different reactions of individuals characterized as innovators or adaptors. Kirton's findings suggest that innovators are likely to respond favorably to readiness programs designed to prepare the target for fundamental change (i.e., change that requires job incumbents to use different mental processes and to develop new skills) while adaptors are more likely to respond favorably to readiness programs designed to prepare the target for incremental change (i.e., change that requires incumbents to make minor modifications in thought patterns and to fine tune existing skills). In sum, individual difference theory serves as a reminder that specific individuals may react differently to the same message.

Social differentiation theory argues that the response to influence attempts will be determined by the target's cultural or subcultural membership. Such cultural memberships may polarize the beliefs, attitudes, and intentions of members. Hierarchical differentiation (i.e., executives, managers, supervisors, and workers) or other differentiates (e.g., union/non-union, engineers/non-engineers) shape group membership and result in psychological boundaries that may affect the beliefs, attitudes, intentions, and behaviors of members (cf. Van Maanen & Barley, 1985; Bushe, 1988). These psychological boundaries affect the ease with which readiness is evenly created across the subcultures within the organization.

Finally, social relationships theory suggests that responses to an influence attempt will hinge on the network of relationships individuals have. In particular, the influence of opinion leaders on others' sentiments can be powerful in affecting those others' readiness for change. Identifying and recognizing the influence of opinion leaders in the organization may enable the change agent to more effectively design them into the readiness intervention. Building readiness in these opinion leaders first could allow them to provide social cues for others in the organization and, in effect, act as informal change agents in disseminating the logic of the readiness program. As a result, a social information processing-based *snowball effect* might be generated.

Influence Strategies

Given the above conceptualization of readiness dynamics, how might a change agent intervene in the natural flow of social information processing occurring among organizational members to increase their readiness for change? Two strategies offered by Bandura (1977) and Fishbein and Azjen (1975) for influencing individual cognitions are appropriate for creating readiness for organizational change: persuasive communication (both oral and written) and active participation. A third strategy consists of the management of external sources of information. These three strategies have certain advantages and disadvantages (e.g., timeliness and manageability). The skillful change agent will capitalize on opportunities and the strengths of each strategy and utilize them in concert to influence readiness. Each of these strategies offers a lever for conveying discrepancy and efficacy information.

Persuasive Communication. Persuasive communication is primarily a source of explicit information regarding discrepancy and efficacy. However, the form of persuasive communication employed also sends symbolic information regarding the commitment to, prioritization of, and urgency for the change effort. For example, a CEO who travels to all corporate locations to discuss the need for change sends the message explicitly communicated in his/her comments and the symbolic message that the issues are important enough to take the time and resources necessary to communicate them directly. Oral persuasive communication consists of in-person speeches, either live (e.g., speaking in person or through teleconferencing technology) or recorded (e.g., audio/videotape). Written persuasive communication consists of documents prepared by the organization (e.g., newsletters, annual reports, memos).

Lengel and Daft (1988) have assessed communication media in terms of *richness,* a composite dimension comprising the extent of simultaneous multiple information cues, personal focus, and timeliness of feedback. In-person is the richest medium because it establishes a personal focus and permits multiple information cues and immediate feedback. Written media (e.g., annual reports, newsletters) are considered lean, being impersonal and providing for few information cues, and no direct feedback opportunities. Between these two extremes are other media like audio/videotape and electronic mail. For nonroutine communications (i.e., ones that are emotional and difficult to express) more richness is required. Messages that are simple, straightforward, rational, and logical can be communicated via lean media.

Oral persuasive communication involves direct, explicit message transmission through meetings, speeches, and other forms of personal presentation. Live in-person presentations would be rated high in richness, according to Lengel and Daft's criteria. If this form of presentation is not feasible, a videotape of the presentation may be appropriate. For example, Eden and Kinnar

(1991) recently employed both verbal persuasion and videotape presentation to boost self-efficacy and increase volunteering for a special-forces service. Elsewhere, Barrett and Cammann (1984) describe a case in which the CEO of National Steel Company conducted a series of personal meetings and prepared a videotape that would be available to all employees. The main objective was to communicate that the ongoing downturn in the steel industry (a contextual factor) was not simply a cyclical one. Thus, this CEO was creating readiness using live and video-recorded presentations.

Management of External Information. Sources outside the organization can be used to bolster messages sent by the change agent. For example, a diagnostic report prepared by a consulting firm may be used to add credibility to a message sent by the change agent. Generally, a message generated by more than one source, particularly if external to the organization, is given a greater air of believability and confirmation (Gist, 1987).

The news media is one form of external source that can play an important role in creating readiness for change. Employee knowledge about issues influencing their readiness can be affected through mass media channels like radio and television broadcasts, magazines, and newspapers. Information provided by such sources tends to have an air of objectivity and is therefore often persuasive with regard to creating readiness for change. However, while such information is persuasive, it is not easily managed by the change agent.

There are two ways in which a change agent may attempt to manage such information. First, information can be provided to the external press. Organizations often use press releases in this manner. Warren (1984) described a case involving the president of Antioch College who supplied the press (e.g., *The New York Times, Newsweek,* and the local newspaper) with information regarding the college's fiscal difficulties (i.e., discrepancy) and a plan (i.e., efficacy) to restore Antioch to fiscal stability. A second way a change agent can manage such media information is by making change-relevant information available by disseminating copies of selected articles, books, or film clips to organizational members. For example, many organizations distribute copies of business books which highlight particular desired messages.

Active Participation. Persuasive communication and the management of external information both emphasize the direct communication of readiness messages. Change agents can also manage opportunities for organizational members to learn through their own activities, and thereby send readiness messages indirectly. The message generated by active participation is essentially self-discovered (Fishbein & Azjen, 1975). This source of information is advantageous since individuals tend to place greater trust in information discovered by themselves. It is important to note that while a change agent may manage opportunities for organizational members to be exposed to information which influences readiness, the message is generated through the activity and is therefore outside of the explicit control of the change agent.

One form of active participation is directly involving individuals in activities which are rich in information pertaining to potential discrepancy and efficacy messages. For example, participating in formalized strategic planning activities can lead to self-discovery of discrepancies facing the organization. Answering customer complaints can lead to a similar self-discovery. Furthermore, experiential learning exercises have been recognized as effective in providing change relevant insights in training programs. For example, Kirton's (1980) work suggests that experiential learning exercises may be used to teach *adaptive* style individuals the appropriateness of a more *innovative* style.

Another form of active participation is vicarious learning. For example, a vicarious learning experience can be designed to bolster confidence that new production techniques, not only offer competitive advantages, but can be implemented in their own work environment. Gist, Schwoerre, and Rosen (1989) successfully applied vicarious learning in getting workers to begin using computer software. The act of observing others applying new productive techniques enhances one's confidence in adopting the innovation.

A third form active participation can take is enactive mastery. Enactive mastery can be used to prepare a target for change by taking small incremental steps. Success from the small-scale efforts can generate efficacy with regard to the challenge of implementing changes necessary for large-scale change. This logic has been discussed by Schaffer (1981) and Thompson (1981) in terms of getting clients to buy into, initiate, and sustain needed changes.

Change Agent Attributes

The effectiveness of the influence strategies is dependent upon the change agent wielding them. Attributes, such as credibility, trustworthiness, sincerity, and expertise of the change agent are gleaned from what people know about the agent and/or the agent's general reputation. Clearly, readiness-creating messages will have more influence if the change agent generating those messages has a good reputation in these domains (Gist, 1987). Conversely, when these attributes are unfavorable, the change agent's ability to create readiness for change will be hampered.

Readiness Assessment

To guide readiness building efforts, it is beneficial to assess the system's readiness. Assessments of the perceived discrepancy and efficacy of the target would be performed in gauging the state of readiness. Pond, Armenakis, and Green (1984) and Fox, Ellison, and Keith (1988) provide evidence that readiness can be assessed through survey research methodology. As described in the evaluation literature (cf. Armenakis, Field, & Holley, 1976) assessment methodologies can include the use of questionnaire, interview, and observation methods.

Whatever methods are used in sensing readiness, the change agent must respect the importance of reliability and validity issues (cf. Sackett & Larson, 1990). However, this respect should be tempered by the realization that readiness assessments may be for the purpose of discovery as much as for the purpose of confirmation. Thus, as McCall and Bobko (1990) note, a broader perspective on what is acceptable in the way of methodology may be required by the context in which the assessment is conducted. Qualitative techniques become more necessary in fluid, dynamic contexts. For example, polling opinion leaders or identifying and tracking rumors may help clarify trends that appear in survey data. Domain or taxonomic analyses, which are directed at understanding semantics, symbolic structures, and underlying perceptions of employees (McCall & Bobko, 1990), are other examples of procedures that may be useful in an attempt to determine the collective readiness of the organization. Naturally, the typical constraints of availability of time, funds, and expertise, and the importance placed on the assessment will influence the design. If properly conducted, such assessments can reveal the need to intensify efforts, use additional strategies to create readiness, and offer insights into how readiness messages might be modified.

A Typology of Readiness Programs

The purpose of the preceding discussion was to describe the major components of a program for creating employee readiness for change. However, decisions about leveraging each of the components into a readiness program should be guided by two considerations, the *extent to which employees are ready* (as determined through an assessment) and the *urgency of the change* (the amount of time available before changes must be implemented).

As described, employee readiness is influenced by the message transmitted via the strategies, the change agent attributes, and the interpersonal and social dynamics of organizational members. In addition to these planned efforts, however, employee readiness may be influenced by at least three other factors, *viz.,* unplanned media information, existing organizational conditions, and significance of the change effort. Information disseminated through the media (e.g., industry layoffs, increasing foreign competition, economic conditions) may affect employee readiness for change, heightening awareness of changing external contextual factors. Furthermore, existing organizational conditions affect employee loyalty, commitment, or other feelings toward an organization and its leaders, consequently influencing readiness. Indeed, Fox et al. (1988) found that effective management practices (e.g., planning, delegating, communicating) influenced employee cooperation and perceived equity and were associated with higher employee readiness for implementing improvements in procedures and problem solving. In contrast, ineffective practices were associated with lower readiness.

In addition, some changes are more intense and potentially more threatening. Fundamental change, such as changing from a functional form to a strategic business unit organization or from an assembly line to an autonomous workgroup arrangement, requires different mental processes and the development of new skills. In contrast, incremental change, such as rearranging work stations to capitalize on a more efficient plant layout (without re-engineering jobs), requires lesser modifications of thought processes and a simple fine-tuning of job skills. Thus, employees may be less ready for fundamental than for incremental change.

Sometimes organizational changes are urgently needed and require rapid implementation. In such cases, a readiness program will have to be implemented which utilizes the most effective and efficient strategies. Thus, a change agent may only utilize a persuasive communication strategy. In other situations, needed changes may not be so urgent, permitting the implementation of a readiness effort broader in scope and more thorough in detail. Such a program may involve persuasive communication as well as active participation (e.g., vicarious learning) and the management of external information (e.g., press releases).

By combining readiness and urgency, various combinations of change conditions can be hypothesized. Hypothetical programs appropriate for four generic urgency and readiness conditions

TABLE 1

Hypothetical Readiness Programs for Various Combinations of System Readiness and Urgency

Conditions	Program Nomenclature	Salient Characteristics
Low readiness/ low urgency	Aggressive	Persuasive communication. Active participation. External information. Change agent attributes.
Low readiness/ high urgency	Crisis	Persuasive communication. Change agent attributes.
High readiness/ low urgency	Maintenance	Persuasive communication. Active participation. External information.
High readiness/ high urgency	Quick response	Persuasive communication.

are summarized in Table 1. Although readiness and urgency are both continuous dimensions, for the sake of clarity, programs consistent with the combinations of the extreme conditions of readiness and urgency will be described.

Low Readiness/Low Urgency. An *aggressive program* is appropriate when employees are not ready for organizational change yet there is ample time for creating that readiness. A comprehensive readiness program leveraging all components is appropriate for this set of conditions. A variety of rich and lean persuasive communication methods (i.e., in-person presentations, video/audiotapes, newsletters) is suitable. Active participation experiences (e.g., visits to model manufacturing facilities) can be employed. If the organizational changes include introducing new technology (e.g., computerized systems as part of a change to autonomous workgroups) some form of enactive mastery could be appropriate. Furthermore, external information sources (e.g., press releases, speeches by recognized experts) can be incorporated into the program. Some attempt to build the credibility of the change agent may also be fruitful. For example, a CEO or other internal key figure in the change effort may participate in magazine and newspaper interviews describing previous experiences or recent awards so that credibility can be enhanced. When external change agents are involved, organizational leaders will want to select those with established reputations so their involvement will lend credibility to the anticipated changes. These actions will be expected to favorably influence opinion leaders, thus marshalling their support among other members of the change target.

Low Readiness/High Urgency. A *crisis program* may be appropriate when employees are not ready and there is great urgency in implementing needed organizational changes. The organization is in a crisis situation and must react immediately or face severe consequences. Obviously, this is an undesirable situation and requires drastic measures. The system needs to be *jolted,* which may include replacing the current change agent or augmenting this position with key personnel. Any personnel changes may be necessary in order to add credibility, trustworthiness, sincerity, and expertise. In addition, persuasive communication (e.g., in-person presentations) is required. Given time constraints, managing external information and active participation are likely to be infeasible.

High Readiness/Low Urgency. A *maintenance program* may be appropriate when employees are ready for change but there is little urgency in implementing needed organizational changes. The threat in this situation is that readiness may wane before changes are implemented. Therefore, the emphasis should be on maintaining readiness. Efforts should focus on keeping the discrepancy and efficacy messages current and visible. Lean persuasive communication methods (e.g., newsletters) and managed external information (e.g., magazine and newspaper press releases) may suffice as information sources. Active participation is not as critical to this program as in the aggressive program, but may still be appropriate.

High Readiness/High Urgency. A *quick response* program may be appropriate when employees are ready and the time available for implementing needed change is short. Thus, organizational changes can be implemented almost immediately. The challenge here is to maintain readiness energy as the change begins to unfold. Once again, persuasive communication, particularly rich persuasive communication is appropriate. Because of the urgency of the needed changes and the high readiness state, active participation and management of external information may not be suited for this program.

The brief descriptions of these four generic readiness programs provide the salient characteristics for the extremes of the readiness and urgency conditions. For whatever reason, a change agent may elect to vary from the programs described. Attempts to leverage any combination of the components contained in the readiness model would be a matter of whether the conditions are conducive to their use. To provide a detailed comprehensive example of the readiness model, the readiness creating efforts of the Whirlpool Corporation, the world's largest manufacturer of major home appliances, are described. In terms of Table 1, Whirlpool's program can be classified as an aggressive readiness program.

An Integrative Example of Readiness Interventions

Whirlpool's leaders, Jack Sparks in 1983, succeeded by David Whitwam in 1987, began a long-term program designed to improve the company's competitiveness by fundamentally altering the organization to become more aggressive, responsive, innovative, and market-oriented. In the following discussion, a summary of the external contextual factors and the readiness-building activities of Sparks and Whitwam are reviewed.

Contextual Factors

During the 1960s and 1970s, the fierce competition within the appliance industry resulted in the consolidation of numerous companies into relatively few players, namely, Whirlpool, General Electric, Electrolux, and Maytag. The strategy adopted by Whirlpool Corporation leaders was to emphasize cost control and operational efficiency rather than market aggressiveness, growth, and globalization. While the supply of appliances in the U.S. had been largely domestically based, foreign competitors began entering the already competitive market in the 1980s. These increasingly competitive pressures were compounded when the U.S. demand for appliances leveled off. The opportunities for expansion abroad, however, were growing (Stewart, 1990).

The Message

The content of the message Sparks and Whitwam communicated to build readiness for change included discrepancy and efficacy aspects. The discrepancy part of the message was that competitive pressures were mounting and that to remain competitive, Whirlpool would have to become more aggressive, more sensitive to the marketplace, more *lean and mean,* and a global player. To enhance efficacy, Whirlpool employees were sent to observe model manufacturing operations (in Japan and Korea), were reminded of other companies that had successfully implemented changes resulting in classic turnaround examples, and were assured that Whirlpool could make the fundamental changes needed to prosper in the emerging environment.

Active Participation

Three active participation interventions that were implemented to create readiness are particularly noteworthy—formalized strategic planning efforts, the Global Awareness Program, and the 75th Anniversary Celebration and Show.

Formalized Strategic Planning. One of the first actions Sparks initiated in 1983 was a formalized strategic planning process to augment the organization's traditional profit planning activities. This strategic planning activity required managers in all major operational units and functions to identify their strengths and weaknesses and for corporate managers to analyze competitors' strengths

and weaknesses, industry trends, and merge the operational plans. Involvement in such activities had the effect of participants discovering the discrepancy (need for change) as well as enhancing efficacy through developing the plans necessary to capitalize on the opportunities available in the marketplace.

The Global Awareness Program. To further emphasize the increased competitiveness facing the company, the Global Awareness Program was conceived. This program, initiated in 1986, involved sending groups of employees drawn from various levels and functions to visit companies operating in Japan and Korea. The program was designed to allow employees to observe first-hand the nature of the competition they faced as well as build confidence that Whirlpool could implement the same processes. It was hoped that the experience would lead them to conclude that the changes being advocated by Whirlpool leaders were indeed appropriate. Furthermore, the fact that their competitors were operating in this manner was intended to transmit the message "if they can do it, so can we."

In addition to offering an opportunity for active participation by a subgroup of employees, the Global Awareness Program was implemented on the assumption that the participants would return and share their discoveries with their peers. Though an appreciation for the potential of social synergy was evident in several of Whirlpool's readiness interventions, this is perhaps best illustrated with the Global Awareness Program. First, specially selected subgroups (from the lowest to the highest levels in the hierarchy) were formed to participate. Then, these participants were expected to exercise their personal influence and create readiness for change. For example, discussion groups involving participants and nonparticipating co-workers were established. Furthermore, videotape technology was used to expose as many employees as possible to the program. The 13-minute videotape describing the program and capturing the thoughts of participants (Global Awareness Program, 1986) could be viewed not only by those who were absent at the live presentations, but could be viewed in peer groups without supervisors being present.

The 75th Anniversary Celebration and Show. To celebrate the company's 75th anniversary in 1986, an elaborate Broadway-style stage production was developed. The show traveled to company locations throughout the U.S. and played to packed houses of employees. In addition to celebrating the company's history, the show had an implicit efficacy message for all employees. Throughout the production, several points bearing on readiness for change were emphasized: (1) Whirlpool has, and can in the future, succeed against the odds, (2) change and aggressiveness were the bedrock of the company's early history, and (3) Whirlpool cares about its people and will take care of them. While these messages were not explicitly stated, they were under the surface awaiting self-discovery and self-insight by the members of the audience.

Management of External Information Sources

External sources of information used by Whirlpool to help mold readiness consisted of increased coverage of the company's operations in business periodicals and a diagnostic analysis by a well-known consulting firm.

Business Periodical Publicity. In contrast to the traditional low-key approach taken at Whirlpool, Sparks and Whitwam made an effort to increase company coverage in the business media. This visibility effort coupled with the degree of change and increase in competitive activities by Whirlpool resulted in increased coverage and exposure. For example, during the period 1983–1990, the number of magazine articles (not including *The Wall Street Journal*) mentioning Whirlpool increased almost threefold from the average of the previous 10 years. *Business Week* and *Fortune* published articles about the company's change efforts. In addition to this coverage, Whirlpool employees were constantly exposed to media bearing on issues of readiness. For example, articles regarding the company's

activities and broader industry trends were routinely copied and distributed among managers.

The McKinsey and Company Structures Study. In 1987, after Whitwam's move to CEO, the consulting firm of McKinsey and Company analyzed Whirlpool's structure. Several observations were offered about the inadequacies of the current structure, and resulted in a recommended major reorganization. The details of this study remained unannounced until presented by Whitwam in the New Structure Speech described below. When released, the report served to provide an important message regarding the need for change.

Persuasive Communication

In addition to the sharing of knowledge about their overseas experiences by Global Awareness Program participants described above, several other internally generated persuasive communication efforts are notable. The majority of these efforts involved instrumental, high-profile speeches and spoken and written statements of vision.

The New Vision Speech. Probably the most visible example of persuasive communication was the New Vision Speech personally delivered in 1986, 29 times in 13 different locations to approximately 5,500 employees. A 52-minute videotape (New Vision Speech, 1986) of the speech was also made so that all employees could view it as desired. The New Vision Speech was compelling for two reasons: it was the most comprehensive statement of the need for change, plan for change, and encouragement for change, yet offered, and the organization's leaders had expended a great deal of time and effort to share it as widely and personally as possible.

Simply stated, the focus of the new vision message was the need for change at Whirlpool with references to other successful large-scale change efforts. Two significant external contextual factors were cited to support the need for change. First, the increase in foreign competition was described. It was noted that imports in the appliance industry had increased 400 percent from 1982–1986. Second, it was noted that the consolidation among domestic appliance manufacturers had resulted in four fierce competitors, namely, Whirlpool, Maytag, GE, and Electrolux.

Part of the message devoted to efficacy was a brief history of how Whirlpool had successfully experienced change in the past by evolving from one product (a washing machine in 1911) to the multiple product company of 1986. Furthermore, the much celebrated Chrysler Corporation turn-around was used as an example to build efficacy.

The New Structure Speech. At the February 1988, Corporate Quarterly Review (which was attended by most officers, directors, and managers), Whitwam (New Structure Speech, 1988) stressed that the old structure was not permitting Whirlpool to be competitive. Although he did not explicitly report the company's performance, his audience was aware that 1987 company performance was below projections (Zellner, 1988). Whitwam referred to the diagnostic analysis conducted by McKinsey, thus providing additional support for the impending reorganization.

Whitwam explained the company was to reorganize around the strategic business unit concept. The intended result of this reorganization was to increase accountability and stimulate a sense of ownership throughout the company, push decision making closer to the marketplace, and to improve operating effectiveness and efficiency. After describing the benefits of the new structure, he challenged Whirlpool employees telling them the company needed their patience, support, and cooperation. His determination to succeed was reflected in his exclamation that Whirlpool would not fail in the bitterly contested marketplace.

Readiness Assessment

An important part of Whirlpool's change efforts has been an attempt to track the progress of change and assess the degree of readiness and resistance to change. Specifically, Sparks and Whitwam commissioned assessments of the attitudes of the company's leadership regarding these issues. These assessments were conducted by a team of university-based researchers who surveyed the opinions of the top four levels of management throughout the organization. These assessments were used to guide the interventions designed to create readiness for large-scale change. For example, the 1986 assessment suggested that not very many employees, even in the leadership cadre, fully understood the company's vision. This finding helped in the refinement of the influence strategies used to create readiness, including the New Vision Speech.

Epilogue

In March 1988, Whirlpool began the implementation of the SBU reorganization. In addition, in August 1988, Whirlpool completed the negotiations for a new joint venture with N. V. Philips Gloeilampenfabricken of the Netherlands to produce and market appliances in Europe, thus becoming the world's largest global competitor in the home appliance industry. Although the home appliance industry has been sluggish, due to the nationwide downturn in housing construction, Whirlpool has been described several times in the business media as a company aggressively positioning itself to meet the challenges of a slowed domestic economy and to take advantage of the economic unification of Europe (e.g., Woodruff & Kapner, 1991).

Conclusion

This article has emphasized the importance of creating readiness as a precursor to organizational change and examined the influence strategies available to help generate readiness. Some further implications for, and contributions to, the management of organizational change are summarized below.

First, the readiness concept complements previous contributions made by Lawrence (1954), Kotter and Schlesinger (1979), and others regarding resistance to change. The potential causes of resistance should be appreciated in designing the discrepancy and efficacy content of the readiness message and in selecting the strategies for creating readiness. The findings from mass communications research are useful in understanding that individual and cultural differences are influential in the response of the target group to readiness efforts. This information can be coupled with the traditional causes of resistance (e.g., lack of trust) in designing readiness programs to address the pertinent issues in eliciting the necessary support to accomplish successful change.

Second, the readiness model suggests the importance of building readiness within the context facing the organization. For example, Whirlpool's readiness efforts, begun in 1983, were not a response to an immediate crisis but rather to anticipated challenges. Beer and Walton (1987) and Pettigrew (1987) emphasize the role of contextual factors in bringing about change. It is apparent from the Whirlpool experience that company leaders were very deliberate in incorporating the appropriate contextual factors in the message to communicate discrepancy and efficacy information.

Third, decisions about implementing readiness programs should be guided by the urgency of the change and the extent to which employees are ready for the needed change. By conceptualizing high and low urgency to implement needed organizational change in combination with high and low readiness for change, four generic readiness programs (i.e., aggressive, crisis, maintenance, and quick response) were described. This typology of readiness programs is useful because it describes various scenarios faced by change agents. Within the constraints imposed by time limitations and the readiness challenge, a change agent can understand the practicalities of readiness creation.

Fourth, the detailed description of Whirlpool's aggressive readiness program demonstrated the full complement of strategies available to change agents. A change agent can use this program as a basis from which to extract ideas and tailor a readiness program for another organization.

Fifth, this article argues for the active creation of readiness. Recognizing the importance of readiness, some authors have argued that change agents may direct their initial efforts to areas where organization members are ready (cf. Beer & Walton, 1987; Pond et al., 1984). The framework presented

in this article makes a case for identifying where change is needed and then designing a readiness program to influence the appropriate beliefs, attitudes, and intentions so that changes can be successfully implemented. Instruments designed to assess readiness can then be administered to determine the effectiveness of readiness activities. New strategies can be implemented and messages transmitted through existing strategies can be modified to achieve the readiness intended. The creation of readiness is not necessarily a pre-change concern only. Readiness must be maintained throughout the process of large-scale change particularly since such change is composed of smaller changes which are ongoing. A single initial creation-of-readiness effort may not be adequate to maintain the required levels of readiness throughout the duration of the change process. Thus, employees need to be made ready and readiness efforts should be conducted as needed throughout the change effort.

Finally, the concepts presented in this article can be extended to include other change applications. For example, readiness can be aimed at the individual level, taking on more of the appearances of coaching and counseling. That is, a primary change agent, such as a CEO or some key officer, may need to ready other top officers so that they can become effective change agents for the organization as a whole.

The topic of readiness represents a rudimentary issue in the management of change, and as presented here illustrates the need for further refinement in the planned change process. The implications of overlooking the importance of readiness may very well be that an appropriate intervention may not produce the intended organization changes because organization members are simply not ready (cf. Pasmore & Fagans, 1992). It is hoped that this article will stimulate change agents to consciously think about and plan readiness interventions. Furthermore, urgency and readiness are concepts whose values were discussed in relative terms. Currently, the relativity of these concepts must be determined by the change agent. However, more research under conditions permitting experimental control may provide useful findings and needed guidance for the design and implementation of readiness programs.

Acknowledgments

We would like to thank David Whitwam, Chairman and Chief Executive Officer, and E. R. Dunn, Corporate Vice President of Human Resources, for allowing us to observe and report on Whirlpool Corporation's change activities. In addition, we gratefully acknowledge the constructive comments offered by Art Bedeian, Alan Glassman, Bernie Keys, Bob Pond, Alan Randolph, and John Slocum. An earlier version of this article was presented at the 51st Annual Academy of Management Meeting.

References

Armenakis, A., Field, H., & Holley, W. Guidelines for overcoming empirically identified evaluation problems of organizational development change agents. *Human Relations,* 1976, *129,* 1147–1161.

Armenakis, A., Mossholder, K., & Harris, S. Diagnostic bias in organizational consultation. *Omega: The International Journal of Management Science,* 1990, *18*(6), 161–179.

Bandura, A. Self-efficacy: Toward a unifying theory of behavioral change. *Psychological Review,* 1977, *84,* 194–215.

Bandura, A. Self-efficacy mechanism in human agency. *American Psychologist,* 1982, *37*(2). 122–147.

Bandura, A. *Social foundations of thought and action: A social-cognitive view.* Englewood Cliffs, NJ: Prentice Hall, 1986.

Barrett, A., & Cammann, C. Transitioning to change: Lessons from NSC. In J. R. Kimberly and R. E. Quinn (Eds.), *Managing organizational transitions.* Homewood, IL.: Richard D. Irwin, 1984, pp. 218–239.

Bartlem, C., & Locke, E. The Coch and French study: a critique and reinterpretation. *Human Relations,* 1981, *34*(7), 555–566.

Beckhard, R., & Harris, R. *Organizational transitions: Managing complex change.* Reading, MA: Addison-Wesley Publishing Company, 1987.

Beer, M., & Walton, A. Organization change and development. *Annual Review of Psychology,* 1987, *38,* 339–367.

Bennis, W., & Nanus, B. Leaders: *The strategies for taking charge.* New York: Harper & Row, 1985.

Bushe, G. Developing cooperative labor–management relations in unionized factories: A multiple case study of quality circles and parallel organizations within joint quality of work life projects. *Journal of Applied Behavioral Science,* 1988, *24*(2), 129–150.

Coch, L. & French, J. Overcoming resistance to change. *Human Relations,* 1948, *1*(4). 512–532.

DeFluer, M., & Ball-Rokeach, S. *Theories of mass communication,* New York: Longman, 1989.

Eden, D., & Kinnar, J. Modeling Galatea: Boosting self-efficacy to increase volunteering. *Journal of Applied Psychology,* 1991, *76,* 770–780.

Fishbein, M., & Azjen, I. *Belief, attitude, intention, and behavior: An introduction to theory and research.* Reading, MA: Addison-Wesley Publishing Company, 1975.

Fox, D., Ellison, R., & Keith, K. Human resource management: An index and its relationship to readiness for change. *Public Personnel Management,* 1988, *17*(3), 297–302.

Gardner, G. Workers' participation: A critical evaluation of Coch and French. *Human Relations,* 1977, *30*(12), 1071–1078.

Gist, M., Self-efficacy: Implications for organizational behavior and human resource management. *Academy of Management Review,* 1987, *12*(3). 472–485.

Gist, M., Schwoerer, C., & Rosen, B. Effects of alternative training methods on self-efficacy and performance in computer software training. *Journal of Applied Psychology,* 1989, *74*(6), 884–891.

Global Awareness Program (Videotape). Benton Harbor, MI: Whirlpool Corporation, 1986.

Griffin, R. Toward an integrated theory of task design. In L. L. Cummings and B. M. Staw (Eds.), *Research in organizational behavior* (Vol. 9). Greenwich, CT: JAI Press, 1987, pp. 79–120.

Kanter, R. *The change masters.* New York: Simon and Schuster, 1983.

Katz, D., & Kahn, R. *The social psychology of organization.* New York: John Wiley, 1978.

Kirton, M. Adaptors and innovators in organizations. *Human Relations,* 1980, *3,* 213–224.

Kissler, G. *The change riders.* Reading, MA: Addison-Wesley Publishing Company, 1991.

Kotter, J., & Schlesinger, L. Choosing strategies for change. *Harvard Business Review,* 1979, *57*(2), 106–114.

Lawrence, P. How to deal with resistance to change. *Harvard Business Review,* 1954, *32*(3), 49–57.

Lengel, R., & Daft, R. The selection of communication media as an executive skill. *Academy of Management Executive.* 1988, *2*(3), 225–232.

Lewin, K. *Field theory in social science.* New York: Harper and Row, 1951.

McCall, M., & Bobko, P. Research methods in the service of discovery. In M. Dunnette and L. Hough (Eds.), *Handbook of industrial and organizational psychology* (Vol. 1). Palo Alto, CA: Consulting Psychologists Press, 1990, pp. 381–418.

Nadler, D., & Tushman, M. Organizational frame bending: Principles for managing reorientation. *Academy of Management Executive,* 1989, *3*(3), 194–204.

New Structure Speech (Videotape). Benton Harbor, MI: Whirlpool Corporation, 1986.

New Vision Speech (Videotape). Benton Harbor, MI: Whirlpool Corporation, 1988.

Pasmore, W., & Fagans, M. Participation, individual development, and organizational change: A review and synthesis. *Journal of Management,* 1992, *18,* 375–397.

Pettigrew, A. Context and action in transforming the firm. *Journal of Management Studies,* 1987, *24*(6), 649–670.

Pond, S., Armenakis, A., & Green, S. The importance of employee expectations in organizational diagnosis. *Journal of Applied Behavioral Science,* 1984, *20,* 167–180.

Sackett, P., & Larson, J. Research strategies and tactics in industrial and organizational psychology. In M. Dun-

nette & L. Hough (Eds.), *Handbook of industrial and organizational psychology* (Vol. 1). Palo Alto, CA: Consulting Psychologists Press, 1990, pp. 419–490.

Schaffer, R. Productivity improvement strategy: Make success the building block. *Management Review,* 1981, *70,* 46–52.

Schein, E. Personal change through interpersonal relationships. In W. Bennis, J. Van Maanen, E. Schein, and F. Steele (Eds.), *Essays in interpersonal dynamics.* Homewood, IL: The Dorsey Press, 1979, pp. 129–162.

Smelser, N. *Theory of collective behavior.* New York: Free Press, 1963.

Spector, B. From bogged down to fired up: Inspiring organizational change. *Sloan Management Review,* Summer, 1989, 29–34.

Stewart, T. A. Heartland industry takes on the world. *Fortune,* 1990, *121*(6), 110–112.

Thompson, H. Consulting for results. *Business Horizons,* 1981, *24*(6), 62–65.

Turner, A. Consulting is more than giving advice. *Harvard Business Review,* 1982, *60*(5), 120–129.

Van Maanen, J., & Barley, S. Cultural organization: Fragments of a theory. In P. J. Frost, L. F. Moore, M. R. Louis, C. C. Lundberg, and J. Martin (Eds.), *Organizational culture.* Beverly Hills, CA: Sage, 1985, pp. 31–54.

Warren, D. Managing in crisis: Nine principles for successful transition. In J. R. Kimberly and R. E. Quinn (Eds.), *Managing organizational transitions.* Homewood, IL: Richard D. Irwin, 1984, pp. 85–106.

Woodruff, D., & Kapner, F. Whirlpool goes on a world tour. *Business Week,* June 3, 1991, 99–100.

Zellner, W. A. Tough market has Whirlpool in a spin. *Business Week,* May 2, 1988, 121–122.

Reading 29

Defining a Political Model of Organizations

Larry E. Greiner
Virginia E. Schein

The most commonly considered expression of power in organization research and practice is *downward* power, which is the influence of a superior over a subordinate. This kind of influence in the form of one having power over another is a central focus in much of our traditional leadership research and training, such as Theory X versus Theory Y or task oriented versus people oriented styles.

Upward power refers to attempts by subordinates to influence their superiors. Until recently, subordinates were considered relatively powerless. But a small and growing body of research indicates that subordinates can and do influence their superiors in subtle ways. Studies by Kipnis, Schmidt, and Wilkinson (1980) and Schlilit and Locke (1982) have identified subordinate influence strategies such as persistence, logical presentation of ideas, coalition formation, and ingratiation. And Gabarro and Kotter (1980) have argued that the leadership challenge for most subordinates is to learn how to manage one's boss.

A third direction, *sideways* power, refers to influence attempts directed at those people who are neither subordinates nor superiors in one's immediate reporting chain of authority. *Horizontal power, interdepartmental power, external relationships, and lateral relationships* are all terms that reflect expressions of sideways power. Various researchers have called attention to this increasingly important expression of power in organizations—Mintzberg, 1973; Strauss, 1962,

at the individual level and Hickson et al., 1971; Pfeffer and Salancik, 1974, at the subunit level.

Interestingly, the net result of these research studies has been to show that sideways power—the predominant form of power expression outside the formal boss-subordinate relationship—is absolutely essential if managers are to get their jobs done. Downward power—getting work done through subordinates—represents a much smaller portion of a manager's time and effort than heretofore considered. The bulk of a manager's efforts is often spent outside the work unit, dealing with other department heads, divisions, or subsidiaries, over whom he or she has no formal control.

Developing, using, and maintaining multiple sources of power other than formal position becomes essential for today's managers in complex organizations, When managers move outside clean-cut authority relationships to get things done, dependence on others is greater than the formal power and control given to people to do these jobs. According to Kotter (1979), "Power dynamics, under these circumstances, are inevitable and are needed to make organizations function well."

Models of Organization

How we view power directions is often a function of the conceptual model that we use to understand behavior in organizations. All of us utilize our mental maps to determine how organizations actually and ideally should function. Sometimes we use these models as tools for diagnosis and other times we use them as idealized versions of how life should be in organizations. It is not unusual

Source: L. Greiner and V. Schein, *Power and Organizational Development*, (pp. 14–24). © 1988 Addison-Wesley Publishing Company, Inc. Reprinted by permission of Addison Wesley Longman, Inc.

for us to confuse our idealized model with how organizations actually do function.

Our concern in this book is with deciding on a model that comes closer to representing organizational reality, even if it departs from our idealized models. It is this reality that OD consultants have to work with before they attempt to move an organization to some other "reality." Two authors have prepared several models. Baldridge (1971) describes three organizational archetypes—bureaucratic, collegial, and political. Pfeffer (1981) suggests four organizational decision models—rational, bureaucratic, organized anarchy, and political. Distilling from these various alternatives, we present three organizational models of our own and relate them to the power directions discussed in the previous section. As we shall see, our three models treat power directions differently, and thereby affect which types of power we attend to, ignore, or, possibly, try to eliminate.

Rational/Bureaucratic Model

The Rational/Bureaucratic model is most likely to be espoused by traditional management scholars, and one that most of us know well. It emphasizes rationally structured systems, built on division of labor and job specialization in a functional structure. Authority is top down, and utilizes formal communication channels, usually vertical, and well-defined policies and procedures. Organizational goals are clearly specified to direct efforts of employees toward greater efficiency. Formal systems and policies are used to provide control, predictability, and stability.

If we as OD practitioners use or even prefer this model, how are we likely to view power in organization? First, power is seen as hierarchial and so gaining formal approval from top management becomes the sine qua non of successful organizational change. The focus of change is directed toward improving the way superiors use power to manage subordinates. Managerial effectiveness is equated with subordinate performance, and it is achieved through what is known as humanistic management. The leader acts with greater sensitivity to soften the impact of downward power. Al-

though the humanistic leadership labels have changed over the years, Theory Y Management, the Considerate Leader, and the Situational Leader are all concepts that are conditioned by a concern with the exercise and effects of downward power.

Upward power in the Rational/Bureaucratic model is generally seen as disruptive and nonlegitimate. Under limited circumstances, it may be tolerated or even encouraged if its expression is narrowly controlled, such as in the use of Management by Objectives or Quality Circles. Sideways power receives virtually no consideration in this model, since vertical authority is the prescribed decision-making channel; integration occurs only at the apex of the pyramid.

Collegial/Consensus Model

The Collegial/Consensus model places emphasis on interpersonal and small group behavior in organizations (Argyris, 1962). Rules, policies, and procedures are relaxed, or even disbanded, in order to enhance interaction and participation in decision making. In contrast to the Rational/Bureaucratic model, formal authority relationships are minimized in the Collegial/Consensus model. The need for direction and control is replaced by teamwork in the spirit of "all for one, one for all." Individual contributions are highly valued, within a focus on collaboration and integration.

The view here is that human involvement and participation are good for both the organization and the individual. Equalizing the distribution of authority is assumed to lead to better decision making and fuller commitment to decisions.

Upward power is seen as legitimate and encouraged in this model. All forms of power redistribution are part of the organizational "should's," such as an Employee Bill of Rights, profit-sharing, worker councils, and employee representation on the board of directors. A flat organizational structure, appropriate to a professional group, reflects the high priority given to upward power.

In the Collegial/Consensus model, downward power is barely tolerated, and then only in limited situations in which peer pressure proves ineffective, such as in firing a troublesome employee.

Sideways power proves unnecessary because consensus and collaboration are the accepted norms.

Pluralistic/Political Model

The Pluralistic/Political Model sees organizations as composed of differing interest groups. Each party pursues its own goals, sometimes on selfish grounds but often for well-intended reasons based on its view of what is best for the organization as a whole. Conflict is viewed as inevitable and a normal part of the way things get done. Political behavior results when an attempt at influence is countered by another interested party or group.

According to Cyert and March (1964) (among the first to espouse a political theory of organizations), the objectives of the firm are arrived at through a process of bargaining among and between coalitions as they respond to environmental changes. Basic to the idea of a coalition is the expectation that those with similar interests will band together to influence the direction of the organization toward goals attributed to it by the coalition. Power becomes the intervening variable between desired outcomes and actual results.

Kotter (1977, 1985) sees power and political behavior arising naturally out of the inherent interdependency in most managerial jobs. Power and political behavior are dependent on a wide range of people outside the formal authority chain to get decisions made and work accomplished— for example, in dealing with suppliers, government officials, bankers, and technical experts. Lacking formal authority over these people, the use of power and influence becomes essential for effective managerial functioning.

The Pluralistic/Political Model allows for all forms of power expression. Power is truly everywhere and naturally used by those desiring to fulfill their work-related objectives. The arena of work activity expands beyond the traditional superior-subordinate relationship to include the entire organization. For example, a product manager in the marketing department may discover that one plant in manufacturing is producing defective products. The product manager may go directly to the VP of manufacturing (sideways and upwards power) and convince him to fix things. This VP will then have to influence his subordinates to correct the problems (downward power). The product manager may even have to involve his boss (upward power) to bring about the change.

Sideways power is recognized as a necessary and frequently exercised component of managerial effectiveness. Groups across the organization must compete for scarce resources, and they are horizontally dependent on one another to perform their jobs on schedule. Similarly, upward power takes on importance as individuals lower on the organization chart attempt to exercise influence over senior managers with greater control over needed resources.

Downward power is important, too, to assure that the needs of the overall organization, as perceived by the powerholders at the top, are being considered in decision making at lower levels. Sometimes downward power is required to force a solution on conflicting parties. However, downward power can lose its potency when lower level units also possess significant power, such as found in conflicts with a labor union or with a group of prima donna research scientists.

Organizational Realities

Which of the three models, or archetypes, comes closer to matching organizational reality? We agree with Cyert and March (1964), Baldridge (1971), and Pfeffer (1981), among other organizational theorists, who advance the Pluralistic/Political Model as a more accurate representation of how organizations and managers really function. It is not because people in organizations are greedy or corrupt, but simply because people are different and resources are scattered and limited. A compromise must be reached if the organization is to continue to function.

Moreover, Kotter (1985, 1986) contends that today's organizations possess even greater diversity and interdependence than companies of a few years ago. Technologies have proliferated, economic resources have become constrained, and competition has intensified. Unfortunately, according to Kotter, "The recentness of these changes is one of the key reasons why many people are only partially aware of the realities" of the Pluralistic/Political model.

The Pluralistic/Political model is, in our opinion, a less idealized model than the other two models. These other models may be worth striving for in certain situations, because research evidence suggests that the Rational/Bureaucratic model may be more effective in dealing with simple technologies and stable environments, while the Collegial/Consensus model fits better with more complex and uncertain environments (Lawrence and Lorsch, 1967).

However, these two "desirable" models for unique situations often work out differently in practice (Greiner and Schein, 1981; Schein and Greiner, 1977). The Rational/Bureaucratic model can produce overly restrictive formal systems that stifle initiative and reduce responsiveness to change. And the Collegial/Consensus model can create anarchic behavior at lower levels that undermines teamwork and, ultimately, the firm. We also know from research on human personality that not all people want to work in teams; some people prefer greater structure (Lorsch and Morse, 1974). The point is that both models, even in their most perfect states, will always contain strong threads of the Pluralistic/Political perspective.

Therefore, the key to understanding power in organizations is to acknowledge the pervasive reality of political behavior across and throughout all organizational forms. It means accepting power as natural and necessary to decision making regardless of formal structure. By using a Pluralistic/Political model, we can diagnose the many and varied expressions of power in a broader and more unbiased way. Adhering to either the Rational/Bureaucratic or Collegial/Consensus models may blind us to many aspects of power-oriented behavior.

• • • •

Implications for OD

Warren Bennis, in his book, *Organization Development* (1969), predicts what can happen to OD if it does not acknowledge the reality of the Pluralistic/Political model. "The organization development consultant tends to use the truth-love model when it may not be appropriate and has no alternative model to guide his practice under conditions of distrust . . . and conflict. . . . This means that in pluralistic power situations . . . organization development may not reach its desired goal. . . . This may explain why OD has been reasonably successful where power is relatively centralized . . . organization development has not met with success in diffuse power structures."

Understanding the realities of power with one's blinders off is essential for the healthy survival of the OD field. We have listed three directional expressions of power and their relationship to three models in use so that we can reexamine our own ways of diagnosing organizations, as well as question our own attitudes toward various expressions of power in them.

Few would deny that OD's model in use has for many years been dominated by the Collegial/Consensus model. OD has focused mainly on upward power within formal work groups, thereby ignoring or denying other expressions of power. If OD categorizes other forms of power as neurotic, selfish, or even unnecessary, it fails to recognize that work-related power is expressed naturally in a variety of ways across the entire work environment. The Pluralistic/Political model, in contrast, assumes that the expression of power is essential in reaching a trade-off between vested interests and organizational goals.

For OD to let go of the Collegial/Consensus model as a primary model for understanding and influencing behavior in organizations does not mean abandoning OD's traditional values of trust, openness, and collaboration or its techniques of team building and interpersonal feedback. Instead, these values and techniques must be treated as limited expressions of power to be supplemented by many other forms of influence that are selectively applied in a particular political context.

References

Argyris, C. 1962. *Interpersonal Competence and Organizational Effectiveness.* Homewood, IL: Irwin-Dorsey.

Baldridge, J. V. 1971. *Power and Conflict in the University.* New York: John Wiley.

Bennis, Warren. 1969. *Organization Development.* Reading, MA: Addison-Wesley.

Cyert, Richard M., and James G. March. 1964. *A Behavioral Theory of the Firm.* Englewood Cliffs, NJ: Prentice Hall.

Gabarro, John I., and John P. Kotter. 1980. "Managing Your Boss*.*" *Harvard Business Review,* January–Febuary, 92–100.

Greiner, Larry E., and Virginia E. Schein. 1981. "The Paradox of Managing a Project-Oriented Matrix: Establishing Coherence within Chaos." *Sloan Management Review,* Winter, 17–22.

Hickson, D. J., C. A. Lee, R. E. Schneck, and J. M. Pennings. 1971. "A Strategic Contingency Theory of Intraorganizational Power." *Administrative Science Quarterly,* 16, 216–229.

Kipnis, D., S. M. Schmidt, and I. Wilkinson. 1980. "Intraorganizational Influence Tactics: Exploration in Getting One's Way." *Journal of Applied Psychology,* 65, 440–452.

Kotter, John P. 1986. "Why Power and Influence Issues Are at the Very Core of Executive Work." In *Executive Power,* ed. by S. Srivastva Assoc. San Francisco: Jossey-Bass, 20–32.

Kotter, John P. 1985. *Power and Influence.* New York: Free Press.

Kotter, John P. 1979. *Power in Management.* New York: Amacom.

Kotter, John P. 1977. "Power, Dependence and Effective Management." *Harvard Business Review,* July–August, 125–136.

Lawrence, Paul, and Jay Lorsch. 1967. *Organization and Environment.* Boston: Division of Research, Harvard Business School.

Lorsch, Jay, and John Morse. 1974. *Organizations and Their Members: A Contingency Approach.* New York: Harper and Row.

Mintzberg, Henry. 1973. *The Nature of Managerial Work.* New York: Harper and Row.

Pfeffer, J. 1981. *Power in Organizations.* Marshfield, MA: Pitman.

Pfeffer, J. and G. R. Salancik. 1974. "Organizational Decision Making as a Political Process." *Administrative Science Quarterly,* 19, 135–151.

Schein, V. E., and L. E. Greiner. 1977. "Can Organization Development Be Fine-Tuned to Bureaucracies?" *Organizational Dynamics,* Winter, 48–61.

Schlilit, W. K., and E. A. Locke. 1982. "A Study of Upward Influence." *Administrative Science Quarterly,* 27, 304–316.

Strauss, G. 1962. "Tactics of Lateral Relationships: The Purchasing Agent." *Administrative Science Quarterly,* 7, 161–186.

Reading 30

Functional Roles of Group Members

Kenneth D. Benne
Paul Sheats

The Relative Neglect of Member Roles in Group Training

Efforts to improve group functioning through training have traditionally emphasized the training of group leadership. And frequently this training has been directed toward the improvement of the skills of the leader in transmitting information and in manipulating groups. Little direct attention seems to have been given to the training of group members in the membership roles required for effective group growth and production. The present discussion is based on the conviction that both effective group training and adequate research into the effectiveness of group training methods must give attention to the identification, analysis, and practice of leader *and* member roles, seen as co-relative aspects of overall group growth and production.

Certain assumptions have undergirded the tendency to isolate the leadership role from membership roles and to neglect the latter in processes of group training. (1) "Leadership" has been identified with traits and qualities inherent within the "leader" personality. Such traits and qualities can be developed, it is assumed, in isolation from the functioning of members in a group setting. The present treatment sees the leadership role in terms of functions to be performed within a group in helping that group to grow and to work productively. No sharp distinction can be made between leadership and membership functions, between leader and member roles. Groups may operate with various degrees of diffusion of "leadership"

Source: Kenneth D. Benne and Paul Sheats. Reprinted with permission of *The Journal of Social Issues,* Spring 1948, pp. 41–49.

functions among group members or of concentration of such functions in one member or a few members. Ideally, of course, the concept of leadership emphasized here is that of a multilaterally shared responsibility. In any event, effectiveness in the leader role is a matter of leader-member relationship. And one side of a relationship cannot be effectively trained in isolation from the retraining of the other side of that relationship. (2) It has been assumed that the "leader" is uniquely responsible for the quality and amount of production by the group. The "leader" must see to it that the "right" group goals are set, that the group jobs get done, that members are "motivated" to participate. On this view, membership roles are of secondary importance. "Membership" is tacitly identified with "followership." The present discussion assumes that the quality and amount of group production is the "responsibility" of the group. The setting of goals and the marshalling of resources to move toward these goals is a group responsibility in which all members of a mature group come variously to share. The functions to be performed both in building and maintaining group-centered activity and in effective production by the group are primarily member roles. Leadership functions can be defined in terms of facilitating identification, acceptance, development, and allocation of these group-required roles by the group. (3) There has frequently been a confusion between the roles which members enact within a group and the individual personalities of the group members. That there are relationships between the personality structures and needs of group members and the range and quality of group membership roles which members can learn to perform is not denied. On the contrary, the importance of studies designed to describe and explain and to increase our control of these relationships is affirmed. But, at the level of group functioning, member roles, relevant to group growth and accomplishment, must be clearly distinguished from the use of the group environment by individuals to satisfy individual and group-irrelevant needs, if clear diagnosis of member-roles are to be advanced. Neglect of this distinction has been associated traditionally with the neglect of the analysis of member roles in group growth and production.

A Classification of Member Roles

The following analysis of functional member roles was developed in connection with the First National Training Laboratory in Group Development, 1947. It follows closely the analysis of participation functions used in coding the content of group records for research purposes. A similar analysis operated in faculty efforts to train group members in their functional roles during the course of the laboratory.[1]

The member-roles identified in this analysis are classified into three broad groupings.

1. Group task roles. Participant roles here are related to the task which the group is deciding to undertake or has undertaken. Their purpose is to facilitate and coordinate group effort in the selection and definition of a common problem and in the solution of that problem.

2. Group building and maintenance roles. The roles in this category are oriented toward the functioning of the group as a group. They are designed to alter or maintain the group way of working, to strengthen, regulate, and perpetuate the group as a group.

3. Individual roles. This category does not classify member-roles as such, since the "participations" denoted here are directed toward the satisfaction of the "participant's" individual needs. Their purpose is some individual goal which is not relevant either to the group task or to the functioning of the group as a group. Such participants

are, of course, highly relevant to the problem of group training, insofar as such training is directed toward improving group maturity or group task efficiency.

Group Task Roles

The following analysis assumes that the task of the discussion group is to select, define, and solve common problems. The roles are identified in relation to functions of facilitation and coordination of group problem-solving activities. Each member may of course enact more than one role in any given unit of participation and a wide range of roles in successive participations. Any or all of these roles may be played at times by the group "leader" as well as by various members.

a. The *initiator-contributor* suggests or proposes to the group new ideas or a changed way of regarding the group problem or goal. The novelty proposed may take the form of suggestions of a new group goal or a new definition of the problem. It may take the form of a suggested solution or some way of handling a difficulty that the group has encountered. Or it may take the form of a proposed new procedure for the group, a new way of organizing the group for the task ahead.

b. The *information seeker* asks for clarification of suggestions made in terms of their actual adequacy, for authoritative information and facts pertinent to the problem being discussed.

c. The *opinion seeker* asks not primarily for the facts of the case but for a clarification of the values pertinent to what the group is undertaking or of values involved in a suggestion made or in alternative suggestions.

d. The *information giver* offers facts or generalizations which are "authoritative" or relates his own experience pertinently to the group problem.

e. The *opinion giver* states his belief or opinion pertinently to a suggestion made or to alternative suggestions. The emphasis is on his proposal of what should become the group's view of pertinent values, not primarily upon relevant facts or information.

f. The *elaborator* spells out suggestions in terms of examples or developed meanings, offers a rationale for suggestions previously made, and tries to deduce how an idea or suggestion would work out if adopted by the group.

g. The *coordinator* shows or clarifies the relationships among various ideas and suggestions, tries to pull ideas and suggestions together, or tries to coordinate the activities of various members or subgroups.

h. The *orienter* defines the position of the group with respect to its goals by summarizing what has occurred, points to departures from agreed-upon directions or goals, or raises questions about the direction which the group discussion is taking.

i. The *evaluator-critic* subjects the accomplishment of the group to some standard or set of standards of group-functioning in the context of the group task. Thus he may evaluate or question the "practicality," the "logic," the "facts," or the "procedure" of a suggestion or of some unit of group discussion.

j. The *energizer* prods the group to action or decision, attempts to stimulate or arouse the group to "greater" or "higher quality" activity.

k. The *procedural technician* expedites group movement by doing things for the group—performing routine tasks (e.g., distributing materials) or manipulating objects for the group (e.g., rearranging the seating or running the recording machine, etc.)

l. The *recorder* writes down suggestions, makes a record of group decisions, or writes down the product of discussion. The recorder role is the "group memory."

Group Building and Maintenance Roles

Here the analysis of member-functions is oriented to those participations which have for their purpose the building of group-centered attitudes and orientation among the members of a group or the maintenance and perpetuation of such group-centered behavior. A given contribution may involve several

roles and a member or the "leader" may perform various roles in successive contributions.

a. The *encourager* praises, agrees with, and accepts the contribution of others. He indicates warmth and solidarity in his attitude toward other group members, offers commendation and praise, and in various ways indicates understanding and acceptance of other points of view, ideas, and suggestions.

b. The *harmonizer* mediates the differences between other members, attempts to reconcile disagreements, relieves tension in conflict situations through jesting or pouring oil on the troubled waters, etc.

c. The *compromiser* operates from within a conflict in which his idea or position is involved. He may offer compromise by yielding status, admitting his error, by disciplining himself to maintain group harmony, or by "coming half-way" in moving along with the group.

d. The *gate-keeper and expediter* attempts to keep communication channels open by encouraging or facilitating the participation of others ("We haven't got the ideas of Mr. X yet," etc.) or by proposing regulation of the flow of communication ("Why don't we limit the length of our contributions so that everyone will have a chance to contribute?", etc.)

e. The *standard setter* or *ego ideal* expresses standards for the group to attempt to achieve in its functioning or applies standards in evaluating the quality of group processes.

f. The *group-observer* and *commentator* keeps records of various aspects of group process and feeds such data with proposed interpretations into the group's evaluation of its own procedures.

g. The *follower* goes along with the movement of the group, more or less passively accepting the ideas of others, serving as an audience in group discussion and decision.

"Individual" Roles

Attempts by "members" of a group to satisfy individual needs which are irrelevant to the group task and which are nonoriented or negatively oriented to group building and maintenance set problems of group and member training. A high incidence of "individual-centered" as opposed to "group-centered" participation in a group always calls for self-diagnosis of the group. The diagnosis may reveal one or several of a number of conditions— low level of skill-training among members, including the group leader; the prevalence of "authoritarian" and "laissez faire" points of view toward group functioning in the group; a low level of group maturity, discipline, and morale; and inappropriately chosen and inadequately defined group task, etc. Whatever the diagnosis, it is in this setting that the training needs of the group are to be discovered and group training efforts to meet these needs are to be defined. The outright "suppression" of "individual roles" will deprive the group of data needed for really adequate self-diagnosis and therapy.

a. The *aggressor* may work in many ways— deflating the status of others, expressing disapproval of the values, acts, or feelings of others, attacking the group or the problem it is working on, joking aggressively, showing envy toward another's contribution by trying to take credit for it, etc.

b. The *blocker* tends to be negativistic and stubbornly resistant, disagreeing and opposing without or beyond "reason" and attempting to maintain or bring back an issue after the group has rejected or bypassed it.

c. The *recognition-seeker* works in various ways to call attention to himself, whether through boasting, reporting on personal achievements, acting in unusual ways, struggling to prevent his being placed in an "inferior" position, etc.

d. The *self-confessor* uses the audience opportunity which the group setting provides to express personal, nongroup-oriented, "feeling," "insight," "idealogy," etc.

e. The *playboy* makes a display of his lack of involvement in the group's processes. This may take the form of cynicism, nonchalance, horseplay, and other more or less studied forms of "out of field" behavior.

f. The *dominator* tries to assert authority or superiority in manipulating the group or certain members of the group. This domination may take the form of flattery, of asserting a superior status or right to attention, giving directions authoritatively, interrupting the contribution of others, etc.

g. The *help-seeker* attempts to call forth "sympathy" response from other group members or from the whole group, whether through expressions of insecurity, personal confusion or depreciation of himself beyond "reason."

h. The *special interest pleader* speaks for the "small business man," the "grass roots" community, the "housewife," "labor," and so forth, usually cloaking his own prejudices or biases in the stereotype which best fits his individual need.

The Problem of Member Role Requiredness

Identification of group task roles and of group building and maintenance roles which do actually function in processes of group discussion raises but does not answer the further question of what roles are required for "optimum" group growth and productivity. Certainly the discovery and validation of answers to this question have a high priority in any advancing science of group training and development. No attempt will be made here to review the bearing of the analyzed data from the First National Training Laboratory in Group Development on this point.

It may be useful in this discussion, however, to comment on two conditions which effective work on the problem of role-requiredness must meet. First, an answer to the problem of optimum task role requirements must be projected against a scheme of the process of group production. Groups in different stages of an act of problem selection and solution will have different role requirements. For example, a group early in the stages of problem selection which is attempting to lay out a range of possible problems to be worked on, will probably have relatively less need for the roles of "evaluator-critic," "energizer," and "coordinator" than a group which has selected and discussed its problem and is shaping a decision. The combination and balance of task role requirements is a function of the group's stage of progress with respect to its task. Second, the group building role requirements of a group are a function of its stage of development—its level of group maturity. For example, a "young" group will probably require less of the role of the "standard setter" than a more mature group. Too high a level of aspiration may frustrate a "young" group where a more mature group will be able to take the same level of aspiration in its stride. Again, the role of "group observer and commentator" must be carefully adapted to the level of maturity of the group. Probably the distinction between "group" and "individual" roles can be drawn much more sharply in a relatively mature than in a "young" group.

Meanwhile, group trainers cannot wait for a fully developed science of group training before they undertake to diagnose the role requirements of the groups with which they work and to help these groups to share in such diagnosis. Each group which is attempting to improve the quality of its functioning as a group must be helped to diagnose its role requirements and must attempt to train members to fill the required roles effectively. This describes one of the principal objectives of training of group members.

The Problem of Role Flexibility

The previous group experience of members, where this experience has included little conscious attention to the variety of roles involved in effective group production and development, has frequently stereotyped the member into a limited range of roles. These he plays in all group discussions whether or not the group situation requires them. Some members see themselves primarily as "evaluator-critics" and play this role in and out of season. Others may play the roles of "encourager" or of "energizer" or of "information giver" with only small sensitivity to the role requirements of a given group situation. The development of skill and insight in diagnosing role requirements has already been mentioned as an objective of group member training. An equally important objective is the development of role flexibility, of skill and security in a wide range of member roles, on the part of all group members.

A science of group training, as it develops, must be concerned with the relationships between the personality structures of group members and the character and range of member roles which various personality structures support and permit. A science of group training must seek to discover and accept the limitations which group training per se encounters in altering personality structures in the service of greater role flexibility on the part of all members of a group. Even though we recognize the importance of this caution, the objective of developing role flexibility remains an important objective of group member training.

Methods of Group Member Training

The objectives in training group members have been identified. Some of the kinds of resistances encountered in training group members to diagnose the role requirements of a group situation and to acquire skill in a variety of member roles have been suggested. Before analyzing briefly the methods used for group member training in the First National Training Laboratory, a few additional comments on resistances to member training may be useful. The problem of group training is actually a problem of retraining. Members of a training group have had other group experiences. They bring to the training experience attitudes toward group work, more or less conscious skills for dealing with leaders and other members, and a more or less highly developed rationale of group processes. These may or may not support processes of democratic operation in the training group. Where they do not, they function as resistances to retraining. Again, trainees are inclined to make little or no distinction between the roles they perform in a group and their personalities. Criticism of the role a group member plays is perceived as criticism of "himself." Methods must be found to reduce ego-defensiveness toward criticism of member roles. Finally, training groups must be helped to make a distinction between group feeling and group productivity. Groups which attain a state of good group feeling often perceive attempts to diagnose and criticize their level of productivity as threats to this feeling of group warmth and solidarity.

1. Each Basic Skill Training group in the Laboratory used self-observation and diagnosis of its own growth and development as a primary means of member training.

a. Sensitization to the variety of roles involved in and required by group functioning began during the introduction of members to the group. In one BST group, this early sensitization to member role variety and role requiredness began with the "leader's" summarizing, as part of his introduction of himself to the group, certain of the member roles in which he was usually cast by groups and other roles which he found it difficult to play, even when needed by the group. He asked the group's help in criticizing and improving his skill in those roles where he felt weakest. Other members followed suit. Various members showed widely different degrees of sensitivity to the operation of member roles in groups and to the degree of their own proficiency in different roles. This introduction procedure gave the group a partial listing of member roles for later use and supplementation, initial self-assessments of member strengths and weaknesses, and diagnostic material concerning the degree of group self-sophistication among the members. The training job had come to be seen by most members as a retraining job.

b. A description of the use of training observers in group self-evaluation sessions is given in the next paper in this issue (David H. Jenkins, "Feedback and Group Self-Evaluation"). At this point, only the central importance which self-evaluation sessions played in member training needs to be stressed. Research observers fed observational data concerning group functioning into periodic discussions by the group of its strengths and weaknesses as a group. Much of these data concerned role requirements for the job the group had been attempting, which roles had been present, which roles had probably been

needed. "Individual" roles were identified and interpreted in an objective and nonblaming manner. Out of these discussions, group members came to identify various kinds of member roles, to relate role requiredness to stages in group production and in group growth, and to assess the range of roles each was able to play well when required. Out of these discussions came group decisions concerning the supplying of needed roles in the next session. Member commitments concerning behavior in future sessions also came out of these evaluations. These took the form both of silent commitments and of public commitments in which the help of the group was requested.

c. Recordings of segments of the group's discussion were used by most Basic Skill Training groups. Groups listened to themselves, diagnosed the member and leader functions involved, and assessed the adequacy of these.

2. Role-played sessions in each group, although they were pointed content-wise to the skills of the change agent, offered important material for the diagnosis of member roles and of role-requiredness. These sessions offered an important supplement to group self-diagnosis and evaluation. It is easier for members to get perspective on their participation in a role-played episode of group process than it is on their own participation in a "real" group. The former is not perceived as "real." The role is more easily disengaged for purposes of analysis and evaluation from the person playing the role. Ego-defensiveness toward the role as enacted is reduced. Role-playing sessions also provided practice opportunity to members in a variety of roles.

3. Practice by group members of the role of *observer-commentator* is especially valuable in developing skill in diagnosing member roles and in assessing the role requirements of a group situation. In several groups, each member in turn served as observer, supplementing the work of the research observers in evaluation sessions. Such members worked more or less closely with the anecdotal observer for the group on skill-problems encountered. Practice opportunity in the *observer-commentator* role was also provided in clinic group meetings in the afternoon.

Summary

Training in group membership roles requires the identification and analysis of various member roles actually enacted in group processes. It involves further the analysis of group situations in terms of roles required in relation both to a schema of group production and to a conception of group growth and development. A group's self-observation and self-evaluation of its own processes provides useful content and practice opportunity in member training. Practice in enacting a wider range of required roles and in role flexibility can come out of member commitment to such practice with help from the group in evaluating and improving the required skills. Member training is typically retraining and resistances to retraining can be reduced by creating a nonblaming and objective atmosphere in group self-evaluation and by using role-playing of group processes for diagnosis and practice. The training objectives of developing skill in the diagnosis of group role requirements and developing role flexibility among members also indicate important research areas for a science of group training.

Endnote

1. A somewhat different analysis of member-participations, in terms of categories used by interaction observers in observation of group processes in the First National Training Laboratory, is described in the *Preliminary Report* of the laboratory, pages 122–32. The number of categories used by interaction observers was "directed primarily by limitations of observer load."

Reading 31

Choosing the Depth of Organizational Intervention

Roger Harrison

Since World War II there has been a great prolif-eration of behavioral science-based methods by which consultants seek to facilitate growth and change in individuals, groups, and organizations. The methods range from operations analysis and manipulation of the organization chart, through the use of Grid laboratories, T-groups, and non-verbal techniques. As was true in the development of clinical psychology and psychotherapy, the early stages of this developmental process tend to be accompanied by considerable competition, criticism, and argument about the relative merits of various approaches. It is my conviction that controversy over the relative goodness or badness, effectiveness or ineffectiveness, of various change strategies really accomplishes very little in the way of increased knowledge or unification of be-havioral science. As long as we are arguing about what method is better than another, we tend to learn very little about how various approaches fit together or complement one another, and we cer-tainly make more difficult and ambiguous the task of bringing these competing points of view within one overarching system of knowledge about human processes.

As our knowledge increases, it begins to be ap-parent that these competing change strategies are not really different ways of doing the same thing—some more effective and some less effective—but rather that they are different ways of doing *different* things. They touch the individual, the group, or the organization in different aspects of their function-

Source: Roger Harrison, "Choosing the Depth of Organizational Intervention" in *Journal of Applied Behavioral Science* (6, no.2), pp. 182–202, copyright © 1970 by NTL Institute of Applied Behavoiral Science. Reprinted by permission of Sage Publications, Inc.

ing. They require differing kinds and amounts of commitment on the part of the client for them to be successful, and they demand different varieties and levels of skills and abilities on the part of the practitioner.

I believe that there is a real need for conceptual models which differentiate intervention strategies from one another in a way which permits rational matching of strategies to organizational change problems. The purpose of this paper is to present a modest beginning which I have made toward a conceptualization of strategies, and to derive from this conceptualization some criteria for choosing appropriate methods of intervention in particular applications.

The point of view of this paper is that the depth of individual emotional involvement in the change process can be a central concept for differentiating change strategies. In focusing on this dimension, we are concerned with the extent to which core ar-eas of the personality or self are the focus of the change attempt. Strategies which touch the more deep, personal, private, and central aspects of the individual or his relationships with others fall to-ward the deeper end of this continuum. Strategies which deal with more external aspects of the indi-vidual and which focus on the more formal and public aspects of role behavior tend to fall toward the surface end of the depth dimension. This di-mension has the advantage that it is relatively easy to rank change strategies upon it and to get fairly close consensus as to the ranking. It is a widely discussed dimension of difference which has meaning and relevance to practitioners and their clients. I hope in this paper to promote greater flexibility and rationality in choosing appropriate depths of intervention. I shall approach this task by examining the effects of interventions at various depths. I shall also explore the ways in which two important organizational processes tend to make demands and to set limits upon the depth of intervention which can produce effective change in organizational functioning. These two processes are the autonomy of organization members and their own perception of their needs for help.

Before illustrating the concept by ranking five common intervention strategies along the dimension of depth, I should like to define the dimension somewhat more precisely. We are concerned essentially with how private, individual, and hidden are the issues and processes about which the consultant attempts directly to obtain information and which he seeks to influence. If the consultant seeks information about relatively public and observable aspects of behavior and relationships, if he tries to influence directly only these relatively surface characteristics and processes, we would then categorize his intervention strategy as being closer to the surface. If, on the other hand, the consultant seeks information about very deep and private perceptions, attitudes, or feelings, and if he intervenes in a way which directly affects these processes, then we would classify his intervention strategy as one of considerable depth. To illustrate the surface end of the dimension let us look first at operations research or operations analysis. This strategy is concerned with the roles and functions to be performed within the organization, generally with little regard to the individual characteristics of persons occupying the roles. The change strategy is to manipulate role relationships; in other words, to redistribute the tasks, the resources, and the relative power attached to various roles in the organization. This is essentially a process of rational analysis in which the tasks which need to be performed are determined and specified and then sliced up into role definitions for persons and groups in the organization. The operations analyst does not ordinarily need to know much about particular people. Indeed, his function is to design the organization in such a way that its successful operation does not depend too heavily upon any uniquely individual skills,

abilities, values, or attitudes of persons in various roles. He may perform this function adequately without knowing in advance who the people are who will fill these slots. Persons are assumed to be moderately interchangeable, and in order to make this approach work it is necessary to design the organization so that the capacities, needs, and values of the individual which are relevant to role performance are relatively public and observable, and are possessed by a fairly large proportion of the population from which organization members are drawn. The approach is certainly one of very modest depth.

Somewhat deeper are those strategies which are based upon evaluating individual performance and attempting to manipulate it directly. Included in this approach is much of the industrial psychologist's work in selection, placement, appraisal, and counseling of employees. The intervener is concerned with what the individual is able and likely to do and achieve, rather than with processes internal to the individual. Direct attempts to influence performance may be made through the application of rewards and punishments, such as promotions, salary increases, or transfers within the organization. An excellent illustration of this focus on end results is the practice of management by objectives. The intervention process is focused on establishing mutually agreed-upon goals for performance between the individual and his supervisor. The practice is considered to be particularly advantageous because it permits the supervisor to avoid a focus on personal characteristics of the subordinate, particularly those deeper, more central characteristics which managers generally have difficulty in discussing with those who work under their supervision. The process is designed to limit information exchange to that which is public and observable, such as the setting of performance goals and the success or failure of the individual in attaining them.

Because of its focus on end results, rather than on the process by which those results are achieved, management by objectives must be considered less deep than the broad area of concern with work style which I shall term instrumental process analysis. We are concerned here not only with performance but with the processes by which that performance is achieved. However, we are primarily concerned with styles and processes of work rather than with the processes of interpersonal relationships which I would classify as being deeper on the basic dimension.

In instrumental process analysis we are concerned with how a person likes to organize and conduct his work and with the impact which this style of work has on others in the organization. Principally, we are concerned with how a person perceives his role, what he values and disvalues in it, and what he works hard on and what he chooses to ignore. We are also interested in the instrumental acts which the individual directs toward others: delegating authority or reserving decisions to himself, communicating or withholding information, collaborating or competing with others on work-related issues. The focus on instrumentality means that we are interested in the person primarily as a doer of work or as a performer of functions related to the goals of the organization. We are interested in what facilitates or inhibits his effective task performance.

We are not interested per se whether his relationships with others are happy or unhappy, whether they perceive him as too warm or too cold, too authoritarian or too laissez-faire, or any other of the many interpersonal relationships which arise as people associate in organizations. However, I do not mean to imply that the line between instrumental relationships and interpersonal ones is an easy one to draw in action and practice, or even that it is desirable that this be done.

Depth Gauges: Level of Tasks and Feelings

What I am saying is that an intervention strategy can focus on instrumentality or it can focus on interpersonal relationships, and that there are important consequences of this difference in depth of intervention.

When we intervene at the level of instrumentality, it is to change work behavior and working relationships. Frequently this involves the process of bargaining or negotiation between groups and individuals. Diagnoses are made of the satisfactions or dissatisfactions of organization members with one another's work behavior. Reciprocal adjustments, bargains, and trade-offs can then be arranged in which each party gets some modification in the behavior of the other at the cost to him of some reciprocal accommodation. Much of the intervention strategy which has been developed around Blake's concept of the Managerial Grid is at this level and involves bargaining and negotiation of role behavior as an important change process.

At the deeper level of interpersonal relationships the focus is on feelings, attitudes, and perceptions which organization members have about others. At this level we are concerned with the quality of human relationships within the organization, with warmth and coldness of members to one another, and with the experiences of acceptance and rejection, love and hate, trust and suspicion among groups and individuals. At this level the consultant probes for normally hidden feelings, attitudes, and perceptions. He works to create relationships of openness about feelings and to help members to develop mutual understanding of one another as persons. Interventions are directed toward helping organization members to be more comfortable in being authentically themselves with one another, and the degree of mutual caring and concern is expected to increase. Sensitivity training using T-groups is a basic intervention strategy at this level. T-group educators emphasize increased personalization of relationships, the development of trust and openness, and the exchange of feelings. Interventions at this level deal directly and intensively with interpersonal emotionality. This is the first intervention strategy we have examined which is at a depth where the feelings of organization members about one another as persons are a direct focus of the intervention strategy. At the other levels, such feelings certainly exist and may be expressed, but they are not a direct concern of the intervention. The transition from the task orientation of instrumental process analysis to the feeling orientation of interpersonal process analysis seems, as I shall suggest later, to be a critical one for many organization members.

The deepest level of intervention which will be considered in this paper is that of intrapersonal analysis. Here the consultant uses a variety of methods to reveal the individual's deeper attitudes, values, and conflicts regarding his own functioning, identity, and existence. The focus is generally on increasing the range of experiences which the individual can bring into awareness and cope with. The material may be dealt with at the fantasy or symbolic level, and the intervention strategies include many which are non-interpersonal and non-verbal. Some examples of this approach are the use of marathon T-group sessions, the creative risk-taking laboratory approach of Byrd (1967), and some aspects of the task group therapy approach of Clark (1966). These approaches all tend to bring into focus very deep and intense feelings about one's own identity and one's relationships with significant others.

Although I have characterized deeper interventions as dealing increasingly with the individual's affective life, I do not imply that issues at less deep levels may not be emotionally charged. Issues of role differentiation, reward distribution, ability and performance evaluation, for example, are frequently invested with strong feelings. The concept of depth is concerned more with the *accessibility* and *individuality* of attitudes, values, and perceptions than it is with their strength. This narrowing of the common usage of the term *depth* is necessary to avoid the contradictions which occur when strength and inaccessibility are confused. For instance, passionate value confrontation and bitter conflict have frequently occurred between labor and management over economic issues which are surely toward the surface end of my concept of depth.

In order to understand the importance of the concept of depth for choosing interventions in organizations, let us consider the effects upon organization members of working at different levels.

The first of the important concomitants of depth is the degree of dependence of the client on the special competence of the change agent. At the surface end of the depth dimension, the methods of intervention are easily communicated and made public. The client may reasonably expect to learn something of the change agent's skills to improve his own practice. At the deeper levels, such as interpersonal and intrapersonal process analyses, it is more difficult for the client to understand the methods of intervention. The change agent is more likely to be seen as a person of special and unusual powers not found in ordinary men. Skills of intervention and change are less frequently learned by organization members, and the change process may tend to become personalized around the change agent as leader. Programs of change which are so dependent upon personal relationships and individual expertise are difficult to institutionalize. When the change agent leaves the system, he may not only take his expertise with him but the entire change process as well.

A second aspect of the change process which varies with depth is the extent to which the benefits of an intervention are transferable to members of the organization not originally participating in the change process. At surface levels of operations analysis and performance evaluation, the effects are institutionalized in the form of procedures, policies, and practices of the organization which may have considerable permanence beyond the tenure of individuals. At the level of instrumental behavior, the continuing effects of intervention are more likely to reside in the informal norms of groups within the organization regarding such matters as delegation, communication, decision making, competition and collaboration, and conflict resolution.

At the deepest levels of intervention, the target of change is the individual's inner life; and if the intervention is successful, the permanence of individual change should be greatest. There are indeed dramatic reports of cases in which persons have changed their careers and life goals as a result of such interventions, and the persistence of such change appears to be relatively high.

One consequence, then, of the level of intervention is that with greater depth of focus the individual increasingly becomes both the target and the carrier of change. In the light of this analysis, it is not surprising to observe that deeper levels of intervention are increasingly being used at higher organizational levels and in scientific and service organizations where the contribution of the individual has greatest impact.

An important concomitant of depth is that, as the level of intervention becomes deeper, the information needed to intervene effectively becomes less available. At the less personal level of operations analysis, the information is often a matter of record. At the level of performance evaluation, it is a matter of observation. On the other hand, reactions of others to a person's work style are less likely to be discussed freely, and the more personal responses to his interpersonal style are even less likely to be readily given. At the deepest levels, important information may not be available to the individual himself. Thus as we go deeper the consultant must use more of his time and skill uncovering information which is ordinarily private and hidden. This is one reason for the greater costs of interventions at deeper levels of focus.

Another aspect of the change process which varies with the depth of intervention is the personal risk and unpredictability of outcome for the individual. At deeper levels we deal with aspects of the individual's view of himself and his relationships with others which are relatively untested by exposure to the evaluations and emotional reactions of others. If in the change process the individual's self-perceptions are strongly disconfirmed, the resulting imbalance in internal forces may produce sudden changes in behavior, attitudes, and personality integration.

Because of the private and hidden nature of the processes into which we intervene at deeper levels, it is difficult to predict the individual impact of the change process in advance. The need for clinical sensitivity and skill on the part of the practitioner thus increases, since he must be prepared to diagnose and deal with developing situations involving considerable stress upon individuals.

The foregoing analysis suggests a criterion by which to match intervention strategies to particular organizational problems. It is *to intervene at a level no deeper than that required to produce enduring solutions to the problems at hand.* This criterion derives directly from the observations above. The cost, skill demands, client dependency, and variability of outcome all increase with depth of intervention. Further, as the depth of intervention increases, the effects tend to locate more in the individual and less in the organization. The danger of losing the organization's investment in the change with the departure of the individual becomes a significant consideration.

Autonomy Increases Depth of Intervention

While this general criterion is simple and straightforward, its application is not. In particular, although the criterion should operate in the direction of less depth of intervention, there is a general trend in modern organizational life which tends to push the intervention level ever deeper. This trend is toward increased self-direction of organization members and increased independence of external pressures and incentives. I believe that there is a direct relationship between the autonomy of individuals and the depth of intervention needed to effect organizational change.

Before going on to discuss this relationship, I shall acknowledge freely that I cannot prove the existence of a trend toward a general increase in freedom of individuals within organizations. I intend only to assert the great importance of the degree of individual autonomy in determining the level of intervention which will be effective.

In order to understand the relationship between autonomy and depth of intervention, it is necessary to conceptualize a dimension which parallels and is implied by the depth dimension we have been discussing. This is the dimension of predictability and variability among persons in their responses to the different kinds of incentives which may be used to influence behavior in the organization. The key assumption in this analysis that the more unpredictable and unique is the individual's response to the particular kinds of controls and incentives one can bring to bear upon him, the more one must know about that person in order to influence his behavior.

Most predictable and least individual is the response of the person to economic and bureaucratic controls when his needs for economic income and security are high. It is not necessary to delve very deeply into a person's inner processes in order to influence his behavior if we know that he badly needs his income and his position and if we are in a position to control his access to these rewards. Responses to economic and bureaucratic controls tend to be relatively simple and on the surface.

Independence of Economic Incentive

If for any reason organization members become relatively uninfluenceable through the manipulation of their income and economic security, the management of performance becomes strikingly more complex; and the need for more personal information about the individual increases. Except very generally, we do not know automatically or in advance what styles of instrumental or interpersonal interaction will be responded to as negative or positive incentives by the individual. One person may appreciate close supervision and direction; another may value independence of direction. One may prefer to work alone; another may function best when he is in close communication with others. One may thrive in close, intimate, personal interaction; while others are made uncomfortable by any but cool and distant relationships with colleagues.

What I am saying is that, when bureaucratic and economic incentives lose their force for whatever reason, the improvement of performance *must* involve linking organizational goals to the individual's attempts to meet his own needs for satisfying instrumental activities and interpersonal relationships. It is for this reason that I make the assertion that increases in personal autonomy dictate change interventions at deeper and more personal levels. In order to obtain the information necessary to link organizational needs to individual goals, one must probe fairly deeply into the attitudes, values, and emotions of the organization members.

If the need for deeper personal information becomes great when we intervene at the instrumental and interpersonal levels, it becomes even greater when one is dealing with organization members who are motivated less through their transactions with the environment and more in response to internal values and standards. An example is the researcher, engineer, or technical specialist whose work behavior may be influenced more by his own values and standards of creativity or professional excellence than by his relationships with others. The deepest organizational interventions at the intrapersonal level may be required in order to effect change when working with persons who are highly self-directed.

Let me summarize my position about the relationship among autonomy, influence, and level of intervention. As the individual becomes less subject to economic and bureaucratic pressures, he tends to seek more intangible rewards in the organization which come from both the instrumental and interpersonal aspects of the system. I view this as a shift from greater external to more internal control and as an increase in autonomy. Further shifts in this direction may involve increased independence of rewards and punishments mediated by others, in favor of operation in accordance with internal values and standards.

I view organizations as systems of reciprocal influence. Achievement of organization goals is facilitated when individuals can seek their own satisfactions through activity which promotes the goals of the organization. As the satisfactions which are of most value to the individual change, so must the reciprocal influence systems, if the organization goals are to continue to be met.

If the individual changes are in the direction of increased independence of external incentives, then the influence systems must change to provide opportunities for individuals to achieve more intangible, self-determined satisfactions in their work. However, people are more differentiated, complex, and unique in their intangible goals and values than in their economic needs. In order to create systems which offer a wide variety of intangible satisfactions, much more private information about individuals is needed than is required to create and maintain systems based chiefly on economic and bureaucratic controls. For this reason, deeper interventions are called for when the system which they would attempt to change contains a high proportion of relatively autonomous individuals.

There are a number of factors promoting autonomy, all tending to free the individual from dependence upon economic and bureaucratic controls, which I have observed in my work with organizations. Wherever a number of these factors obtain, it is probably an indication that deeper levels of intervention are required to effect lasting improvements in organizational functioning. I shall simply list these indicators briefly in categories to show what kinds of things might signify to the practitioner that deeper levels of intervention may be appropriate.

The first category includes anything which makes the evaluation of individual performance difficult:

A long time span between the individual's actions and the results by which effectiveness of performance is to be judged.

Nonrepetitive, unique tasks which cannot be evaluated by reference to the performance of others on similar tasks.

Specialized skills and abilities possessed by an individual which cannot be evaluated by a supervisor who does not possess the skills or knowledge himself.

The second category concerns economic conditions:

Arrangements which secure the job tenure and/or income to the individual.

A market permitting easy transfer from one organization to another (e.g., engineers in the United States aerospace industry).

Unique skills and knowledge of the individual which make him difficult to replace.

The third category includes characteristics of the system or its environment which lead to independence of the parts of the organization and decentralization of authority such as:

An organization which works on a project basis instead of producing a standard line of products.

An organization in which subparts must be given latitude to deal rapidly and flexibly with frequent environmental change.

I should like to conclude the discussion of this criterion for depth of intervention with a brief reference to the ethics of intervention, a problem which merits considerably more thorough treatment than I can give it here.

The Ethics of Delving Deeper

There is considerable concern in the United States about invasion of privacy by behavioral scientists. I would agree that such invasion of privacy is an actual as well as a fantasized concomitant of the use of organizational change strategies of greater depth. The recourse by organizations to such strategies has been widely viewed as an indication of greater organizational control over the most personal and private aspects of the lives of the members. The present analysis suggests, however, that recourse to these deeper interventions actually reflects the greater *freedom* of organization members from traditionally crude and impersonal means of organizational control. There is no reason to be concerned about man's attitudes or values or interpersonal relationships when his job performance can be controlled by brute force, by economic coercion, or by bureaucratic rules and regulations. The "invasion of privacy" becomes worth the cost, bother, and uncertainty of outcome only when the individual has achieved relative independence from control by other means. Put another way, it makes organizational sense to try to get a man to *want* to do something only if you cannot *make* him do it. And regardless of what intervention strategy is used, the individual still retains considerably greater control over his own behavior than he had when he could be manipulated more crudely. As long as we can maintain a high degree of voluntarism regarding the nature and extent of an individual's participation in the deeper organizational change strategies, these strategies can work toward adapting the organization to the individual quite as much as they work the other way around. Only when an individual's participation in one of the deeper change strategies is coerced by economic or bureaucratic pressures, do I feel that the ethics of the intervention clearly run counter to the values of a democratic society.

Role of Client Norms and Values in Determining Depth

So far our attention to the choice of level of intervention has focused upon locating the depth at which the information exists which must be exchanged to facilitate system improvement. Unfortunately, the choice of an intervention strategy cannot practically be made with reference to this criterion alone. Even if a correct diagnosis is made of the level at which the relevant information lies, we may not be able to work effectively at the desired depth because of client norms, values, resistances, and fears.

In an attempt to develop a second criterion for depth of intervention which takes such dispositions on the part of the client into account, I have considered two approaches which represent polarized orientations to the problem. One approach is based upon analyzing and overcoming client resistance; the other is based upon discovering and joining forces with the self-articulated wants or "felt needs" of the client.

There are several ways of characterizing these approaches. To me, the simplest is to point out that when the change agent is resistance-oriented he tends to lead or influence the client to work at a depth greater than that at which the latter feels comfortable. When resistance-oriented, the change agent tends to mistrust the client's statement of his problems and of the areas where he wants help. He suspects the client's presentation of being a smoke screen or defense against admission of his "real" problems and needs. The consultant works to expose the underlying processes and concerns and to influence the client to work at a deeper level. The resistance-oriented approach grows out of the work of clinicians and psychotherapists, and it characterizes much of the work of organizational consultants who specialize in sensitivity training and deeper intervention strategies.

On the other hand, change agents may be oriented to the self-articulated needs of clients. When so oriented, the consultant tends more to follow and facilitate the client in working at whatever level the latter sets for himself. He may assist the client in defining problems and needs and in working on solutions, but he is inclined to try to anchor his work in the norms, values, and accepted standards of behavior of the organization.

I believe that there is a tendency for change agents working at the interpersonal and deeper levels to adopt a rather consistent resistance-oriented approach. Consultants so oriented seem to take a certain quixotic pride in dramatically and self-consciously violating organizational norms. Various techniques have been developed for pressuring or seducing organizations' members into departing from organizational norms in the service of change. The "marathon" T-group is a case in point, where the increased irritability and fatigue of prolonged contact and lack of sleep move participants to deal with one another more emotionally, personally, and spontaneously than they would normally be willing to do.

I suspect that unless such norm-violating intervention efforts actually succeed in changing organizational norms, their effects are relatively short-lived, because the social structures and interpersonal linkages have not been created which can utilize for day-to-day problem solving the deeper information produced by the intervention. It is true that the consultant may succeed in producing information, but he is less likely to succeed in creating social structures which can continue to work in his absence. The problem is directly analogous to that of the community developer who succeeds by virtue of his personal influence in getting villagers to build a school or a community center which falls into disuse as soon as he leaves because of the lack of any integration of these achievements into the social structure and day-to-day needs and desires of the community. Community developers have had to learn through bitter failure and frustration that ignoring or subverting the standards and norms of a social system often results in temporary success followed by a reactionary increase in resistance to the influence of the change agent. On the other hand, felt needs embody those problems, issues, and difficulties which have a high conscious priority on the part of community or organization members. We can expect individuals and groups to be ready to invest time, energy, and resources in dealing with their felt needs, while they will be relatively passive or even resistant toward those who attempt to help them with externally defined needs. Community developers have found that attempts to help with felt needs are met with greater receptivity, support, and integration within the structure and life of the community than are intervention attempts which rely primarily upon the developer's value system for setting need priorities.

The emphasis of many organizational change agents on confronting and working through resistances was developed originally in the practice of individual psychoanalysis and psychotherapy, and it is also a central concept in the conduct of therapy groups and sensitivity training laboratories. In all of these situations, the change agent has a high degree of environmental control and is at least temporarily in a high status position with respect to the client. To a degree that is frequently underestimated by practitioners, we manage to create a situation in which it is more unpleasant for the client to leave than it is to stay and submit to the pressure to confront and work through resistances. I believe that the tendency is for behavioral scientists to overplay their hands when they move from the clinical and training situations where they have environmental control to the or-

ganizational consulting situation where their control is sharply attenuated.

This attenuation derives only partially from the relative ease with which the client can terminate the relationship. Even if this most drastic step is not taken, the consultant can be tolerated, misled, and deceived in ways which are relatively difficult in the therapeutic or human relations training situations. He can also be openly defied and blocked if he runs afoul of strongly shared group norms; whereas when the consultant is dealing with a group of strangers, he can often utilize differences among the members to overcome this kind of resistance. I suspect that, in general, behavioral scientists underestimate their power in working with individuals and groups of strangers, and overestimate it when working with individuals and groups in organizations. I emphasize this point because I believe that a good many potentially fruitful and mutually satisfying consulting relationships are terminated early because of the consultant's taking the role of overcomer of resistance to change, rather than that of collaborator in the client's attempts at solving his problems. It is these considerations which lead me to suggest my second criterion for the choice of organization intervention strategy: *to intervene at a level no deeper than that at which the energy and resources of the client can be committed to problem solving and to change.* These energies and resources can be mobilized through obtaining legitimation for the intervention in the norms of the organization and through devising intervention strategies which have clear relevance to consciously felt needs on the part of the organization members.

The Consultant's Dilemma: Felt Needs versus Deeper Levels

Unfortunately, it is doubtless true that the forces which influence the conditions we desire to change often exist at deeper levels than can be dealt with by adhering to the criterion of working within organization norms and meeting felt needs. The level at which an individual or group is willing and ready to invest energy and resources is probably always determined partly by a realistic assessment of the problems and partly by a defensive need to avoid confrontation and significant change. It is thus not likely that our two criteria for selection of intervention depth will result in the same decisions when practically applied. It is not the same to intervene at the level where behavior-determining forces are most potent as it is to work on felt needs as they are articulated by the client. This, it seems to me, is the consultant's dilemma. It always has been. We are continually faced with the choice between leading the client into areas which are threatening, unfamiliar, and dependency-provoking for him (and where our own expertise shows up to best advantage) or, on the other hand, being guided by the client's own understanding of his problems and his willingness to invest resources in particular kinds of relatively familiar and nonthreatening strategies.

When time permits, this dilemma is ideally dealt with by intervening first at a level where there is good support from the norms, power structure, and felt needs of organizational members. The consultant can then, over a period of time, develop trust, sophistication, and support within the organization to explore deeper levels at which particularly important forces may be operating. This would probably be agreed to, at least in principle, by most organizational consultants. The point at which I feel I differ from a significant number of workers in this field is that I would advocate that interventions should *always* be limited to the depth of the client's felt needs and readiness to legitimize intervention. I believe we should always avoid moving deeper at a pace which outstrips a client system's willingness to subject itself to exposure, dependence, and threat. What I am saying is that, if the dominant response of organization members indicates that an intervention violates system norms regarding exposure, privacy, and confrontation, then one has intervened too deeply and should pull back to a level at which organization members are more ready to invest their own energy in the change process. This point of view is thus in opposition to that which sees neg-

ative reactions primarily as indications of resistances which are to be brought out into the open, confronted, and worked through as a central part of the intervention process. I believe that behavioral scientists acting as organizational consultants have tended to place overmuch emphasis on the overcoming of resistance to change and have underemphasized the importance of enlisting in the service of change the energies and resources which the client can consciously direct and willingly devote to problem solving.

What is advocated here is that we in general accept the client's felt needs or the problems he presents as real and that we work on them at a level at which he can serve as a competent and willing collaborator. This position is in opposition to one which sees the presenting problem as more or less a smoke screen or barrier. I am not advocating this point of view because I value the right to privacy of organization members more highly than I value their growth and development or the solution of organization problems. (This is an issue which concerns me, but it is enormously more complex than the ones with which I am dealing in this paper.) Rather, I place first priority on collaboration with the client, because I do not think we are frequently successful consultants without it.

In my own practice I have observed that the change in client response is frequently quite striking when I move from a resistance-oriented approach to an acceptance of the client's norms and definitions of his own needs. With quite a few organizational clients in the United States, the line of legitimacy seems to lie somewhere between interventions at the instrumental level and those focused on interpersonal relationships. Members who exhibit hostility, passivity, and dependence when I initiate intervention at the interpersonal level may become dramatically more active, collaborative, and involved when I shift the focus to the instrumental level.

If I intervene directly at the level of interpersonal relationships, I can be sure that at least some members, and often the whole group, will react with anxiety, passive resistance, and low or negative commitment to the change process. Furthermore, they express their resistance in terms of norms and values regarding the appropriateness or legitimacy of dealing at this level. They say things like, "It isn't right to force people's feelings about one another out into the open"; "I don't see what this has to do with improving organizational effectiveness"; "People are being encouraged to say things which are better left unsaid."

If I then switch to a strategy which focuses on decision making, delegation of authority, information exchange, and other instrumental questions, these complaints about illegitimacy and the inappropriateness of the intervention are usually sharply reduced. This does not mean that the clients are necessarily comfortable or free from anxiety in the discussions, nor does it mean that strong feelings may not be expressed about one another's behavior. What is different is that the clients are more likely to *work with* instead of *against* me, to feel and express some sense of ownership in the change process, and to see many more possibilities for carrying it on among themselves in the absence of the consultant.

What I have found is that, when I am resistance-oriented in my approach to the client, I am apt to feel rather uncomfortable in "letting sleeping dogs lie." When, on the other hand, I orient myself to the client's own assessment of his needs, I am uncomfortable when I feel I am leading or pushing the client to operate very far outside the shared norms of the organization. I have tried to indicate why I believe the latter orientation is more appropriate. I realize of course that many highly sophisticated and talented practitioners will not agree with me.

In summary, I have tried to show in this paper that the dimension of depth should be central to the conceptualization of intervention strategies. I have presented what I believe are the major consequences of intervening at greater or lesser depths; and from these consequences I have suggested two criteria for choosing the appropriate depth of intervention: first, *to intervene at a level no deeper than that required to produce enduring solutions to the problems at hand;* and second, *to intervene at a level no deeper than that at which the energy and resources of the client can be committed to problem solving and to change.*

I have analyzed the tendency for increases in individual autonomy in organizations to push the appropriate level of intervention deeper when the first criterion is followed. Opposed to this is the countervailing influence of the second criterion to work closer to the surface in order to enlist the energy and support of organization members in the change process. Arguments have been presented for resolving this dilemma in favor of the second, more conservative, criterion. The dilemma remains, of course, the continuing tension under which the change agent works is between the desire to lead and push, or to collaborate and follow. The middle ground is never very stable, and I suspect we show our values and preferences by which criterion we choose to maximize when we are under the stress of difficult and ambiguous client-consultant relationships.

References

Byrd, R. E. "Training in a Nongroup." *Journal of Humanistic Psychology* 7, no. 1 (1967), pp. 18–27.

Clark, J. V. "Task Group Therapy." Unpublished manuscript, University of California, Los Angeles, 1966.

Reading 32

Rules of Thumb for Change Agents

Herbert A. Shepard

The following aphorisms are not so much bits of advice (although they are stated that way) as things to think about when you are being a change agent, a consultant, an organization or community development practitioner—or when you are just being yourself trying to bring about something that involves other people.

Rule I: Stay Alive

This rule counsels against self-sacrifice on behalf of a cause that you do not wish to be your last.

Two exceptionally talented doctoral students came to the conclusion that the routines they had to go through to get their degrees were absurd, and decided they would be untrue to themselves to conform to an absurd system. That sort of reasoning is almost always self-destructive. Besides, their noble gesture in quitting would be unlikely to have any impact whatever on the system they were taking a stand against.

This is not to say that one should never take a stand, or a survival risk. But such risks should be taken as part of a purposeful strategy of change, and appropriately timed and targeted. When they are taken under such circumstances, one is very much alive.

But Rule I is much more than a survival rule. The rule means that you should let your whole being be involved in the undertaking. Since most of us have never been in touch with our whole beings, it means a lot of putting together of parts

that have been divided, of using internal communications channels that have been closed or were never opened.

Staying alive means loving yourself. Self-disparagement leads to the suppression of potentials, to a win-lose formulation of the world, and to wasting life in defensive maneuvering.

Staying alive means staying in touch with your purpose. It means using your skills, your emotions, your labels and positions, rather than being used by them. It means not being trapped in other people's games. It means turning yourself on and off, rather than being dependent on the situation. It means choosing with a view to the consequences as well as the impulse. It means going with the flow even while swimming against it. It means living in several worlds without being swallowed up in any. It means seeing dilemmas as opportunities for creativity. It means greeting absurdity with laughter while trying to unscramble it. It means capturing the moment in the light of the future. It means seeing the environment through the eyes of your purpose.

Rule II: Start Where the System Is

This is such ancient wisdom that one might expect its meaning had been fully explored and apprehended. Yet in practice, the rule—and the system—are often violated.

The rule implies that one should begin by diagnosing the system. But systems do not necessarily *like* being diagnosed. Even the term *diagnosis* may be offensive. And the system may be even less ready for someone who calls himself or herself a change agent. It is easy for the practitioner to forget that the use of jargon, which pre-

Source: Herbert A. Shepard, "Rules of Thumb for Change Agents," *Organization Development Practitioner*, November 1975, pp. 1–5. (Publication of the National Organization Development Network, P.O. Box 69329, Portland, OR 97201.)

vents laymen from understanding the professional mysteries, is a hostile act.

Starting where the system is can be called the Empathy Rule. To communicate effectively, to obtain a basis for building sound strategy, the change agent needs to understand how the client sees himself and his situation, and needs to understand the culture of the system. Establishing the required rapport does not mean that the change agent who wants to work in a traditional industrial setting should refrain from growing a beard. It does mean that, if he has a beard, the beard is likely to determine where the client is when they first meet, and the client's curiosity needs to be dealt with. Similarly, the rule does not mean that a female change agent in a male organization should try to act like one of the boys, or that a young change agent should try to act like a senior executive. One thing it does mean is that sometimes where the client is, is wondering where the change agent is.

Rarely is the client in any one place at any one time. That is, she or he may be ready to pursue any of several paths. The task is to walk together on the most promising path.

Even unwitting or accidental violations of that Empathy Rule can destroy the situation. I lost a client through two violations in one morning. The client group spent a consulting day at my home. They arrived early in the morning, before I had my empathy on. The senior member, seeing a picture of my son in the living room, said, "What do you do with boys with long hair?" I replied thoughtlessly, "I think he's handsome that way." The small chasm thus created between my client and me was widened and deepened later that morning when one of the family tortoises walked through the butter dish.

Sometimes starting where the client is, which sounds both ethically and technically virtuous, can lead to some ethically puzzling situations. Robert Frost[1] described a situation in which a consultant was so empathic with a king who was unfit to rule that the king discovered his own un-

fitness and had himself shot, whereupon the consultant became king.

Empathy permits the development of a mutual attachment between client and consultant. The resulting relationship may be one in which their creativities are joined, a mutual growth relationship. But it can also become one in which the client becomes dependent and is manipulated by the consultant. The ethical issues are not associated with starting where the system is, but with how one moves with it.

Rule III: Never Work Uphill

This is a comprehensive rule, and a number of other rules are corollaries or examples of it. It is an appeal for an organic, rather than a mechanistic approach to change, for a collaborative approach to change, for building strength and building on strength. It has a number of implications that bear on the choices the change agent makes about how to use him/herself, and it says something about life.

Corollary 1: Don't Build Hills as You Go

This corollary cautions against working in a way that builds resistance to movement in the direction you have chosen as desirable. For example, a program which has a favorable effect on one portion of a population may have the opposite effect on other portions of the population. Perhaps the commonest error of this kind has been in the employment of T-group training in organizations: turning on the participants and turning off the people who didn't attend, in one easy lesson.

Corollary 2: Work in the Most Promising Arena

The physician-patient relationship is often regarded as analogous to the consultant-client relationship. The results for system change of this analogy can be unfortunate. For example, the organization development consultant is likely to be greeted with delight by executives who see in his specialty the solution to a hopeless situation in an outlying plant. Some organization development consultants have disappeared for years because of the irresistibility of such challenges. Others have whiled away their time trying to counteract the Peter Principle by shoring up incompetent managers.

Corollary 3: Build Resources

Don't do anything alone that could be accomplished more easily or more certainly by a team. Don Quixote is not the only change agent whose effectiveness was handicapped by ignoring this rule. The change agent's task is an heroic one, but the need to be a hero does not facilitate team building. As a result, many change agents lose effectiveness by becoming spread too thin. Effectiveness can be enhanced by investing in the development of partners.

Corollary 4: Don't Overorganize

The democratic ideology and theories of participative management that many change agents possess can sometimes interfere with common sense. A year or two ago I offered a course, to be taught by graduate students. The course was oversubscribed. It seemed that a data-based process for deciding whom to admit would be desirable, and that participation of the graduate students in the decision would also be desirable. So I sought data from the candidates about themselves, and xeroxed their responses for the graduate students. Then the graduate students and I held a series of meetings. Then the candidates were informed of the decision. In this way we wasted a great deal of time and everyone felt a little worse than if we had used an arbitrary decision rule.

Corollary 5: Don't Argue If You Can't Win

Win-lose strategies are to be avoided because they deepen conflict instead of resolving it. But the change agent should build her or his support constituency as large and deep and strong as possible so that she or he can continue to risk.

Corollary 6: Play God a Little

If the change agent doesn't make the critical value decisions, someone else will be happy to do so. Will a given situation contribute to your fulfillment? Are you creating a better world for yourself and others, or are you keeping a system in operation that should be allowed to die? For example, the public education system is a mess. Does that mean that the change agent is morally obligated to try to improve it, destroy it, or develop a substitute for it? No, not even if he or she knows how. But the change agent does need a value perspective for making choices like that.

Rule IV: Innovation Requires a Good Idea, Initiative, and a Few Friends

Little can be accomplished alone, and the effects of social and cultural forces on individual perception are so distorting that the change agent needs a partner, if only to maintain perspective and purpose.

The quality of the partner is as important as the quality of the idea. Like the change agent, partners must be relatively autonomous people. Persons who are authority-oriented—who need to rebel or need to submit—are not reliable partners: the rebels take the wrong risks and the good soldiers don't take any. And rarely do they command the respect and trust from others that is needed if an innovation is to be supported.

The partners need not be numerous. For example, the engineering staff of a chemical company designed a new process plant using edge-of-the-art technology. The design departed radically from the experience of top management, and they were about to reject it. The engineering chief suggested that the design be reviewed by a distinguished engineering professor. The principal designers were in fact former students of the professor. For this reason he accepted the assignment, charged the company a large fee for reviewing the design (which he did not trouble to examine), and told the management that it was brilliantly conceived and executed. By this means the engineers not only implemented their innovations but also grew in the esteem of their management.

A change agent experienced in the Washington environment reports that he knows of only one case of successful interdepartmental collaboration in mutually designing, funding, and managing a joint project. It was accomplished through the collaboration of himself and three similarly minded young men, one from each of four agencies. They were friends and met weekly for lunch. They conceived the project and planned strategies for implementing it. Each person undertook to interest and influence the relevant key people in his own agency. The four served one another as consultants and helpers in influencing opinion and bringing the decision makers together.

An alternative statement of Rule IV is as follows: Find the people who are ready and able to work, introduce them to one another, and work with them. Perhaps because many change agents have been trained in the helping professions, perhaps because we have all been trained to think bureaucratically, concepts like organization position, representatives, or need are likely to guide the change agent's selection of those he or she works with.

A more powerful beginning can sometimes be made by finding those persons in the system whose values are congruent with those of the change agent, who possess vitality and imagination, who are willing to work overtime, and who are eager to learn. Such people are usually glad to have someone like the change agent join in getting something important accomplished, and a careful search is likely to turn up quite a few. In fact, there may be enough of them to accomplish general system change, if they can team up in appropriate ways.

In building such teamwork the change agent's abilities will be fully challenged, as he joins them in establishing conditions for trust and creativity; dealing with their anxieties about being seen as subversive; enhancing their leadership, consulting, problem solving, diagnosing, and innovating

skills; and developing appropriate group norms and policies.

Rule V: Load Experiments for Success

This sounds like counsel to avoid risk taking. But the decision to experiment always entails risk. After that decision has been made, take all precautions.

The rule also sounds scientifically immoral. But whether an experiment produces the expected results depends upon the experimenter's depth of insight into the conditions and processes involved. Of course, what is experimental is what is new to the system; it may or may not be new to the change agent.

Build an umbrella over the experiment. A chemical process plant, which was to be shut down because of the inefficiency of its operations, undertook a union-management cooperation project to improve efficiency, which involved a modified form of profit sharing. Such plans were contrary to company policy, but the regional vice president was interested in the experiment and successfully concealed it from his associates. The experiment was successful; the plant became profitable. But in this case, the umbrella turned out not to be big enough. The plant was shut down, anyway.

Use the Hawthorne effect. Even poorly conceived experiments are often made to succeed when the participants feel ownership. And conversely, one of the obstacles to the spread of useful innovations is that the groups to which they are offered do not feel ownership of them.

For example, if the change agent hopes to use experience-based learning as part of his or her strategy, the first persons to be invited should be those who consistently turn all their experiences into constructive learning. Similarly, in introducing team development processes into a system, begin with the best-functioning team.

Maintain voluntarism. This is not easy to do in systems where invitations are understood to be commands; but nothing vital can be built on such motives as duty, obedience, security seeking, or responsiveness to social pressure.

Rule VI: Light Many Fires

Not only does a large, monolithic development or change program have high visibility and other qualities of a good target, it also tends to prevent subsystems from feeling ownership of and consequent commitment to the program.

The meaning of this rule is more orderly than the random prescription—light many fires—suggests. Any part of a system is the way it is partly because of the way the rest of the system is. To work toward change in one subsystem is to become one more determinant of its performance. Not only is the change agent working uphill but, as soon as he turns his back, other forces in the system will press the subsystem back toward its previous performance mode.

If many interdependent subsystems are catalyzed and the change agent brings them together to facilitate one another's efforts, the entire system can begin to move.

Understanding patterns of interdependency among subsystems can lead to a strategy of fire-setting. For example, in public school systems it requires collaboration among politicians, administrators, teachers, parents, and students to bring about significant innovation, and active opposition on the part of only one of these groups to prevent it. In parochial school systems, on the other hand, collaboration between the administration and the church can provide a powerful impetus for change in the other groups.

Rule VII: Keep an Optimistic Bias

Our society grinds along with much polarization and cruelty, and even the helping professions compose their world of grim problems to be "worked through." The change agent is usually flooded with the destructive aspects of the situations he or she enters. People in most systems are impressed by one another's weaknesses, and

stereotype each other with such incompetencies as they can discover.

This rule does not advise ignoring destructive forces. But its positive prescription is that the change agent be especially alert to the constructive forces, which are often masked and suppressed in a problem-oriented, envious culture.

People have as great an innate capacity for joy as for resentment, but resentment causes them to overlook opportunities for joy. In a workshop for married couples, a husband and wife were discussing their sexual problem and how hard they were working to solve it. They were not making much progress, since they didn't realize that sex is not a problem but an opportunity.

Individuals and groups locked in destructive kinds of conflict focus on their differences. The change agent's job is to help them discover and build on their commonalities, so that they will have a foundation of respect and trust which will permit them to use their differences as a source of creativity. The unhappy partners focus on past hurts and continue to destroy the present and future with them. The change agent's job is to help them change the present so that they will have a new past on which to create a better future.

Rule VIII: Capture the Moment

A good sense of relevance and timing is often treated as though it were a "gift" or "intuition," rather than something that can be learned, something spontaneous, rather than something planned. The opposite is nearer the truth. One is more likely to "capture the moment" when everything one has learned is readily available.

Some years ago my wife and I were having a very destructive fight. Our nine-year-old daughter decided to intervene. She put her arms around her mother and asked: "What does Daddy do that bugs you?" She was an attentive audience for the next few minutes while my wife told her, ending in tears. She then put her arms around me: "What does Mommy do that bugs you?" and listened attentively to my response, which also ended in tears. She then went to the record player and put on a favorite love song ("If Ever I Should Leave You") and left us alone to make up.

The elements of my daughter's intervention had all been learned. They were available to her, and she combined them in a way that could make the moment better.

Perhaps it's our training in linear cause-and-effect thinking and the neglect of our capacities for imagery that makes us so often unable to see the multiple potential of the moment. Entering the situation "blank" is not the answer. One needs to have as many frameworks for seeing and strategies for acting available as possible. But it's

not enough to involve only one's head in the situation: one's heart has to get involved, too. Cornelia Otis Skinner once said that the first law of the stage is to love your audience. You can love your audience only if you love yourself. If you have relatively full access to your organized experience, to yourself, and to the situation, you will capture the moment more often.

Endnote

1. Robert Frost, "How Hard It Is to Keep from Being King When It's in You and in the Situation," *In The Clearing* (New York: Holt, Rinehart & Winston, 1962), pp. 74–84.

Reading 33

Shining a New Light on Organizational Change:
Improving Self-Efficacy Through Coaching

John W. Malone

Abstract

Organizations do not change, people do! This is a commonly held belief among organizational researchers and practitioners in the behavioral sciences. We see over and over again that individual behavior change precedes all measurable improvements in organizational performance. Or put another way, organizational change fails without individual behavior change.

Social Cognitive Theory (SCT) has demonstrated the importance of self-efficacy in behavior change. Individuals with high self-efficacy perform new tasks at much higher levels of success than do individuals with lower self-efficacy. Building self-efficacy should, therefore, become a primary focus of management—especially in the context of planned organizational change.

This article explains self-efficacy and presents coaching techniques for improving it during the process of leading change. Coaching techniques are well suited for the management activities associated with improving self-efficacy. Coaching is suggested as the best way to enable the following five self-efficacy strengthening approaches: self-thought, mastery experiences, modeling, social persuasion, and physiological states. The article then concludes with practice tips that every practitioner should know.

Source: John W. Malone, "Shining a New Light on Organizational Change: Improving Self-Efficacy Through Coaching," *Organization Development Journal,* Summer 2001, Vol. 19, No. 2, pp. 27–36. Reprinted by permission.

Introduction

Organizations do not change, people do! Organization Development (OD) and Human Resources (HR) professionals commonly repeat this refrain as part of selling the human dimension of planned change. Or more frequently, perhaps, when asked to explain the latest failed change program! Individual behavior change is a prerequisite for major improvements in organizational performance (Robinson, Roberts, & Porras, 1993). Effective models of planned organizational change account for this fact. However, pressures for low cost, high-speed change often force organizations to overlook the human and behavioral aspects of change, typically leading to disastrous results. This article not only advocates a behavioral model; it introduces new thinking on approaches to integrating more effective behavioral change techniques into the planned change process.

The behavior change techniques are based on social cognitive theory (SCT) and self-efficacy (Bandura, 1997). Stajkovic and Luthans (1998a) highlighted the power of self-efficacy in a meta-analysis applied to two decades of research. Their results demonstrate that self-efficacy explains a 28% increase in performance. This compares to 10.39% for goal setting, 13.6% for feedback interventions and 17% for organizational behavior modification (O.B. Mod.) (Stajkovic & Luthans, 1998a). Organization Development and HR practitioners should become very familiar with such a powerful concept and should support a coaching environment that enables management to bring about higher levels of self-efficacy—especially in the context of change!

The remainder of this article is structured to that end. First, self-efficacy will be defined and its power in the organizational context will be further explained. This will be followed by recommended coaching techniques to bring about higher self-efficacy. Finally, a section called practice tips will highlight the do's and don'ts that no practitioner should be without.

Social Cognitive Theory and Self-Efficacy

Self-efficacy is a psychological construct advanced by the prominent Stanford psychologist Albert Bandura in his social cognitive theory. Briefly, SCT is built from a combined behaviorist and social learning framework and advances our understanding of psychology and organization behavior. It explains behavior as a triadic reciprocal causation operating through the bi-directional relationship between (1) the employee's cognitive and other personality factors; (2) the employee's behavior (e.g. past successful or unsuccessful performances); and (3) the employee's environment (e.g. perceived consequences from the organization environment). These relationships are illustrated in Figure 1 (Wood & Bandura, 1989; Stajkovic & Luthans, 1998b).

Self-efficacy is defined as employees' beliefs in their capabilities to mobilize the motivation, cognitive resources, and courses of action needed to exercise control over events in their lives (Bandura and Wood, 1989). Self-efficacy plays a central role in regulating a wide array of motivation and performance attainments. Employees' belief in their efficacy influences the choices they make, their aspirations, the level of effort they will sustain on a given task, how positively or negatively they think, the amount of stress they experience when coping with change, and even their vulnerability to depression (Bandura, 1991).

It is no surprise to OD and HR practitioners that two individuals with exactly the same skills will often produce different organizational results. This is because it is one thing to have the skills, and another to use them consistently under difficult circumstances—such as those typically created during major change. Social cognitive theory has taught us that success depends on having both the required skills and a resilient self-belief in one's ability to apply the skills in such a way as to control events and achieve desired goals. Although SCT and self-efficacy take it much further, most experienced managers and practitioners will know at the gut level that employees with higher confidence and a positive belief in their abilities will perform better than those without them. Social cognitive theory now gives us greater knowledge and confidence to leverage this experience, as well as a scientific understanding of the factors that contribute to increased self-efficacy. Perhaps Henry Ford was onto this when he said; "If you think you can or think you can't, you are right" (Frank, 1999).

Coaching to Strengthen Self-Efficacy

Given the power of self-efficacy to influence individual behavior, HR and OD practitioners must help their customers tap into it as a tool to help drive organizational change and improve business results. Coaching is ideally suited to bring this about. Coaching here is defined as a relationship that focuses on improving both skills and behavior in pursuit of better individual and organizational

FIGURE 1

Triadic Relationship of Social Cognitive Theory

Employee

Environment   Behavior

FIGURE 2

Source: Adapted from
Evered & Selman,
1989.

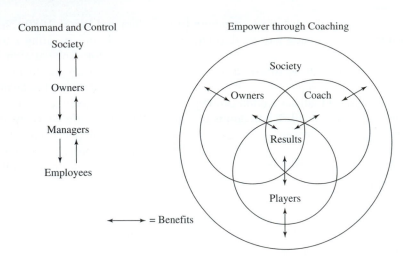

Command and Control

Empower through Coaching

performance. The term coach and the coaching process represent a departure from the traditional command and control management function. Figure 2 contrasts the traditional management function with coaching, indicating that coaching is a more collaborative and empowering process, deriving organizational benefits through synergistic relationships between key stakeholders. The deeper relationships and trust that are built in the coaching process are a requirement for helping individuals understand and strengthen their self-efficacy.

It cannot be done to someone; the individual must do the inner work his/her self (Hudson, 1999). Also, in an organizational change context, the manager, the change agent, or the HR or OD practitioner can potentially play the role of coach. In the situation where the manager is the coach, an OD or HR practitioner could, in turn, coach the manager in the background. In fact, Evered and Selman (1989) argue that most organizations would benefit from a cultural change that is driven by managers transforming themselves into coaches. Therefore, the self-efficacy strengthening techniques described next could also be used to help managers become coaches.

Strengthening Self-Efficacy

The level of self-efficacy that employees believe they possess can be instilled or strengthened in a number of practical ways. Five of them will be discussed here: self-thought, mastery experiences, modeling, social persuasion, and physiological states.

Self-Thought

The power of self-thought is summed up well by Charles Swindol: "life is 10% what happens to you, and 90% how you react to what happens to you." Manz and Neck (1991) refer to this as inner leadership, suggesting that behavioral choice and experiences of life largely reside in the mind. This poses a significant new challenge to OD and HR professionals (as well as to our line management clients) by pushing us to prioritize the cognitive processes of employees in support of change. This must be a facilitative process, however, because only the individual knows what is going on inside one's own head. Nonetheless, using self-thought techniques, coaches can facilitate employees to (1) challenge destructive thinking, (2) establish constructive thought patterns, (3) improve their internal self-talk and (4) leverage mental imagery. (Manz & Neck, 1991)

1. Challenging Destructive Thought Patterns

As many as 10 categories of destructive thinking have been identified by researchers (Burns, 1980). Two of these that are very frequently identified in the workplace are "Jumping to Conclusions" and "Magnifying and Minimizing." Chris Argyris (1996) suggests that OD and HR practitioners must learn to help people see and understand the master programs in their heads, which shape their thinking and behavior. "Jumping to negative conclusions," for example, is the thinking pattern that draws negative conclusions regarding situations despite lacking concrete evidence to support these conclusions. This thinking pattern is very harmful to self-efficacy beliefs, and will typically manifest itself as resistance to new ideas and ways of working. Coaching employees to recognize and understand this type of thought pattern should become part of the role of OD and HR practitioners.

2. Establish Constructive Thought Patterns

This is the process of replacing the erroneous thought patterns with constructive ones. Having identified the destructive thoughts, it is a matter of discipline to replace the old thinking with new productive thinking. The following example will illustrate such a process. Most change agents have experienced the situation where an employee group blames another group, typically "management," for all the negatives associated with changing their work process or structure. This "jumping to negative conclusions" thinking, once identified, can be corrected by facilitating a discussion of more realistic, alternative root causes for the change, and then gaining consensus on a replacement. Once the replacement thinking is finalized, everyone in the employee group must catch one another using old thinking, and then reinforce the new.

3. Improve Internal Self-Talk

This technique alters internal dialogue to improve personal effectiveness. It is based on research that suggests that what we tell ourselves about our en-vironments and ourselves can become a self-fulfilling prophecy through its effect on our emotional state (Manz & Neck, 1991). Individuals and teams should be coached to monitor their internal dialogue and, much as in steps one and two above, identify and correct negative self-talk with positive self-talk. A typical example of this occurs when employees facing a major change in their work processes speak (internally and with others) negatively about the change requirements. Statements such as "they are just trying to give us more work" or "I'll never be able to learn this new system" should be surfaced and corrected. Another example applies to coaches and managers, many of whom identify executive level presentations as the most difficult and least desirable aspect of their job. By simply paying attention to the self-talk messages you send yourself internally, you can identify negative messages like, "I'm not a good public speaker" and replace them with messages like, "I am a good public speaker and I am consistently improving every time I speak."

4. Leveraging Mental Imagery

This is a very widely researched technique, especially in sports psychology, as evidenced in a meta-analysis of sixty different studies (Feltz & Landers, 1983). The idea here is to imagine yourself, in great detail, actually accomplishing the selected goal in your mind before doing it in reality. Mental rehearsal of this kind has been shown to increase the effectiveness of actual results.

The four self-thought techniques just reviewed addressed the first of the five self-efficacy strengthening techniques.

Guided Mastery

The second self-efficacy strengthening technique is guided mastery. This involves the process of intentionally creating opportunities for employees to be successful at undertaking new activities and then reinforcing that success as due to their efforts. This is sometimes referred to as generating quick-hits or celebrating small victories, which is accomplished first by demonstrating early performance improvements associated with a change initiative. Secondly, the coach reinforces individual and organizational confidence in the ability to repeat the success on an ongoing basis. Interestingly, changes in self-efficacy do not occur as a result of performance accomplishment, but rather occur based on how employees process the information created by the success (Stajkovic & Luthans, 1998b). This point reinforces the importance of the coaching role of the practitioner or manager. Here the practitioner must reinforce the link between the performance improvement and the effort of the individual or team generating the improvement, thus making sure the employees process the information correctly.

Modeling

The third self-efficacy strengthening technique is modeling. Modeling occurs when one employee observes another competent employee successfully perform an activity and then receive positive reinforcement for their performance from the coach. This technique is based on the social learning process all individuals employ, whether consciously or unconsciously, as part of working in a social organization. The role of the coach is to enable individuals and groups to observe others doing the desired new activities well, along with the positive outcomes associated with the effective performance. During a planned change process, practitioner coaches should ensure that a number of project team members become highly competent performing new roles and activities, and ensure that these individuals conduct simulations and training in such a way that the employees can learn to model what they observe.

Social Persuasion

The fourth self-efficacy strengthening technique to be employed by HR and OD practitioners through coaching is called social persuasion. Social persuasion is the combined process of providing realistic encouragement while also ensuring that individuals are not prematurely placed into situations where success in unlikely. The combi-

nation of verbal reinforcement and managed exposure to increased task complexity will raise individual willingness to exert greater effort and become successful.

Psychological States

The fifth and final strengthening technique is called psychological states. This refers to the fact that individuals rely on their judgements of their stress and anxiety levels as indicators of probable success. Individuals that are stressed and anxious will attribute these states to the task at hand, resulting in a sense of vulnerability to failure and a loss of confidence in their ability. Coaches must encourage employees to take good care of themselves physically, to reduce stress, and to not necessarily associate feelings of uncertainty with the immediate activity at hand. Coaches should also pay close attention to the physical environment of the individuals concerned. Employees are more likely to feel an improved sense of self-efficacy if they are not preoccupied with stress. Therefore, eliminating environmental stresses, and ensuring that new tools provided to do new activities work effectively, are important during planned organizational change.

Practice Tips

The following list of coaching practice tips can aid the OD or HR practitioner in the process of coaching individuals or groups to strengthen their self-efficacy in the pursuit of planned change objectives.

Tip #1: Be Very Clear about Activity Descriptions and Standards

The research has shown that efficacy perceptions are based on comparing actual to expected performance outcomes (Bandura, 1997). Employees must understand the specific requirements of the activity and expected outcomes if they are to accurately assess efficacy. Efficacy will be perceived even in the absence of descriptions and measures. Highly efficacious performance can be misinterpreted due to a lack of understanding of requirements and a lack of standards—which should obviously be avoided.

Tip #2: Continue to Use Contingent Consequences

Employees may have no incentive to accurately assess their perceived self-efficacy if no consequences exist. Bandura (1997) sums it up by saying that, "it is because people see outcomes as contingent on the adequacy of their performance, and care about those outcomes, that they rely on efficacy beliefs in deciding which course of action to pursue and how long to pursue it" (p. 24).

Tip #3: Provide Self-Efficacy Training

Task and activity training conducted in support of planned change should be expanded to include self-efficacy training (Gist & Mitchell, 1992). The goal here is to go beyond traditional skill building in an effort to raise employees' beliefs about what they can do with both current and new skills. A three-step strategy may be helpful for accomplishing this tip. First, initial classroom education about the five self-efficacy strengthening techniques described above should be conducted to introduce the concepts and approaches. Second, the coaching techniques for each of the five strengthening activities should be built into the project plan for the planned change process and managed accordingly. Third, the efficacy building activities should be monitored on an ongoing basis and techniques adjusted based on feedback and measurement.

Conclusion

Much common sense wisdom has been espoused over the years by gurus encouraging us to be all we can be, or to become the person of our dreams. Examples include: Dale Carnegie's *How to Win Friends and Influence People,* first copyrighted in 1936 with over 15 million copies sold; Norman Vicent Peale's *The Power of Positive Thinking,* copyrighted in 1952 with over 5 million copies in print; Stephen Covey's many popular books; not to mention Zig Ziglar, Wayne Dyer, Deepak Chopra and Anthony Robbins! We clearly have an inner drive, often considered our spiritual nature, compelling us to maximize our potential. In many ways, SCT and self-efficacy have taken the soundings of these gurus and provided a scientific basis for their application in the organizational setting. The magnitude of the research on self-efficacy should provide the most skeptical practitioner sufficient confidence. There is now both theory and research that suggest that employees who perceive themselves as highly efficacious will activate sufficient effort, which if well executed, will produce desired outcomes, as well as reinforce expectations of self confidence (Stajkovic & Luthans, 1998). This simple but sometimes overlooked fact of human psychology must become a primary tool in the coaching tool kit of HR and OD practitioners, especially in the process of driving planned organizational change initiatives.

References

Anderson, A.C., Argyris, C., de Bono, E., Dechant, K., et al. (1996). Can you teach your people to think smarter? *Across the Board, 33*(3), 16–37.

Bandura, A. (1991). Social Cognitive Theory of Self-Regulation. *Organizational Behavior and Human Decision Processes, 50,* 248–287.

Bandura, A. (1997). *Self-Efficacy: The Experience of Control.* New York: W. H. Freeman.

Burns, D. (1980). *Feeling Good: The New Mood Therapy.* New York: William Morrow.

Carnegie, D. (1936). *How to Win Friends and Influence People.* New York: Pocket Books.

Evered, E.D., & Selman, J.C. (1989). Coaching and the Art of Management. *Organizational Dynamics, 18*(2), 16–32.

Feltz, D.L., & Landers, D.M. (1983). The Effects of Mental Practice on Motor Skill Learning and Performance: A Meta-Analysis. *Journal of Sports Psychology, 5,* 25–57.

Fran, L.R. (1999). *Quotationary.* New York: Random House.

Gist, M.E., & Mitchell, T.R. (1992). Self-Efficacy: A Theoretical Analysis of Its Determinants and

Malleability. *The Academy of Management Review,* 17(2), 183–207.

Hudson, F. M. (1999). *The handbook of Coaching.* San Francisco, CA: Jossey-Bass.

Manz, C. C., & Neck, C. P. (1991). Inner Leadership: Creating Productive Thought Patterns. *Academy of Management Executive,* 5(3), 87–95.

Peale, N. V. (1952). *The Power of Positive Thinking.* New York: Fawcett Columbine.

Robertson, P. J., Roberts, D. R., & Porras, J. I. (1993). Dynamics of Planned Organizational Change: Assessing Empirical Support for a Theoretical Model. *Academy of Management Journal,* 36(3), 619–634.

Stajkovic, A. D., & Luthans, F. (1998a). Self-Efficacy and Work-Related Performance: A Meta-Analysis. *Psychological Bulletin,* 124(2), 240–261.

Stajkovic, A. D., & Luthans, F. (1998b). Social Cognitive theory and Self-Efficacy: Going Beyond Traditional Motivational and Behavioral Approaches. *Organizational Dynamics,* Spring 1998, 62–74.

Wood, R., & Bandura, A. (1989). Social Cognitive Theory of Organizational Management. *The Academy of Management Review,* 14(3), 361–383.

Part 6

Examples and Special Situations

We believe that organizations and their members are in a decade of continuous/discontinuous change and the challenge for leaders will be to make a paradigm shift to OT and design the dynamically stable organization.[1] This organization of the future is called by many different names. Some of the more popular are the horizontal organization,[2] the knowledge and technology-based organization; and the learning organization;[3] and the 1993 Academy of Management annual meeting even had the theme of "Managing the Boundaryless Organization."

We believe all of these organizations have more similarities than differences, and, although some authors describe limited successes, these organizations are still in the experimental stages. Figure 1 is an overview of the "old organization" and the "future organization." This model first appeared in *Business Week,* and we modified it to include the main patterns from the models listed above. OD and OT is the application of behavioral science theory and practice to help organizations make the paradigm shift to the future organization.

Readings in Part 6

The first article, by Leonard Goodstein and Warner Burke, examines large-scale and fundamental change, often called *organizational transformation.* In this essay, Goodstein and Burke apply Kurt Lewin's model of unfreezing, movement, and refreezing to a major change effort at British Airways. They describe how considerable use was made of all of the usual OD methodologies such as team building, process consultation, role clarification, and negotiations.

Reading 35 by Gary J. Young is included in this book because we believe it is an example of a successful large-scale change (OT) in a public agency. This large Veterans Health Administration organization is worthy of careful review because it is

FIGURE 1
The Mature Organization and the Future Organization

Source: This is a modification of *Business Week,* October 23, 1992, pp. 62–63, and Robert A. Zawacki, Carol A. Norman, Paul A. Zawacki, and Paul Applegate, *Transforming the Mature Information Technology Organization* (Colorado Springs: EagleStar Publishing, 1995), p. 28.

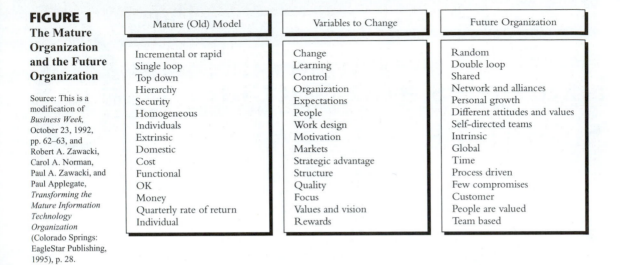

Mature (Old) Model	Variables to Change	Future Organization
Incremental or rapid	Change	Random
Single loop	Learning	Double loop
Top down	Control	Shared
Hierarchy	Organization	Network and alliances
Security	Expectations	Personal growth
Homogeneous	People	Different attitudes and values
Individuals	Work design	Self-directed teams
Extrinsic	Motivation	Intrinsic
Domestic	Markets	Global
Cost	Strategic advantage	Time
Functional	Structure	Process driven
OK	Quality	Few compromises
Money	Focus	Customer
Quarterly rate of return	Values and vision	People are valued
Individual	Rewards	Team based

one of the largest public agencies and it overcame many substantial obstacles during the transformation. Further, this is a longitudinal study over a five-year period that is rich with insights and examples of OT. The author concludes this essay with lessons learned.

We follow up the above longitudinal case study of large-scale change with an article written especially for this 6th edition, by Kathleen Dannemiller and Sylvia James, that presents some of the history of large-scale change and a step-by-step plan for a change journey. This article gives another perspective on the large-scale systems change projects at Ford Motor Company and the Boeing Company reported by Gary Jusela in Reading 24. Dannemiller and James's "reflections" enrich our understanding of what was happening during these ground-breaking change efforts. Further, the authors give many excellent insights and lessons learned that should prove helpful to practicing OD/OT consultants and students of OD.

Most of the growth in new jobs has been in small entrepreneurial firms during the past 10 years. We see that pattern of job growth continuing at least for the remainder of this decade. Because of this recent emphasis and interest in small firms, we included the article by W. Gibb Dyer, which articulates an OD framework for diagnosis and intervention in small entrepreneurial firms. Further, Dyer discusses interventions at the start-up, growth, and succession stages of the firm.

Two of the drivers of change in organizations today are time-based competition and reduced costs. Because of these drivers, change agents are working with more and more organizations that are merging with other organizations or are in turnaround situations. Can OD efforts add value to the bottom line of a business during mergers and turnaround situations? The final reading, by Gregory W. Pacton, attempts to answer the question of the applicability of OD during the crises of turnaround situations.

Endnotes

1. Andrew C. Boynton and Bart Victor, "Beyond Flexibility: Building and Managing the Dynamically Stable Organization," from a paper dated June 27, 1991, and forthcoming in the *California Management Review.*

2. "The Horizontal Organization," *Information Week,* August 27, 1992, pp. 32–40.

3. Peter M. Senge, "Transforming the Practice of Management," paper presented at the Systems Thinking Conference, November 14, 1991.

Reading 34

Creating Successful Organization Change

Leonard D. Goodstein
W. Warner Burke

Buffeted at home and abroad by foreign competition that appears to produce higher-quality goods at lower prices, corporate America has now largely forsaken (at least publicly and momentarily) the traditional analogy of the organization as a machine and its organizational members as parts designed to work effectively and efficiently. Instead, many American corporations are accepting the "New Age" view of organizations as "a nested set of open, living systems and subsystems dependent upon the larger environment for survival."

What is surprising about this quote is not its viewpoint, which has been normative in the organizational psychology and behavioral literature for several decades, but its source: *The Wall Street Journal.* And it is typical to find such articles in virtually every issue of most recent American business publications: articles on corporate culture, on the changing attitudes of American workers, on the need for greater employee participation in managerial decision making, and on the place of employees as an important (if not the most important) asset of the corporation.

We are not suggesting that traditionally managed organizations are now extinct in America. Corporate executives, however, have definitely begun to recognize that managing the social psychology of the workplace is a critical element in the success of any organization.

Source: Leonard D. Goodstein and W. Warner Burke, "Creating Successful Organization Change." Reprinted, from *Organizational Dynamics,* Spring 1991. Copyright ©1991 American Management Association International. Reprinted by permission of American Management Association International, New York, NY. All rights reserved. http://www.amanet.org.

Organizational Change

Organizations tend to change primarily because of external pressure, rather than an internal desire or need to change. Here are a few all-too-familiar examples of the kinds of environmental factors requiring organizations to change:

- A new competitor snares a significant portion of a firm's market share.
- An old customer is acquired by a giant conglomerate that dictates new sales arrangements.
- A new invention offers the possibility of changing the organization's existing production technology.

Other examples include (1) new government regulations on certain health care financing programs and (2) economic and social conditions that create long-term changes in the availability of the labor force. The competent organization will be so alert to early warning signs of such external changes that it can move promptly to make internal changes designed to keep it viable in the changing external world. Competent organizations are those that continue to change and to survive.

Thus it is practically a cliché to state that change in organizations today is a way of life. And clearly it is not saying anything new to comment that executives and managers today are more finely attuned to change or that they more frequently view their role as that of change agent.

But even though we often state the obvious and spout clichés about change, this does not mean that we have an in-depth understanding of what we are talking about. We are only beginning to understand the nature of change and how to manage the process involved, especially with respect to organizations. The purpose of this article is to improve our understanding of organizational change by providing both some conceptual clarification and a case example that illustrates many of the concepts involved.

It is possible to conceptualize organizational change in at least three ways—levels of organizational change, strategies of organizational change, and, more specifically and not mutually exclusive of strategies, models and methods of organizational change. (First we will present the concepts, second the case example, and finally some implications.)

Levels of Organizational Change

A broad distinction can be made between (1) fundamental, large-scale change in the organization's strategy and culture—a transformation, refocus, reorientation, or "bending the frame," as David A. Nadler and Michael L. Tushman have referred to the process—and (2) fine-tuning, fixing problems, making adjustments, modifying procedures, and so on; that is, implementing modest changes that improve the organization's performance yet do not fundamentally change the organization. By far most organizational changes are designed not to transform the organization but to modify it in order to fix its problems.

In this article we address more directly the large-scale, fundamental type of organizational change. (A word of caution: "Organizational transformation," "frame bending," and other expressions indicating fundamental change do not imply wholesale, indiscriminate, and complete change. Thus when we refer to "fundamental change," we do not mean "in any and all respects.")

We are concerned with transformation when an organization faces the need to survive and must do things differently to continue to exist. After polio was licked, for example, the March of Dimes had to change its mission in order to survive as an organization. Although its mission changed from one of attacking polio to one of trying to eradicate birth defects, the organization's core technology—fund raising—remained the same.

A corporate example of transformation is seen in the transition of International Harvester to Navistar. Facing bankruptcy, the company downsized drastically, completely restructured its financial situation, and overhauled its corporate culture. Although many of the company's technologies were sold off, it, too, retained its core technology: producing trucks and engines. Once internally focused, its culture is now significantly market-oriented—and the company is operating far more efficiently than it did in the past.

Although organizational members experience such transformations as a complete change, they rarely if ever are. Theory would suggest that if fundamental—or even significant—change is to occur with any success, some characteristic(s) of the organization must *not* change. The theory to which we refer comes from the world of individual change: psychotherapy. For organizational transformation to be achieved—for the organization to survive and eventually prosper from such change—certain fundamentals need to be retained. Some examples: the organization's ultimate purpose, the previously mentioned core technology, and key people. The principle here is that for people to be able to deal with enormous and complex change—seeming chaos—they need to have *something* to hold on to that is stable.

Conceptually, then, we can distinguish between fundamentally changing the organization and fine-tuning it. This distinction—which is a matter of degree, not necessarily a dichotomy—is useful in determining strategies and methods to be used in the change effort. When fine-tuning, for example, we do not necessarily need to clarify for organizational members what will not change—but in the case of transformation, such clarity is required for its successful achievement.

Strategies of Organizational Change

Organizational change can occur in more than one way. In a 1971 book, Harvey A. Hornstein and colleagues classified six ways: individual change strategies, technostructural strategies, data-based strategies, organization development, violent and coercive strategies, and nonviolent yet direct-action strategies. All of these strategies have been used to attempt, if not actually bring about, organizational change. Senior management usually chooses any one or various combinations of the first four and manages them internally. The last two—violent, coercive strategies and nonviolent yet direct-action strategies—are more often than not initiated by actions outside the organization, and the organization's executives typically manage in a reactive mode.

In this article we address some combination of the first four strategies. Yet, as previously indicated, we are assuming that the overwhelming majority of organizational changes are motivated by *external* factors—that executives are responding to the organization's external environment. But even when it is not a reaction to some social movement, organizational change is nevertheless a *response*—a response to changes or anticipated changes in the marketplace, or changes in the way technology will affect the organization's products/services, or changes in the labor market, etc.

This assumption is based on the idea that an organization is a living, open system dependent on its environment for survival. Whether it is merely to survive or eventually to prosper, an organization must monitor its external environment and align itself with changes that occur or will occur in that environment. Practically speaking, the process of alignment requires the organization to change itself.

Models and Methods of Organizational Change

Models of change and methods of change are quite similar in concept and often overlap—so much so that it is not always clear which one is being discussed. Kurt Lewin's three-phase model of change—unfreeze, move (or change), refreeze—also suggests method. Organization development

is based on an action-research model that is, at the same time, a method.

More on the model side is the relatively simple and straightforward framework provided by Richard Beckhard and Reuben T. Harris. They have suggested that large-scale complex organizational change can be conceptualized as movement from a present state to a future state. But the most important phase is the in-between one that they label *transition state*. Organizational change, then, is a matter of (1) assessing the current organizational situation (present state), (2) determining the desired future (future state), and (3) both planning ways to reach that desired future and implementing the plans (transition state).

Methods of implementing the change—for example, a new organizational strategy—include the following:

- Setting up a comprehensive training program (individual change strategy).
- Modifying the structure, individuals' jobs, and/or work procedures (technostructural strategy).
- Conducting a companywide survey to assess organizational culture for the purpose of using the data to pinpoint required changes (data-based strategy).
- Collecting information from organizational members about their views regarding what needs to be changed and acting accordingly (organization development strategy).
- Combining two, three, or all of these methods.

The case example we will discuss here illustrates organizational transformation in response to change initiated in the institution's external environment—excluding, however, the violent, coercive strategies and the nonviolent, direct ones. The example, which is analyzed according to Lewin's three-phase model/method, highlights the use of multiple methods for change—in fact, it presents in one form or another a specific method from each of the four other change strategies mentioned earlier.

Case Example

In 1982 Margaret Thatcher's government in Great Britain decided to convert British Airways (BA) from government ownership to private ownership. BA had regularly required large subsidies from the government (almost $900 million in 1982), subsidies that the government felt it could not provide. Even more important, the Conservative government was ideologically opposed to the government's ownership of businesses—a matter they regarded as the appropriate province of private enterprise.

The growing deregulation of international air traffic was another important environmental change. Air fares were no longer fixed, and the resulting price wars placed BA at even greater risk of financial losses.

In order to be able to "privatize"—that is, sell BA shares on the London and New York Stock Exchanges—it was necessary to make BA profitable. The pressures to change thus exerted on BA by the external environment were broad and intense. And the internal organizational changes, driven by these external pressures, have been massive and widespread. They have transformed the BA culture from what BA managers described as "bureaucratic and militaristic" to one that is now described as "service-oriented and market-driven." The success of these efforts over a five-year period (1982–1987) is clearly depicted in the data presented in Figure 1.

This exhibit reflects BA's new mission in its new advertising slogan—"The World's Favorite Airline." Five years after the change effort began, BA had successfully moved from government ownership to private ownership, and both passenger and cargo revenues had dramatically increased, leading to a substantial increase in share price over the offering price, despite the market crash of October 1987. Indeed, in late 1987 BA acquired British Caledonian Airways, its chief domestic competitor. The steps through which this transformation was accomplished clearly fit Lewin's model of the change process.

Lewin's Change Model

According to the open-systems view, organizations—like living creatures—tend to be homeostatic, or continuously working to maintain a steady state. This helps us understand why organizations require external impetus to initiate change and, indeed, why that change will be resisted even when it is necessary.

Organizational change can occur at three levels—and, since the patterns of resistance to change are different for each, the patterns in each level require different change strategies and techniques. These levels involve:

1. Changing the *individuals* who work in the organization—that is, their skills, values, attitudes, and eventually behavior—but making sure that such individual behavioral change is always regarded as instrumental to organizational change.

2. Changing various organizational *structures and systems*—reward systems, reporting relationships, work design, and so on.

FIGURE 1 The British Airways Success Story: Creating the "World's Favorite Airline"

	1982	1987
Ownership	Government.	Private.
Profit/(loss)	($900 million).	$435 million.
Culture	Bureaucratic and militaristic.	Service-oriented and market-driven.
Passenger load factor	Decreasing.	Increasing—up 16% in 1st quarter 1988.
Cargo load	Stable.	Increasing—up 41% in 1st quarter 1988.
Share price	N/A	Increased 67% (2/11/87–8/11/87).
Acquisitions	N/A	British Caledonian.

3. Directly changing the organizational *climate or interpersonal style*—how open people are with each other, how conflict is managed, how decisions are made, and so on.

According to Lewin, a pioneer in the field of social psychology of organizations, the first step of any change process it to *unfreeze* the present pattern of behavior as a way of managing resistance to change. Depending on the organizational level of change intended, such unfreezing might involve, on the individual level, selectively promoting or terminating employees; on the structural level, developing highly experiential training programs in such new organization designs as matrix management; or, on the climate level, providing data-based feedback on how employees feel about certain management practices. Whatever the level involved, each of these interventions is intended to make organizational members address that level's need for change, heighten their awareness of their own behavioral patterns, and make them more open to the change process.

The second step, *movement,* involves making the actual changes that will move the organization to another level of response. On the individual level, we would expect to see people behaving differently, perhaps demonstrating new skills or new supervisory practices. On the structural level, we would expect to see changes in actual organizational structures, reporting relationships, and reward systems that affect the way people do their work. Finally, on the climate or interpersonal-style level, we would expect to see behavior patterns that indicate greater interpersonal trust and openness and fewer dysfunctional interactions.

The final stage of the change process, *refreezing,* involves stabilizing or institutionalizing these changes by establishing systems that make these behavioral patterns "relatively secure against change," as Lewin put it. The refreezing stage may involve, for example, redesigning the organization's recruitment process to increase the likelihood of hiring applicants who share the organization's new management style and value system. During the refreezing stage, the organization may also ensure that the new behaviors have become the operating norms at work, that the reward system actually reinforces those behaviors, or that a new, more participative management style predominates.

According to Lewin, the first step to achieving lasting organizational change is to deal with resistance to change by unblocking the present system. This unblocking usually requires some kind of confrontation and a retraining process based on planned behavioral changes in the desired direction. Finally, deliberate steps need to be taken to cement these changes in place—this "institutionalization of change" is designed to make the changes semipermanent until the next cycle of change occurs.

Figure 2 presents an analysis of the BA change effort in terms of Lewin's model. The many and diverse steps involved in the effort are categorized both by stages (unfreezing, movement, and refreezing) and by level (individual, structures and system, and climate/interpersonal style).

Unfreezing. In BA's change effort, the first step in unfreezing involved a massive reduction in the worldwide BA workforce (from 59,000 to 37,000). It is interesting to note that, within a year after this staff reduction, virtually all BA performance indices had improved—more on-time departures and arrivals, fewer out-of-service aircraft, less time "on hold" for telephone reservations, fewer lost bags, and so on. The consensus view at all levels within BA was that the downsizing had reduced hierarchical levels, thus giving more autonomy to operating people and allowing work to get done more easily.

The downsizing was accomplished with compassion; no one was actually laid off. Early retirement, with substantial financial settlements, was the preferred solution throughout the system. Although there is no question that the process was painful, considerable attention was paid to minimizing the pain in every possible way.

A second major change occurred in BA's top management. In 1981, Lord John King of Wartinbee, a senior British industrialist, was appointed chairman of the board, and Colin Marshall, now

FIGURE 2 Applying Lewin's Model to the British Airways (BA) Change Effort

Levels	Unfreezing	Movement	Refreezing
Individual	Downsizing of workforce (59,000 to 37,000); middle management especially hard hit. New top management team. "Putting People First."	Acceptance of concept of "emotional labor." Personnel staff as internal consultants. "Managing People First." Peer support groups.	Continued commitment of top management. Promotion of staff with new BA values. "Top Flight Academies." "Open Learning" programs.
Structures and systems	Use of diagonal task forces to plan change. Reduction in levels of hierarchy. Modification of budgeting process.	Profit sharing (3 weeks' pay in 1987). Opening of Terminal 4. Purchase of Chartridge as training center. New, "user-friendly" MIS.	New performance appraisal system based on both behavior and performance. Performance-based compensation system. Continued use of task forces.
Climate/interpersonal style	Redefinition of the business: *service,* not *transportation.* Top-management commitment and involvement.	Greater emphasis on open communications. Data feedback on work-unit climate. Off-site, team-building meetings.	New uniforms. New coat of arms. Development and use of cabin-crew teams. Continued use of data-based feedback on climate and management practices.

Sir Colin, was appointed CEO. The appointment of Marshall represented a significant departure from BA culture. An outsider to BA, Marshall had a marketing background that was quite different from that of his predecessors, many of whom were retired senior Royal Air Force officers. It was Marshall who decided, shortly after his arrival, that BA's strategy should be to become "the World's Favorite Airline." Without question, critical ingredients in the success of the overall change effort were Marshall's vision, the clarity of his understanding that BA's culture needed to be changed in order to carry out the vision, and his strong leadership of that change effort.

To support the unfreezing process, the first of many training programs was introduced. "Putting People First"—the program in which all BA personnel with direct customer contact participated—was another important part of the unfreezing process. Aimed at helping line workers and managers understand the service nature of the airline industry, it was intended to challenge the prevailing wisdom about how things were to be done at BA.

Movement. Early on, Marshall hired Nicholas Georgiades, a psychologist and former professor and consultant, as director (vice president) of human resources. It was Georgiades who developed the specific tactics and programs required to bring Marshall's vision into reality. Thus Georgiades, along with Marshall, must be regarded as a leader of BA's successful change effort. One of the interventions that Georgiades initiated—a significant activity during the movement phase—was to establish training programs for senior and middle managers. Among these were "Managing People First" and "Leading the Service Business"—experiential programs that involved heavy doses of individual feedback to each participant about his or her behavior regarding management practices on the job.

These training programs all had more or less the same general purpose: to identify the organization's dysfunctional management style and begin the process of developing a new management style that would fit BA's new, competitive environment. If the organization was to be market-driven, service-based, and profit-making, it would require an open, participative management style—one that would produce employee commitment.

On the structures and systems level during the unfreezing stage, extensive use was made of diagonal task forces composed of individuals from different functions and at different levels of responsibility to deal with various aspects of the change process—the need for MIS (management information systems) support, new staffing patterns, new uniforms, and so on. A bottom-up, less centralized budgeting process—one sharply different from its predecessor—was introduced.

Redefining BA's business as service, rather than as transportation, represented a critical shift on the level of climate/interpersonal style. A service business needs an open climate and good interpersonal skills, coupled with outstanding teamwork. Off-site, team-building meetings—the process chosen to deal with these issues during the movement stage—have now been institutionalized.

None of these changes would have occurred without the commitment and involvement of top management. Marshall himself played a central role in both initiating and supporting the change process, even when problems arose. As one index of this commitment, Marshall shared information at question-and-answer sessions at most of the training programs—both "to show the flag" and to provide his own unique perspective on what needed to be done.

An important element of the movement phase was acceptance of the concept of "emotional labor" that Georgiades championed—that is, the high energy levels required to provide the quality of service needed in a somewhat uncertain environment, such as the airline business. Recognition that such service is emotionally draining and often can lead to burnout and permanent psychological damage is critical to developing systems of emotional support for the service workers involved.

Another important support mechanism was the retraining of traditional personnel staff to become internal change agents charged with helping and supporting line and staff managers. So, too, was the development of peer support groups for managers completing the "Managing People First" training program.

To support this movement, a number of internal BA structures and systems were changed. By introducing a new bonus system, for example, Georgiades demonstrated management's commitment to sharing the financial gains of BA's success. The opening of Terminal 4 at Heathrow Airport provided a more functional work environment for staff. The purchase of Chartridge House as a permanent BA training center permitted an increase in and integration of staff training, and the new, "user-friendly" MIS enabled managers to get the information they needed to do their jobs in a timely fashion.

Refreezing. During the refreezing phase, the continued involvement and commitment of BA's top management ensured that the changes became "fixed" in the system. People who clearly exemplified the new BA values were much more likely to be promoted, especially at higher management levels. Georgiades introduced additional programs for educating the workforce, especially managers. "Open Learning" programs, including orientation programs for new staff, supervisory training for new supervisors, and so on, were augmented by "Top Flight Academies" that included training at the executive, senior management, and management levels. One of the academies now leads to an MBA degree.

A new performance appraisal system, based on both behavior and results, was created to emphasize customer service and subordinate development. A performance-based compensation system is being installed, and task forces continue to be used to solve emerging problems, such as those resulting from the acquisition of British Caledonian Airlines.

Attention was paid to BA's symbols as well—new, upscale uniforms; refurbished aircraft; and a new corporate coat of arms with the motto "We fly to serve." A unique development has been the creation of teams for consistent cabin-crew staffing, rather than the ad hoc process typically used. Finally, there is continued use of data feedback on management practices throughout the system.

Managing change. Unfortunately, the change process is not smooth even if one is attentive to Lewin's model of change. Changing behavior at both individual and organizational levels means inhibiting habitual responses and producing new responses that feel awkward and unfamiliar to those involved. It is all too easy to slip back to the familiar and comfortable.

For example, an organization may intend to manage more participatively. But when a difficult decision arises, it may not be possible to get a consensus decision—not at first, at least. Frustration to "get on with" a decision can lead to the organization's early abandonment of the new management style.

In moving from a known present state to a desired future state, organizations must recognize that (as noted earlier) the intervening *transition* state requires careful management, especially when the planned organizational change is large and complex. An important part of this change management lies in recognizing and accepting the disorganization and temporarily lowered effectiveness that characterize the transition state.

In BA's change effort, the chaos and anger that arose during the transitional phase have abated, and clear signs of success have now emerged. But many times the outcome was not at all clear, and serious questions were raised about the wisdom of the process both inside and outside BA. At such times the commitment and courage of top management are essential.

To heighten involvement, managing such organizational changes may often require using a transition management team composed of a broad cross-section of members of the organization. Other techniques include using multiple interventions, rather than just one—for example, keeping the system open to feedback about the change process and using symbols and rituals to mark significant achievements. The BA program used all of these techniques.

Process consultation. In addition to the various change strategies discussed above, considerable use was made of all the usual organization development (OD) technologies. Structural changes, role clarification and negotiations, team building, and process consultation were all used at British Airways to facilitate change.

In process consultation—the unique OD intervention—the consultant examines the pattern of a work unit's communications. This is done most often through direct observation of staff meetings and, at opportune times, through raising questions or making observations about what has been happening. The role of the process consultant is to be counternormative—that is, to ask why others never seem to respond to Ruth's questions or why no one ever challenges Fred's remarks when he is clearly off target. Generally speaking, process consultation points out the true quality of the emperor's new clothes even when everyone is pretending that they are quite elegant. By changing the closed communication style of the work teams at British Airways to a more open, candid one, process consultation played an important role in the change process.

The Research Evidence

Granted that the BA intervention appears to have been successful, what do we know generally about the impact of OD interventions on organizations and on their effectiveness? Over the past few years, the research literature has shown a sharp improvement in both research design and methodological rigor, especially in the development of such "hard criteria" as productivity and quality indices. The findings have been surprisingly positive.

For example, Raymond Katzell and Richard Guzzo reviewed more than 200 intervention studies and reported that 87 percent found evidence of significant increases in worker productivity as a result of the intervention. Richard Guzzo, Richard Jette, and Raymond Katzell's meta-analysis of 98 of these same studies revealed productivity increases averaging almost half a standard deviation—impressive enough "to be visible to the naked eye," to use their phrase. Thus it would appear that the success of BA's intervention process was not a single occurrence but one in a series of successful changes based on OD interventions.

The picture with respect to employee satisfaction, however, is not so clear. Another meta-analysis—by Barry Macy, Hiroaki Izumi, Charles Hurts, and Lawrence Norton—on how OD interventions affect performance measures and employee work satisfaction found positive effects on performance but *negative* effects on attitudes, perhaps because of the pressure exerted by new work-group norms on employee productivity. The positive effects on performance, however, are in keeping with the bulk of prior research A recent comprehensive review of the entire field of OD by Marshall Sashkin and W. Warner Burke concluded, "There is little doubt that, when applied properly, OD has substantial positive effects in terms of performance measures."

Implications and Concluding Remarks

We very much believe that an understanding of the social psychology of the change process gives all of us—managers, rank-and-file employees, and consultants—an important and different perspective for coping with an increasingly competitive environment. Our purpose in writing this article was to share some of this perspective—from an admittedly biased point of view.

The change effort at BA provides a recent example of how this perspective and this understanding have been applied. What should be apparent from this abbreviated overview of a massive project is that the change process at BA was based on open-systems thinking, a phased model of managing change, and multiple levels for implementing the change. Thus both the design and the implementation of this change effort relied heavily on this kind of understanding about the nature of organizations and changing them.

The change involved a multifaceted effort that used many leverage points to initiate and support the changes. The change process, which used transition teams with openness to feedback, was intentionally managed with strong support from top management. Resistance to change was actively managed by using unfreezing strategies at all three levels—individual, structural and systems, and interpersonal. Virtually all of the organizational change issues discussed in this article emerged in some measure during the course of the project.

It is quite reassuring to begin to find empirical support for these efforts in field studies and case reports of change efforts. Moreover, the recent meta-analyses of much of this work are quite supportive of what we have learned from experience. We need to use such reports to help more managers understand the worth of applying the open-systems model to their change efforts. But we also need to remember that only when proof of the intervention strategy's usefulness shows up on the firm's "bottom line" will most line managers be persuaded that open-systems thinking is not necessarily incompatible with the real world. The BA success story is a very useful one for beginning such a dialog.

As we go to press, it seems clear that many of the changes at British Airways have stabilized the company. Perhaps the most important one is that the company's culture today can be described as having a strong customer-service focus—a focus that was decidedly lacking in 1982. The belief that marketing and service with the customer in mind will have significant payoff for the company is now endemic to the corporate culture. Another belief now fundamental to BA's culture is that the way one manages people—especially those, like ticket agents and cabin crews, with direct customer contact—directly impacts the way customers will feel about BA. For example, during 1990, Tony Clarry, then head of worldwide customer service for BA, launched a leadership program for all of his management around the globe to continue to reinforce this belief.

Yet all is not bliss at British Airways, which has its problems. Some examples:

- American Airlines is encroaching upon BA's European territory.
- The high level of customer service slips from time to time.
- Those who can afford to ride on the Concorde represent a tiny market, so it is tough to maintain a consistently strong customer base.
- Now that BA has developed a cadre of experienced managers in a successful company, these managers are being enticed by search firms to join other companies that often pay more money.

Other problems, too, affect BA's bottom line—the cost of fuel, effectively managing internal costs, and the reactions of the financiers in London and on Wall Street, to name a few. It should be noted that since 1987 and until recently, BA's financials have remained positive with revenues and profits continuing to increase. During 1990 this bright picture began to fade, however. The combination of the continuing rise in fuel costs, the recession, and the war in the Persian Gulf have taken their toll. Constant vigilance is therefore imperative for continued success.

It may be that BA's biggest problem now is not so much to manage further change as it is to manage the change that has already occurred. In other words, the people of BA have achieved significant change and success; now they must maintain what has been achieved while concentrating on continuing to be adaptable to changes in their external environment—the further deregulation of Europe, for example. Managing momentum may be more difficult than managing change.

References

The *Wall Street Journal* article referred to at the outset, "Motivate or Alienate? Firms Have Gurus to Change Their Cultures,'" was written by Peter Waldbaum and may be found on p. 19 of the July 24, 1987, issue.

With respect to levels of organizational change, see the article by W. Warner Burke and George H. Litwin, "A Causal Model of Organizational Performance," in the 1989 Annual published by University Associates of San Diego. These authors describe the differences between transformational and transactional change. Along the same conceptual lines is the article by David A. Nadler and Michael L. Tushman—"Organizational Frame Bending: Principles for Managing Reorientation" (*The Academy of Management Executive,* August 1988, pp. 194–204).

Regarding strategies of organizational change, see Harvey A. Hornstein, Barbara B. Bunker, W. Warner Burke, Marion Gindes, and Roy J. Lewicki's *Social Intervention: A Behavioral Science Approach* (The Free Press, 1971).

Concerning models and methods of organizational change, the classic piece is Kurt Lewin's chapter "Group Decisions and Social Change," in the 1958 book *Readings in Social Psychology* (Holt, Rinehart & Winston), edited by Eleanor E. Maccobby, Theodore M. Newcomb, and Eugene L. Hartley. For an explanation of organization development as action research, see W. Warner Burke's *Organization Development: Principles and Practices* (Scott, Foresman, 1982). The framework of present state-transition state-future state is explained in *Organization Transitions: Managing Complex Change,* 2nd ed. (Addison-Wesley, 1987), by Richard Beckhard and Reuben T. Harris. A recent article by Donald C. Hambrick and Albert A. Cannella, Jr.—"Strategy Implementation as Substance and Selling" (*The Academy of Management Executive,* November 1989, pp. 278–85)—is quite helpful in understanding how to implement a change in corporate strategy.

A point made in the article is that, for effective organizational change, multiple leverage is required. For data to support this argument, see W. Warner Burke, Lawrence P. Clark, and Cheryl Koopman's "Improving Your OD Project's Chances of Success" (*Training and Development Journal,* September 1984, pp. 62–68). More on process consultation and team building may be found in two books published by Addison-Wesley: Edgar H. Schein's *Process Consultation, vol. 1: Its Role in Organization Development,* 1988, and W. Gibb Dyer's *Team Building: Issues and Alternatives,* 1987.

References for the research evidence are: Richard A. Guzzo, Richard D. Jette, and Raymond A. Katzell's "The Effects of Psychologically Based Intervention Programs on Worker Productivity: A Meta-Analysis" (*Personnel Psychology* 38, no. 2 (Summer 1985), pp. 275–91); Raymond A. Katzell and Richard A. Guzzo's "Psychological Approaches to Worker Productivity" (*American Psychologist* 38 (April 1983), pp. 468–72); Barry A. Macy, Hiroaki

Izumi, Charles C. M. Hurts, and Lawrence W. Norton's "Meta-Analysis of United States Empirical Change and Work Innovation Field Experiments," a paper presented at the 1986 annual meeting of the Academy of Management, Chicago; John M. Nicholas's "The Comparative Impact of Organization Development Interventions on Hard Criteria Issues" (*The Academy of Management Review* 7, no. 4 (October 1982), pp. 531–43; John M. Nicholas and Marsha Katz's "Research Methods and Reporting Practices in Organization Development" (*The Academy of Management Review,* October 1985, pp. 737–49); and Marshall Sashkin and W. Warner Burke's "Organization Development in the 1980s" (*Journal of Management,* no. 2 (1987), pp. 205–29).

Reading 35

Managing Organizational Transformations: *Lessons from the Veterans Health Administration*

Gary J. Young

Many U.S. organizations in both the public and private sectors are undergoing some type of transformation to improve their performance. These organizations face a daunting challenge. Although no studies document comprehensively the outcomes of such large-scale change efforts, experts seem to agree that most organizations are left with disappointing results.[1] Yet some organizations do succeed and their experiences can provide valuable lessons for future transformation efforts.

The lessons learned from the transformation of the Veterans Health Administration (VHA) are worthy of careful study for several reasons. First, the VHA overcame substantial obstacles to make remarkable progress during its transformation. In this regard, the transformation is a potential source of best practices for other organizations undergoing transformation. Second, the VHA's transformation, while generally a success, has not been without shortcomings that when examined offer insight into the challenges and tensions that underlie many transformations. Third, the VHA is one of the largest agencies in the federal government, and the size and scope of its transformation is itself a remarkable story of large-scale organizational change in the public sector.

This article is adapted from a report prepared for the Pricewater-houseCoopers Endowment for the Business of Government. The report is based on a case study that was supported financially in part by the National Science Foundation (#9529884). Several individuals helped collect data for the case study: Martin Charns, Carol Van Deusen Lukas, Geraldine McClynn, and Richard Coffey. Their support is gratefully acknowledged.

Source: *California Management Review,* 43, no. 1 (Fall 2000), pp. 66–82. Used with permission.

The article is based on a longitudinal case study of the first five years of the VHA's transformation. Data for the case study were drawn from several sources.[2] The primary source of data was interviews conducted with VHA employees at all levels of the agency's hierarchy. Interviews were also conducted with individuals who have observed the transformation as members of organizations that interface with the VHA, including the U.S. General Accounting Office, congressional oversight committees for the VHA, and veterans service organizations. Another source of data was employee surveys, which were conducted periodically during the transformation and focused on employee perceptions about the implementation and impact of the change effort.[3] Additional data were obtained from internal VHA documents, reports, and databases. To identify key lessons from the transformation, standard methods of content analysis were used to identify themes and patterns from the interview data. The analysis entailed coding transcribed interviews for key concepts and tabulating how frequently the concepts were mentioned and the type of interviewee that mentioned them (e.g., network director, staff physician).

VHA Background

The VHA is a federally funded and centrally administered health care system for veterans.[4] The agency is a primary component of the Department of Veterans Affairs, a cabinet-level department within the executive branch of the federal government.[5] It is currently one of the country's largest health care delivery systems with 172 hospitals, 132 nursing homes, 73 home health care programs,

40 residential care programs, and more than 600 outpatient clinics. Through this nationwide health care system, the VHA provided services to 3.6 million veterans in 1999, approximately 14 percent of the more than 25 million veterans in the United States. Most veterans who use VHA services meet at least one of two criteria that qualifies them for priority status under the agency's patient eligibility rules, namely, a disability that is connected to military service or low income.

The VHA also encompasses extensive research and teaching activities. Research programs exist in biomedical sciences, rehabilitative medicine, and health services delivery systems. With respect to teaching, the agency has academic affiliations with many of the country's medical schools and schools of allied health professions. In particular, the agency is an integral component of the country's system for graduate medical education, providing financial support and clinical training to approximately one-third of the country's medical residents.

In 1999, the VHA operated with a budget of over $17 billion. The agency's workforce, which has undergone substantial reductions in recent years, now consists of approximately 180,000 individuals. The senior official for the VHA, who carries the title "undersecretary for health," is appointed by the president of the United States for a term of four years.

Context for VHA Transformation

At the time the VHA embarked on its transformation in 1995, several external developments had placed its future in peril.[6] Specifically, the VHA had become out of synch with prevailing trends in the delivery of health care services. By the early 1990s, the advent of health maintenance organizations and developments in medical technology had shifted resource priorities in the delivery of health care services away from inpatient-oriented tertiary care to outpatient-oriented primary care. The VHA, however, had much of its material and intellectual resources invested in the delivery of inpatient care. Most of the VHA's hospitals, which

historically have served as the agency's primary operating units, were large, technology-intensive, and often underutilized facilities. VHA physicians who staffed these hospitals were medical specialists with little expertise or interest in primary care medicine. Moreover, the VHA lacked a well-developed infrastructure for providing services in the community. The agency was gradually becoming a health care dinosaur in danger of extinction.

In addition, the VHA faced the prospect that it could lose many of its patients to the private sector. Historically, the VHA has served as an important public safety net for uninsured veterans since more than half of those who use VHA services have low incomes and typically lack alternative sources of health care. However, the VHA's safety net status was placed in jeopardy during the early 1990s following a series of national and state-level health care reform proposals that included provisions to expand the accessibility of low-income individuals to private-sector health care. Although these reform proposals did not come to pass, VHA officials were left to ponder the agency's ability to compete with private-sector health care organizations should such reforms come to pass in the future. VHA officials knew the agency would have to its advantage a strong reputation for excellence in many areas of specialty medicine, but they also knew that unless changes occurred, the agency would have—to its disadvantage—a reputation for long waiting times, fragmented care, and a cumbersome bureaucracy for accessing services.

Two other external developments also threatened the agency's long-term viability. One development took the form of growing fiscal constraints on the agency. Although the VHA had been searching for ways to achieve cost savings for some time, the issue became much more pressing in 1995 when Congress indicated its intention to freeze the agency's budget. Another development was an unfavorable demographic trend in the agency's patient population. Over time the VHA's patient population was becoming increasingly older and sicker than the general U.S. population. In the absence of any future military conflicts, this trend would result in the agency caring for a sicker but dwindling patient population.

The sum total of these external threats created a black cloud over the VHA's future. To ensure its viability into the next century, the VHA needed to significantly refocus its approach to the delivery of health care services, improve patient satisfaction, and increase the efficiency of its operations. Several barriers to change existed. First, like many large, established organizations, the VHA was not oriented to flexibility and innovation. The agency's management systems and culture were deeply rooted in a command-and-control, military-style mind set. Decision making was highly centralized and bureaucratic. VHA headquarters tended to micro-manage many of the decisions and activities of the agency's hospitals and other operating units. This decision-making structure impeded operating units from adapting to local circumstances in a timely manner. Additionally, the VHA's system for allocating resources to operating units, which was based largely on units' historical costs, did not provide incentives for the efficient delivery of health care services to the patient population.

Second, as a public-sector health care system, the VHA has multiple stakeholders including Congress, medical schools, labor unions, and various veterans service organizations. Any change effort the VHA undertakes is complicated by the fact that these stakeholders have different and sometimes conflicting interests regarding agency priorities and activities. Third, as a federal agency, the VHA operates within a framework of extensive rules and regulations. At the time of the transformation, a number of these rules and regulations were barriers to the agency's ability to adapt to its changing circumstances. In particular, complex patient eligibility rules for VHA services limited the agency's ability to treat patients on an outpatient basis. The agency also operated under rules that limited its ability to contract for services with private-sector organizations. This restriction impeded the VHA from expanding community-based services to meet the needs of its patients.

Lessons Learned

Despite formidable obstacles, the VHA has demonstrated much progress during the first five years of its transformation (from 1995 to 1999). Indicators of the VHA's progress, which speak to the general success of the transformation, are presented selectively in Exhibit 1. In general, these data reveal a substantial shift in agency priorities and activities relative to ambulatory care and primary care. They also reveal substantial improvements in the efficiency and quality of VHA services. Indeed, the U.S. General Accounting Office, which has monitored the VHA transformation closely, recently reported to Congress that the VHA transformation has made "significant progress."[7] In addition, the VHA has become a national leader among health care organizations in the effort to improve patient safety.[8] The agency's ability to assume this leadership role appears at least in part attributable to the transformation and its positive impact on innovation at the agency.

Although all transformations are somewhat unique, the VHA's experience provides a number of useful lessons for managing large-scale organizational change. Based on the study, the following seven lessons emerge.

Lesson 1: Appoint Leaders Whose Backgrounds and Experiences Are Appropriate for the Transformation

As is often the case with organizational change efforts, the VHA's transformation began with new leadership. Toward the end of 1994, Dr. Kenneth W. Kizer assumed the position of VHA undersecretary for health with a mandate from Congress to transform the agency. Dr. Kizer, a physician trained in emergency medicine and public health, proved to be a highly effective leader for the VHA transformation. According to interviewees, Dr. Kizer's effectiveness was largely a result of the match between his professional experience and qualifications and the needs of the transformation.

EXHIBIT 1 VHA Transformation: Selected Indicators of Progress

Outpatient-Oriented Primary Care

- Annual inpatient admissions have declined by more than 32 percent while ambulatory care visits have increased by more than 45 percent.
- Percent of surgeries performed on an outpatient basis has increased from approximately 35 percent to over 70 percent.
- Approximately 60 percent of hospital beds have been eliminated.
- Percent of patients receiving cancer screening for early detection of several types of cancers has increased substantially (e.g., colorectal cancer screening from approximately 34 percent to 74 percent).
- Percent of patients receiving treatments for preventing or controlling disease has increased substantially (e.g., cholesterol management for heart disease from approximately 74 percent to almost 100 percent).

Convenience and Accessibility of Care

- Over 300 new community-based outpatient clinics have been established.
- Telephone-linked care has been established at all hospitals.

Operational Efficiency

- The number of full-time equivalent employees has been reduced by more than 14 percent while the number of patients treated per year has increased by more than 25 percent.

Patient Satisfaction

- Patient satisfaction scores for outpatient care (based on the VHA's own national surveys of patients) have improved by more than 15 percent.

Source: VHA internal documents and databases; U.S. General Accounting Office, *Veteran's Affairs: Progress and Challenges in Transforming Health Care,* GAO/T-HEHS-99-109 9, April 1999.

Three of Dr. Kizer's qualifications appear to have been particularly relevant to his effectiveness. First, he was an outsider. Unlike many of his predecessors, he assumed the under secretary position without progressing through the agency hierarchy. Because of his outsider status, he was not a captive to entrenched interests within the agency. According to interviewees, when previous VHA leaders proposed making large-scale changes to the agency, they would find themselves constrained from going forward by loyalties to old colleagues who opposed the changes. Dr. Kizer was beholden to no one inside the agency. After assuming the under secretary position, Dr. Kizer selected several insiders for his senior leadership team, an action that reportedly helped him compensate for his own limited knowledge of the inner workings of the agency. In selecting insiders for his senior leadership team, Dr. Kizer focused on two primary criteria: credibility with VHA employees and leadership experience within the agency. The selection process involved teams of VHA managers that Dr. Kizer assembled to screen candidates.

Second, although Dr. Kizer was new to the VHA, he did have substantial leadership experience in the public sector. In particular, Dr. Kizer had served as director of the California Department of Health Services where he reportedly learned how to work effectively with both policy makers and career civil servants. His style of leadership could be at times hard hitting. Indeed, from his discussions with members of Congress about the VHA's transformation, Dr. Kizer developed a reputation for being "unusually candid and direct for an agency official." However, he also gained the trust of many members of Congress by keeping them well informed of all major changes he was planning to make at the agency. Dr. Kizer also had prior experience as a medical school department chair within the University of California system, a position that helped prepare him to manage the VHA's important but complicated relationships with its affiliated medical schools.

Dr. Kizer was, as noted by a staff member of the Senate Committee on Veterans' Affairs, "exceptionally well qualified for the job."

Third, Dr. Kizer was an enthusiastic student of innovations in the financing and delivery of health care services. He had witnessed many innovations firsthand through his professional experiences in California, a state that has led the country in cutting-edge approaches to the organization and financing of health care services. Dr. Kizer brought this spirit of innovation and experimentation to the VHA. He emphasized managed care principles, preventive medicine, and outpatient-oriented care. Above all, he emphasized experimentation that, in the words of one interviewee, "challenged old-line bureaucrats to search for better ways to provide care to veterans."

It should also be noted that Dr. Kizer had good timing. He took the helm of the VHA at a time when Congress, the veterans service organizations, and the agency's own employees were ready to see the agency undergo change. As a result, Dr. Kizer had a window of opportunity to remake the agency without some of the constraints and close scrutiny that would certainly have impeded his predecessors. He appears to have capitalized on this opportunity to its fullest. Nevertheless, the difficulties of reconciling the interests of so many different stakeholders also took its toll on him politically. His reappointment to a second term as under secretary proved to be a contentious matter in Congress. As the end of Dr. Kizer's initial appointment approached, members of Congress extended the appointment nine months so they could further deliberate on the matter of reappointment. When the nine-month period expired without resolution about his reappointment, Dr. Kizer, rather than endure the process further, stepped down as undersecretary.

The VHA's transformation demonstrates the importance of having leaders whose background and experiences fit the needs of the transformation. For some organizations undergoing transformation new leadership may be necessary, but the focus should be on ensuring that leaders have the right backgrounds and experiences for the transformation.

Lesson 2: Follow a Focused and Coherent Transformation Plan

Most transformations encompass many different activities and initiatives. Although this is also true of the VHA's transformation, the senior leadership team for the transformation focused on four interrelated initiatives that formed a coherent and effective transformation plan: creation of a vision, adoption of a new organizational structure, establishment of an accountability system, and modification of agency rules and regulations.

Creation of a Vision for the Agency

It has become a well-established principle that successful transformations require a clear and comprehensive vision for the organization's future.[9] Early on in the transformation effort the VHA's senior leadership team developed such a vision. After his appointment as undersecretary, Dr. Kizer held several months of planning meetings with representatives from different parts of the agency. Based on these meetings, the senior leadership team prepared a document entitled *Vision for Change*.[10] The document articulated the basic philosophy, principles, and organizational framework to which a transformed VHA would adhere. As a follow-up to *Vision for Change*, the senior leadership team prepared two other related documents that provided greater operational guidance to VHA managers regarding the transformation.[11]

The vision documents provided a comprehensive statement of purpose and goals for the transformation. The documents made clear that the "transformation would fundamentally change the way veterans health care is provided" and that this would include "increasing ambulatory care access points and a marked emphasis on providing primary care, decentralizing decision making, and integrating the delivery assets to provide a seamless continuum of care." Interviewees referred to the documents as forming a "true charter" for the transformation. The vision documents also established high standards for the transformation. The

VHA was to provide care at a level that "must be demonstratively equal to, or better than, what is available in the local community." Although the VHA officials had always spoken with pride in the quality of care that the agency offered veterans, the vision documents (as interviewees repeatedly emphasized) presented a direct challenge to the agency to provide the best care available anywhere in the country.

Adoption of a New Organizational Structure

Within the first year of the transformation, the VHA's senior leadership team implemented a sweeping change in the agency's basic organizational structure. The new structure entailed the reorganization of all VHA operating units into 22 networks known as Veterans Integrated Service Networks (networks). The design of the networks was intended to reflect actual and potential patient referral patterns among VHA operating units.

Within this structure, the networks replace hospitals as the primary planning and budgeting units within the VHA. In addition, much of the authority for operational decision making was effectively transferred from headquarters to the networks. The role of the VHA headquarters, which as part of the transformation had its staff cut by more than one-third, was to set overall policy and to provide technical support to network managers. The senior leadership team selected a director for each network. Of the first group of 22 directors, about one-third were drawn from outside the agency. In addition, changes were made to the agency's internal resource allocation methods so that a network's budget depended on the number of veterans served rather than its historical costs (which was the case for hospitals in the past).

The sweeping change in organizational structure appears to have affirmed the emergence of a new era in the VHA's history. Prior to the transformation, VHA employees had witnessed other attempted change efforts only to see them abandoned before they were fully implemented. The expression "this too shall pass" became a rallying cry for VHA employees who opposed the transformation. However, the dramatic change in structure could not be overlooked; it provided a strong signal that the transformation was not a passing fad. One long-time VHA manager summed up the comments of many interviewees about the sweeping change in structure: "VHA needed clear, decisive action that would leave no doubts that the agency would never return to its past." Still, shortly after the new structure was implemented, long-time headquarters' staff tested the boundaries of the new power structure by attempting on several occasions to impose central policy initiatives on network directors. When this occurred, members of the senior leadership team stepped in and reaffirmed the transfer of decision-making authority to the network directors.

In addition, the new structure stimulated experimentation and entrepreneurial activity. For example, in an effort to save money and streamline care, network directors consolidated hospitals in more than 45 locations where two or more facilities operated in close proximity to each other. Network directors also implemented many innovative organizational arrangements to coordinate patient care across operating units within the same network. Three networks reorganized their services substantially into network-wide product lines for the purpose of facilitating population-based (rather than operating unit-based) resource allocation decisions. Other arrangements often featured managed care principles related to primary care and preventive services. One network director, a long-time VHA manager with over 20 years experience with the agency, commented, "I saw more innovation at the agency during the first three years of the transformation than I had seen during all of my previous years combined." Another director, who had been a longtime hospital manager within the agency, remarked, "The new freedom I had to make decisions was absolutely invigorating."

Establishment of an Accountability System

As another key transformation initiative the senior leadership team established an accountability system for network directors. Performance contracts served as the centerpiece of the new accountability system. Each director was required to sign a contract that stipulated a set of performance goals to which he or she would be held accountable. The contracts provided directors with financial incentives in the form of a bonus for achieving performance goals. The goals changed each year to reflect new agency priorities. Some performance goals required network directors to implement new programs or functions, some called for directors to achieve quantitatively measurable improvements in key efficiency and quality indicators for their network (e.g., patient satisfaction), and some goals required network directors to develop core competencies in such areas as interpersonal effectiveness. To monitor performance, the senior leadership team used existing data sets and measurement systems and also created new ones. Reports were routinely generated and disseminated that provided feedback on each network's relative performance on key measures for the transformation.

The accountability system linked strategically a network director's performance goals to the agenda set forth in the vision documents. The agency had not previously had an accountability system that integrated the performance goals of operating units with agency-wide strategic goals. As one interviewee noted, "the accountability system created a very sustained focus on the ultimate goals of the transformation at levels of the agency where the goals could best be translated into action."

Modification of Agency Rules and Regulations

The VHA transformation also included reforms to agency rules and regulations. Some of these reforms entailed changes by Congress in legislatively defined regulations for the VHA, while others entailed changes by the senior leadership team in the agency's own internal policies. The primary reforms pertained to patient eligibility requirements that provided the agency with more flexibility to shift patient care to outpatient settings. These legislative reforms also gave the agency expanded authority to contract with private-sector organizations and to market its services to veterans who lacked priority status under the traditional eligibility requirements.

In addition, the senior leadership team eliminated a long-standing agency policy that prevented dismissal of physician employees except for clinical incompetence. Although this reform created some bitter feelings on the part of VHA physicians, it also conveyed a necessary message to all VHA employees that they needed to change their attitudes and behaviors to serve the goals of the transformation. On this point, Dr. Kizer remarked to us: "It always was our hope to achieve compliance by offering employees a carrot, but we could ill afford not to have a sick available to us."

These four initiatives—creation of a vision, adoption of a new organizational structure, establishment of an accountability system, and modification in agency rules and regulations—formed the basic transformation framework for the agency. Other activities undertaken during the transformation were typically linked to one or more of the four initiatives. The senior leadership team's ability to develop and implement each one of the four initiatives was central to the overall success of the transformation.

Lesson 3: Persevere in the Presence of Imperfection

All transformations generate controversy and criticism. Such criticism and controversy often distract leaders of transformations from focusing on the central goals of the transformation. In the case of the VHA, the senior leadership team kept its sights fixed on key transformation goals while making mid-course corrections to address technical problems as they were recognized.

For example, the VHA's senior leadership team became deeply embroiled in controversy over the accountability system it had established for upper-level managers. The new accountability system entailed the development of new performance measures and data sets. Initially, managers complained bitterly about the adequacy of the data sets, reliability of the measures, and potential opportunities for gaming the accountability system.

They also raised objections based on the number and attainability of performance goals.

Certainly many of the complaints were valid and efforts were made to improve databases and measures. The senior leadership team, however, believed the value of the new accountability system exceeded its functional capabilities. Indeed, the new accountability system's emphasis on performance data had a symbolic significance that reverberated throughout the agency. Managers at lower levels of the agency began developing data sets for measuring the performance of their own units or departments in ways that supported the transformation agenda. These new performance systems often came to be know by such clinically oriented nicknames as pulse points and vital signs. The result was a substantial shift in focus among VHA managers, a shift away from inputs (i.e., how large is my budget and how many staff do I have) to that of outputs as defined by the goals in network directors' performance contracts. Moreover, the focus of the senior leadership team was reportedly not on whether network directors precisely met each and every goal stipulated in their contracts but rather whether they met the spirit of their contracts in the sense that performance was moving in a direction that promoted the transformation agenda.

No transformation will be perfect and those who oppose the changes will often seek to derail the effort by exploiting its flaws and limitations. Leaders of transformations need to be responsive to legitimate criticisms but they also must avoid being swallowed up in technical details.

Lesson 4: Match Changes in the External Environment with Changes in the Internal Environment

Leaders of transformations are often consumed with managing the internal changes of an organization. The VHA's transformation reveals the importance of managing external changes to complement internal ones. As noted, the transformation included legislative reforms to long-standing agency regulations that impeded internal changes. To accomplish these important reforms, the VHA's senior leadership team collaborated with other interested parties to lobby for the reforms as part of the transformation effort.

Patient eligibility reforms provide a case in point. Although eligibility reforms had been in the planning stage long before the transformation began, the reforms had met substantial opposition from several influential members of Congress who raised concerns about the impact of the reforms on agency expenditures. Dr. Kizer countered this opposition by presenting the reforms as a necessary step to achieving the goals of the transformation such as shifting service orientation from inpatient care to outpatient care. He maintained that in the absence of the reforms he could not hold his own managers accountable for accomplishing many of the goals in their performance contracts. Congress proceeded to adopt the reforms that became part of the Veterans Eligibility Reform Act of 1996. This legislation also expanded the VHA's authority to market its services to a wider population of veterans (i.e., those without a service-connected disability or low-income) and to contract with private-sector entities for various services, facilitating the agency's ability to build its infrastructure for outpatient care. Interviewees familiar with these events noted Dr. Kizer's "political acumen in reframing the debate over the reforms from one of agency expenditure to one of agency accountability."

Leaders of a transformation will typically have far more control over their organization's internal environment than they will its external environment. Nevertheless, change initiatives that capitalize on interdependencies between external and internal environments may contribute substantially to a successful transformation.

Lesson 5: Develop and Manage Communication Channels from the Highest to Lowest Levels of the Organization

The VHA's transformation offers another of many examples where conventional communication strategies did not work to keep frontline employees well informed about the change effort. To inform employees about the transformation, the senior leadership team distributed written notices and videotapes, held town meetings, and conducted videoconferences. These communication efforts were not effective in reaching frontline employees. The employee surveys that were conducted as part of the case study indicate that after the first year of the transformation frontline employees, including physicians in nonsupervisory positions, had substantially less understanding of the purpose and nature of the transformation than did those to whom they reported. For example, one of the survey questions asked employees to indicate on a five-point scale the degree to which they understood the goals the transformation was intended to accomplish (where 5 was very strong understanding and 1 was no understanding). The mean score for frontline employees on this question was slightly below two whereas the mean score for employees occupying managerial or supervisory positions was slightly above four.

Interview data also indicate that the VHA's communication efforts had limited success in reaching frontline employees. In a series of focus groups with frontline employees at the end of the first year of the transformation, employees repeatedly expressed frustration about communication issues. One employee appeared to sum up the sentiments of many of the focus group participants when she remarked that "[frontline] employees had too much rumor and too few facts about the change process." Although the communication problems reportedly had a number of different adverse effects on the transformation, employees most frequently mentioned adverse effects on morale and job satisfaction.

What strategies can managers use to communicate effectively with their employees during a transformation? Some management consultants advocate that organizations plan for communication to be handled face-to-face between frontline employees and the supervisors to whom they report directly. Along these lines, at Ford Motor Corporation the CEO has embraced the concept of what change expert Noel Tichy calls the teachable point of view. This philosophy calls for a carefully planned initiative whereby managers at each level of an organization, from highest to lowest, spend time with the employees they supervise directly to convey and discuss key organizational principles. Under this approach, frontline employees meet to discuss a change effort with their immediate supervisors who have had similar meetings with their own immediate supervisors.[12]

Although the initiative underway at Ford Motor Corporation appears promising, there is not likely to be one best way to communicate with employees during a transformation effort. Much may depend on the size, scope, and structure of the organization. What would seem most important is that those leading a transformation be attentive to the challenges of communicating to frontline employees. Clearly, effective communication with frontline employees requires a well-planned and highly focused effort.

Lesson 6: Do Not Overlook Training and Education

As noted, the VHA's senior leadership team implemented a sweeping change in organizational structure as part of the transformation. Although this sweeping change in structure helped achieve credibility for the transformation and helped stimulate innovations, it also placed managers in a trial by fire situation. Many managers struggled in their efforts to adapt to a structure that now called for them to make innovative and strategic decisions in a turbulent environment. Such decision making was not the common experience of most VHA managers who had spent much of their careers carrying out directives from agency headquarters.

The difficulty that some VHA managers had in adapting to the new structure was compounded by a lack of educational and training resources. Although the VHA's senior leadership team did plan for several educational initiatives as part of the transformation, most of these initiatives were not in place at the time the agency was undergoing its sweeping change in structure. Managers reportedly needed but often lacked the skills to conduct sophisticated analyses for strategic and marketing plans, capital investment decisions, and contract negotiations with private-sector organizations. In a report to Congress, the U.S. General Accounting Office took note of this problem after reviewing a number of poorly developed feasibility studies for hospital consolidations.[13] It appears that in setting priorities, the VHA's senior leadership team may have placed too little emphasis on education and training.

In this regard, the VHA's experience speaks to a long-standing debate over how quickly a transforming organization should implement major changes in organizational structure.[14] Some experts argue against dramatic changes in organizational structure or management systems on the ground that employees will be mentally and emotionally unprepared to adapt to the new job requirements that such changes entail. These experts often recommend that organizations make gradual changes to allow employees to adjust to their new circumstances. Other experts, however, contend that dramatic changes in structure are sometimes needed to overcome the inertia that often attends transformation efforts. These experts contend that sweeping changes in organizational structure can "unfreeze" the organization from its existing state and allow the transformation to proceed. Although the VHA experience cannot resolve this debate, it does highlight the potential need for education and training during a transformation. Accordingly, in situations where dramatic or swift change is deemed necessary, senior managers should not overlook the importance of education and training to support employees in developing needed skills in a timely manner.

Lesson 7: Balance System-Wide Unity with Operating Unit Flexibility

Leaders of all multiunit organizations must struggle with the issue of how much decision-making authority should be given to operating units and how much should be reserved for headquarters. The issue is often central to transformations, which are often undertaken by organizations in part to improve the fit between their decision-making structure and business requirements.[15]

In the case of the VHA transformation, a dramatic push occurred to decentralize decision making after years of micro management on the part of headquarters. However, the VHA's sudden swing from centralized to decentralized management appears to have allowed little opportunity for careful planning in the reorganization of certain functions and programs at agency headquarters. Some programs were left in disarray without clear lines of responsibility or system-wide criteria for coordinating activities across networks and operating units. Functions and activities were also sometimes eliminated without careful review and evaluation. As noted by one VHA manager who played a prominent role in the transformation process: "We were moving so quickly that we probably in some instances could not help but throw out the baby with the bathwater."

A related problem was a lack of central oversight to ensure that networks followed consistent data collection and reporting procedures. This problem was noted in reports by the Senate Committee on Veterans' Affairs, the U.S. General Accounting Office, and the VHA's own Office of Inspector General.[16] In particular, the Senate Committee on Veterans' Affairs criticized the agency for not maintaining a cohesive, system-wide quality management program, commenting that "headquarters does not require that its hospitals and clinics use uniform methods for collecting data."[17] Although problems in the comparability of data among VHA operating units had existed before the transformation, the network structure had both exacerbated and magnified these problems.

Further, interviewees remarked that the new structure provided limited opportunities for sharing best practices among the networks. Although the senior leadership team held monthly group meetings for network directors, these meetings have largely focused on administrative matters. The agency did not appear to be capitalizing on its system-level resources to promote learning and innovation. As such, the VHA's experience reveals the need to carefully plan decentralization efforts so that an appropriate balance is struck between system-level coordination and control and operating unit flexibility.

Conclusion

On balance, the VHA transformation is a wonderful story of large-scale organizational change. While mistakes and oversights can be found, the agency has made remarkable progress during its transformation, particularly when one considers where the organization was only five short years ago. The VHA has shifted its resources substantially toward outpatient and preventive care, streamlined the efficiency of its operations, and improved service quality. Future challenges, of course, lie ahead. Since this case study was completed, the pace of change at the VHA has slowed and the agency appears to be transitioning toward a state of maintenance where the focus is on formalizing and standardizing the policies and practices that have emerged from the transformation. Although such a transition is inevitable and necessary, the future viability of the VHA will depend on its ability to be responsive to future shifts in the patterns of service delivery within the health care industry. Following a successful transformation, organizations can become mired in their new structural arrangement, leaving them vulnerable once again to subsequent changes in their external environment. The leadership of the VHA must guard against such organizational paralysis by keeping alive within the agency a spirit of experimentation and innovation.

Clearly, a general lesson that emerges from the VHA transformation is that organizations and the people who work in them can change. The keys to successful change are more open to debate as is the generalizability of the VHA's transformation. Certainly, the VHA's transformation is distinguishable in at least several respects from the change efforts of many other organizations. In particular, the agency's sheer size and scope of operations were somewhat unique factors that undoubtedly increased the difficulty of maintaining effective communication with frontline employees. It is also true that the VHA, unlike most private-sector or-

ganizations undergoing transformation, was able to conduct a change effort without the immediate concern of direct competitors who would be in a position to exploit mistakes. Still, the VHA confronted the same basic challenges that other complex organizations do during a transformation including developing a vision to revitalize the organization, motivating and empowering employees to adopt new behaviors, and creating an infrastructure to monitor the organization's progress. All transforming organizations face these challenges regardless of whether they operate within the public sector or private industry, whether their key stakeholders are members of Congress or members of the board of directors. Thus, to the extent that the VHA's experience is generalizable, it points to the importance of selecting leaders who are well prepared to articulate a vision for the transformation and to develop and implement a coherent transformation plan. The VHA's experience also reveals the importance of focusing on transformation goals while faced with numerous distractions during the implementation process. This said, future leaders of organizational change efforts would do well by studying the VHA transformation as a prelude to their own.

Endnotes

1. See, for example, J. P. Kotter, "Leading Change: Why Transformation Efforts Fail," *Harvard Business Review,* 73/2 (March/April, 1995); 59–67; G. Hall, J. Rosenthal, and J. Wade, "How to Make Reengineering Really Work," *Harvard Business Review,* 71/6 (November/December 1993): 119–130. Some evidence suggests that change efforts in public-sector organizations are less likely to succeed than change efforts in private-sector organizations (e.g., P. J. Robertson and S. J. Seneviratne, "Outcomes of Planned Organizational Change in the Public Sector: A Meta-Analytic Comparison to the Private Sector," *Public Administration Review,* 55/16 (1995): 547–558).

2. The collection and analysis of data were guided by a model of the change process that was originally proposed by Kurt Lewin. In this model, transforming organizations are conceptualized as moving through three stages or states of equilibrium—frozen

unfrozen, and refrozen. The model does not consider strategies or tactics that move organizations from one stage to another. K. Lewin, "Group Decision and Social Change," in G. E. Swanson, T. N. Newcomb, and E. L. Hartley, eds., *Readings in Social Psychology,* rev. ed. (New York, NY: Holt, 1952).

3. The surveys were conducted by selecting a random sample of employees from each VHA operating unit. During each wave of the survey, completed questionnaires were obtained from over 10,000 members of the agency's workforce for a response rate that was consistently above 60 percent.

4. Information contained in this section was drawn from both published sources as well as internal VHA documents. For published sources, see generally K. W. Kizer, "The 'New VA': A National Laboratory for Health Care Quality Management," *American Journal of Medical Quality,* 14/1 (1999): 3–19; E. S. Fisher and H. G. Welch, "The Future of the Department of Veterans Affairs Health Care System," *Journal of the American Medical Association,* 273/8 (1995): 651–667; K. W. Kizer, "Re-engineering the Veterans Healthcare System," in P. Ramsaroop and J. Ball, eds., *Advances in Federal Sector Health Care* (New York, NY: Springer, 2000).

5. The Department of Veterans Affairs was formed in 1988. The Department subsumed the former Veterans Administration, which was established in 1930 to consolidate most veterans' programs within a single agency. Through its two other components, the Department of Veterans Affairs administers on behalf of veterans a program for disability benefits and a national system of cemeteries.

6. Information contained in this section was drawn from a number of sources. See Paralyzed Veterans of America, *The VA Responsibility on Tomorrow's National Health Care System: Strategy 2000,* Washington, D.C., 1992; Mission Commission, *Report of the Commission on the Future Structure of Veterans Health Care,* Washington, D.C., 1991; E. S. Fisher and H. G. Welch, op. cit.; J. K. Iglehart, "Reform of the Veterans Health Care System," *New England Journal of Medicine,* 335/18 (1996): 1407–1411; K. W. Kizer, "Health Care, Not Hospitals: Transforming the Veterans Health Administration." In G. W. Dauphinais and C. Price, eds., *Straight from the CEO* (New York, NY: Simon & Schuster, 1998); S. Findlay, "Military Medicine: The Image and the Reality of Veterans' Hospitals," *U.S. News & World Report* (June 1992); Department of Veterans Affairs (Management Decision and Research Center), "Analysis and Recommendations for Reorganization of Veterans Health Administration," October 1993; Task Force on the Reorganization of VHA Central Office, "Veterans Health Administration Central Office Reorganization," September 1994; Northwestern University (Kellogg Graduate School of Management), "Analysis of the Organizational Structure and Management Functioning of VA's Health Delivery System, 1991; Kizer (2000), op. cit.

7. U.S. General Accounting Office, *Veterans' Affairs: Progress and Challenges in Transforming Health Care,* GAO/T-HEHS-99-109 9, April 1999.

8. The VHA is among the first health care organizations to conduct a comprehensive self-examination of medical errors and adverse events. The agency has also initiated several research and operational activities to reduce the frequency of medical errors and adverse events. These initiatives are serving as models for other health care organizations. See R. Pear. "Report Details Medical Errors in VA Hospitals," *Sunday New York Times,* December 18, 1999.

9. For a recently published book that discusses the concept, see R. M. Miles, *Leading Corporate Transformation* (San Francisco, CA: Jossey-Bass, 1997).

10. Veterans Health Administration, *Vision for Change: A Plan to Restructure the Veterans Health Administration,* Washington, D.C., February 1995.

11. Veterans Health Administration, *Prescription for Change: The Strategic Principles and Objectives for Transforming the Veterans Healthcare System,* Washington, D.C., January 1996; Veterans Health Administration, *Journey for Change,* Washington, D.C., April 1997.

12. See T. J. Larkin and S. Larkin, "Reaching and Changing Frontline Employees," *Harvard Business Review,* 74/3 (May/June 1996): 95–104; S. Wetlaufer, "Driving Change: An Interview with Ford Motor Company's Jacques Nasser," *Harvard Business Review,* 77/2 (March/April 1999): 76–88.

13. U.S. General Accounting Office, *Major Management Challenges and Program Risks: Department of Veterans' Affairs,* GAO/OCG-99-15, January 1999.

14. See, generally, L. E. Greiner, "Patterns of Organizational Change," *Harvard Business Review,* 45/3 (May/June 1967): 119–128; M. Beer, R. A. Eisenstadt and B. Spector, *The Critical Path to Corporate Re-*

newal (Boston, MA: Harvard Business School Press, 1990); D. A. Nadler, R. B. Shaw, and A. E. Walton, eds., *Discontinuous Change* (San Francisco, CA: Jossey-Bass, 1995); R. K. Reger, L. T. Gustafson, S. M. Demarie, and J. Mullane, "Reframing the Organization: Why Implementing Total Quality Is Easier Said Than Done," *Academy of Management Journal,* 19/3 (1994): 565–584.

15. The management literature recommends a number of factors that organizations should consider in addressing this issue, such as the magnitude and pace of technological and market changes in the external environment. See, generally, P. Leatt, S. Shortell, and J. Kimberly, "Organization Design," in S. Shortell and A. Kaluzny, eds., *Health Care Management: Or-* *ganizational Design and Behavior* (Albany, NY: Delmar, 2000).

16. U.S. Senate, Minority Staff of the Committee on Veterans' Affairs, op. cit.; U.S. General Accounting Office, *Major Management Challenges and Program Risks;* Department of Veterans Affairs, Office of the Inspector General, *Quality Management in the Department of Veterans Affairs Veterans Health Administration;* Office of Healthcare Inspections, Report 8HI-A28-072, Washington, D.C., February 1998.

17. U.S. Senate, Minority Staff of the Committee on Veterans' Affairs, "Staff Report on Quality Management in the Veterans Health Administration," Department of Veterans Affairs, December 1997.

Reading 36

Innovation in Whole-Scale™ Change: Past, Present and Future

Kathleen D. Dannemiller
Sylvia L. James

Learning from Our Past and Present

Kathleen's Story

The roots of the processes now known as Whole-Scale Change[1] go back to the early days in the development of "organization development"—to the 1950s at the National Training Labs (NTL) in Bethel, Maine. Ron Lippitt was one of the founders of NTL and had begun doing "community development" as an expansion of what he had learned about group processes in his work with small groups. This expansion was the work he was doing to help communities create a systemwide view of the future the participants yearned to achieve for their own communities. I had the privilege to learn from him both at NTL and in his community work during the 1960s until his death in 1985.

In the early 1980s Bruce Gibb, Al Davenport, Chuck Tyson and I were invited to Ford Motor Company to talk with an Executive Vice President, Tom Page, who was convinced that the downturn Ford Motor Company was experiencing was not just the usual cyclical change in the industry. He was aware that the industry itself was being permanently challenged in the United States, and indeed must change if it were to survive the Japanese competition. He had been exposed to a quality circle program developed at Ford between the UAW and the Employee Relations office in the late 1970s.

Many of Mr. Page's manufacturing plants had been involved in the quality circle programs. Mr. Page became very impressed as he watched and received results from the program. His most important learning was how knowledgeable hourly workers were about what would make the plants more effective. He began to see how little of this knowledge had been utilized in the past. He suspected that keeping this knowledge alive and growing in the future could be a secret weapon for change. His dilemma was that in those days Ford leaders were archetypes for a "command and control" type of leadership—a cultural style that could diminish employee empowerment if it continued unchecked.

The request, therefore, from Mr. Page was to build a training program to teach the "top of the house" how to manage participatively. The four of us as consultants replied:

> A training program won't work. The leaders have been trained to be the way they are. They've been rewarded and promoted because they were good at a "Read my lips" style of leadership. We as consultants could put together the best training program imaginable and the leaders would finish the training saying that it was an interesting way of leading—and it was too bad it wouldn't work at Ford. They would walk away with new ideas, but with the traditional Ford mindset unchanged.

Tom Page's response was: "Then what can we do?" And the four of us said that we would go home and work together to answer that question. We worked over the next several months with Nancy Badore and Cynthia Holmes, internal consultants at Ford, to design a proposal we believed would work.

Source: Written especially for this volume.

As we learned more about the hierarchy of Ford Motor, we began to understand what made it so difficult for an organization of Ford's size to respond to a turbulent environment. The structure and age of the organization led us to compare it to an aging human body. As we get older, we often develop osteoarthritic build-ups (calcium deposits) at the "joints." That development causes a reduced flexibility. Each division was a pyramid, with functional "chimneys" going up and down and levels of job titles going across the chimneys. This model causes each person, at whatever level and whatever "chimney," to be locked into an "arthritic box" where people can't see what's going on above, below, or beside their own box. The arthritis blocks the view beyond my box.[2] In order to get people connected around a radical new style of managing and/or different strategy, we decided we would need to pull the top five levels together outside the pyramid. We needed to enable people to see a common database (customers, suppliers, corporate leaders, each other) and therefore be able, as a whole, to uncover what changes would be called for. We came to see that we can influence as far as we can see—and no farther. Therefore we needed to get each and all of them to arrive at a whole common picture, internal and external.

The answer was to use what we knew about small group work and expand it to fit larger groups. Our idea was to work with one division at a time, pulling together the top five layers of management in each division, from the General Manager to the direct reports of the plant managers. We had this group be together with us for five days. The five days consisted of two sessions: a three-day seminar and another two-day seminar after a six-week interval in which they returned to their "real world" to try to change things in their own realms. We would not "teach" participative management. Instead, we would give them the experience of being participative, using their own division's data. Over the next six months we

planned and implemented this work within each of Tom Page's business divisions. We began to refer to the work we were doing as "Large Group Intervention Processes" (LGIP)—a way to help a large organization shift in its heart and head quickly enough to survive radical changes in the environment.

The results from the different divisional meetings were astonishing to all of us. In every five-day meeting, we were surprised to discover that each division's purpose for the five days of planning together was achieved. The purpose was slightly different for each division, and yet it basically aimed at this reason for having the gathering:

To work together as the leaders of the _____ division to unleash and combine the wisdom, knowledge and skills of all of our people in order to be able to create an organization of our own choosing.

The secret to the results we were achieving turned out to be in bringing all of the leadership of the division together in one room for five days to engage in conversations about what each person knew and yearned to be able to create. In order to have helpful conversations, we used everything we had learned about group process, such as:

- We created smaller microcosms by having "max-mix" table groups of eight persons. *That seating enabled a table to hold a systemwide conversation.* Several times during the five days we changed seating arrangements to create the group that needed to be talking together for a particular assignment, e.g., a max-mix of leaders within a Program, or a "back-home" group to make commitments for change at home.

- We gave clearly written assignments to small microcosm tables, with part of the assignment being to manage themselves by choosing a facilitator, recorder and reporter. These assignments helped them to have more effective meetings. One important assignment was to listen to each other without judgment: "Listen to see the world through the speaker's eyes. Remember that each person's truth is truth." When the group is able to listen to each other, to see what each of them sees, the group will have built a complex truth instead of arguing with each other.

- We kept the conversations going from the individual level to the table to the total group, and back again. We made sure to be focused in each assignment on expanding the database at every step. We invented a process we called an "Open Forum," designed to shift the balance of power from a speaker or panel to a table discussion of what they have heard and what they want to know more about. Tables then asked questions of understanding, to be able to see the world through the stakeholder's eyes.

- We invented a method of getting data shared amongst the people in the room, where a table would brainstorm, "What's working/not working" in the organization right now? These data are created anonymously to document a table's picture. The data are posted and each individual indicates by checkmarks what he/she agrees is working or not working. The items that received large numbers of checkmarks were reported out to the whole group to ensure that everyone was building a systemic database.

- We built a common database, where everyone could see the same challenges. A key element in building that common database was to bring in a variety of stakeholders (such as customers, suppliers and corporate leaders) who enabled the group to see the world through their eyes.

- We followed what we knew about action learning to architect a change journey. Our plan called for three stages:

Stage I. Spend three days together creating a common database, a preferred future, and the first steps to move forward. . . .

Stage II. Followed by an interval of six weeks, in which the leaders went home to their arthritic boxes and tried to bring about the changes they had uncovered.

Stage III. This back-home interval was followed by a two-day reunion with the same people. The agenda was based on action learning principles we learned from Edwards Deming. Plan/Do/Check/Act[3] was described by Dr. Deming as the same stages we use in Action Learning—"What did you say you'd do when you left? What did you actually do? What surprised you? What did you learn from all of that? The interim phase had the leaders back in their home base with the intent to change. They often felt as if nothing worked.

Coming back for the third phase, we began in back-home groups agreeing on the answers to Dr. Deming's time-honored questions. Astonishing stories emerged. Though they had arrived with a somewhat cynical view that nothing had happened, they uncovered the data that told them of the many changes that were occurring because of the first three days together. They had begun new ways of managing without even consciously knowing they had changed until they explored the questions and answers together.

In designing the flow of needed discussions, we used a model for change that Dick Beckhard[4] first articulated as DxVxF>R: Dissatisfaction with things as they are (D); a vision of what we (individually and together) yearn to have in our organization's future and in our own (V); and the first systemwide actions we must take together in order to move us in the direction (F). If all of those elements have been discussed and created, the product of DxVxF will be greater than resistance to change (R). If any one of the elements has not been explored and combined, the sum will be zero, and you will find that you can't overcome the very natural resistance to change. In that eventuality, the consultant and the microcosm group will need to diagnose what is missing. When all three elements are in place, change will begin in a moment. Six months into the change process (LGIP) we realized that the astonishing results were the direct response to creating a paradigm shift. The DVF formula was a description of what was needed to get a paradigm shift . . . literally seeing the world through new "eyes" and therefore being able to act in new ways.

And what we had uncovered was a way to ensure that the whole organization saw the world differently and was committed, individually and together, to making the change happen. What we learned in that early work with Ford was the power of a "one-head/one-heart" paradigm shift happening in a way that creates resonance—a physics concept where all of the energy unleashed will enable the "waves to get in phase." The same process in human beings is expressed in our phrase describing becoming "one-brain and one-heart." When we all (as a microcosm of the whole organization) see the world differently, and we know that we are all on the same path, the organization as a whole will begin to shift behavior. When the microcosms began to shift in their new ways back home, it was like a "positive virus" moving through the large organization.

In order to re-enforce what had happened with the leaders, we created several more stages: (1) "diffusion events" for the "bottom" of each division—from plant managers all the way through to hourly workers. We trained internal Ford people to carry out that diffusion; and (2) moving the LGIP up to the top of Tom Page's Ford organization, creating wholeness in the views across divisions. We also took the work to Europe for Ford. The most important thing we learned from those experiences is that once a group, division or person has made a paradigm shift, the person or people cannot go back. That fact doesn't mean it's easy. Leadership changes in the company can break the spirit for a while, with people ducking down for cover until the right leaders emerge again. And most of the time people are ready and eager to respond to that new leadership, even some years later. The spirit is strong.

Many years after leaving Ford, while we were writing a book about our processes, we were searching for the answer to why the concept of "microcosm" was so critical to the success of the

processes we now thought of as "robust processes." *They always worked, far beyond what we originally expected.* We, as a company ourselves, began to hear stories about the power of stem cell transplants. Stem cells are human blood cells which represent the basic cell types in the body and are capable of transforming themselves into cells needed for the heart, muscles, brain, skin and other tissues. A complex stem cell contains the DNA of the whole body. Medical research is finding ways to transplant cells into the human bone marrow. Our exposure to this way of creating blood cells has come from several friends who had been diagnosed as having terminal cancer. In the early stages of their treatment they were each given stem cell transplants from relatives or similar blood types. The next stage, if that didn't work, was to do chemotherapy on a level that killed the cancer cells for a brief period of time, allowing the doctors to harvest the person's own stem cells without including the cancer cells. This treatment appeared to take the patient to the edge of death. The medical world has uncovered a process that enables a doctor to take some of a person's own stem cells (a process called harvesting), and re-plant those cells in the same person's body. Because the cells are actually the person's own cells, the whole body system is able to "ask" for whatever it needs in order to get healthy. If the body needs red blood cells, the stem cell transplant will transform itself to supply them; if the body needs white blood cells, that can happen also.

It seemed like a magic trick when we first heard about it, and our anecdotal education is certainly flawed, but it captured our imagination. We realized that it was the same process we had been using with organizations to bring about the paradigm shift. When a "microcosm" began to develop a common picture of what was needed in the future, with a common understanding of "why," the change began to happen *at that moment*. And when it began to happen with the microcosm group, we found that the new way of "being" would spread to the wider organization. It often felt as if we were unleashing a "virus" that spread naturally in a way that caused people to know the answers they needed to have in order to change. Starting with the Ford work, we began to experience something that felt like magic: the people unite with the right answer and they are on fire to bring it about.

One of the places where we cemented our learnings about the importance of microcosm was when we uncovered a new way to design events. We called it an "Event Planning Team." We asked for and got a group of people who were representative of the participants who would be called together for an event. This Event Planning Team was a microcosm of the participants for the event. Previously we had tried to gather the data with interviews. We discovered that by getting a microcosm of the real group together for two days, we were able to get data and answers that we, as outsiders, would not know how to discover. This microcosm planning team, as they developed the Purpose ("what has to be different in the world because we will pull all these people together?") became truly connected as a team, thinking as a mini-whole system to design the agenda. At the end of the two days, the Event Planning Team would have prepared an event that was predictable in achieving the purpose, because they knew what the conversations needed to be, what decisions were needed, what follow-through should look like. As they struggled to grow together over the two days, that struggle (or conversation) would be a precursor to what will happen in the actual meeting . . . exactly because they are a microcosm. They notice this and design the meeting in ways that would work for them as a group.

We spent five years at Ford Motor, around the United States and abroad, running large group events and teaching internal consultants how to create this rapid change. Then Chuck Tyson and I were called to work at Boeing Company. One of the things we have been clear about is that the "magic" is in the people, so we listened carefully to clients and adjusted our processes to fit the particular need. At Boeing we began to use what we had learned in our work with Ford to help leaders create new strategy and get all their people engaged around the head and heart to bring about fast new results. During the mid-80s with Boeing, we invented the phrase "Real Time Strategic Change" because we realized that the Large Group Interventions processes we had invented during our Ford work enabled people at all levels of the organization to connect around a common strategic direction, and as soon as they all got it, they began to change. We realized that change truly happened in "real time."

After three years working with Boeing, we were called on by several industries facing the most serious need for change at any given time to help them change quickly. These clients included organizations in the changing areas of banking, health systems, education, telecommunications, and (of course) the defense industry. The pain in organizations became endemic, spreading now, in the new century, to e-businesses. As we modified our work to respond to these critical challenges, we began to truly understand the need for whole system thinking as organizations redesign their structures, their processes, and their global interactions. We learned constantly from our clients, and we continued to expand what we had learned at Ford and Boeing into what we now call "Whole-Scale Change." For us, Whole-Scale means "always thinking whole" (whole systems) at any scale (from a large group of thousands or a small group of 15–100). We found that it always works as long as the participants are a microcosm of the larger system . . . and the Event Planning Team is always a smaller microcosm of the participants.

Whole-Scale is based on the theory, values, and processes we had been using all along. Our work became more conscious of the importance of "system focused" work, and the incredible magic continued to unfold. As clients' convening issues became increasingly complex, we joined them in the journey to create whole-systems solutions faster and faster. People were able to redesign their organizations, and their process flows within the organization, together, enabling the "real time" magic to continue to take place. The moment a microcosm saw how it could work, the people began to do it.

Sylvia's Story

Today I can refer to myself as a "pioneer in large group, systemwide change" because I was fortunate enough to be in the right place at the right time . . . wise enough to notice that fact! . . . and curious enough to explore what I saw! In 1981, I was an internal consultant with Ford Aerospace, a subsidiary of Ford Motor Company, when 120 of our managers attended the "Participative Management" three-day session Kathie describes. I was there to learn and to work with the organization on its interim and reunion experiences. I remember standing in the room as all those previously disparate voices reached consensus on the future they saw and the actions to move them forward. All the individual (and often conflicting) stories of dissatisfaction that I had heard in previous management meetings and skill workshops became a powerful force to do something!

Of course, the aerospace management dutifully "saluted" their parent company Ford and embarked on the change journey to become more participative. More importantly, managers saw the power of breaking through cross-functional barriers and began to see all kinds of opportunities for a different approach to managing their own government programs. Instead of designing, and then throwing designs "over the wall" (an arthritic barrier) to manufacturing, and quality controlling and fixing, they could launch new programs *together* and engage every function in the conversations to design, manufacture, and deliver products—what later was termed Concurrent Engineering. They saw the possibilities to ensure on-time delivery, within budget and to continue to position themselves for future government's defense contracts.

I was fortunate to work inside an organization that "noticed" the power of the microcosm and these large group engagements around "real work." They were quick to "trust the process." They had endless ideas for staying agile and competitive even though they were already highly profitable and a winning team for defense contracts. (This was before the drastic cuts in defense budgets.) Over the next ten years, I had all kinds

of "invitations" to integrate concepts like Concurrent Engineering, Total Quality Management, SEI levels of Excellence[5] and Product Development Teams. I was asked by a new Human Resource leader to help transform the Human Resource organization from a procedure-centered staff to a consultative partner in the business. All these were opportunities to engage microcosms (small and large groups) in improving processes, structures, shared information, and organizational learning.

My own learning was from those managers and employees who kept asking, "Could we use that process to . . . ?" I just kept working with them to figure it out. They let me know when we were "out of bounds" for the situation or culture. I learned reliability, the scalability and the adaptability of those original processes and principles which we began to articulate. Again and again, I trusted DxVxF as the frame work for conversations with leaders, for agenda designs, for training, for living my life. I surrounded myself with "max-mix microcosms" to do the work and to uncover the right work to be doing along the way to support my internal customers.

Since that time, I have worked with all types of organizations around the world. I continue to discover both participative and "command and control" leaders who see these processes as "an efficient way of managing"—from aligning an entire organization to managing major programs, to leading staff meetings or project reviews. They see their organization shift from blaming to learning, to routinely engaging microcosm groups to develop creative next steps, and to listening to the wisdom of diverse viewpoints and backgrounds. They incorporate these processes for engaging microcosms into their Project Management in order to launch one integrated team with shared goals, agreement on schedules, and connected relationships capable of providing each other with what is truly needed, on time.

In the early 1990s, I received a telephone call from an engineer from my former aerospace days who was now a contractor to NASA. He knew he was involved in another task so complex that it required those robust processes he had experienced with Kathie and me at Ford Aerospace. He asked me to help NASA approach the task of overhauling the "Columbia," the oldest orbiter in their fleet of shuttles. She also needed to be fully x-rayed and retro-fitted with a new parachute. Talk about complexity! This was the first overhaul ever tackled on a shuttle. The task involved approximately five contractors (who are all competitors with each other, vying for follow-on business), three NASA centers, and two government regulatory agencies. The task would start in a month and had to be accomplished within a non-negotiable (and short) time frame in order to ensure that the next "payload" was launched into space on time. The launch schedule could not be delayed without affecting the entire "shuttle business."

Over three days we worked with key stakeholders to understand their picture of success and the obstacles they saw for getting there. Everyone wanted to collaborate, yet each group "did its own thing," and saw the other group(s) as being in the way by having unreasonable and inflexible procedures. We listened, and then asked them if they were to come to a meeting to sort all this out and make decisions, what would need to be accomplished, who would need to be there? "Impossible," they thought. I trudged on in the conversations with each one: "Say it is possible, what needs to happen right now and who needs to be at the meeting?" Quickly each one joined me in solving the puzzle, answering these questions and arranging for me to meet with others to build the meeting outcomes and participant list. Those with the influence assured me they would get the right people there!

We worked together to create a roadmap for when and how to engage a microcosm through the life of the project to ensure on-time delivery. While the details of that journey unfolded as the project progressed, it became clear that everyone needed to launch with one shared picture of success, as well as a clear picture of all of the complexity needing to be addressed to make it come together. Over four months, three whole-system events were held. Each event brought together a microcosm of these contractors, NASA personnel, and government regulatory agencies. At the first session, the group created a shared vision of how they would work together, what they would need to do differently to ensure the short turnaround, and when they would check back to ensure they were on track.

At the end of the first session the NASA and contractor leaders stood side-by-side to talk about what they had accomplished and what would happen next. They were serious about the critical importance of having the shuttle not only be on time but be safe. At the same time they were light-hearted about the energy produced by the meeting and the "partnerships" formed—they referred to the meeting as a kind of marriage ceremony!

Each work session engaged only about 60–80 people; however, they were a "microcosm" with clear purpose and processes for the conversations they needed to have at each phase. Each work session was designed by a subset of the microcosm using the current state of affairs (what is working, what isn't working) and their needs at this stage (next steps). Between each large-group work session, normal project status meetings were held and special task teams met—all designed to include a microcosm for whole-system solutions. Based on this continuous flow, the "tuned-up" Columbia was successfully launched in time, complete with parachute.

I poured every learning I had from the last 10 years into working with the NASA/Contractor community on the Columbia overhaul. And I did not work alone; I partnered with colleagues who also had experience in these large group processes. I was reminded of the power of embracing the complexity of a situation, pushing back against traditional views of getting things done, seizing each glimmer of a leader's hopefulness and learning from their doubts (wisdom), using my own adrenalin to stay focused, and staying curious to figure out each engagement. Finally, I trusted the thinking of the microcosm and the robust processes for engaging people.

Innovating into the Future: Kathleen and Sylvia

The beat goes on. The speed of change, worldwide, has called all of us into new challenges and excitement.

And now as we move forward into this century, we join our clients in discovering new approaches, including helping a global company connect around the "head and heart" when it's not possible to get everyone in the room. We are finding those answers together, because both the clients and we, as consultants, know how revolutionary it will be when we figure it out.

As we move ahead and innovate with our clients, we know that some things must remain absolute if we are to be successful together.

First is our underlying principles and beliefs—about people, empowerment, integrity and trustworthiness—that shape every facet of our work. These principles are, indeed, the "heart" of the work, and no compromise of the principles is possible for us.

We disturb the universe with every breath, and every breath/word/action must be intentional. We are constantly asking ourselves, "What is the purpose? What truly needs to be different in the world because of . . . this event, this change effort, this conversation . . ."?

Wisdom is in the people of the organization. That wisdom is developed through helping participants get to one-brain (all seeing the same data) and one-heart (all connected around common yearnings). When this has come to pass, people will be bonded together as a "whole," and will be capable of acting separately, yet in a unified way—to combine and release their own system-wide wisdom.

Each person's truth is truth. Creating a common database of truths is the work of the consultant and the organization. From the complexity of all those diverse "truths," organizational wisdom will emerge and make sense. If you create that organizational wisdom in a microcosm of the whole organization, you will find that they are able to move back into the larger organization and act as a catalyst to evoke change in the virtual "blood stream" of the whole organization.

It's about living out of our hearts. We freely share the wealth of our experiences and processes with others, in the faith that those who receive the wealth will do the same, thus creating an ongoing, positive force for change in the world.

Let's uncover this together. As Kathie Dannemiller says, "I am not the expert with 'answers.' It's easy to keep from acting as if I know everything because I don't! The biggest clue that I am inappropriately 'taking over' is when I get irritated at others for not doing the 'right' things." Consultants, internal or external, can be experts on process and adult education, that's all. Clients must fight for processes which they believe will work and must be flexible and creative at the same time. Organization members are the real experts on their own world. If the organization says a particular process (e.g., a presentation or open forum) will be wrong there, we must be willing to say "Okay. Let's work together to invent another way to achieve the purpose."

This work is about a sincere, deep abiding, unwavering view of democracy and empowerment within a system-wide view of reality. The wisdom is in the "whole." Help to release and combine the diverse beliefs and voices, and the answers will always be the right ones. Leaders[6] help everyone be as good as they can be by getting them to see the whole picture of reality—inside and outside the organization.

Be authentic in everything we do, with client systems as a whole, with others in our organizations and communities, with students, and with our own families. This belief system is not a "part time" thing.

Life is an Action Research Project. Everything we do or say becomes data for action learning and insight.

Second, and equally important to innovation in our work, we need to continue to build on our "robust processes" which are capable of addressing the complexity of today's environment. Whole-Scale change processes are built from the wisdom that had become part of our field of organization development: process consultation, action learning, systems theory, preferred futuring, community building, social-technical-systems, adult learning, strategic planning, and chaos theory.

As we move into the chaotic future, we know that we must always remember that the answers to the emerging questions are in the collective wisdom of the people. If we remember that and behave accordingly, we will all be successful beyond our wildest dreams. Ron Lippitt would have been very proud to see that the wisdom he awakened in all of us continues to be expanded and utilized in the ways we now do our work. Life has always been an action research project to us, which is what enables us to stay alive and growing. The "work" is always in process, never "finished" . . . and we are grateful for that unfolding of learning in our lives.

Appendix A: Roots and Theories Underlying Whole-Scale: Selected Readings

Action Research

Frohman, M., M. Sashkin, and M. Kavanagh (1976). "Action Research as Applied to Organization Development." In *Organization and Administrative Sciences,* Vol. 7, Nos, 1 and 2: 129–42.

Adult Learning

Knowles, M. (1980). *The Modern Practice of Adult Education.* New York: Cambridge, The Adult Education Company.

Knowles, M., E. Holton, and R. Swanson (1998). *The Adult Learner: The Definitive Classic in Adult Education and Human Resource Development.* 5th Edition. Houston: Gulf Publishing Company.

Kolb, D. (1984). *Experiential Learning: Experience as the Source of Learning and Development.* Old Tappen, N.J.: Prentice-Hall.

Chaos Field Theory

Gleick, J. (1987). *Chaos: Making a New Science.* New York: Penguin.

Wheatley, M. (1992). *Leadership and the New Science.* San Francisco: Berrett-Koehler.

Community Building

Lippitt, G., and R. Lippitt (1978). *The Consulting Process in Action.* San Diego: University Associates.

Preferred Futuring

Beckhard, R., and R. Harris (1987). *Organizational Transitions: Managing Complex Change.* Reading, MA: Addison-Wesley.

Lippitt, Lawrence (1998). *Preferred Futuring: Envision the Future You Want and Unleash the Energy to Get There.* San Francisco: Berrett-Koehler.

Lippitt, Ron (1983). "Future Before You Plan." In *The NTL Manager's Handbook.* Arlington, VA: NTL Institute.

Socio-Technical Systems

Trist, E. (1981). "The Evolution of Socio-Technical Systems." In *Perspectives on Organizational Design and Behavior* by Andy Van de Ven and William Joyce. Wiley Interscience.

Systems Thinking

Deming, W. (1986). *Out of the Crisis.* Cambridge, Mass.: Massachusetts Institute of Technology, Center for Advanced Engineering Study.

Scherkenbach, William W. (1988). *The Deming Route to Quality and Productivity.* Washington D.C.: CEE Press Books.

Endnotes

1. Whole-Scale is a registered international trademark of Dannemiller Tyson Associates

2. Dannemiller, K. "Team Building at a Macro Level, or 'Ben Gay' for Arthritic Organizations." In *Team Building: Blueprints for Productivity and Satisfaction.* W. B. Reddy & K. Jamison, eds. Alexandria, VA: NTL Institute, 1988.

3. Deming (1986), p. 86 and Scherkenbach (1988), pp. 35–36.

4. Beckhard and Harris (1987).

5. Software Engineering Institute, Carnegie Mellon University

6. Dannemiller, Kathleen D., Peter F. Norlin, and Therese Fitzpatrick. "Unleashing the Magic in Organizations, Some New Rules for Leaders." *Executive Excellence,* September 2001.

Reading 37

Organization Development in the Entrepreneurial Firm

W. Gibb Dyer, Jr.

Organization development (OD), a field that applies behavioral science knowledge to the problems facing organizations, has been created and shaped by theorists and practitioners whose work has been grounded in large institutions. For example, much of Kurt Lewin's pioneering work at the Massachusetts Institute of Technology (MIT) was based on his efforts to train leaders of various community organizations. Other notables in the field such as Douglas McGregor, Herbert Shepard and Robert Blake, and Richard Beckhard developed their ideas while consulting with Union Carbide, Esso Standard Oil (later Exxon), and General Mills, respectively. And even today, when writers cite companies that practice OD, names such as TRW, Honeywell, General Electric, and other large organizations are frequently mentioned (Cummings & Worley, 1993). Indeed, most of the theories and methods used by OD practitioners are based on the experience of large corporations (Cummings & Worley, 1993; French, Bell, & Zawacki, 1994; Glassman & Cummings, 1991).

In the past decade, however, we have witnessed the rise of the entrepreneurial firm. In the United States there are about 21 million businesses. Of those businesses, only 80,000 employ 100 or more people (Birch, 1987; Dennis, 1993). Small businesses grew faster than the historical trend during the past two decades, and entrepreneurial

This article was originally presented as a paper at the Academy of Management Meetings, Vancouver, British Columbia, August 9, 1995.

Source: W. Gibb Dyer, Jr., "Organization Development in the Entrepreneurial Firm" in *Journal of Applied Behavioral Science* (vol. 33, no. 2) 1997, pp. 190–208. Copyright © by NTL Institute of Applied Behavioral Science. Reprinted by permission of Sage Publications, Inc.

firms have created more net new jobs during this period than have large corporations (Birch, 1987; Kirchoff & Greene, 1995). In fact, large corporations (more than 500 employees) have had a net loss of jobs in recent years, ascribable to corporate restructuring and downsizing. The Bureau of Labor Statistics also notes that small business will be the predominant organizational form in those industries projected to grow during the next 10 years (Dennis, 1993).

Given this dramatic change in the structure of American industry, along with similar trends in other parts of the world, we must wonder how well the traditional theories and methods in the field of OD fit these "new" organizations: Do present diagnostic models capture the essence of an entrepreneurial firm? Can interventions such as team building be applied similarly in both large corporations and in entrepreneurial firms? Are change processes similar in large corporations and small, entrepreneurial firms? The purpose of this article is to explore these issues by presenting a diagnostic model and framework for managing change in entrepreneurial organizations. Such a framework comes from others' research and practice as well as my own experience attempting to introduce change into these kinds of organizations.

Theory and Conceptual Framework

The Nature of "Large" Versus "Small" Systems

Before outlining a framework for diagnosing and intervening in entrepreneurial firms, we first need to briefly explore how these new, relatively small, entrepreneurial ventures differ from larger systems that are typically the targets of OD activities. Over the years, numerous scholars have noted how organizational dynamics change and evolve as organizations grow and mature (e.g., Adizes, 1979; Greiner, 1972; Schein, 1985). Indeed, even some of the early OD practitioners recognized some of the differences between large and small systems and defined their practice as "large system change" (Beckhard, 1975; Miller & Rice, 1967). I have summarized the characteristics of large systems and smaller, entrepreneurial organizations in Table 1. Although there may be exceptions, these dimensions reflect the significant differences between the two.

Large systems typically have a history that provides a backdrop for the norms, values, and behaviors of organizational members. Well-developed routines and traditions serve as guides for present behavior as well as orient the organization toward the future. In contrast, new ventures have little in the way of ingrained traditions and routines. In the early stages of an entrepreneurial firm's development, the creation of traditions plays a significant role in organizational dynamics. Moreover, although entrepreneurial firms may have more "freedom" given that they are not bound by tradition, the lack of timeworn routines can also prove to cause inefficiency and a poor use of resources as members of the organization try to develop routines that "work" and are effective.

The leadership dimension also presents numerous differences between these types of firms. Previous work by Schein (1983), Kets de Vries (1977), and others has already outlined how entrepreneurs and founders differ from managers in the way they lead others. Such work suggests that managers lead by using a variety of analytic tools, are conservative in their orientation, and tend to follow the tenets of "professional management." Entrepreneurs, on the other hand, tend to be impulsive, highly emotional, and have high needs for control. They tend to be "visionaries" who have the ability to create excitement and commitment among their followers. Such differences in

TABLE 1   The Differences between "Large" and "Small" Systems

Dimension	Large Systems	Small Systems
History	Relatively long history as compared with small entrepreneurial systems; have developed traditions, routines, and so on.	Short history; lack traditions, routines, and so on.
Leadership systems	Led by those with a managerial orientation. Typically have developed formal information, reward, human resource systems, and so on.	Led by entrepreneurs and founders. Informal or no systems.
Structure	Hierarchical and bureaucratic.	Flat, informal, and particularistic.
Ownership	Often dispersed through public ownership, C-corporation. Stock price is important.	Closely held, private, family owned; typically proprietorship, partnership, LLC,* or subchapter S. Stock price not as important as earnings.
Governance	Well-defined board of directors. "Outside" directors often play a role.	Based on founder's decisions. Rarely is there a functioning board.
Family	Little if any involvement by leader's/manager's families.	Family of founders/leaders often work in the business.

* LLC = limited liability company.

leadership styles have a tremendous impact on the behaviors and cultures of each type of organization (Kets de Vries, 1977).

Large organizations, by their very nature, generally need more formal systems to coordinate their activities. Because problem solving and coordination generally cannot be done through frequent face-to-face contact as is the case in smaller systems, large organizations require formal policies and procedures, information systems, and other formal systems to regulate behavior. New organizations generally function by following informal rules of thumb and tend to avoid the creation of formal systems until absolutely necessary. In my own studies of entrepreneurial firms, I have found that founders and employees in these firms preferred informal ways of doing work because they disdained the bureaucratic procedures they had encountered in large organizations (Dyer, 1992).

The structure of large systems also tends to be more hierarchical and bureaucratic than that of smaller, entrepreneurial firms. Much like Weber's bureaucratic model, employees in large systems tend to be evaluated on the basis of merit, rise through a series of relatively well-defined hierarchical positions, and are oriented to a particular career path. An organization chart helps provide the framework outlining hierarchical movement as well as career paths. Entrepreneurial organizations have what is known as a "wheel" or "spider web" structure, with the founder at the hub or center controlling all of the activities of the organization (Dyer, 1992). Evaluation of employees' performance is informal and based on the expectations of the founder. Employees often are required to do several different tasks—they must be generalists rather than specialists—and therefore a clear, formal career path is not possible when an organization is newly founded.

Large systems are frequently public corporations (C-corporations) where the stock is widely held. Shareholders are concerned about the stock price and make a concerted effort to influence the management team to make quarterly goals to maintain or increase the price of their shares. Entrepreneurial organizations are generally propri-etorships, partnerships, limited liability companies (LLCs), or subchapter S corporations where the stock is privately held. The reason for using such forms has to do with questions of liability and the fact that the owners avoid the double income taxation of the C-corporations because they are only taxed at their individual tax rate. The number of shareholders is typically quite small with these forms of organizations, and the stock price is not as critical as earnings because the stock is not publicly traded.

These two types of organizations are also governed quite differently. Large organizations generally have a well-defined board of directors, frequently composed of company outsiders. The board meets regularly and provides overall direction and sets policy for the firm. In entrepreneurial firms, the founder makes all the key decisions and thus a board is viewed as either unnecessary or redundant (Ward, 1991). Founders find outside review of their decisions anathema and therefore avoid using a board that would provide such review and oversight.

Large organizations often have strict policies against nepotism, and with few exceptions (e.g., Ford, IBM) family relations play little role in the firm. In contrast, often family members are the only ones who are willing to work for the new venture and therefore become an important source of labor. However, hiring family members makes relationships complex given that the entrepreneur may not know how to treat family members: Should they be treated like all other employees or like family (Dyer, 1986)? This potentially creates conflicts and dilemmas in managing the firm's human resources that are not found in large organizations.

Having discussed some of the more prominent differences between large and small systems, the reader, it is hoped, will be able to recognize that these organizations do indeed function quite differently and have different dynamics. Given this backdrop, we can now begin to develop a framework that will help to more effectively diagnose the problems and dynamics of entrepreneurial organizations.

A Diagnostic Framework for Entrepreneurial Firms

Traditional diagnostic models such as those developed by Cummings and Worley (1993), Weisbord (1978), Hanna (1988), Peters and Waterman (1982), Nadler and Tushman (1977), and Kotter (1978) focus exclusively on work systems in the context of the managerial hierarchy, describing various organizational systems (e.g., information, structure, reward) and processes (e.g., communications, decision making, leadership). Moreover, most of these systems and processes are assumed to be well developed and routinized, reflecting the dynamics of larger corporations.

However, these diagnostic models are found wanting when it comes to diagnosing the dynamics of entrepreneurial firms. The behavior of entrepreneurial firms is not only a function of firm dynamics but should also be seen in light of the firm's governance structure and also in light of the dynamics of the founder's family (Lansberg, 1983). Indeed, these three interdependent systems: (*a*) business, (*b*) governance, and (*c*) family, and their relationship to one another, must be part of any diagnostic framework for entrepreneurial firms. Even open-systems diagnostic frameworks often do not reflect the dynamics of governance or of family systems because OD practitioners generally assume that a governance structure such as a board of directors is not accessible as a system in which to initiate change, and family dynamics are often assumed to be "nonrational" and therefore should not be a subject of serious consideration or should be merely eliminated (Dyer, 1994). However, those who have attempted to initiate change in entrepreneurial firms have described the importance of understanding these three systems and their interrelationships (Hollander & Elman, 1988: Lansberg, 1983). The diagnostic model presented in Figure 1 presents the basic elements of each of these systems.

The model in Figure 1 presents a skeletal framework outlining a few of the structures and processes that are a part of each of the three systems. In the business system, for example, strat-

FIGURE 1   Systems of an Entrepreneurial Firm

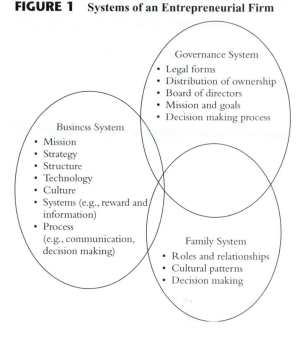

egy, structure, technology, and culture are key factors that drive behavior. Reward and information systems, along with communications and decision-making processes, are also key to understanding firm behavior. A diagnosis of the governance system begins with an understanding of what kind of formal structure is in place. Typical forms include the following: (*a*) a proprietorship, (*b*) a partnership, (*c*) an S-corporation, (*d*) a C-corporation, (*e*) a limited-liability company, or (*f*) a trust. Each form has somewhat different issues and dynamics because the distribution of ownership and responsibility for decision making vary depending on the type of governance structure. For any governance system, it is also important to understand who makes what decisions. For example, if a board of directors is established, there are a number of issues related to board composition and decision making that need to be understood (Ward, 1991). In terms of the family system, it is important to understand the culture of the family; the nature of family relationships and decision making; as well as the family's relationship to, and assumptions about, the business and the governance systems (Dyer, 1986). Those consulting with entrepreneurial firms may find the values underlying these systems in conflict. For example, a family exists to develop and support family members, whereas a business exists to generate profits and operate efficiently. Family members are rewarded for who they are, whereas businesses conditionally reward employees on the basis of their performance. Such conflicting value systems often create significant tensions as they clash in an entrepreneurial firm.

Although some entrepreneurs may insist that their family plays no role in the firm, I find that it is important for any diagnosis to examine current and possible future family involvement in the business. For example, in most cases, were the founder to die, his or her ownership in the business would be passed to his or her family. With such an event, the family is thrust into a critical role regarding the business. Thus the family needs to be prepared for such a contingency. Also, as the founder's family grows and evolves, family members may begin to play a significant role in the ownership or management of the business even if they had no role in the founding of the business. Thus family dynamics (or the potential for family dynamics) should be explored in all diagnoses of entrepreneurial organizations regardless of whether or not they are currently defined as "family firms."

Organizational Patterns in Entrepreneurial Firms

As we examine the systems in entrepreneurial firms, there appear to be common patterns that are largely a function of the founder's personality, experience, and skills. Kets de Vries (1977) and Dyer (1986) have noted that because founders often distrust others, the systems that they create are based on an authoritarian model. For example, in a previous study, I discovered that most entrepreneurial firms I studied had the following systems patterns (Dyer, 1986).

1. The business was paternalistic in nature. The founder "took care" of employees in return for their loyalty. The founder also made all key decisions, supervised employees closely, and carefully controlled all information disseminated to employees.

2. The business was governed by either a "paper" or "rubber stamp" board. These boards existed only on paper or to ratify decisions that the founder had already made. These boards reflected the disdain that the founders had for outside review.

3. The family was patriarchal (matriarchal) in nature. The founder also exhibited an authoritarian presence in the family. Children were taught not to question the founder and were generally left in a dependent relationship.

This particular configuration of these three systems had significant implications for the functioning of these entrepreneurial firms. Innovation and creativity in the firm were often stifled. Little employee development took place. Employees were in the dark regarding company goals and objectives. Little information was shared regarding employee performance. Without the oversight of a board, founders made decisions in a vacuum. Furthermore, their families were of little help because they were also kept in the dark regarding the firm's operations and had to rely almost totally on the founders for direction. Under these conditions, strategic planning, succession planning, or any sort of change planning was either not done or done quite poorly.

Other, less common patterns reflect more professional orientations to running an enterprise. The board may actively advise the founder. Decisions may be based more on formal systems rather than the personality of the founder. The family may not play a role in the firm if the founder decides that merit should be the only criterion used in making employment decisions. Such a pattern has different consequences for the founder and the business. Thus the role of the OD consultant working with an entrepreneurial firm is not only to discover the nature of each system but to see the holistic pattern: to understand the relationships between systems and recognize that the patterns in these systems lead to certain outcomes.

Criteria of Effectiveness in Entrepreneurial Firms

For OD consultants to function effectively, they must have the ability to work with a client to ascertain the criteria to be used to evaluate the system under scrutiny and to develop normative models to determine what the system should look like in the future. With any organization, developing criteria to determine effectiveness is a difficult issue, but it is a particularly thorny problem in entrepreneurial firms. Common criteria for business success might include such things as stock price, profits, or market share, but these criteria may need to be weighed against such things as family harmony and solidarity, providing employment for family members, and family wealth. Moreover, the needs of family and nonfamily shareholders may also need to be considered. How to increase shareholder wealth when there is no market for the company's stock is often a difficult question to answer.

Each system tends to have different criteria that determine effectiveness, and unfortunately in many cases they are in conflict. For example, should a founder employ an incompetent family member if this enhances family relationships at the expense of the firm's performance? Unless OD consultants are able to see the "big picture" and work through these issues related to the effectiveness question, they may end up using criteria that meet their own expectations and therefore not serve their clients well.

With these ideas in mind, I will now describe how the framework presented in Figure 1 can be used to diagnose the problems afflicting entrepreneurial firms at various developmental stages.

Methodology for Diagnosis

The "clinical approach" I use for gathering data to diagnose an entrepreneurial firm relies on work done by Berg and Smith (1985), Schein (1987), and McCollom (1990). This approach to data gathering is a process of generating and testing hypotheses through working with members of the organization being studied and by using their categories and systems of meaning to interpret the data. Moreover, with the clinical approach, the consultant becomes the research instrument and therefore should be aware of, and take into account, his or her reactions, feelings, biases, and emotions while gathering the data. Schein notes that the consultant should focus initially on the presenting problem of the client and then organize an inside-outside team to gather and analyze data. In the context of an entrepreneurial firm, such a team is generally composed of the founder(s), the consultant(s), and several key employees, board members, and family members. The process involves gathering data and having the insiders articulate the meaning of the data from their perspective and the outside consultants looking for "surprises" and interpreting the data with their knowledge of behavioral science. On the basis of their analysis, the team develops various hypotheses to be tested and a theory of firm behavior.

I have found the following to be key sources of data:

1. The firm's founders (whether currently working at the firm or not).
2. Family members of the founders or other employees with equity ownership.
3. Key managers—particularly those who joined the firm during the founding period.
4. A cross section of employees from different functions and levels.
5. Company records: articles of incorporation, partnership agreements, histories, organization charts, policy manuals, sales, productivity, or other records.
6. The layout and design of the offices/plant.
7. Regular activities and meetings.
8. The organization's customers and suppliers.

Through interviewing, observation and a review of archival records, the inside-outside team attempts to gather data from these sources. The key to an effective diagnosis, in my opinion, is to initially cast a broad net—gather data from all sources available. What might initially seem irrelevant or unimportant may prove crucial at a later stage of the diagnosis. In my own experience, lengthy interviews (2–4 hours) with the founders tend to provide the best initial source of data. There are often little archival data to analyze and, depending on the organization, little to observe. Thus "getting inside the heads" of the founders is my preferred starting point. The kinds of questions that might be asked in such interviews are described in detail in Dyer (1986, pp. 138–141).

Diagnosis across the Entrepreneurial Life Cycle: Three Case Studies

To illustrate how I have used the diagnostic framework and methods previously outlined, I will describe three entrepreneurial firms and my attempts to help them. I have found that the issues facing entrepreneurial firms are quite different depending on their stage of development. Thus the three firms that I will use for illustrative purposes will be a start-up company, a growth company, and an entrepreneurial firm making a transition from the founder to the next generation of leadership.

The Dilemmas of Start-Ups: The Phillips Company

Entrepreneurial start-ups face a number of problems unique to founding an enterprise. The governance structure needs to be defined and its role delineated. New firms may fail because of the inability of founding partners or board members to develop effective working relationships (Ward, 1991). Because start-ups have a "liability of newness" without established resource networks, only half of these firms survive five years (Dyer, 1992). Moreover, an efficient work system has to be created for the firm to function. Cummings and Worley (1993) suggest that in such "underorganized systems," defining work roles, decision-making processes, authority, and communications

patterns is key to organizational effectiveness, and the role of the OD specialist is to help management define these roles. Entrepreneurs often rely on family members to fill positions in their start-up companies because finding personnel is a serious problem. This creates the problem of "institutional overlap" because the norms of doing business that emphasize profitability and efficiency are often in conflict with familial norms of love and support (Lansberg, 1983).

The case of the Phillips company (all names disguised) illustrates how these issues are brought to bear in the founding of a business. The Phillips family had made initial plans to start a small software business. The father, Fred Phillips, a Ph.D. in electrical engineering, had made a decision to leave a firm that he had helped found and start a new enterprise with his sons and son-in-law. However, as they began to have meetings to launch this new enterprise, conflicts began to emerge in the family. It was at this point that I was asked by one of the sons to intervene to help the family work through these conflicts. Initially, I interviewed the founder, his four sons, his son-in-law, and their spouses. Because my client was strictly the Phillips family, I decided to gather the data myself rather than create a team. Gathering data in this manner would allow family members to be more candid in giving information without another family member present. Upon analyzing these interviews, several business, governance, and family issues emerged.

Business Issues
1. The new business was not going to be capitalized sufficiently for it to succeed. Thus the founder needed to seek additional sources of capital.
2. Fred Phillips' son-in-law had some technical expertise and one son had an MBA degree and some managerial experience, but the other three had little expertise related to software development. It was unclear how they would contribute to the firm.
3. A business plan had not been clearly formulated that examined all of the marketing and production problems that the new firm would face.

Governance Issues

1. Although the family had decided that the new company would be a subchapter S corporation, the composition of the governing board was unclear. Two of the sons wanted all family members participating in the business to be on the board, the father assumed that the board would follow his lead and not play an active role, whereas the son with the MBA degree was encouraging the family to include some nonfamily board members.

Family Issues

1. The father wanted the business to be a "family business" that would help strengthen family relationships. However, the spouse of one of the sons felt that such an arrangement would "smother" her independence. She wanted to have a life independent of her in-laws and was concerned that if her husband worked in the business with his family, her own family would become a mere extension of her husband's family as well as the business.

2. The son with the MBA degree, who it was assumed would be the general manager, wanted to be compensated on the basis of his position and expertise. This would mean that he and his father would be the highest paid employees in the company. The other brothers and the son-in-law, however, wanted all family members to receive the same salary. All family members are equal, they reasoned, thus salaries should be equal as well.

After gathering these data, I met with all family members and their spouses to present these issues and to discuss ways to resolve them. Given that the issues affected the entire family, I brought the entire family together initially to provide the feedback. In presenting the data to a client, I prefer to start with the less emotionally charged issues first (usually business issues) to allow the client some success in working through a problem and to set some norms for problem solving. In this case, the business issues were relatively easy to manage: The father was able to identify other sources of capital, an organization chart was developed and roles defined, and the son with the MBA degree was able to articulate a clear business plan. However, the family was not able to resolve the family and board issues. Some were adamant that all family members should be on the board, whereas others felt that the board should only include those with experience and outside board members should be considered. The compensation issue caused heated debate, because compensation not only affected their standard of living but was a reflection of one's self-worth and standing in the family. My role in the discussion was to help the family clarify the issues, to understand the options available to them, and to understand the potential consequences of their actions. As a result of these discussions, the son with the MBA degree decided not to participate in the business and took a job with a large high-technology firm.

Even though Fred Phillips recognized that it would be quite risky to start the business without the assistance of his son with the MBA degree, he decided to start the new venture anyway. Almost immediately the new firm ran into difficulty with product development and manufacturing. Without quality products to ship to customers, the company experienced increasing cash flow problems. As a result, one of Fred's sons and his son-in-law left the business. In a consulting role, the son with the MBA degree has recently attempted to help Fred develop a plan to make the company profitable, but it is teetering on the brink of bankruptcy.

Managing a Growth Company: The Bills Company

As an entrepreneurial firm expands and grows, a different set of issues and dilemmas emerges for the entrepreneur to grapple with. As the firm grows more complex, the governance structure often must change to include a functioning board that oversees company strategy, capital requirements, and management practices. Few start-up entrepreneurial firms have functioning boards, and those that do often find them relatively ineffective (Schwartz & Barnes, 1991; Ward, 1991; Ward & Handy, 1988). Most entrepreneurial firms are highly centralized, authoritarian systems that are not conducive to growth (Kets de Vries, 1977; Schein, 1983). Hence other forms of control via budgets, information systems, delegation, and shared values may need to be developed (Dyer, 1992). Professional management may enter the entrepreneurial firm as it grows, creating a clash of values and operating system (Dyer, 1989; Schein, 1983). Finally, family members and other employees may become incompetent as the firm develops and higher skills are required. Thus the entrepreneur must make decisions regarding the entry and development of family members who may wish to be involved in the business.

The case of the Bills Company (all names disguised) illustrates many of the problems that afflict the typical entrepreneurial growth company. My involvement with the Bills Company began when I was invited by the director of human resources to help them deal with several problems related to their human resource practices. The Bills Company, a retail organization, had grown rapidly since its inception. The company had been doubling or tripling its size each year, both in terms of revenue and number of employees. This posed some significant problems for the president of the firm, John Larson, and his cofounders. The following is a list of issues that emerged after I interviewed the key founders and a sample of company employees and examined various historical documents. I should note that the interviews were generally conducted with a representative from human resources as part of an inside/outside team effort.

Business Issues

1. Because the firm was hiring so many employees to handle its growth, little thought had been given to the selection and training of these employees (employees joked that all someone needed was a pulse to be hired). Thus many new employees were mismatched with their jobs and, as the firm grew, were unable to perform effectively. For example, no one in the human resource department (about 20 employees) had any formal training in human resources. Although these employees did the best they could under the circumstances, the level of performance needed to improve significantly in human resources in order to support company growth.

2. The company's growth had exceeded the founders' wildest expectations. However, in a volatile industry, they knew that competitors would start encroaching on their markets. Thus company strategy, which had been highly successful, needed to be refined to meet these new competitive conditions. Moreover, the strategy needed to be communicated effectively to employees who often complained that they were in the dark regarding the future direction of the company.

3. As the company expanded into foreign markets, issues related to organizational structure and control began to emerge. The question they were asking was, How much control should be given to the foreign subsidiaries and how much should be left to company headquarters? Moreover, the company now needed managers who had a global perspective, and preparing managers for overseas assignments and keeping expatriates motivated and productive were key issues.

Governance Issues

1. The board of directors, composed of the original founders, met irregularly to discuss company issues. Larson found the board meetings generally to be unproductive and therefore he believed the fewer meetings the better.

2. The firm had no clear succession plan in the event of the death of any of the key founders, particularly Larson. It was also unclear how a stock buyback would be financed in the event of the death of one of the founders—particularly those with large numbers of shares. Thus future control of the firm was uncertain.

Family Issues

1. The Larson family had several family members working in the business in significant positions, whereas other founders had family members as employees to a lesser extent. As the firm grew, most of these family members were reassigned to positions that fit their capabilities, and professional managers were hired to take their places. This "changing of the guard" created some confusion on the part of employees as expectations and demands changed with new management.

2. Larson and the other founders have several children. Although currently young, some of the founders seem to want their children to have opportunities to participate in the business. Thus requirements for the entry and evaluation of family members needed to be developed in the future.

In my role as a consultant, I have spent most of my time helping the firm work on the business issues. Some of the activities that have taken place include the following:

- Developing a strategic plan for continued growth.
- Restructuring several departments and reevaluating their mission.
- Developing management training programs.
- Team building in departments to clarify roles and expectations.
- Clarifying roles between family and nonfamily employees.

Future OD activities will need to focus on helping the company improve the functioning of its board, clarifying its succession plan, and developing a plan to involve future generations of family members in the business.

Exiting the Entrepreneurial Firm: The Williams Company

All entrepreneurs will eventually be replaced as leaders of their organizations through death or retirement. Succession brings a whole new set of dy-

namics and issues for business, governance, and the family. It is at this stage of the entrepreneurial firm's evolution that the training and development of future leadership become a significant issue; however, "letting go" on the part of the founder often proves to be a most difficult problem to resolve (Dyer, 1986; Lansberg, 1988). As the firm matures, bureaucracy and other related problems of organizational rigidity may inhibit growth and innovation. Thus new leadership and paradigms for management may be needed to transform the firm into a more competitive enterprise. During succession, the question of governance can become even more problematic because the founder(s) and other key shareholders and board members may be asked to play different roles. Estate planning also becomes a key issue as the entrepreneur attempts to transfer assets and ownership to the next generation of family members.

Several years ago, I was asked by Steve Williams, son of Peter Williams, founder of the Williams Company, to help them manage the succession process (all names disguised). Unfortunately, the family had not done any planning regarding succession. The firm had grown rapidly in recent years, growing from 1 small store in the 1960s to 15 stores in the 1990s. The company was known as a "high-end" company, one with quality products that commanded premium prices. Peter Williams's four sons, Alan, Steve, Lee, and Matt, all worked in the business; however, only Steve, who had recently obtained an MBA degree, had expressed much interest and aptitude in taking over for his father. One sister, Jean, had worked in the business briefly but was now staying at home raising her four children. As I interviewed all of the family members and some nonfamily managers, the following issues emerged:

Business Issues

1. There was little coordination and consistency in policies across the various stores. This created some confusion among the store managers and among customers who patronized more than one store.

2. Store managers requested more feedback regarding their performance.

3. Quality control needed to be improved.

4. Advertising programs needed to be coordinated.

5. Employee training needed to be standardized.

6. The company needed to develop a marketing strategy to compete against lower priced competitors that had recently been able to improve their product quality.

Governance Issues

1. Although Peter Williams, his wife, and his four sons were designated as members of the governing board and were, in fact, equal owners, the board did not function. Peter Williams made all of the decisions regarding the business. Thus there was no regular forum for family members to express their concerns regarding the business.

Family Issues

1. The sons did not trust Peter to turn over the business to them. They felt he would still control all the major decisions.

2. Peter Williams, now in his early 60s, did want to turn the business over to his sons but wanted his sons to recognize his contributions to the business and still wanted some input regarding the firm's operations, because the value of his shares and the income he received from property that he was leasing to the business were contingent on the firm's performance.

3. Peter Williams's daughter, Jean, wanted to feel "equal" to the other brothers because she did not own any stock in the business. Family members recognized this inequity but did not know how to resolve it.

4. One son was going through a divorce. His wife was claiming that she should be given half of his stock in the business, thus complicating the governance system.

5. Another son had a substance abuse problem and was having difficulty functioning in his role in the firm.

To deal with these issues, the following steps were taken:

1. A family team-building session was held to deal with the trust issue. This proved to be a very difficult session, but in the end, misunderstandings were clarified, and the trust level was restored.

2. A board of directors was formally established. Peter Williams was named as board chairman, and Steve Williams was named chief executive officer. This arrangement satisfied Peter's need for recognition and some involvement, and Steve felt comfortable because he was given the responsibility for making executive decisions. Board meetings were held on a regular basis and Steve developed financial reports to update each board member on the firm's progress.

3. The board started with strategic planning to deal with the business issues. A comprehensive marketing and operational plan was developed and carried out. As a result, sales reached an all-time high.

4. Working with the accountants and lawyers, along with myself, the family worked out a plan to transfer assets (not ownership) to Jean so she would feel more equal, and a plan was developed to give assets, and not stock, to the one son's ex-wife.

5. Working with a professional counselor, the family confronted the son with the substance abuse problem and was able to get him into treatment. He has made good progress thus far.

As was the case with the previous companies, the diagnosis and intervention focused on all three systems simultaneously. However, in the case of the Williams Company, improvements in the business and the governance system could only be made after trust was restored in the family. Once trust was restored, creating an effective process for governing the firm was the next step. This allowed the family to focus all of its resources and energies in solving the business problems along with the other problems that were afflicting the family.

Managing Change in the Entrepreneurial Firm

Managing change in an entrepreneurial firm also presents some unique challenges. Typical models for managing change suggest that the change agent, whether a manager or consultant, needs to build broad support in order to initiate change (Beckhard & Harris, 1977; Cummings & Worley, 1993; Quinn, 1980). In the context of entrepreneurial firms, however, the key figures are the founders. Their support is critical to achieve success. Moreover, because they generally are involved in all aspects of the business, they are in a position to implement any plans for change. Thus the role of the change agent is to prepare entrepreneurs and coach them in the art of managing change. In entrepreneurial firms, key people in a change effort may not even work in the business. Family members and board directors may be able to help to initiate change or could serve to undermine any change effort. Thus, by looking at all three systems, the change agent can better plan for change by identifying those people whose support is critical.

As the field of organization development emerged, one of the primary technologies was "process consulting" pioneered by Edgar Schein (1988) of MIT. The assumption underlying process consulting was that the consultant need not have any specific knowledge about an organization's products, markets, technologies, and so on but needed only to have an understanding of what constituted effective organizational processes such as decision making, communications, or problem solving. If consultants were to help clients improve these processes, then clients would be more effective at solving other, more technical problems facing them. What I have found in working with entrepreneurial firms is that their leaders need both process and content consulting. Consultants need to be able to provide entrepreneurs with road maps regarding how to solve specific problems, such as succession planning or the creation of a board of directors, along with helping them improve organizational processes. Also, the problems related to the family are often highly emotional and sensitive. Thus they may require more expertise than a typical OD consultant might have. Hence Swartz (1989) has argued that interdisciplinary consulting teams are needed when working with entrepreneurial firms and family businesses. In my own work, I have worked jointly with lawyers, accountants, financial planners, family therapists, and clinical psychologists when working with various clients because many of the problems facing these clients fell outside my level of expertise. Working with other professionals who operate from different paradigms can be somewhat frustrating, but if the members of the consulting team can collaborate successfully with each other, the results can be excellent. For example, I recently helped the founder of a family business work through several business and family problems related to his divorce. His wife wanted joint control of the business, which would have made governing the business very difficult because they had different goals for the business: He wanted to grow the business, whereas she wanted to take funds out of the business for her personal use. A financial consultant who had worked with this family and myself were able to work out a plan with the founder and his wife to leave the founder in control of the business while leaving his wife sufficient assets to ensure financial security for her. Through this plan we were also able to find significant tax savings for the founder. Such a plan would not have been possible unless I had worked with the financial planner to develop this plan.

The types of interventions employed by the OD consultant often require modification (Dyer, 1994). For example, consultants may find themselves conducting team-building and role clarification sessions that include members of the same family or members of the board of directors. These individuals may have long, dysfunctional histories with each other in nonwork contexts, and therefore the issues that emerge may be difficult to resolve. Also, because employees in entrepreneurial firms may have roles in each of the

TABLE 2   Interventions in Entrepreneurial Firms

System	Stage of Development		
	Start-Up	**Growth**	**Succession**
Business	Business planning	Strategic planning Structural change Team building Career development	Strategic planning Succession planning
Family	Family council	Family strategic planning Career development Family therapy	Asset management board Estate planning Conflict management Family therapy
Governance	Partner relationship interventions	Board of directors interventions	Ownership and board transition planning

three systems, clarifying their roles and their goals and objectives can prove a daunting task. Strategic planning is also done quite differently when one is attempting to satisfy the goals and demands of both business and family (Ward, 1987).

The kinds of interventions employed by consultants also change as the entrepreneurial firm evolves (see Table 2). In early-stage entrepreneurial firms, interventions designed to improve the company's business plan, to define roles for those governing the firm, and to help the entrepreneur's family work through the stress of a new business start-up are often used. Growth firms generally require changes in organizational structure and in clarifying roles. Training and career development needs become more important along with developing new forms of control through better systems. Thus structural change, career development, clarifying corporate strategy and values, and helping to engineer new information systems often become the interventions of choice during the growth stage. During the growth stage the family may also need to engage in family strategic planning (Ward, 1987) to plan for family involvement in the firm. Particularly in dysfunctional families, therapy may be the best option. I have also found that the creation of an effective board of directors during the growth stage can help the founder gain the insight and support needed to manage growth success-

fully. Succession and estate planning, whether or not to sell the business, leadership development, and culture change and renewal are the issues facing entrepreneurial firms making the transition to the next generation. These complex issues require the consultant to have considerably different types of expertise to help founders, organizations, and their families manage these changes successfully. Strategic and succession-planning interventions are generally needed along with interventions to manage the founder's estate and the potential conflicts that accompany such planning. Firm ownership and board composition often change during succession, and therefore planning needs to take place to ensure a smooth transition.

Conclusion

The purpose of this article has been to suggest that the models and methods typically employed by OD consultants do not necessarily apply to entrepreneurial firms. More complex theories and diagnostic models are needed that take into account the dynamics of the business, the governance system, and the family. Consultants often find themselves working in and between these systems and therefore need to develop interventions that are appropriate for each system. Also entrepreneurial firms are not all the same. Depending on their stage of development, the issues they face are very different, requiring very different types of expertise. Thus interdisciplinary consulting teams may be needed. Finally, the consultant needs to be aware of the pitfalls of managing change in these complex systems. Although the entrepreneur is generally the focal point for any change effort, one must also consider the power of individuals in the other systems as well. I have found consulting with entrepreneurial firms to be an extremely rewarding enterprise because change can occur more quickly than in large organizations and therefore it is somewhat easier to test one's theories about organizations and change. Working with entrepreneurial firms can also be very frustrating because of their complexity, but it can also be a highly rewarding learning experience.

References

Adizes, I. (1979, Summer). Organizational passages—Diagnosing and treating life cycle problems of organizations. *Organizational Dynamics,* pp. 3–25.

Beckhard, R. (1975, Winter). Strategies for large system change. *Sloan Management Review,* pp. 43–55.

Beckhard, R., & Harris, R. T. (1977). *Organizational transitions: Managing complex change.* Menlo Park, CA: Addison-Wesley.

Berg, D., & Smith, K. (1985). The clinical demands of research methods. In D. Berg & K. Smith (Eds.), *The self in social inquiry.* Newbury Park, CA: Sage.

Birch, D. (1987). *Job creation in America: How our smallest companies put the most people to work.* New York: Free Press.

Cummings, T. G., & Worley, C. G. (1993). *Organization development and change* (5th ed.). St. Paul, MN: West.

Dennis, W. J., Jr. (1993). *A small business primer.* Washington, DC: The NFIB Foundation.

Dyer, W. G., Jr. (1986). *Cultural change in family firms: Anticipating and managing business and family transitions.* San Francisco: Jossey-Bass.

Dyer, W. G., Jr. (1989). Integrating professional management into a family owned business. *Family Business Review, 2* (3), 221–235.

Dyer, W. G., Jr. (1992). *The entrepreneurial experience: Confronting career dilemmas of the start-up executive.* San Francisco: Jossey-Bass.

Dyer, W. G., Jr. (1994). Potential contributions of organizational behavior to the study of family owned businesses. *Family Business Review, 7* (2), 109–131.

French, W. L., Bell, C. H., Jr., & Zawacki, R. A. (Eds.) (1994). *Organizational development and transformation: Managing effective change* (4th ed.). Burr Ridge, IL: Irwin.

Glassman, A. M., & Cummings, T. G. (Eds.). (1991). *Cases in organizational development.* Homewood, IL: Irwin.

Greiner, L. E. (1972, July/August). Evolution and revolution as organizations grow. *Harvard Business Review,* pp. 37–46.

Hanna, D. P. (1988). *Designing organizations for high performance.* Menlo Park, CA: Addison-Wesley.

Hollander, B. S., & Elman, N. S. (1988). Family-owned business: An emerging field of inquiry. *Family Business Review, 1* (1), 145–164.

Kets de Vries, M. F. R. (1977). The entrepreneurial personality: A person at the crossroads. *Journal of Management Studies, 14,* 34–57.

Kirchoff, B. A., & Greene, P. G. (1995). *Response to renewed attacks on the small business job creation hypothesis.* Working paper, New Jersey Institute of Technology, Newark, NJ.

Kotter, J. P. (1978). *Organizational dynamics: Diagnosis and intervention.* Menlo Park, CA: Addison-Wesley.

Lansberg, I. (1983). Managing human resources in family firms: The problem of institutional overlap. *Organizational Dynamics, 12* (1), 39–46.

Lansberg, I. (1988). The succession conspiracy. *Family Business Review, 1* (2), 119–143.

McCollom, M. E. (1990). Problems and prospects in clinical research on family firms. *Family Business Review, 3* (3), 245–262.

Miller, E. J., & Rice, A. K. (1967). *Systems of organization.* London: Tavistock.

Nadler, D. A., & Tushman, M. L. (1977). A diagnostic model for organizational behavior. In J. R. Hackman, E. E. Lawler III, & L. W. Porter (Eds.), *Perspectives on behavior in organizations* (pp. 85–98). San Francisco: McGraw-Hill.

Peters, T. J., & Waterman, R. H., Jr. (1982). *In search of excellence: Lessons from America's best-run companies.* San Francisco: Harper & Row.

Quinn, J. B. (1980). Managing strategic change. *Sloan Management Review, 21*(4), 3–20.

Schein, E. H. (1983). The role of the founder in creating organizational culture. *Organizational Dynamics, 12* (1), 13–28.

Schein, E. H. (1985). *Organizational culture and leadership.* San Francisco: Jossey-Bass.

Schein, E. H. (1987). *The clinical perspective in fieldwork.* Newbury Park, CA: Sage.

Schein, E. H. (1988). *Process consultation* (2nd ed.). Reading, MA: Addison-Wesley.

Schwartz, M. A., & Barnes, L. B. (1991). Outside boards and family businesses: Another look. *Family Business Review, 4*(3), 269–285.

Swartz, S. (1989). The challenges of multidisciplinary consulting to family-owned businesses. *Family Business Review, 2* (4), 329–339.

Ward, J. L. (1987). *Keeping the family business healthy.* San Francisco: Jossey-Bass.

Ward, J. L. (1991). *Creating effective boards for private enterprises: Meeting the challenges of continuity and competition.* San Francisco: Jossey-Bass.

Ward, J. L., & Handy, J. L. (1988). A survey of board practices. *Family Business Review, 1* (3), 289–308.

Weisbord, M. (1978). *Organizational diagnosis: A workbook of theory and practice.* Reading, MA: Addison-Wesley.

Are Organizational Development Interventions Appropriate in Turnaround Situations?

Gregory W. Pacton

Introduction

Turnarounds vary considerably in the type, the conditions leading to the critical situation, the degree of severity, and the resources available. Turnaround firms are those which have deteriorated beyond the level where they are simply underperforming. They are in need of significant and immediate improvements in their performance levels. "Workout specialists" are frequently hired to manage firms in the more advanced stages of deterioration. These specialists are narrowly focused on "stopping the bleeding"; if the "bleeding" cannot be stopped, these individuals are skilled in maximizing the liquidation value of the firm. Generally, turnaround firms differ from companies which are engaged in renewal or rejuvenation efforts in the respect that turnarounds require crisis management in order to simply survive. Daily business reports and news briefings contain a wealth of information regarding the actions taken by managers in an attempt to accomplish turnarounds at ailing companies. Most of this information is geared toward the investment communities and deals with balance sheet and cash flow issues. The investment community closely scrutinizes the actions of turnaround managers and the short term performance results of these actions as a way to assess risks and credit worthiness. The business community is similarly preoccupied with the strategic and market implications of turnarounds. Much of the attention given to turnarounds is focused on the "hard" financial, strategic, market, and operational business issues.

Academic and popular business literature abound with case studies of successful OD transformations. Much has been written recently about the rejuvenation of businesses which have been subject to mergers, acquisitions, divestitures, and changes in strategic direction. The volume of popular business literature dealing with this subject would imply a growing acceptance of OD in the business community as an integral and vital element in achieving organizational change and making organizations more competitive. Despite this growing acceptance however, questions remain regarding the applicability of OD during the crises of turnaround situations.

Problem

Turnaround endeavors stand apart from typical business change processes in the respect that the magnitude and rapidity of the changes required are critical to the organization's survival.

The focal point for firms which are essentially sound, profitable, but underperforming, will be different than that for firms which are unprofitable and at the brink of insolvency. The firm near insolvency will be struggling with an acute shortage of critical resources, namely cash and time. Relative to an underperforming company, a turnaround firm will typically require drastic and immediate actions by the CEO to keep the firm solvent. Such actions may include large-scale workforce reductions, elimination of all nonessential spending, wholesale

Source: Reprinted with permission of *Organization Development Journal.* "Are Organizational Development Interventions Appropriate in Turnaround Situations?" by Gregory W. Pacton, vol. 16, no. 2, Summer 1998, pp. 43–53.

liquidation of inventories, disposal of nonessential assets, restructuring of debt with creditors, and negotiation of extended terms with suppliers.

The underperforming firm is analogous to a person whose health might be characterized by obesity, high blood pressure, and a general lack of fitness. This person's condition has seriously deteriorated, and though not life-threatening at the moment, may become life-threatening in the future unless actions are taken to improve the situation. The turnaround firm is analogous to a person who has suffered cardiac arrest, is in cardiac intensive care, and requires immediate bypass surgery. The cardiac patient, like the turnaround firm, must first be stabilized before the journey back to wellness can begin. It makes little sense for the turnaround firm to concern itself with longer term activities such as R&D or capital investment if the firm cannot survive the immediate crisis. It would also seem to make little sense for the turnaround firm to be concerned with OD efforts which may have long term benefits but do not aid in immediate crisis survival.

The CEO, as doctor of the ailing firm and its chief change agent, must provide selective and intensive attention to the few critical elements which will provide immediate improvements in the firm's condition. This paper explores several questions regarding the relevance and applicability of OD under turnaround conditions. Should OD efforts be part of the selective and intensive focus of the turnaround CEO? Are OD interventions applicable and appropriate to turnaround situations? Does OD contribute materially toward achievement of the turnaround? Does OD improve the likelihood of success or the rate at which success is achieved? What kinds of OD interventions might be appropriate for turnaround situations?

Prior Research and Literature Review

Before the applicability of OD to turnaround situations can be addressed, it is necessary to establish an operational definition of a turnaround.

There is a wealth of literature dealing with organizational decline. Unfortunately the definitions of organizational decline, and more specifically, of turnaround situations vary considerably. Sloma (1985) takes a broad perspective that turnarounds include any initiatives aimed at improving the company's performance. His definition includes companies who are facing imminent bankruptcy as well as those who are currently profitable but have hints of an impending future problem.

A broad but more clinical view of a company turnaround is taken by Pant (1991) in her definition of a turnaround effort as one which strives to achieve "a substantial improvement in the firm's return on assets relative to the average return of its industry." Her research found that of 835 firms which had ROA's in the bottom quartile for their industries during the period 1970 through 1976, only 64 successfully executed a turnaround by improving their ROAs to the upper quartile during the ensuing four year period. Of the remaining firms, 369 remained in the lowest quartile while 402 indicated some improvement but still well short of a successful turnaround. Pant's work focuses on technical aspects of turnarounds but illustrates that a large percentage of companies which undertake turnarounds do not achieve the desired results. Of those which are not successful, some demonstrate improvement but remain underperforming companies, some continue to barely survive, and others are liquidated.

In the Weitzel and Jonsson (1989) model, organizational decline progresses through five stages of increasing severity. The first two stages in their model are characterized by decreasing margins, profits, and capital investment. The third and fourth stages are characterized by operating losses and cash flow crises respectively. The final stage is liquidation of the firm's assets and beyond the point of potential turnaround. Winn (1993) adds a dimension to the five-stage decline model by proposing that the type of turnaround can vary, with each type incurring a different degree of difficulty. Companies which are operating in stages one and two are considered underperforming, whereas only those companies which have deteriorated to stages three or four are considered turnaround situations. Her research indicates that a successful turnaround will generally require one to five years depending upon the type and degree of decline.

The need to immediately address financial issues is confirmed by Hoffman's (1989) extensive research on turnarounds. He found that most successful turnaround managers rank cost control as first in importance, followed by changes in employee attitudes. Successful turnaround managers aggressively and actively managed financial, strategic, marketing, and operational issues with the objective of accomplishing very short term improvements in the firm's performance. He also found that these turnaround leaders actively engaged in making political and symbolic changes within the firm, developed new team members, and consulted with large numbers of the organization's members. Schaffer and Thomson (1992) found through their studies of numerous companies that turnaround situations required management to shift away from activity-centered efforts to a results-driven focus. They concluded that only a results-driven approach will yield the desired bottom-line business results in the timeframe required. Their work suggests that turnaround efforts aimed at establishing organizational development processes such as widespread employee training or team-building may be misdirected because these processes will not yield the immediate and tangible results required. Their work, however, indicates that a results-driven approach may be the basis for reorienting the organization for its future existence.

Finkin (1985, 1988) also stressed the requirement to address both strategy and control of operating costs, but acknowledges the importance of addressing the "drastic psychological and cultural changes" in a turnaround. He argues that employees must feel a sense of urgency, cooperation, involvement in achieving the turnaround, and certainly commitment to the turnaround. Finkin also points out that successful turnarounds are not accomplished by consensus; although employees must be involved, the radical changes necessary require a strong leader with the will to do whatever is necessary to assure the success of the turnaround effort.

Unfortunately, as organization deterioration continues, many incumbent CEOs are unable to make the drastic changes required for a turnaround. Levinson (1994) found that many incumbent CEOs in declining businesses either failed to grasp the firm's situation or were unable to bring themselves to making the radical changes required. Similarly, Castrogiovanni's (1992) research indicates that as the organization progresses to more severe levels of deterioration, the potential benefits of changing the CEO increase. The benefits of such an action are all related to gaining the support of the organization stakeholders. New CEOs can provide a fresh perspective on the business and its environment, provide a skill set or competency needed to navigate the turnaround, and to provide a signal to the organization that change is imminent. Castrogiovanni argues that long term change strategies are irrelevant if the business is not able to survive the short term crisis. His work indicates indirectly that OD intervention efforts become less applicable as the stages of organizational decline become more grievous. When a company's situation becomes sufficiently serious to necessitate a turnaround specialist, OD change efforts become subordinated to other issues such as cost cutting, financial restructuring, large scale downsizing, and maximizing the business' liquidation value.

Implementing the financial and operational changes required in a turnaround requires a strong willed CEO capable of making difficult decisions. However, there are far too many detailed actions for an individual to carry out single-handedly. Therefore, widespread involvement of employees would intuitively provide the vehicle for accomplishing a rapid turnaround. Reger, Mullane, Gustafson, and DeMarie (1994) point out a flaw in this intuitive conclusion. They argue that other members of the organization may not share the CEO's mental model about what must be done, the actions required to accomplish such, and the time frame in which the results must be realized. Turnarounds require actions which challenge members' basic assumptions and beliefs about the organization and its business. However, Reger, Mullane, Gustafson, and DeMarie also imply that the fundamental and radical levels of business change typically required in turnarounds cannot be accomplished without a deliberate organizational development effort.

Similarly, Tushman, Newman, and Romanelli (1986) argue that concurrent "frame-breaking" organizational changes may be required in strategy, structure, people, and processes for firms in a turnaround situation. Frame-breaking changes are revolutionary and involve discontinuous changes throughout the organization. They argue that rapid frame-breaking may be healthier than slower evolutionary organizational efforts because the old organization including its culture, practices, perspectives, are dismantled faster than they can reform. This creates a void in the organization which primes it for new attitudes and behavior, and provides the basis for establishing a new organization. The preponderance of research literature regarding organizational development deals with the broad topic of change, e.g. the need to become something different and perform differently in the future. However, there is little in the prior research which addresses the applicability and relative importance of OD as an integral component in time-critical turnaround efforts. The applicability of OD change initiatives would seem to be obvious for underperforming firms. The applicability of organizational development change efforts in or approaching the crisis stage of organizational decline and the relative contributions of OD to actually achieving a successful turnaround are less clear.

Implications for Organization Development

The five-stage model of organizational decline proposed by Weitzel and Jonsson (1989) can be adapted to provide a framework for discussing the relevance of OD in a turnaround situation. The first stage of decline may yield symptoms that a problem exists in the form of decreasing product margins, increasing inventories, and decreases in capital investment. Company profits may remain stable and mask the symptoms. The second stage of decline will generally occur because management does recognize the symptoms and does not perceive that a problem exists. This stage involves an initial decrease in company profit levels which management erroneously interprets as a one time event due to extraordinary circumstances. The third stage is characterized by a pattern of declining profits and possibly occasional operating losses. It is at this stage that it is recognized that the business is in serious trouble and that deliberate actions to correct the situation are required. Companies in the fourth stage of decline begin to experience problems with cash flow. The organization has reached the crisis stage where it is now at the brink of insolvency and must take immediate and radical steps to preserve its existence. The fifth and final stage in the organizational decline model involves liquidation of the firm's assets. Obviously turnaround efforts and organizational development do not apply. Businesses which reach this final stage are no longer viable concerns and are beyond the point of salvage.

All companies in any of the first four stages of decline would provide fertile ground for OD work. However, as businesses progressively deteriorate from the first to the fifth stages, their condition becomes increasingly critical, and greater levels of attention need to be given to the fundamental financial, strategic, and operational aspects of the business. In early stages of deterioration, cash flow may not yet be a problem. The firm may still be profitable even though signs of imminent distress are beginning to form on the horizon. It is not likely that a firm at this stage would be considering radical steps such as liquidation of nonessential assets which might be required of firms at the brink of insolvency. Firms at the early stages of decline would not require severe remedial actions because their condition is not yet life-threatening. It is at these early stages that organizational development change efforts would be most appropriate as preventive actions aimed at avoiding further decline and ultimately reversing it. Recognizing the early signs of trouble gives the company additional time to react and avoid becoming a turnaround candidate. Recruiting the workforce as participants in the change effort takes time. Sharing the vision of the future, development of a supportive constituency among the stakeholders, gaining trust and buy-in of organization members will require time—a critical resource which may be in very short supply as the business approaches the final stages of decline. Unfortunately, when a firm reaches levels three and four, the firm may be in such a critical state financially, that nearly all of the available management resources must be focused on financial issues. If the firm cannot pay its creditors, organizational development becomes irrelevant. The value of OD efforts would seem to diminish as the firm approaches these latter stages of decline. Figure 1 provides a graphical model depicting the relative importance of financial management issues versus organizational development in the various stages of decline.

For firms which have already reversed the momentum of decline and which are beginning to realize the financial benefits of a turnaround effort, OD becomes a more valuable tool in continuing

and reinforcing the turnaround. Management has more latitude in the reallocation of their time and effort; management of financial issues becomes less demanding thereby allowing increased attention to change interventions which will propel the firm toward its renewal. The need to first focus on cost controls until the firm is back on safe footing is supported by Hoffman's research (1989). Only after the business is again financially viable can the CEO begin to work on employee attitudes and behavior.

However, it seems that for all but the most severe cases of deterioration, focusing only on financial, strategic, or operational issues may "stop the bleeding" but does not necessarily prepare the firm to again become successful. The cardiac patient may have survived the coronary crisis, but survival is not synonymous with fitness or wellness. It would therefore appear that some other type of managerial impetus will also be required to move the organization back to health. Organizational development change efforts are the logical therapy. The turnaround firm, like the cardiac patient, must begin a rehabilitation program which involves significant changes in attitudes and lifestyle. Conversely, OD alone does not appear to be sufficient to save the most critically ill

FIGURE 1   Model of Relative Importance between Financial Management Issues and Organizational Development Efforts during Progressive Stages of Decline

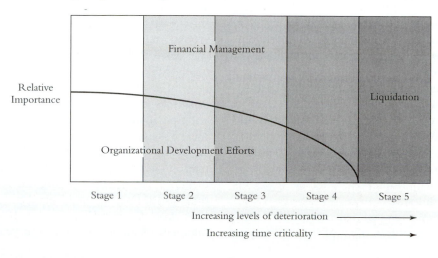

firms; OD efforts are irrelevant to bankrupt firms. The most effective approach to achieving material results quickly appears to be a combination of aggressive management of business issues and focused short term organizational development efforts. The correct combination will depend upon the circumstances and the many variables as noted by Winn (1993). It may be helpful to examine this model via case studies.

The priority of financial concerns over OD in a turnaround effort was illustrated in Clausen's (1990) turnaround methodology at BankAmerica Corporation. From 1981 to 1986, the company's situation deteriorated rapidly as a result of several environmental forces. In 1986, when his turnaround efforts began, the company was losing money at a rapid rate, had suspended its common stock dividend, was facing a hostile takeover attempt by First Interstate Bankcorp, and was being pressured by regulators to address its deteriorating capital structure. He employed a five-step approach in his efforts—three of the steps were focused at producing immediate and tangible results in business performance while the remaining two steps focused on organization development.

The severity of BankAmerica's financial situation required short term actions to "stop the bleeding" including the sale of assets to improve capital ratios. Assets were reduced by $9.6 billion, from $113.8 billion to $104.2 billion, in a 78-day period from September 30 to December 31, 1986. Clausen was also able to raise $425 million to improve primary capital ratios by offerings of notes, warrants, and convertible preferred stocks to Japanese financial institutions. Further, the organization's cost structure required immediate reductions in expenses. Expense reductions were accomplished by a reduction in employment of 21,700 people (30 percent) and closure of over 200 branches to reduce occupancy costs from $513 million to $420 million. The corporation returned to profitability in the third quarter of 1987, within one year after he began his turnaround efforts.

Though the financial aspects of the turnaround efforts captured most of the publicity in the popular press, BankAmerica employed several actions specifically aimed at organizational development issues. A new management team of outstanding performers was formed. Clausen noted that the management skills required in a turnaround situation differ from those needed under normal circumstances. Clausen indicated that success would be achieved only as a team and that every employee needed to fully understand the corporation's objectives and to feel personally involved in the recovery. Specific programs such as the "one new customer" program were aimed at improving the corporation's customer base and at simultaneously involving every employee in the effort. As the turnaround effort progressed and yielded results, the corporation awarded each employee 10 shares of stock in the company. Clausen noted the value in such an action as a symbolic recognition of those who were instrumental in the turnaround and in creating a stronger sense of ownership in the corporation's future. OD efforts were apparently a component of the turnaround strategy at BankAmerica, but significant attention to organizational development issues were not undertaken until the financial issues had been adequately addressed. The relative importance of OD efforts (vs. technical business) and relative contributions of these efforts to the eventual success are unclear.

The immediate attention to financial issues is also illustrated in Navistar's recovery. In their case study, Borucki and Barnett (1990) examined the role of organizational development in the turnaround and renewal at Navistar Corporation. In the early 1980s International Harvester was nearly bankrupt. The firm was characterized by a lack of cost controls, obsolete manufacturing processes and equipment, excessive debt, and widespread mismanagement of fundamental technical business elements. A series of environmental factors including a workforce labor strike, high interest rates, poor conditions in the farm segment of the economy, and trucking industry deregulation pushed International Harvester to the edge of extinction. Corporation sales in 1983 were less than half of the levels from four years prior; the firm had also accumulated losses in excess of $2 billion during the same period.

Immediate actions were required to avoid imminent bankruptcy. First, IH was able to negotiate restructuring of its debt with more than 200 lenders. However, many of Harvester's business units were still losing money. IH also restructured in order to reduce operating costs and generate vital revenues. The turnaround effort at IH suffered a near fatal blow in its first start toward recovery. Archie McCardell was initially given the assignment of leading the firm back to prosperity. He embarked on a cost-cutting program which alienated employees and resulted in a 180-day strike. His focus on cost-cutting blinded him to fundamental restructuring of the market and industry, and by 1980, pushed IH to the brink of extinction. Don Lennox was subsequently given the assignment to salvage IH, which had deteriorated even further under McCardell. Radical and immediate change was necessary. One of the most visible and difficult decisions was the divesture of the agricultural business operations. This particular action resulted in the sale of approximately one-half of the company and its original founding heritage. Facilities were reduced from 42 to 7. Corporate employment declined from 95,000 to 13,000—an 86 percent reduction.

Technical actions which yielded substantial impact in both magnitude and speed were required for IH to survive. It was apparent to top management that the required transformation could not be accomplished on technical actions alone. IH made OD an immediate and integral part of its survival strategy. IH provided outplacement services, severance packages with extended health and life insurance, job search assistance workshops, retraining services, relocation financial assistance, and a variety of other benefits to ease the transition of exiting employees. IH spent a total of $5.2 million to aid displaced workers.

Fortunately, Don Lennox had a more global perspective on the company's situation than his predecessors. As part of his initial turnaround efforts, he commissioned a study of the company's policies, management practices, and culture, to determine to what extent these factors would inhibit the turnaround efforts at IH. The conclusion of this study was that the hierarchical style and bureaucratic management would stifle the turnaround efforts unless dealt with. Business divestitures, downsizings, and plant closures were quickly undertaken. The firm also undertook OD efforts to aid the survivors in the form of team-building training and team effectiveness workshops. These type of efforts were aimed clearly at the short term adjustments required of survivors. Concurrently, Navistar undertook longer term organizational development initiatives, including decentralization of operating authority to the business unit levels, a formalized effort among top management to manage corporate culture, a name change from IH to Navistar, and a formalized mission statement to aid the firm in its transition to a new identity. By 1987, five years after its initial turnaround efforts in earnest, Navistar had successfully navigated beyond its pure survival concerns. Borucki and Barnett concluded that OD efforts were vital to Navistar's short term turnaround and longer term renewal.

The OD interventions employed at Navistar included the development of a corporate values statement, redefinition of the HR function to move it toward a pro-active, service oriented group, decentralization of decision making, and implementation of a dynamic strategic planning process with involvement down to the operating levels. After the company was stabilized, additional OD interventions were employed with an eye toward renewal and revitalization. The company established team-building and team facilitation initiatives which evolved into Continuous Improvement Teams. A process to address issues of employment security and competitiveness was installed. New performance management methodologies were introduced. A formal mission statement was also developed.

In their case study, Sorensen, Head, Scoggins, and Larsen (1990) cite OD interventions as a critical element in the SAS turnaround. SAS lost market share between 1975 and 1980 in an increasingly turbulent environment. In 1981, the company lost $8 million and recruited Jan Carlzon to lead the turnaround. Carlzon's technical changes were heavily focused on creation of market niches which would attract business passengers. Specific programs included the creation of the "Euro-class" of travel, increased passenger seating space, dramatic improvements in on-time performance, and differentiated pricing structures to attract new leisure travelers.

They also found that from the onset of the turnaround effort, SAS began a transition from a bureaucratic culture to a service-oriented one. Carlzon replaced 13 of 15 top managers in the company as a way of communicating to the workforce in a very visible way that the firm had moved beyond its old approaches. He used top management behavior and symbolism as vehicles to demonstrate change. The rewards and performance appraisal systems were modified to reinforce the desired behaviors throughout the workforce. SAS also used extensive employee training to develop a favorable self-image, to cultivate the desired service orientation among all employees, and to establish a culture with a bias toward achieving results versus simply engaging in processes. SAS was returned to profitability in a little more than one year. It is noteworthy that SAS was able to reverse its financial plight within a very short period of time without reducing its total employment. In fact, employment increased and 25 percent of administrative personnel were redeployed to areas of direct customer service. Sorensen argues convincingly that OD interventions were a vital component in the turnaround endeavors and the speed with which the turnaround was accomplished.

In a more recent case, Gil Amelio (1996) led the turnaround at National Semiconductor. Amelio claims that the transformation was accomplished in two steps. The first step required nursing the company back to financial health with "tactical actions" such as plant closures, aggressive cost slashing, and downsizing the workforce. Once accomplished, the company could then divert its attention to transformation of the organization into a "great company." Unfortunately, he

left National Semiconductor after concluding only "Phase 1" to join Apple Computer with a similar challenge.

Amelio (1996) asserts that "You cannot save your way into success." Cost-cutting measures alone will not achieve a turnaround. At best, such actions may stop the deterioration and stabilize the company, but will not restore it to levels of outstanding performance. Amelio argues that the aggressive financial management must be supplemented with other initiatives in order to achieve organizational transformation. Some of these initiatives are strategic in nature such as development of a thorough understanding of customers' needs, knowing your own firm's core competencies and competitive advantages. Other turnaround initiatives are clearly OD oriented. Among the initiatives he believes need to be immediately undertaken in a turnaround are the creation of a clear vision of the company's future, inviting employees to share in the vision and to contribute to it, clearly defining what constitutes success, identification of critical success factors, taking bold steps to reverse the negative momentum, and active communication of the new direction to all employees.

Does the needed attention and priority to tactical turnaround issues imply that ignoring OD initiatives during early turnaround efforts is appropriate? It appears that the answer is "no." All of the aforementioned turnarounds engaged in some type of OD change intervention during the initial turnaround actions. All of the OD change interventions were geared toward simultaneously modifying the firms' cultures, attitudes, and behaviors in parallel with the changes occurring in the financial, strategic, and operational elements of the businesses.

Is there a pattern in the type and application of OD interventions used in successful turnarounds? There does appear to be a pattern. Table 1 provides a comparative view of the tactical/financial actions and the OD intervention employed in each of the turnaround case studies discussed. Clearly, all firms utilized OD interventions. Would the turnarounds have been successful without the use

TABLE 1   Comparison of the Financial and OD Turnaround Actions of Four Successful Companies

Company	Turnaround Financial/Operational Actions	Initial Organizational Interventions	Time to Achieve Turnaround (return to profitability)
Bank America	Aggressive cost-cutting Location closures Sale of assets Suspended stock dividend Issued preferred capital Workforce reductions	CEO replaced Established new management team Aggressive communication campaign	1 year
Navistar	Plant closures Downsizing Debt restructuring Strategic market realignment Divestitures	CEO replaced Corporate values statement Redefinition of HR function Install dynamic and participative strategic planning process	7 years
SAS	Focused on market niches Differentiated pricing structures	CEO replaced Replaced 13 of 15 top managers Modified rewards and performance appraisal system Extensive employee training Redeployed 25% of administrative workforce	1 year
National Semiconductor	Plant closures Downsizing Workforce reduction Aggressive cost-cutting Realignment of manufacturing plants	CEO replaced Active communication to employees Creating clear vision of future Define key success factors	2 years

of these OD interventions? It is impossible to say if each would have otherwise been successful. However, the chief change agents in each situation make a convincing case for OD efforts as a key component in the turnaround initiative.

Conclusions

The empirical evidence would seem to indicate that OD efforts do complement turnaround efforts and to a degree improve the likelihood of success in all but the most severe situations. The firm must first survive the immediate financial crisis for OD to be effective.

Case studies of successful turnarounds acknowledge organizational development efforts, but it is difficult to ascertain the relative impor-

tance of these OD efforts to the success. Conversely, case studies of failed turnaround efforts usually cite the cause of the failure as the inability to stem the firm's liquidity problems. Although cost-cutting and aggressive financial management may be able to forestall bankruptcy, it appears that such actions need to be supplemented with other strategic and organizational changes in order to materially move the firm back toward rejuvenation and renewal. Future research might be appropriate to statistically validate whether deliberate inclusion of OD interventions in the turnaround effort yields a greater likelihood of success. Future research might also explore whether turnarounds are achieved faster when supplemented by OD change efforts despite the generally accepted wisdom that OD change efforts take time.

References

Amelio, Gil, & Simon, William L. (1996). *Profit from experience: the story of National Semiconductor and transformation management.* New York: Van Nostrand Reinhold.

Borucki, Chet, & Barnett, Carole K. (1990). Restructuring for self-renewal: Navistar International Corporation. *Academy of Management Executive, 4*(1), 36–49.

Castrogiovanni, Gary J., Baliga, B. R., & Kidwell, Roland E. Jr., (1992). Curing sick businesses: changing CEOs in turnaround efforts. *Academy of Management Executive, 6* (3), 26–41.

Clausen, A. W. (1990). Strategic issues in managing change: The turnaround at BankAmerica Corporation. *California Management Review, 32,* 98–105.

Finkin, Eugene F. (1985). Company turn around. *Journal of Business Strategy, 6,* 14–24.

Finkin, Eugene F. (1992). Structuring a successful turnaround. *Journal of Business Strategy, 13,* 56–58.

Hoffman, Richard C. (1989). Strategies for corporate turnarounds: What do we know about them? *Journal of General Management, 14* (3), 46–66.

Levsinson, Harry (1994). Why the behemoths fell: Psychological roots of corporate failure. *American Psychologist, 49,* 428–436.

Pant, Laurie W. (1991). An investigation of industry and firm structural characteristics in corporate turnarounds. *Journal of Management Studies, 28,* 623–643.

Reger, Rhonda K., Mullane, John V., Gustafson, Loren T., & DeMarie, Samuel M. (1994). Creating earthquakes to change organizational mindsets. *Academy of Management Executive, 8* (4), 31–46.

Schaffer, Robert H., & Thomson, Harvey A. (1992). Successful change programs begin with results. *Harvard Business Review, 70,* 80–89.

Sloma, Richard S. (1985). *The turnaround managers handbook.* New York: Free Press.

Sorensen, Peter F., Head, Thomas C., Scoggins, Helen, & Larsen, Henrik Holt (1990). The turnaround of Scandinavian Airlines: An OD interpretation *Organization Development Journal, 8* (1), 1–6.

Tushman, Michael L., Newman, William H., & Romanelli, Elaine (1986). Convergence and upheaval: Managing the unsteady pace of organizational evolution. *California Management Review, 24* (1), 29–44.

Winn, Joan (1993). Performance measures for corporate decline and turnaround. *Journal of General Management, 19* (2), 48–63.

Part 7

Challenges and Opportunities for the Future

Organization development and organization transformation face opportunities and challenges that will greatly test practitioners and scholars in the years ahead. This is partly because it is a young field, partly because of its eclectic nature, and partly because of the dramatic changes occurring in the nature of work, organizations, and society. Contemporary OD & T practices borrow from social psychology, counseling psychology, organization theory, family group therapy, human resources management, systems theory, group dynamics, management, and other disciplines. Any attempt at an amalgamation of insights from such a spectrum of fields to develop effective interventions for ongoing organizations is bound to create many challenges. For example, how nondirective can the OD consultant afford to be if the client is talking about establishing benefits or privileges in one group without being cognizant of potential perceived inequities by other groups? Counseling psychology has something to say about the utility of a supportive nondirective consultation style, but human resources management and social psychology have something to say about cognitive dissonance and inequity. Reconciling the two conflicting action implications may be difficult in such a situation. How does OD relate to various movements or contemporary areas of emphasis like "quality of work life" or the learning organization? Is OD the same thing? Different? How can one articulate the differences or similarities? What are the consequences of not doing so?

But OD & T practices are also beset with many problems and issues because they inevitably affect people's lives, and sometimes deeply. We would like to think that people are usually affected positively, and we believe this to be so; but questions of ethics, of values, of what is helpful and what is hurtful, must and do arise. How much manipulation is there in the particular OD intervention in the particular context; that is, to what extent is there a hidden agenda in the use of the intervention, or to what extent is the nature of the technique or its consequences kept from the participants? What should be the depth of an intervention in order to be both efficacious and at the same time not harmful? Should the consultant attempt to interpret and surface resistances? Under what circumstances is feedback constructive? How much, or should, the OD consultant be aligned with the exercise of power in the organization? What should the OD consultant's training be? And how does one know when a consultant is qualified to practice? These are not simple matters.

Opportunities and challenges also arise from tectonic shifts taking place in technology, science, demographics, industrial and world economics, cultures, competition, and the nature of change itself. Only the fittest (and fastest, smartest, most nimble, most adaptive, most proactive, and luckiest) organizations will survive. And only the fittest organizational effectiveness strategies will survive, too. How must the field of organization development and transformation change to become more effective, viable, and valuable in these turbulent times? What first-order (incremental) and second-order (revolutionary) changes must be made to keep OD relevant and useful to organization leaders and members? OD has changed a lot since its beginnings; it must continue to do so. Innovation, adaptation, experimentation, and a lot of hard work—that's the agenda for today's and tomorrow's practitioners and theorists.

Readings in this part explore the relevance and efficacy of OD, ethics, team empowerment, sources of environmental turbulence, productivity-enhancing human resource practices, and a future agenda for the field.

Readings in Part 7

In the first reading, Jane Galloway Seiling interviews Peter Vaill, a well-known, highly regarded OD practitioner. Vaill raises several issues for consideration: Is it possible to integrate individual goals and organizational goals, as OD consultants claim? Are OD's theories of planned change adequate given today's conditions of constant change and "permanent white water"? Is OD even relevant in today's environment? These are serious questions that merit serious reflection and analysis.

In the second essay, "Ethics and Organizational Change," Warren Nielsen, Nick Nykodym, and Don Brown emphasize that along with pressures for change have come critical questions about the ethics of change. These issues, they assert, must be acknowledged and confronted by those involved in change processes. One of the most provocative questions they raise is the following: *"Is it ethical to hold on to the nondirective philosophy?"* They go on to say that "organizations recognize the need for process consultants, but, because of external pressures for change, need consultants who can also function in the task and expert areas."

Empowered teams—what they are, how to create them, what they deliver in terms of performance and member satisfaction—is the topic of "Powering Up Teams" by

Bradley Kirkman and Benson Rosen. A study of 100 teams in four different organizations, in which the teams possessed varying levels of team empowerment, was conducted to discover the antecedents and consequences of empowered work teams. The results are interesting and exciting: empowered team members have a sense of potency, meaningfulness, autonomy, and impact; and this in turn leads to increased team effectiveness. As the authors suggest, Why settle for self-managed teams when you can have empowered teams?

In the essay, "Managing Discontinuities," C. K. Prahalad describes major discontinuities he sees facing *all managers* as the world moves into the next millennium. Trends we have seen in the past may be interrupted, or will be juxtaposed with conflicting trends that must be accommodated, or will converge to create major new challenges and opportunities. While Prahalad does not refer to OD & T directly, some of the challenges he mentions certainly cry for OD-type help, for example, dislocation of employees, mergers, the creation of teams from several different cultures; the formation of temporary alliances; speed in disseminating and absorbing new knowledge; the introduction of new skills into organizations; the need for "processes that improve the ability of teams to develop special skills," and dealing with four levels of diversity: "race, gender, cultural, and intellectual."

In the fifth essay, "Seven Practices of Successful Organizations," Jeffrey Pfeffer describes seven dimensions he sees as characterizing "most if not all of the systems producing profits through people." All are congruent with successful OD & T efforts; some like "self-managed teams and decentralization of decision making" may be outcomes of OD & T efforts. Pfeffer's seven practices are "employment security," "selective hiring of new personnel," "self-managed teams and decentralization of decision making," "comparatively high compensation contingent on organizational performance," "extensive training," "reduced status distinctions and barriers, including dress, language, office arrangements, and wage differences across all levels," and "extensive sharing of financial and performance information through the organization."

W. Warner Burke, in his "The New Agenda for Organization Development," reminds us that OD traditionally has emphasized such values as human development, fairness, openness, choice, and balance of autonomy and constraint. He goes on to say, "A number of senior practitioners in OD, i.e., those with 20 or more years of experience, believe that the profession has lost its way—that its values are no longer sufficiently honored, much less practiced, and that the unrelenting emphasis on the bottom line has taken over." In particular, Burke finds these values largely absent in reengineering and downsizing practices and discusses the appropriate role for the OD practitioner when the client is contemplating moving in one or both of these directions. Of even more importance, Burke believes, is for OD practitioners to become involved with the deep issues of "community," the "employer-employee social contract," the concept of "employability," "trust," "culture clash," and "corporate power."

Reading 39

An Interview with Peter Vaill

Jane Galloway Seiling

Setting

Peter B. Vaill, D.B.A., holds the Distinguished Chair in Management Education at the University of St. Thomas, Minneapolis, MN. He is considered to be one of the leading authorities on organization development. He is a consultant and author of a number of books including: *Management as a Performing Art* (1989); *Learning As a Way of Being* (1996); and *Spirited Leading and Learning* (1998).

In Dr. Vaill's book *Management as a Performing Art* he introduced us to the term *permanent white water*. He said, "We live in a time of permanent white water . . . Permanent white water consists of events that are surprising, novel, messy, costly, and unpreventable . . . With this there seems to be widespread agreement: permanent white water conditions are regularly taking us all out of our comfort zones and asking things of us that we never imagined would be required. Permanent white water means permanent life outside one's comfort zone." Permanent white water is even more obvious and overwhelming now than it was then—and is impacting the field of organization development significantly. After reading a chapter of an edited book written by Dr. Vaill, I approached Dr. Vaill and he consented to the following interview.

Dr. Vaill, I recently read a book chapter you wrote titled, "Change as Growth" and I was impressed with your thinking on this subject. The writing

Source: "An Interview with Peter Vaill," by Jane Galloway Seiling, *Organization Development Journal,* Vol. 20, No. 3, Fall 2002, pp. 100–106. Reprinted by permission.

suggests OD has been on the wrong track and trying to do an inherently undoable task for the past 40 years. Could you tell us more about this?

Peter: Thank you, Jane. I'm glad that idea caught your eye, because I have wanted to get some feedback from the profession about whether it makes any sense. In *The Human Side of Enterprise,* McGregor said that management's job is ". . . the creation of conditions such that the members of the organization can achieve their own goals *best* by directing their efforts toward the success of the enterprise." He calls this the "principle of integration." Old timers will know that this single statement functioned as a call to arms all through the early years of O.D. It provides the foundation for the idea that an organization can be both very prosperous itself, and be a thoroughly satisfying place for people to live and work. In the 1960s and 1970s, I heard it quoted constantly as a fundamental statement of what we should be trying to do in O.D. Yet, I now think it's a mistaken notion in two ways. First, it breaks a rule of logic. Second, even if it doesn't break any rules, I think it has been overtaken by events.

The statement, I believe, contains what logicians call a "category error." We know it more simply as an effort to compare apples and oranges. The two kinds of goals are those of persons, and those of the organization, which are not the same order of things. If one inadvertently compares apples and oranges, you will constantly find yourself trying to make things fit that don't fit. For example, is McGregor saying that all of a person's goals can best be reached by pursuing the goals of the enterprise? Is he saying that his principle applies to all of the goals of the enterprise? Would he make any allowance for the fact that sometimes organization do dangerous, noxious things as part of their mission? Does his principle apply to those things? Or are some personal goals selfish, indulgent, and even harmful? Does his principle apply there? If not, where would he draw the line?

In the succeeding forty years, the pace of change has picked up substantially, and the manager's environment has become much more complex and unstable. But do we still insist on the integration? As you know, I like to say we're living in "permanent white water." Goals are not stable, tangible things any more. At best they are tendencies and approximations. "Integration" is literally a mechanistic concept. What about the dynamism of the two categories? They both change and evolve, but is he saying they must change and evolve in step with each other? What about how personal goals are much more concrete than organizational goals? At the personal level we can feel those goals, taste them, and describe them specifically. Organizational goals, on the other hand, are much more abstract and aggregated. They also differ widely in meaning depending on where you are sitting in the organization. A plant manager may think the principle of integration is working fine, whereas a foreman on the shop floor may be much more aware of how the principle is not working for a given group of people.

Net, the integration principle sounds great, but when you actually push on its meaning, it turns out not to be a very helpful guide to action. Yet thousands of managers, consultants, and professors have bought into it as a valid principle of management. Millions of dollars have been spent on change efforts aimed at fulfilling the principle of integration.

My perception is that most change programs don't stick. Return five years later, and it's usually hard to detect their effects on the organization. Perhaps this is due, at least in part, to an ill-conceived change effort in the first place. An effort that thought personal goals and organizational goals could be aligned.

Of course, if I'm right in this critique of McGregor, the big question is what should be the basis for doing O.D. in an organization? If it is not alignment and integration, then what?

In my days in graduate school, O.D. was defined by French and Bell as "planned, systematic, long-range efforts focused on the culture and its human and social process." These efforts to make change happen, as you note, were at times short-lived and even disastrous. I sense that you see "change" as different than what the O.D. definition called for. In your view, what is change? Especially in view of the words "planned change"?

Peter: Once again, I wonder if we are giving as much attention to the new conditions under which O.D. is operating. When we used the phrase "planned change" forty years ago, we meant moving from one stage to another. Kurt Lewin's famous definition of "unfreezing, moving, refreezing" says exactly that. Today's organization is permanently unfrozen! It is gyrating in all kinds of ways—in its products and markets, its work force, the technologies it employs, its forms of financing, even its statement of its principal mission and purpose. What is "planned change" under such conditions? Moreover, it always amuses me to read an O.D. textbook and realize that it is written as though the reader is the only person in the organization who is trying to foster change. I can't think of any text that says flatly, "Look, *everybody* is trying to foster change these days. Your efforts to do what we call 'organization development' are just one set among many. In fact, there may be serious dedicated people in the organization who are trying to undo the very changes you're trying to foster!" That would be a much more honest way of talking, but I don't recall hearing anyone in O.D. say that out loud.

For example, I remember hearing many TQM people say that what they were doing was definitely not O.D., and some of the socio-tech folks used to talk that way also. I've heard people who seek "organizational transformation" say that what they're doing is not O.D. Certainly some of those who are beginning to imagine a thoroughly virtual organization unlike anything that has ever existed would probably not say they are doing O.D.

So we have these things called organizations, which have become the objects of change for several different professions, quasi-professions, and schools of thought. I'm not even sure O.D. is on the leading edge anymore. Yet, I must quickly add that the historic vision of O.D. that focuses so much on improving human relationships in the organization is, I think, still of strategic validity and necessity. It's just that O.D. is no longer the only game in town, and maybe not even the most glamorous one!

What everyone needs is a more adequate theory of the change process than Kurt Lewin's original formulation. How O.D. could have gone on this long without a theory of the change process is kind of amazing, but it has. The result is that an O.D. person is always feeling his or her way, "makin' it up as you go along," "writing the book as you go." Maybe it has to be that way, but we won't know until we try for a more powerful theory of the change process. I'll say one thing: I think a better theory of the process lies in the direction of what we would call a political process, yet a lot of us in the field get nervous when we hear that word.

You can't get off the hook that easy: what would "a political process" look like as a theory of the process of change?

Peter: Jane, I'm not sure exactly what an adequate theory of the change process would look like. But the reason I say it would be more "political" is because I think any change process of any real significance in a complex organization is going to involve a lot more intense persuasion, bargaining, influencing, exchange of rewards, and a lot more back-and-forth tugging and hauling than O.D. has historically assumed. Now in that last sentence I am trying to get at a descriptive theory of the process. A descriptive theory of what it's actually

going to be like, as opposed to O.D.'s tendency to hold itself to very pristine standards of behavior. "Political" action doesn't have to be dirty tricks and manipulation. In fact, it must not be. It must play fair: it must have an ethos of fairness. However it is still "political" in recognizing power realities, that there are multiple interests in play that are not always in harmony. Also, that there is intense consciousness among players of the resources and rewards that exist and a desire on their part not to be slighted or outmaneuvered as these resources and rewards are distributed. O.D. has historically been officially disapproving of all of this. Though it must quickly be said that there are plenty of O.D. practitioners who know exactly what I'm talking about and who are comfortable defining their work in a political frame, rather than a moralistic frame.

You have written in the past about high performing systems (HPS) and also of spirituality being a significant part of leader development. HPS has been a highly "acceptable" topic for years, but spirituality as part of leading? This would be a new way of thinking for many leaders. Could you elaborate more about this?

Peter: Back in the 1970s and 1980s, I used to do a lot of writing and speaking about what I called "high performing systems" (HPS). I love those things to this day, but I don't actively do research on them anymore. Partly because the "excellence" writers have made the whole subject so glitzy and commercial, but mainly because I don't think just describing an HPS is helpful. The real question is how a group or organization achieves that transcendent level of performance. And guess what? When you study that, you discover that it was not by some super rational piece of strategic management, but rather it was by a process marked by great courage, political skill, and luck.

Every effective leader of an HPS I've ever seen has a wonderful ability to navigate the permanent white water, keeping clear on the purpose of the activity. At the same time imparting some measure of faith and hope to the members of the system so that they trust that things are going to turn out all right. The "political" part of it is in knowing who needs to be on board, how to get them and keep them on board, and who is potentially a blocker or destroyer of the effort and how to deal with them, ethically, but firmly. The political part also lies in the ability to negotiate and finagle the resources the system needs, whether it's officially in the budget or not. HPSs engage in what I called "non-guilty exploitation of their environments." They don't sit around moping about not having the resources they need. It's all "political" because often the HPS is vulnerable to being crushed by the larger system, and "stayin' alive" becomes a top priority. That's when the political process of change comes alive.

Many men and women who are navigating successfully in these turbulent environments feel very vulnerable, and have found they need a faith in some kind of higher power or reality that will sustain them through what can be dangerous and pretty stressful times. I think this is why we've discovered "spirituality" in the last decade or so. We feel the need for something to put our faith in, and we see other leaders and managers in organizations feeling a similar need. Moreover, many of us have had the unpleasant experience of having put our faith in something material and instrumental, only to find it undercut by the white water. Our salaries and fees, our advanced degrees, our robust bodies and workaholic life styles, our dedication to our profession, our supposedly secure jobs in our supposedly secure organizations, all our supposed resources we have found can dissolve on us in a twinkling. That's the great, unnoticed experience of the last decade and particularly since 9–11. We Americans have finally discovered all our supposed material strength is in fact a fragile bubble we've been walking around in. In recent years in various ways we've discovered how permeable our bubble actually is.

So now here we are out in the open. Do we still have the faith and courage to try to instigate positive change in these organizations of ours? Are we willing to go through what you have to go through to stay with a complex change process? I don't

know if I can do it, but I certainly know I can't do it without continual spiritual practice and development on my part. I think we're all like this in some kind of a situation. Just today, a consultant friend of mine said he was finding more and more that fearlessness is becoming a requisite in his work. Well, I don't know about him. However, for me my fearlessness, to the extent I have it, is under-girded by faith in the transcendent truth, goodness, beauty, and love I have learned to see all around me.

Here is a tough one, Dr. Vaill: I would like to hear more about your thoughts regarding "change as growth." Organization members certainly do feel "out in the open" and vulnerable when faced with continual change. Under these circumstances, how does change become (meaningful) growth for the people experiencing it?

Peter: That is indeed a key question and it's another way that McGregor's principle of integration may get us into trouble. Most organizations these days are trying very hard to change. The changes they are pursuing are driven by market realities and financial realities, not by efforts to make themselves more healthy and growthful environments for their people. They may say that they want to be positive, supportive environments, but the first priority is survival under conditions of ferocious competitive pressure and resource constraints. And so organization members are left to adapt to these conditions. This is when courage is really called for.

The question then is, what is O.D. under these conditions? Can it continue to pursue its historic function of helping organization managements create a more positive, supportive climate for organization members? Can it help organizations become flatter, more democratic places? Can it foster more authentic communication among organization members? I am starting to wonder if O.D. can continue to play this kind of role in present and future organizations.

The very fabric of the organization is a different thing than it was when O.D. was invented.

People are spread so thinly, and organizations are so thoroughly decentralized and stove-piped that it's not even easy to find the client any more!

You used to be able to walk into a department, where most of the members were present most of the time, and look at the way they were working together. Maybe do some survey feedback, maybe convene a few focus groups, maybe take everybody on an off-site, and come out of it with an understanding (a "diagnosis") of how they were impeding themselves and of what they might do to be more effective together. Less and less is it possible to do this kind of O.D. Less and less is there anything very tangible to consult to!

Of course, it is also the case that continual change is occurring. People are being moved around, functions redefined and reorganized, new leadership appearing continually (only to be then gone in a year or two), the organization buying or being bought by other organizations with consequent mergers of organization cultures going on, rampant technological change of all kinds but especially in information systems technologies, plus a host of more specific, local kinds of changes. This "permanent white water" is where the O.D. is going to go on, and it is where "change as growth" is going to occur if it is going to occur at all.

How does McGregor's integration principle fit in here, or does it?

Peter: I don't think it is going to occur by McGregor's principle, because that principle requires too much stability and too much control.

The bugaboo is control. Every O.D. person has had clients who are control freaks, who have to be on top of every detail, who want to plan things out to the proverbial gnat's eyebrow. There's the wonderful saying about the manager who can't resist continually pulling the plant up to see if it was growing. Our whole managerial culture is one of control that's what we're teaching for the most part in business schools. We teach how to get control of things and keep control; how to find out what is going wrong and "take charge" of it and "straighten it out." It's all very macho, very mas-

culine (which doesn't mean there aren't plenty of women who like to control things too). Control is the dominant mental model of American management. Even "leadership," which has become probably the most popular management topic there is, has become a kind of code word for control. Instead of saying someone needs to take control of a situation, we say the situation needs leadership, but we mean the same thing.

We call people who want to control everything, "control freaks." A more exact term would be "cyberholic," one who is compulsively addicted to trying to control things. It is a compulsion. Think of the clients we've had who just can't resist taking control of meetings, even if it is not needed or even appropriate. Or think of the clients we've had who have to win every argument, always have the last word. Many of them cannot stop from behaving this way. If it is an addiction, then we know we are up against a very tough problem.

The longer I have reflected on what permanent white water calls for, the more I think the ability to let go and move with the energy of the system is key. We say "don't push the river." Interestingly enough, one of my early observations about high performing systems, almost thirty years ago, taught me the same thing. That they find a groove, get on a roll, get in sync, get on the same page, get in their rhythm. They invariably had favorite phrases for conveying this feeling of smooth, effortless movement. They'd use these phrases to convey the idea that minimizing control was the secret to the extraordinary effectiveness they displayed.

Yet we can all think of plenty of cyberholic clients who would be very nervous about relinquishing control, and you can understand why. They're personally under crushing performance pressure. It is paradoxical that they might be able to perform better if they would let go of more control, and they have trouble even contemplating the idea, much less trying to learn to practice it. Steve Rhinesmith, a well-known Washington DC O.D. consultant, said at a conference a few years ago, "In order for significant change to occur, you have to be willing to let things get more out of control than you're comfortable with." I think he's exactly right, but what a tough lesson!

This is a point at which an O.D. consultant might be extremely helpful. To help the client experiment with ways of relinquishing control, finding the latent energy in the system and seeking to *release* it rather than battle against it, or trying to trick it into appearing with reward schemes and sweet talk. Learning to dramatically reduce the amount of control one exerts *is* change that is growth, and as I say, it is a kind of change that is widely needed. I think it would be of strategic value for an O.D. consultant to focus his or her practice on developing ways of helping a client to let go and reduce the amount of control they are exerting on the system.

Here is where yet another paradox appears, many O.D. folks themselves have cyberholic tendencies. I certainly do not exempt myself! Some of the O.D. pioneers were very strong personalities who definitely wanted to have their way about things. There is the constant temptation in O.D. work to replace the client's judgment with one's own, to accede to the client's desire for a cookbook by giving them one. Many clients think that is what you hire a consultant for, to tell you how to do things. In the long run, we're of much greater value if we help a client learn to create and develop solutions themselves rather than rely on someone else's cookbook. But we have to grow out of our needs for control, if we are going to help clients grow out of theirs. I know there are plenty of O.D. people who understand this problem and are continually engaging in the learning and growth that is required. I think this challenge ought to be one of the main ingredients of O.D. training. Edwin Olson and Glenda Eoyang's recent book, "Facilitating Organization Change" (Jossey-Bass, 2001), for which I had the honor of writing the "Introduction," is focused directly on this question of how to help the client let go and work with the energy that is already in the system.

So, you are saying that growth means giving up as well as moving forward—not to be as strong and controlling as we have practiced being in the past—that growth is often learning to let go of the things we learned long ago that was part of getting the job done. These are tough things to do when the permanent white water is up to our hips and climbing fast. Is there anything else we should know about growth?

Peter: I have to emphasize that I learned long ago that it is hard to come up with an elaborate technical definition of growth. I am talking about change that is more than tinkering with symptoms, more than resolving problems that one thought had been put to rest. Certainly "growth" has to be change on one's own preferred terms, rather than change just to please someone else or to stay out of trouble. Growthful change brings a person into a fuller, richer mode of thinking and feeling. It seems to involve greater balance among a person's various priorities and needs. A major dimension of growth certainly must be a reduction in excessive worry and fear, something both the addiction recovery movement and many management writers have emphasized. Growth must mean fuller, richer, more satisfying relationships with others, better communication, more trust and empathy, a clearer feeling of being valued by others. Finally, increased openness and thus greater learning and creativity are characteristic of growth, with a corresponding reduction in the kind of denial which recovery writers have shown to characterize addiction. So growth, perhaps, is an outcome of all the letting go and working well with others that happens in high performance systems. The important thing is to keep doing the growth thing. Don't stop or it gets replaced with the anxiety I talked about before.

You are suggesting, I think, that as practitioners and academics we must give up some of our most cherished sources of meaning and stability—especially control—in order to continue to grow. You've said, "Permanent white water forces me to rethink the meaning of what I am doing including the basic foundations that give my life and work meaning." Expand on this for us?

Peter: Well, the short answer is what I've been saying—simply that with things in constant motion, what I had been counting on to supply meaning and purpose is constantly in danger of being profoundly altered or swept away entirely. For example, the first wave of layoffs and downsizing in the 1980s made this point dramatically to many thousands of people. To the extent that their sense of meaning rested on employment security, a layoff suddenly left them without an anchor. It wasn't just the loss of a job: it was that for many of these people getting downsized was unthinkable. Well, it is very "thinkable" today, and as a result we've learned as a society not to put quite as much faith in security of employment. This same point applies to many of the material "anchors" we have relied upon to give significance and purpose to our lives.

A longer answer goes in two directions. The first direction is toward transcendent sources of meaning. Sources that can't be negated just because the market turns down or our house burns down. I think the upsurge of interest in spirituality expresses this search. I like to say that spirituality involves a turning away not just from all the materialistic props we've used to give ourselves significance and meaning, but also from the self that would do the propping! Preoccupation with self, we're finding, blocks spiritual growth.

That direction is pretty well understood and has profound validity so I'll not say more about it for the moment. The other direction is less often remarked on, but I think it is equally important. I'm not sure I can put this very well because it's just an intuition gleaned from watching myself and others cope with white water. Permanent white water offers us the opportunity to rethink what it means to have "foundations" in the first place. I can illustrate the difference by referring to the difference in mentality between the Hawkeye and Radar characters on M.A.S.H., and the Frank Burns and Hotlips characters. One pair is heavily dependent, laughingly dependent, on the traditional structures of the Army and of organized medicine for meaning and purpose. In real life, the Frank Burns and Hotlips kinds of folks be-come intensely anxious when the world does not behave the way they think it should. The other pair, Hawkeye and Radar, grew past this dependence and is able to deal here and now with what *is*. The pair draws their sense of meaning and purpose from what is actually occurring, rather than from some presumption about what should be occurring. They have not given up their commitment to performing good medicine and maintaining an effective military unit; nor are they wedded to forms that are clearly inappropriate on the front lines of battle.

The dance metaphor has become very popular in O.D. to convey the ability to engage with the flow of events, stay present, stay interested, stay calm, still perform the needed actions, and have some fun in the process. Linda Ackerman-Anderson has put the phrase "flow state" into our vocabularies, and I remember back in the early 1980s when she first started talking this way. I'd say, "Linda, the term 'flow state' is self contradictory!" She'd say, "Uh huh," and smile. Well, she had it and I didn't at that point. She had the realization that we have to let our foundations flow and that *that* is a "state" different from clinging desperately to supposed fixities of structure, role, tradition, or mandate. Gordon Allport wrote a wonderful little book called *Becoming* about twenty-five years ago that develops the psychology of one whose "foundations" are fluid and evolving. Of course, T.S. Eliot in *Burnt Norton* said it more profoundly than perhaps it has ever been said:

> At the still point of the turning world. Neither flesh nor fleshless; Neither from nor towards; at the still point there the dance is, But neither arrest nor movement, and do not call it fixity, Where past and future are gathered. Neither movement from nor towards, Neither ascent nor decline. Except for the point, the still point, There would be no dance, and there is only the dance. I can only say there *we have been*: but I cannot say where.

I find ". . . there we have been . . ." thrilling. He's inviting me to reflect on my experience to see if I can discover *my* dance involving *my* still point of *my* turning world. Permanent white water has brought me into this awareness. Without its dynamism, I come to take my turning world for granted. I do not gather my past and future. I am asleep. Permanent white water is therefore a blessing, not a curse. Even at its most turbulent, it offers me the challenge of continual reflection on the meaning of my existence.

This poem symbolizes another part of the answer to your question, Jane. The arts, at their best, enlarge my awareness, give me the resiliency Daryl Connor writes about, in ways that "applied behavioral science" never can. I define an art as the attempt to wrest coherence and meaning out of more reality than we ordinarily try to deal with. Well, so does white water. It thrust more reality on me than I'd perhaps prefer to deal with. Thank God for the artists who have been there before me, who have struggled to interpret the meaning of the profound events of life, and to do it in a way that is unforgettable. David Whyte says, "A poem is not about experience; a poem *is* the experience." I do not look to the arts for instruction; "applied behavioral science" can do that. The arts are where my growth occurs, where I have my sudden insights and thrilling discoveries. The arts upend me. You might say they are white water of and for the soul!

Finally, your question reminds me to stay loose, and the way we do that is to have some fun with all the craziness of our lives. George Vaillant, a psychiatrist who specializes in adult development, says humor is an adult's supreme coping mechanism. Humor gives us perspective; it puts a "twist" on experience that makes us laugh out loud. It helps us take delight in paradox and contradiction. It blindsides us with ideas we didn't see coming. White water destroys perspective and makes us hate paradox and contradiction. If we can't have some fun with all this crazy stuff, it can really mess us up. Humor is also one of humanity's most powerful and probably oldest bonding mechanisms. When I realize that you find the same things funny that I do, I instantly feel that you and I have something important in common.

(And the reason there are so many jokes about sex and the eliminative functions, I'm convinced, is because we all share problems with those two things!) White water drives people apart. It gets us feeling lonely and unloved. "Nobody's got it as bad as I do," we feel. Humor helps us get over this loneliness and see that we're all struggling with the same kinds of things.

On these last two points, the arts and the role of humor, O.D. can play a key leadership role. If we realize that a given client group needs to become more comfortable with all the turbulence they're in, maybe we can help them have a shared experience with arts, and have some fun together. The client itself may tend to dismiss these two areas as not sufficiently "business related," even though secretly wishing it could be done. The consultant can support the client in taking the first steps into these two realms, so that they become more standard parts of the client's way of working.

It seems, Dr. Vaill, that it is timely for your reminder to us to "stay loose" and that "if we can't have some fun with all this crazy stuff, it can really mess us up." We get tied too tight into our work lives and don't remember this enough. Thank you so much for sharing your thoughts on "change as growth." It is definitely significant to our need to appreciate the permanent white water we experience every day on the job and in our every day lives. It has been great fun talking to you about this.

Peter: Thank you, Jane, for the opportunity to talk about these things. O.D. has one unique asset that is very precious in my opinion. It is a profession that is uniquely qualified to think through what our organizations and the people in them need to survive and prosper in the new century. I perceived this very early in my career, and thus it has always been a pleasure to make whatever contribution to the profession that I can. This conversation has been one of the most enjoyable and stimulating opportunities I have had.

Reading 40

Ethics and Organizational Change

Warren R. Nielsen
Nick Nykodym
Don J. Brown

Introduction

Within the United States we are seeing the demise of once large and powerful organizations; the rapid birth, growth and death of many high technologically oriented organizations; large numbers of mergers in an attempt to diversify or generate a stronger financial base; the introduction of, and growth of franchises offering some market stability; and the attack on the once unquestioned military/industrial complexes.

With these changes in society and organizations have come numerous individuals, groups, and fields of study, which offer assistance to organizations in both managing and instigating internal change. The successes, failures, contributions, and inadequacies of management consulting in providing organizations with methodology and technology to improve organizational effectiveness and health and improve the quality of work life for employees have been reviewed in the literature for nearly 20 years.

In any approach there are a number of ethical issues which have been previously considered by Walton and Warwick (1973), Miles (1979), Frame, Hess, and Nielsen (1982), the OD Institute (1985), Nykodym, Nielsen, and Christen (1985), and Nykodym, Ruud, and Liverpool (1986). Un-

fortunately, many involved in the field of organizational change have been so busy collecting data for research, attempting to have a positive impact so consulting operations may continue; or trying to develop and implement new change strategies, that little real attention has been paid to the ethical issues involved in the process of change.

The purpose of this paper is threefold: first, to review the ethical issues which have already been raised; second, to outline some new considerations which have developed over the past few years; and finally, to make some suggestions relative to the ethics of organization change for both the researcher and the practitioner.

In drawing attention to ethical issues already raised, an attempt to not re-invent the wheel will be made by drawing upon Walton and Warwick (1973), Miles (1979), and the OD Institute (1985). The framework used to specify the issues will be to separate them into issues faced before, during, and after the application of any change intervention(s).

Before Intervention

A major ethical issue facing those involved in organizational change is actually engaging in a discussion of the ethics that will provide the overall parameters within which the client, practitioner, or researcher will act. Such action appears to be relatively simple, but experience to date would indicate that it is seldom done. Too often ethical issues are raised during the project, frequently in a conflict situation, when major work must be set aside until differences are resolved. Even whole projects which had great potential for positive im-

Note: The authors would like to acknowledge the comments of two anonymous reviewers and those of Larry Pate, Colleen Bement, and Rachel Call on previous drafts of this paper.

Source: Warren R. Nielsen, Nick Nykodym, and Don J. Brown (1991), "Ethics and Organizational Change," *Asia Pacific HRM*, vol. 29, no. 1, pp. 82–93; reprinted with permission of *Asia Pacific Journal of Human Resources*.

pact on organizational effectiveness, health, and quality of work life have been discontinued because of ethical issues between clients, practitioners, and researchers not dealt with before the project began. It may be that some of those involved in organizational change may be reluctant to openly examine the change objectives of the practitioner because of fear that the client would not be willing to proceed if they were known. On the other hand, it may be that the client's ethics regarding change are not examined because of the belief that the change process itself will change them sufficiently so that they will be consistent with the project and/or the underlying values and beliefs of the strategy being applied.

By far the most important ethical issue that should be dealt with before any change strategy is implemented is that of defining the goals, behavioral outcomes, or expected change objectives. Those involved in the field of organizational change are, at times, painfully aware of the vague unspecified goals used to launch an organization change effort. Probably, over the years, most practitioners have been, at one time or another, so anxious to get a major project started and underway that they have deluded themselves and their clients that the work is an `emerging' process and that the goals will become clear as more and more is learned regarding the organization. Though it would be foolish to imply that all goals could be established before the change process is undertaken, it would be a breach of ethics to not do everything possible to insure that the client and practitioner know where the change process is likely to lead. Too often, attempts at organizational change appear as the proverbial "Christopher Columbus voyage." Kubr (1986) emphasizes the need for the client and consultant to define the problem together. The clients, immersed in the situation, may be too involved to see the problem objectively. Consultants will make greater progress if they work directly with the client on problem definition. From this basis, clients and consultants will be able to effectively work together to clarify what results are desired from the consulting process.

Another critical issue is that of who will be involved in the establishment of the goals and behavioral objectives. Walton and Warwick (1973), Miles (1979), and the OD Institute (1985) all warn of not solely relying on the higher level managers and administrators to establish the goals. They argue that, since most organizational participants could, at some time, be dramatically impacted by the process, those lower in the organization should also have input. Philosophically, it is difficult to argue with such a position, particularly given the underlying values of the field of organizational change. The difficulty with this issue is the ability to get real involvement on the part of all participants, particularly if the change project is in a very large system. When the authors first began working with one large automotive corporation, that organization employed over one million individuals. To even take a sample of what the employees believed should be the goals would have been a major undertaking and would have taken so long that the change effort would never have been undertaken. Also, in some organizations in which unions exist, and where there is a strong adversarial relationship, consultants and researchers may not be permitted to talk to employees at lower levels.

The authors' feeble solution to this issue is to start with overall goals developed primarily by the top, but with an agreement that new, though consistent goals would be established as each new part of the organization becomes involved. Also, in large projects, we have built in provisions for goal review and modification on at least a quarterly basis. As we have struggled with this issue, we found ourselves coming to the position that as many of the participants as possible should be involved in setting goals; however, the value of high involvement must be considered against the possibility of the occurrence of more serious organizational problems developing during the goal-setting process. To move quickly on goals established by only part of the organization and to have positive impact on the organizational variables that will insure a positive position and provide greater flexibility may be more ethical than attempting to involve the entire organization (at least at the beginning) in the goal-setting process.

Another issue that needs to be considered is that of the process utilized to determine the initial targets for intervention. Should top management make the decision or should it be made with input from the rest of the organization? If people have input there is more support; however, given certain information and perspective, the top may, in fact, be in a better position to establish the target area. The size of the organization also affects this dilemma. In a small organization, it may be relatively easy to get input from all potential participants; whereas, in a large organization, this is much more difficult. In either case, the issue needs to be discussed and the reason for how an area is selected should be made very clear.

Prior to the activation of a change process in any organization, the practitioner or researcher should confront some very personal ethical questions such as:

- What are my own personal values, and how will they impact on this project?
- What are my skills and abilities, and are they sufficient to promote the required change?
- Am I willing to accept the responsibility for the consequences of my decisions and acts upon the organization?
- Am I willing to share all "need to know" data with the client?

It is the authors' perception that the whole field of organizational change would be more effective and would have had a greater positive impact on organizations over the past 20 years had these questions been asked and dealt with honestly. It should be noted, however, that clients can also put pressure on change practitioners to accept and direct projects which are beyond their skill level. The authors are acquainted with a current case where the external consultant does superb team building and has a very positive image with the division management group of a particular manufacturing corporation. This consultant, because of the relationship, was forced upon the management of one

of the corporation's assembly plants by division management. The assembly plant, if it is to continue, requires an extensive sociotechnical transformation. Unfortunately, the plant is now involved in a great deal of team building which will likely have little, if any, impact on the real problems of the organization. In addition, the plant has been given a three-year period to move from a negative to a positive position in nearly every measurable organizational performance indicator. If such a turnaround does not occur, the facility is to be sold. The sale of the facility could result in the termination of approximately 4,000 employees.

Another issue that needs to be clarified prior to the initiation of a change project is the projected costs involved. For this issue to be adequately dealt with, the practitioner needs to be very clear with the prospective client regarding fees, travel expenses, material costs, and lost-time cost for participants who will have to be away from their normal work assignments. Currently the authors are involved in a project in Mexico where the travel expenses far exceed the daily fees. Fortunately, the possibility of this situation occurring was openly discussed and agreed to prior to the initiation of the project.

Another crucial issue facing the field of organizational change is that of claims made by practitioners and, to some degree, researchers. Unfortunately, there are few descriptions of failures in the literature, but most practitioners and researchers know of at least several. Too often, those interested in the field, and prospective clients, are faced with the problem of exaggerated claims relative to the viability of organizational change methodologies. If the claims had been more realistic, would the field today have greater credibility in the eyes of prospective clients? Also, would there be more opportunities of learning how to change organizations had the exaggerated claims not led to the demise of many projects? The authors have found high-level managers and administrators more willing to experiment when they were aware, prior to the beginning of a project, that untested interventions and methods were to be utilized.

Miles (1979) and the OD Institute (1985) raise the issue that all organizational participants should have a choice in launching an organizational change process. They argue that all participants should have full information relative to outcomes and costs prior to committing to a full-scale organizational change project. As with the development of change goals, an ethical statement or position such as this sounds appropriate, but becomes very difficult to accomplish in an organization of any size. Certainly, an attempt to keep everyone up to date through the use of newsletters, group meetings, etc., can and should be made. However, in a large organization the process is likely to be weak at best and may break down and become a deterrent, rather than a help. No doubt, most practitioners and some researchers would question the validity of trying to inform all organization participants prior to intervention and may argue that, to do so, might generate expectations or resistance which could not be dealt with adequately. Many of those involved in change strategies argue for intervening into the organization one part at a time. There may be cases where informing the whole organization could be disruptive to the specific project.

Because change projects can go very well or very poorly, depending on numerous situations, circumstances, and decisions, a specific question needs to be raised for the protection of both the client and practitioner—"How can the relationship be discontinued?" The authors have very strong feelings that, if a project is going very poorly, due to reasons outside the consultant's control, the consultant should not be forced to continue an effort which is clearly doomed. On the other hand, the client should not have to continue an effort which is seen as harmful to the organization, its employees, and cash flow. Based on the above, the authors always utilize a contract which allows either party to withdraw with a 30-day written notice. The result has been a greater level of trust between the parties and an assurance that both will genuinely try to make the project a success.

During the Activity

As is the case before intervening in a system to produce change, once a project is launched ethical issues arise which need to be recognized and dealt with by both practitioners and researchers.

Relative to issues during a change project, Walton and Warwick (1973), Miles (1979), and the OD Institute (1985) all focus on the collection and use of data which is obtained from organizational participants. They raise such questions as:

- What data are collected?
- What format is utilized?
- What happens to the data?
- Who gets the data?
- Is the anonymity of the providers protected?

There are still pertinent ethical questions that need to be asked and resolved prior to the collection of any data. There is no question that data can be used to punish organizational participants, and steps must be placed in the process to help prevent such behavior. On the other hand, it is possible that the questions above reflect an old bias from the days of sensitivity training and the use of team-building models which were very interpersonal in nature. In today's setting, some slightly different questions need to be asked, such as:

- Will the data be collected and processed in such a manner that the source(s) of problems can be recognized?
- Will the data be given to individuals who can best solve the problems?
- Will the format used facilitate an understanding of the data (allowing those who furnished the data to explain what it means)?
- Will the format facilitate the obtaining of further data which could more specifically define the problems?

Surely practitioners and researchers must be beyond the point of collecting data where anonymity is guaranteed, and the data are processed solely for the review by upper-management personnel who can make little sense of the data and have great difficulty in trying to resolve any issues that may be contained therein.

A few years ago, the authors were involved in a major organizational change project with a large engineering organization. The organization employed nearly 3,000 engineers and support personnel and was part of a multinational corporation. The project was directed by a steering committee made up of individuals from all levels and functions. The steering committee wanted to collect some data utilizing a format which would insure that the data could be acted on. The result was a survey instrument designed to identify data by work group and through which the providers of the data could explain their perceptions and be involved in problem resolution. The survey also provided an opportunity for the respondents to sign the questionnaire if they so desired. All of the employees were brought into a meeting where the purpose of the format of the survey was explained and questions could be asked. The participants were told that problems could only be solved if it was possible to discern the location of the problems, and the individuals in those areas had an opportunity to develop and implement solutions. The survey was given out and each employee was asked to complete the form and mail it to the consultant's office several states away. We have always believed that it was very significant that 100 percent of the questionnaires were returned, and 95 percent were signed.

The point of the above illustration is that the wrong questions relative to data may be being asked. Rather than asking, "Will anonymity be protected?" the question should be, "Will the data make it possible for the organization to act on and solve problems, whether they be technical, social or interpersonal?"

Another issue that is raised, but often ignored, is that of "Who is the client?" Most change practitioners and researchers are brought in, given access to various aspects of the organization, and paid by the senior management of the organization. Argyris (1970) and Beckhard (1969) take the position that a change effort should, in fact, be directed by the top of the organization. On the other

hand, Kubr (1986) realizes that those whose work will be affected by the change process should also be taken into consideration. While guidance from upper-level management is necessary, implementation will require cooperation of the workers. Walton and Warwick (1973) also raise the issue as to the freedom of individuals to participate in the change process. They discuss the necessity of informed consent, lack of coercion, lack of manipulation, and avoiding the misuse of data. Though these issues may be relevant, they again seem to apply more to the highly interpersonal interventions of the past. As change consultants attempt, as they are now, to facilitate large-scale systems change, these issues seem to fade somewhat. In fact, if large-scale systems change is to be accomplished, all organizational participants must participate in the process and cannot have the option of sitting on the sidelines and watching. Also, there simply may not be sufficient time to insure every individual the freedom of choice in the change process.

One model for dealing with some of these issues has been initiated in the General Motors Corporation (GM) where the change teams consist both of salaried employees and employees represented by the United Auto Workers Union (UAW). Before launching change projects at any particular location, there is an agreement that approval will be given both by GM and the UAW. This model may have great potential in dealing with the issue of freedom of participation; however, it has not been in place a sufficient length of time to determine the real results and impact.

Another issue which has particularly faced practitioners using primarily interpersonal change models has been whether the client system is really interested in change or just the achievement of stability. If the practitioner is restricted to interpersonal models, real change is unlikely to occur (Pate 1979). This being the case, the practitioner could be entrapped into a situation where the real reason for the project is to appease or mollify employees in the organization. Therefore, two factors appear to be critical. First, the practitioner and client must come to a firm agreement that actual change is the goal, and its achievement is to be monitored on a regular basis throughout the project. Second, the project must be so designated that it is not limited to a single organizational variable. Given the interdependencies between organizational variables, work on one area may produce short-run change, but in the long run the organization will most likely return to its prior condition or state.

While working as consultants within a large U.S. insurance firm, the authors became aware of a particular situation which was most troubling and appeared to be a major issue of ethics in organizational change. As change consultants, we were becoming so enthralled with the process of change that we were actually pushing the client system into a position of overplanning and over-intervening. The question of how the organizational participants could plan and implement major change and, at the same time, continue the accomplishment of regular tasks and processes, was not asked. As the project continued, it became apparent that pushing the organization to change too many things at one time was leading to failure. In this situation, organizational participants who genuinely wanted to plan for and initiate change were becoming overloaded to the point where they gave up on change plans and went back to doing only their normally assigned tasks. The ethic then is: *Don't push an organization for more change than that which can be handled within the organization's parameters and constraints.* This is not to say that, in a large transformation effort, normal tasks and duties may not be set aside completely and total attention, time, and skills given to the change effort.

The practitioners must assist those ultimately responsible for the change process to establish specific but attainable goals and priorities within realistic time periods. In addition, these goals, priorities, and time frames need to be carefully monitored to insure that there is consistency between goals and the organization's ability to attain those goals.

The argument has repeatedly been made that an organization is an open system and, therefore, change methodologies and technologies must be based on a systems approach. Unfortunately, an examination of consulting projects (Pate, Nielsen, & Bacon, 1977) shows little evidence that a systems approach to organization change has been utilized. Most projects have focused on one or two variables at the most. In working with client systems, the authors have used a particular descriptive model of organizations to assist those directing the change process in recognizing all the variables which will require anywhere from major change to slight modification. The model is illustrated in Figure 1.

Using the model with clients has helped to insure that a systems approach is taken and that sufficient variables are changed which will, in turn, produce real measurable organizational change.

As a project moves down through an organization, particularly one of any size, another serious question with major ethical implications must be asked and answered. The question is—"How much say will those who are directly or even indirectly affected by the change(s) have in the direction of the change?" It would appear as though this concern is currently being more appropriately dealt with by consultants than in the past. Most current projects with which the authors are familiar require and have built-in mechanisms to involve organizational participants in planning and directing the required change at their level. Again, the joint GM/UAW consulting team is a good illustration of getting all levels of an organization involved and participating in the process. One of the most significant factors in the design of GM's highly acclaimed Saturn project was the extensive planning involvement of the manufacturing facility system and culture, by individuals from all organizational levels.

The last issue which needs to be mentioned is that of the length of the project itself and how long the organization will need to rely on outside resources. One of the original purposes of organizational change consulting was to build an organization capable of continually monitoring the need for and initiating appropriate change to respond to changing environments. The ethic of

FIGURE 1 **Interaction of Organizational Variables**

Source: Frame, Hess, and Nielsen, *The OD Source Book,* 1982.

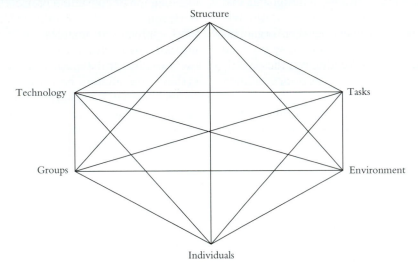

assisting the organization in its attempts to change, but not building dependent relationships, still seems appropriate today. Greiner and Metzger (1983) point out that dependency between the client and the consultant is inherent in long-term relationships. The client depends on the consultant's availability and advice, and the consultant depends on a steady income. But when the consultant begins doing work that could be performed by the client, or when the consultant depends solely on the client for income, the situation is unhealthy and should be discontinued. Kubr (1986) emphasizes that consultants can cause problems by both leaving too early or terminating too late, and that they should discuss withdrawal with the client before intervention and continue discussions periodically throughout the assignment.

After Major Change Interventions

If those who intervene in organizations for the purpose of producing real organizational change have faced and adequately dealt with the ethical issues prior to and during the effort, there are few issues left once the practitioner has left the system. Having said this though, there are some issues that need to be considered by both practitioners and researchers.

One such issue was raised by Miles (1979)—that being possible harm occurring to individuals who have participated in the project. It appears that practitioners who have been in this field for any length of time have made a real effort not to have change strategies primarily utilized for the purpose of reducing headcount, or simply implementing plans which enable fewer people to do more work, thus creating an excess of employees who are subject to employee reductions. Unfortunately, this issue may not be raised prior to intervening in a system and assurances obtained from top management that reduction of employees would not be the primary goal of the change activity. If practitioners are successful in improving the organization, there may well be less employees required, and individuals who lack necessary skills may be identified. In the past, this problem was primarily experienced at the lower levels of organizations; but as practitioners and consultants have become more proficient, the impact of change strategies, as noted by Naisbitt and Aburdene (1985), is being felt by large numbers of middle managers. A conclusion that may be drawn is that, when starting change projects, practitioners and researchers should insist that this issue be brought into the open and that the organizations involved develop and implement effective outplacement programs or changes in retirement programs so that a potential reduction in force is not a devastating experience for organizational participants.

The second issue noted, which has ethical ramifications, is that of unintended negative results. An illustration may serve to clarify this point. Several years ago the authors were involved in a change effort in a large manufacturing firm with approximately 5,000 employees. The early stages of the project were focused primarily on the production manager and his immediate staff. Through the change activities, the production group became more and more effective and more organizationally powerful. The effect was that other interdependent departments began to interact less and less with the production group. The other departments felt powerless in relation to the production management team and, out of fear, decreased the necessary interaction and supply of services to them. The answer to this problem may be considerably oversimplified, but it appears as though, if potential negative consequences are identified and discussed, plans can be developed to avoid or reduce them.

The problem which has continued to cause the authors the greatest concern over the years is that of working with an organization, seeing great benefits come from the effort, and then, from a distance, watching the organization revert back to previous patterns and outcomes. One such project has been of particular concern. In brief summary: through a great deal of work, the authors, with other outside consultants, were able to bring a major function of one of the world's largest corporations from the position of being the worst to the best on every performance measure and to significantly assist in obtaining a $14 million savings. Unfortunately, today the function has lost at least 50 percent of the gain obtained. The issue that must be dealt with is that of maintenance.

Those involved in organizational change could be subject to criticism for not including actions and procedures which adequately maintain and protect gains.

The way in which the authors have attempted to deal with this dilemma is not to accept contracts which do not include the assurance from top management that an appropriate number of internal resource personnel will be hired or trained to work with the authors and to assure the necessary follow up and maintenance.

One final concern is directed at those involved in research and evaluation. The field of organizational change continues to lack appropriate evaluation and assessment. Data regarding success or failure continues to be primarily anecdotal in nature. Closely controlled, rigorous studies are needed if practitioners are to be able to evaluate their effectiveness, make necessary modifications, and develop new interventions and strategies. Kubr (1986) proposes that evaluation of the consultation process should be a joint effort between client and consultant. He points out that by evaluating specific benefits to the client, such as new capabilities, new systems, and behavior, and new performance, interpretations of the outcome become clearer. Evaluations are also needed which do not stop after one intervention measurement. Evaluations are desperately needed which track the impact of our work with organizations over a significant time.

Current Issues

As mentioned at the beginning of this paper, most companies and industries in the United States are facing the critical need to change quickly. In the last few years, once-strong organizations have disappeared and whole industries have become very weak because of their inability to compete with both domestic and foreign entities. This environmental condition has raised questions for which solutions are required.

First, those involved in changing organizations must focus on more than the human variable. Though few would argue that the human variable is extremely important in the total change process, this is not the only variable which must be changed. Therefore, if practitioners, executives, and researchers are to be successful, they must have skills in dealing with and changing many organizational variables simultaneously. Therefore, three of the current ethical questions that need to be asked by practitioners, consultants, and researchers are:

- Am I ready and do I have the skills to work with numerous variables?

- Am I prepared to obtain and utilize support of other professionals in areas of the change project where I lack the necessary skills?

- If we take on projects without the necessary skills in this new environment, are we being ethical relative to clients, organizational participants, communities, and maybe even societies?

Second, foreign competition has become so fierce that U.S. organizations, if they are to survive, must change and change quickly. This very need for speed in the change process brings current needs into conflict with some of the older ethical statements, such as that everyone in the organization should be informed of the process so they can "have" free choice in terms of participating. A particular ethical issue that may supersede the above mentioned is:

"Am I, as a consultant, researcher, or manager, prepared to do as much as possible in a short time frame to enable organizations and, possibly whole industries to survive?"

Third, whereas ethical concerns of the past have focused primarily upon the organization involved in the change process, growing interdependencies are mandating a broader view. The issue of the potential impact of change interventions on communities, geographical areas, other organizations, and society need to be acknowledged. In addition, as change efforts are initiated which involve multiple organizations and possibly whole industries, the following ethical question needs to be asked: *"Are organizational change practitioners helping to establish new ethics and values in society, and is that their role?"*

Certainly we are bringing about value shifts without getting input from all those impacted upon by our work.

Fourth, organizational change, in the past, has been a relatively slow, deliberate process. Practitioners were facilitators and operated primarily out of a nondirective model. However, the question that can now be raised as the need for fast and extensive change becomes more and more the need of organizations is: *"Is it ethical to hold on to the nondirective philosophy?"*

It may be possible that the ethical question now is whether or not the practitioner has the skills and is ready to provide facilitative content, as well as expert roles. The authors' recent experience would indicate that organizations recognize the need for process consultants, but, because of external pressures for change, need consultants who can also function in the task and expert arenas.

Fifth, current organizational change requirements are pushing those involved in the field to not just talk about systems approaches but to actually use system models in their change activities. No longer can having done teambuilding or conducted experiential training in all parts of the organization be, in any way, considered a systems approach.

Sixth, there is a growing need for consulting teams made up of individuals who are particularly trained to provide options for impacting on specific variables. The question to be asked is: *"Is a change team being utilized which provides for dealing with and impacting on several variables simultaneously?"*

Seventh, overall change strategies with goals, objectives, time frames, change targets, responsibilities, and assessment methods must be developed and utilized. OD practitioners and consultants have had the luxury, in the past, of implementing one phase of a change effort and then determining the next phase or steps. Given the enormous pressure on organizations, a one step at a time process is inconsistent with the needs. This is not to say that flexibility and a commitment to appropriate modification through the change process should be abandoned. However, to enter into a major organizational change effort without a change strategy is, indeed, unethical.

Suggestions and Conclusions

In conclusion, the authors offer a series of suggestions to both the practitioner and the researcher. This is not intended to be an exhaustive list but, rather, a small base upon which others might build.

Relative to practitioners, seven suggestions are offered. First, be aware of and sensitive to the ethical issues in the field of organizational change, as well as the source and strength of these issues. Second, include a discussion and obtain agreement from the client relative to the ethics which will guide the change effort. Third, recognize that the ethics and ethical questions of the past may not fit the current need for rapid and extensive change and that new ethics are emerging. Fourth, discard old variable change models. They may have fit and produced positive results in the past, but are totally inadequate in our current environment. Fifth, insist on more assessment of the impact of interventions. The field of organizational change has once again moved into a time frame where new interventions and approaches are being developed, utilized, and nearly being marketed as the "cure-all" answer to the problems of change. As practitioners and consultants, do not allow a repeat of the past by becoming dependent on anecdotes and continuing to use interventions that have little or no value. Sixth, develop and be able to use the skills necessary to build organizational change strategies. Seventh, stop talking about and begin to truly utilize systems models to produce actual and measurable organizational change.

To the researchers, the authors include some suggestions as well. Again, these are not offered as an exhaustive list but, rather, some areas which need work and which could lead to more and improved assessment. First, produce quality, valid research on organizational change in terms of impact on various variables, intervention effectiveness in accomplishing stated objectives, and identification of real and potential negative consequences as a result of change projects. Second, be willing to provide more than just assessment studies. Assist practitioners by becoming more familiar with organizations in order to provide useful input into the design and implementation of change projects. Third, provide comparison data on the impact of organizational change where different change strategies have been utilized. Fourth, develop longitudinal studies which will provide insights into why particular change projects remain viable and effective over time, while others diminish or die.

In conclusion, the field of organizational change is extremely value-laden. Clients, practitioners, and researchers come into change projects with both individual and organizational values. Interventions come out of values. Interventions in the organization are nearly always based on some value judgment, and the way our results are assessed is often the result of the researchers' value regarding what organizational measures should be assessed.

Those in the field of organizational change are being called upon more than ever to assist organizations to survive and become viable once again. What is done in organizations may have profound impact on society. Those involved in organizational change must acknowledge, deal with, and test the underlying ethics that affect every change project undertaken.

References

Argyris, C. *Intervention Theory and Method.* Reading, MA: Addison-Wesley, 1970.

Beckhard, R. *Organization Development: Strategies and Models.* Reading, MA: Addison-Wesley, 1969.

Bermant, G.; Kelman, H. C.; and Warwick, D. P. *The Ethics of Social Intervention.* Washington: Hemisphere, 1978.

Frame, R. M.; Hess, R. H.; and Nielsen, W. R. *The OD Source Book: A Practitioners Guide.* California: University Associates, 1982.

Greiner, L. E., and Metzger, R. O. *Consulting to Management.* Englewood Cliffs, NJ: Prentice Hall, 1983.

Kubr, M. *Management Consulting: A Guide to the Profession.* Geneva: International Labour Office, 1986.

Miles, M. B. "Ethical Issues in OD Interventions." *OD Practitioner* 2, no. 3 (1979).

Naisbett, J., and Aburdene, P. *Reinventing the Corporation.* New York: Warner Books, 1985.

Nykodym, N.; Nielsen, W. R.; & Christen, J. C. (1985) "Can Organizational Development Use Transactional Analysis?" *Transactional Analysis Journal* 15 (1985), pp. 278–84.

Nykodym, N.; Ruud, W. N.; & Liverpool, P. R. (1986) "Quality Circles: Will Transactional Analysis Improve Their Effectiveness?" *Transactional Analysis Journal* 16 (1986), pp. 182–87.

O.D. Institute. "A Statement of Values and Ethics for Professionals in Organization and Human System Development." Organization Development Institute, April 1985.

Pate, L. E. "A Longitudinal Study of the Intervention Process within an Insurance Firm Using Quasi-Experimental Research Designs." Unpublished thesis, University of Illinois, 1979.

Pate, L. E.; Nielsen, W. R.; and Bacon, P. C. "Advances in Research on Organization Development." In *Contemporary Issues in Human Resource Management.* Schuster F. E., Reston Publishing, 1980.

Walton, R. E., Warwick, D. P. "The Ethics of Organization Development." *Journal of Applied Behavioral Science* 9, no. 6 (1973), pp. 681–98.

Reading 41

Powering Up Teams

Bradley L. Kirkman
Benson Rosen

It's midnight. It's 15 degrees outside the plant we are visiting. Everything around our building is dark and desolate. We are in Warsaw . . . North Carolina. We are eagerly awaiting the arrival of a third-shift work team in a textile manufacturing plant. Inside the building we hear the constant hum of cotton spinning machines that were constructed in Germany and Italy. The cotton that is made in this plant will be shipped to Mexico where workers will assemble cotton products such as T-shirts and briefs. The finished products will be sold in the United States.

Our task is to interview a third-shift team to determine its sense of empowerment. As the members of the team file slowly in, each holding an extremely high-caffeine-laced soft drink, we brace ourselves for the task at hand. The interview starts slowly and uncomfortably. As the caffeine begins to take effect, our team begins to open up. Members sit close together, support each other's comments, and beam with pride as they talk about previous and current team successes. This team produces yarn from raw cotton from midnight to 7:00 A.M. every night in what has to be one of the most rural and isolated locations imaginable. And yet, several weeks later, after we complete all our interviews with almost 100 teams in four organizations, we conclude that this is one of the most empowered teams in our study.

What accounts for the high level of team empowerment for teams who work under these conditions? In *Organizational Dynamics* since 1972

(volumes 1–27), 15 articles have been published on teams and four articles on empowerment. However, no articles have examined the interaction of these two important and widely used organizational practices—team empowerment. In this article, we first describe what it means to be an empowered work team and what outcomes result from empowered teams. We then describe the distinction between empowered teams and self-managing teams. We go on to discuss the components of each of the support systems that must be in place to maximize the effectiveness of empowered work teams. Our discussion builds on our recent empirical research examining the antecedents and consequences of empowered work teams. The study is among the largest and most comprehensive examinations of empowered teams conducted to date. The teams in our study made yarn, manufactured silicon wafers, and processed insurance claims. They were made up of men and women of many races, ages, and educational backgrounds. The research methodology included both traditional, quantitative (i.e., survey) measures of the variables of interest as well as intact team interviews. We also include specific examples from our work with other companies using empowered teams that were not in our original study such as Conoco Inc., the Houston-based energy company, and Motorola.

What Exactly Is an Empowered Work Team and What Does It Do?

Much has been written about the potential of work teams to transcend the collective performance of individual members. We define a work

Source: Bradley L. Kirkman and Benson Rosen, "Powering Up Teams," *Organizational Dynamics,* Vol. 28, Winter 2001, pp. 48–66. Reprinted by permission.

team as a group of individuals working interdependently toward common goals and whose members are mutually accountable for task achievement. Well-known management expert Peter Drucker notes that the wonderful music created by a symphony orchestra far exceeds the aggregated talents of the individual musicians. Similarly, a basketball team playing together wins more games than could be predicted from the statistical profiles of the individual players. In organizations, there are many examples of work teams that produce breakthrough innovations, solve impossible problems, achieve new heights of quality, or set records for productivity. Theoretically, by collective effort, teams can achieve goals far beyond the sum of their individual members' efforts. In other words, successful teams achieve synergy.

What these winning teams have in common is the ability of each group member to make his or her teammates better. The dynamics of team effectiveness are not always obvious to the casual observer. In the basketball world, the willingness of players to engage in self-sacrificing behaviors to put their teammates in scoring position are subtle, but crucial for team success. Blocking out on rebounds, setting picks, and creating screens are behaviors that don't show up in the box score, but each contributes to team effectiveness. In the business world, sharing knowledge, suggesting contacts, providing resources, easing tensions, arbitrating conflicts, and many other subtle acts each enable teammates to contribute to their full potential. Clearly, the willingness to make personal sacrifices on behalf of team success plays a critical part in generating synergy. So does the ability to blend the talents, skills, and efforts of team members to generate new ideas, solve complex problems, politick for external support, and implement change. Effective teams develop mechanisms to maximize their performance.

Like previous studies on teams, our research suggests that teams differ in their performance. Some are clear winners, others muddle along, and still others are outright losers. In contrast to previous research, our study of teams indicates that a sense of team empowerment is closely associated with team effectiveness. Our research suggests that team empowerment is a complex, multidimensional construct. To better understand empowered teams, we studied 100 teams in four organizations with varying levels of team empowerment. We learned that empowered teams share four experiences: potency, meaningfulness, autonomy, and impact.

A Sense of Potency

Team members who share a sense of potency believe in themselves. They exhibit a confident, can-do attitude. We have seen dramatic examples of potency or confidence in the cockiness of world champion basketball teams, in the quiet confidence of a team of astronauts, and among the management teams of new technology start-ups and fast companies.

Teams in our study varied with respect to how much potency members felt. How would you know a potent team if you saw one? The teams that demonstrated a sense of potency displayed much more confidence and team assuredness in their speech and body language than did teams lacking potency. During team interviews, high-potency team members sat close to one another, supported each other in conversation, and talked about their accomplishments with pride. Potent teams clearly knew their capabilities as a team, separate and apart from their individual abilities. Team members that lacked a sense of potency spread themselves out around the interview room, laughed uncomfortably when asked about their accomplishments, and frequently derided each other's attempts to answer questions about their team. High-potency team members talked about "we" and "us"; low-potency team members talked about "I" and "they."

A Sense of Meaningfulness

Teams with a sense of meaningfulness have a strong collective commitment to mission. They work with a sense of purpose and they have an intrinsic caring about their tasks. They see their goals as valuable and worthwhile. From surgical teams to military units, from theatrical groups to political protesters, and from product development teams to corporate cost-cutting task forces, these teams all share a strong belief in the importance of their cause.

Not all team members in our study found their tasks meaningful. Team members who did experience a high degree of meaningfulness talked about the inner pride that comes from doing their jobs well. They discussed times when they helped each other solve complex problems or meet a deadline. They insisted that even the most mundane aspects of their jobs are viewed as integral to overall team success. These are not surgical team members whose intrinsic interest comes from saving lives daily. These are teams that spin yarn, make silicon wafers, and handle customer complaints. Yet, they recognize the significance of their work. Teams high on the meaningfulness dimension of empowerment, individually and collectively, experience ordinary tasks in an extraordinary way.

A Sense of Autonomy

Autonomy refers to the freedom, discretion, and control that teams experience. Team members that have the responsibility to establish their own work processes experience autonomy. These teams have the freedom to allocate resources, seize opportunities, and make rapid decisions without approval from on high. In some auto manufacturing operations, teams have the authority to halt production for the entire plant. On Wall Street, portfolio management teams make billion-dollar investments in a matter of minutes. At the airport, teams of gate agents, baggage handlers, and ground maintenance personnel collaborate to get planes out on time. What these teams have in common is the discretion to make important decisions.

Among the teams we studied, we found varying amounts of autonomy across plants and organizations. We saw the highest level of autonomy in a yarn-making plant. There were only three levels at the plant: the general manager, a very small number of external team leaders, and the team members themselves. The high level of autonomy at this plant led the former CEO of this organization to tell us: "Pure and simple, the employees run that plant!" Indeed, we saw line-level employees problem-solving quality issues with customers, engaging in strategic discussions with company management, and taking full control of shut-down situations. At most of the other facilities we studied, team members reported less than full autonomy experiences. Perhaps the difficulty for managers to let go remains a key stumbling block on the road to empowerment.

A Sense of Impact

Impact is experienced when teams see the effect of their labors on other stakeholders. A design team experiences impact when it attends a focus group discussion and hears the reaction of potential customers to its newest creation. On the shop floor, a production team experiences impact when it reviews quality data for the past week. Human resource managers develop a sense of impact from the comments of employees to their new flexible benefit plan. Feedback from internal and external customers contributes to a sense of impact.

In our study, teams varied with respect to their knowledge of customer impact. While many of the teams received regular feedback from internal customers, other teams had absolutely no sense of their impact on customers outside the organization. Team members who did experience a sense of impact talked about how knowing their customers and getting feedback made their work more important to them. One team member, who had recently been hired away from a more traditional work environment, said that in her old job "it was easy to let things slip by and lose interest when we didn't know our customers." In her new job on an empowered team, that same worker stated, "My pride is on the line; I don't want my customers thinking I'm up here just trying to get by. I want them to know I'm doing a good job."

Exhibit 1 shows the four dimensions of our team empowerment model. The double-sided arrows in our diagram imply that the four dimensions of team empowerment are likely to be mutually reinforcing. For example, if a team's

EXHIBIT 1

The Four Dimensions of Team Empowerment and Their Relationship to Team Effectiveness

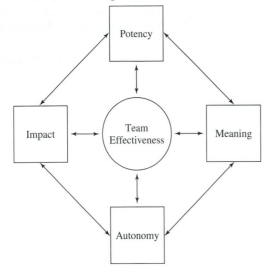

members experience impact by talking to customers about how the team's work affects them, they are likely to care more about their tasks (i.e., enhanced meaningfulness) and develop a better sense of the team's capabilities (i.e., a heightened sense of potency). When team members experience potency, they are also more likely to take on additional responsibilities and desire higher levels of discretion. Thus, the team empowerment dimensions exhibit a dynamic interplay of powerful team experiences that will likely lead to higher and higher levels of team effectiveness.

The double-sided arrows between the four dimensions of empowerment and team effectiveness also imply a reciprocal relationship. For example, we have learned that teams that develop greater levels of potency are also more likely to be effective. However, higher team effectiveness will also generate greater potency experiences. In short, members on teams fresh off successful performances will develop stronger beliefs in their team's capabilities. As our diagram implies, these reciprocal relationships are likely to hold for all four dimensions of team empowerment and team effectiveness.

Exhibit 2 shows the level of team empowerment in each of the organizations in our study. Not surprisingly, even within the same facility, teams differed in the degree to which they felt empowered. And, as we will see shortly, external leaders saw clear differences in the effectiveness of teams reporting to them. In summary, we refer to work teams that develop a sense of potency, meaningfulness, autonomy, and impact as empowered work teams. Regarding the outcomes of empowered teams, our research shows that empowered work teams are organizational winners. They are more productive, more proactive, and more capable of providing excellent customer service. Moreover, empowered work teams share a very strong esprit de corps. Collectively, empowered team members report very high levels of job satisfaction, organizational commitment, and commitment to their teams. Before turning to what it takes to create empowered teams, we briefly discuss the key differences between empowered teams and another widely used organizational structure: self-managing teams.

Empowerment Versus Self-Management: What's the Difference?

In contrast to his earlier thinking, Drucker has recently cast doubt on the staying power of work teams, and specifically self-managing work teams, in industry. He makes this argument not because he believes that teams are not right for industry, but because he believes that they are too limited in their use. It is just this reasoning that led us to begin to think about what might lie beyond existing models of team effectiveness such as self-managing work teams. While research has demonstrated that self-managing teams have strong effects on employee satisfaction and commitment, only modest effects (or none at all) have been found for productivity. What might account for these mixed findings?

We found several factors that may explain Drucker's concern about the staying power of

EXHIBIT 2
Team Empowerment Levels of Organizations in Our Study

Organization and Location	Team Empowerment Level
Fortune 50 Insurance Organization, Southwestern United States	High
Fortune 50 Textile Manufacturer, Southeastern United States	
Plant A	Extremely high
Plant B	Moderately low
High-Technology Silicon Wafer Manufacturer, Southeastern United States	Moderate
Small Textile Manufacturer, Southeastern United States	
Plant A	Low
Plant B	Moderately low
Plant C	Low
Plant D	Low

self-managing work teams. First, we found that self-management is a necessary, but not sufficient, condition for empowerment. Self-management is synonymous with only one of the four dimensions of team empowerment: autonomy. In fact, some use the terms *self-managing* teams and *autonomous* teams interchangeably. As we noted, it is very important for team members to experience autonomy, but they must also experience potency, meaningfulness, and a sense of impact to feel fully empowered. Our analyses revealed that potency, meaningfulness, and impact enhance team outcomes *beyond* the effects of autonomy alone.

We also observed that some self-managing work teams are swimming upstream against a very strong current. When leadership styles, production/service systems, human resources policies, and organizational social structures all pose significant obstacles to team effectiveness, even highly empowered work teams risk becoming entangled in the corporate seaweed. At the extremes, empowered work teams caught in the undertow of micromanagement, inflexible production or service schedules, centralized human resource practices, and disempowering social structures risk drowning in corporate bureaucracy—exactly as Drucker predicted.

For example, in our work with the small textile manufacturer, we saw the company embrace the concept of teams on the surface. Through employee interviews, however, we discovered that team leaders did not encourage teams to take control of their work, nothing had changed in the way employees were being rewarded or appraised, and team members did not feel that they could obtain resources or information necessary to be high-performing. One frustrated team member exclaimed, "Nothing has really changed around here. It's the same old people doing the same old thing. They're just calling it something different." In our view, the company had implemented a very narrow version of work teams without regard to the larger organizational context. Those who have implemented and led teams over the past two decades might have seen greater benefits had they broadened their conceptualization of what a high-performing team is and what is required to support these types of teams. We next describe aspects of the organizational context that are crucial for helping teams reach full power.

What Does It Take to Become an Empowered Team?

Given the dramatic differences between empowered work teams and their less empowered counterparts, it is an organizational no-brainer to power up teams—to create the conditions where teams experience a sense of empowerment. Indeed, some organizations have already embraced the concept of empowered work teams. For example, AES Corporation, a global electricity company based in Arlington, Virginia, uses empowered teams in facilities located all over the world. Chairman Roger Sant explains," [The employees] have total responsibility for decisions.

They are accountable for results. What they do every day matters to the company . . . every AES person is a mini-CEO."

In addition to the organizations in our original study, we assessed the level of team empowerment and examined how it was developed in other organizations including Motorola, Conoco, and Genencor International (an Eastman Chemical Company joint venture with Finland-based Cultor and one of the largest biotechnology companies in the world). One of the more impressive examples of empowered teams that we have seen was in our visit to a Motorola microchip-making plant in the Philippines. With team names such as the Last Maverick, Path Finder, Revival X, and Be Cool, the Filipino teams have been consistent finalists (appropriately referred to as the "Magic 10") in Motorola's worldwide team recognition program, the Total Customer Satisfaction (TCS) showcase. Winning teams are flown, all expenses paid, to locations such as Disney World in Florida to display and discuss examples of how they achieve breakthrough results. Team accomplishments are regularly reported in an in-house quarterly magazine. As a result of this "publicity," teams at other Motorola facilities around the world can learn about and incorporate these valuable team ideas. As one member stated, "When teams first started here, members were not that close. But when we went to the U.S. and won [the TCS], members felt like brothers and sisters, and this family feeling has remained ever since." Indeed, that kind of success works to enhance feelings of empowerment, which in turn breeds even higher levels of excellence.

Like the companies discussed above, organizations often engage consultants to reengineer work processes and capture team synergies. Typically, the rollout of organizational efforts to install empowered work teams begins with visionary statements by top management, the formation of work teams, team-building exercises, and a variety of efforts to establish team identity, including the creation of team names like those at Motorola and the development of team mission statements. At Genencor International, team mission statements are exhibited on the walls as a constant reminder of the team's purpose and goals. The companies we worked with also emphasized the importance of involving employees from the very beginning of the transition. Instead of traditional supervisors, managers are encouraged to play the role of coach or facilitator. At Conoco's LiquidPower™ flow improver plant in Bryan, Texas, associates (not employees) produce material that increases the flow of crude oil through pipelines. The few managers in the plant are called "resources" and they are expected to act not like supervisors, but more like advisers and coaches to fully unleash the "power" in empowered teams. Paul Chomka, plant manager, explains, "Everybody in the plant reports to the plant manager. You can't get any flatter than that." Are these changes enough to empower work teams?

According to our research, sustaining empowered work teams requires much more. The success of empowered work teams requires realignment of leader roles, production and service responsibilities, human resource management policies, and the social structure within the organization. Anything less than comprehensive organizational realignment risks undermining team empowerment. We provide examples of actions taken in each of these areas in Exhibit 3.

David Nelson, manager of worldwide organizational development and director of Conoco University, the internal training and development arm of Conoco, told us, "Getting empowered teams is not easy. It takes a commitment from all levels of the organization to succeed. Every day I hear new stories about how our teams have provided innovative solutions and breakthrough results that would not have been possible without truly empowered employees." Next, we discuss the specific changes needed to get teams to full power.

Leadership

Leading empowered work teams requires managers to rethink their philosophies of management. For decades, managers viewed their roles as planning, motivating, evaluating, and rewarding

EXHIBIT 3 Organizational Levers of Team Empowerment

External Leader Behavior

1. Make team members responsible and accountable for the work they do.
2. Ask for and use team suggestions when making decisions.
3. Encourage team members to take control of their work.
4. Create an environment in which team members set their own team goals.
5. Stay out of the way when team members attempt to solve work-related problems.
6. Generate high team expectations.
7. Display trust and confidence in the team's abilities.

Production/Service Responsibilities

1. The team sets its own production/service goals and standards.
2. The team assigns jobs and tasks to its members.
3. Team members develop their own quality standards and measurement techniques.
4. Team members take on production/service learning and development opportunities.
5. Team members handle their own problems with internal and external customers.
6. The team works with a whole product or service, not just a part.

Human Resource Management System

1. The team gets paid, at least in part, as a team.
2. Team members are cross-trained on jobs within their team.
3. Team members are cross-trained on jobs in other teams.
4. Team members are responsible for hiring, training, punishment, and firing.
5. Team members use peer evaluations to formally evaluate each other.

Social Structure

1. The team gets support from other teams and departments when needed.
2. The team has access to and uses important and strategic information.
3. The team has access to and uses the resources of other teams.
4. The team has access to and uses resources inside and outside the organization.
5. The team frequently communicates with other teams.
6. The team makes its own rules and policies.

the work of their subordinates. Given that managers were ultimately accountable for the performance of their direct reports, it is not surprising that many managers were quite proactive in setting goals, delineating work processes, and closely monitoring individual and group performance. However, empowering work teams requires a 180-degree shift in philosophy and behavior. Leaders of empowered teams must play the role of coaches and facilitators, helping teams define tasks, structure activities, and monitor their own progress.

Relinquishing power and control does not come easily for many leaders. Some view the transfer of responsibilities to teams as simply losing power. As a result, many of the changes surrounding the transition to work teams may end up being directed solely at team members. At Levi Strauss, an adopter of work teams in the early 1990s, word leaked out that "some managers don't like having sewing-machine operators challenge their authority."

At some of the companies we visited, it seemed that supervisors were expected to become team leaders who would "know what to do when the time comes." One team leader we spoke to reinforced our observations by stating, "Teams are really something we brought in for the employees. None of us really think it's something that was brought in to improve or change what we do."

Alternatively, many leaders cognitively accept the importance of changing their modus operandi and are willing to do so, but they lack the skills and experience required. Becoming a team leader requires a careful balancing act—team leaders need to know when to step in and, more importantly, when to get out of the way. Organizations need to establish the equivalent of coaching clinics or workshops designed to help leaders build the skills needed to empower and support work teams. From our observations, providing leaders with their own mentors and coaches seems to help. Assuring leaders that, rather than losing power, they actually gain power as they are freed to pursue more strategic (and thus more visible) activities is important. Without gaining the trust and support of leaders, empowerment efforts are handicapped from the start.

Specifically, our research discovered several leader behaviors that are associated with high levels of team empowerment. Those behaviors include:

- Generating high team expectations.
- Creating an environment in which team members set their own team goals.
- Encouraging team members to take control of their work.
- Staying out of the way when team members attempt to solve work-related problems.
- Displaying trust and confidence in the team's abilities.
- Holding teams responsible and accountable for the work its members do.

At both of the *Fortune* 50 companies in our study, managers are not allowed to become team leaders until they have completed extensive training programs designed to teach coaching and facilitating behaviors. Both companies contracted with external training firms initially to deliver the training until sufficient numbers of internal company trainers were certified to train in-house. Training sessions included role playing, behavioral modeling, and the use of videotapes and simulations to transfer the training of the new behaviors required. In contrast, at the silicon wafer manufacturer and the smaller textile producer (with lower levels of team empowerment), we saw little in the way of supervisor training. Again, managers were expected to learn "on the fly" the necessary skills to make the transition from traditional supervisor to coach.

Our findings suggest that managers cannot be expected to simply start behaving differently because they are told they are now in a team-based organization. Those companies willing to invest in education have a much greater chance at successful empowered teams. Those who do not invest have almost no chance. Our findings are in-line with much that has been written about successful transitions to self-managing work teams. Descriptions of coaching behaviors have included allowing team members to manage themselves, enhancing the problem-solving skills of teams, and not undermining team authority. Because we view empowered teams as much broader than self-managing ones, we think these skills are even more crucial in empowered teams. Those leaders that exhibit the skills identified here will have a much greater chance of creating empowerment experiences for their teams than those who do not.

At Genencor International and Conoco, team leaders receive quite a bit of training before they are "thrown in" to a coaching or facilitating role. Genencor has been using empowered teams in its U.S. facilities since 1991 and has since expanded their use to sites in Belgium and Finland. A Finnish team leader we spoke to emphasized the importance of leading by example: "I would never ask anyone to do something I wouldn't do. The team members have to trust me and I have to trust them." At Conoco, leaders receive a large amount of training up front, and, as one manager put it, "It's like getting four years of training in 18 months, but we believe in the benefits of intensive training." Conoco also advocates the concept of "felt leadership." Chomka, the Bryan, Texas, plant manager explains that "everyone at Conoco has the ability to lead and is expected to lead at certain times." Chomka also added that such a system invites positive "push back," or the expression and resolution of conflicting ideas that are so important to unleashing the innovative power of empowered teams.

Production/Service Responsibilities

Line-level operating systems can either reinforce or drain team empowerment. The total quality management (TQM) movement was a catalyst for organizations to redesign operating systems and procedures. Continuous improvement, the mantra of TQM, required individuals and teams to take responsibility for solving quality problems throughout the organization. In order to respond quickly, employees needed ready access to a full range of quality indicators. Fortunately, breakthroughs in information technology provided an easier means for furnishing rapid feedback. Organizations that embraced TQM seized the opportunity to transform operating procedures and systems, increasing the flow of information across the organization.

When operating systems readily provide data on productivity, quality, and customer service, teams can monitor their performance, diagnose problems, and make adjustments. Similarly, when operations include built-in coordinating systems permitting integration across functional boundaries, teams experience greater autonomy and control Conversely, teams at the mercy of operating system constraints are sapped of their sense of empowerment.

Teams that we studied at Plant A of the *Fortune* 50 textile manufacturer had production responsibilities that far exceeded the other manufacturing plants in our study (including Plant B which had, surprisingly, implemented teams at the same time as its sister plant). The move to empowered teams now allows employees complete control over the yarn-making facility. Team members rotate the responsibility for job assignments and coverage when anyone is absent or in training. Team members spend an average of three days in training each month. One team leader explained, "Our team members know the value of training. They don't moan or complain when someone is upstairs in training. They know that person will bring new skills back to the floor, and they're willing to take up the slack until that person gets back. And they are intensively cross-trained for situations just like this."

Organizational changes in operating systems must be accompanied by corresponding changes in control systems for empowerment efforts to succeed. Knowing about problems is a necessary but hardly a sufficient condition for increasing organizational effectiveness. Individuals must also have the authority to act quickly to resolve quality problems. For example, visitors at the Texas Conoco plant were stunned to see team members take action to solve an automation problem during a recent plant tour. One observer explained, "People came out of nowhere, nobody gave any orders, there was no supervision, everyone did the work that needed to be done, and when they were finished they all went back to their normal routine. And the most impressive part was that no one at Conoco seemed to think it was that big of a deal! What would have taken most facilities two or three hours to fix took only about 20 minutes."

Roger Sant, chairman of AES, echoes the Conoco example by stating, "We want people to take ownership of the whole—the way you care about your house. You run it; you keep it up; you fix it. When something goes wrong, you own the problem from start to finish. And nobody has to tell you to do it because the responsibility is all yours." For some teams, action may involve negotiations with internal and external suppliers, designers, and producers. In other instances, immediate action may be needed to resolve customer concerns. As the Conoco example above shows and Sant confirms, control systems must provide teams with the authority to respond to problems rapidly and decisively.

In another example, the shrill whistle of a team member's pager interrupted our interview at the yarn-making facility of the *Fortune* 50 company. We stopped the interview while the member responded to the message. The member made the call on a speaker phone in the interview room. When the problem was communicated to the team, the entire team called the customer who had originally called in with a complaint. Once reached, the irate customer notified the team that she had received a yarn shipment of incorrect size (i.e., the diameter of the yarn was larger than ordered). We observed the team "huddling" in response to this unexpected problem. Through a series of decisive phone calls, the team acquired raw material from a different team in another part of the plant, scheduled several periods of overtime, and assured the customer in a subsequent call that the correct size yarn would be delivered in a matter of days. In order for the team to satisfy this customer (and as a result experience true empowerment), organizational control systems had to be in place that allowed the acquisition of raw materials and the scheduling of overtime. Such an event clearly demonstrated the "power" in an empowered team.

In the *Fortune* 50 insurance company, customers are no longer moved from claims person to claims person as had been done in the past. The company completely reengineered its information technology system to allow empowered claims teams to handle every aspect of a customer problem or request. Team members now have the power to solve customer problems. Instead of being responsible for just a small part of the service, claims teams now experience higher levels of potency, meaningfulness, autonomy, and impact as a result of their job redesign. As one employee put it, "I like knowing that our team can really help our customers and their families. There's no more passing the buck here. If we can't solve it, it can't be solved. And I don't think there's ever been a problem this team couldn't solve."

Teams are embedded in a larger organizational framework. When the framework includes production/service responsibilities that facilitate and support ownership and control, team empowerment is strongly reinforced. Our findings suggest that team empowerment experiences are more likely when production and operation systems require teams to:

- Set their own production standards
- Develop and monitor their own quality standards and measurement techniques
- Take on production/service learning and development opportunities
- Handle their own problems with internal and external customers
- Work with a whole product or service, not just a few elements.

Human Resource Management Policies

Can work teams be trusted to internally assume human resource management functions? Some organizations have delegated important human resource decisions to teams. In many instances, teams screen applicants and select new members. In the Texas Conoco plant, associates do all the hiring. Prospective new hires are evaluated, not so much on skills as on behavior. Plant manager Chomka adds, "Empowered teams are not right for everyone. We can train people on the skills but we're looking for people who 'fit' with our empowered system. No one can assess that better than our associates." A Genencor International team member in the United States echoed this by stating that "people want to work in a company that reflects their values so they will want to be a part of it. That way, it won't compromise you."

Once new members are on board, teams take responsibility for orienting them to team norms and processes. In addition, some teams provide both informal and formal training for each other. And teams in many organizations are charged with creating their own procedures for evaluating individual contributions, recommending rewards for deserving teammates, and sanctioning free riders. For example, Conoco's commercial marketing team based in Houston, Texas, was given a budget and then developed a process for allocating their own salary. Sixty percent of compensation is based on meeting team goals while the remaining 40 percent is allocated for individual goals. "We wanted to send a signal that team goals have a higher priority than individual ones," commented team member, Jim Hamilton.

Commercial marketing team members also developed the performance appraisal process, which takes customer feedback into account, and the specific content items for their own peer appraisals. Team members provide each other with direct, face-to-face feedback in team appraisal sessions. Hamilton adds, "It took a while to get used to getting such direct feedback from peers. We struggled at first, but have become much more comfortable with the process over time. Keeping our eye on the overall success of the team, rather than our own personal success, helped tremendously." Commercial marketing's team champion (Conoco's name for a high-level team sponsor), Bob Stone, states, "The performance evaluation system, because it was developed by the team itself, has been very effective at motivating all of the team members." Taking ownership of the human resource management function provides teams an important source of internal control. It heightens team perceptions of potency, meaningfulness, and autonomy—core dimensions of empowerment.

Our research showed that the following human resources policies are linked to higher levels of team empowerment:

- Team-based reward systems
- Cross-training of team members on jobs within their team
- Responsibility for hiring, training, punishment, and firing
- Peer evaluations.

The *Fortune* 50 Plant A facility has moved exclusively to team-based pay. Each week, all team members take home exactly the same amount of money based on the performance of the team as a whole. While some would argue that both team and individual compensation should be included in team-based organizations, management (in conjunction with employee task forces) adopted a total team-based pay structure. The organization wanted to send a strong signal to existing employees and potential new hires that team members are expected to carry out tasks with the welfare of the team as their primary concern.

Did doing away with individual pay and incentives cause grumbling among high performers and company stars? "Yes," says plant management. The general manager commented, "We did lose a few of our strongest producers to our competitors and that bothered me at first. But after seeing other good producers sharing and helping their teammates and after seeing our numbers re-

cover and even go up after falling at first, I was convinced that team pay was the way to go." Tying team performance to take-home pay increases team empowerment by enhancing potency experiences. Team members can see the results of their performance in a concrete, measurable way. As one Motorola team member in the Philippines put it, "When we win, we all win. When we fail, we all fail. That's what teamwork means here."

Team members at the *Fortune* 50 insurance company play a role in recruiting, selecting, and training new employees. As many team members as possible interview prospective new hires depending on their work-related duties. Such a practice might be a little intimidating at first for some potential employees, as some recent hires confirmed. However, both the existing team members and new hires feel that this is the best way to give prospective employees a realistic job preview in a team-based organization. One team member commented, "I like having a say in deciding who works here. I feel like we are the best ones to judge who will fit in here and who will be best for the team." And there are other benefits. Chairman Roger Sant describes AES's hiring process as one in which "teams interview candidates, and there are multiple meetings in which they try to get the sense of the person and whether he or she will be comfortable in the AES environment." Letting team members hire also has a dynamic effect on the new hires themselves. AES CEO Bakke commented, "I am always amazed at how well some people who have just been hired understand what we are doing and how well they manage to spread the news."

Extending employee empowerment experiences to the human resources function allows employees more autonomy, adds meaning to their jobs, and lets members have a visible impact on their team and organization as a whole. However, of the four factors that enhance team empowerment experiences, we found that organizations struggled the most with human resources policies. Regarding hiring, discipline, and firing, these organizations were quick to point out the need to balance their excitement over empowerment with conformance to employment labor laws and the decisions set forth by the National Labor Relations Board (NLRB). Regarding team pay, one manager stated, "People started to doubt this team thing when the changes began to affect their paychecks. Our people went wild. They couldn't believe that they would have to rely on nine other people for their take-home pay." The concerns expressed by these managers are real. In Finland, for example, tight union restrictions prevented Genencor International from aggressively moving to team-based pay. There are legal issues yet unresolved regarding how much control can be exerted by employees over fellow team members. Some employees in the companies we visited exerted a tighter form of control than might have been present in a traditional, supervisor-led work environment. In any change effort, pay and evaluations systems are "where the rubber meets the road." Resistance will be most evident in these types of changes. However, there are ways to overcome these roadblocks.

For example, team members at Motorola struggled initially with peer evaluations. Team members told us that the Filipino culture, in general, does not promote direct confrontation, especially in the workplace. To give someone negative feedback in front of other people in a team setting has the potential to generate feelings of shame and loss of dignity on the part of the recipient. How did the team members handle this cultural "barrier" to empowered teams? "We give feedback more indirectly," one team member explained. "We give examples without names, and the people know who they are." If direct feedback is a must, it is normally done on a one-to-one basis rather than openly in a team meeting as would be the case in Motorola facilities in the United States. We observed that Filipino employees at Motorola were quite adept at making small adjustments to managerial practices while retaining the overall spirit (and, more important, the impact) of empowered teams. A similar situation existed at Genencor's Finland operation. One team leader explained that "there are traditional boundaries in the Finnish culture that make it hard for

us to give each other honest feedback. These are breaking down slowly over time here in Genencor because we understand how important it is to the overall success of empowered teams."

Keeping in mind these difficulties, companies that have radically changed human resource systems to support team-level performance have benefited most from extremely high levels of team empowerment and, in turn, team effectiveness. Finding ways to address the roadblocks creatively will be key and, of course, there will be no one right answer for every organization.

Social Structure

Organizations are political entities. Every effective politician knows the importance of understanding the needs of his or her constituents, networking with others, cultivating support, tapping valuable information sources, forming coalitions, and building consensus. Organizational politics requires many of the same skills. Teams embedded in a hospitable political climate have the opportunity to strengthen their sense of empowerment.

Our research indicates that political climates differ across organizations. When the political climate encourages sharing of resources, building coalitions, and working cooperatively toward common goals, teams readily find sources of support and assistance for reaching their objectives. When the political climate is "cutthroat," team effectiveness can be seriously undermined. According to our study, aspects of the social structure that enhance team member empowerment experiences include:

- Support from other teams and departments
- Sharing important strategic information
- Access to the resources of other teams
- Frequent communication with other teams
- Team development of rules and policies

In our work with team-based organizations, we have heard complaints about how, rather than improving the flow of communication and coordination across organizations (which, in theory, teams are designed to do), teams create mini-empires that divide rather than integrate. Without a proper social structure, this is exactly the result one would expect when employees are broken up into small groups, given names and separate areas of responsibility, and even encouraged to compete with other teams.

In the organizations we studied with high levels of team empowerment, efforts were taken at the organizational level to reinforce superordinate (i.e., organizational) goals and open communication channels. In the insurance company, a few members of each team in the organization also belonged to what the company called "bridge" teams—also known as "ring" or "linking" teams.

Bridge teams are composed of members from different teams that must integrate their efforts and are charged with facilitating communication and coordination among their teams. In our observations of bridge team meetings, we saw team members seeking creative ways to share information and supporting each other. Our research indicates that access to other teams' resources and a high degree of interteam communication is critical to forming team empowerment experiences. Team members have to know that they can get the "stuff" to get things done even if it means occasionally calling in political favors and IOUs from other teams (not unlike the earlier example of the resolution of the customer complaint in the yarn-making plant). At Motorola, for example, individual teams come together every quarter to share team progress and get feedback from other teams. Such meetings build effective communication, cut down on unhealthy interteam conflict, and keep team members focused on bigger issues. In the *Fortune* 50 textile organization, team members have access to the company's financial status and competitive information at a moment's notice. In organizations of the past, such sharing was considered inappropriate and possibly even dangerous. Openness with regard to big picture information is critical for team empowerment. Sharing information signals top management trust and helps teams align their decisions with organizational priorities. As one team leader explained,

"We used to only discuss our strategy and competition in management meetings. Some of that might have trickled out to the floor, but keeping it quiet was just part of the culture around here. We found out that our associates were not only interested in this information, but now see it as an important part of the whole team experience." Our study findings show that creating a social structure at the organizational level that regularly shares information, provides team resources, and encourages cooperation across teams goes a long way to foster team empowerment.

Are Empowered Teams Right for Every Company, Team, and Task?

In response to whether teams are always right for every situation, the answer is unequivocally "no." Just as with self-managing work teams, organizational decision makers will want to weigh the costs and benefits of implementing empowered teams. Every organization we studied was clear about the long-term investment needed to move ahead with empowered teams. In addition, all our data came from permanent work teams. We did not examine management teams, cross-functional teams, project teams, or virtual teams. There are certainly conditions under which empowered teams might be less appropriate. Before deciding on empowered teams, managers and employees must get answers to important questions regarding organization, team, and individual factors. Exhibit 4 contains some of the more important questions we identified in our research.

At the organization level, managers should understand the system requirements necessary for a change to empowered work teams. Assessments will have to be made regarding top management commitment, organizational resource availability, goal clarity, information technology capabilities, change strategies, anticipated boundaries of team empowerment, and the flexibility to allow the team empowerment system to change and grow based on team member input. At the team level, managers should ascertain the permanency of teams, resource availability, the nature of the

EXHIBIT 4 **Diagnostic Questions to Assess Appropriateness of Empowered Teams**

Organizational Level

1. Is the organization fully committed to aligning all management systems with empowered work teams including leader behaviors, team-based rewards, and open access to information?
2. Will top management support such a change and the requisite system changes?
3. Does the organization have sufficient resources to invest in significant training and development for both managers and employees?
4. Is human resources ready/equipped to commit to changes in pay systems and performance management systems and to give up control over traditional selection and evaluation functions?
5. Are organizational goals and the expected results from empowered teams clearly specified?
6. Will the organization share strategic/competitive information and have systems (e.g., an enterprise-wide information system) accessible to empowered team members?
7. Does the organization have a plan to manage the transition including timetables for the transfer of managerial responsibilities and known boundaries or limits on the level of team empowerment expected or desired?
8. Will the organization support continued monitoring and adjustment of team empowerment implementation by team members (or as Chris Argyris states, will the "do your own thing—the way we tell you" mentality prevail)?

Team Level

1. Are the teams designed to be long-term, permanent work teams?
2. Will the teams have access to the resources they need for high performance?
3. Will team members carry out interdependent tasks (i.e., tasks that require a high degree of coordination and communication)?
4. Are team tasks complex and nonroutine in nature? If not, can the tasks be enlarged or enriched to get optimal benefits from team empowerment?
5. Can systems be designed to facilitate a high degree of interteam coordination?

Individual Level

1. Will employees be receptive to, and benefit from, cross-training?
2. Do employees have the necessary maturity levels to effectively carry out peer evaluations, selection and discipline decisions, conflict management, and other administrative tasks?
3. Are employee ability levels currently sufficient for handling increased responsibility and, if not, will increased training result in appropriate ability levels?
4. Do employees intended for empowered teams have appropriate personality characteristics such as high growth needs, preferences for autonomy, preferences for teamwork, a high tolerance for ambiguity, flexibility, and an internal locus of control?
5. Will employees be open to examining their own behavior in the context of empowered teams?

team's tasks, the degree of likely interteam cooperation and coordination. At the individual level, managers must decide whether employees will benefit from and use cross-training, are mature enough to handle increased responsibility such as peer evaluations, have the necessary ability levels to assume managerial tasks, have personality traits consistent with empowered teams, and are open to examining and changing behavior in light of the requirements of team empowerment.

If the answer to a majority of the questions in Exhibit 4 is "yes" (or if the organization can transition itself in order to answer yes to most of the questions), then empowered teams will likely be right for the organization, the teams, and the individuals. If the answer to most of the questions is "no," empowered teams are probably not right for your organization—at least not right now. One of the strongest pieces of advice we can give to managers and employees is to be very leery of anyone who insists teams are right for your company when there has been no attempt to gather detailed information about the organizational context or the tasks that employees do. Consultants who "sell teams" as their wares will only make money if you "buy" teams. Many of the failures of self-managing and empowered teams can probably be attributed to implementing them when the situation does not call for teams or when there is not adequate organizational support or systems alignment.

Clearly, some tasks are better suited to be carried out by individuals in a more traditional work environment. Examples include tasks that do not require employee interdependence or highly routine tasks that do not involve a high degree of decision-making discretion. Managers must also determine the "readiness" of their organizations for working in empowered teams. It is much better to find out that empowered teams are not right for your organization *before* significant investments are made rather than after the money has been spent.

Levi Strauss spent millions of dollars in installing work teams in the early 1990s. In 1993, after morale and productivity plunged, Levi Strauss called in Sibson & Company, a Princeton, New Jersey, consulting firm, to analyze the problems. Their conclusion? Start over—*from scratch.* Ralph Pollard, a former Levi's manufacturing manager, stated, "We created a lot of anxiety and pain and suffering in our people, and for what? We bet the farm on team manufacturing, but the whole system wasn't ready to take advantage of it." Levels of stress, infighting, and personal threats became so intense at a Tennessee plant that Levi's stationed an off-duty sheriff's deputy at the plant's front entrance. Levi Strauss learned a hard lesson about work team implementation. Much of the difficult and important work is done *before* teams are implemented. And employees must be involved every step of the way. Levi's experience further reinforces the importance of aligning organizational systems behind empowered work teams.

Piecing Together the Empowerment Puzzle

To overcome many of the problems associated with teams, we recommend that managers take a much broader view of teams than the label "self-managing" might suggest. Our study findings suggest that getting teams to reach optimal performance levels requires much more than handing over the managerial reins to the team and getting out of the way. In addition to giving teams more

freedom and discretion, team members must believe in their team's capabilities, find meaning in their team's tasks, and fully realize the impact that their team's work has on customers if they are to become truly high-performance teams.

Our findings also suggest that creating the conditions for empowered work teams to survive and thrive is a complex and challenging assignment. As Conoco's Chomka put it, "I don't believe you ever actually finish implementing empowered teams. As soon as we get to where we think we should be, we redefine the vision, it becomes more complex, and we keep changing and growing as our market demands." Adds Conoco University director, David Nelson, "The success of our teams is really a testament to both the team leaders, who had the courage to let go and trust, and the team members that have embraced not only increased autonomy but increased accountability as well." One team member from Conoco's commercial marketing team also commented, "Some days it would just be easier to have a boss—but those days are far outnumbered by the ones when I feel a real sense of pride in what we accomplished as a team without direct supervision."

In summary, teams need supportive leaders who will trust them to make important decisions, celebrate their successes, and learn from their mistakes. Leaders must take on the roles of coaches, teachers, and advisers, helping teams to set high expectations for themselves and working hard to fulfill them. Production/service responsibilities and the systems that support them must be aligned with empowerment concepts, providing teams with coordination mechanisms, access to internal and external customers, and rapid feedback on a full range of quality indicators. Teams must receive training and support to manage many of their human resource management functions internally. Empowered teams function best in a political climate that stresses resource sharing, consensus building, and cooperation in achieving meaningful organizational goals.

As CEO Bakke of AES states, "[Our structure] is like an ecosystem. Everything about how we organize gives people the power and the responsibility to make important decisions, to engage with their work as business-people, not as cogs in a machine." And as one of the team members in Genencor International's Finnish plant put it, "When people are given responsibility, and everyone does their share, it's a feeling that you can't explain in words." Well said. When all of the pieces of the empowerment puzzle fit tightly together, teams will be ready to work at full power.

References

For a more comprehensive review of the literature on empowered teams and a measure of team empowerment, see Bradley Kirkman and Benson Rosen's chapter entitled "A Model of Work Team Empowerment," in *Research in Organizational Change and Development,* Volume 10 (JAI Press, 1997); and for a test of the team empowerment model, see their article entitled "Beyond Self-Management: Antecedents and Consequences of Team Empowerment," in *Academy of Management Journal,* February, 1999.

To read about Peter Drucker's thoughts on teams, see Mike Verespej's article entitled "Drucker Sours on Teams," in *Industry Week,* April 6, 1998, and Patricia Panchak's article entitled "The Future of Manufacturing: An Exclusive Interview with Peter Drucker," in *Industry Week,* September 21, 1998. For an example of a company that has successfully transitioned to empowered teams, see Suzy Wetlaufer's interview with executives at AES in an article entitled, "Organizing for Empowerment: An Interview with AES's Roger Sant and Dennis Bakke," in *Harvard Business Review,* January/February, 1999. For more information on the Levi Strauss experience with teams, see Ralph King, Jr.'s article entitled "Levi's Factory Workers Are Assigned to Teams, and Morale Takes a Hit," in *The Wall Street Journal,* May 20, 1998, p. A1.

To learn more about implementation issues regarding empowerment, see Alan Randolph's article entitled "Navigating the Journey to Empowerment," in *Organizational Dynamics,* Spring 1995; Chris Argyris's article en-

title "Empowerment: The Emperor's New Clothes," in *Harvard Business Review,* May–June, 1998; and Robert Simons's article entitled "Control in an Age of Empowerment," *Harvard Business Review,* March–April, 1995.

For more information about the leadership requirements in empowered and self-managing work organizations, see Robert Quinn and Gretchen Spreitzer's article entitled "The Road to Empowerment: Seven Questions Every Leader Should Consider," in *Organizational Dynamics,* Autumn 1997; Charles Manz and Henry Sims's article entitled "Leading Workers to Lead Themselves: The External Leadership of Self-Managing Work Teams," in *Administrative Science Quarterly,* March 1987; and Kimball Fisher's book, *Leading Self-Directed Work Teams: A Guide to Developing New Team Leadership Skills* (McGraw-Hill, 1993).

More information about creating the proper structure for work teams can be found in Ruth Wageman's article entitled "Critical Success Factors for Creating Superb Self-Managing Teams," in *Organizational Dynamics,* Summer 1997; Richard Wellins, William Byham, and Jeanne Wilson's book entitled *Empowered Teams: Creating Self-Directed Work Groups That Improve Quality, Productivity, and Participation* (Jossey-Bass, 1991); and Susan Mohrman, Susan Cohen, and Allan Mohrman Jr.'s book, *Designing Team-Based Organizations: New Forms for Knowledge Work* (Jossey-Bass, 1995).

More information about the impact of self-managing work teams on employee attitudes and productivity can be found in Toby Wall, Nigel Kemp, Paul Jackson, and Chris Clegg's article entitled "Outcomes of Autonomous Workgroups: A Long-Term Field Experiment," in *Academy of Management Journal,* April, 1986; John Cordery, Walter Mueller, and Leigh Smith's article, "Attitudinal and Behavioral Effects of Autonomous Group Working: A Longitudinal Field Study," in *Academy of Management Journal,* April, 1991; and Susan Cohen, Gerald Ledford, Jr., and Gretchen Spreitzer's article entitled "A Predictive Model of Self-Managing Work Team Effectiveness," in *Human Relations,* May, 1996.

Reading 42

Managing Discontinuities: The Emerging Challenges

C. K. Prahalad

As we move into the next millennium, all managers will face a new set of competitive challenges—challenges that represent *major discontinuities*. The critical managerial tasks are more than just becoming good (e.g., TQM), fast (e.g., cycle time) or lean (e.g., agile). Managers recognize that these attributes are necessary but not adequate goals for survival in the next millennium.

Increasingly, the ability to recognize the impending discontinuities and learning how to be innovative are becoming the real challenges for senior managers. Most firms do not have good track records. To the contrary, there is evidence that established firms are not very adept at coping with or managing discontinuous change.[1]

Discontinuities translate some core competencies into core rigidities.[2] At the same time, new core competencies have to be built to exploit the new opportunities that emerge. Managers have to simultaneously "forget" selectively and "learn" aggressively. This is the challenge.

This article outlines the basic discontinuities that all firms will face during the next decade. Next, the critical managerial challenges and tasks that result from these discontinuities are described. The creation of new competencies by integrating the old processes with newly acquired knowledge and skills follow. Finally, the basic steps for building a program to implement the new competencies are provided, along with the nature and impact of the new demands on the maintenance of a corporate core competency profile.

Source: C. K. Prahalad, "Managing Discontinuities: The Emerging Challenges." Reprinted from *Research Technology Management*, May–June 1998, pp. 14–22. Copyright © 1998 Industrial Research Institute, Inc.

The Emerging Competitive Landscape

The eight discontinuities described below constitute the emerging competitive landscape. Taken one at a time, they do not tell the whole story. What is not obvious is the collective pressure these discontinuities exert on a management group.

1. *Global.* During the 1980s, "global" meant new and aggressive competition from Japan and South Korea. Increasingly, it also means global customers, as is the case of the auto industry.

During the last decade, over 3 billion people abandoned the ideology of a planned economy and moved toward variants of a market economy. This generated new opportunities for established firms. However, global expansion also produces geographical asymmetries in growth patterns. China and India may be growing at 7–10 percent per year, while Western Europe may be growing at less than 2 percent. Asymmetrical growth can lead to dramatic shifts in resources within a multinational (MNC) firm. By the year 2010, it would not be surprising if most of the Western MNCs had more than 50 percent of their assets in China, Southeast Asia and India. This would have a dramatic effect on how products are developed and how human resources are managed within the MNC. Needless to say, the composition of the top management in these firms will also be different.

Further, there is an emerging geographical focus to industry expertise. For example, Taiwan produces more than 50 percent of all computer monitors, 72 percent of all mouses, and about 60 percent of all the motherboards.[3] The California

Bay area (Silicon Valley) remains the heart of the software industry. London and its environs dominate the video game software development industry. Movies and music industries are still dominated by the United States and the United Kingdom. This geographical foci means that firms must be present in the "place where the music is made" to keep themselves up-to-date.

It is not surprising that all high-tech firms—European, Japanese or South Korean—have made investments in the Bay area. While these investments, initially, tended to be small and of a "sensing post" variety, increasingly they represent significant investments. For similar reasons, most electronics and financial services companies are also investing in Bangalore and other centers in India to access software talent. Thus, globalization will have a significant impact on both the resource and skill configuration of the MNC.

2. *Deregulation and Privatization.* There appears to be an unstoppable trend toward deregulation and privatization. Starting from the breakup of "Ma Bell," the trend is clear—in both the developed and developing countries.

Telecommunications, utilities, airlines, financial services, and health care are but a few of the traditionally regulated industries that are undergoing traumatic change. For example, in most of these industries, mergers and acquisitions are endemic. There is a race to extract value out of the inefficiencies that are inherent in regulation-induced local and regional monopolies. There is also a race to globalize. For example, utility firms such as Enron are expanding into other countries. Relieved from local regulatory restrictions, these industries (e.g., power, telecommunications) are rapidly becoming global. Further, there is a significant amount of de-verticalization of the industries—separating, for example, power generation from transmission and marketing. There is also an emerging spot market for power. Recently, there has been an attempt to differentiate and brand products and services, such as power, which have been traditionally managed as commodities.

In tandem with deregulation, there is a significant move toward privatization of public sector firms. This trend is obvious worldwide—from China, India, Chile, Poland, France, and Germany. Privatization produces a significant amount of social disruption as the inefficient public sector firms shed obsolete assets, consolidate their businesses and resize their firms. These efforts significantly impact capital flows, unemployment and the need for growth to absorb the workforce rendered surplus by the restructuring of the public sector.

The implications of deregulation/privatization are:

- Most industries that were local will become regional, national and global.
- The economics of these businesses will change dramatically.
- There is likely to be significant unemployment generated by these efforts to rationalize regulated industries. The U.S. and U.K. telecommunications industry demonstrates the level of resizing that may be required worldwide in a wide variety of industries.

3. *Volatility.* Almost all industries are experiencing a new level of volatility—the need for scaling up and scaling down and significantly reducing the cycle time for product development.

Volatility and seasonality combined create a new set of demands on management. For example, it is hard to justify "focused factories" dedicated to a single business line when that business is subject to great volatility. As the demand for products and services fluctuates, focused factories will have to dramatically scale up or be closed down. This dilemma is increasingly forcing firms to create "flexible factories" that can serve multiple, related business units.

Further, privileged access to suppliers is also becoming a major source of concern. Firms must maintain a close relationship with their suppliers to ensure that they will support the marketplace volatility of their end products.

4. *Convergence.* The convergence of multiple technologies represents a major discontinuity. Although the convergence of computing, communications, consumer electronics, and entertainment is often cited as an example, convergence is a lot more pervasive. For example, increasingly:

- Personal care products such as shampoo and face creams will have to incorporate the disciplines of pharmaceutical technologies, including clinical trials. Hair growth and anti-aging, for example, will change the nature of the personal care products industry. The fashion industry must marry science.

- Soybeans, corn, potatoes, cotton, and other "commodity" products will have to contend with new developments in plant genetics. Monsanto's introduction of Roundup, for example, along with pest-resistant seeds, brings a new level of technological sophistication to a traditional business—in the application of fertilizers and insecticides, as well as in primary processing.

- Chemical and electronic technologies are co-mingling. Digital cameras, printers and copiers are interesting combinations of material science, chemistry, electronics, and software.

- Automobiles are a combination of "engineered" materials, electronics and software combined with traditional mechanical engineering.

A large number of similar convergences can be identified. The key issue is that very distinct "intellectual heritages" will have to be managed and seamlessly integrated. For example, a company such as Kodak, steeped in chemical imaging, can find managing such a transition (chemical engineering + electronics + software) to be daunting. Revlon, Procter & Gamble and others have to manage an equally difficult transition—from traditional fashion to "cosmaceuticals," and from traditional food to "health and wellness diets," respectively.

Digitalization has probably had the most profound significant impact on all types of industries, from movie-making to financial services. There is not one industry that can postpone the need to understand and exploit the benefits of digital (information) technology.

5. *Indeterminate Industry Boundaries.* As a result of such convergences, many of the traditional industry boundaries are changing. For example, the dividing line between personal computers and television is uncertain. So too is the boundary between communication and computing or entertainment. The distinction between what constitutes a professional business and a consumer business is increasingly hard to delineate. Microsoft, AT&T, Sears, Sainsbury, or Tesco could all be the next competitors in the financial services industry. These indeterminate sector boundaries suggest:

- There are no clearly identifiable competitors.

- Competitors will approach selected opportunities from their own vantage points. For example, Dell computers can see the opportunity as PC–TV, while Sony or Philips see it as TV–PC, reflecting their different starting points. Therefore, there will be multiple migration paths—Dell and Philips may not approach the migration to a PC–TV the same way, much less Microsoft or Intel. The same can be argued for banks—insurance firms, banks, retailers, and communication companies will not approach the market the same way.

- Competition for "migration paths" may be as critical as the end game itself.

Traditional analytical tools used to determine where value is created may be inappropriate in this new and emerging industry environment.[4] For example, in the traditional view of strategy, we have associated size with market influence. In the emerging competitive landscape, size does not lead to industry influence. Similarly, incumbency provides no rights; indeed, it may be a disadvantage.

One cannot assume clear industry boundaries. The boundaries between suppliers, competitors, customers, and collaborators are very porous. There are no permanent competitive positions. The structure of these industries is in a state of constant flux. The strategic question is not about optimizing but retaining the *capability for flexible and quick response.* The goal is to create a robust competitive position.

As the resource configurations of individual firms tend to be inadequate to meet the growing and changing demands, a wide variety of collaborative arrangements have become the norm in most industries. Increasingly, firms large and small have a higher propensity to form alliances. Many of them may be temporary. As industry structures evolve, the importance of an alliance does change. Firms will form new alliances and opt out of old ones. Forming and learning from alliances and disbanding those that are no longer strategic may be a learned skill itself.

6. *Standards.* New industries produce new standards as markets evolve. What are the standards for DVD or Minidisk? What are the standards we need for security and privacy before E-Commerce can flourish? What are the communication standards for creating a seamless exchange of images and video over the Internet? Questions such as these are critical in the evolution of markets. Increasingly, issues of this kind are resolved by market forces, not by governmental mandates. Several interesting phenomena created by these changes are:

- Competitors collaborate to establish standards. Vendor standards do not become industry standards unless one standard gains enough market power to implicitly enforce it. This means that a coalition of firms subscribing to the standard proposed by one vendor (e.g., Java by Sun) will have to support it over other vendor standards (e.g., NT by Microsoft). This is "inter-coalition" competition.
- Multiple industry standards may coexist for some time, and this is very expensive, creat-

ing uncertainties for both the consumer and the firms. Over time, one dominant industry standard evolves.

- Inter-coalition competition for setting standards is different from "intra-coalition" competition for profits. For example, while Philips and Sony collaborated in creating the DVD standard, they also compete for profits in the DVD business.

Standards can evolve through market-based competition (as against standards imposed by public policy). Such market-based standards involve competition between a cluster of firms supporting a standard against another cluster supporting an alternate standard. In an important sense, this competition is about competition among coalitions of firms. All firms involved in this process will have to take a position on the basis for supporting one standard over another. For the firm proposing the standard, the question is "What makes the standard attractive to the largest number of firms? What core competence can be used as a bargaining tactic with potential supporters?"

7. *Disintermediation.* In almost all industries, the distance between the producer and the end-user is shrinking. The multiple distribution steps—wholesalers, dealers and retailers—are being reduced to a single distribution step. New channels are emerging. The World Wide Web provides an opportunity for producers to go directly to the end-user. This phenomenon is pervasive, be it in brokerage (e.g., Charles Schwab), garments (e.g., Levi Strauss) or computers (e.g., Dell, Gateway).

With the proliferation of manufacturers offering their wares electronically, there is unlikely to be a dearth of information available to the end-user. However, information, by itself, does not guarantee the ability to make good decisions. It is likely that a new form of intermediary—the expert—will emerge. Experts (electronic equivalent of Consumer Reports) will act as intermediaries who will verify quality and cost and make recommendations.

The process of disintermediation has significant implications for the traditional cost structure of industries, especially the selling and administrative costs. Disintermediation will also have an impact on the levels of finished goods, inventories and accounts receivables required for a unit of revenue. The implication is that there will be both profit and loss and balance sheet impacts. Firms will have to fundamentally rethink their business models.

8. *Eco-Sensitivity.* This will become a major issue in the next millennium. Firms will move away from a compliance-oriented perspective to a business-opportunity-driven viewpoint of environmental issues.

For example, the growing affluence of mainland China will influence the mix of food consumed. (Invariably, affluence is associated with more meat and sugar consumption.) China has a shortage of water and arable land. Therefore, most of the additional demand for food—in the form of corn, chickens or hogs—must be imported. This implies that China will become a major importer of food during the next decade. This is ecologically sensible; China gets all the food it needs, without straining its scarce water resources. The abundant water resources and land in the Americas get used. This is an ecologically sensible solution for the world as a whole.

The New Economy

Any of the individual discontinuities can be managed. But the New Economy is about all these forces impacting the firm simultaneously (see Figure 1). Businesses will be affected differently; however, all of them will be subject to the impact of a subset of these forces. Taken as a whole, these discontinuities will force all firms to:

- Be concerned about doing business worldwide. This implies that all firms will have to worry

FIGURE 1 **Eight Discontinuities Are Shaping the New Economy**

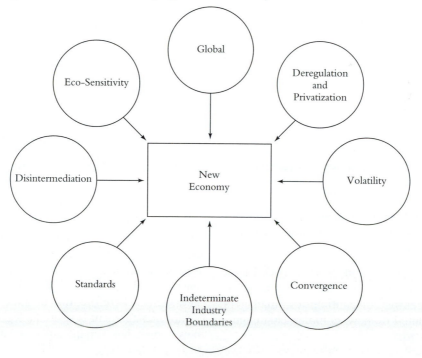

about multiple locations, multiple cultures, multiple skill sets, and multiple business perspectives.

- Be concerned about temporary alliances— alliance and collaborative agreements that are designed to transfer skills across firms. In these alliances, learning is as important as protecting critical intellectual property, demanding that people be open to new ideas while protecting vital company interests.

- Focus on speed as a major issue—not just speed in product development, but also in knowledge transfer across markets and businesses. To remain competitive, companies will have to absorb this new knowledge and reconfigure their businesses accordingly.

- Reevaluate the business model used in the developed world. Current beliefs about the "capital intensity" of a business or the "profit model" associated with it may not be sustainable. The business model needs to be reevaluated and adapted to meet the requirements of the New Economy.

The discontinuities that constitute the New Economy will demand new skill sets among management teams.

Revisiting Core Competencies of the Firm

The idea is widely accepted that in addition to being a portfolio of distinct businesses, the diversified firm is a portfolio of core competencies.[5] Core competencies are a combination of:

- Multiple technologies (hard and soft).
- Collective learning (multilevel, multifunctional).
- Capacity to share (across business and geographical boundaries).

A core competency can be represented as a multiplicative function of these three elements. To manage competitive discontinuities, managers will be confronted by new, complex challenges. They will have to:

- Incorporate new bundles of technologies— new to the traditional businesses of the firm. A bundle of related technologies, or a *knowledge stream,* such as software, needs to be blended with more traditional technologies (e.g., electronics and software in a chemical firm). This means that managers must recognize that they have to work with a new logic (e.g., electronics in a traditional chemical firm).

- The composition of teams will also change. Globalization requires that team members *from multiple cultures* must learn as a group.

- The redeployment of core competence across a number of applications at high speed will force firms to *collaborate and transfer knowledge across multiple business units and geographical locations.*

The task of managing competencies in the new global market place is complex. There are at least five distinct tasks:

1. Gaining Access to, and Absorbing New, Knowledge

The most obvious way to gain access to the new knowledge stream is to recruit people with the required (new) knowledge (e.g., mathematicians in a bank, geneticists in a traditional pharmaceutical firm, or software engineers in a hard-core manufacturing firm). Anyone who has been through this process of new skills acquisition knows how hard it is to have these new skills accepted and made welcome in an organization. While bankers have to learn the new tools that mathematicians bring to the game, mathematicians also have to learn banking.

This two-way knowledge transfer is critical before a useful blending can occur. However, the tendency in most organizations is to reject these new skills—similar to the response of an immune system to an invading virus. Left to its own devices, the organization is unlikely to absorb these new skills. Therefore, one of the critical roles of senior management is to create legitimacy for the new knowledge. Top managers must not only constantly present the strategic direction of the firm to all employees, but also identify the new knowledge that will help to create that future. Further, several levels of the organization must learn and apply the "culture" of that new knowledge. For example, software has a different culture from manufacturing.

The intellectual heritage limits and restricts what a management team can do. For example, why do we not have software upgrades in automobiles? It is equally difficult for those who have operated in a regulated environment to understand the culture and discipline of the capital market. One senior manager from the Eastern bloc, perplexed by the changes in the stock prices on a daily basis, asked: "Which organization fixes the price?" In his country, governmental agencies fixed all prices until recently.

It is not enough that the need for new knowledge is recognized and steps are taken to acquire them (including alliances), but fundamental legitimacy and urgency must be assigned to that task. In order to be successful, the progress of the task of instituting and melding the new knowledge into the different traditional intellectual cultures must be continually monitored.

2. Integrating Multiple Streams of Knowledge

Acquiring new knowledge is a difficult process, and actively integrating it into traditional knowledge to create new business opportunities is even harder. For example, at Kodak, knowledge of chemical imaging must be integrated with electronics and software knowledge to create new hybrid products. Photo compact disks and digital cameras demand a seamless and careful integration of multiple streams of knowledge. Over time, the commingling of these streams creates a new competence.

Organizations learn by doing. Therefore, it is critical that top managers set up specific, bite-size projects. Projects are the carriers of new learning. They focus the organization's attention on solving the problems of integrating the new knowledge

with the old. Project teams with cross-disciplinary membership are critical for successful learning and application.

3. Sharing across Cultures and Distance

While the focus thus far has been on intellectual diversity—the culture of various knowledge streams—in a global firm, there is yet another dimension to cultural diversity. This is a result of *multiple country cultures.*

Different cultures have different implicit priorities. For example, the product development philosophy—the priorities placed on quality, cost, time, safety, and performance—among U.S.-trained, European, Japanese, and Chinese designers is likely to be different. No manager lives in a vacuum. She/he lives in a culture that values some characteristics more than others. This is a result of deep socialization. In some cultures, for example, learning is a linear process. It is primarily analytical and based on individual effort. In other societies, learning is much more sequential, experiential and a team-oriented effort in which intuition plays an important role.

When collaboration is initiated in the context of evolving knowledge, across multiple cultures (i.e., collaboration with teams from three different continents), conflicts and misunderstandings emanate. A deeper and explicit understanding of the socialization patterns of groups involved becomes a necessity. Moreover, managers must avoid stereotyping the other groups. Cross-cultural collaborative activity is emerging as a critical skill in the New Economy.

4. Learning to Forget

It is easy to exhort an individual or an organization to learn. But forgetting may be equally important.[6] The dominant logic of the firm,[7] or the recipes people use to learn, can become a major impediment to learning. Firms (managers) must first learn to forget, and forgetting is more difficult than learning. In most organizations, the forgetting curve is flat; in an age of discontinuities, a flat forgetting curve is a serious problem.

For example, it takes an enormous amount of effort to move from a "cost plus" view of the business to a "price minus" view of the business. The two formulas are: (1) Cost + Profit = Price; and (2) Price – Profit = Cost.

The traditional Department of Defense (DoD)–type businesses are characterized by mindsets, processes and skill sets appropriate to (1). Commercial businesses are characterized by (2). The transition for DoD-driven firms to the commercial arena has been one of deep frustration, with few successes. Participants in this different business culture need to forget their old patterns and replace them with new ones.

A similar situation exists in deregulated industries. Previously, the market was the "regulators"; some would argue that competition was also the "regulators." Senior managers paid a lot of attention to regulators, and the process of regulation made most of the firms in the industry look and act the same. The genetic variety, if any, was minimal. In market-based competition, the game is about consumers, differentiation, price-performance, innovation, and competition. This is a very different competitive milieu. To compete in the New Economy, it is essential to forget the old patterns.

5. Deploying Competence across Business Unit Boundaries

The more that the large organizations move toward business unit (BU)–based strategies, measurement systems such as EVA, and rewards, the harder it is to focus on sharing across BU boundaries. The motivation for sharing is removed from the BUs and the competence base becomes fragmented.

In order to have a system of deployment of competencies, all BUs must have a common understanding of the patterns of market and technology evolution. Without such understanding, the conceptual framework for sharing does not exist.[8] But a conceptual framework, without organizational support systems, is unlikely to work. Many firms invest time and energy developing

perspectives on the future while clinging to administrative systems that reinforce the BU orientation to the exclusion of all others. It is as if we were approaching the fourth-generation strategy with a third-generation knowledge base, second-generation managers, and first-generation administrative systems. There is a clear mismatch between "desire," rhetoric and reality in most firms across this dimension.

Composition of Competencies

The creation of new competencies by integrating a firm's existing knowledge base with new knowledge streams creates the need to reevaluate the elements that collectively create the system of competencies. Two broad elements can be recognized:

1. People-embodied knowledge—both tacit and explicit.[9]
2. Capital-embodied knowledge—both proprietary and vendor-based.

It is the combination of both people-embodied and capital-embodied knowledge that represents the totality of the competence base within an organization. In many industries, such as semiconductor manufacturing, access to vendor-based knowledge (and learning to work with them creatively) tends to be as important as the internally-generated proprietary knowledge (see Figure 2).

The relative importance of the various elements in the overall composition of a firm's competence profile is important to understand, in order to manage it effectively. The balance is likely to be different between:

- Established and new firms in the same industry (e.g., General Motors and Samsung).
- Traditional and new industries (e.g., cement manufacture vs. digital imaging).
- Firms with one location and multiple locations around the world (e.g., the tacit-to-explicit balance is critical in managing multiple locations, which demand more explicit knowledge).

FIGURE 2 It Is the Combination of Both People-Embodied and Capital-Embodied Knowledge that Represents the Totality of an Organization's Competence Base

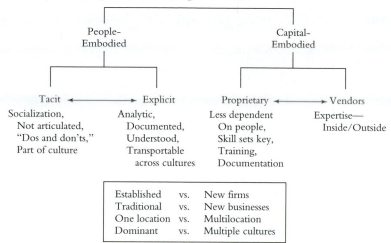

Competence Progression

Competence development is about learning, but learning takes place at three levels: (1) individual; (2) family groups; and (3) the firm as whole. The focus of learning is not just analytical, but also processes and values. Process and behavioral learning are as much a requirement as the analytical or scientific capabilities of individuals. The concepts of a team and a family group are embedded in the framework of competence. Therefore, processes that improve the ability of teams to develop special skills are critical.

- Dominant and multiple cultures (e.g., if most of the development work is done in one dominant culture, say in Japan, then the group can work with more tacit knowledge).

Needless to say, the balance between the elements is a moving target. As the discontinuities in the competitive landscape evolve, they will have an impact on the nature and composition of the elements of the competence base of the firm. Senior managers will have to constantly evaluate and calibrate these shifts and adjust their focus accordingly.

Deploying competence into creating new "white space" opportunities embraces the idea of inter-team transfer and sharing. Therefore, individuals, teams (family groups) and the total organization (inter-team collaboration) are important aspects of competence management. But the cornerstone of the concept is the quality and the centrality of individuals.

The development of a new competence must explicitly recognize the role of individuals, teams, the whole organization, and the process by which individual excellence, scientific knowledge, creativity, and imagination are transformed into team expertise and organizational capability. The competence progression is illustrated in Figure 3.

The challenge to senior managers is to develop specific managerial steps to manage this transformation. While many of these steps will be somewhat firm-specific, there are some universally beneficial steps.

Building New Competencies: First Steps

Building new competencies and selectively leveraging and protecting existing competencies are difficult organizational tasks. The difficulties are

FIGURE 3   **The Challenge to Senior Management Is to Develop Specific Steps to Manage the Competency Development Process**

Competence Progression		
Technology ✕ **Collective Learning** ✕ **Sharing across Boundaries**		
1. Individuals	Teams	Organization
2. Tacit/explicit	Tacit/explicit	Explicit/tacit
3. Personal excellence	Team expertise	Organizational capability
4. Scientific knowledge	Understanding specific applications	Building competence
5. Creativity and imagination	Projects/special capabilities	New way to build businesses, and compete

as much organizational as intellectual. A minimum program would include:

1. Investment in extensive socialization within the firm. Extensive international travel and job assignments help managers become more culturally sensitive. In addition to training in interpersonal competence, there should be training in intercultural competence. Managers during the next decade will have to deal with four levels of diversity: race, gender, cultural, and intellectual. Each aspect of these areas needs training.

2. Development of language skills. European firms do a better job than U.S. firms in language training, at least of their expatriate managers. Language will be a critical aspect of competence transfer. It is easy to recognize that tacit knowledge cannot be easily transferred across language barriers. As the tacit component of the competence profile increases, language skills become critical.

3. Extensive documentation—not a bureaucracy—is critical to transfer from the tacit to explicit. This means that there must be a concern for standards and standardization, such as a commitment to a common CAD system, common IT architecture, common and shared glossary of terms, and a common design philosophy. Basically, there is a need for a common, shared managerial framework. Top managers must clearly identify what is not negotiable within

the firm. But left to their own devices, they are likely to have, for example, incompatible CAD systems or quality processes—a common occurrence in highly decentralized firms. This makes sharing impossible.

4. Extensive commitment to training, in both the analytic and experiential side of management.

These four areas are a basic framework for constructing a program to manage new competencies in the New Economy that is forming. This New Economy will dominate the competitive landscape for the foreseeable future. This competitive landscape is being shaped by major discontinuities. These provide immense opportunities for firms that are alert. Firms will have to rethink the nature of their core competencies and acquire new competencies that will shape their future.

The future belongs to the imaginative, those that have the courage to overcome the discontinuities and reshape their firms to meet the challenges of the New Economy.

Endnotes

1. Christensen, Clayton M. *The Innovator's Dilemma: When Technologies Cause Great Firms to Fail.* Harvard Business School Press, 1977.

2. Leonard-Barton, Dorothy. "Core Capabilities and Core Rigidities: A Paradox in Managing New Product Development." *Strategic Management Journal,* Vol. 13, Special Issue, Summer 1992 (pp. 111–125).

3. See for example, Chin Chung: "Division of Labor across the Taiwan Strait: Macro-overview and Analysis of the Electronics Industry," in *The China Circle.* Barry Naughton, (ed), Brookings Institution Press, 1997.

4. See Porter, M. E. *Competitive Strategy: Techniques for Analyzing Industries and Competitors,* Free Press, New York, 1980.

5. Prahalad, C. K. and Gary Hamel. "The Core Competencies of the Corporation," *Harvard Business Review.* May–June, 1990.

6. Hamel, Gary and C. K. Prahalad. *Competing for the Future* (Chapter 3), Harvard Business School Press, 1994.

7. Prahalad, C. K. and Richard Bettis. "Dominant Logic: A New Linkage between Diversity and Performance." *Strategic Management Journal,* Volume 7, Number 6, November–December 1986 (pp. 485–501).

8. The need for such a framework, a strategic architecture, is discussed in C. K. Prahalad and Gary Hamel: *Competing for the Future,* (chapter 5), Harvard Business School Press, 1994.

9. People-embodied knowledge has received a fair amount of attention with the increasing focus on knowledge management. I. Nonaka and H. Takeuchi: *The Knowledge Creating Company,* Oxford University Press, New York, 1995.

Reading 43

Seven Practices of Successful Organizations

Jeffrey Pfeffer

Effective management of people can produce substantially enhanced economic performance. A plethora of terms have been used to describe such management practices: high commitment, high performance, high involvement, and so forth. I use these terms interchangeably, as they all tap similar ideas about how to obtain profits through people. I extract from the various studies, related literature, and personal observation and experience a set of seven dimensions that seem to characterize most if not all of the systems producing profits through people.

- Employment security.
- Selective hiring of new personnel.
- Self-managed teams and decentralization of decision making as the basic principles of organizational design.
- Comparatively high compensation contingent on organizational performance.
- Extensive training.
- Reduced status distinctions and barriers, including dress, language, office arrangements, and wage differences across levels.
- Extensive sharing of financial and performance information throughout the organization.

This list is somewhat shorter than my earlier list of sixteen practices describing "what effective firms do with people,"[1] for two reasons. First, this list focuses on basic dimensions, some of which,

Source: Reprinted by permission of Harvard Business School Press. An excerpt from *The Human Equation,* by Jeffrey Pfeffer, entitled "Seven Practices of Successful Organizations," which appeared in *California Management Review,* Winter 1998.

such as compensation and reduction of status differences, have multiple components that were previously listed separately. Second, some of the items on the previous list have more to do with the ability to implement high-performance work practices—such as being able to take a long-term view and to realize the benefits of promoting from within—than with describing dimensions of the practices themselves. It is, however, still the case that several of the dimensions of high-performance work arrangements listed, for instance employment security and high pay, appear to fly in the face of conventional wisdom. This article outlines these practices, provides examples to illustrate both their implementation and their impact, and explains their underlying logic.

Employment Security

In an era of downsizing and rightsizing—or, as Donald Hastings, CEO of Lincoln Electric, called it in a speech to the Academy of Management in 1996, "dumbsizing"—how can I write about employment security as a critical element of high-performance work arrangements? First, because it is simply empirically the case that most research on the effects of high-performance management systems have incorporated employment security as one important dimension in their description of these systems. That is because "one of the most widely accepted propositions . . . is that innovations in work practices or other forms of worker-management cooperation or productivity improvement are not likely to be sustained over time when workers fear that by increasing productivity they will work themselves out of their jobs."[2]

This was recognized long ago by Lincoln Electric, the successful arc welding and electric motor manufacturer that has dominated its markets for decades. Years ago, it began offering guaranteed employment to workers after two (and now three) years on the job. It has not had a layoff since 1948. Nor is it the case that this is just because the company has never faced hard times. In the early 1980s, a recession and high interest rates caused Lincoln's domestic sales to fall about 40 percent over an eighteen-month period. Nevertheless, it did not resort to layoffs. One thing the company did to avoid laying off people was to redeploy them. Factory workers who had made Lincoln's products were put in the field with the task of selling them, in the process actually increasing Lincoln's market share and penetration. Over the years, Lincoln has enjoyed gains in productivity that are far above those for manufacturing as a whole, and its managers believe that the assurance workers have that innovations in methods will not cost them or their colleagues their jobs has significantly contributed to these excellent results. Similarly, when General Motors wanted to implement new work arrangements in its innovative Saturn plant in the 1990s, it guaranteed its people job security except in the most extreme circumstances. When New United Motors was formed to operate the Fremont automobile assembly plant, it offered its people job security. How else could it ask for flexibility and cooperation in becoming more efficient and productive?

Many additional benefits follow from employment assurances besides workers' free contribution of knowledge and their efforts to enhance productivity. One advantage to firms is the decreased likelihood that they will lay off employees during downturns. How is this a benefit to the firm? In the absence of some way of building commitment to retaining the work force—either through pledges about employment security or through employment obligations contractually negotiated with a union—firms may lay off employees too quickly and too readily at the first sign of financial difficulty. This constitutes a cost for firms that have done a good job selecting, training, and developing their work force: Layoffs put important strategic assets on the street for the competition to employ. When a colleague and I interviewed the Vice President for People at Southwest Airlines, she noted that the company had never had a layoff or furlough in an industry where such events were common. When we asked why, she replied, "Why would we want to put our best assets, our people, in the arms of the competition?" Seeing its people as strategic assets rather than as costs, Southwest has pursued a careful growth strategy that avoided overexpansion and subsequent cuts in personnel.

Employment security policies will also lead to more careful and leaner hiring, because the firm knows it cannot simply let people go quickly if it has overestimated its labor demand. Leaner staffing can actually make the work force more productive, with fewer people doing more work. The people are often happy to be more productive because they know they are helping to ensure a result that benefits them—having a long-term job and a career. Furthermore, employment security maintained over time helps to build trust between people and their employer, which can lead to more cooperation, forbearance in pressing for wage increases, and better spirit in the company. Herb Kelleher, the CEO of Southwest, has written:

> Our most important tools for building employee partnership are job security and a stimulating work environment . . . Certainly there were times when we could have made substantially more profits in the short term if we had furloughed people, but we didn't. We were looking at our employees' and our company's longer-term interests . . . [A]s it turns out, providing job security imposes additional discipline, because if your goal is to avoid layoffs, then you hire very sparingly. So our commitment to job security has actually helped us keep our labor force smaller and more productive than our competitors'.[3]

For organizations without the strategic discipline or vision of Southwest, a guarantee of employment security can help the firm avoid making a costly decision to lay people off that has short-term benefits and long-term costs.

If you want to see just how costly such layoff decisions can be, consider Silicon Valley. Executives from the semiconductor and electronics industries often write newspaper and magazine articles and testify before Congress in favor of permitting immigration of skilled workers. These executives favor immigration because they manage companies that are frequently short of necessary talent. The executives complain about their difficulty in recruiting qualified personnel in their expanding industry.

What you won't see in their articles or testimony, but what you will find if you look at newspapers from a few years ago, is that many of these very same firms laid off engineers, technicians, and other skilled workers in some instances just two or three years—or even less—before subsequently complaining about labor scarcity. Think about it. My friends in the valley have perfected the art of buying high and selling low. When times are tough in the industry, common sense suggests that that is exactly the time to recruit and build your work force. Competition for talented staff will obviously be less, and salaries need not be bid up in attempts to lure people from their existing jobs. By hiring when times are poor and developing a set of policies, including assurance that people will be retained, a firm can become an employer of choice, and the organization will not have to enter the labor market at its very peak to acquire the necessary work force. Instead, many firms do exactly the opposite. They lay people off in cyclical downturns and then, when the entire industry is booming and staff is scarce, they engage in often fruitless bidding contests to rehire the skills that they not that long ago sent packing.

Employment security can confer yet another benefit, in that it encourages people to take a longer-term perspective on their jobs and organizational performance. In a study of the financial performance of 192 banks, John Delery and Harold Doty observed a significant relationship between employment security and the bank's return on assets, an important measure of financial performance: "The greater the employment security given to loan officers, the greater the returns to banks."[4] Why might this be? In a bank that hires and lays off loan officers quickly to match economic fluctuations, the typical loan officer will worry only about booking loans—just what they have typically been rewarded for doing. With employment security and a longer-term perspective on the job, the bank officer may be more inclined to worry as well about the repayment prospects of the loan and about building customer relationships by providing high levels of service. Although a specific loan officer's career may prosper by being a big loan producer and moving quickly from one bank to another, the bank's profitability and performance are undoubtedly enhanced by having people who take both a longer term and a more comprehensive view of their jobs and of the bank's financial performance. This is likely to occur, however, only with the prospect of long-term continuity in the employment relationship.

The idea of employment security does not mean that the organization retains people who don't perform or work effectively with others—that is, performance does matter. Lincoln Electric has very high turnover for employees in their first few months on the job, as those who don't fit the Lincoln culture and work environment leave. Southwest will fire people who don't provide the level of customer service the firm is well-known for delivering and don't want to improve. Employment security means that employees are not quickly put on the street for things, such as economic downturns or the strategic mistakes of senior management, over which they have no control. The policy focuses on maintaining total employment, not on protecting individuals from the consequences of their individual behavior on the job.

The idea of providing employment security in today's competitive world seems somehow anachronistic or impossible and very much at variance with what most firms seem to be doing. But employment security is fundamental to the implementation of most other high-performance management practices, such as selective hiring, extensive training, information sharing, and delegation. Companies are unlikely to invest the resources in the careful screening and training of new people if those people are not expected to be with the firm long enough for it to recoup these investments. Similarly, delegation of operating authority and the sharing of sensitive performance and strategic information requires trust, and that trust is much more likely to emerge in a system of mutual, long-term commitments.

Selective Hiring

Organizations serious about obtaining profits through people will expend the effort needed to ensure that they recruit the right people in the first place. This requires several things. First, the organization needs to have a large applicant pool from which to select. In 1993, for example, Southwest Airlines received about 98,000 job applications, interviewed 16,000 people, and hired 2,700. In 1994, applications increased to more than 125,000 for 4,000 hires. Some organizations see processing this many job inquiries as an unnecessary expense. Southwest sees it as the first step toward ensuring that it has a large applicant pool from which to select its people. Similarly, Singapore Airlines—frequently listed as one of Asia's most admired companies, one of the most profitable airlines in the world, and consistently ranked quite high in ratings of service quality—is extremely careful and selective in its recruiting practices. Flight attendants are an important point of contact with the customer and one way in which Singapore Airlines differentiates its service. Consequently, senior management becomes personally involved in flight attendant selection. Prospective generalist staff, from which the ranks of managers will come, must pass a series of tests and clear two rounds of interviews, including interviews with a panel of senior management. "From an initial pool of candidates, about 10 percent are short-listed and only 2 percent [one out of 50] are selected."[5]

Nor is such selectivity confined to service organizations. When Subaru-Isuzu opened its automobile assembly plant in the United States in the late 1980s, it received some 30,000 applications for employment. The Japanese automakers have consistently emphasized selecting good people as critical to their success, and they have been willing to expend the resources required on the selection process. It has always fascinated me that some people see selectivity on the part of elite universities or graduate schools as a mark of the school's prestige but see the same selection ratios on the part of companies as a waste of resources. It isn't.

Second, the organization needs to be clear about what are the most critical skills and attributes needed in its applicant pool. The notion of trying to find "good employees" is not very helpful—organizations need to be as specific as possible about the precise attributes they are seeking. At Southwest Airlines, applicants for flight attendant positions are evaluated on the basis of initiative, judgment, adaptability, and their ability to learn. These attributes are assessed in part from interviews employing questions evoking specific instances of these attributes. For instance, to assess adaptability, interviewers ask, "Give an example of working with a difficult co-worker. How did you handle it?"[6] To measure initiative, one question asks, "Describe a time when a co-worker failed to pull their weight and what you did about it."

Third, the skills and abilities hired need to be carefully considered and consistent with the particular job requirements and the organization's approach to its market. Simply hiring the "best and the brightest" may not make sense in all circumstances. Enterprise Rent-A-Car is today the largest car rental company in the United States, with revenues in 1996 of $3 billion, and it has expanded at a rate of between 25 and 30 percent a year for the past eleven years. It has grown by pursuing a high customer service strategy and emphasizing sales of rental car services to repair garage customers. In a low wage, often unionized, and seemingly low employee skill industry, virtually all of Enterprise's people are college graduates. But these people are hired primarily for their sales skills and personality and for their willingness to provide good service, not for their academic performance. Dennis Ross, the chief operating officer, commented "We hire from the half of the college class that makes the upper half possible . . . We want athletes, fraternity types . . . people people." Brian O'Reilly interpolates Enterprise's reasoning:

> The social directors make good sales people, able to chat up service managers and calm down someone who has just been in a car wreck . . . The Enterprise employees hired from the caboose end of the class have something else going for them . . . a chilling realization of how unforgiving the job market can be.[7]

Fourth, organizations should screen primarily on important attributes that are difficult to change through training and should emphasize qualities that actually differentiate among those in the applicant pool. An important insight on the selection process comes from those organizations that tend to hire more on the basis of basic ability and attitude than on applicants' specific technical skills, which are much more easily acquired. This has been the practice of Japanese organizations for some time. "Japanese recruitment seeks to find the individual with the 'proper character whom it can train.' . . . Instead of searching for applicants with necessary skills for the job, the focus is on social background, temperament, and character references."[8]

Sophisticated managers know that it is much more cost-effective to select on those important attributes that are difficult or impossible to change and to train people in those behaviors or skills that are more readily learned. At Southwest Airlines, a top pilot working for another airline who actually did stunt work for movie studios was rejected because he was rude to a receptionist. Southwest believes that technical skills are easier to acquire than a teamwork and service attitude. Ironically, many firms select for specific, job-relevant skills that, while important, are easily

acquired. Meanwhile, they fail to find people with the right attitudes, values, and cultural fit—attributes that are harder to train or change and that are quite predictive of turnover and performance. To avoid having to retrain or resocialize people that have acquired bad habits at their previous employers, companies like Southwest prefer to hire individuals without previous industry experience. Many also prefer to hire at the entry level, obtaining individuals who are eager to prove themselves and who don't know what can't be done.

It is tempting to hire on the basis of ability or intelligence rather than fit with the organizations—so tempting that one occasionally observes firms trying to differentiate among a set of individuals who are basically similar in intelligence or ability while failing to distinguish those that will be well suited to the organization from those that will not. One of my favorite examples of this is recruitment at Stanford Business School. Stanford has a class of about 370 MBAs, selected from an initial applicant pool that in recent years has exceeded six thousand. These are obviously talented, motivated, and very intelligent individuals. Distinguishing among them on those criteria would be difficult, if not impossible. But many firms seek to do the impossible—they try to get around the school's policy of not releasing grades in an effort to figure out who are the smartest students and to assess differences in ability among a set of applicants through interviewing techniques such as giving them problems or cases to solve. Meanwhile, although many job recruits will leave their first job within the first two years, and such turnover and the requirements to refill those positions are exceedingly expensive, few firms focus primarily on determining fit—something that does vary dramatically.

Two firms that take a more sensible and pragmatic approach to hiring are Hewlett-Packard and PeopleSoft, a producer of human resource management software. For instance, one MBA job applicant reported that in interviews with People-Soft, the company asked very little about personal or academic background, except about learning experiences from school and work. Rather, the interviews focused mostly on whether the person saw herself as team oriented or as an individual achiever; what she liked to do outside school and work; and her philosophy on life. The specific question was "Do you have a personal mission statement? If you don't, what would it be if you were to write it today?" Moreover, the people interviewing the applicant presented a consistent picture of PeopleSoft as a company and of the values that were shared among employees. Such a selection process is more likely to produce cultural fit. A great deal of research evidence shows that the degree of cultural fit and value congruence between job applicants and their organizations significantly predicts both subsequent turnover and job performance.[9]

Firms serious about selection put applicants through several rounds of interviews and a rigorous selection procedure. At Subaru-Isuzu's U.S. manufacturing plant, getting hired involved going through multiple screening procedures including written tests and assessment center exercises and could take as long as six months or more. The fastest hire took nine weeks.[10] Such a lengthy selection process has several outcomes. First, it ensures that those who survive it have been carefully scrutinized. Second, it ensures that those eventually hired into the firm develop commitment. Applicants selected become committed as a consequence of having gone through such a lengthy and rigorous process—if they didn't really want the job, why would they go through it? At Subaru-Isuzu, the selection process "demanded perseverance," ensured that those who were hired had "the greatest desire and determination," and, since it required some degree of sacrifice on the part of the people, encouraged self-elimination and built commitment among those who survived.[11] Third, this type of process promotes the feeling on the part of those who are finally selected that they are part of an elite and special group, a feeling that causes them to enter the organization with a high level of motivation and spirit. Laurie Graham's participant observa-

tion study of Subaru-Isuzu concluded that "the fact that so much money, time, and effort went into the selection of employees reinforced the belief that the company was willing to go to great lengths to select the best."[12]

Rigorous selection requires a method, refined and developed over time through feedback and learning, to ensure that the firm can identify the skills it is seeking from the applicant pool. At Southwest Airlines, the company tracks who has interviewed job applicants. When someone does especially well or poorly, the organization can actually try to assess what the interviewers saw or missed, and why. It is puzzling that organizations will ensure the quality of their manufacturing or service delivery process by closing the loop on that process through feedback, while almost no organizations attempt to do the same thing with their recruiting process. Sources of applicants, scores on tests or interview ratings, and other selection mechanisms must be validated against the subsequent performance of the people selected if there is to be any hope of improving the effectiveness of the process over time.

The following list summarizes the main points about how to go about selective hiring to build a high-performance organization.

- Have a large number of applicants per opening.
- Screen for cultural fit and attitude—not for skills that can be readily trained.
- Be clear about what are the most critical skills, behaviors, or attitudes crucial for success; isolate just a small number of such qualities and be as specific as possible. Simply seeking "the best and brightest" frequently doesn't make sense.
- Use several rounds of screening to build commitment and to signal that hiring is taken very seriously.
- To the extent possible, involve senior people as a signal of the importance of the hiring activity.
- Close the loop by assessing the results and performance of the recruiting process.

Self-Managed Teams and Decentralization as Basic Elements of Organizational Design

Organizing people into self-managed teams is a critical component of virtually all high-performance management systems. Numerous articles and case examples as well as rigorous, systematic studies attest to the effectiveness of teams as a principle of organization design. One researcher concluded that "two decades of research in organizational behavior provides considerable evidence that workers in self-managed teams enjoy greater autonomy and discretion, and this effect translates into intrinsic rewards and job satisfaction; teams also out-perform traditionally supervised groups in the majority of . . . empirical studies."[13]

In a manufacturing plant that implemented high-performance work teams, for example, a 38 percent reduction in the defect rate and a 20 percent increase in productivity followed the introduction of teams.[14] Honeywell's defense avionics plant credits improved on-time delivery—reaching 99 percent in the first quarter of 1996 as compared to below 40 percent in the late 1980s—to the implementation of teams.[15] A study of the implementation of teams in one regional Bell telephone operating company found that "self-directed groups in customer services reported higher customer service quality and had 15.4% higher monthly sales revenues."[16] In the case of network technicians, the implementation of self-directed work teams saved "an average of $52,000 in indirect labor costs for each self-directed team initiated."[17] Moreover, membership in self-directed work teams positively affected employee job satisfaction, with other factors that might also affect satisfaction statistically controlled. "More than 75% of surveyed workers who are currently in traditional work groups say they would volunteer for teams if given the opportunity. By contrast, less than 10% who are now in teams say they would like to return to traditional supervision."[18]

Teams offer several advantages. First, teams substitute peer-based for hierarchical control of work. "Instead of management devoting time and energy to controlling the workforce directly, workers control themselves."[19] Peer control is frequently more effective than hierarchical supervision. Someone may disappoint his or her supervisor, but the individual is much less likely to let down his or her work mates. At New United Motor Manufacturing (NUMMI), the work process is organized on a team basis with virtually no buffers of either in-process inventories or employees. As a consequence, "all the difficulties of one person's absence fall on those in daily contact with the absentee—the co-workers and immediate supervisor—producing enormous peer pressure against absenteeism."[20] Team-based organizations also are largely successful in having all of the people in the firm feel accountable and responsible for the operation and success of the enterprise, not just a few people in senior management positions. This increased sense of responsibility stimulates more initiative and effort on the part of everyone involved.

The tremendously successful natural foods grocery store chain, Whole Foods Markets, organized on the basis of teams, attributes much of its success to that arrangement. Between 1991 and 1996, the company enjoyed sales growth of 864 percent and net income growth of 438 percent as it expanded, in part through acquisitions as well as internal growth, from ten to sixty-eight stores. In its 1995 annual report, the company's team-oriented philosophy is clearly stated.

> Our growing Information Systems capability is fully aligned with our goal of creating a more intelligent organization—one which is less bureaucratic, elitist, hierarchical, and authoritarian and more communicative, participatory, and empowered. The ultimate goal is to have all Team Members contributing their full intelligence, creativity, and skills to continuously improving the company . . . Everyone who works at Whole Foods Market is a Team Member. This reflects our philosophy that we are all partners in the shared mission of giving our customers the very

best in products and services. We invest in and believe in the collective wisdom of our Team members. The stores are organized into self-managing work teams that are responsible and accountable for their own performance.[21]

Each store is a profit center and has about ten self-managed teams in it, with team leaders and clear performance targets. Moreover, "the team leaders in each store are a team, store leaders in each region are a team, and the company's six regional presidents are a team."[22] Although store leaders recommend new hires, teams must approve hires for full-time jobs, and it takes a two-thirds vote of the team members to do so, normally after a thirty-day trial period. Through an elaborate system of peer store reviews, Whole Foods encourages people to learn from each other. By sharing performance information widely, the company encourages peer competition. "At Whole Foods, pressure for performance comes from peers rather than from headquarters, and it comes in the form of internal competition."[23]

Second, teams permit employees to pool their ideas to come up with better and more creative solutions to problems. The idea, similar to brainstorming or group problem solving, involves pooling ideas and expertise to increase the likelihood that at least one member of the group will come up with a way of addressing the problem. In the group setting, each participant can build on the others' ideas, particularly if the members are trained in effective group process and problem solving. Teams at Saturn and at the Chrysler Corporation's Jefferson North plant "provide a framework in which workers more readily help one another and more freely share their production knowledge—the innumerable 'tricks of the trade' that are vital in any manufacturing process."[24]

Third, and perhaps most importantly, by substituting peer for hierarchical control, teams permit removal of layers of hierarchy and absorption of administrative tasks previously performed by specialists, avoiding the enormous costs of having people whose sole job it is to watch people watch people who watch other people do the work. Ad-

ministrative overhead is costly because management is typically well-paid. Eliminating layers of management by instituting self-managing teams saves money. Self-managed teams can also take on tasks previously done by specialized staff, thus eliminating excess personnel and, just as important, putting critical decisions in the hands of individuals who may be closer to the relevant information.

The AES Corporation is an immensely successful global developer and operator of electric power and steam plants, with sales of more than $835 million and six thousand employees in 1996. A 1982 investment in the company of $10,000 would be worth more than $10 million in 1996. The company "has never formed corporate departments or assigned officers to oversee project finance, operations, purchasing, human resources, or public relations. Instead, such functions are handled at the plant level, where plant managers assign them to volunteer teams."[25] Front-line people develop expertise in these various task domains, including finance, and receive responsibility and authority for carrying them out. They do so effectively. Of course, mistakes get made, but learning follows. The AES structure saves on the cost of management—the organization has only five levels—and it economizes on specialized staff. The company developed a $400 million plant in Cumberland, Maryland, with a team of just ten people who obtained more than thirty-six separate permit approvals and negotiated the complex financing, including tax-exempt bonds and ten lenders. Normally, projects of this size require "hundreds of workers, each with small specific tasks to perform within large corporations."[26] The savings and increased speed and flexibility of the AES team-based approach are clear and constitute an important source of the firm's competitive advantage.

At Vancom Zuid-Limburg, a joint venture in the Netherlands that operates a public bus company, the organization has enjoyed very rapid growth in ridership and has been able to win transport concessions by offering more services at the same price as its competitors. The key to this success lies in its use of self-managed teams and the consequent savings in management overhead.

> Vancom is able to [win transport contracts] mainly because of its very low over-head costs. . . . [O]ne manager supervises around forty bus drivers . . . This management-driver ratio of 1 in 40 substantially differs from the norm in this sector. At best, competitors achieve a ratio of 1 in 8. Most of this difference can be attributed to the self-managed teams. Vancom . . . has two teams of around twenty drivers. Each team has its own bus lines and budgeting responsibilities . . . Vancom also expects each individual driver to assume more responsibilities when on the road. This includes customer service (e.g., helping elderly persons board the bus); identifying problems (e.g., reporting damage to a bus stop), and active contributions (e.g., making suggestions for improvement of the services).[27]

How can moving to self-managed teams, possibly eliminating layers of administration and even specialized staff, be consistent with the earlier discussion of employment security? Eliminating positions need not entail the elimination of the people doing these jobs—those individuals can be redeployed to other tasks that add more value to the organization. In the case of Lincoln Electric, recall that, at least temporarily, factory workers became salespeople, something that Mazda Motors also did when it faced a production employee surplus because of low sales in the 1980s. At SAS Airlines, staff that formerly did market research and planning were moved to positions where they had a more direct effect on customer service and operations. At Solectron, a contract manufacturer of electronics, institution of self-managed teams meant that managers, who typically had engineering degrees, could spend more time rethinking the overall production system and worrying about the technology strategy of the company—activities that added a lot more value than directly supervising $7 per hour direct labor. Often many tasks, such as the development of new products and new markets and the evaluation and introduction of new production technologies, require the time and strategic talents of managers, and these activities

and decisions add much more value to the organization by using the knowledge and capabilities of the people. Consequently, a move to self-managed teams is consistent with maintaining employment when other, often more important, things are found for supervisors and specialized staff to do.

Even organizations for which working in formal teams is not sensible or feasible can benefit from one of the sources of team success: decentralization of decision making to front-line people, who have the knowledge and ability to take effective action. The Ritz-Carlton Hotel chain, winner of the Malcolm Baldrige National Quality Award in 1992, provides each of its people with discretion to spend up to $2,500, without any approval, in order to respond to guest complaints. Hampton Inn Hotel, a low-priced hotel chain, instituted a 100 percent Satisfaction Guarantee policy for its guests and permitted employees to do whatever was required to make the guests happy.

> A few years ago while working as a guest services representative at a Hampton Inn Hotel, I overheard a guest at our complimentary continental breakfast complaining quite loudly that his favorite cereal was not available. Rather than dismiss the person as just another disgruntled guest, I looked at the situation and saw an opportunity to make this guest happy. I gave him his money back—not for the continental breakfast, but for the cost of one night's stay at our hotel. And I did it on the spot, without checking with my supervisor or the general manager of the hotel.[28]

These policies may seem wasteful, but they're not. Ritz-Carlton managers will tell you that a satisfied customer will talk to ten people and an unhappy customer to one hundred. Spending money to keep clients satisfied is a small price to pay for good advertising and encouraging guests to return. Similarly, at the Hampton Inn, "company research suggests that the guarantee strongly influences customer satisfaction and loyalty to Hampton Inn, and that guests who have experienced the guarantee are more likely to stay with Hampton Inn again in the future."[29] It is important to realize that successful implementation of guest satisfaction programs or, for that matter, programs to use the ideas and knowledge of the work force require decentralizing decision making and permitting people at all levels to exercise substantial influence over organizational decisions and processes. All of this requires trust, a commodity in short supply in many organizations that have become accustomed to operating with an emphasis on hierarchical control.

High Compensation Contingent on Organizational Performance

Although labor markets are far from perfectly efficient, it is nonetheless the case that some relationship exists between what a firm pays and the quality of the work force it attracts. It is amusing to see firms announce simultaneously that first, they compete on the basis of their people and that their goal is to have the very best work force in their industry, and second, that they intend to pay at (or sometimes slightly below) the median wage for comparable people in the industry. The level of salaries sends a message to the firm's work force—they are truly valued or they are not. After all, talk is cheap and many organizations can and do claim that people are their most important asset even as they behave differently.

I sometimes hear the statement that high compensation is a consequence of organizational success, rather than its progenitor, and a related comment that high compensation (compared to the average) is possible only in certain industries that either face less competition or have particularly highly educated employees. But neither of these statements is correct. Obviously, successful firms can afford to pay more and frequently do so, but high pay can also produce economic success.

When John Whitney assumed the leadership of Pathmark, a large grocery store chain in the Eastern United States in 1972, the company had about ninety days to live according to its banks and was in desperate financial shape. Whitney looked at the situation and discovered that 120 store managers in the chain were paid terribly. Many of them made less than the butchers, who were unionized. He decided that the store managers

were vital to the chain's success and its ability to accomplish a turnaround. Consequently, one of the first things he did was to give the store managers a substantial raise—about 40 to 50 percent. The subsequent success of the chain was, according to Whitney, because the store managers could now focus on improving performance instead of worrying and complaining about their pay. Furthermore, in a difficult financial situation, the substantial raise ensured that talent would not be leaving for better jobs elsewhere, thereby making a turnaround more difficult. Whitney has consistently tried to pay a 15 percent wage premium in the many turnaround situations he has managed, and he argues that this wage premium and the resulting reduced turnover *facilitates* the organization's performance.

The idea that only certain jobs or industries can or should pay high wages is belied by the example of many firms including Home Depot, the largest home improvement and building supply company in the United States, with about 8 percent of the market and approximately 100,000 employees. The company has been successful and profitable, and its stock price has shown exceptional returns. Even though the chain emphasizes everyday low pricing as an important part of its business strategy and operates in a highly competitive environment, it pays its staff comparatively well for the retail industry, hires more experienced people with building industry experience, and expects its sales associates to provide a higher level of individual customer service.

> At Home Depot, clients can expect to get detailed instruction and advice concerning their building, renovation, and hardware needs. This requires a higher level of knowledge than is typical of a retail sales worker. Management considers the sales associates in each department as a team, with wide discretion over department operations. Associates also receive above average pay for this retail segment.[30]

Contingent compensation also figures importantly in most high-performance work systems. Such compensation can take a number of different forms, including gain sharing, profit sharing, stock ownership, pay for skill, or various forms of individual or team incentives. Wal-Mart, AES Corporation, Southwest Airlines, Whole Foods Markets, Microsoft, and many other successful organizations encourage share ownership. When employees are owners, they act and think like owners. Moreover, conflict between capital and labor can be reduced by linking them through employee ownership. Since 1989, Pepsico has offered a broad-based stock option plan available to 100,000 people, virtually its entire full-time labor force. Publix, a supermarket chain with 478 stores in the Southeastern United States, earned 2.75 percent on net sales in 1995 in an industry where the average is 1 percent. The company has enjoyed rapid expansion. It is important to note that the sixty-four-year-old company "has always been owned entirely by its employees and management, and the family of its late founder. . . . Employees become eligible for stock after working one year and one thousand hours . . . [E]mployees . . . wear name badges proclaiming that each is a stockholder."[31] Home Depot, the number one rated *Fortune 500* service company for profit growth, makes sure its managers own stock in the company. At Starbucks, the rapidly growing coffee outlet chain, 100 percent of the employees, even those working part-time, receive stock options in the company.[32] But such wide-spread encouragement of stock ownership remains quite rare. Hewitt Associates, a compensation consulting firm, estimated that in 1993 "only 30 large companies now have stock option plans available to a broad range of employees. Instead, most companies simply give stock options to employees once they reach a certain level in the corporation. Many workers then exercise the options and sell the stock in a single transaction. . . . They do not acquire a stake in the company."[33]

As various schemes for encouraging employee stock ownership have become increasingly trendy, in part because they frequently have tax advantages and, more importantly, are relatively straightforward to implement, it is critical to keep two things in mind. First, little evidence suggests that employee ownership, by itself, affects organizational performance. Rather, employee ownership works best as part of a broader philosophy or culture that incorporates other practices as well.

> An employee ownership culture is . . . a high-performance workplace in which each employee becomes an owner who is afforded certain rights in exchange for assuming new responsibilities. Such a culture is achieved by following the "working for yourself" thrust of employee ownership in conjunction with a battery of practices intended to create a non-bureaucratic, less hierarchical organization focused on performance.[34]

Merely putting in ownership schemes without providing training, information sharing, and delegation of responsibility will have little effect on performance because even if people are more motivated by their share ownership, they don't necessarily have the skills, information, or power to do anything with that motivation.

Second, many organizations treat stock options and share ownership as psychologically equivalent, but they are not. An option is just that—the potential or option to acquire shares at some subsequent point in time, at a given price. If the stock price falls below the option price, the option has no value. As Bill Gurley, one of the Wall Street's premier technology analysts, has argued. "The main problem with stock options is that they do not represent true ownership." Gurley goes on to describe the two potential negative effects that follow from the option holder's being given the upside but protected from the downside:

> There is a huge incentive for option holders to take undue risk [and] there is an incentive for [people] to roam around. Try your luck at one job, and if it doesn't pan out, move on to the next one. . . . [A]n aggressive stock-option program has many of the same characteristics as leverage. When times are good, they are doubly good . . . when times turn bad, the effects of stock-option compensation can be quite devastating.[35]

If, by contrast, someone purchases stock, even at a slightly discounted price, that person has made a behavioral commitment with much more powerful psychological consequences. The person remains an owner, with psychological investment in the company, even when the stock price falls. Consequently, share ownership builds much more powerful commitments and psychologically binds people to their organizations more than do options, even when the economic consequences of the two schemes are largely similar.

One worry I sometimes hear voiced about share ownership concerns inevitable declines in stock price. When I asked AES people working at the power plant in Thames, Connecticut, specifically about this issue, I was told that people do watch the stock price, but when it goes down, most employees want to buy more. One person stated, "We feel we're part of the entrepreneurs. The fluctuations in stock price reinforces the fact that we're responsible. If there were only upside, we're taking a free ride. The fact that the stock price fluctuates and that people gain and lose accordingly makes people feel like they are more of an owner of the company."

A number of organizations use profit sharing to great effect, particularly when it extends throughout the organization. At Southwest Airlines, profit sharing causes its people to focus on costs and profits because they receive a percentage of those profits. At Hewlett-Packard, quarterly profit-sharing payments are greeted with anticipation and excitement. The enthusiasm of vice presidents and secretaries alike, the excited talk pervading the organization, makes it clear that when profit sharing covers all employees the social pressure to continue producing good results becomes both powerful and widespread.

Profit sharing also makes compensation more variable, permitting adjustments in the labor bill without layoffs. At Lincoln Electric, profit sharing averages around 70 percent of individual employee salaries. When business falls, profit-sharing payments fall and labor expenses decrease—without having to break the firm's commitment to employment security. This variable component of wage costs, achieved through profit sharing, has permitted Lincoln to ride out a substantial sales decrease without laying off anyone covered by its guaranteed employment policy.

Paying for skill acquisition encourages people to learn different jobs and thereby to become more flexible. Gainsharing differs from profit sharing in that it is based on incremental improvements in the performance of a specific unit. Levi Strauss, for instance, has used gainsharing in its U.S. manufacturing plants. If a plant becomes more efficient in its use of labor and materials, the people share in the economic gains thereby achieved. They share in these gains even if profits in the firm as a whole are down. Why should employees in a plant in which they have achieved efficiency gains be penalized for problems in the general economy that have adversely affected sales or, for that matter, by the performance of other parts of the organization over which they have no control?

For a number of reasons, contingent compensation is important. First, simply, it is a matter of equity and fairness. If an organization produces greater returns by unharnessing the power of its people, justice suggests that some proportion of those gains should accrue to those who have produced the results as opposed to going solely to the shareholders or management. If people expend more effort and ingenuity, observe better results as a consequence of that effort, but then receive nothing, they are likely to become cynical and disillusioned and to stop trying.

Second, contingent compensation helps to motivate effort, because people know they will share in the results of their work. At Whole Foods, a gainsharing program "ties bonuses directly to team performance—specifically, sales per hour, the most important productivity measurement."[36] Teams, stores, and regions compete on the basis of quality, service, and profitability, with the results translating into bonuses. At Solectron, the implementation of self-managed teams positively affected quality and productivity. But when bonuses based on team performance were instituted, productivity and quality improved yet again.

Managers sometimes ask how to prevent employment security from turning into something resembling the civil service, with people just marking time. The answer is by coupling employment security with some form of group-based incentive, such as profit or gainsharing or share ownership. The organization thus unleashes the power of the team, whose economic interests are aligned with high levels of economic performance. Explaining Whole Foods' exceptional performance record, their CEO, John Mackey, stated the following:

> Whole Foods is a social system. . . . It's not a hierarchy. We don't have lots of rules handed down from headquarters in Austin. We have lots of self-examination going on. Peer pressure substitutes for bureaucracy. Peer pressure enlists loyalty in ways that bureaucracy doesn't.[37]

Peer pressure is stimulated by profit sharing and stock ownership that encourages team members to identify with the organization and to work hard on its behalf.

Training

Virtually all descriptions of high-performance management practices emphasize training, and the amount of training provided by commitment as opposed to control-oriented management systems is substantial. Training in steel minimills, for example, was almost 75 percent higher in mills relying on commitment as opposed to those relying on control. The previously cited study of automobile assembly plants showed that training was substantially higher in flexible or lean compared to mass production systems. Training is an essential component of high-performance work systems because these systems rely on front-line employee skill and initiative to identify and resolve problems, to initiate changes in work methods, and to take responsibility for quality. All of this requires a skilled and motivated work force that has the knowledge and capability to perform the requisite tasks.

> [H]aving a work force that is multiskilled, adaptable to rapidly changing circumstances, and with broad conceptual knowledge about the

production system is critical to the operation of a flexible production system. The learning process that generates these human capabilities is an integral part of how the production system functions, not a separate training activity.[38]

Training is often seen as a frill in many U.S. organizations, something to be reduced to make profit goals in times of economic stringency. Data from the worldwide automobile assembly plant study, in this instance, from fifty-seven plants, are particularly instructive in illustrating the extent to which U.S. firms, at least in this industry, underinvest in training compared to competitors based in other countries. Table 1 presents information on the amount of training provided in automobile assembly plants operating in various countries and with different ownership.

The data in the table are startling. In terms of the amount of training provided to newly hired production workers, U.S. firms operating either in the U.S. or in Europe provide by far the least. Japanese plants in North America provide about 700 percent more training, and plants in newly industrialized countries such as Korea, Taiwan, and Brazil provided more than 750 percent more training than do U.S. plants. Only the amount of

TABLE 1

Amount of Training for Production Workers in Automobile Assembly Plants

Source: John Paul MacDuffie and Thomas A. Kochan, "Do U.S. Firms Invest Less in Human Resources? Training in the World Auto Industry." *Industrial Relations* 34 (1995): 156.

Ownership/ Location	Hours of Training in the First Six Months for New Workers	Hours per Year for Those with > 1 Year Experience
Japanese/Japan	364	76
Japanese/North America	225	52
U.S./North America	42	31
U.S./Europe	43	34
European/Europe	178	52
Newly industrialized countries	260	46
Australia	40	15

training provided in Australia compares with U.S. levels. Similar, although not as dramatic, differences exist in the training provided for experienced production workers. Once again, the United States and Australia lag, with Japanese firms operating in Japan providing more than twice as much training to experienced workers. It is, of course, possible that U.S. firms' training is so much better and so much more efficient that it accomplishes just as much with a small fraction of the effort. This explanation cannot be definitively ruled out because the study did not measure (which would be almost impossible in any event) the consequences or the effectiveness of training. Although this explanation for the differences is possible, it is not very plausible. Rather, the differences in training reflect the different views of people held by the different firms and their corresponding production systems. "The Japanese-owned plants appear to train a lot because they rely heavily on flexible production, while the U.S.-owned plants in Europe and the Australian plants appear to train very little because they follow traditional mass production practices and philosophies."[39] U.S. automobile plants serious about pursuing profits through people show substantially larger training expenditures. Workers coming to Saturn initially "receive between 300 and 600 hours of training and then at least 5 percent of their annual work time (92 hours)" goes to training.[40]

The difference in training levels also reflects differences in time horizon—the Japanese firms and Saturn, with their policies of employment security, intend to keep their people longer, so it makes more sense for them to invest more in developing them. This illustrates a more general point—that the returns from any single high-performance management practice depend importantly on the entire set of practices that have been implemented. A firm that invests a lot in training but considers its people to be expendable costs to be quickly shed in times of economic difficulty will probably see little return from its training investment.

Studies of firms in the United States and the United Kingdom consistently provide evidence of inadequate levels of training and training focused on the wrong things: specialist skills rather than generalist competence and organizational culture. For instance, a case study of eight large organizations operating in the United Kingdom found one, W. H. Smith, a retailing and distribution organization, in which less than half of the people received *any* training at all in the past year. Furthermore, in only two of the organizations "did more than half the respondents indicate that they thought they received the training they needed to do their jobs well,"[41] and less than half of the organizations had a majority of employees who felt they were encouraged to develop new skills. What training is provided frequently focuses narrowly on specific job skills. "One Lloyds Bank senior manager said, 'People's perceptions of development would be that it is inadequate. But of course they are looking at being developed as generalists and I want them to be specialists more and more.'"[42] And all of this is occurring in a world in which we are constantly told that knowledge and intellectual capital are critical for success. Knowledge and skill *are* critical—and too few organizations act on this insight.

Training can be a source of competitive advantage in numerous industries for firms with the wisdom to use it. Consider, for instance, the Men's Wearhouse, an off-price specialty retailer of men's tailored business attire and accessories. Because four of the ten occupations expected to generate the most job growth through 2005 are in the retail trade sector, and in 1994, 17.9 percent of all American workers were employed in retail trade, this industry has some importance to the U.S. economy.[43] Yet the management of people in retailing is frequently abysmal. Turnover is typically high, as is the use of part-time employees, many of whom work part-time involuntarily. Employees are often treated poorly and subjected to arbitrary discipline and dismissals. Wages in retailing are comparatively low and are falling compared to other industries, and skill and career development and training are rare. The industry is characterized by both intense and increasing competition, with numerous bankruptcies of major retailing chains occurring in the last decade.

The Men's Wearhouse went public in 1991 and in its 1995 annual report noted that since that time it has achieved compounded annual growth rates in revenues and net earnings of 32 and 41 percent respectively. The value of its stock increased by approximately 400 percent over this period. In 1995, the company operated 278 stores with a total revenue of $406 million. The key to its success has been how it treats its people and particularly the emphasis it has placed on training, an approach that separates it from many of its competitors. The company built a 35,000 square-foot training center in Fremont, California, its headquarters. In 1994, some 600 "clothing consultants" went through Suits University, and that year the company added "Suits High and Selling Accessories U to complement our core program."[44] "New employees spend about four days in one of about thirty sessions held every year, at a cost to the company of about $1 million."[45] During the winter, experienced store personnel come back to headquarters in groups of about thirty for a three- or four-day retraining program.

The Men's Wearhouse has invested far more heavily in training than have most of its competitors, but it has prospered by doing so.

Our shrink is 0.6 percent, only about a third of the industry average. And we spend zero on monitors in our stores. We have no electronic tagging and we spend nothing on security . . . We feel that if you create a culture and an environment that is supportive of employees, you don't have to spend money on security devices. . . . My sense is that our rate of turnover is significantly lower than elsewhere.[46]

Not only does the typical U.S. firm not train as much, but because training budgets often fluctuate with company economic fortunes, a perverse, procyclical training schedule typically develops: Training funds are most plentiful when the firm is doing well. But, when the firm is doing well, its people are the busiest and have the most to do, and consequently, can least afford to be away for training. By contrast, when the firm is less busy, individuals have more time to develop their skills and undertake training activities. But that is exactly when training is least likely to be made available.

Training is an investment in the organization's staff, and in the current business milieu, it virtually begs for some sort of return-on-investments calculations. But such analyses are difficult, if not impossible, to carry out. Successful firms that emphasize training do so almost as a matter of faith and because of their belief in the connection between people and profits. Taco Inc., for instance, a privately owned manufacturer of pumps and valves, with annual sales of under $100 million, offers its 450 employees "astonishing educational opportunities—more than six dozen courses in all,"[47] in an on-site learning center. It cost the company $250,000 to build the center and annual direct expenses and lost production cost about $300,000. Asked to put a monetary value on the return from operating the center, however, the company's chief executive, John Hazen White, said "It comes back in the form of attitude. People feel they're playing in the game, not being kicked around in it. You step to the plate and improve your work skills; we'll provide the tools to do that."[48]

Even Motorola does a poor job of measuring its return on training. Although the company has been mentioned as reporting a $3 return for every $1 invested in training, an official from Motorola's training group said that she did not know where these numbers came from and that the company is notoriously poor at evaluating their $170 million investment in training. The firm mandates forty hours of training per employee per year, and believes that the effects of training are both difficult to measure and expensive to evaluate. Training is part and parcel of an overall management process and is evaluated in that light.

Reduction of Status Differences

The fundamental premise of high-performance management systems is that organizations perform at a higher level when they are able to tap the ideas, skill, and effort of all of their people.

One way in which they do this is by organizing people in work teams, a topic already briefly covered here. But neither individuals nor teams will feel comfortable or encouraged to contribute their minds as well as their physical energy to the organization if it has sent signals that they are not both valuable and valued. In order to help make all organizational members feel important and committed to enhancing organizational operations, therefore, most high-commitment management systems attempt to reduce the status distinctions that separate individuals and groups and cause some to feel less valued.

This is accomplished in two principal ways—symbolically, through the use of language and labels, physical space, and dress, and substantively, in the reduction of the organization's degree of wage inequality, particularly across levels. At Subaru-Isuzu, everyone from the company president on down was called an Associate. The company's literature stated, "SIA is not hiring workers. It is hiring Associates . . . who work as a team to accomplish a task."[49] It is easy to downplay the importance of titles and language in affecting how people relate to their organization—but it is a mistake to do so.

> The title "secretary" seems subservient, Wilson [a consultant at Miss Paige Personnel agency in Sherman Oaks, California] said, "whereas administrative assistant sounds more career-oriented, and they like that." . . . Paul Flores . . . said employees at the Prudential Insurance Co. of America treat him better because of his new title. . . . When he moved to the supply unit, he became a SIMS (supply inventory management system) technician. . . . [I]nstead of people saying, "I want it now," they say, "Get it to me when you can."[50]

At NUMMI, everyone wears the same colored smock; executive dining rooms and reserved parking don't exist. Lincoln Electric also eschews special dining rooms—management eats with the employees—as well as reserved parking and other fancy perquisites. Anyone who has worked in a manufacturing plant has probably heard the expression, "The suits are coming." Differences in dress distinguish groups from each other and, consequently, help to inhibit communication across internal organizational boundaries. At Kingston technology, a private firm manufacturing add-on memory modules for personal computers, with 1994 sales of $2.7 million per each of its three hundred people (a higher level of revenue per employee than Exxon, Intel, or Microsoft), the two cofounders sit in open cubicles and do not have private secretaries.[51] Solectron, too, has no special dining rooms and the chief executive, Ko Nishimura, does not have a private office or a reserved parking space. Parking has become quite tight as the company has expanded, and shuttle buses ferry employees in from more distant parking lots. Ko Nishimura rides these same shuttles and has said that he learns more riding in with the employees than from almost anything else he does. The reduction of status differences encourages open communication, necessary in an organization in which learning and adaptation are encouraged.

Status differences are reduced and a sense of common fate developed by limiting the difference in compensation between senior management and other employees. Whole Foods Markets, whose sales in 1996 were over $800 million and which has enjoyed substantial growth and stock price appreciation, has a policy limiting executive compensation. "The Company's publicly stated policy is to limit annual compensation paid to any executive officer to eight times the average full-time salary of all Team Members."[52] In 1995, the CEO, John Mackey, earned $130,000 in salary and a bonus of $20,000. Nor does Whole Foods circumvent this restriction on executive compensation through grants of stock options or by giving executives shares in the company. In 1995, Mr. Mackey received options at the market price on four thousand shares of stock.

Herb Kelleher, the CEO of Southwest Airlines who has been on the cover of *Fortune* magazine with the test, "Is he America's best CEO?" earns about $500,000 per year including base and bonus. Moreover, when in 1995 Southwest negotiated a five-year wage freeze with its pilots in exchange for stock options and occasional profitability bonuses, Kelleher agreed to freeze his base salary at $395,000 for four years.

> Southwest's compensation committee said the freeze, which leaves Mr. Kelleher's salary unchanged from his 1992 contract, "is pursuant to a voluntary commitment made by Mr. Kelleher to the Southwest Airlines Pilots' Association." . . . The . . . compensation committee said the number of options granted Mr. Kelleher, at his recommendation, was "significantly below" the number recommended by an independent consultant as necessary to make Mr. Kelleher's contract competitive with pay packages for rival airline chief executives.[53]

Sam Walton, the founder and chairman of Wal-Mart, was typically on Graef Crystal's list of one of the most underpaid CEOs. These individuals are, of course, not poor. Each of them owns stock in the companies they manage. But stock ownership is encouraged for employees in these companies. Having an executive's fortune rise and fall together with those of the other employees differs dramatically from providing them large bonuses and substantial salaries even as the stock price languishes and people are being laid off.

Clearly, practices that reduce status differences are consistent with rewards contingent on performance—as long as these contingent rewards are applied on a group or organizational level so that the benefits of the performance of the many are not awarded to the few. Reducing status differences by reducing wage inequality does limit the organization's ability to use individual incentives to the extent that the application of individual rewards increases the dispersion of wages. But this is not necessarily a bad thing. Many managers and human resource executives mistakenly believe that placing *individual* pay at risk increases overall motivation and performance, when it is actually the contingency of the reward itself, not the level at which it is applied (individual, group, or organizational) that has the impact. Contingent rewards provided at the group or organizational level are at least as effective, if not more so, than individual incentives and, moreover, they avoid many of the problems inherent in individual merit or incentive pay.

Sharing Information

Information sharing is an essential component of high-performance work systems for two reasons. First, the sharing of information on things such as financial performance, strategy, and operational measures conveys to the organization's people that they are trusted. John Mackey, the chief executive of Whole Foods Markets, has stated, "If you're trying to create a high-trust organization . . . an organization where people are all-for-one and one-for all, your can't have secrets."[54] Whole Foods shares detailed financial and performance information with every employee—things such as sales by team, sales results for the same day last year, sales by store, operating profits by store, and even information from its annual employee morale survey—so much information, in fact, that "the SEC has designated all 6,500 employees 'insiders' for stock-trading purposes."[55] AES Corporation also shares detailed operational and financial information with its employees to the extent that they are all insiders for purposes of securities regulation. But Whole Foods goes even further, sharing individual salary information with every employee who is interested.

> The first prerequisite of effective teamwork is trust. . . . How better to promote trust (both among team members and between members and leaders) than to eliminate a major source of distrust—misinformed conjecture about who makes what? So every Whole Foods store has a book that lists the previous year's salary and bonus for all 6,500 employees—by name.[56]

This idea may at first seem strange. But think about your organization. If it is anything like mine, where salaries are secret, when it's time for raises people spend time and effort attempting to figure out what others got and how their raise (and salary) stacks up. This subtle attempt to find out where you stand takes time away from useful activities. Moreover, individuals frequently assume the worst—that they are doing worse than they actually are—and in any event, they don't have enough information to trust the salary system or, for that matter, the management that administers it. John Mackey of Whole Foods instituted the open salary disclosure process to signal that, at least this company had nothing to hide, nothing that couldn't be seen—and questioned—by any team member.

Contrast that organization with *Fortune* magazine, where a now-retired senior editor told me that after the Time-Warner merger when the company was saddled with debt, senior personnel were called together and told to "cut expenses by 10 percent." When the editor asked to see the expense budget and how it was allocated, he was told he could not. He resigned soon after. What message does an organization send if it says "Cut expenses, but, by the way, I don't trust you (even at senior levels) enough to share expense information with you?"

A second reason for sharing information is this: Even motivated and trained people cannot contribute to enhancing organizational performance if they don't have information on important dimensions of performance and, in addition, training on how to use and interpret that information. The now famous case of Springfield ReManufacturing beautifully illustrates this point. On February 1, 1983, Springfield ReManufacturing Corporation (SRC) was created when the plant's management and employees purchased an old International Harvester plant in a financial transaction that consisted of about $100,000 equity and $8.9 million debt, an 89–1 debt to equity ratio that has to make this one of the most leveraged of all leveraged buy-outs. Jack Stack, the former plant manager and now chief executive, knew that if the plant was to succeed, everyone had to do their best and to share all of her or his wisdom and ideas for enhancing the plant's performance. Stack came up with a system called "open-book management" that has since become a quite popular object of study—so popular that SRC now makes money by running seminars on it. Although the method may be popular as a sem-

inar topic, fewer organizations are actually willing to implement it.

The system has a straightforward underlying philosophy, articulated by Stack:

> Don't use information to intimidate, control or manipulate people. Use it to teach people how to work together to achieve common goals and thereby gain control over their lives. . . . Cost control happens (or doesn't happen) on the level of the individual. You don't become the least-cost producer by issuing edicts from an office. . . . [T]he best way to control costs is to enlist everyone in the effort. That means providing people with the tools that allow them to make the right decisions.[57]

Implementing the system involved first making sure that all of the company's people generated daily numbers reflecting their work performance and production costs. Second, it involved sharing this information, aggregated once a week, with all of the company's people, everyone from secretaries to top management. Third, it involved extensive training in how to use and interpret the numbers—how to understand balance sheets and cash flow and income statements. "Understanding the financials came to be part of everyone's job."[58]

Springfield ReManufacturing has enjoyed tremendous financial success. In 1983, its first year of operation, sales were about $13 million. By 1992, sales had increased to $70 million, the number of employees had grown from 119 at the time of the buy-out to 700, and the original equity investment of $100,000 was worth more than $23 million by 1993.[59] No one who knows the company, and certainly not Jack Stack or the other managers, believes this economic performance could have been achieved without a set of practices that enlisted the cooperation and ingenuity of all of the firm's people. The system and philosophy of open-book management took a failing International Harvester plant and transformed it into a highly successful, growing business. Similarly impressive results have been reported in case studies of Manco, a Cleveland-based distributor of duct tape, weather stripping, and mailing materials; Phelps County Bank, located in Rolla, Missouri; Mid-States Technical Staffing Services, located in Iowa; Chesapeake Manufacturing Company, a packaging materials manufacturer; Allstate Insurance; Macromedia, a software company; and Pace Industries, a manufacturer of die cast metal parts.[60]

If sharing information makes simple, common sense, you might wonder why sharing information about operations and financial performance is not more widespread. One reason is that information is power, and sharing information diffuses that power. At an International Harvester plant, "the plant manager's whole theory of management was 'Numbers are power, and the numbers are mine.' " [61] If holding performance information is the critical source of the power of a firm's leaders, however, let me suggest that the organization badly needs to find some different leaders.

Another rationale for not sharing information more widely with the work force is managers' fears that the information will leak out to competitors, creating a disadvantage for the organization. When Bob Beck, now running human resources at Gateway 2000, a manufacturer of personal computers sold largely by mail order, was the Executive Vice President of Human Resources at the Bank of America in the early 1980s, he told his colleagues that the organization could never improve customer service or retention until it shared its basic business strategy, plans, and measures of performance with its entire work force. When his colleagues on the executive committee noted that this information would almost certainly leak out to the competition, Beck demonstrated to them what ought to be common knowledge—in most instances, the competition already knows.

When organizations keep secrets, they keep secrets from their own people. I find it almost ludicrous that many companies in the electronics industry in the Silicon Valley go to enormous lengths to try to keep secrets internally, when all you have to do to penetrate them is to go to one of the popular bars or restaurants in the area and listen in as people from different companies talk

quite openly with each other. When people don't know what is going on and don't understand the basic principles and theory of the business, they cannot be expected to positively affect performance. Sharing information and providing training in understanding and using it to make better business decisions works.

Conclusion

Firms often attempt to implement organizational innovations, such as those described here, piecemeal. This tendency is understandable—after all, it is difficult enough to change some aspect of the compensation system without also having to be concerned about training, recruitment and selection, and how work is organized. Implementing practices in isolation may not have much effect, however, and, under some circumstances, it could actually be counterproductive. For instance, increasing the firm's commitment to training activities won't accomplish much unless changes in work organization permit these more skilled people to actually implement their knowledge. If wages are comparatively low and incentives are lacking that recognize enhanced economic success, the better trained people may simply depart for the competition. Employment security, too, can be counterproductive unless the firm hires people who will fit the culture and unless incentives reward outstanding performance. Implementing work teams will probably not, by itself, accomplish as much as if the teams received training both in specific technical skills and team processes, and it will have less effect still if the teams aren't given financial and operating performance goals and information. "Whatever the bundles or configurations of practices implemented in a particular firm, the individual practices must be aligned with one another and be consistent with the [organizational] architecture if they are ultimately to have an effect on firm performance."[62] It is important to have some overall philosophy or strategic vision of achieving profits through people, because an overall framework increases the likelihood of taking a systematic, as contrasted with a piecemeal, approach to implementing high-commitment organizational arrangements.

Clearly, it requires time to implement and see results from many of these practices. For instance, it takes time to train and upgrade the skills of an existing work force and even more time to see the economic benefits of this training in reduced turnover and enhanced performance. It takes time not only to share operating and financial information with people, but also to be sure that they know how to understand and use it in decision making; even more time is needed before the suggestions and insights implemented can provide business results. It certainly requires time for employees to believe in employment security and for that belief to generate the trust that then produces higher levels of innovation and effort. Consequently, taking a long-term view of a company's development and growth becomes at least useful if not absolutely essential to implementation of high-performance organizational arrangements. One way of thinking about various institutional and organizational barriers and aids to implementing high-performance management practices is, therefore, to consider each in terms of its effects on the time horizon that characterizes organizational decisions.

Endnotes

1. See chapter 2 in Jeffrey Pfeffer, *Competitive Advantage through People: Unleashing the Power of the Work Force* (Boston, MA: Harvard Business School Press, 1994).

2. Richard M. Locke, "The Transformation of Industrial Relations? A Cross-National Review," in Kirsten S. Wever and Lowell Turner, eds., *The Comparative Political Economy of Industrial Relations* (Madison, WI: Industrial Relations Research Association, 1995), pp. 18–19.

3. Herb Kelleher, "A Culture of Commitment," *Leader to Leader,* 1 (Spring 1997): 23.

4. John E. Delery and D. Harold Doty, "Modes of Theorizing in Strategic Human Resource Management: Tests of Universalistic, Contingency, and Configurational Performance Predictions," *Academy of Management Journal,* 39 (1996): 820.

5. Ling Sing Chee, "Singapore Airlines: Strategic Human Resource Initiatives," in Derek Torrington, ed., *International Human Resource Management: Think Globally, Act Locally* (New York, NY: Prentice Hall, 1994), p. 152.

6. "Southwest Airlines," Case S-OB-28, Graduate School of Business, Stanford University, Palo Alto, CA, 1994, p. 29.

7. Brian O'Reilly, "The Rent-a-Car Jocks Who Made Enterprise #1," *Fortune,* October 28, 1996, p. 128.

8. Laurie Graham, *On the Line at Subaru-Isuzu* (Ithaca, NY: ILR Press, 1995), p. 18.

9. See, for instance, C.A. O'Reilly, J.A. Chatman, and D.E. Caldwell, "People and Organizational Culture: A Profile Comparison Approach to Assessing Person-Organization Fit," *Academy of Management Journal,* 34 (1991): 487–516; J.A. Chatman, "Managing People and Organizations: Selection and Socialization in Public Accounting Firms," *Administrative Science Quarterly,* 36 (1991): 459–484.

10. Ibid.

11. Ibid.

12. Ibid.

13. Rosemary Batt, "Outcomes of Self-directed Work Groups in Telecommunications Services," in Paula B. Voos, ed., *Proceedings of the Forty-Eighth Annual Meeting of the Industrial Relations Research Association* (Madison, WI: Industrial Relations Research Association, 1996), p. 340.

14. Rajiv D. Banker, Joy M. Field, Roger G. Schroeder, and Kingshuk K. Sinha, "Impact of Work Teams on Manufacturing Performance: A Longitudinal Field Study," *Academy of Management Journal,* 39 (1996): 867–890.

15. "Work Week," *The Wall Street Journal,* May 28, 1996, p. Al.

16. Batt, op. Cit., p. 344.

17. Ibid.

18. Ibid., p. 346.

19. Ibid., p. 97.

20. M. Parker and J. Slaughter, "Management by Stress," *Technology Review,* 91 (1988): 43.

21. Whole Foods Market, Inc., *1995 Annual Report,* Austin, TX, pp. 3, 17.

22. Charles Fishman, "Whole Foods Teams," *Fast Company* (April/May 1996), p. 104.

23. Ibid., p. 107.

24. Harley Shaiken, Steven Lopez, and Isaac Mankita, "Two Routes to Team Production: Saturn and Chrysler Compared." *Industrial Relations,* 36 (January 1997): 31.

25. Alex Markels, "Team Approach: A Power Producer Is Intent on Giving Power to Its people," *The Wall Street Journal,* July 3, 1995, p. A1.

26. Kirsten Downey Grimsley, "The Power of a Team," *Washington Business, The Washington Post,* February 12, 1996, p. F12.

27. Mark van Beusekon, *Participation Pays! Cases of Successful Companies with Employee Participation* (The Hague: Netherlands Participation Institute, 1996), p. 7.

28. Rhonda Thompson, "An Employee's View of Empowerment," *HR Focus* (July 1993), p. 14.

29. Ibid.

30. Thomas R. Bailey and Annette D. Bernhardt, "In Search of the High Road in a Low-Wage Industry," *Politics and Society* (1997, in press).

31. Glenn Collins, "In Grocery War, the South Rises," *The New York Times,* April 25, 1995, p. C5.

32. Verne C. Harnish, "Company of Owners," *Executive Excellence* (May 1995), p. 7.

33. Mary Rowland, "Rare Bird: Stock Options for Many," *The New York Times,* August 1, 1993, p. F14.

34. David Jacobson, "Employee Ownership and the High-Performance Workplace," working paper no. 13, National Center for the Workplace, Berkeley, CA, 1996.

35. Bill Gurley, "Revenge of the Nerds: The Stock Option Square Dance," World Wide Web, www.upside.com/texis/Columns/atc/article.html?UID=970314003, March 14, 1997.

36. Fishman, op. cit., p. 105.

37. Ibid., p. 104.

38. John Paul MacDuffie and Thomas A. Kochan, "Do U.S. Firms Invest Less in Human Resources? Training in the World Auto Industry," *Industrial Relations,* 34 (1995): 153.

39. Ibid., p. 163.

40. Shaiken, Lopez, and Mankita, op. cit., p. 25.

41. Catherine Truss, Lynda Gratton, Veronica Hope-Hailey, Patrick McGovern, and Philip Stiles, "Soft and Hard Models of Human Resource Management: A Reappraisal," *Journal of Management Studies,* 34 (1997): 60.

42. Ibid., pp. 60–61.

43. Bailey and Bernhardt, op. cit., p. 5.

44. Men's Wearhouse, *1994 Annual Report,* Fremont, CA. p. 3.

45. Michael Hartnett, "Men's Wearhouse Tailors Employee Support Programs," *Stores* (August 1996), p. 47.

46. Ibid., p. 48.

47. Thomas A. Stewart, "How a Little Company Won Big by Betting on Brainpower," *Fortune,* September 4, 1995, p. 121.

48. Ibid., p. 122.

49. Graham, op, cit., pp. 107–108.

50. Suzanne Schlosberg, "Big Titles for Little Positions," *San Francisco Chronicle,* April 29, 1991, p. C3.

51. "Doing the Right Thing," *The Economist,* May 20, 1995, p. 64.

52. Whole Foods Market, Inc., *Proxy Statement,* January 29, 1996, p. 15.

53. Scott McCartney, "Salary for Chief of Southwest Air Rises After 4 Years," *The Wall Street Journal,* April 29, 1996, p. C16.

54. Fishman, op. cit., p. 106.

55. Ibid., p. 104.

56. Ibid., p. 105.

57. "Jack Stack (A)," Case 9-993-009, Business Enterprise Trust, Stanford, CA, 1993, pp. 2–4

58. Ibid.

59. Ibid., p. 5.

60. Tim R.V. Davis, "Open-Book Management: Its Promise and Pitfalls," *Organizational Dynamics,* 25 (Winter 1997): 7–20.

61. "Jack Stack (A)," op. cit., p. 3.

62. Brian Becker and Barry Gerhart, "The Impact of Human Resource Management on Organizational Performance: Progress and Prospects," *Academy of Management Journal,* 39 (1996): 786.

Reading 44

The New Agenda for Organization Development

W. Warner Burke

Founded on a value base circa 1960 that emanated from the human relations movement, in general, and the sensitivity training (T group) movement, in particular, organization development (OD) has always operated within a framework of humanistic and ethical concerns for people. Although not all practitioners would agree on the specific values that guide the field, most would concur that OD has tended to emphasize such concerns as:

Human development—It is worthwhile for people in organizations to have opportunities for personal learning and for growth toward a full realization of their individual potentials.

Fairness—It is important that people in organizations are treated equitably without discrimination and with dignity.

Openness—It is imperative that communication in organizations be conducted with forthrightness, honesty, and integrity.

Choice—It is critical that people in organizations are free from coercion and the arbitrary use of authority.

Balance of autonomy and constraint—It is significant that people in organizations have autonomy and freedom to perform their work responsibilities as they see fit, yet execute these responsibilities within reasonable organizational constraints. The OD practitioner's responsibility is to see that these two forces—autonomy and constraint—are in balance.

Source: Reprinted from *Organizational Dynamics,* Summer 1997. Copyright © 1997 American Management Association International. Reprinted by permission of American Management Association International, New York, NY. All rights reserved. http://www.amanet.org.

While this list may fall short of expressing the value system that guides OD, it likely comes close. The problem we face today is not so much agreeing on the specifics, but rather living the values we do espouse.

A number of senior practitioners in OD, i.e., those with 20 or more years of experience, believe that the profession has lost its way—that its values are no longer sufficiently honored, much less practiced, and that the unrelenting emphasis on the bottom line has taken over. Moreover, such management techniques—fads, if you will—as reengineering and downsizing have taken the country by storm, hurt people, and violated the values associated with OD. In the meantime, OD practitioners have stood on the sidelines and watched—or themselves become victims. Regardless of how valid these observations may be, it does seem true that OD has lost some of its power, its presence, and perhaps its perspective.

The purpose of this paper, then, is to address some of these issues, first by examining what we know about the efficacy of reengineering and downsizing and, second, by articulating a current and future agenda for OD practitioners with respect to these techniques. Reengineering and downsizing were selected for examination as opposed to, say, total quality management (TQM), because the former represent a greater challenge to the practice of OD—they more directly impact the field's underlying values.

To be clear about the direction of this paper: It begins by examining reengineering and downsizing to determine the OD practitioner's agenda vis-à-vis these two interventions, but it does not leave it at that. The overriding purpose is to propose a deeper agenda for OD and to consider six additional intervention domains—community, the employer-employee social contract, employability, trust, culture clash, and corporate power.

Reengineering, Downsizing, and Organization Development

To begin, let's review what is known about the efficacy of reengineering and downsizing and, for each, ask if the technique should even continue to be used. Answering these questions allows us to focus on the implications for OD practitioners, i.e., the agenda.

Reengineering—Does It Work?

Even though reengineering as we know it today (similar practices were previously labeled "business process redesign") has been in evidence for about a decade, we do not as yet have enough research to draw sound conclusions about its validity. Part of the problem is that reengineering has taken on the trappings of a fad—a rapid surge in popularity in the early 1990s, fueled by Michael Hammer and J. Champy's book on the subject, which rode the best-seller list for months. Organizations rapidly initiated reengineering projects; then, faced with disappointing early results, abandoned the effort just as quickly. Likely, the results would have been better had companies stayed with the ship longer. Most of the evidence so far (much of it anecdotal) builds a case for a low success rate. Some recent evidence provides encouragement, but the jury is still out.

Reengineering—Should It Be Done?

There's nothing inherently wrong with the idea. To consider a set of workplace activities and processes at their most basic levels in an effort to improve the activities, eliminate them altogether, and/or add new procedures and processes can be highly beneficial. Like so many other organizational change ideas, the problems come with implementation.

Typically, these problems arise for several reasons. Rather than fine-tune work processes, reengineering has focused on a radical redesign of work—a reinvention of how tasks get done. By emphasizing the details of specific procedures, the designers lose sight of the bigger picture—how changes at the work unit level will affect the larger business or organizational unit. In addition, reengineering has frequently been associated with downsizing and therefore vehemently resisted by many organizational members, much to Michael Hammer's dismay.

The Agenda for the OD Practitioner

If reengineering is a passing fad, why bother to set an agenda? There are two answers to this.

First, much of what is involved in reengineering is not new. Its roots can be traced to Frederick Taylor, and before that, to the very foundation of industrial engineering. This discipline, after all, has been around for 90 years. Its fundamentals are basic to any and all work organizations and, moreover, are not likely to pass from the scene. Other labels for the practice may come into vogue, just as "reengineering" superseded "work redesign," but the knowledge of how to redesign work processes, even radically, will remain useful.

Second, reengineering means change, and there is much to be said for starting with a clean slate and redesigning work for the good of workers and the organization. It should even be alluring for OD practitioners. Moreover, OD practitioners are in a position to contribute. In their study of 20 organizations involved in reengineering (at least three of these achieving successful implementations), Gene Hall, Jim Rosenthal, and Judy Wade identified six crucial organizational elements, or depth levers as they call them, that must be the focus of change if reengineering is really going to work: roles and responsibilities, organizational structure, measurements and incentives, shared values, skills, and information technology.

With the possible exception of the last item, OD practitioners provide (or should provide) ballast for all these levers and thus play a key role in any reengineering effort. And by being organizationally focused (as opposed to working exclusively with certain individuals and selected work processes), the OD practitioner can be highly useful in keeping the larger business or organizational units, and their intricate relationships, in mind. To the extent that OD ignores or, even worse, challenges reengineering, it loses an important opportunity to make an impact and to be true to its values.

Downsizing—Does It Work?

The short answer is "no." The amazing fact about downsizing is that, in most cases, the action produces the opposite of what is intended. Consider, for example, cost reduction—a primary goal for most downsizing plans. Although this may occur in the short run, a longer term scenario usually shows either no cost reduction or, in a number of instances, actual cost increases.

Another typical goal, productivity improvement, proves equally elusive. The evidence shows either no improvement or even a deterioration in productivity!

To add to the evidence, research by R.E. Cole found nine additional organizational problems resulting from downsizing: loss of personal relationships between employees and customers, increases in rules and procedures (therefore addition to bureaucracy), and loss of a common organizational culture, to name three. And a study of over 200 organizations by Kim Cameron and his colleagues added a dozen other problems to Cole's list.

The toll taken on individuals is immense. For a flavor of the consequences on individual and family lives, see the recent *New York Times Special Report: The Downsizing of America* and David M. Noer's book, *Healing the Wounds*. The pictures painted are not pretty. In fact, our American experience with downsizing is similar to cancer; practically every family we know has been touched.

The history of downsizing, now 16 or so years in the making, has left its legacy. The American workplace will never be quite the same.

Downsizing—Should It Be Done?

We might well ask if there is ever any justification for downsizing. The short answer is maybe.

We know that most large organizations employ people with "non jobs" and continue to support useless if not downright wasteful activities. There is some evidence that when downsizing is done carefully it can have positive consequences. Poor outcomes result from poor implementation and a lack of supporting activities such as counseling, training, severance packages, and outplacement. The way downsizing is carried out seems to be more important than the decision itself. Also, downsizing is more likely to be associated with positive outcomes when it works as part of an overall strategic plan.

Regardless of the potential for positive results, many would argue that downsizing is harmful to the economy, devastating to both its victims and the corporate survivors, and plainly and simply immoral. But not everyone would so argue.

In a carefully crafted and balanced article in *The New Yorker*, John Cassidy points to evidence supporting a net gain over the past decade in American jobs rather than a loss. He refers to two important reports, one by Joseph Stiglitz, chairman of the Council of Economic Advisors, the other by Princeton economics professor Henry Farber. These two reports independently concur that downsizing has not had the dire consequences on our economy and the country as a whole that the popular press and other anecdotal writings would lead us to believe.

Cassidy points out that these reports "should permit a more dispassionate discussion of downsizing." He goes on to emphasize that downsizing is real, that there are victims, and that these victims should not be ignored. Furthermore, layoffs and downsizing have been with us a long time, as our economy ebbs and flows. Ask any blue collar worker.

The two reports by Stiglitz and Farber on which Cassidy relies suggest "that what is really new about the downsizing phenomenon is not its absolute scale as much as its impact on the upper echelons of society. An increasing number of its victims are middle-aged, educated, and affluent." Labor Department statistics show that while displacement has indeed occurred, there has been little change in overall job stability in the United States. Job loss, then, while serious (just ask a recent victim), does not appear to be any more serious today than 10 or 15 years ago.

And to quote Cassidy one last time: "The ability of the United States economy to create jobs at a rate matching its rapid population growth distinguishes it sharply from many other industrial economies, especially those in Europe. . . . While American commentators worry about downsizing, the talk in Paris and Berlin is about how best to mimic American job creation."

So perhaps what we are experiencing is not "the downsizing of America" (the title of *The New York Times* book) but the "job shifting of America." And maybe we are not losing our middle class, but rather our middle class is changing its work affiliations, from the bulk employed by large corporations—each person for an entire career—to a more dispersed and diverse group of Americans. This group may include more people than before working in small to mid-size companies (many starting their own enterprises), more working in nonprofit organizations, and some living off their severance packages or working in temporary situations until they discover what they want to do next with their lives.

The Downsizing Agenda for the OD Practitioner

It's tempting for the OD practitioner to want absolutely nothing to do with downsizing. After all, downsizing hurts people, and the act itself can border on (if not blatantly constitute) immorality.

Yet, if OD practitioners are employed by or contracted to work with an organization, are they not obligated to help? If they are capable of providing help, are they not obligated to do so? Isn't this provision to help a value of higher priority than avoiding involvement in a situation where people may be hurt, if not treated immorally?

These queries beg the question of what we mean by *help*. For the good of the organization and its individual members, consultative help may mean confrontation, questioning, and challenging.

Let's consider downsizing from a different point of view, namely, why so many executives stick to their decision to reduce headcount in the face of so much negative evidence regarding the outcomes. William McKinley, Carol M. Sanchez, and Allen G. Schick provide insights on this issue. Building on institutional theory from sociology and simplifying the language, they cite three social forces that support an executive's downsizing rationale: "constraining," "cloning," and "learning."

Constraining forces pressure executives to conform to what is the "right thing" to do at a particular time. Although previously associated with decline, a negative force, downsizing is now seen as "the right step." Large organizations mean bureaucracy, rigidity, and resistance to change. Today's fashion is to be lean, mean, and nimble, and thus more competitive. To capture the essence of this social force, the authors refer to a *Fortune* article in which the writer stated that "The chiefs of America's biggest companies seem caught in the grip of what might be called wee-ness envy—my company's workforce is smaller than yours."

Organizational cloning can take a number of forms; for example, mimicking other organizations with respect to such management techniques as TQM, reengineering, self-directed groups and, of course, downsizing. Cloning is particularly prominent within industries, each company wanting to mimic what the best in its field is doing. And when executives want to measure how well their cloning process is going, they call it benchmarking.

Learning occurs via educational institutions and conferences sponsored by professional associations, as well as by finding "lessons" in the actions of apparently successful peers at other companies. Academic courses in cost accounting, for example, teach (at least by implication) that downsizing is an efficient form of doing business. And when one CEO sees another turn companies around with a "slash and burn" strategy (e.g., Albert J. Dunlap, previously at Scott Paper and [at the time of this writing] at Sunbeam), there is a temptation to duplicate the practice.

McKinley et al. go on to identify four conditions that enhance the power of these social pressures for downsizing: (1) dependence, (2) ambiguous standards, (3) uncertain core technologies, and (4) frequent corporate interaction patterns. In other words, the more dependent a company is on other organizations for resources, especially when those other organizations are dominant partners, the greater the ambiguity regarding what should be proper performance. Also, the greater the uncertainty about what a company's core technologies are, and the more interactive a company is with its constituents and competitors, the more susceptible that company is to conformity, cloning, and learning. And the more likely to downsize, if that is what others are doing.

The point, then, is as follows: When an OD practitioner's client is contemplating downsizing, the intervention of choice is to test the wisdom of such a decision. Testing the degree to which the potential decision seems to be a response to the social forces that McKinley et al. define (and within the context of their four conditions that enhance the power of these forces) would be highly appropriate—because this testing, or intervention, would be grounded in relevant theory and would confront forces to which the client may be oblivious.

There are other reasons for challenging a potential act of downsizing. Consider, for example, the consequences in terms of organizational memory loss and erosion of valued skills and experience. Service companies are highly susceptible to such loss. An example:

One insurance group, having slimmed its claims department, found itself settling larger claims both too swiftly and too generously. Belatedly, the group discovered that it had sacked a handful of long-term employees who had created an informal—but highly effective—way to screen claims. The company was eventually forced to reinstate them.

Moreover, there are alternative models to follow. For example, Sara Lee, under the leadership of its CEO, John Bryan, seems to compete quite well in a tough business and to do so globally without laying off hundreds or thousands of people when times are tough. Sara Lee takes pride in being socially responsible, a good corporate citizen.

For corporate leaders, perhaps the model regarding downsizing is Bill Flynn, the former CEO, now chairman, of Mutual of America. Mr. Flynn stated at an annual employee meeting that if the company ever had to institute a corporate layoff policy, it would not be because someone in the mail room had made a mistake. Rather, it would be because he had made a mistake—and he would put his name first on the layoff list. Not surprisingly, Flynn's statement earned him the trust of the employees attending that meeting.

OD practitioners have a twofold role to play in the downsizing arena. First, to challenge a potential downsizing decision by asking "why" and to test for the impact of social forces. This includes searching for other ways to control and reduce costs and to become a key player in implementing those alternatives. Second, if other options have been thoroughly explored and downsizing is the only remaining choice, to push for dignity, humane treatment, and ultimate fairness in how the victims and survivors are dealt with.

The OD Practitioner's Deeper Agenda

Rather than become obsessed with reengineering and downsizing, it is more important that practitioners understand and become involved with issues that are deeper, longer lasting, and more critical to the bigger picture. Six issues in particular merit attention.

Community

Each summer, we conduct a two-week conference for public school superintendents at Teachers College, Columbia University. Participants come from all pockets and corners of the United States—large, medium, and small districts from urban, suburban, and rural areas. My colleague, Professor Tom Sobol, runs the program. In his summary report of the 1996 summer conference, the following paragraph was a jolt:

> It's not easy being a public school superintendent these days, so cataloging their mutual problems was easy: lack of money, too many conflicting public demands, public hostility, uncertain tenure. But surprisingly, once these matters were acknowledged, they were not what superintendents wanted to spend time on. The problem that gripped their attention was the decline of community in America—the role of the public school in creating and sustaining that community.

I suspect that the assessment is accurate. Downsizing may hurt victims much more today than a few decades ago when communities were stronger. Support now comes from professionals (e.g., outplacement counselors), not so much from friends and neighbors. More of the burden is placed on one's family, and some families have not survived the ordeal. Moreover, downsizing has hit the white collar worker harder and, compared with a layoff of hourly wage earners, is more permanent. And white collar workers have no labor union for support, to help serve in the community's role of providing sustenance.

This lack of community is not likely to change anytime soon. As a culture, we Americans are clearly an independent lot. This independence seems to have become more pronounced in recent years, in part because of two trends. One is an apparent increase in self-orientation, the "what's in it for me?" syndrome. Christopher Lasch has written about the syndrome in his 1978 book, *The Culture of Narcissism*. Similarly, a national survey by Donald L. Kanter and Philip H. Mirvis identified what they subsequently labeled "the cynical Americans"—a group that made up 43 percent of those surveyed. Consider, also, that 58 percent of the survey respondents agreed or strongly agreed with this statement, "People pretend to care more about one another than they really do."

A second trend, growing stronger as technology marches onward, is that for daily living, we literally do not need other people as much as in the past. We can live alone quite comfortably, thank you, especially in large urban areas. We can have almost anything—from a mattress to pizza—delivered. And with Blockbuster Video, who needs friends for entertainment? Besides, we have the Internet.

There are, no doubt, other trends that help explain the decline in community—crime, geographical dispersion of family members, and less personal time, to name a few. Suffice it to say, the superintendents are probably right.

Agenda for the OD Practitioner: Organizational effectiveness depends on interactions and interrelationships among employees at all levels. The OD practitioner plays a significant role by bringing people together. This means initiating and arguing for, if not calling and conducting meetings themselves—not just facilitating them. This means, especially, promoting activities such as cross-functional teams and helping self-directed groups to actually self-direct.

Is it not true that the lack of community in society carries over into the organization? Also, employees today are incredibly busy just keeping up with their individual tasks and responsibilities. They spend considerably more time with a computer terminal (with troublesome software and poor interactive systems) than with people. They are reluctant to get together; they have too much to do. By promoting community via small and large group meetings, the OD practitioner helps with organizational effectiveness and also improves individuals' quality of worklife.

The Employer-Employee Social Contract

We know that the relationship between employer and employee has changed. Company loyalty—especially in large corporations—is a thing of the past. True, in small and family-owned businesses, loyalty may still be strong. But with the pervasiveness of downsizing, and with the message that one can no longer expect a lifetime career with a single employer ringing clear, the weakening of the bond between the organization and its employees comes as no surprise.

In fact, a recent study by Chip Walker and Elissa Moses shows that a "self-navigation" subculture has emerged in America, representing about 26 percent of those sampled, half of them being under the age of 35. Members of this group hold strongly to the value "I must take care of myself." They tend to reject tradition and conformity and are more likely to start their own businesses.

The self-navigators, however, are not the majority. A far larger number of workers would prefer to stay with their companies, if possible, yet feel insecure about the prospects. The popular press continues to report that in spite of low unemployment and a strong economy, people continue to express an unease about the security of practically any workplace. Even the Federal government (e.g., NASA) and employee-owned companies have downsized.

In addition to doing away with loyalty, downsizing has affected another aspect of the employer-employee social contract. A new work relationship falling under the banner of "rent an employee" has recently emerged. The so-called contract worker has been around for a long time but many of the new contracts return former employees to their old jobs, some as consultants, others as employees of temp agencies or leasing companies. Approximately 20 percent of those who were victims of downsizing fall into this category, another version of the changing employer-employee relationship in which the two parties feel less obligation to one another. As *The New York Times* reported,

> Not having careers to advance, some praise the liberation from enervating office politics, and from the stress of competing for raises and promotions. They talk of a greater flexibility to work when they please. But their altered status cuts at their self-esteem. They are sometimes shunned by co-workers. They are often less effective than they had been. Many find themselves no longer going the extra mile to get a job done or acquire a new skill.

The new arrangement is attractive to companies because they can immediately place experienced workers into their former jobs, sidestepping the need for training. But these workers are not likely to be as motivated as before. Consequently, productivity suffers. If the rental employee trend continues, productivity will be adversely affected nation-wide.

While most of these "rental" workers reported that they enjoyed their increased freedom, they regretted the loss of pension and health benefits. Although portability is not fully in place as yet, it looks as though employees will be able to carry these benefits from one employer to another sometime in the near future. This kind of portability should help bolster their feeling of security. But rental employees will have to find other means for their benefits.

Agenda for the OD Practitioner: The agenda for the OD practitioner in this domain concerns at least the following:

1. *Expectations.* The greater an employee's ambiguity regarding the employer's expectations related to role and task responsibilities, the more likely the employee is going to experience feelings of job insecurity, if not reduced motivation. OD practitioners can help by cajoling and coaching managers to be clear with their people about goals, objectives, and task requirements and about what they as managers want.

2. *Performance Feedback.* The absence of feedback also contributes to insecurity and reduced motivation. Again, urging and coaching managers to provide feedback to their people will help clarify employees' understanding of their social contract with the organization.

3. *Reward Systems.* If employers want to keep their above-average performers but cannot guarantee long-term employment, then they must make it worthwhile for these employees to stay with the organization. OD practitioners can help with the development and sustainability of a true pay-for-performance system. What discourages employees is a reward system that (*a*) does not base pay appropriately on the level of work and/or skills required, and (*b*) provides incentives based on some seemingly arbitrary process.

Employability

A recent opinion survey of bank employees, conducted by our organization, revealed very clear attitudes concerning training and development. These employees, the survey showed, want opportunities for training and development and are very likely to take advantage of these. Consider this in the context of the "employability clause" many companies are adding to the social contract, along the lines of "if we have to let you go some time in the future, we will ensure that you are employable." If these bank employees are representative, they intend to hold their employer to that promise.

Whether employees work for a large bank, General Motors, or for a variety of companies as contract labor, they need to think of themselves as self-employed in the sense that they are in charge of their own careers. As Edward E. Lawler III recently put it:

> . . . individuals must be able to develop marketable skills, assess and compare their skill levels with those of others, and manage their own careers.

In other words, few employers today and in the future are going to take responsibility for career management.

Agenda for the OD Practitioner: The employability arena is, of course, all about career development, but not exactly as we have known it in the past. Rather, it is about one's career per se, as a professional, as a specialist, as an expert, regardless of organizational affiliation. The OD practitioner's job is to help individuals understand more clearly what they (*a*) are good at, i.e., their unique set of skills and talents; (*b*) want in their work life, e.g., one career, multiple careers, etc.; and (*c*) feel about the balance of work and other activities in life, e.g., family, hobbies, community service, etc.

It would behoove us as OD practitioners to revisit such sources as Edgar Schein's writings on career anchors; J. Kotter, V. Faux, and C. McArthur on self-assessment and one's career; Herb Shepherd's life planning exercise; Morgan McCall, Michael Lombardo, and Ann Morrison's "lessons of experience"; and Warren Bennis's "invented life." In addition, we can help individuals by being knowledgeable about continuing education and distance learning opportunities as well as the broad array of training and development programs.

Trust

In a consultant's private interviews with employees sooner rather than later, the subject of trust (or more accurately, distrust) is likely to surface. This topic rarely appeared in my interviews a dozen or more years ago. Today, the issue seems pervasive. Why? While there are multiple reasons, three stand out: (1) the widening gap between "haves" and "have nots," (2) a diminished congruence between words and deeds, and (3) a lack of openness.

1. As we know, there is an increasing disparity between the wealthy and the poor in our society. Corporations clearly contribute to this: the disparity between a CEO's compensation and the average worker's has, in some instances, reached the incredible ratio of 140 to 1 in the United States. This gap remains regardless of the CEO's or the organization's performance. And with a merger or acquisition, the CEO and others at the top become multimillionaires while the rank and file continue to worry about their jobs, pensions, and health insurance. In time, the tremendous wage gap may begin to deflate, but the damage to trust has been done.

2. Not unrelated is another gap that I hear about time and again in my consulting interviews—the difference between what managers and executives say and what they do. We Americans cannot abide hypocrisy.

On this issue, Warren Bennis refers to the special case of empowerment, that is, executives espousing empowerment on the one hand and downsizing on the other. He puts it this way:

> . . . empowerment is an increasingly Orwellian term, not simply a lie, but an infuriating inversion of the truth. A demoralizing sense of powerlessness is what many jobholders are feeling

(as they worry about being downsized) . . . How can you have workplace empowerment in the absence of trust? . . . Empowerment and restructuring are on a collision course. It's impossible for a company to reengineer and empower at the same time, even though many firms are attempting it.

3. And, finally, distrust comes from a lack of openness. Executives rarely believe that it is wise to tell employees anything about an impending change until they have all the facts in hand and their ducks in a row. Yet I have never encountered an organization where executives are accurate in their assessment of what employees know. Invariably, employees know more than executives think they do. So, when executives delay or communicate in an ambiguous manner, they breed distrust.

Agenda for the OD Practitioner: The trust issue is fundamental. Trust, after all, is an outcome, a result of certain behaviors. But the prime behavioral precursor to trust is openness, and openness is one of the fundamental values guiding OD. We practitioners must espouse and push for openness in the organization(s) we serve. We might begin by modeling the behavior ourselves. And, of course, coach and provide feedback for executives on this dimension of their behavior.

Culture Clash

Attempts to integrate very distinct organizational cultures as part of a merger or acquisition is not uncommon today and will become even more prevalent in the future. Even though the merging companies may be in the same business, the difference in their respective cultures can be remarkable. Putting the two cultures together is a monumental task and will take years, not mere months.

A merger or acquisition provides an obvious example of the cultural issue. Not so obvious is, say, outsourcing, often a result of downsizing or some other form of restructuring. The outsourced unit is not a formal member of the organizational family, but the relationship has to be nurtured and managed nevertheless. And the relationship is not dramatically different from the partnering dynamics of a strategic alliance or joint venture.

The ability to recognize and manage the effects of cultural differences constitutes a strategic advantage in today's environment. Culture influences the negotiation process, management in general, performance monitoring and control, and work and information-sharing norms. Cultural differences can be assets or liabilities, depending on the strategic goals for the interorganizational relationship. Cultural characteristics should therefore be considered as important determinants of relationship viability when assessing the potential partner's compatibility.

Several revealing insights on this subject emerged from a recent interview with a group of seven senior bank executives. The executives had been through a merger some 18 months earlier and were about to enter a second, considerably larger and more complicated merger. I asked what they had learned from their previous experience that, when applied, would make this upcoming merger more effective. The following is a synopsis:

1. First and foremost, they stressed the importance of having a vision of what the merged bank should be. This emphasis is similar to what social psychologists refer to as a superordinate goal, that is, a goal that can only be achieved through the cooperation of the two parties.

2. People in the merged organization need to understand the "why" behind the vision—the rationale for the merger and how individual action supports and contributes to a realization of the vision.

3. Related to the previous point, they talked about the importance of employee communications, especially being open and truthful with all employees. For example, if people are going to be forced to leave the firm and find jobs elsewhere, the sooner they can be told, the better.

4. Establishing relationships with one's merged partners beyond the workplace is helpful: for example, having lunch together, going to a ballgame together, etc.

5. The executives believed that having a few off-site meetings together early in the process to work on critical issues was highly useful. Getting

together on neutral territory and away from the daily grind of their respective offices expedited the communication and decision-making processes.

6. These executives also believed that proximity was key. Being in separate geographical locations was detrimental to a successful merger, they maintained.

7. Also key was rapid decision making, particularly in the early days of a merger. These executives believed that "getting on" with the new organization as rapidly as possible, even though some corrections might have to made later, was more important because people needed clarity and structure to begin the long and arduous process of making the merger work.

8. Again on the theme of openness, these executives stated that in order for them to gain the respect of their people in the merged organization, they had to "walk the talk," that is, say what they mean, mean what they say, and be highly congruent in word and deed.

9. Most importantly, the executives stressed that the customer must not be forgotten. Prior to and in the midst of a merger, everyone becomes insular, discussing in great detail the new organization and forgetting the business, especially the customer.

This list of nine principles comes from these executives' collective experiences and does not constitute research. Yet in the area of interorganizational relations, practice continues to outpace research. It is therefore sensible that lessons from experience such as these should guide both practice and research about interorganizational relations.

Agenda for the OD Practitioner: Instead of focusing on organizational culture change as I advocated back in 1982, the work of OD should now emphasize the interrelationships of cultures. To some extent, this is an extension of our diversity work at the interpersonal and group level. But at the same time it is different, in that culture, from an organizational perspective, is related more to general systems theory, social psychology, and organizational sociology than to interpersonal psy-

chodynamics and the dynamics within and across small groups.

I do not mean to advocate an either/or scenario here—either culture change or emphasis on cultural interrelationships. Rather, there needs to be a different theoretical perspective and consequently a difference in certain action steps. For example, an early step in a merger is putting together two, usually different, compensation systems. This requires expertise of a different order from what an OD practitioner would normally bring to the table, although the OD person could contribute by helping participants become aware of the assumptions and values that underlie the two systems.

Back to the main point. The agenda for the OD practitioner is *inter,* working in between persons and systems. OD skills that need to be honed, therefore, include negotiation, mediation, conflict management, and conflict resolution. Add to this a good dose of understanding about organizational cultures for good measure. Increasing our knowledge about cross-cultural dynamics, general systems theory, and organizational psychology and sociology would help as well.

Corporate Power

My final agenda item is simply to call attention to two important books: David Korten's *When Corporations Rule the World* and Ralph Estes' *Tyranny of the Bottom Line.* Our agenda here is to read these books and to think about values. Our actions, whatever they may be, will come later. My urging at this stage is to read, think, and feel.

With strong credentials and considerable documentation, Korten contends that global corporations are becoming more powerful than nation states and, therefore, are not sufficiently monitored or regulated. Driven predominantly by financial goals, global corporations contribute significantly to (1) widening the gap between the haves and have-nots throughout the world, (2) destroying the middle class, and (3) weakening local economies. With all the hype about globalization, Korten's perspective is sobering. Not

EXHIBIT 1   **Summary of Organizational Consulting Issues and the OD Practitioner's Agenda**

Organizational Consulting Issue	OD Practitioner's Agenda
Reengineering	Focus on specific change targets that are critical to the success of a reengineering effort, e.g., roles and responsibilities, the larger systemic picture, etc.
Downsizing	Confront reasons for decision and test for constraining, cloning, or learning forces; push for humane treatment, dignity, and fairness.
Community	Bring people together; initiate meetings, not just facilitate them.
Employer-employee social contract	Seek clarity regarding task expectations and goals/objectives; help to provide feedback for employees; promote reward system based on merit and perhaps pay for performance.
Employability	Foster career development by helping people to understand what they (a) are good at, (b) want in their work, and (c) desire concerning balance of work and other aspects of life. Review career development literature and related sources.
Trust	Espouse and live the value of openness; provide coaching and feedback for executives regarding the congruence of their words and actions.
Culture clash	Place emphasis on the interrelationships of cultures and consult in the domain of "in-between-ness."
Corporate power	Read the two books by Korten and Estes, and think about the implications for OD work and feel the values that are confronted.

everyone agrees with Korten, particularly global executives—see, for example, a book by a former global company executive, Henry Wendt, titled *Global Embrace: Corporate Challenges in a Transnational World.* In any case, as you read Korten's book, think about where you stand vis-à-vis the issues he raises, especially if you work with a global corporation.

Even those who have not as yet read Estes's book can predict much of its content—corporations being driven by short-term profits and working to please stockholders more than customers and certainly more than employees. Estes makes these points and more. He addresses the fundamental purpose of a corporation, raises the question of who controls the corporation and, of course, discusses accountability. Again, not all would agree with Estes. But he raises the right questions—important questions for us to consider and . . . use in determining our own position.

It is equally important, as we read Estes, to clarify for ourselves what the primary causal factors are for a positive bottom line—what organizational behaviors contribute to profitability,

which hinder. Our job is to determine the antecedents, then decide which ones we should get behind, which ones to fight against.

This final agenda, then, is one that confronts our values. My purpose has been to raise awareness. Joining a picket line, a march on Washington, D.C., or storming the gates of a global corporation *is* your business.

Exhibit 1 provides a summary of the eight organizational consulting issues that have been covered, plus brief statements of the OD practitioner's agenda.

The Tao of OD

There are at least two primary criteria for a professional practice. One is to have a theoretical basis for the practice and the other is to act within the bounds of a set of ethics.

The way for OD is in place. It is more a matter of owning the theories and values of OD and, with strong commitment, putting them into practice. As we say to our clients: "If you own the decision, you're likely to implement it."

And, finally, back to the purpose of this paper, that is, to argue in favor of a deeper agenda for OD. In an attempt to be relevant to "real" business issues, such as downsizing, we have neglected many of the fundamental values of our field, values that are integral to community, the organization-individual interface, the development of people, trust, interorganizational relations, especially concerning cross-cultural dynamics, and how power is addressed and exercised.

It is time—indeed, past time—for OD practitioners to challenge issues and actions that we know to be wrong, to run counter to the very foundation of our field, and to cause us to wake up in the middle of the night and question ourselves.

References

This paper is based on a presentation given for the combined preconference on "Restructuring, Reengineering, and Downsizing: A Crossroads for Society" and "The Bottom Line: Defining Our Values for the Future" at the Annual Conference of the Organization Development Network, Orlando, Florida, October 5, 1996. I am grateful to Billie Alban, Dennis Gallagher, Len Goodstein, Dick Powell, and Lisa Tolliver for their feedback on an earlier draft of this paper.

The wave of reengineering began with M. Hammer and J. Champy's book, *Reengineering the Corporation: A Manifesto for Business Revolution* (New York: Harper Business, 1993). Some case examples of successful and unsuccessful reengineering have been described by G. Hall, J. Rosenthal and J. Wade in a 1993 *Harvard Business Review* (Vol. 71, No. 6, pp. 119–131) article, "How to Make Reengineering Really Work," but more comprehensive reviews have been provided by Kim Cameron, "Techniques for Making Organizations Effective," a chapter in D. Druckman, J. E. Singer, and H. P. van Cott (eds.) *Enhancing Organizational Performance* (Washington, D.C.: National Academy Press, 1997) and by J. P. Womack and D. T. Jones in their 1996 book, *Lean Thinking* (New York: Simon & Schuster). *The Economist* article recording Michael Hammer's defense of reengineering was in the November 5, 1994 issue on page 70.

For articles showing the ill effects on productivity as a result of downsizing, see A. Bennett, "Downsizing Doesn't Necessarily Bring an Upswing in Corporate Profitability," *The Wall Street Journal,* June 6, 1991, pp. B1, B4; R. E. Cole, "Learning from Learning Theory: Implications for Quality Improvements of Turnover, Use of Contingent Works, and Job Rotation Policies," *Quality Management Journal,* 1993, Vol. 1, pp. 9–25; and R. Henkoff, "Getting Beyond Downsizing," *Fortune,* January 10, 1994, pp. 58–64. Kim Cameron's work concerning downsizing is published in a number of sources; the one referred to in this paper is K. S. Cameron, S. J. Freeman, and A. K. Mishra, "Best Practices in White-Collar Downsizing: Managing Contradictions," *Academy of Management Executive,* 1991, Vol. 5, No. 3, pp. 57–73. For a current and more extensive coverage, see his chapter in the Druckman et al. book referred to above. And for yet another review, see Wayne Casio's article, "Downsizing: What Do We Know? What Have We Learned?" *Academy of Management Executive,* Vol. 7. No. 1, pp. 95–104. For publications about the effect of downsizing on individuals, victims, and survivors, see the 1996 book, *New York Times Special Report: The Downsizing of America* (New York: Times Books, Random House), and David M. Noer's book, *Healing the Wounds: Overcoming the Trauma of Layoffs and Revitalizing Downsized Corporations* (San Francisco: Jossey-Bass, 1993). For a recent article claiming that downsizing is not over, see L. Uchitelle's piece in *The New York Times,* "Despite Drop, Rate of Layoffs Remains High," August 23, 1996, pp. 1, D2.

Studies showing the importance of *how* downsizing is implemented and demonstrating the possibility of some positive outcomes include S. W. J. Kozlowski, G. T. Chao, E. M. Smith, and J. Hedlund, "Organizational Downsizing: Strategies, Intervention, and Research Implications, "*International Review of Industrial & Organizational Psychology,* 1993, Vol. 8; J. Brockner, S. Grover, T. Reed, R. DeWitt, and M. O'Malley, "Survivors' Reactions to Layoffs: We Get By With A Little Help From Our Friends," *Administrative Science Quarterly,* 1987, Vol. 32, pp. 526–554; G. D. Bruton; J. K. Keels, and C. L. Shook, "Downsizing the Firm: Answering the Strategic Questions," *Academy of Management Executive,* 1996, Vol. 10, No. 2, pp. 38–45; and Cameron's chapter in Druckman et al. (see above). *The New Yorker* article by J. Cassidy was in the April 22, 1996 issue, pp. 51–55.

For information on the ebb and flow of the American middle class, at least from an economics perspective, see the article by E. Kacapyr, "Are You Middle Class?" *American Demographics,* 1996, Vol. 18. No. 10, pp. 30–35.

The W. McKinley, C. M. Sanchez, and A. G. Schick article is "Organizational Downsizing: Constraining, Cloning, Learning," *Academy of Management Executive,* 1995, Vol. 9, No. 3, pp. 32–42. The "wee-ness envy" article is by L.S. Richman in the September 20, 1993 issue (pp. 54–56) of *Fortune* and entitled, "When Will the Lay-offs End?"

The articles about the downsized insurance group and the CEO of Sara Lee are both from *The Economist:* the former "Fire and Forget," April 20, 1996, p. 51, and the latter "The Cecil Rhodes of Chocolate-Chip Cookies: How to Be a Good Corporate Citizen in a World of Globalized Markets," May 25, 1996, p. 74. The anecdote about Bill Flynn comes from an article by the current CEO of Mutual of America—T. J. Moran, "What Leaders Owe," *Leader to Leader,* 1996, Vol. 1, No. 2, pp. 15–17.

The "me-syndrome" was expounded in Christopher Lasch's book, *The Culture of Narcissism: American Life in an Age of Diminishing Expectations* (New York: Norton, 1978), and the cynical Americans in the D. L. Kanter and P. H. Mirvis book, *The Cynical Americans: Living and Working in an Age of Discontent and Disillusion* (San Francisco: Jossey-Bass, 1989).

The "age of self-navigation" study is by C. Walker and E. Moses and reported in *American Demographics,* 1996, Vol. 18, No. 9, pp. 36–42. For an article about downsizing in employee-owned companies see L. Uchitelle, "Downsizing Comes to Employee-Owned America," *The New York Times,* July 7, 1996, p. E3. Also by Uchitelle is *The New York Times* article about rental employees, "More Downsized Workers Are Returning as Rentals," December 8, 1996, pp. 1, 34.

Ed Lawler's thinking and advice about career self-management can be found in his latest book, E. E. Lawler III, *From the Ground Up: Six Principles for Building the New Logic Corporation* (San Francisco: Jossey-Bass, 1996, Chapter 12). And sources for OD practitioners regarding careers and career development include E. H. Schein's *Career Dynamics: Matching Individual and Organizational Needs* (Reading, MA: Addison-Wesley, 1978); the book by J. Kotter, V. Faux, and C. McArthur, *Self-Assessment and Career Development* (Englewood Cliffs, NJ: Prentice Hall, 1978); a description of Herb Shepherd's life-planning exercise can be found in Chapter 13 of W. L. French and C. H. Bell, Jr., *Organization Development: Behavioral Science Interventions for Organizational Improvement,* 5th Ed. (Englewood Cliffs, NJ: Prentice-Hall, 1995); "lessons of experience" is recorded in the book by M. W. McCall, M. M. Lombardo, and A. M. Morrison, *The Lessons of Experience: How Successful Executives Develop on the Job* (Lexington, MA: Lexington Books, 1988); and the "invented life" is W. G. Bennis' *An Invented Life: Reflections on Leadership and Change* (Reading, MA: Addison-Wesley, 1993).

The quote from Warren Bennis about empowerment comes from an article in the February 20, 1996 *Los Angeles Times.*

With respect to interorganizational relations and culture clash, see W. W. Burke and N. W. Biggart, "Interorganizational Relations," in D. Druckman, J. E. Singer, and H. P. Van Cott (eds.) *Enhancing Organizational Performance* (Washington, D.C.: National Academy Press, 1997). In 1982 in W. W. Burke, *Organization Development: Practices and Principles* (Boston: Little, Brown) I argued that OD practitioners should focus on culture change.

With respect to corporate power, see D. C. Korten, *When Corporations Rule the World* (West Hartford, CT: Kumarian Press, and San Francisco: Berrett-Koehler, 1995) and R. Estes, *Tyranny and the Bottom Line: Why Corporations Make Good People Do Bad Things* (San Francisco: Berrett-Koehler, 1996). A counter-argument is provided by H. Wendt's *Global Embrace: Corporate Challenges in a Transnational World* (New York: Harper Business, 1993).

Name Index

Subject Index